BYRON: *A Biography*

VOLUME II

A BIOGRAPHY

By

Leslie A. Marchand

VOLUME II

ALFRED A. KNOPF : NEW YORK : 1957

© *Leslie A. Marchand, 1957*

L. C. catalog card number: 57–7547

THIS IS A BORZOI BOOK,
PUBLISHED BY ALFRED A. KNOPF, INC.

FIRST EDITION

CONTENTS

VOLUME ONE

VOLUME TWO

VOLUME THREE

ILLUSTRATIONS

VOLUME ONE

VOLUME TWO

VOLUME THREE

BYRON : *A Biography*

VOLUME II

CHAPTER XIII

1814

Engaged

BYRON was at first shaken by Annabella's acceptance of his proposal. His thoughts turned immediately to Lady Melbourne. "May I hope for your consent, too?" he asked. "In course I mean to reform most thoroughly, and become 'a good man and true,' in all the various senses of these respective and respectable appellations." [n]

Whatever mental reservations she may have had about the compatibility of the couple, Lady Melbourne readily gave her blessing. She probably congratulated herself that she had had nothing to do with the second proposal, though Byron credited her with having brought them together. "After all it is a match of *your* making, and better had it been had *your* proposal been accepted at the time. I am quite horrified in casting up my moral accounts of the two intervening years. . . ." But after this seriousness he could not resist a little flippancy of the kind his confidante had grown accustomed to. "I wish one or two of one's idols had said No instead; however, all that is over. I suppose a married man never gets anybody else, does he? I only ask for information." [n]

When Lady Melbourne taxed him with lack of serious interest in the business, however, he replied: "You very much mistake me if you think I am lukewarm upon it . . . if I think she likes me, I shall be exactly what she pleases; it is her fault if she don't govern me properly, for never was anybody more easily managed. . . . You can't conceive how I long to call you Aunt." [n]

Lady Melbourne would have been surprised indeed had she known with what earnestness and what frequency and at what length he wrote to his fiancée. He was determined to convince Annabella (and himself) that her confidence had not been misplaced, that he would try to be everything she wished. Their dispositions were not so different as perhaps she had supposed, he said, and even if they were, that need be no obstacle to their happiness. He wanted much to see her, and yet, he confessed, ". . . I feel more tremblingly alive to that meeting than I quite like to own to myself. When your letter arrived, my Sister was sitting near me and grew frightened at the effect of its contents—which was even painful for a moment—not a long one—nor am I often so shaken." [n]

And the next day he resumed his clarification and apologia, taking up the matter of religion, on which he knew she was anxious on his behalf. "I am rather bewildered by the variety of tenets than inclined to dispute their foundation. In a word, I will read what books you please, hear what arguments you please. . . . You shall be 'my Guide, Philosopher, and Friend'; my whole heart is yours. . . ." [n]

All Annabella's reserves were broken. "I offered my existence to him," she said years later. "The reply [his first letter following her acceptance] was gratifying beyond words to describe—it made me feel inspired with the purest happiness." [n] And after receiving his next letter she wrote: "Had I *known* that you suffered, the baseless fabric would sooner have fallen. . . . I have been very foolish, and if you had not been wiser, we might both still have been without hope." And then she proceeded to tell him the whole story of the phantom suitor she had set up between them, first George Eden and more recently Hugh Montgomery, a casual friend with whom she had been corresponding. But her self-assurance had melted now, and she too was a little frightened at the prospect of their meeting. Could she live up to the ideal he had built from her letters? His confidence in her consistency and his insistence that she should be his guide now gave her some uneasiness too. Now that she had surrendered she wanted him to do the leading. ". . . my ideas wait to be fixed by yours," she told him. "My pursuits easily adapt themselves, and to share them, of whatever kind, must be my greatest pleasure." [n]

But, despite his genuine desire to please in every way and to adapt himself to the wishes of his fiancée, Byron soon began to feel uncomfortable in his new role as a man legitimately engaged to an innocent and inexperienced girl. All his serious love affairs since his idealized boyish attachment to Mary Chaworth had had something of the forbidden or the clandestine in them. He knew better how to make love to a married woman than to a single girl, especially one who had never had a serious attachment, who had grown up under indulgent parents, and who knew more of books than of life. At the same time that he was writing so seriously to Annabella, he revealed some of his inner disquietude in announcing the event to Moore, who, like some of his other sophisticated friends, would not approve of the match. He covered up his embarrassment with flippancy: "My mother of the Gracchi (that *are* to be), *you* think too strait-laced for me. . . . Miss Milbanke is the lady, and I have her father's invitation to proceed there in my elect capacity,—which, however, I cannot do till I have settled some business in London, and got a blue coat. . . . I must, of course, reform thoroughly. . . . She is so good a person, that—that—in short, I wish I was a better." [n]

Annabella and her doting parents did not delay in spreading the news in quite a different vein to their friends and relatives. But, knowing that Byron's reputation in the world had spread for other reasons than his poetic fame, they were at first defensive. Annabella wrote to her friend Emily Milner: "It is not in the great world that Lord Byron's true character must be sought; but ask of those nearest to him—of the unhappy whom he has consoled, of the poor whom he has blessed, of the dependents to whom he is the best of masters." Byron might have smiled sheepishly had he seen her next sentence, though he himself had allowed her to form that complacent opinion: "For his despondency I fear I am but too answerable for the last two years." Then she added piously: "I have a calm and deep security,—a confidence in God and man." [n]

In the meantime, Byron, never precipitate in moving, lingered a few days at Newstead. Augusta had urged him to go to Seaham at once, but he was in no hurry. He must journey to London first, not only to outfit himself properly for the trip, but to get Hanson to put his affairs in shape and arrange to sell Newstead so that he could make a proper settlement on his bride-to-be. Besides, he hated to leave, perhaps for the last time, the ancestral estate he had always loved better than anything else in England. The freshness of early autumn was already enlivening the beauty of the great oaks in the park. As he wandered with Augusta by the lake" or in the cool woods, the melancholy of parting, of upheaval and change, seized him. The new step he was taking would part him not only from the ruined hall and its memories, but also from the only woman who had ever really understood him, who had given him unselfish and undemanding love and appreciation. They walked into the "Devil's Wood" back of the Abbey, where the "Wicked Lord" in his misanthropic solitude had set up his leering satyrs. There they carved their names deeply into the bark of an old elm."

The next day (the 21st) they left for London, Augusta returning to Six Mile Bottom." Back in town on the 23rd, Byron felt concern for the trouble that Caroline Lamb might make when she heard the news. He was disappointed to learn that the report that she had gone to France was not true. The anxiety drove him to write immediately to Lady Melbourne: "If Annabella has any firmness, if she has even any *woman* in her composition, *C.* will only lose her labour by trying to mar the match." " And when on October 5 the *Morning Chronicle* printed a paragraph contradicting the announcement of the engagement which had appeared in a Durham paper, Byron, imagining Caroline was at her tricks again, told Lady Melbourne: ". . . it could only be *her,* no one else has the motive or the malignity to be so *petty.*" " But after the editor, Perry, had sent him the anonymous letter, he discovered it was not in her hand."

Caroline, in fact, took the news calmly and decided to be romantic instead of troublesome. It was not that her interest in Byron had subsided. But she had known that this day would come and she was tragically resigned to it. She had written to

Murray earlier (possibly while Byron was engaged in some mild
flirtations in the spring): "I think that I shall live to see the
day when some beautiful and innocent Lady Byron shall drive
to your door. . . . I really believe that when that day comes
I shall buy a pistol at Manton's and stand before the Giaour
and his legal wife and shoot myself. . . ." [n]

But when the event actually happened, Caroline, after an
interval, eschewed the pistol and took up the pen, writing in her
most sentimental and self-sacrificing vein: "Do you remember
the first rose I gave you? The first rose you brought me is still
in my possession. . . . Now God bless you—may you be very
happy. I love and honour you from my heart as a friend may
love—no wrong I hope—as a sister feels—as your Augusta feels
for you." [n]

Byron was relieved, and he wrote her with a guarded kindness
which he hoped would not upset the delicate balance of her
impulsive mind. Though she found his letter icy and conde-
scending, she spared him and sought relief in writing to Murray:
"How has he disposed of the other unfortunates? I speak of
them by dozens, you see." [n] She gave a grudging compliment to
Annabella: "She is very learned and very good, and the top of
her face is handsome. . . ." [n] But in another mood she said
that Byron would "never be able to pull with a woman who
went to church punctually, understood statistics and had a bad
figure." [n] And she later wrote to Murray: "Her [Annabella's]
character is spotless—her understanding sensible accurate intelligent but when you talk of playfulness I comprehend not
your meaning—if Fulvia sporteth it must be like the dance of
the Elephant that would vainly attempt to rival the Antelope." [n]

Lady Melbourne was now more concerned with Augusta, however, than with Caroline. Could she be trusted to withdraw
gracefully from Byron's life? When he delayed his visit to Seaham,
his confidante was inclined to lay the blame on Augusta, but
Byron replied: "X never threw obstacles in the way; on the
contrary, she has been more urgent than even you, that I should
go to S[eaham] and wished me to set out from N[ewstead]
instead of London. She wished me much to marry, because it was

the only chance of redemption for *two* persons. . . ." [1] And when
Lady Melbourne's anxiety continued, Byron assured her: "X is the
least selfish person in the world. . . . her only error has been my
fault entirely, and for this I can plead no excuse, except passion,
which is none." "

Lady Melbourne was justified in her suspicion that Byron's
passion would not die so lightly, but she did not know Augusta
as well as did the brother. Indeed, Augusta loved Byron quite non-
possessively, and wanted genuinely to see him happy. Now she
was perfectly willing to go on loving him as a sister with over-
tones of motherly concern for his welfare. What had happened
scarcely embarrassed her and made no difference in her feeling
for him.

Hanson, who had been busy at his son-in-law's, where all
was not going well—marriage to a young wife had not steadied
the wavering senses of Lord Portsmouth—did not return to London until October 7. Byron wanted to put his finances in order
before he paid his respects at Seaham. He proposed to make a
settlement of £60,000, or £3,000 a year, on Annabella, to be
secured on Newstead, which he still intended to sell. His most
pressing debts had been paid from the money forfeited by
Claughton, and Hanson thought the Abbey would still sell for
£120,000."

Byron had made no inquiries as yet concerning the financial
status of his prospective father-in-law, though he had heard that
Sir Ralph was "dipped." The fact is that "old twaddle Ralph,"
as his relations called him, had overspent himself foolishly in
electioneering as early as 1812." Annabella's chief prospects were
from her uncle, Lord Wentworth.[2] But Hanson could not fix a

---

[1] *LBC*, I, 273–4. Letter of Oct. 4, 1814. (Corrected from Murray MSS. In
LBC the sentence begins: "I never threw. . . .") In this same letter Byron
told Lady Melbourne: "X has written to A. to express how much all my relations are pleased by the event, &c. &c." (*LBC*, I, 275.) Augusta expressed
the hope that she might soon be able to call Annabella *"my sister,"* and
added: "If I could possibly express how deservedly dear my Brother is to
me, you might in some degree imagine the joy I have felt in the anticipation
of an event which promises to secure his happiness." (Fox, p. 75. Letter of
Oct. 1, 1814.)

[2] Annabella wrote her friend Lady Gosford: "My ready money is £16,000.
I should think his annual income between 5 and 6 thousand—so we shall do

time to meet with Sir Ralph's agents, and Byron did not want to leave London until that was arranged.

Byron soon began to fret, first at the rapid spreading of the news by Annabella's family, and then at the thought of the public ceremony of the wedding itself, from which in his shyness he rebelled. "I don't much admire this kind of publicity," he told his "Aunt," "on account of the fuss and foolery it produces. It has always seemed to me very odd that so much ceremony should be made of a thing so very simple in itself. . . ." ⁿ On top of all this he had to weather the comments of his facetious friends. Augusta told him that Colonel Leigh reported that "they are '*betting* away at Newmarket, whether I am to be married or not.' " And soon some bets made in his rash minority that he would never marry began to catch up with him. In August 1808, at Brighton, Byron had received a guinea each from several drinking companions for which he was to forfeit a hundred to one, and fifty, as he recalled the agreement, to another. As soon as the news broke, these were upon him for their forfeits.ⁿ

In the meantime, the engaged couple wrote so often that their letters crossed. Byron's letters to Annabella gave evidence of an honest effort to reshape his character and habits. Realizing his own weaknesses, he still relied on her to help him form a more rational pattern of life. All the things he had striven for in his pictures of the ideal he tried to see embodied in her. Perhaps with her aid he could escape from the constant battle of opposing forces in his nature. Shortly after arriving in London he wrote her: "Sir W. Knighton brought Spurzheim (I believe is the name) the *craniologist* to see me—a discoverer of faculties and dispositions from heads.³ He passes his hand over the head & then tells you—curious things enough, for I own he has a little

very well, as I am not of an extravagant disposition." (Mayne: *Lady Byron*, p. 455.) But she miscalculated Byron's income, having no doubt based it on his statement of the value of Newstead. Actually the rents, though they had been raised, were not bringing him above three or four thousand, and were not always easily collectable.

³ Johann Christoph Spurzheim (1776–1832), a German phrenologist, came to England in 1813 and for four years had considerable success as a lecturer on the then supposed science of determining character by the bumps on the head.

astonished me. He says all mine are strongly marked—but very antithetical; for every thing developed in & on this same skull of mine has its *opposite* in great force, so that to believe him my good & evil are at perpetual war. Pray heaven the last don't come off victorious." [n]

Later the same day he reconstructed for her his recollection, somewhat idealized, of his first meeting with her at Melbourne House. "I set you down as the most puzzling person there—for there was a quiet contempt of all around you & the nothings they were saying & doing in your manner that was so much after my own heart I could hardly refrain from telling you so. . . . There was a simplicity—an innocence—a beauty in your deportment & appearance. . . ." And then—oh, what gross rationalizations love can make—he continued: "In very truth—from my heart of hearts, dearest Annabella—I can now tell you that then—at the very time when I became unworthy of being yours —it was to you my attachment had turned—it was you from whom it was wrenched. . . . I yet wish to be good—with you I cannot but be happy; but I never shall be what I would have been."

He concluded with an appeal that must have been disconcerting to a girl who had waited so long for a man whom she could esteem and look up to as superior to herself: ". . . I am whatever you please to make me. I am at least above the paltry reluctance of not submitting to an understanding which I am sure is superior to mine." [n]

Lady Melbourne, who half suspected that he was delaying his visit to Seaham deliberately, did not know all that was going on behind the scenes. Byron felt that he would be no nearer marriage if he did not get Hanson to confer with Sir Ralph's lawyer before he went. His plan was to set out two days after the attorney and to stop at Newstead on the way. But two days before Hanson's scheduled arrival at Durham on the 19th the attorney had skipped off without notice to Ilfracombe, Devon, on business and left Byron with embarrassing explanations to make. He wrote with restrained irritation to Hanson urging haste, but when a week had passed and there was no

more definite prospect of Byron's appearance at Seaham, Annabella could no longer conceal the impatience of her parents,
though she tried to soften the news. "My Uncle [Lord Went-
worth] is obliged to leave us next week," she wrote on the 22nd,
"and is in despair lest you should not arrive before he *must*
go. It is odd enough that my task should be to pacify the old
ones, and teach *them* patience. They are growing quite ungovernable, and I must have your assistance to manage them." [n]

After receiving this letter Byron lost patience with Hanson
and wrote him with some asperity: "It is now *five* weeks since
I announced to you Miss M's resolution and mine, and, since
that period, little or nothing has been done towards the object
of our wishes. . . . It looks like trifling on my part, and on yours
does not appear very attentive to me as a client or friendly as
a man." [n] When he learned that Hanson had been ill, he was
scarcely less severe. ". . . this marriage will be broken off, and,
if so, whether intentional or accidental, I can't help it, but, by
God, I can never look upon any one again as my friend, who
has even been the innocent cause of destroying my happiness." [n]

It is difficult to believe, after reading this letter, that Byron
was delaying of his own accord, though it is probable that his
irritation at the delay was caused chiefly by a fear of its consequences within his own unstable nature. His uneasiness, however, was not caused by any doubts of himself or Annabella, but
only by the annoyance of practical arrangements. On the 17th
he had written to ask Hobhouse to be his "groomsman" and
stand up with him at the marriage ceremony which he dreaded.
"I confess that the character of wooer in this regular way does
not sit easy upon me. I wish I could wake some morning, and
find myself fairly married . . . . if you would but take a wife
and be coupled then also, like people electrified in company
through the same chain, it would be still further comfort." [n]

While Byron was thus distracted, he had received a letter
from a young lady who signed herself "Eliza." There was nothing
very novel about it. Like so many others, she praised the "exquisite touches of feeling" that melted her heart when she read
his poetry. The letter was dated "Oct. 21, 1814" and signed

"Your young admirer & enthusiastic friend Eliza." She gave a cautious return address, probably that of some trusted friend: "Miss Horatia Somerset, Post Office, Clifton, nr. Bristol." ⁿ

According to her own story, written fifty years later when she was an old woman, Eliza had in her letter requested Byron's subscription for a poem she had written. Three days later she took her courage in her hands and called at his chambers in the Albany. Her narrative of what followed has a naïve charm which shows Byron in a mellow and yet realistic light.

"It was the 24th of October 1814 when I rang at his bell," she wrote; "it was about three o'clock in the afternoon, and the door was opened by his faithful attendant Fletcher. . . ." She asked him to "tell his Lordship that it is the Lady who wrote to him on Friday." In her confusion she had quite forgotten that other ladies might have written him on Friday. Byron, apparently cautious, asked her to explain her wishes in writing. She was nearly crying with agitation when Fletcher finally led her into the presence of the poet. He was standing by the fireplace when she entered, but he seated himself at a large writing-desk before he asked her to sit down.[4]

She confessed with embarrassment that it was family distress which brought her. Byron paid her the compliment of saying she looked seventeen or eighteen, but she replied:

"Oh my Lord—I am five and twenty— . . . and because I look so young I cannot get a situation—I have tried for twenty two of different kinds—. . . ."

Byron rang for Fletcher and asked him to bring a red leather trunk, out of which he took his checkbook. Eliza saw that it resembled her own school trunk in which she kept her papers and exclaimed naïvely: "I have a trunk too!"

Byron smiled and said: "Oh! you think I keep my Manuscripts in this Box, but there is nothing in it but some old Letters and odd papers—I never keep my Mss—by me."

While they talked of various things, he wrote a check, folded it, and handed it to her. She objected to Miss Edgeworth's

---

[4] Byron's seating himself at his desk before the lady was seated was probably not a gesture of impoliteness but an instinctive movement to conceal his lameness from a stranger.

novels, saying that they had no heart, to which Byron smiled but agreed: "Oh! *heart*—no more heart than a post—but she writes well and cleverly."

Eliza stayed talking for two hours and left with his promise that she might bring her book of poems to him. She was overwhelmed when she found that the check he had given her was for fifty pounds. When she called on the 26th with her poem she surprisingly got Byron's consent to look over another poem of hers in manuscript, though that was the one thing he liked least. As she shook hands with him at parting, she was "electrified by his touch."[5]

Eliza began to realize the nature of her feeling for Byron, and the next day passed slowly until she was back at the Albany and had laid her papers on his table. He said some polite things about her poem that quite elated her, the finest compliment to her ears being: ". . . you must have known much sorrow." He advised her to select the best pieces for publication and then turned to other matters.

Emboldened by his friendliness, she asked him to call on her. " 'My dear Child,' he replied, 'I cannot; I will tell you how I am circumstanced and then you will see it is impossible—*I am going to be married.*'

[5] Elizabeth Francis (afterward Smith, for apparently she did marry despite her own assertion that she could never find anyone to suit her after the encounter with Byron) was born December 9, 1788, and thus was only a few months younger than Byron. Her father, Samuel Francis, rose from clerk to partner in the bank of John Morlock, political boss of Cambridge in the late eighteenth century, and was elected alderman and then mayor of the town (both elections were contested) before bankruptcy subjected his proud family to hard times. (See Origo: "The Innocent Miss Francis and the Truly Noble Lord Byron," 2–3.) For the narrative of Eliza's interviews with Byron I am indebted to the Marchesa Origo's generosity in lending me her copy of Eliza's manuscript found among the Gamba papers and now in the Biblioteca Classense at Ravenna. Eliza in 1863-4 entered into a long correspondence with another of Byron's idolizing worshippers, the Countess Teresa Guiccioli, and sent her a detailed narrative of her half-dozen interviews with the poet in 1814. Teresa Guiccioli repaid her confidence by devoting a whole chapter of her *My Recollections of Lord Byron* (Chapter XIV, "Virtues of His Soul: His Generosity a Virtue") to a summary of Eliza's story, though much distorted to fit her picture of the angelic and faultless form she had conceived Byron to be. Eliza's own narrative gives a much more lifelike picture of him.

"At these words the glow of delight which had warmed my mind vanished in an instant, my heart sank like lead in my bosom. . . ."

She could scarcely articulate the words "Are you! I wish you happy." Byron looked at her with concern, and seeing how her hands trembled when she tried to roll up her manuscripts, he offered to assist her. With the utmost courtesy he took her in his own carriage and, after getting down himself at Douglas Kinnaird's, sent her home in it."

Two days later (on Saturday, October 29) Byron left for his first visit to his fiancée. He could not wait for Hanson, but urged him to proceed to Durham with all convenient speed." He had announced his departure to Annabella on the day of Eliza's last visit, saying that he was stopping to see his sister on the way."

Byron arrived at Six Mile Bottom on Saturday and remained until late Sunday. A germ of uneasiness about the marriage which might separate him from Augusta began to grow in his mind. He left in a very bad humor, proceeding northward by slow degrees. On the way he had much time to think. His late correspondence with Annabella had not been too reassuring, though he doubted himself more than her. She had begun to feel uneasy under the burden of the reputation she had gained for perfection and feared she could not live up to it when she met him. She recalled to him their last meeting, when she had nearly lost her presence of mind." And Byron had tried to explain his own coldness on that occasion, and to make her less fearful of his awful presence.

Then he had thought to please her with an account of his "present avocations." Douglas Kinnaird had applied to him to write the words for a musical composer "who is going to publish the *real old undisputed Hebrew melodies,* which are beautiful & to which David & the prophets actually sang the 'songs of Zion'—& I have done nine or ten on the sacred model—partly from Job &c. & partly my own imagination. . . . It is odd enough that this should fall to my lot, who have been abused as 'an infidel.' " [6]

[6] Mayne: *Lady Byron,* pp. 468–9. Letter of Oct. 20, 1814. This is Byron's

Their correspondence had too much self-consciousness in it, too much tortured reflection. Why couldn't the girl be easy and natural? He needed that to overcome his own shyness. Only Augusta could do that, and they could laugh together quite un-restrainedly. He half wished, he told Lady Melbourne, that they had run away together. Writing from Newark the second night, he confessed: "I am proceeding very slowly to S[eaham]. . . . I shall not stay above a week, if I can help it; don't write till you hear from me *there*, for I am not sure I shall go now, as Newstead is so near, and I have something to do there. . . . I am in very ill humour. . . ."[n]

At Seaham, Annabella was doing her best to keep her anxious parents from perceiving how agitated she was. Byron had not said when he would arrive. If he had been in any great haste, he could have been there Monday evening. She tried to hide from them too her chagrin that he had not overwhelmed her with poetry and presents. Annabella would have been even more distressed had she known how lavish he had been in gifts of jewelry and pictures to other women.

He had gone to Newstead, after all, and did not arrive at Seaham until Wednesday, November 2. The patience of the parents was strained, almost exhausted. Annabella was in her room reading (she could not have told what) with one ear to the driveway when she heard the carriage. The suspense (his last letter, announcing his departure, had been written on the 27th) had put her on edge. She put out the candles and "deliber-ated what should be done." She decided she could not face him while others were watching, and contrived to come down to the drawing-room when he was alone there. She recalled later that he was "standing by the side of the chimney-piece. He did not move forwards as I approached him, but took my ex-

---

first mention of the *Hebrew Melodies*. Isaac Nathan, a Hebrew musical composer, had written to Byron in June proposing that he write some songs for him to set to music (Letter of Nathan to Byron, June 30, 1814, Murray MSS.), but Byron took no interest in the project at that time, being other-wise occupied and believing that he could write nothing to order. It was not until Kinnaird interested himself in the project in October that Byron finally consented to try his hand at the melodies.

tended hand and kissed it." For a time neither could speak, but at length he said in a low voice: "It is a long time since we met." ⁿ She was too overcome to answer coherently, but made calling her parents the excuse to leave the room.

She did not think at all then, or perhaps she would have been hurt that he had not advanced to meet her, though she would have realized later that he was embarrassed by any movement that showed his lameness. If her parents had been there, they would have observed this slight as they probably did notice that he brought no presents and no engagement ring.

Two days later, after he had had time to observe the household, Byron wrote to Lady Melbourne of Annabella: "She seems to have more feeling than we imagined; but is the most *silent* woman I ever encountered; which perplexes me extremely." ⁿ Fortunately, the ice was broken by the others, who were quite voluble. The first night was spent in general conversation, and whatever qualms her parents had were soon dissipated, for when Byron made an effort to be charming he always charmed. Besides, he did not monopolize the conversation, but listened to Sir Ralph's tedious stories. And the others were, at least at first, eager enough to hear his experiences of the wider world and to pay deference to his fame. All that Annabella remembered of the first evening was that he talked of Kean. On retiring, he asked her at what time she generally appeared in the morning. She said about ten and went to bed, her imagination fired with the hope of taking him on one of her favorite walks before the others were stirring. But she waited until twelve and he had not appeared. She felt a cold chill creeping up her heart, though she would not admit it, and walked on the beach alone to collect herself. But she did take him later on her favorite walk along the cliff that faced the cold northern sea. She "tremblingly prest" his arm as he gazed on the rolling waters.ⁿ But, though he did not say it, the seas he loved washed warmer shores.

When she did not talk, Byron felt uncomfortably that she was watching him with a critical eye. He told Lady Melbourne: "I like them to talk, because then they *think* less. Much cogitation will not be in my favour. . . . I am studying her, but can't boast of my progress in getting at her disposition. . . . However,

the die is cast; neither party can recede; the lawyers are here—
mine and all—and I presume, the parchment once scribbled, I
shall become Lord Annabella." [n]

So ill at ease had she made him by her silence that he thought
she did not love him, and he was so "strange, moody, and unaccountable" [n] that she thought the same thing about him. After
the first two days he reported to his confidante: "I can't yet
tell whether we are to be happy or not. I have every disposition
to do her all possible justice, but I fear she won't govern me;
and if she don't it will not do at all. . . . I never could love but
that which *loves;* and this I must say for myself, that my attachment always increases in due proportion to the return it meets
with, and never changes in the presence of its object. . . ." [n]

With her parents he got on well enough, though he took an
early dislike to Annabella's mother. At first "old twaddle Ralph"
seemed but an amusing and harmless country squire. By the
fourth day he thought he had thawed Annabella to a certain
degree, but was not sure yet that he understood her. His report
to his "Tante" was encouraging but not ecstatic: "Annabella and
I go on extremely well. . . . She is, as you know, a perfectly
good person; but I think, not only her feelings and affections,
but her *passions* stronger than we supposed. Of these last I
can't as yet positively judge. . . ." [n]

Everything seemed to be going smoothly. The lawyers even
had agreed without any quibbling. Annabella was to have
£20,000 settled on her, and she had expectations from her uncle,
Lord Wentworth.[7] But after a week the engaged couple were no
further ahead in understanding. She found him "so peculiar" in
his treatment of her, and could not comprehend his moods,
though they were often caused by her own emotional ups and
downs. He talked much of Augusta, "with sorrowful tenderness,"

[7] *LBC,* I, 289. Letter of Nov. 6, 1814. Actually, only £16,000 was raised as
a charge upon the Halnaby estate of Sir Ralph Milbanke, and the other
£4,000 Sir Ralph covenanted to pay. Only £6,200 was raised in cash, and
interest at five per cent (£690 per year) was charged against the remaining £13,800. Of this income from the dowry Lady Byron was to receive an
annual sum of £300 for pin money. The whole of the complicated agree-
ments of the marriage settlement and of the separation are given in manuscripts drawn up by Hanson in the Murray collection.

and said that no one would ever have as much of his love as she did. She later recalled: "I felt an instant's pain—it was perceptible only to myself." And when he told her: "You remind me of her when you are playful," she tried to take that as a cue to her own behavior, but found it impossible to drop her self-consciousness with him as she could with others. He said: "If you had married me two years ago, you would have spared me what I can never get over." [n] Into this statement, made in a moment of pique, she worked all kinds of sinister meanings.

She came to the conclusion that he did not love her, and her overwrought imaginings led her to make a scene and offer to break off the engagement. She told two different people in later years that on that occasion Byron "fainted entirely away." And she added with an effort: "Then I was *sure* he must love me." [n]

Byron described the scene to Lady Melbourne as "not altogether out of C's [Caroline's] style; it was too long and too trifling, in fact, for me to transcribe, but it did me no good." [n] His report to his confidante on the 13th was anything but reassuring. It looked as if the match might, after all, be broken off. "Do you know I have grave doubts if this will be a marriage now? Her disposition is the very reverse of *our* imaginings. She is overrun with fine feelings, scruples about herself and *her* disposition (I suppose, in fact, she means mine), and to crown all, is taken ill once every 3 days with I know not what. . . . I hear of nothing but 'feeling' from morning till night, except from Sir Ralph, with whom I go on to admiration. L[y] M[ilbanke] too, is pretty well; but I am never sure of A. for a moment. . . . The least word, or alteration of tone, has some inference drawn from it. Sometimes we are too much alike, and then again too unlike. This comes of system, and squaring her notions to the devil knows what."

Byron had found one way of quieting her upsurges of "feelings" —a silent way which he had tried very successfully with other women, though he had never attempted it before with a girl so innocent as Annabella. He told Lady Melbourne: "For my part, I have lately had recourse to the eloquence of *action* (which Demosthenes calls the first part of oratory), and find it succeeds very well, and makes her very quiet; which gives me some hopes of the efficacy of the 'calming process,' so renowned in 'our philosophy.' In fact, and entre nous, it is really amusing; she is like a child in that respect, and quite *caressable* into kindness. . . ." [n]

Annabella, frightened probably at what these caresses might lead to, apprehensive that her parents might sense what was going on, and dreading further scenes before the wedding, urged Byron to leave after he had been there just two weeks. She had the excuse of hurrying that event; there was still business to be done. Byron had to get a blue coat and make other preparations. Sir Ralph and Lady Milbanke had no idea of what turmoil lay under the calm surface of their daughter's behavior, and she was determined that they should not know. Aside from the disappointing fact that he was averse to any elaborate ceremony or guests at the wedding, they were quite taken with their prospective son-in-law. As for Annabella, she was not sure that she could control Byron or herself in his presence, though she foolishly told herself that it would be different after they were married.

And events seemed at first to prove her right. Byron left Seaham on the 16th and wrote the same night from Boroughbridge a letter which he meant to be agreeable, but which had a few barbs in it showing that he was slightly piqued at being pushed away: "My Heart—We are thus far separated, but after all one mile is as bad as a thousand—which is a great consolation to one who must travel six hundred before he meets you again. If it will give you any satisfaction, I am as comfortless as a pilgrim with peas in his shoes, and as cold as Charity, Chastity, or any other virtue. . . ." [n]

If she winced at his pointed references to Charity and Chastity, she had the presence of mind to restrain her feelings. She quieted the seeds of unrest and of doubt and told him and herself that all would turn out well.

Now that he was gone, she would write him freely; she had so long loved the man of her imagination that she was more at ease with him. "Are you quite sure that I love you? Why did you doubt it?" she asked. "It is *your* only trespass. As for *my* trespasses I must not think of them—I wish we were married, and then I could do my best, and not quarrel with myself for a thousand things that you would not mind." [n]

After hearing from him, she wrote: "My own dearest, there is not a moment when I would not give my foolish head to see you. I knew it would be so, and think it a salutary chastisement for all my misdemeanors." [n] She tried to convince him in her next letter that she was not always the emotional and tragic character she had appeared to him. "Those who have seen me *quite* as a domestic animal have had more reason to complain of my nonsense than my sense." [n]

Byron arrived in Cambridge on his way to Six Mile Bottom the evening of the 18th, and there ran into Hodgson. They supped together and talked until a late hour. From the time he heard of Byron's engagement to Miss Milbanke, Hodgson had been in transports of joy for his friend. Byron discussed the whole situation with him, keeping, of course, his doubts to himself. Apparently he showed her latest letter, for Hodgson wrote him the next day when he had gone on to Six Mile Bottom that "from the whole of Miss M's conduct in this affair, from the first letter you showed me to that glorious and openhearted offering of female affection which I saw last night, I have formed the most *exalted* idea of her I ever did of any woman in my life." [n]

Hodgson wrote his fiancée after this meeting with Byron in Cambridge: "Oh! how I glowed with indignation at the base reporters of his *Fortune-hunting*. . . . *entre nous,* he is sacrificing a great deal too much." Hodgson blamed it on the parents. "Her fortune is *not* large at present, but he settles £60,000 upon her. This he cannot do *without selling Newstead again;* and with a look and manner that I cannot easily forget he said: 'You know we must think of these things as little as possible.' 'But,' I replied, 'I am certain, if she saw Newstead she would not let you part with it.' 'Bless her! she has nothing to do with it.' . . . Now where, where are the hearts of those who can under-value, who can depreciate this man?" [n] A further evidence of Byron's disinterestedness, Hodgson said, was the fact that, though Miss Milbanke's chief expectations were from Lord Wentworth, Byron would not go out of his way to call on that worthy gentleman, whose estate at Kirkby Mallory in Leicestershire was not very far from Newstead.

Byron was easily persuaded to remain in the vicinity of Cambridge until Wednesday (the 23rd) to vote for Dr. Clarke, the Eastern traveler, who was a candidate for the professorship of anatomy. He spent the intervening days at Six Mile Bottom. Stricken by indolence and conflicting emotions, Byron wrote only once from his sister's, putting off on her the task of keeping Annabella pacified. Letters continued to come from Seaham, still with an undertone of self-distrust and uneasiness, though professing the greatest devotion and hope for the future.

Byron was back in Cambridge on the 23rd. Hobhouse had come up to vote for Dr. Clarke also. He recorded that Byron was applauded by the students in the gallery when he walked into the Senate House to cast his vote and again when he left the house. "This is, they tell me, unique. He looked as red as fire. Mansel [then Master of Trinity and Bishop of Bristol] and Dr. Clarke contended for the honour of escorting him. This is well for a bishop."

Byron and Hodgson dined with Dr. Clarke, and in the evening they joined a party including Scrope Davies, Hobhouse, and Henry Matthews at Trinity to hear a declamation.[n] The subsequent conviviality left Byron, as he told Annabella, with "that infallible next-day's headache ever attendant upon sincere Friendship."[n] The following day he and Hobhouse left for London, where Byron settled again into his bachelor life at the Albany. On the eve of leaving it forever, he found it good. On the 26th he went with Hobhouse to Drury Lane to see Kean in *Macbeth*. On December 2 the two friends dined *intime* at Kinnaird's with the great actor, who was in fine form and full of anecdotes.[n] This was the kind of evening Byron enjoyed, and he may well have compared it with the evenings at Seaham when he had listened to Sir Ralph's tedious stories.

Annabella wrote again, trying to whip up her hopes and dispel the forebodings that lurked in the background of her mind: "I wish for you, want you, Byron mine, more every hour. All my confidence has returned—never to sink again, I believe. A confidence in the power of my affection to make me anything, everything that you and I wish." [n]

But she soon began to fret again because Byron could not set a definite date for his return and for the wedding. She remembered the long delay before his first visit and wrote: "Tell me the latest, not the earliest, day that you think to arrive here, for my Philosophy likes not 'hope deferred.' " [n] He could only reply that Hanson had the papers and was dealing with them, but was distracted by Lord Portsmouth's affairs, and that he wanted to see what Claughton intended about Newstead. She announced that there was a wedding cake in preparation "which 'makes Ossa like a wart.' " [n] She no doubt would have liked a big church wedding, as would her parents, with all the squirearchy of the county invited to sample the cake and drink to their health, but Byron put a quiet damper on that in a few words. Speaking of the license, he said: "I will have it special —if you please—because I think it will be quieter to be married in a room, and mamma will lend us a cushion each to kneel upon." [n]

For all his reassurances, Annabella was troubled by a vague disquietude which she could not wholly conceal. "I begin to think," she wrote, "that after the great cake is baked, and the epithalamium composed, with all other prologues to the performance, the part of Spouse, like that of Hamlet, will be omitted 'by particular desire.' " [n] She was not much reassured by the statement that Hanson would be ready in ten days, and was scarcely made happier by what followed: "I am sure I wish we had been married these two years [a little gibe at her first refusal]; but never mind—I have great hopes that we shall love each other all our lives as much as if we had never married at all." [n]

In the meantime, Byron was not without distractions in London. Eliza Francis had not forgotten him. Her visits to him in the Albany had spoiled all ordinary company for her.

When she called on him following his return, *"all was sunshine,"* Eliza wrote, for her youthful benefactor, "pleased with my gratitude, and charmed with my artless regard for himself treated me with a kindness beyond what he had ever evinced before. . . . Lord Byron started from his chair and held out both his hands to me—and impulsively I put both mine into his —then he expressed his wish to be of service to me if he only knew how—he then struck his forehead with one of his hands and tearing his hair, he ejaculated 'I wish to God you had come sooner! then I might have managed for you, and we should have been happy!' " When the carriage was announced and she arose to go, Byron stopped her and said: "I was thinking of giving you a letter of introduction to the Duke of Devonshire but we must wait until he returns from the Country—but call again in a day or two."

On her next visit she ventured to express a wish that he would introduce her to Lady Byron after his marriage. To that he gave an explicit negative, "lest *though* amiable and unsuspecting herself, those about her might put some jealous nonsense into her head which she would not otherwise think of."

While they were talking she heard a noise behind the wainscot and asked what it was. " 'Oh, only rats—we have a great many.' It seemed to me wonderful that rats should invade the Albany, but I remarked, 'Well, at any rate you have no children here.' " 'Children!' cried Lord Byron, 'don't talk of them[;] you put me in a fever.' "

But he put out his hands once more "and again I placed mine in them. . . . As we stood together I ventured to ascertain the colour of his eyes, and I saw that though the finest eyes in the world they were not *dark* as I had fancied, but the large grey eye—the 'Mary Queen of Scots eye,' which is so beautiful—and his long dark eye-lash made them appear black—I never did behold such eyes before or since, and how long we should have stood—I looking up, and he looking down, I know not, but the door-bell rung, and he let go my hands."

The next two times when Eliza called at the Albany, Byron was occupied with lawyers, and when she was finally admitted to him there was a great change in his demeanor. She had entered radiantly, but "his voice and manner were chilling—his countenance in general averted, and when I could catch a glimpse of it, freezing to my heart."

On her next visit, three days later, Eliza fancied that his coldness was only assumed. He seemed struggling against his feelings. Once he relented into kindness, but said: "You know how I am situated—and were I to interest myself as I really feel a wish to do, it might do you an injury instead of a service." But he froze up again. As she left, she sighed deeply and, turning at the door, she saw Byron "standing by the fire-place looking after myself with such an expression of passionate love in his countenance as at once astonished and pained me. I hastened away and once at home relieved my heart by shedding tears."

Ten days passed and she heard nothing. In the interim, her mind constantly on him, she had a vision of Miss Milbanke coming to her in a cloud and kneeling in supplication. She could wait no longer. It was the middle of December.

"'Yes, I will go once more just to convince him that he is mistaken and that I am *not in love* with him. . . .'"

She reached his door with foreboding, and Byron confirmed her worst fears:

"Oh! about the Letter to Devonshire . . . I have considered the matter, and I think I had better not appear in it." He advised her to call herself on the Duke, or have her father call. Her voice nearly broke as she confessed it was her farewell visit. She was shocked still further by his reply.

"'Be it so—perhaps it is as well!'—I looked surprised at his ejaculation—he then took my hand and added—'perhaps had we met much oftener, our adventure might have ended as most such adventures do—. . . .'

"'I did not think there was any *danger*,' I replied timidly.

"'Danger!' reechoed Lord Byron, in a tone of pique—'no, *you* were in no danger—the danger was for me.'" But then he apologized for his coldness.

"I now made an effort to go away," Eliza recalled, "but my tremor increased—I reeled, and had he not promptly extended his arm, I should have fallen at his feet. . . .

"When I recovered myself a little, I tried to withdraw from the arm which supported me but he still detained me, and as I could hardly stand I was glad to remain with his other arm around my waist, while he held my hand."

When she confessed that she had written a reply to some verses attacking him in the *Morning Post,* he gave a start, but pressed her to him.

"Somehow though he always said *never* defend me, he looked rather pleased, and as I stood with my head bent down, he lightly put aside some little curls which had escaped from under my cap behind, and kissed my neck—this completely roused me and I struggled to free my hand, but he then clasped me to his bosom with an ardour which terrified me. . . .

" 'Let me go my Lord! you never behaved thus before.' I exclaimed.

" 'Well—but—but—you are not angry with me?' said he anxiously.

" 'Oh! no—I am more angry with myself—let me go!' I said again, alarmed. . . .

" 'Don't tremble, don't be frightened you are safe—with *me* you are safe,' said he impetuously, and throwing himself into an arm-chair he drew me towards him—for a moment I clung to him—I loved for the first time and this must be my final parting with this transcendent Being. . . . he had drawn me down upon his knee, his arms were round my waist, and I could not escape —clasping me tightly he said—'So then, *you hate me*—'

" 'Yes,' replied I, for I knew he meant not hate.

" 'Thank you, that is kind,' [he said.] I answered by a smile which probably did not express *hatred*—for he kissed my cheek with impetuosity, and was about to kiss my lips. . . . I started up, saying, "I will go now,' but he clasped me to his bosom with frenzied violence while his passionate looks showed what his feelings were. But he was recalled to his senses by a few gentle words. . . . He opened wide his arms—'Go then,' he said, 'not for the world would I distress you.' I extended my hand in silence. 'Will you not come again,' he said.

" 'No, oh, no. I must not.'

"—'Are you sure you will not. You are right—but do come, *yet you are very right.*'

"I advanced towards the door, however his voice arrested me—'Stay,' he said in a tone which betrayed his emotion. 'Stay a moment, Eliza—have you all your papers?'—'I did not bring any to-day'—replied I—Lord Byron had now approached me, and folding me in his arms he said in a hurried manner, 'Then you will not come again—yes do—I want you to come and talk to me. Then your father is to call at the Duke's, you will not go yourself.' A negative even more strongly pronounced than my refusal to come again, was my reply—he released me and I reached the door—but I turned to gaze once more at that Being I was resigning for ever and he stood near with a countenance so expressive of grief that I again flung myself into his open arms. 'Then your father is to go to Devonshire'—'Yes—oh—yes'—another wild embrace, and with a desperate effort I tore myself for ever from the truly noble Lord Byron." [n]

At the moment of this touching farewell, Byron was waiting for a special license, for which he had applied to the Archbishop of Canterbury. "I prefer it," he told Annabella, "because we can be married at any hour in any place without fuss or publicity." [n] Annabella hid as well as she could her growing feeling that the pretext of business was not the real reason for Byron's lingering in town. And what he told her of his activities could not have made her too easy. On the 7th he had written: "Moore is in town. I was so glad to see him again that I am afraid I was rather too 'exquisite in my drinking' at dinner yesterday—for I find my head in a whirlwind and my fingers bitten by the abominable parrot this morning." [n]

Then came the announcement that Claughton could not purchase Newstead, and Byron too readily put the question to Annabella whether they should postpone the wedding. "Well—'to marry or not' that's the question—or will you wait? . . . Do as you please." [n] Thinking to amuse him and to suggest the eagerness of her neighbors for the event, she had written that in near-by Sunderland bells were rung in their honor in the belief that the wedding had already taken place. Byron replied rather testily: "I must needs say that your bells are in a pestilent hurry. . . . I am very glad that I was out of hearing—deuce take them." [n]

Augusta, the dear "Goose," had to remind him of the bells too, but then she reminded him of much else that was more pleasant. One of her talkative visitors, she wrote, had "found out a likeness in your picture to Mignonne [8] who is of course very good humoured in consequence + I want to know dearest B + your plans—when you come + when you go—umph! when the writings travel—when ye Cake is to be cut—when the Bells are to ring &c. &c. &c.—by the bye my visitors are acquainted with *a* & did praise her to the skies—They say her health has been hurt by *studying.* . . ." [9]

How easy and casual this was, compared to Annabella's tortured letters. Byron's announcement to his fiancée that he hoped to come "this week *or the next*" was too much for her. She must speak out for the sake of her parents at least. And she would not be put off by his suggestion that until Newstead was sold they would be very poor. "Let us marry then as soon as the writings are done, and we will disperse 'the clouds.' I feel nothing but sunshine in the thought of being thine—thy wife. . . . You still leave your own wishes in sublime mystery. . . . if you won't, I must take the responsibility of speaking plain—only—don't let me marry you against your will. If assured that I shall not, I desire with all my heart to give myself to you." [n]

It was not until the 18th that he announced a date of departure, the following Saturday, December 24. But this was dampened by the possibility that he might have to be a witness in the Lord Portsmouth lunatic trial. He tried to soothe her: "Dearest—all my anxieties have been principally on your account —but if you are satisfied it is enough. I shall have you and Hope —which are as much as mortal man can require." [n]

On the 22nd, Byron wrote her that he had been to Doctors' Commons for the license, "swearing my way to you," and expressed no more than a hope that he would set out on Saturday.

---

[8] Lord Lovelace (*Astarte*, p. 37 n.) gives a letter of Lady Byron to Mrs. Villiers, March 6, 1817, as authority for this note: "Mignonne or Mignon was Byron and Augusta's pet name for Medora, then a few months old. About the end of 1816 or beginning of 1817, the name of Medora was altogether disused, and her other name of Elizabeth or Libby solely employed. . . . Lord Byron was godfather."

[9] *Astarte*, pp. 37–8. This letter, one of the few of Augusta's to Byron that have been preserved, was signed with the peculiar circular scrawl which they used in letters to each other.

In lieu of the eager phrases of a lover Annabella received only
this: "I have your letter sans date—with doubts in itself, and
questions in the postscript. . . ." " And to her suggestion that
they talk things over after he arrived, Byron replied bluntly the
next day: "If we meet let it be to marry. Had I remained at S. it
had probably been over by this time. With regard to our being
under the same roof and *not* married—I think past experience
has shown us the awkwardness of that situation. I can conceive
nothing above purgatory more uncomfortable. If a postponement
is determined upon, it had better have been decided at a distance. I shall however set out tomorrow, but stop one day at
Newmarket.

"Hobhouse, I believe, accompanies me—which I rejoice at;
for if we don't marry, I should not like a 2d journey back quite
alone, and remaining at S. might only revive a scene like the
former—and to that I confess myself unequal." "

What an unhappy Christmas it must have been at Seaham!
Annabella, and still more her parents, had counted on having
him there for that festival. There was the wedding cake growing
stale, the noble effort of Sir Ralph at an epithalamium wasting
in his desk, Lady Milbanke's plans and hopes shattered, Annabella guarding within herself the secret of her disappointment,
refusing to let either her parents or herself look full-face at her
heart's misgivings.

On the 24th, Hobhouse came up to London from his father's
house at Whitton, and at noon he set out with the reluctant
bridegroom on what Hobhouse called "his matrimonial scheme." "
They parted at Chesterford, Hobhouse going on to Cambridge
and Byron to Six Mile Bottom. It was not a very happy Christmas
there either, for Colonel Leigh was at home and Byron felt
restrained. He could play with the children, but his sister had to
divide her time with a sick and complaining husband. Freezing
weather prevented them from going out of the house. On
Christmas Day he wrote Annabella a letter filled with comfortless
facetiousness: "I am thus far on my way and as warm as Love
can make one with the thermometer below God knows what." "

Byron did not leave until late the next day. While he was at
Six Mile Bottom he wrote another letter withdrawing from the

engagement, but Augusta persuaded him not to send it.[1] He left in a most melancholy mood, and did not pick Hobhouse up in Cambridge until three in the afternoon. They went only as far as Wansford. Hobhouse recorded in his diary that night: "Never was lover less in haste." [n]

They set out at noon the next day, the weather bitterly cold. Hobhouse later recalled that the ground was covered with snow when they arrived at Newark (their second day's halt), and ". . . the frost was so biting that the servants could with difficulty support themselves on the box of the carriage. Lord Byron frankly confessed to his companion that he was not in love with his intended bride; but at the same time he said that he felt for her that regard which he believed was the surest guarantee of continued affection and matrimonial felicity. He owned that he had felt considerable repugnance in marrying before his pecuniary affairs were arranged, so as to insure a sufficient income to his wife and himself immediately upon their marriage. . . ." [n] Byron told Hobhouse that he had offered to wait a year or two, considering himself engaged, but Annabella had not wanted to delay.

They were reading with delight the new edition of Gibbon which John Murray had sent Byron just before he left London. Hobhouse that night wrote in his diary: "The bridegroom more and more *less* impatient." [n]

The third night they slept at Ferrybridge, only twenty-seven miles beyond Sheffield, and on the 29th they proceeded only as far as Thirsk, a few miles north of York. That night Hobhouse recorded his friend's feelings toward his fiancée as "indifference, almost aversion." [n]

At eight o'clock in the evening of Friday, December 30, a week after Byron had left London, they finally arrived unannounced. The strain of waiting had been very great upon everyone at Seaham. The travelers were shown to their rooms. Hobhouse came out first. What occurred subsequently is best told in his diary:

---

[1] Mayne: *Lady Byron,* p. 154. According to Miss Mayne, who gives Lady Byron's manuscript Narrative as her authority, Byron told Annabella this during their visit to Six Mile Bottom on their way to London after the wedding, adding to Augusta: "So you see it is all your fault."

"Miss. came to me when alone in the library and with great frankness took me by the hand at once—presently in tottered her father—Miss is rather dowdy looking & wears a long & high dress (as B had observed) though she has excellent feet & ancles —the lower part of her face is bad, the upper expressive but not handsome—yet she gains by inspection. She heard B. coming out of his room—ran to meet him—threw her arms round his neck and burst into tears—she did this not before us—Lady M. was so much agitated that she had gone to her room—our delay the cause—indeed I looked foolish in finding out an excuse for our want of expedition—Miss before us was silent & modest but very sensible & decent and inspiring an interest which it is easy to mistake for love. With me she was frank & open without little airs and affectations—of my friend she seemed doatingly fond, gazing with delight on his bold & animated bust—regulated however with the most entire decorum.

"B. loves her when present and personally as it is easy for those used to such indications to observe. Old Sir R. is an honest red faced spirit a little prosy but by no means devoid of humour. My lady who has been a dasher in her day & has ridden the grey mare is pettish & tiresome but clever—both are doatingly fond of Miss. There were in the House a family of Mr. Hoare [Hoar] of Durham confidential counsel & agent of Sir R. M. and the Revd Thomas Noel, Rector of Kirkby Mallory and illegitimate son of Lord Wentworth, Miss M's uncle maternal, a brisk parson of the better sort. B. won his heart by his kindness & open manners." [n]

The next day Hobhouse walked by himself on the seashore, reflecting on his friend's fate. "The sight of the water had an indescribable effect upon me—it was a fine sunshiny day—I had some private talk with Hoare & Miss Milbanke on Lord B's affairs & I began to entertain doubts of Hanson's probity." Hobhouse had come to see Miss Milbanke in a new light. "The young woman is most attractive—we had a dinner at 6 and jollified a little upon the signing the settlements . . . I put my name to a deed which is to provide for the younger children of the marriage. . . . I talked and talked in the evening which concluded jollily with a mock marriage, *I* being Lady B., Noel parsonifying & Hoare giving me away. Shook hands for new year."

The 1st of January was a Sunday, and the wedding had been set for the next day. Hobhouse walked on the shore again. The Hoars left, and he recorded: "We had not quite so jolly a dinner as yesterday, but tolerable considering. Byron at night said ['] Well, H. this is our last night—tomorrow I shall be Annabella's['] (absit omen!!)"

Monday morning came, and Byron was up and dressed before Hobhouse, but not in his wedding suit. If we may trust Moore's recollections of the burned Memoirs, ". . . he described himself as waking, on the morning of his marriage, with the most melancholy reflections, on seeing his wedding-suit spread out before him. In the same mood, he wandered about the grounds alone, till he was summoned for the ceremony. . . ."[2]

Hobhouse recorded more details: "I dressed in full dress with white gloves and found Byron up and dressed with Noel in canonicals. Lady M. & Sir R. soon came—also dressed. Her ladyship could not make tea—her hand shook. Miss did not appear—the Rev[d] Wallace came in also in canonicals—at half past ten we parted company. B. & I went in to his room—the others up stairs—in ten minutes we walked up into the drawing room and found kneeling mats disposed for the couple & the others. The two clergymen the father & mother & myself were in waiting when Miss M came in attended by her governess the respectable Mrs. Clermont.[3] She was dressed in a muslin gown trimmed with lace at the bottom with a white muslin *curricle* jacket very plain indeed with nothing on her head." Noel was decent & grave—he put them B & Miss upon their cushions. Lady M. placed Sir R. next to his daughter. I stood next to Sir R. My lady & Mrs. Clermont were rather opposite in the corner. Wallace read the responses. Miss M. was as firm as a rock and during the whole ceremony looked steadily at Byron—she repeated the words audibly & well. B. hitched at first when he said 'I George Gordon' and when he came to 'with all my worldly goods I thee endow' looked at me with a half smile." They were married at eleven."

[2] Moore, I, 599. Years later in Italy, when Byron found Sandys's *Ovid* among Leigh Hunt's books, he exclaimed: "God! what an unpleasant recollection I have of this book! I met with it on my wedding-day; I read it while I was waiting to go to church [sic]." (Hunt: *Lord Byron*, I, 78.)

[3] Mrs. Clermont had been Anabella's nurse and later her governess, and had considerable influence over her by reason of her devotion.

The ring which he placed on her finger was the one found in the garden at Newstead, his mother's wedding ring. The heavy gold band, made for the chubby digit of Mrs. Byron, was too big for the delicate finger of Miss Milbanke." Her mother was on the verge of hysterics, for she had inner misgivings about this son-in-law who would have no proper wedding. She later wrote: "Neither before or *since* Marriage has he made any present to Lady B., not even the *common one* of a diamond Hoop ring. . . ." "

Hobhouse continued: "I shook Lady Byron by the hand after the parson and embraced my friend with unfeigned delight— he was kissed by my lady Milbanke. Lady M. & Mrs. C. were much affected." He did not record whether or in what manner Byron kissed the bride. "Lady B. went out of the room but soon returned to sign the register which Wallace & I witnessed—she again retired hastily her eyes full of tears when she looked at her father and mother—and completed her conquest her innocent conquest. She came in her travelling dress soon after a slate coloured satin pellice trimmed with white fur & sate quietly in the drawing room. Byron was calm and as usual—I felt as if I had buried a friend."

There was no reception. No one has recorded anything of the then stale wedding cake, and Sir Ralph's epithalamium must have remained in his desk. The carriage was already waiting. The bridal couple had forty wintry miles to travel before nightfall. Hobhouse put a complete collection of Byron's poems bound in yellow morocco into the carriage as a wedding gift to Lady Byron. His diary continues: "At a little before twelve I handed Lady B down stairs and into her carriage—when I wished her many years of happiness—she said [']if I am not happy it will be my own fault[']—Of my dearest friend I took a melancholy leave. He was unwilling to leave my hand and I had hold of his out of the window when the carriage drove off."

As Hobhouse drove off a few minutes later, "Lady M. asked me if she had not behaved well—as if she had been the mother of Iphigenia." Hobhouse had one more detail to add: "The little bells of Seaham Church struck up after the wedding and half a dozen fired muskets in front of the house."

CHAPTER XIV

1815

Marriage

THE RIDE to Halnaby was as grim as the winter day. Both Byron and his bride were high-strung, and the excitement had left them emotionally tense. Byron, longing for the warmth of Mediterranean lands, disliked the cold intensely and did not relish the tiresome journey in the jolting carriage to the bleak Yorkshire hall. He had time for reflection on the freedom he had lost, the innocent girl he had married, the settled routine that was expected of him. Annabella, still upset at leaving the home where she had been the adored and spoiled child for so long, was on the edge of tears, sensitive to every nuance of his mood and ready to take offense at the seeming coldness of his self-absorption. With nothing to thaw the ice of their mutual guardedness, the chilling ride increased the irritability of the one and the sensitivity of the other.

Of what really happened in the carriage during that dismal journey we have only the conflicting statements of several witnesses, some of them at second hand. Annabella later said that they rode in silence until Byron, to relieve his feelings, broke out into "a wild sort of singing,"[1] perhaps one of the Albanian songs with which he later startled the Shelleys on Lake Geneva. As the

---

[1] Ethel C. Mayne (*Lady Byron*, p. 159 ff.) gives a running account with quotations supposedly from Lady Byron's own Narratives among the Lovelace papers, but unfortunately she has interwoven with this a good many details and quotations from secondary and less reliable sources without specific references to distinguish them.

carriage clattered into Durham, where they had been awaited, bells rang out for the wedding day of Miss Milbanke. Byron, who had been annoyed before by the bells that rang prematurely for the event, said ironically: "Ringing for our happiness, I suppose?" ⁿ As they proceeded on their way he turned on her ferociously: "It *must* come to a separation! You should have married me when I first proposed." ²

When they came to the inn at Rusheyford he said: "I wonder how much longer I shall be able to keep up the part I have been playing!" ⁿ Then, exasperated by her silence perhaps, he went on to say how he detested her mother, how discontented he was with the settlements, "speaking of me," Annabella wrote, "as if I were a beggar." ⁿ He added that he had longed to break off the engagement but was told that as a man of honor he must fulfill it. He had done so and now she was in his power, "and I shall make you feel it." ⁿ

This was Lady Byron's recollection of the events and conversation, as recorded by herself and by others in whom she confided. But, countering a story that was apparently common gossip after the separation, Byron told Medwin: "I have been accused of saying, on getting into the carriage, that I had married Lady Byron out of spite, and because she had refused me twice. Though I was for a moment vexed at her prudery, or whatever you may choose to call it [a reference to her having taken her lady's-maid into the carriage with them], if I had made so uncavalier, not to say brutal a speech, I am convinced Lady Byron would instantly have left the carriage to me and the maid (I mean the lady's). She had spirit enough to have done so, and would properly have resented the affront." ⁿ

Why should the tensions of a cold wedding-day ride that

---

² Mayne: *Lady Byron*, p. 160. Presumably this is quoted from Lady Byron's reminiscences among the Lovelace papers, though Miss Mayne does not say so specifically. Lady Byron in later years told Henry Crabb Robinson the same thing. (Robinson, II, 746.) There are more details of the conversation in the carriage in the *ricordi*, or private family memoirs, of Lady Anne Barnard, quoted by Lord Lindsay in a letter to *The Times* (London), Sept. 7, 1869. (Reprinted in Stowe: *Lady Byron Vindicated*, p. 305.) It should be remembered that this is third-hand evidence, and obvious errors in it should be sufficient warning to take it with some reservations.

provoked them to resentful speeches have spoiled the honeymoon
of Byron more than that of another? The resilience of lovers
who quarrel was not less then than now. Byron knew how to
please, and when he did not brood on the trap he conceived
himself to have fallen into he found his bride not unattractive.
It was not all unpleasantness. Annabella, of course, remembered
the bitter part later and brooded on it, as did Byron, but she
confessed to Lady Anne Barnard: "He laughed it over when he
saw me appear hurt: and I forgot what had passed, till forced
to remember it. I believe he was pleased with me, too, for a little
while. I suppose it had escaped his memory that I was his wife." [n]
Byron, on his side, told Medwin: "Our honeymoon was not all
sunshine; it had its clouds . . . but it was never down at zero." [n]

It was long after dark when the weary pair arrived at Halnaby
Hall. The old butler who received them recalled Lady Byron's
"attitude of despair when she alighted from the carriage on the
afternoon of her marriage-day." Traces of tears on her cheeks
won his sympathy. "The bridegroom jumped out of the carriage
and walked away. The bride alighted, and came up the steps
alone, with a countenance and frame agonized and listless with
evident horror and despair." [n]

Mrs. Minns, who had been Annabella's maid for ten years and
had consented to come back and serve her again during the
temporary stay at Halnaby, gave quite a different picture. She
too saw them alight from the carriage, and she said that "Lady
Byron was as buoyant and cheerful as a bride should be, and
kindly and gaily responded to the greetings of welcome which
poured upon her." [n]

Even these two contradictory accounts may each have some
truth in them. Byron was sensitive about his lame foot and
would not make a spectacle of himself before a group of curious
servants. And no doubt Annabella was on the threshold of tears
from the excitement of the wedding and the long ride, but she
had the strength to respond to the welcoming servants and ten-
ants.

Mrs. Minns presently led them upstairs to their connecting
rooms. They were not the largest bedrooms in the house and
they faced north, but they were perhaps cozier in winter than

the more commodious ones, and coal fires had been started. One
of the fourposter beds was curtained with red moreen.[n]

Byron must have soothed his bride's feelings by the silent
method he had learned was most effective during his first visit
to Seaham, for Moore later told Hobhouse that Byron had recorded in his Memoirs how he "*had* Lady B. on the sofa before
dinner on the day of their marriage."[n]

Dinner and wine helped the evening to pass, and Byron was
pleased by a glimpse of the library, which was snug and faced
south.[n] But he again became bitter and resentful. Perhaps it was
because he was overcome with his old aversion to seeing a woman
eat and with the prospect of facing the silent Annabella alone
in the empty house. It had begun to snow during their long
drive, and Byron was not made more amiable by the fact that
he had caught a cold.[n] He taunted her with the thought that he
would be to her as Caroline Lamb was to her husband's heart,
"a perpetually falling drop of water. It ruins and petrifies."[3]

Alone again after dinner, Byron asked his wife "with every
appearance of aversion" whether she intended to sleep in the
same bed with him. "I hate sleeping with any woman, but you
may if you choose."[n] And he added that, provided a woman
was young, one was as good as another. Again she must have
been convinced that it was a bad jest, or he must have repented
and with the charm he knew how to command persuaded her
that his irritation was only a passing mood, for they retired at
last within the crimson curtains. Roused from his first sleep and
seeing the firelight shining through the red cloth, he thought
while looking at his wife "that he was fairly in hell with Proserpine
lying beside him!"[n] Byron confessed to Hobhouse after the separation that on that first night he had been seized with a sudden
fit of melancholy and had left his bed.[n]

When Byron finally went back behind the red curtains he
stayed until near noon. Annabella crept downstairs to await his

---

[3] Maurois: *Byron*, p. 224. Maurois, like Miss Mayne, had an opportunity to
read Lady Byron's journal, which he calls "a moving piece of writing, with
the ring of truth in it." He quoted a few passages from it not given by Miss
Mayne, but, like her, he has not indicated when he is quoting from other
sources.

coming. She later confessed that it was then that "perhaps the deadliest chill fell on my heart." He awoke to look out on the open park covered with snow and the pond frozen over. When he hobbled down to the library, Annabella came to him. "He met me repellently, and uttered words of blighting irony: 'It is too late now. It is done, and cannot be undone.' I told him I did not repent, and tried to inspire a hope which was almost extinguished in my own heart." [n]

But he grew animated when he was handed a letter from Augusta. Annabella noted that "it affected him strangely—and excited a kind of fierce and exulting transport. He read to me the expression, 'Dearest, first and best of human beings,' and then said with suspicious inquisitiveness, 'There—what do you think of that?' " [n] Then he read aloud Augusta's description of her emotion and agitation at the hour of his wedding: "As the sea trembles when the earth quakes." [n] Annabella did not know what to think of it; she no doubt supposed that he was merely trying to arouse her jealousy.

But Annabella was in love with Byron, and she forgave him readily when he was kind to her. What frightened her was that his moods changed so unpredictably and so rapidly, and she seemed unaware that her own primness and impeccable system often maddened him. When she relaxed and was no longer the infallible Miss Milbanke, they had moments of pleasure as poignant as those which had pained her. They read together in the library. He became playful and called her "Pippin" because of her round and rosy face. And in return she called him "Dear Duck," an endearment perhaps suggested by "Goose," his pet name for Augusta.[n] Byron was probably not aware how much his melancholy and savage moods frightened his bride. A good deal of the time he found her a pleasant and intelligent companion and felt that they were getting on admirably.

This first day at Halnaby he wrote in a facetious but amiable style to Lady Melbourne: "You would think we had been married these 50 years. Bell is fast asleep on a corner of the sopha, and I am keeping myself awake with this epistle—she desires her love, and mine you have had ever since we were acquainted." [n]

And on the 7th he wrote again: "Bell and I go on extremely

well so far, without any other company than our own selves. . . .
I have great hopes this match will turn out well. I have found
nothing as yet that I could wish changed for the better; but
time does wonders, so I won't be too hasty in my happiness."
And he added in a postscript, lest she should be too guarded in
her reply: "Lady Byron sends her love, but has not seen this
epistle; recollect, *we* are to keep our secrets and correspondence
as heretofore, mind that." [n]

Byron and Annabella spent much of their time in the library,
reading and discussing books, including Scott's *Lord of the Isles,*
which Murray had just sent them.[n] Byron set to work again on
the *Hebrew Melodies,* which he had promised to Isaac Nathan.
The sad bewailing complaints of the Old Testament, which he
had read through and through before his eighth year, struck a
responsive chord in Byron's being. And the Hebraic strain, bound
up with his Calvinistic fatalism, was congenial to his present
mood. Several of the pieces, including "Herod's Lament for
Marianne" and "By the Rivers of Babylon We Sat Down and
Wept," were composed at Halnaby, and Lady Byron, pleased no
doubt that he should turn his talents to Biblical subjects, copied
them out for him in her precise hand.

There is no indication of strain in Byron's genial letters of the
early part of January. On the 10th he wrote to Moore: "I was
married this day week. The parson has pronounced it—Perry
has announced it—and the *Morning Post,* also, under the head
of 'Lord Byron's Marriage'—as if it were a fabrication, or the puff-
direct of a new stay-maker." [n]

Still, there was an undercurrent of touchiness on both sides
that subtly vitiated the relationship of the couple. The ease with
which Annabella could be hurt only accentuated Byron's sense of
guilt in having married her and made him brusque despite himself. His moments of tenderness and calm could not dispel the
anxiety she felt when he had disturbing nightmares and rose
from his bed to roam the gallery armed with dagger and pistol
as if awaiting the attack of some unknown assailant. One night,
Ethel Mayne records, he came back to her "exhausted and
piteously haggard. 'Seeking to allay his misery,' she moved her
head until it rested on his breast. He said, more gently than

usual but with piercing bitterness: 'You should have a softer
pillow than my heart.'

"'I wonder which will break first, yours or mine,' she answered   √
—in 'the only words of despair he ever heard me utter.'" [n]

Writing of this period later, Lady Byron said: "At Halnaby
that which at the moment seemed to prevail with him occasioned
him to say—as he has often said—that if I had married him two
years before, I should have spared him that for which he could
never forgive himself. He said he could tell it me but it was
another person's secret. I asked, most innocently of any intention
to discover what had only once for a few minutes entered my
mind, if——[Augusta] knew it. He appeared terrified and
agitated, and said, 'O, for God's sake don't ask her.'" [n] Seeing
the desperation of his mood, she dropped the subject, but he
could not. Like a man irresistibly drawn to the brink of a precipice, he constantly hinted at the thing that obsessed him.

One day not long after their arrival at Halnaby she innocently
asked him a question while reading *Don Sebastian*, Dryden's
tragedy which revolves about a theme of unwitting incest. His
first impulse was to suppose the question designed to draw out
his secret, and he said angrily: "Where did you hear that?" She
recalled later: "I looked up and saw that he was holding over
me the dagger which he usually wore. I replied, 'Oh, only from
this book.' I was not afraid—I was persuaded he only did it to
terrify me. He put the dagger down and said . . . 'If anything
could make me believe in heaven, it is the expression of your
countenance at this moment.'" [n]

From that time forward she went in continual fear that he
would suppose she was trying to pry into his secrets, and yet
she knew not what subjects to avoid.[n] Still, she recalled, "the
intensity of his sufferings absorbed my feelings in his, almost
to self-forgetfulness." [n] His wild speeches and his hovering over
the forbidden topic could not but arouse suspicions which she
fought against.[4]

Annabella brooded over his words spoken in ill-humor:

[4] It was about this time that Byron began *Parisina*, his poem based on an
account in Gibbon of a fifteenth-century tragedy of incest. (*Poetry*, III, 443,
503.)

"I was a villain to marry you. I could convince you of it in three words."

"I only want a woman to laugh, and don't care what she is besides. I can make Augusta laugh at anything. No one makes me happy but Augusta." [5]

She attempted to win him by devotion and sacrifice. That maddened him the more, she recorded, and he tried to assault her impeccable virtue by acquainting her with his own past crimes. She later affirmed that he told her he had attempted to seduce Lady Oxford's twelve-year-old daughter, the Ianthe of *Childe Harold*.[n] He urged her, she wrote, to say that she would condone his unfaithfulness,[n] and he was enraged because she kept a calm temper through it all. He wanted to terrify her into "running back to your father like the spoiled child you are." [n]

Occasionally Annabella assumed some cheerfulness and softened him so that he talked familiarly of his "little foot," saying pathetically that some allowance must be made to him on the Judgment Day, for he had often wished to revenge himself on Heaven for it.[6] She learned to play up to his petty vanities such as his alarm at a gray hair or a blemished tooth.

But she felt the utter misery of her position and could not refrain from confessing everything to Mrs. Minns, the maid who had cared for her in childhood. In the empty house, when Byron shut himself off to reflect or compose, she had no one else to turn to. He sometimes sent her out of the room, saying: "I don't want you. I hope we are not always to be together—that won't do for me, I assure you." [n]

Mrs. Minns was so alarmed by the savagery of Byron's treat-

[5] Mayne: *Lady Byron*, p. 165. It is well to remember, however, that Lady Byron's recollections of her husband's words were recorded after the separation. It is possible that Annabella preserved Byron's words without concern for the tone and the circumstances of their utterance.

[6] Mayne: *Lady Byron*, p. 167. Lord Lovelace recorded that Lady Byron wrote, while living with her husband: "He has horror of being observed by any eye to which he is not accustomed, and in the country when I forced him to walk with me, he would turn pale & tremble if he were to pass any one on the road—and hide himself if possible—if not he would stand still till the person was gone—or run past him." (Marginal note in the proof sheets of Byron's *Poetry* [Murray MSS.] opposite "I would I were a careless child.")

ment of his spouse that she strongly recommended her young mistress to confide everything to her father and then take his advice as to her future conduct." Under the stress of her emotion Annabella apparently contemplated returning to her parents, but in her calmer moments she repented. And she made Mrs. Minns promise never to breathe a word on the subject." Annabella determined with sheer force of will not to believe his gross insinuations. But there was something of the martyr in her resolution to stick by her firm principles and be a friend to her husband even though she was unloved—something that maddened him the more and drove out even the pity he sometimes felt for her. "Poor thing!" he would say while the tears welled in his eyes, but her clearly evidenced resolute aim of saving him from himself drove him frantic. She saw it, but was unable to avoid irritating him. She said later: "If he had not felt, I might have hoped to move him. But he pitied, and was inexorable." "

All his suppressed resentments of her prudish and didactic attitudes before their marriage surged up to choke him with rage. One night he brought out her letters written before and during the engagement, reading passages that now particularly disturbed him. He reproached her again for delaying to accept him, and his anger was so great that she feared he might strike her.

Thinking back on that rueful time, Annabella later felt that his remorse was largely due to his unhappy religion of fear. Sometimes he would attempt to prove to her that there was no truth in religion or morality, ending with the challenge: "Now convert me!" She evaded a direct reply, trying to convince him by her own Christian conduct, which only made him more bitter. Voltairean skepticism, which before marriage she had believed was the source of his Satanic pose, she now saw influenced only the surface of his intelligence; whereas deeply ingrained in his unconscious mind a gloomy Calvinism made him feel that the majority of men and himself in particular had the mark of Cain on them and were slated for damnation. After exhausting his powers of reason, wit, and ridicule in trying to refute the arguments of religion, he would often say with violence: "The worst of it is, I *do believe*." "

As Byron recognized later with bitterness, she could analyze his weaknesses very well, but that did not help to make their relationship any smoother. For with all her sagacity she lacked the intuitive perceptions of a more frivolous woman like Augusta. She was eager to please and studied his every word and mood with a searching intensity. And sometimes he would say, half in exasperation and half in pity: "If you wouldn't mind my words, we shall get on very well together." [n] When he saw that she took everything literally he played up to her credulity, occasionally in deviltry and often in desperation. He would declare that he was a fallen angel and that she had married an exile from heaven, or that he was driven by an invincible force of evil and would, like Zeluco, end by strangling their child.[n] Or he would try to persuade her that he was mad. Referring to her list of qualities for a husband, which Lady Melbourne had shown him, he said: "You were determined that you would not marry a man in whose family there was derangement. You have done very well indeed —my maternal grandfather shot himself, a cousin on the Gordon side was insane and set fire to a house." [n]

Instead of laughing at his superstitions, she let him see that she was shocked, and he dramatized them the more. Before she married him she had thought him a skeptic; now she discovered that he believed in omens. It was dangerous to wear a black gown; he never started anything on Friday; the future, he felt, was governed by portents. Annabella had wound a black ribbon around the too large wedding ring he had given her to make it stay in place. But when Byron saw this he exclaimed: "A black ribbon!" and urged her to remove it. It was an evil omen. And when, as she was standing near the mantel a few minutes later, the ring dropped from her finger into the fire, he was upset and did not regain his equanimity for hours.[n]

The maddening procrastinations of Hanson in the sale of New-stead and the prosecution of the Rochdale business caused distractions enough to ruffle the temper and disturb the tranquillity of a more sanguine honeymooner than Byron. Hobhouse, to whom Byron had communicated the whole story of the vagaries and delays of Hanson, had strongly advised putting a competent barrister in charge of his concerns, with authority to look into

Hanson's accounts and the conduct of Byron's business, and had promised to look for one as soon as he returned to London. In the meantime, Byron had written once more to urge Hanson to dispose of Newstead.

Just before leaving Halnaby, Byron wrote again to Moore in an exuberant humor: "So, you want to know about milady and me? But let me not, as Roderick Random says, 'profane the chaste mysteries of Hymen.' . . . I like Bell as well as you do (or did, you villain!) Bessy—and that is (or was) saying a great deal." He was frank to confess, however, that he did not look forward with pleasure to more evenings with Sir Ralph and Lady Milbanke. "Address your next to Seaham, Stockton-on-Tees," he continued, "where we are going on Saturday (a bore, by the way,) to see father-in-law, Sir Jacob, and my lady's lady-mother." [n]

Annabella was rather relieved when the decision was made to return to Seaham after less than three weeks at Halnaby. Her ostensible reason for their leaving so soon was that her parents wished him to spend his birthday (January 22) with them. They had intended to leave on the 20th, but when Byron discovered that the day fell on a Friday he flatly refused to start until the next day. [n] Seeing Annabella's faint smile, he stated in what seemed to her complete seriousness that Friday was the Moham- medan sabbath, which he observed. But when they finally left on Saturday, the 21st, he was in a good enough humor, believing that he was getting on as well as could be expected with a wife. Looking across at her, he said: "I think you now know pretty well what subjects to avoid." [n]

Annabella was glad to be home again, and they both relaxed somewhat from the tensions of the first days of their new relation- ship. She was no longer forced to be alone with him on what she later referred to as his "black days," and he could sometimes forget that she was his wife and consider her an ally against the greater boredom of her parents and the routine of Seaham. Not that he was openly lacking in respect to the old people. In fact, he had a kind of Spanish punctilio when he was in a reasonably pleasant humor which had quite won them and their guests.

On his birthday he wrote Lady Melbourne: "Mine Aunt,—

This day completes my 27th year of existence, and (save a day) my 'three weeks after marriage.' I am four years and three months older than Bell, who will be twenty-three on May 27th.[n] I suppose this is a fair disproportion.

"Yesterday I came here somewhat anent my imperial will. But never mind, you know I am a very good-natured fellow, and the more easily governed because I am not ashamed of being so; and so Bell has her own way and no doubt means to keep it. . . ." [n]

Byron settled into a routine easily enough, even when he was bored with it, but there is adequate evidence that he was not bored with Annabella. In fact, he was growing rather fond of her, and she was beginning to feel it. It was their situation that galled him on occasion, the interminable ennui of the evenings in the drawing-room, with Sir Ralph repeating his jokes and his speeches, and the thought of his being married, of having given up the bachelor freedom which had spiced his evenings in London with Kinnaird, or Moore, or Hobhouse.

After a few days he wrote to Moore: ". . . the treaclemoon is over, and I am awake, and find myself married. My spouse and I agree to—and in—admiration. Swift says 'no *wise* man ever married;' but, for a fool, I think it the most ambrosial of all possible future states. I still think one ought to marry upon *lease;* but am very sure I should renew mine at the expiration, though next term were for ninety and nine years." But then nostalgia for the world he had lost surged up. "Pray tell me what is going on in the way of intriguery, and how the w——s and rogues of the upper Beggar's Opera go on—or rather go off. . . ." [n]

To Hobhouse, who was trying to prod Hanson and get some action in Byron's affairs, and who had ventured to mention the "expectations" of property from his marriage, he wrote: ". . . don't talk to me of 'expects,'. . . the Baronet is eternal, the Viscount immortal, and my Lady (*senior*) without end. They grow more healthy every day, and I verily believe Sir R[alph] L[ad]y M[ilbanke], and Lord We[ntworth] are at this moment cutting a fresh set of teeth. . . ." [n]

In this environment Byron found some pleasure in being alone occasionally with his wife. During a walk by the seashore, as they approached a great rock known as the Feather-bed, he challenged her to climb it as quickly as he could, and scrambled up ahead of her with boyish dexterity, for when he could run he was never self-conscious about his lameness.[n] He took pleasure also in his favorite pastime of pistol-shooting, and one day, to the amazement and discomfiture of Lady Milbanke, split a walking-stick at a distance of twenty paces in the garden.[n]

Sometimes, Annabella recalled, "but very rarely," he showed a tender gratitude to her for small favors—for handing him a book, or getting up in the night to bring him lemonade. She treasured his words on such an occasion: "You are a good kind Pip—a good-natured Pip—the best wife in the world." And she felt sorry for him in his harsher moods. "He inflicted misery, but I felt that he suffered more than he inflicted." Of all his humors during this second, and for her in many ways more happy, honeymoon, she remembered with most pleasure his "child-side": "He would then speak of himself, as little children do, in the third person, as 'B,' and forget entirely all that belonged to later years . . . but after a few minutes it often happened that some careless word of his own would strike some painful chord, and then the man's mind returned with all its wretchedness. He would say 'B's a fool'—'Yes, he *is* a fool,' bitterly—or 'poor B— poor B.' . . ."[n]

As for the old people, they were still enthusiastic about their newly acquired son-in-law. Lady Milbanke wrote to her brother-in-law, Sir James Burges: "The Byrons returned here last Saturday, and I hope will make some stay with us. They are both well, and as happy as youth and love can make them. He appears to prefer a quiet domestic circle to any other, and neither of them seems in any haste to visit London."[n]

Byron's reports to Lady Melbourne at this time indicate a resigned contentment in his new state. "The *moon* is over," he wrote on February 2; "but Bell and I are as lunatic as heretofore. . . ."[n] The confidante of his bachelor days had enjoined him: "Write to me, *mon cher Neveu, et choisissez mieux votre temps.* [Byron had written his last letter to Lady Melbourne in his dressing-room while Annabella was waiting for him in bed.] I

am inclined to think that gave some *ombrage*, but keep faith
with me, and say nothing." [n]

But while Byron had acquiesced in the routine of family life,
he was disturbed when visitors arrived. It was the interruption
of routine, rather than the routine itself, that was most distasteful to him. Annabella he could now consider his best ally against
the annoying boredom of social life, and she contributed to his
comfort in many ways. On February 6 he reported to Lady Melbourne that, the night before, his dressing-room fire "was so
diabolically pregnant with charcoal, that I was taken almost to
lady-like fainting, and if Bell had not in the nick of time postponed Old Nick for the present, and sluiced me with Eau de
Cologne, and all sorts of waters besides, you might now have
been repairing your latest suit of black to look like new for your
loving nephew. . . . this is in favour of matrimony, for had I
been single, the lack of aid would have left me suffocated." [n]

Annabella remembered some more dramatic aspects of the
episode: "As soon as he recovered his consciousness, the idea
that he was dying presented itself to his imagination, and he
broke forth into the wildest ravings of despair, saying that he
knew he was going to Hell, but that he would defy his Maker
to the last, with other expressions of a revengeful nature. . . .
Afterwards, recovering, he became softened, and said 'I have
tried everything—I will try virtue, I think. Perhaps I shall go to
Heaven, holding by the hem of your garment.'" [n]

Annabella put the fairest face she could on their life together
in her letters to Augusta. And Augusta's description, for Francis
Hodgson, of the situation at Seaham mingled anxiety and op-
timism: ". . . I really hope *most confidently* that all will turn
out very happily. It appears to me that Lady B. *sets about*
making him happy quite in the right way. It is true I judge at a
distance, and we generally *hope* as we *wish*, but I . . . will own
to you, what I would not scarcely to any other person, that I
HAD *many fears* and much anxiety founded upon many causes
and circumstances of which I cannot *write*." [n]

Augusta wrote sisterly and encouraging letters to Annabella
in which, as Miss Mayne indicates, may be seen here and there

a hint of malice: "I am so glad he is spoiled at Seaham, because he would have it no one could spoil him but *me*." ⁿ

Certainly Annabella could not forget that Byron had a peculiar sensitivity concerning his sister. One of their amusements in the long evenings was writing *bouts-rimés*. Some accidental coincidence in the verses caused Byron to say: "You must send those to Guss." But when she said she would distinguish his from hers by crosses, he turned pale and exclaimed: "For God's sake don't—it would frighten her to death!" ⁷

One of the reasons for Byron's irascibility during his marriage, as he later told Lady Blessington,ⁿ was that he was constantly bothered by money difficulties. This was true from the very beginning, for while he was marking time in Seaham he felt that, despite the best efforts of Hobhouse, his affairs were being neglected in London. Soon after the return from Halnaby he had written to Hobhouse: "My debts can hardly be less than thirty thousand: there is *six* thousand charged on N. to a Mr. Sawbridge; ⁿ a *thousand* to Mrs. B. at Nott[ingha]m; a *Jew debt*, of which the interest must be more than the principal, and of which H. must get an account from *Thomas;* another Jew debt, six hundred prin[cipa]l and no interest (as I have kept that down), to a man in New Street—I forget his name, but shall know on half year's day,—a good deal still before majority . . . a good deal of tradesmen, &c, &c."ⁿ

"You know I have paid off *Scrope;* that is £6000 and more; nearly £3000 to *Hans* [Hanson?] carnal; then I lent rather more than £1600 to Hodgson, £1000 to 'bold' Webster, and nearly £3000 to George L[eigh], or rather Augusta. The *last* sum I never *wish* to see again, and the others I *may wish*. I have W's bond, which is worth a damn or two, but from Hodg. I neither asked nor wanted security. . . .

"I think I have now accounted for a good deal of Clau.'s disbursements; the rest was swallowed up by duns, necessities, luxuries, fooleries, jewelleries, 'whores, and fidlers.' " ⁿ

---

⁷ Maurois, p. 231. Ethel Mayne quoted the same passage, but with the addition, after four dots, of "I never wrote anything about *love* to Guss." (Mayne: *Lady Byron*, p. 171.)

Hobhouse had been doing his best to find a suitable barrister to look into Hanson's accounts, but it was well into February before the services of Benjamin Winthrop, an outstanding lawyer recommended by Sir John Nichol and well thought of by Sir Samuel Romilly, were secured.[n] In the meantime, Byron was growing increasingly restive. Until something was done about his business affairs he was stranded in the country; in fact, the couple did not feel that they could establish themselves in London until some decisive steps were taken to clear away debts, for they had only Lady Byron's small income to live upon.

In these circumstances, Byron was susceptible to any thoughts that offered escape from the present quandary. And still he contemplated escape to the sunny south. On February 10 he wrote to Moore: "By the way, don't engage yourself in any travelling expedition, as I have a plan of travel into Italy, which we will discuss. . . . If I take my wife, you can take yours; and if I leave mine, you may do the same."[n]

His boredom at Seaham grew measurably as the weeks passed. He wrote Moore on March 2: "I am in such a state of sameness and stagnation, and so totally occupied in consuming the fruits —and sauntering—and playing dull games at cards—and yawning—and trying to read old Annual Registers and the daily papers—and gathering shells on the shore—and watching the growth of stunted gooseberry bushes in the garden—that I have neither time nor sense to say more. . . ."[n] But there is no suggestion in any of Byron's correspondence that Annabella had ceased to please him, and there is much to indicate that, except in moments of irritation, he was growing to like her more and to feel a relative contentment in his married state.

The desire to get away from Seaham, however, and the anxiety about his business affairs finally made Byron feel that going up to London was imperative, though he would have preferred to go with money in his pocket and his debts cleared away. He wrote to Hobhouse on February 28: "I shall set off from this place on Monday next at furthest—and *solus*—any letters after that you had best address to Six Mile Bottom, Newmarket, & if I come up to London, you will perhaps give me a bed and a book at Whitton."[n]

But Annabella would not consent to his going alone, and he flew into a violent rage." Apparently he calmed down, however, and acquiesced in her desire to accompany him. While Hobhouse was negotiating for the lease of the London house of the Duchess of Devonshire for his friend," Byron and his bride decided to visit Augusta on their way to town. On the eve of their departure Byron wrote genially to Moore: "Bell is in health, and unvaried good-humour and behaviour. But we are all in the agonies of packing and parting; and, I suppose, by this time tomorrow I shall be stuck in the chariot with my chin upon a bandbox. I have prepared, however, another carriage for the abigail, and all the trumpery which our wives drag along with them." "

In spite of his ups and downs, he had grown fonder of Annabella than he would generally admit; one night before they left he told her: "I think I love you." " His earlier determination to go alone to Six Mile Bottom and to London had probably not been motivated by a desire to leave his wife, but only by a feeling of trepidation about her meeting with Augusta and a desire to get the business settled in London before establishing a residence there.

As they were getting into the carriage on the 9th, Lady Milbanke called out to him: "Take care of Annabella." " At this he took sudden umbrage, possibly more at his mother-in-law than at Annabella, though she bore the brunt of his ill-humor as they drove away. "What on earth does your mother mean," he exclaimed, "by telling me to take care of you? I suppose you can take care of yourself? I didn't want you. . . ." "

Byron's ill-temper did not subside for some time, but Annabella had learned something of his moods, and instead of cowering in the carriage as she had done on the ride to Halnaby, she managed, before the journey was over (they did not arrive at Six Mile Bottom until the 12th), "to get him 'less disagreeable,' as Augusta would say." " She could even laugh at the explanation he gave for his irritability as he began to calm down: "I feel as if I were just going to be married." "

At Wansford, the night before their arrival, "He spoke the kindest words I could ever have wished to hear." He said: "You married me to make me happy, didn't you?" When she agreed, he continued, speaking with "passionate affection": "Well then, you do make me happy." "Then again," Annabella recalled, "he seemed to pity me for some impending, inevitable misery." [n]

That misery came in full measure during the visit at Six Mile Bottom, which Annabella was to remember with acute anguish through the rest of her life. No one was there to greet them when they arrived, and Byron said: "You stay in the carriage; I will go in and prepare Guss." But, not finding Augusta downstairs, he returned soon "in great perturbation" to escort his wife into the house. They waited, Annabella observing everything with a su-persensitive eye while Byron read his mail. As Augusta de-cended the stairs, the two women met for the first time (they had seen each other at a party in 1813 but had not been intro-duced). Both were no doubt keyed up to the occasion, each ob-serving the other with the intensest curiosity and watchfulness. Augusta, with her high Byronic forehead, silky dark-brown hair, large brown eyes set in a Grecian countenance, and soft, ample figure, displayed a self-conscious shyness but did not conceal her easygoing kindly disposition. She greeted Annabella with cordiality but did not kiss her. Annabella and Byron both no-ticed that. When Augusta turned to greet her brother, she ob-served that he was in one of his blackest humors. Annabella re-corded that "He accounted for it by a letter about Newstead which he had just opened." [8]

That night and every night of their stay was a nightmare for Annabella. Byron insisted on staying up with Augusta after his wife had gone to bed. If she lingered, he would take savage de-light in insulting her into retiring. "We don't want *you*, my charmer." [n]

There is no evidence of any intimate relationship with his sis-ter at this time, for his cruelty turned upon Augusta as well. In the morning he would greet "Guss" with such pointed allusions to her "inflammable temperament," and so on, as, in Annabella's

[8] Mayne: *Lady Byron,* p. 175. Almost all the details of this visit to Six Mile Bottom come from Lady Byron's later accounts, from which Miss Mayne has quoted. While allowances must be made for Annabella's tendency to read literalness into Byron's peevish words, there is no reason to doubt her record of the impression they made upon her at the time.

)+❖ *ELIZABETH, VISCOUNTESS MELBOURNE*

❯❯ *BYRON* (1814)

words, "sometimes made Augusta ready to sink." " Two or three
days after their arrival Byron received from a London jeweler
"two gold brooches, containing his hair and hers [Augusta's],
with three crosses on them." He presented one to Augusta and
he wore the other, and in Annabella's presence he said to his
sister: "If she knew what these mean! Do you remember our
signs at Newstead?" Then he said: "Well, Guss, I am a reformed
man, ain't I?" " Augusta turned off his taunt with: "I have observed some improvements already." "

Of the misery of her nights Annabella later wrote: "I could
not go to my restless bed till near the time of his leaving A, and
I trembled as I heard his terrible step. He swore at Fletcher as he
was undressing with a degree of rage that seemed to threaten his
life, and every night he came to my room in the same mood, except once or twice, when I heard the freezing sound of heartless
professions—more intolerable than his uncontrolled abhorrence." " Once when some movement in her sleep had brought
her nearer to him, he woke her with the cry "Don't touch me!"
uttered in a voice of "raging detestation." She got up and went
to her own room. "There I wept myself into some peace." "

Annabella did not make allowance for the fact that Byron was
probably drunk on these occasions. And she never learned, as
Augusta had long since, to mind his saner admonition—not to
pay too much attention to his words. Nevertheless, her anguish
was real, and Augusta felt genuinely sorry for her and showed
her every kindness—"she seemed to have no other view but that
of mitigating his cruelty to me," Annabella confessed." Once or
twice Augusta seemed on the point of making a confession: "You
are kind to me because you do not know me," and "He can never
respect *me*." " Mainly she gave Annabella advice on how to han-
dle him, saying that his furies sprang from indigestion caused
by his habit of starving himself to grow thin, then gorging, and
finally trying to relieve the discomfort by taking overdoses of
magnesia." But Annabella wrote later: "She gave me little encouragement to think he loved me." Still, Byron's resentment toward them both established "a sort of tacit understanding between us." "

Augusta did succeed in bringing him to a better temper part

of the time. On March 18, writing to Hodgson at Byron's request, she had only "*agreeables* to communicate." "I think I never saw or heard or read of a more perfect being in mortal mould than she [Annabella] appears to be, and scarcely dared flatter myself such a one would fall to the lot of my dear B. He seems quite sensible of her value, and as happy as the present alarming state of *public* and the tormenting uncertainties of his own private affairs will admit of." She concluded: "My bairns are well, and delighted at being able to scream, 'Oh, Byron!' again, and approve much of their new aunt." [n]

Lady Byron noticed that the children softened Byron more than anything else. One evening when he had relaxed from baiting the two women, they were looking at some portraits of him, and Annabella said: "I should like to have him painted when he is looking at Medora." [n]

But in his blacker moods Byron's impulse to torment both women increased to a kind of mania. His sole pleasure came to be, as he said, "to work them both well." [n] The evasions of the one and the pious martyred innocence of the other poisoned all his normal impulses to kindness. The hopelessness of his financial affairs and his own self-dissatisfaction and feelings of remorse added to his frenzy. He drank to forget,[n] and that made him more uninhibited in his speech. It is not surprising that toward the end of their visit Augusta longed for release from the strain. Byron was reluctant to move, but Annabella observed that Augusta "evidently wished for our departure." [n]

Meanwhile, news arrived that Napoleon had escaped from Elba and had landed in France. Hobhouse, eager to get near the scene of action, wrote Byron that he was preparing to go abroad and wished to see his friend before he left. Gone was the time when he might have hoped for Byron's companionship on such an exciting voyage, but when he failed to hear from Six Mile Bottom he began to worry.[n] He did not leave on the 26th as he had planned, and wrote in his diary: "I am still undecided what to do. . . . in a foolish state of apprehension with respect to Byron, my friend Byron, whose silence annoys me beyond what I can express." [n] But that same day Byron finally bestirred himself to write, and on the 27th, Hobhouse recorded with relief: "Heard from Byron: all my suspicions groundless." [n]

On the eve of departure from Six Mile Bottom, Byron wrote to Moore, expressing his sorrow at the death of his godchild, Olivia Byron Moore, and then turned abruptly to the subject of Napoleon. "I can forgive the rogue for utterly falsifying every line of mine Ode. . . . It is impossible not to be dazzled and overwhelmed by his character and career." [n]

Speaking of his own affairs, he announced quite casually that Lady Byron showed "some symptoms which look a little gestatory. It is a subject upon which I am not particularly anxious, except that I think it would please her uncle, Lord Wentworth, and her father and mother." [9]

On March 28 the Byrons set out for London. Annabella recalled that Byron looked back as they drove away and waved passionately to Augusta as long as he could see her. Then he sank back beside his wife with his dark look and asked: "What do you think of her?" [n]

Annabella was no doubt relieved to escape, and felt some hope that in their own house things would be better. Now, too, there was the possibility that he would soften to the child that was coming, for she remembered how he had looked at Medora. Augusta was relieved, too, to see them go. She loved her brother, but the anxieties and tensions of the visit had exhausted her.

Byron's mood did change as soon as they reached London and settled in the Duchess of Devonshire's house, despite the fact that the address in Piccadilly Terrace was No. 13 and he was superstitious. Annabella recorded that "For ten days he was kinder than I had ever seen him." [n] Hobhouse, who had postponed his journey until their arrival, called on them the next day and had a confidential chat with his friend. He recorded in his diary: "he advises me not to marry though he has the best of wives." [n]

[9] *LJ*, III, 188. Lady Byron later remembered vividly her husband's wild words about an heir: "I mean to live, like a worm on the earth, to propagate my kind, and then I shall put an end to my existence." (Mayne: *Lady Byron*, p. 179.)

Byron was soon drawn into business and publishing affairs. Besides the still unsettled business of Newstead, he had meetings with Kinnaird, who was fostering the publication of the *Hebrew Melodies,* and with John Murray, who was eager for more from Byron's pen than he had had in the past months (Byron had written little since his engagement). Byron's literary reputation was still high. During Easter Week, Samuel Taylor Coleridge had written him a long and flattering letter asking for his assistance with the booksellers in getting a volume of his poetry published to advantage. With a kind of dignified obsequiousness he apologized for intruding on one with whom he had no personal acquaintance except through his works. He touched lightly on Byron's satire of his early poems in *English Bards,* at which he was not offended, and hinted that Byron might be of service by appealing to Murray.[n]

Soon after his arrival in Piccadilly, Byron replied that he would be glad to comply with Coleridge's request and encouraged the author of *Remorse* to write more dramas.[n] And in a postscript Byron added an apology for *English Bards and Scotch Reviewers.* "The part applied to you is pert, and petulant, and shallow enough. . . ." [n]

Byron was soon back in the swing of his old London life, going to Murray's in the morning for a conference or a chat with the literary group who gathered there, attending the theater, and calling on Douglas Kinnaird and even on Lady Melbourne. Annabella was uneasy about his friendship with the last two. And the pleasure she enjoyed at Piccadilly Terrace was short-lived. Impelled by a fate as strong as that which Byron felt governed his own destiny, she had invited Augusta to visit them in their new home.

Why could she not have accepted the present fact of Byron's kindness to her as an omen, as a sufficient indication of how to build her happiness with him? It is impossible not to see in this act a characteristic of Annabella which would sooner or later make her life with her husband untenable. A desire for martyrdom must have been mingled with her Hamlet-like compulsion to prove the past before she acted. Byron's attempt to dissuade her was no doubt motivated by a kindness which she could not accept: "You are a fool for letting her come to the house, and you'll find it will make a great difference to *you* in all ways." [n]

Augusta arrived at Piccadilly Terrace early in April. But the tension was lessened in London by Byron's other interests. Walter Scott was in town en route to France. Through Murray's intervention Byron and Scott had corresponded after the publication of *Childe Harold* and had grown to have a warm admiration for each other's works. There was no one whom Byron was more eager to meet, and Murray was just as eager to bring them together.

Murray recorded proudly in his diary: "1815. Friday, April 7. —This day Lord Byron and Walter Scott met for the first time and were introduced by me to each other. They conversed together for nearly two hours." [n] Among those present at different times on the occasion were William Gifford, James Boswell (son of the biographer of Johnson), and William Sotheby. John Murray's son (who later carried on the publishing business as John Murray III) also recalled seeing "the two greatest poets of the age—both lame—stumping downstairs side by side. They continued to meet in Albemarle Street nearly every day, and remained together for two or three hours at a time." [n]

According to Scott, they met often in society. "Our sentiments agreed a good deal, except upon the subjects of religion and politics. . . . I remember saying to him, that I really thought, that if he lived a few years he would alter his sentiments. He answered, rather sharply, 'I suppose you are one of those who prophesy I will turn Methodist.' I replied, 'No—I don't expect your conversion to be of such an ordinary kind. I would rather look to see you retreat upon the Catholic faith, and distinguish yourself by the austerity of your penances. . . .' He smiled gravely, and seemed to allow I might be right." [n]

Scott's high-principled Toryism was apparently a little irked by Byron's libertarian pronouncements, but he smoothed this over in his recollections for Moore, saying: ". . . it appeared to me that the pleasure it afforded him as a vehicle of displaying his wit and satire against individuals in office was at the bottom of this habit of thinking, rather than any real conviction of the political principles on which he talked. He was certainly proud of his rank and ancient family. . . . at heart, I would have termed Byron a patrician on principle." [n]

On other points Scott observed and judged Byron's character astutely. "He was often melancholy,—almost gloomy," Scott recalled. "When I observed him in this humour, I used either to wait till it went off of its own accord, or till some natural and easy mode occurred of leading him into conversation. . . ." [n] Scott, of course, did not know or inquire into the deeper causes of Byron's melancholy, and Byron, as was usual when he entered wholeheartedly into a friendship, sensed the points at which their mutual interests and philosophies collided, and suppressed, without any intention of deception, much in his character and opinions that would have been incompatible with those of the kindly but more conventional Scotsman.

It was a curious mutual admiration which they shared. Byron was flattered by the attention of the distinguished gentleman author from the north; while Scott was equally pleased with the deference of the author of *Childe Harold*. Scott's own generous spirit enabled him to see the best side of his brother poet. And, like Moore, he was inclined to minimize Byron's own account of his sins.

A few days after Byron's first meeting with Scott, news came on April 10 or 11 of the serious illness of Lady Byron's uncle, Lord Wentworth, and she left immediately for Kirkby Mallory to be with him until her mother could come. She was there three nights before Lady Milbanke arrived in London on her way to Kirkby. Byron wrote to Annabella immediately: "Dearest— Now your mother is come I won't have you worried any longer —more particularly in your present situation which is rendered very precarious by what you have already gone through.

"Pray, come home." [n]

She did return, but, despite the uniform kindness of Augusta and Byron's frequent playful tenderness, her mind was already too poisoned to allow her much peace. Lord Wentworth died on April 17. That and a cold contributed to her misery. Byron was sympathetic, but he continued to go out a great deal, especially to the theater.

The yearly payment to Byron from the Milbankes by the terms

of the marriage settlement, £700, was just enough to pay the rent of the Piccadilly house, and, though they did not entertain much (Lady Byron was in mourning), a considerable number of servants was necessary to care for the mansion, and Byron felt obliged to keep a carriage and coachman. Mrs. Mule, his housekeeper, was installed in new finery befitting the more pretentious lodging.

At the first show of opulence in Piccadilly all Byron's creditors descended upon him. On the 15th he had written to Hanson to say that one of them (Randall) had brought action without giving notice for a debt of £257. 8s. 6d.[n] Others followed, and soon duns dogged his every step.

Some time in April the *Hebrew Melodies* were published by Braham and Nathan in a large folio selling for one guinea. Despite the price and some critical carping, the work was highly successful with the public. Ten thousand copies of this and a subsequent edition were sold, resulting in a profit of over £5,000,[n] and before the summer was out John Murray had published an edition of the poems without the music. One twentieth-century critic has aptly remarked: "Pious persons who bought the *Hebrew Melodies* in the expectation of finding sacred poetry by Lord Byron found instead a book almost as secular as *The Bride of Abydos.* Nine of the poems are Biblical in subject but Byronic in treatment; two are love songs; five are reflective lyrics, neither Jewish nor Christian; and five are expressions of what might be called proto-Zionism."[n] But Byron knew his Bible as well as many of his most pious readers and had a skill in turning its phrases to good account in verses that have a haunting melody. Because it was Byron's favorite, Nathan opened the volume with "She Walks in Beauty," which had no proper place in the collection, and which Caroline Lamb thought was a song without sense.[n]

Those who saw the Byrons during the summer thought them a happily married couple. William Harness recorded that "At the beginning of their married life, when first they returned to London society together, one seldom saw two young persons who appeared to be more devoted to one another than they were. At parties, he would be seen hanging over the back of her chair, scarcely talking to anybody else, eagerly introducing his friends to her, and, if they did not go away together, himself handing her to her carriage." [n]

Murray had met Lady Byron soon after the couple arrived at 13 Piccadilly Terrace, and was much impressed by her. "She is a good mathematician," he wrote to James Hogg, "writes poetry, understands French, Italian, Latin, and Greek. . . . She is a most delightful creature, and possesses excellent temper and a most inordinate share of good sense." [n] At home, however, Annabella's good sense often deserted her. By her own confession later, her suspicions of Augusta still plagued her. Some possessiveness or familiarity on the part of the sister, or Byron's own insinuations, may have unbalanced her. She wrote after the separation: "There were moments when I could have plunged a dagger in her heart, but she never saw them. . . ." [n] It was a household resting on explosives, and Byron for the most part chose to ignore the danger, and at times even played with fire as if driven by an involuntary compulsion.

Away from Piccadilly Terrace, Byron continued to have lively interests. A circumstance which drew him further into the whirl of life centering around the theater was his appointment, probably sometime in May, as a member of the Sub-Committee of Management of Drury Lane Theatre. Douglas Kinnaird was responsible for it. [n] He knew Byron's keen interest in theatrical affairs and believed his good judgment would be a valuable asset to the Committee in the matter of selecting scripts. Other members of the Committee were Lord Essex, George Lamb, Douglas Kinnaird, and Peter Moore. Samuel Whitbread was manager of the theater, and Raymond was stage-manager.

Early in June Walter Scott returned from France and Byron lunched with him and the comedian Mathews at Long's in Bond Street. Scott wrote of this occasion later in his Journal: "I never saw Byron so full of fun, frolic, wit, and whim: he was as playful as a kitten." [1]

Though Byron had ceased to hope for much personal or public

[1] *Sir Walter Scott's Journal*, p. 52. It was during that luncheon, apparently, that Scott repeated to Byron a fragment of Coleridge's *Christabel*, read to Scott from the MS. thirteen years before by John Stoddart, Coleridge's friend.

good from politics, he continued to interest himself in the melancholy spectacle of Tory triumph in the conduct of the war and
in the aid of tyranny abroad. On April 12, soon after his arrival
in town, he had gone to the House of Lords to listen to the debate on Bonaparte's escape from Elba,[n] and, partly because he
knew Hobhouse wished it, he had voted on May 23 with the
Whigs in their attempt to censure the part taken in the Congress
of Vienna by the Tory government.[n]

When unruffled by duns and private irritations, Byron could
be as agreeable as cultivated strangers usually found him. On
June 20 a young American named George Ticknor called at
Piccadilly Terrace with an introduction to Byron from William
Gifford. A lawyer with literary inclinations, Ticknor was on his
way to round out his education at Göttingen, and was armed
with letters to some of the leading literary personalities. Ticknor
found that his anticipations, built on what he had heard of the
Byron legend, were mistaken. "Instead of being deformed, as I
had heard," he wrote in his journal, "he is remarkably well built,
with the exception of his feet. Instead of having a thin and
rather sharp and anxious face, as he has in his pictures, it is
round, open, and smiling . . . I found his manners affable and
gentle, the tones of his voice low and conciliating, his conversation gay, pleasant, and interesting in an uncommon degree." [n]

Ticknor was witness to one dramatic episode. While they were
talking, Sir James Bland Burges, Lady Byron's uncle, "came suddenly into the room, and said abruptly, 'My lord, my lord, a great
battle has been fought in the Low Countries, and Bonaparte is
entirely defeated.' 'But is it true?' said Lord Byron,—'is it true?'
'Yes, my lord, it is certainly true; an aide-de-camp arrived in town
last night. . . . He says he thinks Bonaparte is in full retreat towards Paris.' After an instant's pause, Lord Byron replied, 'I am
d——d sorry for it'; and then, after another slight pause, he
added, 'I didn't know but I might live to see Lord Castlereagh's
head on a pole. But I suppose I sha'n't, now.' And this was the
first impression produced on his impetuous nature by the news of
the battle of Waterloo."

Byron continued his gracious hospitality. He took his guest
upstairs and showed him his library and his collection of Romaic

books, including some rich and rare volumes, and offered him letters to various people in Greece. While he was there, Lady Byron came in. "She is pretty, not beautiful," Ticknor recorded, "for the prevalent expression of her countenance is that of ingenuousness. . . . She was dressed to go and drive, and, after stopping a few moments, went to her carriage. Lord Byron's manner to her was affectionate; he followed her to the door, and shook hands with her, as if he were not to see her for a month." [n]

The next day Ticknor saw Byron again at Murray's literary salon. Gifford and other Tories were there. "The conversation turned upon the great victory at Waterloo, for which Lord Byron received the satirical congratulations of his ministerial friends with a good-nature which surprised me." [n] On the 26th, Ticknor spent the greater part of the morning with Byron. Shortly after he arrived, Mrs. Siddons was announced, and Byron took his guest in to be introduced to her. The following evening Ticknor sat with the Byrons in their private box at Drury Lane. "There was nobody there, this evening, but Lord and Lady Byron, and her father and mother." Ticknor parted with the Byrons "with unexpected regret," confessing that he had received from Byron more kindness than from any other person in England.[n]

Ticknor of course did not observe all the domestic undertones in the Byron ménage, but he did see truly one side of Byron's character. It seems that, despite the constant harassment of debts and uncertainties of their financial situation, Byron was in a relatively happy frame of mind during the early summer. Augusta left before the end of June (probably about the 25th),[n] the atmosphere of suspicion was dissipated, and Annabella relaxed into greater ease and cheerfulness.

She wrote afterward of the pleasure Byron could give her in his happier moods: "When he would converse familiarly, there was a sort of conventional language of nonsense between us— which relieved his fears of 'Sermons and Sentiment,' and rather gave play to his Imagination than confined it. In the midst of this childishness, which with Augusta was continual, he would suddenly deliver the deepest reflections and then shrink again into frolic and levity. The transitions had all the grace of Genius, and formed its greatest charm to me, till I learned to consider those light and brilliant effusions only as the foam that might float on the waters of bitterness." [n]

Leigh Hunt had been released from prison on February 2, and Byron several times called on him during the summer at his house in the Edgeware Road (Maida Vale). Hunt was flattered by the visits and pleased by the simplicity of Byron's manners. In his *Autobiography* Hunt recorded that in a room "at the end of the garden to this house was a magnificent rocking-horse, which a friend had given my little boy; and Lord Byron, with a childish glee becoming a poet, would ride upon it." [n]

"His appearance at that time," Hunt wrote, "was the finest I ever saw it, a great deal finer than it was afterwards, when he was abroad. He was fatter than before his marriage. . . . He sat one morning so long, that Lady Byron sent up twice to let him know she was waiting. Her Ladyship used to go on in the carriage to Henderson's Nursery Ground, to get flowers." [n] Hunt never met Lady Byron, but only caught a glimpse of her at the door once, and thought "she had a pretty earnest look, with her 'pippin' face." [n]

Byron went out of his way to serve Hunt and aid his literary work. He took the trouble to read the manuscript of Hunt's *The Story of Rimini* and make penciled criticisms in the margins, mostly commendatory but occasionally with a tactful suggestion for the deletion of some precious expression. [n]

Byron had tried to resume his easy camaraderie with Lady Melbourne, but it was difficult in his present circumstances, the more so as he was aware that his wife did not approve. Lady Melbourne may have been a little ill at ease with her niece, being already aware of the unwisdom of the match she had helped to bring about. It was probably to Lady Melbourne that Annabella referred when she wrote Augusta after the latter had returned to Six Mile Bottom: "By-the-bye, I believe she is affronted with me. Knowing that I did not voluntarily give cause, I shall not break my heart. She has never called on me, and when I made her a Vis— with my Mother, was very dignified." [n] This visit, made while her mother was still in town, was a trying one

for Annabella, for she met there one of her predecessors in Byron's affections, his earliest romantic attachment. "I never told
you of it [the visit]," she continued, "nor of my meeting with
Mrs. Musters there. She asked after B.? Such a wicked-looking
cat I never saw. Somebody else [Caroline Lamb?] looked quite
virtuous by the side of her." [2] The rival who disturbed her most
was the one who had stirred Byron's romantic imagination. He
had written poems to Mary Chaworth and had courted Annabella with literary and philosophical discussions. She knew she
had nothing to fear from Caroline now, and, besides, Caro Lamb
had for the nonce decided to be discreet. She labored to convince John Murray, who still furnished her with information
about her erstwhile lover, that she was cured of her idolatry.

Byron, she said, "never can be what he appears—he has not
in him that which alone could realize so bright a vision—'he has
not a noble heart.'. . . there is a black speck in our divinity.
. . . out d——ned spot . . . [if] all the waters of the ocean
can wash it away—then I again will bow to my 'sometime' Idol
—& bear the chains whatever of bitter may be mingled with
them—in spight too of Wife and 6 Miles Bottom—but as it is—
I wash my hands from ill deeds. . . ." [n]

In July, Caroline left England to join her mother in Brussels
and nurse her brother Frederick Ponsonby, who had been seri-

---

[2] *LJ*, III, 210 n. The episode described by Medwin (I, 75) may be a confused account of this same meeting, or it is of course possible that Lady
Melbourne and Caroline did return the visit. Medwin makes Byron say: "A
curious thing happened to me shortly after the honey-moon, which was very
awkward at the time, but has since amused me much. It so happened that
three married women were on a wedding visit to my wife, (and in the same
room, at the same time,) whom I had known to be all birds of the same nest.
Fancy the scene of confusion that ensued?"

After Medwin's book was published Caroline wrote him: "Shortly after
he [Byron] married, once, Lady Melbourne took me to see his Wife in Piccadilly. It was a cruel request, but Lord Byron himself made it. It is to this
wedding visit he alludes. Mrs. Leigh, myself, Lady Melbourne, Lady Noel,
& Lady Byron, were in the room. I never looked up. Annabella was very
cold to me. Lord Byron came in & seemed agitated—his hand was cold, but
he seemed kind. This was the last time upon this earth I ever met him."
(*LJ*, II, 453.) Except for her naming Lady Noel (a possible confusion with
the earlier visit of Annabella and her mother to Lady Melbourne?), the details correspond closely enough with Medwin's.

ously wounded at the Battle of Waterloo. From there she passed on to Paris and embarrassed her husband by her flirtations with the Duke of Wellington.[3]

Byron's soberer views on Waterloo were expressed in a letter to Moore on July 7: "In the late battles, like all the world, I have lost a connexion,—poor Frederic Howard,[n] the best of his race. I had little intercourse, of late years, with his family, but I never saw or heard but good of him. Hobhouse's brother is killed.[n] In short, the havoc has not left a family out of its tender mercies. Every hope of a republic is over, and we must go on under the old system. But I am sick at heart of politics and slaughters. . . ."[n]

Hobhouse's entreaties and exciting accounts of what he had seen apparently almost persuaded Byron to join him abroad. Lady Byron wrote to Augusta the following year: "The Paris scheme was *very near* executed in the Summer."[n] It was probably prevented only by his inertia and lack of funds and Hobhouse's early return. When Hobhouse arrived from Paris late in July and Byron learned to what extent the forces of reaction had already entrenched themselves (with English Tory blessing) in France, he relieved his feelings by writing some excoriating paragraphs on Louis XVIII and Talleyrand. He described Louis as "Strict in devotion, skilful in Cookery . . . but a martyr to the Gout," and his chief minister as the "living record of all that public treason, private Treachery, and moral Infamy can accumulate in the person of one degraded being."[n]

[3] In Brussels Caroline encountered another of Byron's admirers, Lady Frances Webster, who had progressed since her innocent flirtation with the poet to become one of the favorites of Wellington. When the Websters and the Lambs moved on to Paris, the magnet of Wellington having drawn both the wives there, Wedderburn Webster was himself attracted by Caroline, but, perhaps remembering Byron's experience, he was a little wary. (*"To Lord Byron,"* p. 112.) Byron was apparently foolish enough to send Caroline a letter through Webster, who warned him: ". . . your letter may awaken what every interest should suppress. . . . She now amazes all Paris by breaking busts of Lord Wellington." (*"To Lord Byron,"* pp. 112–13.) But Byron's letter was a mocking one. Having heard of her escapades with Wellington and the army, he could not resist taunting her. "I had one letter while at Paris from Ld. Byron," Caroline told Medwin; "a jesting one; hoping I was as happy with the regiment as he was with his 'Wife Bell.'" (*LJ*, II, 453.)

Byron's affairs were in a sad way, and the sale of Newstead was constantly postponed. After Hobhouse's departure Byron had been too softhearted to press Hanson, himself badgered by the legal difficulties of his son-in-law, to any effective action. The summer brought increasing embarrassments. The Kirkby Mallory estate of Lord Wentworth, which had gone to Lady Noel [the Milbankes had changed their name to Noel in compliance with Lord Wentworth's will] along with a supposed income of £7,000 a year, "ate itself up," and, despite their property, Annabella's parents were in almost as serious financial difficulties as the Byrons themselves, who gained nothing from the Wentworth inheritance. Indeed, it was positively harmful to their situation, for it immediately brought more creditors upon them."

As early as the middle of June, Byron had commissioned Hanson to draw up a will to supersede the one he had signed on September 29, 1813. This new will, which Byron finally signed on July 29, 1815, provided that the income from the residue of his estate, after all property was sold and the £60,000 of Lady Byron's marriage settlement was paid, should go to his sister and her children. Hobhouse and Hanson were to be the executors.[4] Byron easily convinced Annabella of the justness of these provisions. "Dearest Lei," Annabella wrote, "I must tell you how lovingly B. has been talking of 'dear Goose,' till he had half a mind to cry—and so had I. The conversation arose from his telling the contents of a Will that he has just made—as far as I can judge, quite what he ought to make. . . ."

Annabella's parents, unable to offer the Byrons immediate financial relief, had put Seaham at their disposal as a means of helping them to escape duns and the expenses of London living while at the same time providing Annabella with a more comfortable environment for her lying-in. The Noels were to occupy the Wentworth estate at Kirkby Mallory." These arrangements, made early in July, exactly suited Annabella. She knew that they were spending beyond their present means, and she was uneasy at the temptations which beset Byron in London. In a

[4] This will, given in full in Moore (II, 820–3), with a codicil leaving £5,000 to his natural daughter Allegra, made in 1818 and self-canceled by her death in 1822, was the one which was proved on July 6, 1824, after Byron's death.

letter to Augusta she exclaimed: "O that I were out of this horrid town, which makes me mad! The moving will be a sad business!" But she added: "B. has said something that has gratified me much, as it showed consideration for my Mam. He said he meant to have her at Seaham (not that I should like it) during my Accouchement, because she would be so anxious at a distance. I am as apt to fancy that the sort of things which please me are to be traced more or less to you, as that those which pain me come from another quarter. . . ." [n]

Annabella was pleased, too, that Byron had asked Moore and his wife to visit them at Seaham.[5] But she was not too happy about Byron's absorption in Drury Lane affairs, his close association with Douglas Kinnaird and other cronies, and his familiarity with actors and actresses in the greenroom. Whitbread, the manager, died on July 6. Reporting the event to Moore, Byron said: "He dropped down, and I believe never spoke afterwards. I perceive Perry [editor of the *Morning Chronicle*] attributes his death to Drury Lane,—a consolatory encouragement to the new Committee." [n]

There were other reasons why the Byrons did not leave London. Byron had finally persuaded Hanson to put both Newstead and Rochdale up for auction again at the end of July. Farebrother the auctioneer attempted the sale at Garraway's on July 28. Hobhouse accompanied Byron to the auction, "where N[ewstead] was bought in at 95,000 gs the first lot. the bona fide bidding was 79,000[?] gs. he is much annoyed. Rochdale 16,000 gs. called on Lady Noel who wants B to sell hugely." [n]

Hobhouse recorded that "from the moment of the useless effort to sell the Newstead and other estates, Lord Byron's difficulties began to increase." He added, however: "It was impossible . . . for any couple to live in more apparent harmony; indeed, it was the fear of some friends that his Lordship confined himself too much with Lady Byron, and that occasional separation—for they were never seen apart—might be more conducive to their comfort." [n]

[5] Byron had added an inducement to Moore: ". . . you and I (*without* our *wives*) will take a *lark* to Edinburgh and embrace Jeffrey." (*LJ*, III, 210–11.)

Hobhouse had much opportunity to observe Byron's growing despondency in the months that followed, for they were frequently together. The 79,000 guineas offered for Newstead, after deduction of the £60,000 of the marriage settlement, would have been insufficient to pay even Byron's most pressing debts. The hopelessness of his financial position affected him more deeply than any but a few of his intimates knew. On July 31, Hobhouse wrote in his diary: "B[yro]n is not more happy than before marriage. D[ouglas] K[innaird] is also melancholy. This is the state of man. I shall go mad. . . ." [n] On August 4, Hobhouse "passed night with D. K. & L[ord] B[yron] who tells me he & she have begun a little snubbing on money matters—marry not says he. . . ." [n]

By the end of August, Byron's nerves and temper were frayed. It was exasperating to a man with a penchant for generous prodigality to be constantly hounded by the threat of executions and to have no money in sight. He decided to pay a visit to Augusta, and the consciousness that he ought not to leave his wife with the financial worries of the house in her advanced state of pregnancy may have made him "perfectly ferocious" to her for four days before he left. She recalled later: "As he was starting, he asked my forgiveness, half-earnestly, half-jestingly—but a kind word from him was then too precious to be rigorously examined." [n]

Their notes exchanged in his absence indicate an affectionate intimacy on both sides, and this seems to have been normal when the pressure was lifted from Byron's temper. From Epping, en route, he wrote:

Dearest Pip—The learned Fletcher with his wonted accuracy having forgotten something, I must beg you to forward it. On my dressing table are *two phials labelled "drops,"* containing certain liquids of I know not what pharmacopoly—(*but white* and clear, so you can't mistake, I hope). *One* of these I want in my materia medica. Pray send it carefully packed to me at Goose's per coach on receiving this—and believe me

ever most lovingly thine

B.

(not *frac.*) [6]

[6] Mayne: *Lady Byron*, p. 187. Miss Mayne assumes that the "not *frac.*" refers to his fractiousness or ill-temper before his departure.

Byron arrived at Six Mile Bottom on Wednesday, August 30, and remained until the following Monday, September 4. Colonel Leigh, as usual, was absent. Annabella recorded that when he returned to Piccadilly he was "most kind to me, but offended with Augusta," [n] who had defended Annabella's parents against Byron's petulant abuse of them. In the weeks that followed, Byron's spirits and temper were up and down, his alternating kindness, pity, and exasperated harshness to his wife making his conduct unpredictable. They went out together occasionally and those who saw them still had no inkling of the trouble growing under the surface of their lives.

For the most part, Annabella tried to conceal from her parents all but their money difficulties. Threatened executions by creditors had caused them to give up going to Seaham, and to her mother's invitation to Kirkby, Annabella replied: "The moment B. were to leave town, for a permanency, some measures that are now suspended would immediately ensue. He is in great anxiety about me and would have me go by myself—which I *will not*. As long as I am with him I am comparatively comfortable. . . ." [n]

Byron's unwillingness to leave London was no doubt compounded of his increasing annoyance at his parents-in-law for their failure to provide substantial assistance when it was most desperately needed, his consequent reluctance to accept their hospitality, and his growing interest in the affairs of Drury Lane, which opened on September 9 for the autumn season. Aside from buffooning and sometimes flirting with some of the people in the greenroom, he concentrated on the more important business of getting suitable scripts and first-rate actors for the productions.

Byron's first move was to secure new talent. He first tried William Sotheby, who "obligingly offered *all* his tragedies. . . . Then the Scenes I had to go through!" he recalled. "The authours, and the authoresses, the Milliners, the wild Irishmen, the people from Brighton, from Blackwell, from Chatham, from Cheltenham, from Dublin, from Dundee, who came in upon me! . . . Miss Emma Somebody, with a play entitled the 'Bandit of Bohemia,' or some such title or production. Mr. O'Higgins, then resident at Richmond, with an Irish tragedy, in which the unities could not fail to be observed, for the protagonist was chained by the leg to a pillar during the chief part of the performance." Byron recalled interfering only once in behalf of an actress, deciding a dispute in favor of Miss Smith, a ballet dancer, "because she was like Lady Jane Harley in the face." [n]

Byron had tried in July to get Mrs. Siddons, whom he considered the "*beau idéal* of acting," [n] to come to London for the season, but she would not leave Edinburgh.[n] Drury Lane during Byron's membership of the Committee had in its pay some of the best dramatic talent of the day. In addition to Kean and Miss Kelly,[n] who was widely admired for her acting and who was later toasted by Thomas Hood and Charles Lamb, the Committee had secured the handsome Mrs. Mardyn, who, after making her reputation on the Dublin stage, acted for the first time in London at Drury Lane on September 26, 1815, in *Lovers' Vows*, and continued as a principal support of the theater's repertory.[n]

If the season was not better, it was because of a dearth of good dramatic writing. Byron was constantly searching for new talent in this field. His reading of the hopeless manuscripts on the shelves at Drury Lane convinced him that he must look to poets rather than to professional playwrights. But they were all as reluctant to venture onto the stage as he was. He had appealed to Moore without success, and then he turned to Scott, who recommended Charles Robert Maturin, an Irish novelist and playwright. Byron secured Maturin's *Bertram* for Drury Lane, but when it was produced, with great success, in 1816, Byron had left England.[n]

Remembering Coleridge's drama *Remorse*, and admiring his poetic powers, Byron wrote to him in October and received an enthusiastic reply running to pages, announcing his *Biographia Literaria* and *Sybylline Leaves* and full of plans and promises for a drama for Drury Lane, but the promises, as usual, were never fulfilled.

In replying to Coleridge's letter, Byron took occasion to compliment him on the fragment of *Christabel* which he had heard Scott recite: "I do not know that even 'Love' or the 'Antient

Mariner' are so impressive—and to me there are few things in our tongue beyond these two productions." ⁿ

Coleridge responded at even greater length, expending most of his pages in self-justification for the apparent lack of application of his talents to the best work. He had sent a copy of *Christabel*. After reading it over, Byron confessed that he had apparently unconsciously plagiarized, in *The Siege of Corinth*, not yet published, a dozen lines from his memory of Scott's recitation of it. "If you like," he offered, "I will cut out the passage, and do as well as I can without,—or what you please." ⁷

Byron asked Moore to review Coleridge's volumes favorably in the *Edinburgh Review*. "Praise him I think you must, but you will also praise him *well*,—of all things the most difficult. It will be the making of him." ⁿ How generously Byron could reshape his judgments when faced with a human situation arousing his interest! This was a far cry from his reference to Coleridge in *English Bards and Scotch Reviewers* as one "To turgid ode and tumid stanza dear," who "soars to elegise an ass."

Byron sought compensation in the activities of the Committee and the buffooneries of the greenroom for the hopelessness of his private fortune and the tightening vice of circumstances. Tensed by anxieties, he became the victim again of sleepless nights and nervous fears such as had caused him to walk the floor in the dead of night with his pistols during the honeymoon.

"Once," Annabella recalled, "between 3 and 4 a.m. he fancied a step on the stairs, and lay afraid to stir, suffering so much that I said I would get up and see. He let me, though I was within three or four months of my confinement—but I am convinced it was because he thought *himself* the only one against whom harm was intended." ⁿ

It seems probable that Byron was so absorbed in his own miseries that he was unaware of the extent to which Annabella, herself subject to the moods induced by her pregnancy, exaggerated all the words he spoke in irritation at fate rather than at her, and gave undue significance to every word that sprang from

⁷ *LJ*, III, 229. Letter of Oct. 27, 1815. See above, p. 532 n. The passage was nevertheless published by Byron as the last twelve lines of stanza 19 of *The Siege of Corinth*. Byron added a note on the unintentional plagiarism, but made no attempt to explain or account for it.

his volatile temper. Sometimes, she felt, he spoke to her with a "sterile pity." When she expressed happiness for the few hours he spared her from his daily and nightly sessions at the theater, he said: "Well, poor thing, you are easily pleased, to be sure"; and he added: "I believe you feel towards me as a mother to her child, happy when it is out of mischief." And again: "If any woman could have rendered marriage endurable to me, you would"; "I believe you will go on loving me till I beat you." On another occasion he said: "If I had known you since I was five years old, I might have been happy." But when she said once with a pathetic smile that she believed he would love her yet, he countered with his old reproach: "It is too late now. If you had taken me two years ago. . . . But it is my destiny to ruin all I come near." [n]

Byron found relaxation and forgetfulness in sitting late over brandy with Kinnaird and other cronies. Annabella could only brood at home. When she did go out with him she had no pleasure, though her ladylike demeanor would not have betrayed her critical sensitivity. After one unappetizing dinner she described to her father the absurdities of the young ladies who were determined to talk poetically to Byron. ". . . B. was attacked by ecstasies about 'autumnal tints' in Scotland, which he cruelly answered by raptures about whiskey. In short, they *yelped* and he *snapped*." [n]

Leigh Hunt had written Byron on September 28, apologizing with profuseness for his failure to repay Byron's visits (he had now moved to a new house in Hampstead), and sending the new edition of his *Feast of the Poets*.[n] Byron replied with a long discourse on Wordsworth's poetical blunders and metaphysical moonshine: "I still think his capacity warrants all you can say of *it* only, but that his performances since *Lyrical Ballads* are miserably inadequate to the ability which lurks within him: there is undoubtedly much natural talent spilt over the *Excursion;* but it is rain upon rocks—where it stands and stagnates, or rain upon sands—where it falls without fertilizing. Who can understand him? Let those who do, make him intelligible. Jacob Behmen, Swedenborg, and Joanna Southcote, are mere types of this arch-apostle of mystery and mysticism." [n]

On October 15, Byron sent Hunt his only remaining copy of *English Bards and Scotch Reviewers.* It was the copy of the fourth edition with the manuscript corrections he had intended for the suppressed fifth edition. "There are in it *many* opinions I have altered," he wrote, "and some which I retain; upon the whole, I wish that it had never been written. . . ." [n]

That Byron not only found time for such lengthy correspondence but also completed *The Siege of Corinth* during the month of October (Lady Byron finished copying it for the printer on November 2) [n] indicates that he did not spend all his time at Drury Lane or at dinners with Kinnaird, though it may have seemed so to the oversensitive Annabella. As for the dinners, Byron did not take them so seriously as did his wife. He wrote to Moore on October 31: "Yesterday, I dined out with a large-ish party, where were Sheridan and Colman, Harry Harris of C[ovent] G[arden], and his brother, Sir Gilbert Heathcote, Douglas Kinnaird, and others, of note and notoriety. . . . all was hiccup and happiness for the last hour or so, and I am not impregnated with any of the conversation." [n]

Annabella, who could not take so light a view of these carousings, confessed her anxieties to Augusta: "His [Byron's] misfortune is an habitual *passion for Excitement,* which is always found in ardent temperaments, where the pursuits are not in some degree organised. It is the Ennui of a monotonous existence that drives the best-hearted people of this description to the most dangerous paths, and makes them often seem to act from bad motives, when in fact they are only flying from internal suffering by any external stimulus. The love of tormenting arises chiefly from this Source. Drinking, Gaming &c are all of the same origin." [n]

This was early in November. And then the inevitable and, to Byron, most dreaded thing happened: a bailiff entered the house and camped there. Byron was driven to paroxysms of anger and unreason. He had already sold the furniture at Newstead, [n] and now his precious books would have to go. Yet he had property worth over one hundred thousand pounds! And an heir was coming into the house soon. In his frustration his anger turned upon his wife, the more so because of her philosophic counselings. The next day Annabella wrote again to Augusta:

"Everything is explained by a Bailiff sleeping last night in the house. From the old quarter . . . God knows what I suffered yesterday, & am suffering from B's distraction, which is of the *very worst* kind. He leaves the house, telling me he will at once abandon himself to every sort of desperation, speaks to me only to upbraid me with having married him when he wished not, and says he is therefore acquitted of all principle towards me, and I must consider myself *only* to be answerable for the vicious courses to which his despair will drive him. The going out of the house & the drinking are the most fatal. He was really quite frantic yesterday—said he did not care for any consequences to me, and it seemed impossible to tell if his feelings towards you or me were the most completely reversed; for as I have told you, he loves or hates us together. . . . Things never were so serious—I don't mean the circumstances, for they must mend, but his feelings. . . .

"P.S.—I have waited till the last in hopes of some change, but all is inexorable pride and hardness. O Augusta, will it ever change for me?" "

Annabella continued her account the following day: "B. relented last night, for he returned earlier from the play, and I took the opportunity of attacking him, which I had scarcely had before, as he had never been in my company throughout the day for much more than an hour. He was kind to me again, but still rather odd. . . . He does not think I know the circumstance of our unwelcome guest. I wish George B[yron]or some man friend of common-sense were in the way to laugh B. out of his excessive horrors on this subject, which he seems to regard as if no mortal had ever experienced anything so shocking. . . ." [8]

Poor Annabella, who thought she could read Byron's char-

---

[8] Mayne: *Lady Byron*, p. 195. Byron told Medwin that "an execution was levied, and the bailiffs put in possession of the very beds we had to sleep on." (Medwin, I, 41.) According to Moore, there were eight or nine executions in Byron's house within the year. (Moore, I, 642.) But though Lady Byron found this bailiff a "sad brute," Byron apparently made friends with him and perhaps got off the easier for it. (*LJ*, V, 438–9.)

acter so well, tried to square his actions and his speech with
certain fixed principles, and consequently failed to grasp some
of the simplest keys to his behavior. She was determined to read
method into his madness, when he was merely giving way under
stress to the impulses of a spoiled child and, like the child, was
willing to forgive and be forgiven when the "rage" left him.
Lady Blessington later took note of his "mobility" of temperament,[n] and he himself confessed to her his changeableness, "being
everything by turns and nothing long."[n] She, however, after
knowing him a short while, observed shrewdly: "He gives me
the idea of being the man the most easily to be managed I
ever saw: I wish Lady Byron had discovered the means, and
both might now be happier."[n] And Byron's valet, Fletcher, who
had seen his master in all his moods and had by then been
witness to his relations with dozens of women of all kinds, remarked with naïve wisdom: "It is very odd, but I never yet knew
a lady that could not manage my Lord, *except* my Lady."[n]

Annabella had, Byron told Lady Blessington, "a degree of
self-control that I never saw equalled. . . . This extraordinary
degree of self-command in Lady Byron produced an opposite
effect on me. When I have broken out, on slight provocations,
into one of my ungovernable fits of rage, her calmness piqued
and seemed to reproach me. . . ."[n] At another time he said that
if his marriage was not "founded on love, as love is generally
viewed, a wild, engrossing, and ungovernable passion, there
was quite sufficient liking in it to have insured happiness had
his temper been better."[n]

Yet the surprising thing is that in the midst of all these distractions and maddening provocations Byron could continue to
carry on a correspondence of sense and humor. Murray, quite
unaware of the tortures Byron was suffering and making others
suffer, wrote to Walter Scott on November 8: "Lord Byron is
perfectly well, and is in better dancing spirits than I ever knew
him, expecting every day a son and heir."[n] Actually, Byron felt
himself at the end of his rope. Hobhouse saw some ominous
symptoms when he called on the Byrons on the 11th. He wrote
in his diary: "he is unaltered in any respect dear creature but

owns that marriage makes him selfish. [']I have not written to you, you see['] I forgive him—he does not dine with his wife—well he says don't marry." ⁿ

On the day Hobhouse called, Annabella wrote to Augusta:

"Don't be afraid for my carcase—it will do very well. Of the rest I scarcely know what to think—I have many fears.

"Let me see you the middle of next week—at latest.

"Hobhouse is come—I have great reason to think to arrange a plan for going abroad. . . .

"You will do good, I think—if any can be done—" ⁿ

Annabella was disturbed by Byron's announcement in one of his moods of depression that as soon as the heir was born he meant to go abroad, "because a woman always loves her child better than her husband." Taking him literally as usual, she replied with sharp distress: "You will make me hate my child if you say so!" ⁿ

In bitterness and resignation, while the bailiff was in the house, Byron resolved to sell his library. Annabella herself could have been philosophical about the seizure of their furniture, but for his sake she was concerned about the books because it hurt her "to see him *in agony.*" ⁿ Byron had already discussed the sale with a book-dealer when the matter came to the ears of John Murray, who immediately sent him a check for £1,500, "with the assurance that an equal sum should be at his service in the course of a few weeks, offering, at the same time, to dispose of all the copyrights of his poems for his Lordship's use." ⁿ

Byron's pride would not permit him to accept the money, however. He replied: "I return your bills not accepted, but certainly not *unhonoured.* Your present offer is a favour which I would accept from you, if I accepted such from any man. . . . The circumstances which induce me to part with my books, though sufficiently, are not *immediately,* pressing." ⁹

Lady Byron had not been unaware of the dangers to one of Byron's nature of the daily contact with actresses at the theater. Byron's first, and perhaps his only, liaison of the green-room apparently began in November, about the time that he

⁹ *LJ,* III, 249. Letter of Nov. 14, 1815. Byron's books were not sold until just before he left England in April of the following year.

was most harrowed by family and business affairs. He probably would have shied away from any involvement with a lady of consequence or even with an actress of repute. He had found sufficient occupation for his romantic imagination in poetic composition. All that he wanted from a woman now was physical pleasure, but it was inevitable that he should be harassed by the emotional complications of the simple girl who easily succumbed to his advances. A more heartless rake would have been rid of her sooner; Byron at least preserved her letters. Susan Boyce was a very minor actress at Drury Lane. She was jealous of her theatrical rivals, and her insistence on being treated as a lady was a measure of her vulgarity. That she was genuinely attached to Byron there can be little doubt, and there is evidence that he treated her, within the limits of his own code, not unhandsomely.

In Susan's first letter to Byron, she protested that she wanted his *"confidence* and *esteem."* "If I can ever obtain that, most joyfully would I meet you when you please. . . . I will promise to give myself to you with all my heart, to devote my whole time and affection to you, and you *only."* [n]

It was a most awkward affair from the beginning, and probably because of Miss Boyce's naïveté it was soon, to Byron's great annoyance, the talk of the greenroom. On November 15 she wrote: "I lost my brooch in the carriage last night. . . . I am vexed a good deal about it—not for any particular value I put on the thing itself but I fear it may lead to something unpleasant." But, encouraged by the interest Byron took in her, she left her sister's house and took a room in New Ormonde Street, where he visited her, though not as often as she wished. Her favors were rewarded by a very handsome present, perhaps to replace the lost brooch, but the poor girl was disconcerted that there was no tender message with it: ". . . had the note which accompanied it contained *one* expression congenial to my feelings, I should have valued that ten thousand times more than the gift, generous as it is. . . . I remember you once said of women that the more loving they were the more *troublesome.* *Never* shall you say that of me." [n]

Alas, she was unable to keep that promise. As Susan became

more importunate, Byron grew cooler. She wrote to remind him that she would be home any evening from six to eleven. And when he did not come, she could not endure the suspense: "Why have I not heard from you before this? Since last Thursday I have thought of *nothing else* but you. . . . I shall be in the Prompter's place in the green-room; if you will condescend to speak to me for a minute, pray do so, or I shall be wretched. . . . I cannot flatter myself you will *ever love* me as I *would be loved*, but you shall *respect* me tho' we never meet again." [n]

Then there were scenes in the theater, which only made Byron the more desirous to break the liaison. The situation is made sufficiently clear in one of Susan's tear-splashed letters: "I *must* give vent to my feelings or I shall burst. So unaccountable (was) your conduct to me last night I know not what to say. . . . You never spoke to me at all: *that* I do not mind, but your going away *without* saying goodnight, had I not *run after you*. . . . should I now at this time in my really unhappy state of mind find myself pregnant I won't answer for the consequences." [n]

Susan Boyce continued to annoy Byron until he went abroad in April of the following year, and she appealed for his aid several times while he was in Italy. He could then view the affair with detachment and humor, and at that distance he displayed a willingness to help the foolish girl. In 1821 she wrote him a pathetic letter signed "the wretched but *unchanged* Susan Boyce," in which she appealed to Byron to "save *me* and my *poor Boy* from perishing. I am at the Haymarket Theatre for £2 per week. . . ." [n] Byron sent her letter on to Douglas Kinnaird with the frank comment: "She was a transient piece of mine, but I owe her little on that score, having been myself, at the short period I knew her, in such a state of mind and body, that all carnal connection was quite mechanical, and almost as senseless to my senses, as to my feelings of imagination. Advance the poor creature some money on my account, and deduct it from your books, *quoad* banker, for me." [n]

Byron's feelings were indeed numbed at the time he entered that unsatisfying liaison. Almost frantic with his oppressive financial situation (no one quite understood how small a prov-

ocation was necessary to upset his equilibrium), he became
vindictive and cruel toward those for whom he usually had
the kindest feelings. Augusta, who had arrived at Piccadilly
Terrace on November 15 in response to Annabella's alarming
letters, felt the brunt of it. At first he was chilly toward her,
and then began again his pointed remarks and insults to both
wife and sister. Sometimes he boasted of his conquests of actresses at the theater, "as much to vex Augusta as you," he said
to Annabella.[n] Lady Byron later told Lady Anne Barnard: "One
night, coming home from one of his lawless parties, he saw me
so indignantly collected, and bearing all with such a determined
calmness, that a rush of remorse seemed to come over him. He
called himself a monster, though his sister was present, and threw
himself in agony at my feet. I could not—no—I could not forgive
him such injuries. He had lost me for ever! Astonished at
the return of virtue, my tears, I believe, flowed over his face,
and I said, 'Byron, all is forgotten: never, never shall you hear
of it more!' He started up, and, folding his arms while he looked
at me, burst into laughter. 'What do you mean?' said I. 'Only
a philosophical experiment; that's all,' said he. 'I wished to
ascertain the value of your resolutions.' "[n]

Byron was finishing *Parisina* at this time. As for Annabella,
she could copy the poem and make what she would of it.
Murray, when he received it in December, was delighted. He
wrote: "I tore open the packet you sent me, and have found
in it a Pearl. . . . I have been most agreeably disappointed . . .
at the story, which—what you hinted to me and wrote—had
alarmed me; and I should not have read it aloud to my wife
if my eye had not traced the delicate hand that transcribed it."[n]

Byron replied with a jaunty insouciance: "I am very glad
that the handwriting was a favourable omen of the *morale* of
the piece: but you must not trust to that, for my copyist would
write out any thing I desired in all the ignorance of innocence. . . ."[n]

Byron's heavy drinking contributed to his irrational behavior.
On November 18 he almost came to blows in a drunken argument at Kinnaird's. But the next day he wrote a quite rational
apology to the actor-manager Alexander Rae for the strong lan-

guage he had used in his cups."[n] Byron's language at home was even less controlled. His rages became so terrifying that both women were frightened. Annabella took refuge in the belief that he was suffering from temporary insanity, and Augusta readily acquiesced in this view. Augusta sat up late with him at night to keep him quiet.[1] Since she herself could with difficulty control him, Augusta was filled with pity for her sister-in-law. Lady Byron later told Mrs. Villiers: "He had threatened to bring a mistress into the house during my confinement—and to this moment I believe he would, had she [Augusta] not been there. . . ."[n]

Feeling unable to curb him longer, Augusta appealed to Mrs. Clermont, Annabella's former governess, and George Byron, and they came to live in the house sometime in December before the child was born. Lady Noel had come to London to be with her daughter, but became seriously ill in her hotel and could not be present. Mrs. Clermont later wrote: "Mrs. Leigh intreated me to come and sleep in the house at the time of Lady Byron's confinement, saying 'if he [Byron] continues in this way God knows what he may do!' "[n]

Of this miserable time Annabella recalled: "I was wretched, but I thought her [Augusta] more so." One evening Augusta seemed to be overpowered by remorse: "She said: 'Ah, you don't know *what* a fool I have been about him.' The bitterness of her look as she threw her hair back from her forehead with trembling hand wrung my heart. I kissed that forehead and left the room."[n]

Hobhouse, after calling on Byron on November 25, recorded that "in that quarter things do not go well—strong advices against marriage—talking of going abroad."[n] But Byron did not confide even to Hobhouse the extent to which, driven by his own insecurity, he had made his wife the scapegoat for all his troubles.

The servants, including Fletcher and the night nurse brought in for the confinement, as well as Mrs. Clermont, whose room was next to Annabella's, took quiet precautions to guard Lady

---

[1] Mayne, *Lady Byron*, p. 197. Byron confessed to the Countess Guiccioli that he had discharged a pistol in Lady Byron's room when she was pregnant, but said it was by accident. (Guiccioli, p. 392 n.)

Byron. "Nothing was done, however, to interfere with him ostensibly," Annabella recorded, "and I saw him alone." It is possible that Byron's threats were idle outbursts of frustration and anger, but they were cruel enough to a wife approaching her confinement. Annabella later claimed that only three hours before her labor began, "amid expressions of abhorrence," he told her he hoped she would die and that the child too would perish, and that if it lived he would curse it.[n] It is little to be wondered that she was frightened, though she may have taken too literally her husband's exasperated menaces. She later told Dr. Lushington: ". . . Serjt. Heywood[n] can witness that I consulted him on the subject *the day before my delivery* and proposed the question if I should not then leave the house— this, too, by the desire, or at least full concurrence, of Mrs. Leigh. . . . I also stated to Serjt. Heywood the supposition of insanity as embarrassing my conduct."[n]

While she was in labor, Lady Byron had the impression that Byron was throwing soda-water bottles at the ceiling of the room below the one in which she was lying in order to deprive her of sleep. So she told her physician, Mr. Le Mann, who was brought in to deliver the child. Hobhouse, later investigating this charge, found that "the ceiling of the room retained no mark of blows; and Lord Byron's habit of drinking soda-water, in consequence of taking magnesia in quantities, and of knocking off the heads of the bottles with a poker, sufficiently accounted for the noise. . . ."[n]

Hobhouse also scotched another story which was circulated during the separation proceedings—that of Byron "having asked his wife when in labour whether the child was dead."[n] Hobhouse "put the question to him and his sister. He answered that he was content to rest the whole merits of his case upon Lady Byron's simple assertion in that respect. 'She will not say so,' he frequently repeated, 'though, God knows, poor thing! it seems now she would say anything; but she would not say that—no, she would not say that.'"[n]

At one o'clock in the afternoon of December 10, Lady Byron's labor ended and a baby girl lay beside her.[n] According to Lady Anne Barnard, when Byron "was informed he might see his daughter, after gazing at it with an exulting smile, this was the ejaculation that broke from him: 'Oh, what an implement of torture have I acquired in you!' " " But in reporting the event to Francis Hodgson the next day Augusta said: "B. is in great good looks, and much pleased with his *Daughter*, though I believe he would have preferred a *Son*." " And Mrs. Clermont told Hobhouse "a few days after Lady Byron was brought to bed, that she had never seen a man so proud and fond of his child as Lord Byron. . . . Lady Byron herself more than once said to Lord Byron that he was fonder of the infant than she was, adding also what, to be sure, might have been as well omitted, and 'fonder of it than you are me.' " [2]

On December 20, while Annabella was still not sufficiently well to leave her room, the baptismal registration took place. The child's first name was Augusta, whether selected by Byron or Annabella or mutually agreed upon is not known.[3] Two days later Hobhouse called on Byron (he had been with him until 11:30 the previous night) and "saw his child Augusta Ada—the latter a name of some one who married into his family in the reign of K[ing] John." [4] At first they called the little girl Augusta Junior, but later the first name was dropped.[5]

[2] Broughton, II, 280. Byron later told Medwin: "I was once anxious for a son; but, after our separation, was glad to have had a daughter; for it would have distressed me too much to have taken him away from Lady Byron, and I could not have trusted her with a son's education. I have no idea of boys being brought up by mothers. I suffered too much from that myself. . . ." (Medwin, I, 116.)

[3] At this time Augusta had been named as godmother. On January 23, 1816, Lady Byron told Augusta: "Your God-daughter is very well indeed" (*LJ*, III, 299), but when the time came for the christening (November 1816) Lady Noel and Lady Tamworth (Sophie Curzon) were named as godmothers and Augusta was left out. (*Astarte*, p. 67.)

[4] Hobhouse diary, entry of Dec. 22, 1815. From the original MS., Berg Collection, New York Public Library. (With minor variations, Broughton, I, 324.) Byron wrote to Murray, October 8, 1820: "I found it [the name Ada] in my own pedigree. . . . It was also the name of Charlemagne's sister. It is in an early chapter of Genesis . . . and I suppose Ada is the feminine of *Adam*. It is short, ancient, vocalic, and had been in my family. . . ." (*LJ*, V, 93.)

[5] Mayne: *Lady Byron*, p. 198. When the shift in names came it is difficult to say, but it was probably made sometime during the spring or summer of 1816, after the separation rumors had begun to settle upon Augusta.

However proud Byron was of his daughter, she did not reconcile him to his marriage, as Annabella had for a while vainly
hoped. His erratic behavior increased rather than diminished
after the child was born. He later wrote of Ada as

> *The child of Love! though born in bitterness,*
> *And nurtured in Convulsion! Of thy sire*
> *These were the elements,—and thine no less.*[n]

Hobhouse recalled that about the end of November, Byron
had begun to talk vaguely of the "absolute necessity of his
breaking up his establishment after Lady Byron should have
been confined." And following the birth of the child Byron
"renewed this conversation with his friend, and owned that his
pecuniary embarrassments were such as to *drive him half-mad.*
He said 'he should think lightly of them *were he not married.'* . . .
'My wife,' he always added, 'is perfection itself—the best creature breathing; but, mind what I say—*don't marry.'*"[n]

Lord Lovelace, summarizing Lady Byron's later narratives,
wrote of this period: "About three weeks after Lady Byron's
confinement, the aversion he had already at times displayed
towards her struck everyone in the house as more formidable
than ever. . . . There were paroxysms of frenzy, but a still
stronger impression was created by the frequent hints he gave
of some suppressed and bitter determination."[n]

It is quite possible, however, that Byron was not fully aware
of the cumulative impression his conduct under continued irritations, drinking, and loss of temper must have made on his
wife. She recalled, with what must have been the embellishments
of a hypersensitive imagination making no allowance for Byron's
propensity to jest even in serious situations, certain details of
his conduct which were particularly harrowing. While she was
still recovering from her labor, he sent her, she claimed, a deliberately false message that her mother, dangerously ill at
Mivart's Hotel in Lower Brook Street, had died, an event that he
had told her in the first hours of her confinement he was eagerly
looking forward to.[n] His acts of violence, however, were against
things rather than people. On one occasion he seized a favorite
old watch which he had carried from boyhood and had taken

with him to Greece, and in "a fit of vexation and rage, brought on by some of those humiliating embarrassments to which he was now almost daily a prey, he furiously dashed this watch upon the hearth, and ground it to pieces among the ashes with the poker." [n]

Byron later confessed to only one really brutal outburst against his wife. "One day in the middle of my trouble [money trouble, Hobhouse explained] I came into the room, and went up to the fire; she was standing before it, and said, 'Am I in your way?' I answered, 'Yes, you *are*,' with emphasis. She burst into tears, and left the room. I hopped up stairs as quickly as I could ["Poor fellow," Hobhouse interjected, "you know how lame he was"] —and begged her pardon MOST humbly; and that was the only time I spoke really harshly to her." [n]

But away from provocations, which he was increasingly finding at home, Byron could be agreeable enough. He was still active in the interests of Drury Lane. In the midst of his financial embarrassments he sent fifty guineas to the starving dramatist Maturin, whom Scott had recommended. Before the end of December, Byron had sent off to Murray fair copies of *The Siege of Corinth* and *Parisina*, requesting as usual the opinion of Murray's reader Gifford. Knowing something of Byron's financial difficulties,[6] the publisher sent immediately two notes totaling one thousand guineas, which was his estimate of the worth of the copyrights. Hard-pressed as he was, however, Byron still refused to accept money for his writing." [n]

But behind the scenes the domestic drama was rapidly approaching a crisis. Byron's rages in the presence of his wife and the shocking things he said had already amazed and frightened the household. Annabella was perplexed by his seizures and was willing to accept finally the hypothesis that he was subject to insane delusions, but she wanted some medical proof. She was torn, however, with conflicting opinions concerning both her husband and his sister. She thought of leaving, but post-

---

[6] Byron's creditors had been staved off temporarily by his receiving, supposedly as part of Sir Ralph's £20,000 settlement on his daughter, but actually secured on Newstead because of the precarious state of the Noel property, the sum of £6,200.

꘎ *BYRON (ABOUT 1816?)*

)✤BYRON (1813?)

poned it and changed her plans frequently.[n] A climax came on January 3, when Byron came to her room and talked with "considerable violence" on the subject of his affairs with women of the theater.[n] It was then perhaps that he proposed that they break up the expensive establishment at Piccadilly Terrace and that she precede him to the country.[7]

According to Lord Lovelace, after the scene of January 3, Byron "did not go any more to see her or the child." [n] Annabella had recovered sufficiently to take a drive in the park on January 4.[n] Byron wrote to Moore the next day that his daughter "was, and is, very flourishing and fat, and reckoned very large for her days—squalls and sucks incessantly. . . . Her mother is doing very well, and up again. I have now been married a year on the second of this month—heigh-ho!"

"This is but a dull scrawl," he concluded, "and I am but a dull fellow. Just at present, I am absorbed in 500 contradictory contemplations, though with but one object in view—which will probably end in nothing, as most things we wish do. But never mind,—as somebody says, 'for the blue sky bends over all.' [n] I only could be glad, if it bent over me where it is a little bluer; like the 'skyish top of blue Olympus.' . . ." [n]

Annabella had concealed her anxieties not only from Lady Melbourne and from casual visitors, but also from her parents. She told her mother, who had recovered from her illness and had gone back to Kirkby, that she was "giving suck" while she wrote. "Oh dear! she pinches me," she said, and she tried to keep up her usual playfulness.[n] She had warned her parents that she and her family might descend on them at Kirkby.

On the 6th, Byron wrote to Annabella, having abstained from seeing her personally, perhaps to avoid a scene: "When you are disposed to leave London, it would be convenient that a day should be fixed—and (if possible) not a very remote one for that purpose.—Of my opinion upon that subject you are suf-

[7] Byron's letter of January 6 indicates that the matter of her leaving had already been discussed. Medwin (I, 42) quoted Byron as saying: ". . . it was agreed she should pay her father a visit till the storm had blown over, and some arrangements had been made with my creditors." On December 28 Lady Noel had sent Byron a cordial invitation to Kirkby Mallory. (Fox, pp. 100–1.)

ficiently in possession, & of the circumstances which have led to it—as also to my plans—or rather—intentions—for the future —When in the country I will write to you more fully—as Lady Noel has asked you to Kirkby—there you can be for the present— unless you prefer Seaham—

"As the dismissal of the present establishment is of importance to me—the sooner you can fix on the day the better—though of course your convenience & inclination shall be first consulted—

"The Child will of course accompany you—there is a more easy & safer carriage than the chariot (unless you prefer it) which I mentioned before—on that you can do as you please—" *n*

Byron's story, as told to Hobhouse, was that his wife "had been much offended with this note—that an altercation had ensued of very short duration—that she had declared herself satisfied—and that the affair terminated by a reconciliation that buried the whole matter in silence from that time forwards: that she herself fixed the day of her departure. . . ." *n* But Byron was not aware of all that was going on behind that calm "pippin" countenance. On Sunday, January 7, she wrote him simply: "I shall obey your wishes and fix the earliest day that circumstances will admit for leaving London." *n* According to her later story, this too was only a part of a design to avoid giving him any cause for irritation, for she had already conceived the notion that her husband was suffering from temporary mental derangement. "*With the concurrence of his family,* I had consulted Dr. Baillie," [8] she recalled later, "as a friend (Jan. 8th), respecting this supposed malady. . . . Dr. Baillie thought that my absence might be advisable as an experiment, *assuming* the fact of mental derangement; for Dr. Baillie, not having had access to Lord Byron, could not pronounce a positive opinion on that point. He enjoined that in correspondence with Lord Byron I should avoid all but light and soothing topics." *n*

Hobhouse, who in December was only vaguely aware of what was going on at Piccadilly Terrace, later gave some much more

[8] The same doctor who had been brought into consultation on Byron's foot when the poet was a boy; he was a brother of Annabella's friend Joanna Baillie, the poet and dramatist.

circumstantial, though no doubt in some points biased, details: "Her Ladyship thought she was only doing her duty in investigating *him* and *his* in search of those singularities and obliquities, which she conceived were the proofs and features of that particular insanity under which he laboured. His *drawers* and *trunks*, and *letter-cases*, were the objects of research—[9] in one place, which his Lordship certainly did not intend for the inspection even of his wife, was found a small bottle of laudanum—and in the same place a few volumes of a work which as a curiosity might be kept, but which was certainly not fit for an open library. . . .[1] Her Ladyship had provided herself with a volume of the *Medical Journal* in which she thought a case described of *hydrocephalus* designated the peculiar malady so exactly, that she marked the most prominent and apposite features on the margin with a pencil. Her medical attendant, Mr. Le Mann, who had sent her the book, was consulted on this occasion, and notwithstanding he had entertained apprehensions from the disordered state of his Lordship's liver—that his brain might be partially affected unless the disease was speedily removed—yet he declined giving any decided opinion, or stating those apprehensions to his Lordship." In the meantime, Hobhouse continued, Lady Byron drew up "a statement of Lord

[9] Some of Lady Byron's confidants, though possibly not the lady herself, in looking for "symptoms" of Byron's mental illness may have examined his books and papers. This might have been done without breaking open his writing-desk. But Byron, always suspicious, and more so than usual in this case, believed that his wife had pried into his private papers, for on September 14, 1816, he wrote to Augusta: "You know I suppose that Lady B^n *secretly opened my letter trunks before she left Town. . . .*" (*Astarte*, p. 269.) In the transparent portrait of Lady Byron in the person of Donna Inez in *Don Juan* (I, 28) Byron wrote:

> She kept a journal, where his faults were noted,
> And opened certain trunks of books and letters. . . .

[1] Hobhouse later recorded in his diary (entry for April 26, 1816): "I know she looked at a trunk in which B. kept his black drop [laudanum] and Justine. Mrs. L[eigh] confessed this." The book, which, Byron told Medwin, "did not do much credit to my taste in literature" (Medwin, I, 45), seems to have been the Marquis de Sade's famous suppressed novel *Justine*. Lady Byron would have considered this fact to be ample confirmation of her notions concerning her husband's depraved if not deranged mind.

Byron's conduct, including his *sayings* and singularities of manner and look. Dr. Baillie did come to Lord Byron's own house, and in Lord Byron's own parlour did examine these medical charges preferred against Lord Byron by Lord Byron's own wife. . . . Dr. Baillie also declined giving a decided opinion. . . ." [n]

This conference took place on January 8. Byron, of course, was quite unaware of what was going on. The next day Annabella wrote an urgent note to John Hanson asking for an interview.[n] At the meeting, which took place at Hanson's house, Hobhouse says, she stated her apprehensions "so strongly that Mr. Hanson *actually thought it possible* her Ladyship might have a design of *resorting to personal restraint*. Consequently he took the liberty of warning her most seriously against such a desperate and, as he thought, mistaken measure, which might produce even the very mischief which she dreaded, or perhaps a more terrible catastrophe." [n] On the 12th she sent Hanson the marked pamphlet, and the comment: "The symptoms correspond too well not only with those in the *first*, but also in the *second* stage of the Disease, when an effusion may take place from any act of excess. Not a moment must be lost, and the best medical advice must be insisted on." [n]

At the interview with Hanson, Hobhouse recorded, "Lady Byron mentioned several of Lord Byron's strong expressions, and was otherwise so detailed on this subject that Mr. Hanson thought it his duty to ask her 'what were her actual apprehensions, and *whether she laboured under any personal fear for herself?*' To which Lady Byron answered, without the least hesitation, '*Oh no, not in the least; my eye can always put down his*!!!' and then added that her suspicions were that Lord Byron might make an attempt upon his own life." [n]

Hobhouse's account continues: "Mr. Hanson . . . told Lady Byron . . . that his Lordship was liable to irritation, and, perhaps, sudden bursts of violence and passion; that he had long been in the habit of indulging in a conversation which was not to be taken '*to the letter.*'. . . . At parting she begged Mr. Hanson to use his efforts to induce Lord Byron to follow her as soon as possible to Kirkby, and on getting into her carriage said, 'If I am wanted in London, pray let me know; I will come down at

a minute's warning.' . . ." [2] Hanson wisely said nothing to Byron
about this interview at the time.

The agitation in the household in those last days before Annabella's departure was intense. She had postponed the journey
as long as possible on the ground that she and the child were
not yet strong enough to travel, hoping that something definite
could be determined about Byron's mental health. It was a
positive relief to her, as she later confessed, to be able to believe
that her husband's wicked ravings could be ascribed to a deranged mind.

How Annabella's last days were spent and what the parting
was like must be surmised from little evidence. Byron apparently
thought that everything had been smoothed over by his apologies,
although, he told Hobhouse, he "recollected being occasionally
much annoyed, on lifting up his head, to observe his wife gazing
at him with a mixture of pity and anxiety." [n]

But he and Annabella, according to Hobhouse, "lived on
conjugal terms up to the last moment—and that so far from
not intending to return, she had taken his . . . carriage and
several receipts for large sums belonging to Lord Byron, which
it is not likely a wife resolving to decamp for ever from her
husband should venture to do." [n]

She finally set January 15 for her journey. She would have
remained longer, but Captain Byron, who even more than Annabella herself took Byron's menaces to the letter, "declared he
would not suffer me to remain any longer in the house without
himself informing my parents." [n]

Byron did not like farewells, and particularly eschewed the
sentimental kind. There is enough realism in at least part of
Mrs. Stowe's account to make it seem in its outline credible:
"She went into the room where he and the partner of his sins
[Augusta] were sitting together, and said, 'Byron, I come to say
goodbye,' offering, at the same time, her hand.

[2] Broughton, II, 253–4. Moore (I, 653 n.) says that Lady Byron had drawn
up a list of symptoms (sixteen in number, he believed) in proof of her husband's insanity. In addition to those already mentioned as having been detailed to Hanson "was the emotion, almost to hysterics, which he had exhibited on seeing Kean act Sir Giles Overreach."

"Lord Byron put his hands behind him, retreated to the mantel-piece, and, looking on the two that stood there, with a sarcastic smile said, 'When shall we three meet again?' Lady Byron answered, 'In heaven, I trust.'" " That was no doubt on the 14th; Byron did not rise early enough for her to see him on the morning of her departure. Annabella's own recollection of her last day at Piccadilly Terrace is sentimental:

"I fell into a sound sleep on the last night, as I believe is often surprisingly the case in such cases of deep sorrow. Next morning I woke exhausted. I went downstairs—the carriage was at the door. I passed his room. There was a large mat on which his Newfoundland dog used to lie. For a moment I was tempted to throw myself on it, and wait at all hazards, but it was only a moment—and I passed on. That was our parting." " Byron never saw her again.

CHAPTER XV

1816

The Separation

WHEN Lady Byron left 13 Piccadilly Terrace on January 15 with her unweaned baby for the cold drive to Kirkby Mallory in Leicestershire, her mind was a whirl of conflicting thoughts, but her heart was filled with pity and tenderness for the man she never quite understood, the most fascinating and exasperating of husbands. But it must have been more than pity or concern for the doctor's prescription that she write only on "soothing" topics which prompted her to dash off a note to Byron when they stopped at Woburn.

Dearest B.
  The child is quite well and the best of travellers. I hope you are *good* and remember my medical prayers and injunctions. Don't give yourself up to the abominable trade of versifying—nor to brandy—nor to anything or anybody that is not *lawful* and *right*.
  Though *I* disobey in writing to you, let me hear of *your* obedience at Kirkby.
  Ada's love to you with mine.

Pip.ⁿ

And the day after her arrival ⁿ it was her heart rather than her head that directed her pen when she wrote from Kirkby:

Dearest Duck,
  We got here quite well last night and were ushered into the kitchen instead of drawing-room by a mistake that might have been agreeable enough to hungry people . . . Of this and other incidents Dad wants

to write you a jocose account and both he and Mam long to have the family party completed . . . Such . . . and such a *sitting*-room or *sulking*-room all to yourself. If I were not always looking about for B. I should be a great deal better already for country air. *Miss* finds her provisions increased and fattens thereon. It is a good thing she can't understand all the flattery bestowed upon her—'Little Angel' and I know not what . . . Love to the good goose and everybody's love to you both from hence.

> Ever thy most loving
> Pippin . . . Pip . . . Ip."

But as she reflected about the past months and particularly the past weeks her mind became confused and divided again. Except for Augusta's sympathetic ear she had so far borne her burden all alone, and the strain was visible in her countenance. The same day that she wrote her affectionate note to Byron from Kirkby, Annabella penned two longer ones to Augusta, who had already written to report on things in Piccadilly. In one she confessed:

"I hope Le Mann will write me his opinion after this interview, which must have rendered it more decided. . . . I have made the most explicit statement to my father and mother, and nothing can exceed their tender anxiety to do everything for the sufferer. . . . My father and mother agree that in every point of view it would be best for B. to come here; they say he shall be considered in everything. . . . Has Le Mann advised the country? It will be by means of the *heir* that it can be effected [in his melancholy dejection Byron had said that he would beget an heir (male) and then go abroad], and you will be able to touch that subject skillfully before you go, and give G. B. a hint of it if you can." "

She was wholly dependent on Augusta. She continued: "My mother suggests what would be more expedient about the laudanum bottle than taking it away, to fill it with about three-quarters of water, which won't make any observable difference. . . ." "

How much had she told her parents? Apparently she had revealed only what in her own mind confirmed her theory that his menaces and cruel words were attributable to a mental ailment: his threat of going abroad, his use of laudanum, his paroxysms of rage, and the other symptoms she had assembled for the doctor. Now her unrealistic hope was that his "healing" could be accomplished by getting him away from the temptations of London. On January 17 she wrote to Captain George Byron, urging him to aid with the project of getting Byron to come to Kirkby, where "air and exercise" might alleviate his malady." Annabella recalled at a later time: "With these intentions, my mother wrote on the 17th to Lord Byron, inviting him to Kirkby Mallory." "

Then something happened that changed the whole complexion of events, for on the same day, after the arrival of the post from London, Annabella wrote to Le Mann suggesting that the removal to Kirkby be postponed. She asked him to send further accounts: ". . . I remain ignorant of the bodily disease which you are now led to suppose." " One can only guess, from Annabella's own statements then and later, that in a moment of distrust of the self-hypnosis impelled by her attachment to Byron she saw in a flash that she had been deluding herself into believing in his mental derangement, and that he had been fully responsible for his actions. Some chance remark of one of her correspondents close to Byron—Mrs. Leigh, George Byron, or Mrs. Clermont, who had remained at Piccadilly—could have brought her to a realization of how deeply she had deceived herself. And in her distress she had broken down and told her parents all that she had withheld from them before—all with the important exception of her suspicions of Augusta, which she had now come to think an injustice.[1]

At first it was a relief to throw the burden on her parents, but she soon repented that she had, as Byron at Halnaby suggested she might, run home to her parents like the spoiled child she was. What she in her affection could forgive, they could not, and they became more and more irate, determining then and there that their daughter should never return to the beast who had mistreated her. Her parents induced her to promise that if he proved to be sane, nothing would make her return to him. They decided

[1] In her first letter to Augusta from Kirkby, Annabella had written: ". . . I have much to repair in my conduct towards you. . . . My chief feeling, therefore, in relation to you and myself must be that I *have* wronged you, and that you have never wronged me." (*LJ*, III, 294.)

that she should have legal as well as medical advice, and on the 18th she drew up a statement of her husband's offenses for her mother to take to London. But it is evident from the tone of her letter to Augusta, written the same day, that she still clung to the "hope" of her husband's mental illness."

In the next few days there ensued a heart-consuming battle in Annabella between her "reason" and her unreasoned attachment to Byron. Despite his "naughtiness," he had an irresistible attraction that, if she had let herself go, would have drawn her to him despite all the pain he had caused her. She later wrote: "There were moments when resignation yielded to frenzy—and I would have forgotten myself, my child, my principles, to devote myself to that being who had cast me off." " The foolish Augusta sent daily bulletins of Byron's actions and words and silences, all of which she thought significant of his mental disturbance. On the 19th, Annabella wrote her:

"I think he was so much pleased with my 2nd letter from one expression which acknowledged the power he still has over my affections; and the *love of power* is one principal feature of his Disease or Character. My own conviction of the existence of the former, in any greater degree than many years ago, decreases. . . ." "

After she had written out her indictment of her husband, she was emotionally overwrought to the point of being physically ill. She wrote to Augusta: "I have been endeavouring to write off some of my agonies, and have addressed them to B. in the enclosed, which I wish you to read attentively. . . . God bless you and *him!*" " But she did not send the enclosure. The next day she added: "I mean to break my neck upon my old horse, which is here." " And on the 20th: ". . . my presence has been uniformly oppressive to him from the hour we married—if not before, and in his best moods he has always wished to be away from me. . . . had we continued together he *would* have gone mad." She added plaintively: "Indeed, I have done nothing except on the strictest principle of Duty, yet I feel as if I were going to receive sentence from the judge with his black cap on. . . . O that I were in London, if in the coal-hole." That was the day her mother left for London, carrying the document Annabella felt would seal her doom. On the following Monday (the 22nd) she added a postscript: "Nothing but Conscience to comfort me, and just now it is a Job's comforter." [n]

In London, Byron was quite unaware of what was impending. After parting on what he believed to be perfectly amicable and affectionate terms with his wife, he settled down with a measure of relief to a pleasant bachelor life before taking leisurely steps to break up his expensive establishment (he was already in arrears for half a year's rent for the Piccadilly house). [n] The two affectionate letters he received from Annabella left him with the flattering sense that she missed him, but he had fallen into a lackadaisical state which made letter-writing distasteful, and he delegated Augusta to reply for him, quite heedless of the impression his negligence might make on a sensitive mind.

On the 17th, two days after his wife left, Byron and Hobhouse dined at Tavistock House with Perry, editor of the *Morning Chronicle*. Hobhouse drank too much wine and then "came home with Byron—drank brandy & water till two in the morning— Lady B gone into the country. *B wont go!!!*" [n] In a soberer moment Byron told his friend: "They want me to go into the country. I shall go soon, but I won't go yet. I should not care if Lady Byron was alone, but I can't stand Lady Noel." [n] Hobhouse did not see Byron again for a fortnight, being busy with the last corrections and the attempt to get a publisher for his *Letters* describing the last reign of Napoleon, which he had made up from the substance of his correspondence to Byron and others from Paris the previous year. [n]

In the meantime, Byron was occupied with other business. Sir James Mackintosh, having heard that Byron had refused a large sum offered by Murray for the publication of his poems, wrote to Rogers to propose that, as the poet would not take the money for himself, he might induce Murray to turn over a part of it to William Godwin, "a man of genius, likely, for his independence of thinking, to starve at the age of sixty for want of a few hundred pounds necessary to carry on his laborious occupation." [n] Byron fell in readily with the scheme when Rogers suggested it, and asked Murray to turn over to Godwin six hundred pounds of the thousand guineas first offered, and to divide the remainder between the two needy poets Coleridge and Maturin." Having seen him but once, Byron did not know the facility Godwin had acquired through long experience in easing his conscience in such matters, and he cautioned Rogers to arrange the matter delicately."

But Murray demurred. Byron was surprised and angered by the publisher's resistance to the suggestion, though he might have reflected that it was a bitter pill for Murray, with his Tory leanings, to be forced to contribute to the support of the radical Godwin. Byron countered heatedly, knowing how much Murray had already profited from the Oriental tales he had published: "Had I taken you at your word, that is, taken your money, I might have used it as I pleased; and it could be in no respect different to you whether I paid it to a w[hore], or a hospital, or assisted a man of talent in distress. . . . The things in question shall not be published at all, and there's an end of the matter." " And he asked Murray to return the manuscripts by the bearer.

But a week later he told Leigh Hunt, who was still bargaining with Murray for the publication of *The Story of Rimini*: ". . . I doubt not he [Murray] will deal fairly by you on the whole; he is really a very good fellow, and his faults are merely the leaven of his 'trade.' . . ." "

During the last week of January there was feverish activity in London on the part of Lady Noel and her advisers. She had gone immediately to Sir Samuel Romilly with the catalogue of her daughter's wrongs. Romilly recommended that Byron should not be allowed to remain an instant at Kirkby, if he should come, and that she should put the matter in the hands of a civilian legal adviser. She was then referred to Dr. Stephen Lushington, a distinguished barrister of the Inner Temple, with whom she had a conference a few days after her arrival. In the interval she saw Mr. Le Mann, and also Mrs. Leigh and Mrs. Clermont, who had remained at Piccadilly. Le Mann told her he had never seen any proofs that his patient was insane, "but he *believed* him to be so, from what he had heard from Mrs. Leigh and others, and . . . [what] he had been told of his doings—things at the Theatre, which made people think so." Still, he considered Byron capable of judging between right and wrong. And Mrs. Leigh thought her brother "particularly *acute* in business." ⁿ

But Le Mann had written to Lady Byron the same day her mother arrived in town: "With regard to the state of my patient's mind, I must say that I have discovered nothing like settled lunacy." ⁿ

On January 22, Augusta, who preferred to think it "malady" rather than "*depravity of heart,*" had so far lost her perspective as to see madness in all Byron's actions. "One of the things he did and said last night was desiring George to go and live at Seaham, exactly as if it were his own; and even before our dinner he said he considered himself 'the greatest man existing.' G. said, laughing, 'except Bonaparte.' The answer was, 'God, I don't know that I do except even him.' I was struck previously with a wildness in his eyes." ⁿ

Perhaps Byron was trying to rib his cousin, who was growing a little obstreperous. On Tuesday the 23rd, George, whom Byron felt to be under obligation to him for many favors, openly accused him of cruelty to his wife and threatened that her parents would take up her defense. As Annabella's friend Miss Doyle reported it, Byron "interrupted him with the most animated expressions of exultation and said 'Let them come forward, I'll Glory in it!' " ⁿ

Those who were watching his every move, ready to read deep meaning into his whimsical expressions, noted that at one time he spoke of his wife with great kindness, without actually expressing a wish that she should return, and at another time he would say that the sooner Lady Byron's friends took measures for a separation the better. He talked about his affairs with women at the theater and spoke of marrying Miss Mercer Elphinstone if he could get rid of his present wife.ⁿ George Byron had apparently aroused the spirit of opposition in him and had given him the first hint of what was going on behind the scenes.[2]

[2] But this did not lessen the shock of the emotional reaction when he first got news that Lady Byron was proposing a separation. It was one thing to talk in his usual rattling way of such matters and another to be faced with the cold fact. He, like his wife, was of a divided mind.

Lady Noel, quite beside herself with indignation that grew as she consulted her advisers, was convinced from the beginning of her stay in London that Byron was not mad but bad. When Augusta hinted that the announcement of a separation might cause her brother to take his own life, Lady Noel replied: "So much the better; it is not fit such men should live." [n] Le Mann ceased communicating with Lady Noel in order not to act in a manner prejudicial to his patient.

Le Mann's report of the 20th had left Annabella quite resigned and hopeless, for she knew then that a separation must take place. On the 22nd she wrote her mother: "For Heaven's sake don't let a whisper of my wrongs get abroad. . . . Legal measures ought certainly to be *subsequent* to some direct application to him—and from his regard to appearances, as well as from a strange, though uncertain generosity of character, *I am convinced* that, if he had no reason to suppose harsher measures were in preparation (which would drive him to fury), he would make every requisite acknowledgment of my unexceptionable conduct, and give every security for the child and a due provision. It would be a death-blow to me to be obliged to come forward publicly. . . ." [n]

Lady Noel had consulted again with Dr. Lushington, who had counseled that a proposal for a quiet arrangement should be sent Byron by Sir Ralph. Lushington insisted that Annabella should not see her husband "on *any account*. . . . If you see him voluntarily or he is suffered to remain, you are wholly in his power and he may apply to the Spiritual court for a restoration of *Conjugal Rights*, as they term it, and oblige you to return—neither must you answer any letter he writes." [n]

But Annabella was concerned lest her mother take some irrevocable step without consulting her, and she was fearful that Mrs. Leigh would be treated rudely by the impetuous Lady Noel. Annabella wrote that Augusta had been "the truest of friends to me and I hope you so regard her and *seem* to regard her as such, for I very much fear that she may be supposed the cause of separation by many, and it would be a cruel injustice." [n]

On the same day, when it seemed that an open declaration of her intentions must be imminent, she wrote: "My dearest Au-

gusta,—Shall I still be your sister? I . . . must resign my *rights*
to be so considered. . . . Feelings must not now be indulged;
but whenever I feel at all, it will be as kindly as you could. *Independent* of malady, I do not think of the past with any spirit
of resentment, and scarcely with the sense of injury. God bless
him!" "

Lady Noel, accompanied by Miss Doyle and Mrs. Clermont,
left London on Saturday and arrived at Kirkby Mallory Sunday
evening the 28th." She carried with her a letter proposing a quiet
separation, carefully "corrected" by Sir Samuel Romilly and
other advisers. Sir Ralph immediately copied the proposal and
sent it to London. On the day Annabella expected the letter
would be delivered, her maid, Mrs. Fletcher, noticed that she
"was extremely distressed, and almost insensible." " But Augusta,
already warned by Annabella that such a letter was impending,
feared the effect on her brother and intercepted it, returning it
with a plea for further deliberation." Annabella was relieved and
seemed in much better spirits.

It was determined that Sir Ralph should himself go to London
and see that the letter was delivered. Accompanied by Mrs. Clermont, Sir Ralph arrived at Mivart's Hotel and sent the fatal letter
by messenger on February 2." It was Friday, a day that Byron
ever considered unpropitious. In a sudden change of mood, or
because he had not heard from Annabella directly (Augusta had
been discreetly silent), he had just ordered horses to go to
Kirkby the following Sunday."

His surprise and agitation on opening the letter were wholly
unaffected. He read: "*Very recently*, circumstances have come
to my knowledge, which convince me, that with your opinions it
cannot tend to your happiness to continue to live with Lady Byron, and I am yet more forcibly convinced that after her dismissal from your house, and the treatment she experienced
whilst in it, those on whose protection she has the strongest natural claims could not feel themselves justified in permitting her
return thither." Though Sir Ralph was willing to bring the whole
matter before the public, if necessary, he expressed the hope that
Byron would agree to appoint a *"professional friend"* to consider
with one of his own appointment the terms of a separation."

Remembering the terms on which they had lived during her last days in London and the affectionate and playful tone of her last letters, Byron did not believe that Annabella could have been responsible for such a course of action. He asked Augusta to confront her with the question directly, and to Sir Ralph he replied with forthright candor: "I have received your letter. To the vague and general charge contained in it I must naturally be at a loss how to answer. . . . Lady Byron received no dismissal from my house in the sense you have attached to the word. She left London by medical advice. She parted from me in apparent and, on my part, real harmony, though at that particular time, rather against my inclination. . . .

"It is true that previous to this period I had suggested to her the expediency of a temporary residence with her parents. My reason for this was very simple and shortly stated, viz. the embarrassment of my circumstances, and my inability to maintain our present establishment. The truth of what is thus stated may be easily ascertained by reference to Lady B.—who is truth itself."

During the past year, he said, he had had "to contend with distress without and disease within," which "may have rendered me little less disagreeable to others than I am to myself. I am, however, ignorant of any particular ill-treatment which your daughter has encountered. . . . I must for a few days decline giving a decisive answer. . . . for the present at least, your daughter is my wife; she is the mother of my child; and till I have her express sanction of your proceedings, I shall take leave to doubt the propriety of your interference." ⁿ

Sir Ralph, who was, as Byron had called him, a "good old man," might himself have taken pause at the moderation of this letter had he not been under the strict surveillance of his legal advisers and particularly of Mrs. Clermont, who, on her return to London, remained at Mivart's Hotel as a kind of confidential secretary in all the negotiations.ⁿ

Annabella replied to Augusta's letter promptly, saying that she had given her concurrence to her father's proposal for a separation. She added: "I will only recall to Lord Byron's mind his avowed and insurmountable aversion to the married state, and

the desire and determination he has expressed ever since its com-
mencement to free himself from that bondage, as finding it quite
insupportable. . . ." "

Augusta, seeing her brother's agitated state, withheld this letter from him. Byron, in the meantime, wrote a guarded letter in
his own hand to Annabella.

I feel naturally at a loss how to address you, ignorant as I am how
far the letter I have received has received your sanction. . . . I am
really ignorant to what part of Sir Ralph's letter alludes. Will you explain? . . . I shall eventually abide by your decision; but I request
you most earnestly to weigh well the probable consequences. . . . I
cannot sign myself otherwise than
                        yours ever most affectionately. . . ."

Annabella was forbidden to reply to Byron directly, and wrote
to Augusta after receiving his letter, urging that the indirect reply already sent should not be withheld from him." Byron had
received no word from his wife on February 5 when Hobhouse
called at Piccadilly. He found Byron "exceedingly depressed,
more so than in an intimacy of eleven years he had ever seen."
Byron told him of Sir Ralph Noel's proposition. "He attributed
the determination of his wife, if determination she had taken, to
the influence of Lady Noel, and of Mrs. Clermont. . . . He solemnly protested that Lady Byron and himself had parted friends.
. . . He as solemnly declared, that he could not *guess* at the immediate cause of this resolution." " He showed Hobhouse the
"Dearest Duck" letter, the last he had received from her. Hobhouse wrote in his diary: ". . . he was completely knocked up—
he instantly accepted my offer to write to Lady B. which I did
in great agitation," urging her not to take such a step."

At the same time Byron wrote another short letter to Annabella: "No answer from you yet; but perhaps it is as well; only do
recollect that all is at stake, the present, the future, and even the
colouring of the past. My errors, or by whatever harsher name
you choose to call them, you know; but I loved you, and will not
part from you without your express and expressed refusal to return to, or receive me." "

Lady Noel's activities while she was in London had already

overflowed into the gossip of the town. On the day of Hobhouse's visit Lady Melbourne wrote Byron that she had heard a rumor of a separation. She assured him she knew it was false, but added: "But really, this is so much talked about and believed, notwithstanding my contradictions, that I think you ought to desire her to come to Town, or go to her yourself." [n]

At Kirkby, Annabella was thrown into an emotional state worse than her husband's by his second letter, which arrived on the 6th. Horribly torn between what she considered her duty and her feelings, but irrevocably committed to the former not only by her promise to her parents but also by her own painfully strong sense of reason and consistency, she was nevertheless made to suffer the more acutely because she could not tear from her inner consciousness the attachment which had grown as strong as her sense of having been wronged. It must have been about this time that Mrs. Fletcher reported in a letter to her husband that her mistress's "distress and agony" were "at their height; that she was rolling on the floor in a paroxysm of grief at having *promised* to separate from Lord Byron; that she showed by words and actions that she was compelled by her family to quit her husband. . . ." [n]

The reply which Annabella wrote was dictated, however, not by her parents but by her reason, which left her even less a "free agent": "I have indeed placed myself under the protection of my parents, but I act on my own conviction independently, as they do on theirs. . . . After seriously and dispassionately reviewing the misery that I have experienced almost without an interval from the day of my marriage, I have finally determined on the measure of a separation, which my father was authorised to communicate to you and to carry into effect. It is unhappily your disposition to consider what you *have* as worthless—what you have *lost* as invaluable. But remember that you believed yourself most miserable when I was yours." [n]

The day this was written Hobhouse had dispatched a long letter, which he had spent most of the previous day composing, pleading with Lady Byron to reconsider the step she was about to take. "I am sure I *know the very worst of everything that can be said against my friend*," he wrote, "and in that very worst nothing is comprised which can bear out your friends in the extremity to which they seem inclined to proceed." [n]

But before he could expect a reply, Byron had received Annabella's two letters, Mrs. Leigh having no longer dared to withhold the one addressed to her. The other, arriving soon after, shook him sadly. In response to the first he wrote to Sir Ralph: "My house, while I have one, is open to her, and my heart always —even though I should have no other shelter to offer her. . . . I invite Lady Byron's return . . . I deprecate all attempts which have been made or may be made to part us." [n]

To Annabella's letter directed to him he replied with a resigned desperation: "Were you then *never* happy with me? did you never at any time or times express yourself so? have no marks of affection, of the warmest and most reciprocal attachment, passed between us? or did in fact hardly a day go down without some such on one side and generally on both? . . . had I not— had we not—the days before and on the day when we parted, every reason to believe that we loved each other—that we were to meet again? . . . You are much changed within these twenty days, or you would never have thus poisoned your own better feelings—and trampled upon mine." [n]

This was a terrible letter for Annabella to receive and a great trial for her now irrevocable resolution, for she recognized in it the sincerity which she knew to be basic in the character of her husband. It recalled to her some of the happiest moments of her life with him, now cut off forever by that "consistency" and "undeviating rectitude" to which she had committed herself before she became acquainted with the inconsistencies of Byron and of life. She had already written to decline Hobhouse's proposed visit to Kirkby and all discussion of the subject. [n]

Byron had written with a clarity and reserve which hardly indicated a deranged mind, but her unexpected rejection had shaken him. Hobhouse, who now knew what was yet a secret to others, that Lady Byron had left her husband, was the only one of his friends he had the heart to face. Braving a "tremendous frost, the hardest known for years," Hobhouse went up to town on the 9th and called on Byron, who showed him the two letters from his wife. "Mrs. L[eigh] was questioned before me," Hobhouse recorded, "and owned that not a day passed without some mutual endearment. She sat on his knee she kissed him five thousand times before Mrs. L. rather he kissed her—he never lifted up a finger against her. . . . He told me & told me again & again that he had told me *all*. The matter continued inexplicable." Douglas Kinnaird had told Hobhouse that morning "that the Melbournes are in arms against Lady B. G[eorge] L[amb] called her a d'd fool, but added that C[aroline] L[amb] accused B of —— poor fellow the plot thickens against him." "

Hobhouse had bought a copy of *The Siege of Corinth* and *Parisina* that morning from Murray, whom Byron had forgiven and to whom he had presented the copyright." "It is to be published on Tuesday [the 13th]," Hobhouse wrote. "He showed me that the first was dedicated to John Hobhouse Esq. this poem is inscribed by his Friend. He thought this sublime—I should have liked it better if he had not dedicated Parisina to S. B. Davies. I told him this." " The frost had deepened, and it was twenty degrees below freezing when Hobhouse rode dejectedly away from Piccadilly.

Annabella was stricken by Byron's letter, but in a few days she bolstered herself to reply: "I have determined, *if possible*, not to indulge the language of feeling in addressing you, as it could only be injurious in our present relative situations." Matters that needed discussion, she said, could be settled by "authorised friends." "

Augusta, almost torn in two by her attempt to be loyal to Annabella and yet serve her brother's interests, had not given up hope of a reconciliation. And to aid her she summoned Francis Hodgson to London." Hodgson found "a sincere desire of reconciliation" in Byron, and wrote a long letter to Lady Byron urging his friend's "deep and rooted feeling" of "regret and sorrow" and "the warmest affection" as his excuse for appealing to her, and expressing the fear that in his dejection Byron might destroy himself."

Hobhouse called at Piccadilly again on the 12th: "saw Mrs. L. and George B and from them learnt what I fear is the real truth that B has been guilty of very great tyranny—menaces—furies—neglects & even real injuries such as telling his wife he was *living* with another woman—& actually in *fact* turning her out of the house—G.B. suspected she would leave him & told him so a month before she went—but she had no intention of doing it when she went from London—locking doors—showing pistols—frowning at her in bed—reproaches—every thing she seems to believe him to have been guilty of—but they acquit him—how? by saying that he is mad. . . . Whilst I heard these things Mrs. L. went out & brought word that her brother was crying bitterly in his bed room—poor poor fellow."

Hobhouse resolved that the matter must not come before the public. But he could not conceal what he knew from his friend. "I now thought it my duty to tell Byron I had changed my opinion and to tell him so without compromising my informants." Hobhouse then left and when he came back later "met Lady Melbourne there who abused Lady Noel violently. B was tranquil and jesting—but when I told him what I had heard in *the streets* that day he was astounded indeed and after Lady M. went questioned me—he had heard he was to be accused of cruelty, drunk[en]ness, and *infidelity*—I got him to own much of what I had been told in the morning—he was dreadfully agitated—said he was ruined & would blow out his brains—he is indignant but yet terrified—sometimes says 'and yet she loved me once,' and at other times that he is glad to be quit of such a woman—he said if I would go abroad he would separate at once." [n]

The following morning Augusta wrote to Hanson, whom Byron had authorized to retain counsel: [3] ". . . my Brother is this

---

[3] Hanson and James Farquhar, the Byron family lawyer who had first introduced Byron's mother to Hanson, had retained Dr. Robinson, Dr. Adams, and Dr. Jenner to act for him in Doctors Commons if the matter came to trial. On February 12, Byron wrote to ask Hanson if he was sure that Sir Samuel Romilly was retained for him. (*LJ*, III, 308.) Hanson replied that Sir Samuel had a general retainer for Byron (Broughton, II, 274), but Hanson was unaware that Lady Noel had already consulted him. Not until March 16 did Byron learn that Romilly had been counseling Lady Byron. When Hobhouse confronted Romilly with the fact that he had had a retainer for Byron, he confessed "that he had done a very incorrect thing in being consulted by Lady Byron, but that in the multiplicity of retainers, it was sometimes the case that names were overlooked." (Broughton, II, 307–8.) Sir Samuel then declined to arbitrate the terms of the separation, but Byron never forgave him.

mong. *exactly the reverse* in determination of what he was last night. He is now for *acquiescence* to ye separation having made me write to Ly B. yesterday *nothing on earth should make him resign her willingly;* and the reason he gives for this extraordinary change is having received a Bill from his Coachmaker for £2000, and his affairs being in such a state that if Ly B. came back he should have no where to receive her." [n] Hobhouse, who saw Byron almost daily during this period, found him "a prey to the alternate passions of pity, regret, love, and indignation. . . ." [n]

After her curt reply to Byron's letter of the 8th, Annabella felt impelled to explain to him herself why she had acted on what appeared a reversal of all that was implied in her affectionate behavior before she left him and in her two letters of January 15 and 16. She revealed to him then for the first time that before leaving London she had thought him deranged and could not urge her wrongs at that moment. "From subsequent accounts I found that these particular apprehensions which I, and others, had entertained, were groundless. . . . What then had I to expect? I cannot attribute your 'state of mind' to any cause so much as the *total* dereliction of principle, which, since our marriage, you have professed and gloried in. Your acknowledgements have not been accompanied by any intentions of amendment. I have *consistently* fulfilled my duty as your wife. It was too dear to be resigned till it became hopeless. Now my resolution cannot be changed." [n]

To Augusta she wrote the next day (February 14): "*Happiness* no longer enters into my views, it can never be restored, and the greater or less degree of misery I must endure will depend on the *principles* of my conduct, not on its *consequences*. Now, independent of any advice whatever, I deem it *my duty to God* to act as I am acting. . . ." [4] And to Hodgson's appeal she re-

---

[4] *LJ*, III, 310–11. Augusta perhaps showed this letter to Byron or told him what Annabella said, for in his satiric portrait of his wife in *Don Juan* (I, 27) he wrote:

> For Inez called some druggists and physicians,
>   And tried to prove her loving lord was mad,
> But as he had some lucid intermissions,
>   She next decided he was only bad;

plied: "I know him too well to dread the fatal event which he so often mysteriously threatens. . . . He *does* know—too well—what he affects to enquire." [n]

When Hobhouse called at Piccadilly on the 16th, he saw George Byron, who told him that "in a party the night before what Kinnaird had told me had been said openly by a woman—" Hobhouse then decided that he was going "to work openly to disprove every thing." That night he went to Byron's house again: "sat with him till past one—told him the very worst I had heard against him which he received to my astonishment with very little discomposure—poor fellow." [n]

But Byron's composure was only of the moment and on the surface. The day before he had written to Annabella a last appeal. "And now, Bell, dearest Bell . . . I can only say in the truth of affliction, and without hope, motive, or end in again saying what I have lately but vainly repeated, that I love you, bad or good, mad or rational, miserable or content, I love you, and shall do, to the dregs of my memory and existence."

This was difficult and painful enough for Annabella, though nothing could any longer shake her resolution, but the last paragraph of his letter probably gave her great alarm. He wrote: "I have hitherto avoided naming my child, but this was a feeling you never doubted in me. I must ask of its welfare." [n] What he had meant as an appeal to her sympathy, she took as a hint that he might try to force the child from her by legal means, which Lushington had given her no assurance could be prevented. On February 17, after receiving this letter, she wrote to Dr. Lushington proposing a personal interview with him, saying: "There are things which I, and I only, could explain to you in conversation that may be of great importance to the thorough understanding of the case." Three days earlier she had written: "I could add many facts to my written statement, in which I do not find any exaggeration on the calmest reperusal, but I hope it will not be *necessary* to record them." The following

---

Yet when they asked her for her depositions,
No sort of explanation could be had,
Save that her duty both to man and God
Required this conduct—which seemed very odd.

day (February 15) she wrote to Lushington: "I have thought of Terms, as you desired, and should feel so very happy to be screened from molestation with the child, that I scarcely think of any other advantages. . . ." [n]

In the meantime, Hanson and the other lawyers retained for Byron were gathering evidence against the possibility of the case coming into court. The servants at Piccadilly Terrace were interviewed, and Fletcher asked his wife to return to London from Kirkby that she might give her deposition.[5] Byron wavered so that it was difficult for the lawyers to hold him to his purpose, but on the 21st Hanson sent to Sir Ralph Noel Byron's positive refusal of a separation.[n]

During these days of indecision life went on for Byron, though not even his remarkable resilience could quite stir him to take a very active part in the scenes that generally moved him the most—the gossip at Murray's and the dinners at Kinnaird's together with the activities of the theater. He had, apparently at the suggestion of Sotheby, sent £100 to the needy Coleridge, though the latter had failed to complete his promised tragedy for Drury Lane.[6]

An event recalling one of the tenderest, and at the same time one of the most cynical, of his romantic intrigues roused him momentarily to the fever of composition. Murray wrote Byron that Wedderburn Webster had won his suit against Baldwin, proprietor of the *Morning Chronicle*, for libel (the *Chronicle* had slanderously connected Lady Frances's name with that of the Duke of Wellington). Byron replied ironically: "I thank you for the account of Mr. and Lady F.W.'s triumph; you see

[5] Broughton, II, 262. Lady Byron kept Mrs. Fletcher in her service after she came to London though she was aware of the nature and tendency of her evidence.

[6] Coleridge wrote (letter postmarked Feb. 17, 1816): "Whether, my Lord! it shall be a Loan or not, depends on circumstances not in my power tho' in my hope and expectation. Thank God! this is of the least importance—the debt and the *pleasure* of Love and Gratitude stand unaffected by anything accidental." Then he asked for Byron's works to keep as an "Heir-loom in my Family." (*Unpublished Letters of Samuel Taylor Coleridge*, ed. Earl Leslie Griggs, II, 158-9.) Byron later told Murray that at the time he gave Coleridge £100, "I could not command 150 in the world. . . ." (*LJ*, VI, 113. Letter of Sept. 11, 1822.)

by it the exceeding advantage of unimpeachable virtue and uniform correctness of conduct, etc., etc." [n] But he revived the emotions of the past with the verses:

When we two parted
In silence and tears,
Half broken-hearted
To sever for years,
Pale grew thy cheek and cold,
Colder thy kiss;
Truly that hour foretold
Sorrow to this. . . .
Thy vows are all broken,
And light is thy fame;
I hear thy name spoken,
And share in its shame. . . .

They know not I knew thee,
Who knew thee too well:—
Long, long shall I rue thee,
Too deeply to tell. . . . [n]

Then fare thee well, Fanny,
Now doubly undone,
To prove false unto many
As faithless to one.
Thou art past all recalling
Even would I recall,
For the woman once falling
Forever must fall. [n]

On the 22nd, Lady Byron arrived at Mivart's Hotel in London and had a long private conference with Dr. Lushington, as a result of which he changed his opinion completely on the case. Whereas he had previously considered a reconciliation possible, he now thought a separation inevitable and necessary. [n] What were the "facts utterly unknown . . . to Sir Ralph and Lady Noel" which Annabella revealed to him at that time, and what was her motive for doing so? Lushington never through his long life revealed them,[7] but there is collateral evidence enough

[7] That is, publicly; several people were let into the secret at the time, including Lady Byron's advisers, Robert John Wilmot (Byron's first cousin)

in Lady Byron's own statements and letters and elsewhere to indicate quite clearly that she then for the first time fully confessed her suspicion of the incest, together with details of Byron's own words and actions which tended to confirm it. Her statement of January 18, which she had written out for her mother to take to London, had contained allegations of acts of adultery and cruelty on the part of her husband, but had made no reference to incest. It did, however, contain the unelaborated statement: "His conversation has also (particularly of late) turned on images of the most indelicate nature." [n] What those indelicate images were we have some indication from the several people who saw Annabella's statements written down for Lushington after this visit. All of them seem to indicate that they were of the grossest sort.[8]

Lushington was certain that, with Lady Byron's evidence legally excluded, it would be impossible to prove the charge of incest in court. His advice, therefore, was to seek a separation, in court if necessary, where an adequate case could rest on Byron's "brutally indecent conduct and language." Part of the evidence would be his crude references to intercourse with Mrs. Leigh as a means of torturing his wife, though no effort would be made to establish the fact of incest.

But Annabella was eager, above all else, to avoid a public hearing of the case. For this reason she and her counsel used

---

and Colonel Francis Doyle (see *Astarte*, p. 45), and in conversation with Henry Allen Bathurst, the surviving trustee of Lady Byron's sealed papers, on January 27, 1870, he told the essential facts. Bathurst's memorandum of that conversation was printed for the first time by Fox in *The Byron Mystery* (pp. 57–8). But Lushington's actual papers and records of the separation were destroyed by himself before he died. (Letter of Miss Susan Lushington, his granddaughter, to me, May 1948.)

[8] John Buchan (in *Memory Hold-the-Door*, quoted in *The Notebooks of Henry James*, p. 181 n.) records that "an aunt [Lady Lovelace] of my wife's, who was the widow of Byron's grandson, asked Henry James and myself to examine her archives. . . . So, during a summer week-end, Henry James and I waded through masses of ancient indecency, and duly wrote an opinion. . . . My colleague never turned a hair. His only words for some special vileness were 'singular'—'most curious'—'nauseating, perhaps, but how quite inexpressibly significant.' "

every means possible to get Byron's friends to persuade him to agree to a private settlement and a quiet separation. Their efforts were doubled when in the last week of February the rumors about Mrs. Leigh and her brother began to be widespread and persistent.

It was then that Dr. Lushington, and later Mr. Wilmot, who came to town on March 2, and Colonel Doyle, who was early taken into the secret, urged Lady Byron to cease communication with Mrs. Leigh. This Annabella would not do. Only after she had made a signed statement that would safeguard her position did her advisers reluctantly agree to a limited personal correspondence and an interview with her sister-in-law.

Lushington wrote to Lord Holland, as a friend whom Byron respected, and the latter approached Byron cautiously, asking his permission to act as intermediary.[n] Byron's reply was cordial, but he concluded with a statement of defiance: "In short, they are violent and I am stubborn; and in these amiable tempers matters stand at present. They think to drive me by menacing with legal measures. Let them go into court, they shall be met there."[n]

When Byron learned that Annabella was in London, he asked her for an interview, which she declined. But, with a view to moderate the belligerence of his mood and possibly to prevent him from bringing the matter to court, she wrote in a tone that gave him false hopes that she might relent and consent to a reconciliation: "I regret the necessity of declining an interview under existing circumstances. It must subject my feelings, which are now so much harassed, to a still more distressing trial."[n] But on February 29, Hobhouse recorded in his diary: "Mrs. Leigh has been forbid all intercourse with her [Lady Byron] at her lawyer's request—a story has now got abroad against her & B!!!"[n]

Byron was fully aware of the reports that were circulating. Writing on the 26th to thank Hunt for his dedicatory letter to *The Story of Rimini*, he said: "Your prefatory letter to *Rimini*, I accepted as it was meant—as a public compliment and a private kindness."[n] And in the same letter he said: "Of the 'fifty reports,' [Hunt had mentioned the rumors] it follows that forty-nine must have more or less error and exaggeration. . . ." [n]

On March 3, Byron received through Lord Holland a legal proposal for giving up to Lady Byron £500 a year and half the Noel reversion. The wording of the proposal was such that it suggested he would be gaining £500 a year from the transaction, whereas nothing was said of the £60,000 he had settled on her at the time of the marriage. [n] Byron indignantly rejected the proposal and determined never to sign anything binding him to a definite division of the Kirkby property. [n] Hanson believed Byron would gain a technical advantage by bringing a legal citation enjoining Lady Byron to return to her husband before the other side could enter any suit. But after a conference with Byron and Hobhouse, Byron's legal advisers were unanimous not to cite, though they believed he had a good defendant's case. [n]

When Annabella finally persuaded her lawyers to let her have an interview with Augusta (she could not bring herself to face Byron himself), it was not an indication that she was weakening, but only that she was determined to convince Byron through his sister that she was acting on her own initiative and was not coerced in her determination to seek a separation. [n] For the same purpose she saw George Byron. She assured them both, according to Hobhouse, that she would not return—*"no, not if her father and mother would go upon their knees to her so to do . . . .* she hinted, in pursuance of her former style, *that something had passed which she had as yet told to no one, and which nothing but the absolute necessity of justifying herself in court should wring from her."* [n] To Mrs. Leigh's repeated statement that she could not answer for her brother's life if Annabella did not return, the immovable wife replied: *"she could not help it, she must do her duty."* [n]

Her letter to Byron, which Hobhouse found on his friend's table when he called the next day (March 6), was "decisive but rather milder, & claiming a promise made to Lady B that should she prove the whole to be her own act and will Lord B would consent to a private arrangement." [n] Hobhouse got Byron to admit that he had made that promise through Augusta, and this decided him that Lady Byron had a right to demand its fulfillment. Later the same day Hobhouse learned from Robert Wilmot that Byron had already made overtures to him to act as mediator to bring about a private separation. "This I take to be the first offer of the kind made by Byron." [n]

Caroline Lamb could no longer refrain from giving good advice to the man who had spurned her. As soon as she heard of his refusal of a quiet separation she wrote: ". . . I am sure that a separation nobly and generously arranged by you will at once silence every report spread against either party. . . . They tell me that you have accused me of having spread injurious reports against you. Had you the heart to say this?" [9]

When the rumors touching him and his sister became particularly formidable, and when Caroline was aware that Byron believed she was responsible for them, she wrote again: "Lord Byron hear me & for God sake pause before you rashly believe any report others may make—if letters or reports or aught else has been malignantly placed in the hands of yr wife to ruin you I am ready to swear that I did it for the purpose of deceiving her. There is nothing however base it may appear that I would

[9] *LJ*, II, 449–50. Dated "Thursday," possibly Feb. 15, 1816. On the previous Friday (February 9) Hobhouse had noted in his diary that "C.L. accused B. of ———." Caroline had probably first heard reports of the separation on or before February 5, when Lady Melbourne heard of it, and apparently she told Murray, hoping he would have further information. Shortly after, she wrote him: "For God's sake, tell me—have you breathed what I told you to anyone, and if not, have you heard the reports? Is it really true and do they know why? They say it is certain—everything is rumoured as the cause of it—even the worst. I have been literally ill on account of it." (*"To Lord Byron,"* p. 70.) On March 22, 1816, the Duchess of Devonshire wrote to her son Augustus Foster: "Lady Byron's fate is the most melancholy I ever heard, and he must be mad or a Caligula. Caro [Mrs. George Lamb] will have told you some of the stories. It is too shocking. . . ." (Foster: *The Two Duchesses*, p. 413.)

After Byron's death, when Caroline was trying to recover her letters to Byron, she wrote to Hobhouse: ". . . you know all—I know all—our quarrel was about Mrs. Lei[gh]—yet I do pity her so much. . . . I should very much wish you to get into y[ou]r own hands . . . all letters relating to Mrs. Lei[gh]. Ld. Byron was excessively imprudent. Fletcher was aware of the whole of that business. . . ." (Unpublished letter, undated, Murray MSS. In his diary of May 27, 1824, Hobhouse mentions having received the letter.

not do to save you or yours from this—do not oh do not believe those who would lead you for one moment to think she knows any thing for certain—be firm be guarded. . . ." ⁿ

Byron had tried to see his wife, but in vain, and now that he had accepted her statement that it was by her own wish that she sought a separation and he had acceded, he was resigned, almost relieved. The rest he would leave to his friends and the lawyers. But misfortunes never came singly. The day he received Annabella's final letter, he had news that his library, which had been appraised at £450 and carried away until the books could be sold, had been traced and attached by the sheriff. He now felt obliged to return the £500 Murray had advanced him on them as "a temporary accommodation." Having repaid Murray, he said he had ceased to have any further delicacy in the matter. "This is about the tenth execution in as many months; so I am pretty well hardened. . . ." ⁿ

Moore had written to console him for the separation: "After all your *choice* was the misfortune." ⁿ Byron replied: "I must set you right in one point, however. The fault was *not*—no, nor even the misfortune—in my 'choice' (unless in *choosing at all*) —for I do not believe—and I must say it, in the very dregs of all this bitter business—that there ever was a better, or even a brighter, a kinder, or a more amiable and agreeable being than Lady B." ⁿ

Although Byron appeared to be indifferent to the ugly rumors circulating about him, Hobhouse was determined that before the separation papers were signed he would get a disavowal from the quarter most likely to carry weight, from Lady Byron herself. He consequently drew up a memorandum, "a paper of declarations as preamble to the separation in which Lady B disavowed cruelty, systematic unremitted neglect, gross & repeated infidelities—incest & ——," ¹ all of which had been subjects of current talk that had come to their ears." ⁿ

¹ Hobhouse never committed the word indicated by the dash to his diary (this is from the entry of March 7, 1816, quoted from the MS., Berg Collection, New York Public Library), nor did he mention either that or the incest in the paper that he drew up (quoted from the Lovelace papers, Fox, p. 111), leaving Wilmot to specify them in conveying the paper to Lady Byron, but Byron himself later left the clearest clue to one "enormity" with which

When Wilmot called at Piccadilly the next day, he took Hobhouse into another room "& there in great agitation told me that I knew nothing of the case—that Byron was mad & that something horrid would be proved against him,"ⁿ and urged that Byron be advised not to go into court (there was still the possibility that he would if the negotiations failed). Wilmot then stated the terms of property arrangement acceptable to Lady Byron, and said that when those were agreed upon, she would declare that neither she nor her family had spread any of the rumors prejudicial to Lord Byron's character.

Byron was indignant, and he and his friends protested that the disavowal in that form was only a bribe held out to achieve agreement to the separation. Hobhouse said that such a statement was not sufficient. "Lady B. must not only disown the rumours having been spread but that the specific charges— that is incest & —— made no part of her charges. . . ."² W. it appeared has been partially told Lady B's charge which seems

rumor charged him. Replying to Hobhouse's objection that Donna Inez in the first canto of *Don Juan* was too clear a picture of Annabella, Byron wrote, May 17, 1819, ". . . was it not owing to that 'Porca buzzerena' [a bracketed "her" is substituted for "that 'Porca buzzerena'" in the letter as printed in *LBC*, II, 110], that they tried to expose me upon earth to the same stigma, which . . . Jacopo is saddled with in hell?" (Murray MSS.; Hobhouse proofs.) Jacopo Rusticucci, who ascribed his errors to a shrewish wife (*Inferno*, Canto XVI, line 45), was consigned to the third ring of the seventh circle reserved for sodomites, those who had committed violence against nature. Apparently the rumor that this enormity was the mysterious cause of the separation was half believed, for lack of more specific knowledge, by Lord Holland, and later by Hobhouse himself, who made a significant notation in his copy of Moore opposite this statement: ". . . it has sometimes occurred to me that the occult cause of his lady's separation from him . . . may have been nothing more, after all, than . . . some dimly hinted confession of undefined horrors, which, though intended by the relater but to mystify and surprise, the hearer so little understood him as to take in sober seriousness." (Moore, II, 791.) Hobhouse wrote in the margin: "Something of this sort certainly, unless, as Lord Holland told me, he tried to —— her."
² Many years later Hobhouse told Lord Lindsay: "I wrote down every vice and sin, and crime, and horror in short of which a human being can be capable; and I said, 'Now I shall not stir in this business till you tell me whether you accuse him of any of these things, and which of them it is.' And the answer was, 'It is none of these things.' Then I said, 'What is it?' But they would never say." (Memorandum of conversation with Hobhouse in Lord Lindsay's hand, Murray MSS.)

to fill him with so much horror—he told me it was no enormity
—indeed I told him it never could be or she would have quitted
the house at once—he said I had not a guess at it—we broke
up thinking Lady B. would not consent." *

But the next day (Saturday the 9th) Wilmot appeared at
No. 13 with two documents. One was a memorandum of views
on an equitable property division for the separation: Byron had
proposed to resign the whole of Lady Byron's present fortune
(£1,000 a year), but Lady Byron wished only to receive £200
in addition to her pin money, a total of £500, and to leave the
other £500 to Byron; Lady Byron proposed that her husband
should stipulate, in legal form, that when her parents died, the
Kirkby property should be divided "on fair terms of arbitration." *
This Byron agreed to as a basis for discussion.* The second paper
was a brief statement, signed by Lady Byron and witnessed
by Wilmot, denying that any reports injurious to Byron had been
circulated by her family and adding that "the two reports specifically mentioned by Mr. Wilmot do not form any part of
the charges which, in the event of a Separation by agreement
not taking place, she should have been compelled to make against
Lord Byron." * This statement seemed satisfactory to Byron and
Hobhouse, but they failed to see that it was deliberately worded
so that Annabella did not commit herself to a denial of the
truth of the charges, but only said she would not bring them
forward in court. In fact, her lawyers and advisers who were
in the secret were agreed that she should not bring in the charge
against Byron and Mrs. Leigh, simply because it could not be
proved, but at the same time they were urging her to do something to safeguard her position with regard to her conduct toward her sister-in-law in the event of further disclosures.

In response to this pressure, though she would not give up
her friendship with Mrs. Leigh even when Dr. Lushington
pointed out its prejudicial effects on her case, she drew up a
memorandum of her motives for not acting on her suspicions:

"My principles of conduct in regard to Mrs. Leigh were these.
When I could not help perceiving things which must suggest
dreadful suspicions, I considered that in proportion to the hei-
nous nature of the crime, a stronger evidence was necessary.

I could not adopt a middle line of conduct. I must either have quitted my husband at once upon such a supposition, by which I should have injured her character irreparably—or I must repel the idea as much as possible and act in direct opposition to it. The last alternative, however difficult and painful, appeared to be my duty. . . . But my belief has been so strong that *any* further corroborating evidence would fix it unchangeably." [n]

Delays having ensued from misunderstandings with regard to the terms of the separation agreement, and danger again arising that the issue would be forced to a public trial, she drew up a more formal statement, approved and witnessed by her three inner-council advisers, Dr. Lushington, Mr. Wilmot, and Colonel Doyle. This she signed on March 14, 1816. In addition to the reasons given in the memorandum, she added several others which seemed to justify her conduct toward Augusta:

"Because Mrs L: had from her first acquaintance with Lady B: always manifested towards her the utmost kindness & attention. . . .

"Because Mrs L: at times exhibited signs of a deep remorse. . . .

"Because Lady B: conceived it possible that the crime, if committed might not only be deeply repented of, but never have been perpetrated since her marriage with Lord B:

"It was from these motives & strongly inclining to a charitable interpretation of all that passed that Lady B: never during her living with Lord B: intimated a suspicion of this nature.—

"Since Lady B's Separation from Lord B: the Report has become current in the World of such a connection having subsisted. This report was not spread nor sanctioned by Lady B:. . . . it being intimated that Mrs L:'s character can never be so effectually preserved as by a renewal of intercourse with Lady B: she does for the motives & reasons before mentioned consent to renew that intercourse—" [n]

To Mrs. George Villiers, Augusta's close friend who had defended her when the rumors became persistent but who was soon convinced of their truth by Annabella's evidence, she later wrote: "It must be remembered that my *Conviction* was progressively formed, and not till lately fixed. . . . the *evidence then* rested chiefly on his words & manners, & her *otherwise* unaccountable assent & submission to both." [n]

What woman but Annabella could have denied her instincts and her "wretched doubts" so long for the sake of a mathematical calculation of justice and duty and the "undeviating rectitude" to which in girlhood she had dedicated herself? But she was beginning to show the strain of it. Her mother had written her (March 3, when she was near breaking under appeals from Augusta and Byron and pressure from her advisers): "I neither do, or can expect that you should not *feel* and *deeply feel*— but I have sometimes thought (and that not *only lately*) that Your mind is too *high wrought*—too much so for *this* World— only the *grander* objects engage your thoughts, Your Character is like *Proof Spirits*—not fit for common use—I could almost wish the *Tone* of it *lowered* nearer to the level of *us every day people*. . . ." [n] This is one point on which Byron might have found himself in agreement with his mother-in-law!

Augusta was near a nervous collapse. She was in an advanced state of pregnancy. She had left three of her children at Six Mile Bottom when she went to London in November. The rumors of late February and March had sadly shaken her. On March 13, Hobhouse called on her and "found her in tears and great distress indeed—she thinks she ought in duty to her husband & children to leave B's house—she having staid long enough to give the lie to all rumours respecting herself which Col Leigh has most handsomely discredited in every way—I promised to hint this to Byron. . . ." [n] On March 16, Augusta left 13 Piccadilly Terrace and removed to her rooms in St. James's Palace. [n] (Through some of her friends close to the Queen, Augusta had been appointed a Lady-in-Waiting.)

For several days Byron's moods were alternately up and down, but on the 17th the basis for the legal separation was agreed upon, [n] and on the 22nd Hobhouse found him "in great spirits at prospect of going abroad directly." [n] Though the wound was there, ready to give pain at any sharp turn, he had a sense of relief that the surgery was over. He sent off to Murray a few prints, a silver cup, and "a large screen covered with portraits of actors, pugilists, representations of boxing-matches," [n] etc., to be auctioned off with his books. A devil-may-care mood seized him. He had written to James Hogg, while the struggle was at its height:

"And so you want to come to London? It is a damned place to be sure, but the only one in the world (at least the English world) for fun: though I have seen parts of the globe that I like better, still upon the whole it is the completest either to help one in feeling oneself—alive—or forgetting that one is so." [n]

He wanted alternately to feel again that he was alive, and to forget that he was so. Sometime during the hectic days of March, Byron had received a letter in an unknown feminine hand whose contents were striking enough to excite his curiosity. He had since his first fame in 1812 received dozens, perhaps hundreds, of letters from unknown women, but all of them, even the boldest, had clothed their proposals in the language of conventional sentiments. Here was one which did not proceed by innuendo. Its author indicated that she was not seeking charity and pleaded with him not to scorn her letter, for her mind had been formed by his poetry, and "the Creator ought not to destroy his creature." Then she asked this blunt question:

"If a woman, whose reputation has yet remained unstained, if without either guardian or husband to control she should throw herself upon your mercy, if with a beating heart she should confess the love she has borne you many years . . . could you betray her, or would you be silent as the grave?" [n]

Byron seems not to have replied, for she tried another approach. In a short note dated "Sunday Morning," and signed "G. C. B.," she attempted to get an entry by arousing his curiosity: "Lord Byron is requested to state whether seven o'clock this Evening will be convenient to him to receive a lady to communicate with him on business of peculiar importance. She desires to be admitted alone and with the utmost privacy." [n]

To this Byron replied curtly: "Ld. B. is not aware of any 'importance' which can be attached by any person to an interview with him, and more particularly by one with whom it does not appear that he has the honour of being acquainted. He will however be at home at the hour mentioned." "

The girl who called on him was not yet eighteen. She had a dark, almost Italian appearance, and, while her face was not quite pretty, her youth and the earnestness and flashing intelligence of her brown eyes offset her plain features. With a naïve directness she told him her whole story, and it was not an unromantic one. Her name was Mary Jane Clairmont. Her friends and family called her Jane to distinguish her from her stepsister Mary Godwin,[3] but she called herself Clara or Clare (later to be changed to Claire).[4] She had a precocious intelligence and, particularly with regard to the rights of women, love, and marriage, a bold independence that was always a little repulsive to Byron when he found it in the opposite sex. These ideas she had imbibed by growing up in the household of the philosopher William Godwin, who had married her mother in 1803 after the death of his first wife, Mary Wollstonecraft, author of the *Vindication of the Rights of Women*. Despite his theoretical belief in free love, Godwin had been outraged when the "atheist" author of *Queen Mab*, Percy Shelley, deserted his wife to elope with Godwin's own daughter Mary in 1814. Jane (or Claire) had accompanied Shelley and Mary on their honeymoon elopement, which took them through France to Switzerland. On their return to England she had lived with them, for the most part, being largely dependent on Shelley's bounty. In fact, her too great fondness for him had already made Mary jealous despite her free ideas, and she was desirous of a cessation of this *ménage à trois*. At the moment Claire was spending part of her time with the Shelleys at Bishopsgate and part at Skinner Street with the Godwins. It may have been her desire to show Mary that she too could capture a poet, and one far more famous than Shelley, that first prompted her to beard the literary lion of all London in

[3] Jane Clairmont and Mary Godwin had no blood relationship, Mary being the daughter of Godwin and Mary Wollstonecraft, who died in giving her birth, and Jane being the second Mrs. Godwin's daughter by a former husband.

[4] For the sake of consistency I shall use the spelling "Claire" henceforth, though she continued to sign her letters Clara or Clare for some years.

his den—that and the fact that she had long idolized this apostle of freedom and sympathetic painter of the lawless passions. She had read *Lara* in 1814,[n] and knew something of Byron's reputation for *liaisons dangereuses*, his melancholy reserve, and his irresistible attractiveness to women. Just then, too, she had a desperate desire to escape at any cost from the humdrum life she had been forced into again at Skinner Street. She had perhaps heard that Byron's wife had left him, for the news had now traveled pretty generally through London and even beyond.

She apparently had not made the impression she hoped for on her first visit. Byron listened to her story, but she was not a ravishing beauty, and he was distracted by a thousand irritations. Once having seen him and talked to him, however, she would not give up the pursuit. She may have heard from Godwin of Byron's disposition to help struggling talents in the theater and in literature. She would try that approach. Thinking to get rid of her as he had many another troublesome woman who had applied to him as a member of the Drury Lane Committee, he referred her to Douglas Kinnaird. But he received a long letter in reply.

She had already boasted to him of her acquaintance with the wonder-boy Shelley, who had sent him a copy of *Queen Mab*. Byron had probably never heard of Shelley before, but he apparently had told her of his admiration for the poem, for Claire wrote: "Shelley is now turned three and twenty, and interested as I am in all he does, it is with the greatest pleasure I receive your approbation." She herself had written "half a novel" on which she wanted Byron's opinion, but feared he would be prejudiced on the wrong side, for, she felt, "you rather dislike me." Perhaps she could appeal to him from another angle. She could deride the institution of marriage, the source of his present distress. "I can never resist the temptation of throwing a pebble at it as I pass by." [n]

Still trying to command his attention, she sent him a sample of her writing, something that Byron generally abhorred. She asked: "Will you judge candidly and impartially? Will you make allowance for my years? I do not expect you to approve—all

I wish to know is whether I have talents. . . ." To the ordinary reader, she said, her story "would appear to be written as a warning to young people against extraordinary opinions; a beacon shining along the deep to guide the bark of youth into the safe haven of received opinions and Papa's and Mama's good advice. But Atheists might see and understand my meaning. . . . Gibbon's fifteenth and sixteenth chapters are most admirable models of this kind. . . ." [n]

Certainly the girl showed more originality than most of the authoresses who bedeviled him, whatever Byron might think of the unconventionality of her opinions. Besides, there was an innate gentleness and kindness in his nature which Claire had sensed. Amid the feverish torments of the separation he succumbed to the persistence of this girl whose naïve freshness and candid admiration were a balm to his wounded spirit. He had once told Lady Melbourne: "I could love anything on earth that appeared to wish it." [n] He knew it would be troublesome, but he was leaving England soon. Claire pursued her advantage.

Before long she was calling on him as often as he would let her. When he could not see her, he offered his box at Drury Lane to her and Shelley, but she replied: "I cannot go to the play, much as I wish it, for Shelley declares he could not endure it. . . ." [n] She had a melodious voice, and it may be that she sang to him, and that he was touched as he always was by sentimental ballads.[5]

But other matters were claiming his attention. He was vexed by the legal delays in the arrangement of the separation terms; galled by the silence and what he believed to be the implacable unforgivingness of his wife; and harassed by details of his approaching departure. Soon after they had signed the preliminary agreement for the separation, Byron wrote some verses

[5] It has been conjectured that Byron's poem beginning "There be none of Beauty's daughters" was addressed to Claire because it referred to "thy sweet voice," was dated March 28, and was first published in 1816. But in view of Byron's reiterated statement that he was never in love with Claire, and his failure to mention her anywhere with the slightest sentiment, it seems more likely that the poem has been misdated and misapplied. (See Chapter IX, p. 313 n.)

addressed to his wife, summing up all the sentimental pathos
into which his frustrations and regrets now flowed:

> *Fare thee well! and if for ever,*
> *Still for ever, fare thee well:*
> *Even though unforgiving, never*
> *'Gainst thee shall my heart rebel.*
> *Would that breast were bared before thee*
> *Where thy head so oft hath lain,*
> *While that placid sleep came o'er thee*
> *Which thou ne'er canst know again. . . .*
> *Though my many faults defaced me,*
> *Could no other arm be found,*
> *Than the one which once embraced me,*
> *To inflict a cureless wound?* . . .
> *When our child's first accents flow—*
> *Wilt thou teach her to say "Father!"*
> *Though his care she must forego?* . . .
> *All my faults perchance thou knowest—*
> *All my madness—none can know. . . .*
> *Fare thee well! thus disunited—*
> *Torn from every nearer tie—*
> *Seared in heart—and lone—and blighted—*
> *More than this I scarce can die.*[n]

Shortly after its composition, he sent the poem off to Annabella with a note: "I send you the first verses that ever I
attempted to write upon you, and perhaps the last that I may
ever write at all."[n] If Annabella was affected by the poem or
the letter or both, she kept her emotions to herself, and that
maddening silence probably provoked Byron to send a copy to
Murray, who admired them and showed them to his friends.

Hobhouse, who was constantly trying to restrain Byron from
doing anything rash before the separation papers were signed,
was at Piccadilly Terrace when letters from Rogers, Lord Holland, and Kinnaird testifying that Byron had never said anything but good about her were sent back by Annabella through
Mrs. Leigh, "and without any answer—which made B. furious,"
Hobhouse recorded, "and he was going to write but I stopped
him."[n] But the next night Byron found vent for the vitriol of

his anger in "A Sketch from Private Life," directed against Mrs. Clermont, who, he believed, had been the dominating influence on his wife throughout the proceedings and the cause of her hard determination not to yield to his entreaties or answer his letters. Conceived in rancor, it was the bitterest poem Byron ever wrote:

> Born in the garret, in the kitchen bred,
> Promoted thence to deck her mistress' head; . . .
> Quick with the tale, and ready with the lie,
> The genial confidante, and general spy. . . .
> If like a snake she steal within your walls,
> Till the black slime betray her as she crawls. . . .

Murray, whom he had asked to print fifty copies, had shown both poems, not only to Gifford, but also to Rogers, Canning, and Frere, and secretly to Caroline Lamb, who, it seems, had seen Annabella and heard her story. Caroline told Medwin later that she had met Lady Byron "once only" about this time. "It was just after the separation occurred. She was so altered I could hardly know her—she appeared heart broken. What she then said to me *I may not repeat*—she was however sent away, she did not go willingly. She accused me of knowing every thing, & reproached me for not having stopped the marriage. How could I! She had been shewn my letters, and every one else." [6]

After she had seen the verses, Caroline wrote to Murray in a white heat: "I would rather starve or see my child die for want than I would speak or look or think of Lord Biron but as a poor paltry Hypocrite a mean coward—and a man without a heart. that serpent his sister too. . . ." [n]

Leigh Hunt finally ventured from Hampstead and dined with Byron, Davies, and Hobhouse at Piccadilly Terrace on April 3.[7] "He [Byron] was very ill," Hunt wrote later of this visit,

[6] *LJ*, II, 453–4. The interview between Annabella and Caroline took place on March 27, 1816. Annabella wrote to Dr. Lushington that the interview "changed her strong impression into *absolute* conviction." (Mayne: *Lady Byron*, p. 223.)

[7] Hobhouse, who was with Byron almost daily from this time until his departure, had that day come to stay at 13 Piccadilly Terrace, probably to help him with his preparations for the journey.

"his face jaundiced with bile. . . . The adherence of his old friends was . . . touching. I saw Mr. Hobhouse and Mr. Scrope Davies . . . almost every time I called. Mr. Rogers was regular in his daily visits; and Lord Holland, he said, was very kind to him. Finally, he took the blame of the quarrel to himself. . . . In all this I beheld only a generous nature, subject perhaps to ebullitions of ill-temper, but candid, sensitive, extremely to be pitied, and if a woman knew how, or was permitted by others to love him, extremely to be loved." [n]

Byron showed to Hunt Lady Byron's playful, affectionate letter written just after she had left his house, and Hunt considered it a particular compliment to him until he later discovered with what "singular incontinence" Byron was in the habit "of making a confidant of every body he came nigh." [n] Byron gave Hunt a poem for the *Examiner*,[n] and before he went abroad entertained him several times at Piccadilly Terrace.[n]

On one of his visits Hunt 'found Byron in conversation with Coleridge. According to Hunt's later recollections, Coleridge "recited his 'Kubla Khan' one morning, to Lord Byron, in his Lordship's house in Piccadilly, when I happened to be in another room. I remember the other's coming away from him, highly struck with his poem, and saying how wonderfully he talked." [8]

[8] Hunt: *Lord Byron*, II, 53. Despite Hunt's statement, it has been a moot question whether Byron ever met Coleridge face to face (of course he had seen him at one or two of Coleridge's lectures in 1811 and 1812), for Byron himself never mentioned such a meeting. James Gillman (*Life of Samuel Taylor Coleridge*, I, 266–7) quoted a letter of Coleridge dated April 10, 1816: "If you had seen Lord Byron, you could scarcely disbelieve him—so beautiful a countenance I scarcely ever saw—his teeth so many stationary smiles—his eyes the open portals of the sun—things of light, and for light— and his forehead so ample, and yet so flexible, passing from marble smoothness into a hundred wreathes and lines and dimples correspondent to the feelings and sentiments he is uttering." But Gillman, demonstrably inaccurate in other details of his *Life*, must have erred in this, at least in the date, for on April 10, Coleridge wrote to Byron, apologizing for not sending his tragedy and confessing that he had for years been under the tyranny of the opium habit, which he was then trying to break, and in this letter he said: "Scarcely had I arrived in town when I became indisposed. . . . I am so very weak that it is not in my power at present to wait personally on your Lordship. . . ." (*Unpublished Letters of Samuel Taylor Coleridge*, edited by Earl Leslie Griggs, II, 163–4.) It is possible, however, that Coleridge did recover sufficiently to call on Byron at a later time when Hunt was there.

Byron said later of Coleridge: "Many parts of his 'Memoirs' [*Biographia Literaria*] are quite unintelligible, and were, I apprehend, meant for Kant. . . . If he had never gone to Germany, nor spoilt his fine genius by the transcendental philosophy and German metaphysics, nor taken to write lay sermons, he would have made the greatest poet of the day. . . . Coleridge might have been any thing: as it is, he is a thing 'that dreams are made of.' " [n]

Byron was in a fever of activity during these April days, preparing for his departure, seeing his friends, trying to make some settlement of his business affairs, and plunging into festivities which would save him from too much thought.

On the 8th, Byron's books were sold at public auction. Hobhouse was present and bought thirty-four pounds' worth. Murray bought some for Mrs. Leigh and for Rogers, and also the screen with the portraits of actors and pugilists, which still remains in the Byron Room at 50 Albemarle Street. The total received from the sale came to £723 12s. 6d., which Murray, after deductions, turned over to Byron, who, however, demurred on the ground that his debts to Murray for books and printing exceeded this sum. [n] Hobhouse said that "had B's name been in each book [they] could have sold for *twice* as much—some presentation copies sold very high." [n]

That evening Hobhouse accompanied Byron to Lady Jersey's, where they were introduced by Flahault to Benjamin Constant and his wife—"great compliments de part e[t] d autres." [n] Though Hobhouse does not mention it in his diary, Augusta accompanied Byron on that occasion and was cut by some people, including Mrs. George Lamb, [n] and Byron felt the snubs of the ladies of fashion who had before crowded around him. Some of the men also avoided him. He stood aside, taking mental note of "the various and characteristic ways in which the temperature of their manner towards him was affected by the cloud under which he now appeared." [n] Only Lady Jersey and Miss Mercer Elphinstone went out of their way to be kind to him, and he never forgot it. The latter, who had cast coquettish eyes at Byron in the days of his first fame in the summer of 1812, was a great heiress and independent enough to shake her red hair in the face of public disapproval. According to Hazlitt, Byron "used to tell a story of a little red-haired girl, who, when countesses and ladies of fashion were leaving the room where he was in crowds (to *cut* him after his quarrel with his wife) stopped short near a table against which he was leaning, gave him a familiar nod, and said, 'You should have married *me,* and then this would not have happened to you!' " Byron sent her a book saved from his dispersed library as a memorial.[9]

In the days that followed, while the disputes over the details of the settlement continued, Byron was feted by his old friends in a manner that recalled the London parties of his Cambridge days. On the 9th, Hobhouse recorded that Scrope Davies "gave a dinner [at the Clarendon] to Burdett, D. Kinnaird, Byron & myself. . . . we sat up till six in the morning and had a scene between B & myself at home—poor fellow, he came into my room next morning to ask how I was—he was very sorry and so was I but our regrets originated from different causes."

Byron's volatile temper flared up again on the 13th when— in response to a letter sent by Mrs. Leigh asking Lady Byron for the receipts which she had taken to Kirkby on her departure from Piccadilly and enclosing a ring containing a lock of the hair of Charles I to be saved for his daughter—Augusta received only a formal note from Lady Byron's solicitor." It was the final straw that his wife should snub the sister who had so be-friended her. Hobhouse too was indignant. He wrote in his diary: "This has terminated I believe all correspondence be-tween *my dearest Augusta* and *my dearest Annabella!!!* such are female friendships!!" "

On the 14th, Hobhouse, who had been living at Piccadilly Terrace since April 3, "went down to Whitton that Byron might have a free leave taking of his sister." " Augusta came from St. James's Palace, where she had been living for the past month, and spent the day with her brother. Her pregnancy was far

[9] According to the Countess Guiccioli, Byron, as he was embarking at Dover, put into the hands of Scrope Davies a little parcel which he had forgotten to give Miss Mercer Elphinstone in London, adding: "Tell her that had I been fortunate enough to marry a woman like her, I should not now be obliged to exile myself from my country." (Guiccioli: *My Recollections of Lord Byron,* p. 184.)

advanced, the rumors about her were growing more open and more vicious, she felt the slights at Lady Jersey's ball, and now Annabella apparently had deserted her. There was nothing more she could do, and she was returning the next day to Six Mile Bottom. It was a touching farewell that aroused all of Byron's sincerest and tenderest feelings. In anticipation of her departure he had composed two days before a poem expressing his gratitude to her for standing by him to the last:

> When Fortune changed—and Love fled far,
>   And Hatred's shafts flew thick and fast,
> Thou wert the solitary star
>   Which rose and set not to the last.[n]

Having no shame for the sentiments expressed in these "Stanzas to Augusta" and wanting to proclaim her loyalty to his friends, Byron sent the verses to Murray, who promptly circulated them.[n] Murray had already received confidential gossip from Caroline Lamb, and he foolishly showed her a copy. Shortly thereafter Byron was surprised to receive a frantic letter from Caroline Lamb concerning the verses: "I do implore you for God sake not to publish them. Could I have seen you one moment, I would explain why. I have only time to add that, however those who surround you may make you disbelieve it, you will draw ruin on your own head and hers if at this moment you shew these. I know not from what quarter the report originates. You accused *me,* and falsely; but if you could hear all that is said at this moment, you would believe one, who . . . would perhaps die to save you." [1]

Byron wrote hastily to Murray: "I wished to have seen you to scold you. Really you must not send any thing of mine to Lady *C.L.* I have often sufficiently warned you on this topic—

---

[1] *LJ,* II, 450. Prothero says this letter probably refers to "Fare Thee Well," yet the context shows that that is not true. Moreover, Hobhouse in his diary entry of April 27, 1816, says that Caroline "wrote to Byron the other day desiring him not to publish his poem to his sister—he not knowing what was said of him." At the same time apparently Caroline changed her tone to Murray: "Will you do me one favour—be not over angry with *him* whatever his offenses. . . . change not your adoration let us still pay worship to the Giaour what though he be fallen—it is yet an Angel—promise—swear to me —that you will stand firm to him. . . ." (Murray MSS.)

you do not know what mischief you do by this. Of the copies of things written by me—I wish more particularly the *last* not to be circulated, at present (you know which I mean, those to A.). . . ." [n]

But in spite of Caroline Lamb, he was still ready to defy the world's opinion for the sister who had stood by him. Others may have thought her weak, but Byron had reason to know her firmness. He later told Lady Blessington: "To me she was, in the hour of need, as a tower of strength. Her affection was my last rallying point. . . . Augusta knew all my weaknesses, but she had love enough to bear with them. . . . She has given me such good advice, and yet, finding me incapable of following it, loved and pitied me but the more, because I was erring." [n]

Byron felt genuinely and deeply this farewell to Augusta. "Gussie" was a part of him and understood him more than any other woman he had known, for he had let down the barriers of his inner self to her. Remorse for the grief he had brought to Augusta overwhelmed him.[2] As Byron's premonition told him, on that Easter Sunday they parted never to meet again.[3]

After she had left him, he wrote a final letter to Annabella: "I have just parted from Augusta—almost the last being you had left me to part with—& the only unshattered tie of my existence—wherever I may go—& I am going far—you & I can never meet again in this world—nor in the next—Let this content or atone.—If any accident occurs to me—be kind to *her,* —if she is then nothing—to her children. . . . & recollect though it may be advantage to you to have lost your husband— it is sorrow to her to have the waters now—or the earth here- after—between her & her brother. . . ." [n] Annabella did not reply.

Hobhouse returned to Piccadilly on the 15th and "found Sam Rogers & Leigh Hunt up in arms at the publication of Fare thee well and the Sketch in Scott's Champion of yesterday with violent abuse of Lord Byron." [n] Other papers took up the pub-

[2] Augusta later told Lady Byron that she had "never seen remorse for his guilt towards her in him but once—the night before they last parted, previ- ous to his going abroad." (*Astarte*, p. 65.) But it is probable that neither woman understood the true nature of his remorse.

[3] Before she left, Augusta presented her brother with a Bible that he always carried with him. (*LJ*, V, 391. Letter of Oct. 9, 1821.)

lication of the poems with appropriate comments, and there ensued a wholesale attack on Byron, partly political, partly personal, based on current rumors concerning his treatment of his wife.[4]

Byron's preparations for going abroad had begun in March as soon as the preliminary agreement had been signed. On the 28th of that month he engaged a young Dr. John Polidori, son of an Italian exile, scholar, and language teacher, to accompany him as personal physician. The fact that Polidori spoke English, French, and Italian was not sufficient to make Hobhouse like

[4] Medwin (I, 50–2), probably basing his account on Byron's later exaggerations of the obloquy that was heaped upon him at the time, quoted Byron as saying: "I once made a list from the Journals of the day, of the different worthies, ancient and modern, to whom I was compared. I remember a few: Nero, Apicius, Epicurus, Caligula, Heliogabalus, Henry the Eighth, and lastly the [devil?]. . . . I was abused in the public prints, made the common talk of private companies, hissed as I went to the House of Lords [Byron was last in the House on April 2, at the debate on the state of Ireland —Erdman: "Lord Byron as Rinaldo," p. 194 n.], insulted in the streets, afraid to go to the theatre, whence the unfortunate Mrs. Mardyn had been driven with insult. [A rumor was current about the time Byron left England that he had had an intrigue with Mrs. Mardyn, the actress.] The Examiner was the only paper that dared say a word in my defence, and Lady Jersey the only person in the fashionable world that did not look upon me as a monster." But Hobhouse replied to Medwin: "Lord Byron was never hissed as he went to the House of Lords; nor insulted in the streets. The Examiner was not the only paper that defended Lord Byron." (*The Westminster Review,* Jan. 1825, pp. 25–6.) Hobhouse mentioned the *Morning Chronicle,* but the *News* and the *Independent Whig* also came to Byron's defense. (*LJ,* III, 277 n.) So strong was Byron's impression, however, that he was the object of public and private ostracism and contumely before he left England that he recurred to the subject in his reply to *Blackwood's Magazine* in 1820: "I was accused of every monstrous vice by public rumour and private rancour: my name, which had been a knightly or a noble one since my fathers helped to conquer the kingdom for William the Norman, was tainted. I felt that, if what was whispered, and muttered, and murmured, was true, I was unfit for England; if false, England was unfit for me." (*LJ,* IV, 478–9.) But Sir Francis Burdett, like Hobhouse, did not believe that Byron was under a shadow of general obloquy at the time. He wrote to Douglas Kinnaird shortly before Byron departed: "I have no patience with your saying *poor Byron.* If any man in the world has shower'd upon him all that God and Nature can bestow, it is Byron. *Poor Byron!* What! 'the foremost man of all this World!' . . . Even if he were in the wrong, what an *amende* honourable his 'Farewell!' In my opinion those lines are worth all he ever wrote, and do him, in every way, infinite credit." (*LJ,* VI, 19 n.)

him, but Byron found the Doctor's youthful vanity and cocksureness irresistible.[5] For the voyage Byron had his coachmaker construct a huge coach copied from the one of Napoleon captured at Genappe. According to Pryse Gordon, "Besides a *lit de repos,* it contained a library, a plate-chest, and every apparatus for dining."[n] Byron was straining every resource to raise money for the trip. He even made a futile effort to collect the £1,000 he had loaned to Wedderburn Webster in 1813.[n]

In the first days of April, Byron had been too harried to give much of his time to his persistent new acquaintance Claire Clairmont. When he did admit her, she tried to make the most of the opportunity and it was difficult to persuade her to leave. She wrote: "Since you disappointed me last Evening will you see me to night? If you do not entirely hate me pray do! . . . Now don't send me away with 'now pray go,' 'now will you go' This is the very last Evening I shall see you as I am myself going—not the way of 'all flesh,' but somewhere where you least expect."[n] To entice his interest further, she had promised to bring Godwin's talented daughter Mary to see him.

When Byron finally made an appointment, she wrote a precautionary letter: "Mary has promised to accompany me tonight. Will you be so good as to prepare your servants for the visit, for she is accustomed to be surrounded by her own circle who treat her with the greatest politeness. I say this because on Thursday evening I waited nearly a quarter of an hour in your hall, which though I may overlook the disagreeableness—

[5] Hobhouse diary, entry of March 28, 1816. Dr. John William Polidori, son of Gaetano Polidori, onetime secretary to the dramatist Alfieri, was in his twenty-first year when he was recommended to Byron by Sir Henry Halford (he had received his medical degree from Edinburgh at the unprecedented age of nineteen). The elder Polidori, himself a man of letters, had settled in England as a teacher of Italian and had taken an English wife, a Miss Pierce. Their daughter, sister of Byron's doctor, later married another Italian exile, Gabriele Rossetti, and became the mother of three famous literary children, William Michael, Christina, and Dante Gabriel Rossetti. Dr. Polidori had literary ambitions and was extremely touchy about opinions of his work. He was much flattered to be asked to travel as the companion of the great Lord Byron, and Murray, seeing many guineas in the prospect, offered him before he departed £500 (or guineas) for an account of the forthcoming tour. With this prospect Polidori began to keep a diary from the time they reached Dover.

she, who is not in love would not. . . . She has not the slightest
suspicion of our connection. For pity's sake breathe not a word.
Do not mention my name [perhaps the "Clara" would indicate
a familiarity she didn't want to reveal to Mary]. Talk only on
general subjects. . . . I shall stay a few moments after her departure to receive your last instructions." ⁿ

It was past the middle of April, and Byron was expecting to
leave as soon as the separation papers were ready to sign. His
sister had left and he was eager to be off. Claire had already
proposed her "plan" to meet him alone in Geneva, which ap-
palled him, but now she had a scheme for getting the Shelleys
to accompany her there. Shelley had already determined to
leave England, and Claire could enlist Mary's aid in persuading
him to go to Italy by way of Geneva. After their visit she wrote:

"I steal a moment to write to you to know whether you go
tomorrow. It is not through selfishness that I pray something
may prevent your departure. But tomorrow Shelley's chancery
suit will be decided & so much of my fate depends on the
decision;⁶ besides tomorrow will inform me whether I should be
able to offer you *that* which it has long been the passionate
wish of my heart to offer you." ⁷ Though she later confessed
that she had no passions and that she would rather be his male
companion than his mistress, she was willing to give him the
solace that he felt was the principal function of women and that
his bruised spirit most craved at the moment.

She pursued the subject that was now uppermost in her mind,
the possibility of following him on his travels: "Mary is delighted

⁶ The complicated question to be passed on by the Court of Chancery in
April 1816 is explained by Shelley in a letter to Godwin of Feb. 26, 1816.
(Dowden, I, 547–50.) Shelley had refused to accept his grandfather's leg-
acy, which provided that he renounce his absolute power over the estates
settled on him at his birth in 1792 in order to enjoy a large income for life.
The question was whether his father could buy his interest in the settled
estates at a fair price. The decision went against his father, and therefore
against Shelley. But his father agreed to advance him a sum sufficient to
cover his expenses during the negotiations, and Shelley took Mary abroad as
soon as the decision was given.
⁷ The implication of this statement is not clear. Did she mean to offer herself to Byron? If so, was that offer hinged to Shelley's economic independence or her own?

with you as I knew she would be; she entreats me in private to obtain your address abroad that we may if possible have again the pleasure of seeing you. She perpetually exclaims, 'How mild he is! how gentle! So different from what I expected.' " [n]

Byron had sought relaxation and forgetfulness and, to his embarrassment, found love, unwanted and tedious. But it was against his nature to be rude to her, although he knew that his kindness encouraged the thing he did not want. She was willing to play her last card. It was his final week in England; he was planning to leave the following Monday. She must act now if she was to hold him. Her offer was bold and direct:

"I do not expect you to love me; I am not worthy of your love. I feel you are superior, yet much to my surprize, more to my happiness, you betrayed passions I had believed no longer alive in your bosom. . . . Have you then any objection to the following plan? On Thursday Evening we may go out of town together by some stage or mail about the distance of ten or twelve miles. There we shall be free and unknown; we can return early the following morning. . . . Will you admit me for two moments to settle with you *where?* Indeed I will not stay an instant after you tell me to go. . . . I shall never forget you. I shall ever remember the gentleness of your manners and the wild originality of your countenance." [n]

Whether they went to the country or not, Byron did see her and find momentary solace in the free gift of her embraces. Though his better judgment fought against it constantly and made him impatient and peevish at times, he was weak enough and kind enough to accede to her wishes.

On Sunday the 21st at half past three Hanson brought the deed of separation. Hobhouse, who had signed the deed of the marriage settlement on the last day of December 1814, was a witness. He recorded that Byron "signed it and delivered it in these words at first—'I deliver this as Mrs. Clermont's act and deed.'" Other friends came and, Hobhouse continued, "we had a session—Kinnaird, Mr. & Lord—Sam Rogers—& S. B. Davies—Rogers was afraid to leave the Room & his character behind him—however he went." [n]

Monday came, Byron's final day in London, and the last-minute packing was interrupted by many visitors. He had only time to dash off a note to Augusta: "My own Sweet Sis—The deeds are signed—so that is over.—All I have now to beg or desire on the subject is—that you will never mention nor allude to Lady Byron's name again in any shape—or on any occasion—except indispensable business." *

Byron could not truthfully say that his friends had deserted him. Rogers came to take leave of him. Hobhouse, who took charge of everything, wrote in his diary: "Hanson came in the morning—and told us he had just left Lady Byron [he had taken the deed of separation for her to sign] who looked well—but was torn *here* putting his hand to his breast bone for the place of his heart." * Benjamin Constant also came to pay his respects. [8]

Isaac Nathan, who had been a great admirer of Byron since the days when they worked together on the *Hebrew Melodies*, and who had put a number of Byron's other lyrics to music, including "The Maid of Athens," * was, according to his own story, in and out of the house frequently the last three days before Byron left England. ". . . I expressed my regret at his departure," Nathan wrote, "and desired to know if it was really his intention not to return . . . he fixed his eyes upon me with an eager look of enquiry, exclaiming at the same time, 'Good God! I never had it in contemplation to remain in exile—why do you ask that question?' " *

Through all this Claire Clairmont got little attention, though she made desperate efforts to focus his interest upon her at the last. On Monday morning, the day before he left, she sent him a note: "If amidst your bustle you have a moment to give, pray

[8] Constant's stories of the low morale at Paris may have consoled Byron for his inability to pass through the French capital. Lord Lovelace says, on the authority of a letter from Dr. Lushington to Lady Byron, April 30, 1816 (not quoted): "He was refused permission by the French Government to travel through France except on condition of keeping a prescribed route and avoiding Paris. According to Lady Holland, the ladies of Paris would have received him with open arms had he been allowed to go there." (*Astarte*, p. 52.)

tell me if I may see you an instant this evening. I will only stay one half hour." "

Despairing of seeing him to say farewell, she wrote again later in the day: "Hour after hour & no news of you! . . . I pray give me some explicit direction for I shall be at Geneva soon & it will break my heart if I do not know where you are." She concluded: "And when you read this letter say in that most gentle tone of yours 'poor thing.' Now do not smile contemptuously & call me a 'little fool' when I tell you I weep at your departure. Farewell; you have been kind to me under the most unfavorable circumstances. . . ." " It is improbable that Byron saw Claire on that last hectic day, but he did give her his address: *"Poste restante, à Geneve."*

Despite Byron's dislike of early rising, there was tremendous activity at an early hour on the 23rd in the great house in Piccadilly Terrace. It was important to get started before the bailiffs came. Besides Dr. Polidori, Byron took with him three servants: a Swiss named Berger, William Fletcher, and Robert Rushton, who had accompanied him as far as Gibraltar on his first journey abroad." Hobhouse and Scrope Davies were going to see him off at Dover. Hobhouse chronicled the memorable day: "Up at six—breakfasted—but not off until half past nine— Polidori & I went in S. B. Davies' chaise—B. & S.B.D. in Byron's new Napoleonic carriage—built by Baxter for 500 £—there was a crowd about the door. . . ." " Having followed the route of Chaucer's pilgrims, they stopped at Canterbury to admire the cathedral." They "arrived at Dover by half past 8—dined at Ship and took light French wines." "

The next morning they heard that the bailiffs had entered No. 13 just after they had left and had seized everything. Hobhouse was "in alarm respecting their descent to Dover and the carriage—therefore had it put on board as soon as possible. Mr. Dever[?] the auctioneer has seized for rent for the Duchess of Devonshire." "

The wind was contrary from the eastward and strong, so that they could not leave that day. After a five-o'clock dinner they walked out in the evening to see the grave of Charles Churchill, the satirist, friend of Wilkes, whose *Rosciad* had been one of the admired models which inspired Byron's *English Bards and Scotch Reviewers*. Hobhouse recorded that "Byron lay down on his grave and gave the man a crown to fresh turf it." [n]

News had gone abroad that the celebrated Lord Byron was in Dover, and, Dr. Lushington later reported to Lady Byron, "the curiosity to see him was so great that many ladies accoutred themselves as chambermaids for the purpose of obtaining under that disguise a nearer inspection whilst he continued at the inn. . . ." [n]

The next morning the wind had shifted and the captain was eager to be off, but rousing the travelers was not so easy. Hobhouse was up at eight and reported "all on board except the company—the Captain said he could not wait and B. could not get up a moment sooner—even the serenity of Scrope was perturbed—however after some bustle out came Byron—and taking my arm—walked down to the Quay." [n] They walked through a lane of spectators. [n] Hobhouse continued: "the bustle kept B in spirits—but he looked affected when the packet glided off. I ran to the end of the wooden pier—and as the vessel toss'd by as through a rough sea & contrary wind saw him again—the dear fellow pulled off his cap & wav'd it to me—I gazed until I could not distinguish him any longer—God bless him for a gallant spirit and a kind one. . . ." [9]

[9] Hobhouse diary, entry of April 25, 1816. Hobhouse wished to accompany Byron, but, according to Lord Lovelace, he was unable to get a passport for some time because of his book about the "Hundred Days," which was generally favorable to Napoleon. (*Astarte*, p. 52 n.)

CHAPTER XVI

═══════════

1816

Switzerland

A S THE vessel nosed out of Dover harbor and headed into the waves of the Channel, Byron was both exalted and cast down by the agitations of the parting. But, as he had told Moore, agitation of any kind always gave "a rebound" to his spirits, and his impressions and reflections were vivified and stored for poetic expression. The sea and the wind and the bouncing ship evoked something of the melancholy he had felt the last time he left England's shores, in 1809. He was Childe Harold again, but a matured and altered Harold,

> . . . *grown agèd in this world of woe,*
> *In deeds, not years, piercing the depths of life,*
> *So that no wonder waits him. . . ."*

It was, as Byron half realized already, the end of an epoch in his life, but he was not yet aware to what extent it was the beginning of his maturer literary existence. As he left England never to return, he entered into a freedom of life and expression that transcended the constraints imposed on him by the years of fame. That freedom awoke in him as he headed for the warm lands of the south. Although he planned to stop in Geneva to wait for Hobhouse, his destination was Venice, the "greenest island" of his imagination.[1]

---

[1] *LJ*, IV, 7. Byron had intended ultimately to go on to the eastern Mediterranean. Writing to Lady Byron from Ravenna, December 28, 1820, he said: ". . . I meant to have gone to Turkey and am not sure that I shall not finish with it. . . ." (*Astarte*, p. 112.)

Against head winds the journey to Ostend took sixteen hours. Byron "stomached the sea pretty well," he wrote Hobhouse the next day, "till a damned 'Merchant of Bruges' capsized his breakfast close by me, and made me sick by contagion. . . ." [n] According to Polidori, the Cour Impériale, where they stayed at Ostend, was an excellent inn, and they were astonished at the good treatment they got. "As soon as he reached his room," Polidori recorded indiscreetly, "Lord Byron fell like a thunderbolt upon the chambermaid." [n]

They set off at three in the afternoon (the 26th) with four horses and a postilion. A *calèche* carried their luggage. [n] The picturesqueness of the towns compensated for the flat country, and they had just enough adventures to relieve the monotony.

They did not reach the Hôtel des Pays Bays in Ghent until three in the morning. [n] The next day they visited the cathedral, climbed to the top of the steeple for a view of the surrounding country, and then took a fiacre to the École de Dessin, quite *en touriste*.

Traveling through the flat Flemish landscape, they found it "tiresomely beautiful," as Polidori said. "Level roads," Byron wrote Augusta, "don't suit me, as thou knowest; it must be up hill or down, and then I am more *au fait*." [n] At Antwerp, where they arrived the evening of the 29th, Byron admired the famous basins built for Bonaparte's navy more than he did the Flemish paintings, which they saw in great numbers in the principal churches and museums.

He later wrote to Murray: "The Flemish school, such as I saw it in Flanders, I utterly detested, despised, and abhorred. . . ." [n] But he was particularly severe on its most admired artist. "As for Rubens," he told Hobhouse, ". . . he seems to me . . . the most glaring—flaring—staring—harlotry impostor that ever passed a trick upon the senses of mankind. . . . I never saw such an assemblage of florid nightmares as his canvas contains; his portraits seem clothed in pulpit cushions." [n]

After lunching at Antwerp on the 30th, they started out for Mechlin (Malines). But they had gone only a little way when the carriage, which had given way at Lo-Kristy, broke down again. At Brussels, where they went to have it repaired, Byron met Major Pryse Lockhart Gordon, who had been a friend of the poet's mother in Scotland. Calling on him at the Hôtel d'Angleterre, Gordon, who had not seen Byron since the latter was at Harrow, "found much less change in his appearance than there generally is from youth to manhood. . . ." When the conversation turned to the poet's childhood in Scotland, Byron was fascinated. He was tired of gawking at pictures and let Polidori do the sightseeing while he talked for three hours with the Major."

One thing Byron wanted to see more than cathedrals or museums was the field of Waterloo. Gordon offered to act as "*cicerone*." On the morning of the 4th they started off early, Byron and Gordon in the new *calèche* which the doctor had procured for the servants and baggage, and Polidori and a servant on horseback." Gordon recorded Byron's reactions. "We got out at the Monuments. Lord Byron gazed about for five minutes without uttering a syllable; at last, turning to me, he said—'I am not disappointed. I have seen the plains of Marathon, and these are as fine. . . . He did not seem much interested about the positions of the troops, which I pointed out to him; and we got into our carriage and drove to the Chateau Goumont, the poet remaining silent, pensive, and in a musing mood, which I took care not to interrupt." "

Before leaving, Byron felt he must ride over the field again, and he and Polidori mounted the two saddle horses and galloped away, perhaps imagining themselves in a cavalry charge. Byron, according to Polidori, sang "Turkish or Arnaout riding-tunes." "

At the Gordons' that evening, where "in high spirits and good humor" he charmed the company with anecdotes of his Eastern travels, Byron readily consented to compose some verses for Mrs. Gordon's album, in which Walter Scott had written some lines on Waterloo. Byron took the album home with him and the next day returned it with two stanzas beginning:

Stop!—for thy tread is on an Empire's dust."

Byron had already begun to put down on paper some of the thoughts that had pursued him since he left England, for only in that way could he escape the narrowness and imperfection of existence.

> *'Tis to create, and in creating live*
> *A being more intense that we endow*
> *With form our fancy, gaining as we give*
> *The life we image, even as I do now—* [n]

The excitement of travel stirred up in him again the impalpable longings of his youth, which he now associated with the wild freedom of nature and the landscapes and skies beyond the horizon.

> *Where rose the mountains, there to him were friends;*
> *Where rolled the ocean, thereon was his home. . . .*[n]

And now, having felt while standing on that "place of skulls," "the deadly Waterloo," the vanity of power and the fleetingness of fame, he committed those feelings to paper in the small hours when he had retired to his room in the suite at the Hôtel d'Angleterre. The stanzas on Waterloo and on Napoleon were probably set down in their first draft then. To Byron, Waterloo was not a victory but a melancholy defeat, for Europe was still in fetters and tyranny wielded more power than ever. Yet the individual valor of brave men was memorable and worth recording. And the dramatic contrast of the gaiety at the Duchess of Richmond's ball with the death and destruction that followed made an indelible impression on his mind.

> *There was a sound of revelry by night*

And then

> *Rider and horse,—friend,—foe,—in one red burial blent!* [n]

He must leave his tribute to "young, gallant Howard!"

Above all others, however, one name still remained that had a potency in men's minds: Napoleon. And for Byron it was, as it had been when the news first came of his fall, "impossible not to be dazzled and overwhelmed by his character and career." Now more than ever Byron felt a strong kinship with Napoleon in what he conceived to be the basic springs of his character. He was surely thinking of himself when he wrote:

> *But Quiet to quick bosoms is a Hell,*
> *And* there *hath been thy bane; there is a fire*
> *And motion of the Soul which will not dwell*
> *In its own narrow being, but aspire*
> *Beyond the fitting medium of desire. . . ."*

On the morning of the 6th, when they were ready to depart, Gordon presented Byron with a copy of Abate Giambattista Casti's *Novelle Galanti,* ironic and satiric stories of intrigue and love, which he had never before seen, to beguile the duller hours of his journey.[2] At two they set off for Louvain on the road to the Rhine."

While Byron was trying to forget England, neither his friends nor his enemies in England had forgotten him. Hobhouse, Davies, and Kinnaird were trying to quash the ugly rumors that persisted in London, spread apparently by some of those who had either seen or heard of the depositions of Lady Byron to Dr. Lushington. And at least four women lived daily with the unforgettable image of that handsome face and the memory of the irresistible personality that grew rather than diminished with his absence.

Hobhouse was loyally determined to deny all the charges against his friend. The day after his return from Dover he met a friend (Bambridge) who had heard "that Lady B told that B had boasted to her of going to bed to his sister. I implied that if he had she was more villainous in mentioning it than he in doing it." In his anger Hobhouse added in his diary: "That Lady B will not stick at a trick I know from her having told B that she was in love with another man in order to hook him—she confessed this to B himself." "

Dining that night with Perry, editor of the *Morning Chronicle* —in a large party including Benjamin Constant, Flahault, Turenne (Napoleon's Chamberlain), the Duke of Sussex, Davies, and Kinnaird—Hobhouse found that "Brougham [Lady Byron's legal adviser] has been with him [Perry] telling him that B

---

[2] Byron wrote to Gordon from Geneva: "I cannot tell you what a treat your gift of Casti has been to me; I have almost got him by heart. I had read his 'Animali Parlanti,' but I think these 'Novelle' much better. I long to go to Venice to see the manners so admirably described." (Pryse Gordon: *Personal Memoirs,* II, 328.) Casti was one of the writers who later inspired the rollicking satire of *Beppo* and *Don Juan.*

cheated the Duchess of Devonshire of 500£—I said it was a lie out loud & desired any one present to tell Brougham so for me. . . ." [3]

Later the same day Hobhouse called on Lady Melbourne, who, he wrote, "is in a fright. She is sure that Lady B has seen some of her letters to Lord B., for Caroline Lamb has quoted some passages to her—so that C.L. may be the worthy associate of her Ladyship. . . ." [4] And while he was at Lady Melbourne's the next day, "in came Caroline Lamb. . . . both Lady M & my-self were very kind to this mad creature who is fresh from her *page beating*. . . ." [n]

Caroline Lamb's "page beating" was only another evidence of her unstrung nerves during the weeks before Byron's depar-ture. About the time Byron left England, Caroline in a burst of passion, while she was playing ball with her page in the drawing-room at Melbourne House, threw the ball at his head because he had, contrary to her order, thrown a cracker-like "squib" into the fire. The ball hit him in the temple and made it bleed. "Out of my senses," she wrote later, "I flew into the hall, and screamed 'Oh God, I have murdered the page!' The servants and people in the streets caught the sound, and it was soon spread about. William Lamb would live with me no longer." [n]

It was then that the Melbournes persuaded William Lamb to demand a separation. Caroline would be sent quietly to Brocket, and Melbourne House would no longer be disturbed by

[3] Hobhouse diary, entry of April 26, 1816. Hobhouse had also heard that Brougham had said the cause of the Byron separation was something "too horrid to mention." This gossip of Brougham, which Hobhouse conveyed to Byron, was no doubt the foundation of Byron's undying hatred for "that blackguard Brougham," which was increased tenfold when he later guessed that Brougham was the caustic reviewer of his *Hours of Idleness* in the *Edinburgh Review* in 1808. (See Medwin, I, 176; Rogers, *Table-Talk*, p. 237.)

[4] Hobhouse diary, entry of April 26, 1816. It was perhaps in consequence of these letters having been in a trunk seized when the bailiffs entered 13 Piccadilly Terrace after Byron's departure that Caroline Lamb wrote to Hobhouse: "I have enough trinkets & things to raise about 300£ if the Trunk could be redeemed with this I would gladly part with them. . . ." (Murray MSS.) Needless to say, Hobhouse would have sought money any-where else had it been necessary to redeem the letters, but the bailiffs yielded Byron's personal papers to him.

her madnesses. Caroline acquiesced. The solicitors arrived with
the separation document for William to sign. He went up for
one moment to consult Caroline on the disposition of their son.
She used her seductive wiles so skillfully that half an hour later
they found her sitting fondly by her husband "feeding him with
tiny scraps of transparent bread and butter." [n] The separation
deed was cast aside, and she continued for a time at Melbourne
House, serene on the surface and docile, but determined to seek
revenge on all those who had slighted her.

The unexpected bombshell came on May 9, when Henry
Colburn published her novel *Glenarvon,* a thinly masked satire
on the Holland House and Devonshire House circles linked in
an impossible combination with a romantic gothic narrative involving herself and Byron. She had written it, she told Lady
Morgan later, in one month secretly while the preparations were
going forward to separate her from her husband. [n] As one contemporary reader observed to another: "There is no connection
between any two ideas in the book. . . . Glenarvon is Lord
Byron; Lady Augusta, the late Duchess of Devonshire [Caroline's
aunt]; Lady Mandeville . . . the lady who dictated Glenarvon's
farewell letter to Calantha [Caroline Lamb] is Lady Oxford. . . .
I need not say that the heroine is Lady Caroline's own self." [n]
There were also very thinly veiled satires on the Lamb family
and Lady Jersey and others.

On May 10, Hobhouse wrote in his diary: "Glenarvon—the
hero is a monster & meant for B. . . . I called on the bitch &
was asked whether any harm had been done by her book. . . .
she showed me half bawdy pictures of hers of B." [n] When Hobhouse intimated through Lady Melbourne that he had Caroline's
letters to Byron and might publish them, she countered with a
threat of her own: ". . . let him but publish the tenth part of a
single line in any letter I ever wrote him . . . and if I die for
it I vow to God I will on the instant publish not only all his, but
the whole exact journal I have kept of my acquaintance with
him, and his conduct during the last four years." [5]

Her reply to Hobhouse's further remonstrances was a long

[5] "*To Lord Byron,*" p. 75. It would appear from an undated note to Murray
that this was hardly an idle threat, for she had actually prepared Byron's

letter, half pathetic, half eloquently defiant: "You say in your letter to Lady M. something as if I were Lady Byron's advocate and confidante. I believe you will find yourself utterly mistaken. I do not fancy she would even extend her compassion to a reprobate like me, and though from my soul I pity her, as I knew that which ought to have made me fly to her and prevent her marriage—some day you will find that Lord Byron's imprudence betrayed to her a thousand circumstances which to this hour I believe Lady Noel and Mrs. Clarmont [sic] have not the remotest idea of. . . ." [n]

Caroline had not painted Byron as dark as she might have in the novel. Although she ascribed murder and kidnapping and a few seductions to the character she had created, once she let herself go he became a romantic hero, interestingly melancholy, whose genius and charm thrilled her in the writing as they had in life. Caroline had remarkable talent in the handling of words, but she bungled her opportunity to create the semblance of life in the characters, burying them in the artificialities of an absurd plot and the claptrap conventions distilled from her reading of current novels.

While Caroline Lamb was thus making a fool of herself, another woman whose thoughts were constantly occupied with Byron retired sedately to Kirkby Mallory in Leicestershire. The day that Byron left the shores of England, "Lady Byron too," Sam Rogers said, "went into the country to break her heart." [n] Annabella had ceased to correspond with Augusta after the first week in April, but she was already laying plans for a correspondence on a new footing. As she brooded over the past words and actions of Byron and his sister now that the separation was a *fait accompli,* her opinion that there had been incestuous relations between them became certain and unalterable. The mere fact that she had at last given expression to the grounds of her suspicions gave them a reality they had not had before. Now she

---

letters to her for publication in the hope that she could trick Murray or some other publisher into printing them. "I am about to publish a work," she wrote, "—250 letters from a young Venetian nobleman—addrest to a very absurd English Lady—they are beautiful & might serve all other noblemen." (Murray MSS.)

had two objects in view: one, to establish the fact absolutely, preferably by getting Augusta to confess, and thus to know for certain whether Byron had ever persuaded her to repeat the crime after his marriage (that was important to her); and another, to condition or frighten Augusta against ever again renewing an intimacy with her brother, actually to root out the love she bore him even from her correspondence and her thoughts.

The jealousy which her principles would not permit her to acknowledge found sublimation in a truly sadistic zeal to extract the sin from Augusta's life and save her. The religious-moral tone of her correspondence, interspersed with expressions of love for Augusta and for her spiritual well-being, does not conceal the brutality of her attack upon the foolish, lovable, and impulsive woman. There are few records of the cruelty that wears a benevolent face, of the studied undermining of the peace of mind of a fellow woman, equal to the deliberate assault upon the conscience of Augusta in the correspondence of Lady Byron and Mrs. Villiers, Augusta's intimate friend, in the months that followed the separation.

Mrs. Villiers had at first suggested that Lady Byron make a clean breast of her knowledge to Augusta, but to that Annabella objected. There were certain desired ends and a certain subtlety to be observed: "My great object, next to the Security of my Child," she wrote, "is, therefore, the restoration of her mind to the state which is religiously desirable. I differ from you in regard to the effects of an unequivocal communication. . . . I do not conceive that the repetition of his words to me in private, could make a change in her feelings, if what passed in her presence did not." [n]

Through May the preparations continued, for Lady Byron graciously abstained from launching the attack until after Augusta's confinement. Mrs. Villiers, avid for more details, expressed a willingness to aid in the attainment of Lady Byron's worthy objects.

While this nemesis of righteousness was preparing for her, Augusta, having given birth to her son,[n] cut off from all intercourse with Annabella, and feeling desolate in the loss of her brother's society, turned for news of him to Hobhouse, who might go abroad soon and could carry messages for her. As soon as she recovered, she wrote to thank him for the verses of Byron he had sent her, probably the "Stanzas to Augusta," which she now read for the first time. "I think them most beautiful," she said simply, "and I need not add, they are most gratifying to me, who doat upon dear B." "

Another dark-eyed girl was deeply interested in Byron's journey, and hoped to reach Geneva before him. Claire Clairmont left Dover with Percy Shelley and Mary Godwin on May 3 and wrote to Byron from Paris on the 6th: "In five or six days I shall be at Geneva. I entreat you on receipt of this to write a little note for me directed as Madame Clairville, Poste Restante, saying where you are & how you are. I have taken the name of Clairville because you said you liked the name of Clare but could not bear *mont* because of that very ugly woman. And I chuse to be married because I am so [6] & Madame's have their full liberty abroad. . . .

"I know not how to address you; I cannot call you friend for though I love you you do not feel even interest for me; fate has ordained that the slightest accident that should befall you should be agony to me; but were I to float by your window drowned all you would say would be 'Ah voila.'. . . a few days ago I was eighteen; people of eighteen always love truly & tenderly; & I who was educated by Godwin however erroneous my creed have the highest adoration for truth." "

But Byron had other things to occupy his mind than a foolish, lovesick girl. There were diversions and "novelties" enough as the heavy carriage jolted along toward Cologne and the Rhine. When they reached the kingdom of Prussia, they found the people cleaner, but everything else dirty. Polidori asked a beautiful face in one of the towns whether the "*dames n'aimaient pas beaucoup les Français,*" and got for reply: "*Oui, les dames publiques.*" "

Arriving at Cologne at night on May 8, they secured rooms at the Hôtel de Prague and the next morning visited the cathedral and St. Ursula's Church, "where we were shown virgins' skulls of ninety years old, male and female, all jumbled into a mass of

[6] This seems to indicate that Claire already knew or suspected that she was carrying Byron's child.

11,000 virgins' bones. . . ."" This made a more lasting impression on Byron than all the other sights of Cologne.

And, perhaps merely out of complaisance to Polidori, Byron went picture-gazing again." But he had something more notable to record in his letter to Hobhouse a few days later: "The host of our hotel mistook a German Chambermaid—whose red cheeks and white teeth had made me venture upon her carnally—for his wife, & stood swearing at the door like a Squadron of Cavalry, to the amusement or consternation of all his audience—till the mystery was developed by his wife walking out of her own room & the girl out of mine."

Proceeding up the west bank of the Rhine, the travelers were in ecstasies over the picturesque scenery. But Polidori was scarcely the companion Byron would have preferred on this occasion. He thought of his sister, who shared so many of the Byron sensitivities. "The castled Crag of Drachenfels" would have given him "double joy" if Augusta had been there."

Occasionally Byron thought it necessary to deflate the young Polidori, who felt himself "on the footing of an equal" with the poet who employed him. Byron was reading at a window overlooking the Rhine "when Polidori turning abruptly to him, after having read a great eulogium of his works, said, 'and, pray, what is there excepting writing poetry that I cannot do better than you?'" Byron replied that there were three things—"First . . . I can hit with a pistol the keyhole of that door—Secondly, I can swim across that river to yonder point—and thirdly, I can give you a d——d good thrashing." " Polidori left the room.

At Mannheim they crossed the river to the eastern shore, and kept on that side, Byron told Hobhouse, "to avoid the French segment of territory at Strasburg, as we have not French passports, and no desire to view a degraded country and oppressed people." " There Dr. Polidori was taken very ill with a fever. And they were stopped again at Karlsruhe by the doctor's illness. On the 18th they set out again. Perhaps the sight of the Jura and the Alps revived Polidori, for he seems to have recovered from his fever and his own medicines after they crossed into Switzerland at Basel."

A visit to Aventicum (Avenches), the site of the old Roman

capital of Helvetia, and to the field of Morat near by, where the Swiss defeated the Burgundians in the fifteenth century, gave Byron material for some more stanzas for *Childe Harold*. Like other travelers, he picked up a few bones, "as much as may have made a quarter of a hero," he grimly boasted."

They now headed direct for the Lake of Geneva (or Lake Leman, as Byron preferred to call it), which they came upon first at Lausanne, where they spent the night. The next day (May 25) they set out for Geneva by the road along the lake, which disappointed Polidori but captivated Byron immediately: "Lake Leman woos me with its crystal face." " They passed through Coppet, where Mme de Staël's château was awaiting its chatelaine, but they did not stop. Night had fallen before they arrived at Dejean's Hôtel d'Angleterre on the main road to Geneva, a mile outside the city.

Byron, weary from the journey and probably annoyed by the formality, everywhere required in the Continental hotels, of writing statistical details in the register every night, put down his age as 100. Half an hour later he had a note from the innkeeper, Jaques Dejean, asking him to give the correct information."

Before the entry was changed, however, other observant eyes had seen it. Claire Clairmont had been watching the register eagerly since she had arrived with the Shelleys on May 13. Not knowing Byron's leisurely habits of travel, she had expected him to be there before her. While the Shelleys were exploring Geneva or boating on the lake, she kept an anxious watch, for she now knew that she was pregnant by the most talked-of poet of England.

The exhausted travelers had already retired when she saw Byron's name on the register, and she wrote a note in playful and exuberant relief:

I am sorry you are grown so old, indeed I suspected you were 200, from the slowness of your journey. I suppose your venerable age could not bear quicker travelling. Well, heaven send you sweet sleep—I am so happy.

Clare

Direct under cover to Shelley for I do not wish to appear either in love or curious."

❊ *ANNABELLA MILBANKE, 1812*

:►► *AUGUSTA LEIGH*

But Byron was in no hurry to renew the affair with this importunate girl. After a leisurely breakfast the next morning, he and the doctor ordered a *calèche* to go into Geneva. Byron, who was interested in finding a house or small villa that he could rent for the summer, went to see a house in the village of Cologny, two miles from Geneva on the south shore opposite their hotel.

The Villa Diodati stood back some two hundred yards from the lake on a hill and commanded a magnificent panorama of the blue water, with the city to the left and the snowy Jura Moun-tains furnishing a distant backdrop across the lake in front. The property belonged to Édouard Diodati, a descendant of the Charles Diodati who had been a friend of John Milton. But the rent, twenty-five louis a month, seemed too much, and, besides, it was a little smaller than Byron had hoped for.[n] He expected soon to entertain Hobhouse, Davies, and perhaps other friends. He decided to look further.

Claire, having written two more sentimental letters to Byron, waited the whole day and evening for a note. At a quarter past two the next morning (Monday), she poured out her agony and made what she believed was the best suggestion for a rendezvous safe from prying eyes: "I have been in this weary hotel this fortnight & it seems so unkind, so cruel, of you to treat me with such marked indifference. Will you go straight up to the top of the house this evening at ½ past seven & I will infallibly be on the landing place & shew you the room." [n]

Whether Byron complied with her wishes and limped up the stairs to the top landing that night there is no way of knowing, but through Shelley he did establish relations with her again soon after. On Monday morning Byron and Polidori rowed across to Diodati, but Byron was disappointed to find that the villa had been promised to an English family for three years.[n] As Byron stepped out of the boat on his return, he met Claire and Mary with Shelley. When the two poets made each other's acquaintance then on the shore of the Lake of Geneva, there began one of the most famous friendships in literary history.

There is no record of the poets' first impressions of each other, but Byron had heard much from Claire of the wonderful boy, then only twenty-three, and he had read *Queen Mab*, which

Shelley had sent him in admiration for a fellow iconoclast."
Shelley was shy with strangers. But so was Byron; Mary had
observed in her one meeting with him his mild manners, his
almost feminine gentleness. And Trelawny and others meeting
Shelley for the first time noted that his shyness vanished once
he was launched upon other than commonplace topics. Polidori made a curious record in his diary, perhaps half garnered
from his later conversation with Byron: "P[ercy] S[helley],
the author of *Queen Mab*, came; bashful, shy, consumptive;
twenty-six [*sic*]; separated from his wife; keeps the two
daughters of Godwin, who practise his theories; one L[ord]
B[yron]'s." "

The next day Byron, while hunting for a suitable house, seemed
on the point of being drawn into the social life of Geneva. Marc-
Auguste Pictet, one of the literary and political figures of the
city, asked him and Polidori to go with him to a soiree of Mme
Eynard-Châtelain, wife of a delegate to the Congress of Vienna."
Before they left for the soiree, the banker Charles Hentsch came
in. He had had no idea when he changed their money the day
before that he was talking to one of the most famous literary
men of England. He offered his services, and in fact became
Byron's chief adviser and man of business during his whole
stay in Switzerland. Hentsch was a lively young man of twenty-
six, cultivated (he did some writing in his spare hours), philan-
thropic, and a man of mark in the community. Byron was always
welcome at Hentsch's home and at his bank in the rue de la
Corraterie."

The two guests at Mme Eynard's party who most interested
Byron and with whom he later had most cordial relations were
Pellegrino Rossi, brilliant young economist, law professor, and
statesman, who had fled from Italy and become a naturalized
citizen of Geneva, and Charles Victor de Bonstetten, the venerable liberal patrician whose ideas were entirely congenial to
Byron. Both were friends of Mme de Staël, at whose château
he again met them during the summer. Bonstetten, man of the
world and excellent conversationalist, had sat at the table of
Voltaire and had been an admirer and disciple of Rousseau.
His earlier friendship and correspondence with the English poet

Thomas Gray gave him an aura of the eighteenth century which was pleasing to Byron.

But Byron had seen enough of Genevese society. From this time forward he spent more and more time with the Shelley ménage. Apparently the friendship was cemented, for thereafter until Shelley moved across the lake they always breakfasted together, and in the boat of one or the other they looked for houses along the lake. Shelley too was eager to get out of the expensive and uncongenial hotel.

On the first of June their search for houses seemed ended, for Polidori recorded: "took Necker's house for 100 louis for 8 or 365 days.[7] Saw several houses for Shelley; one good." As it turned out, Byron did not actually take Mme Necker's villa, but the Shelleys settled for a small square two-story house at Montalègre, at the foot of the hill of Cologny, which they rented from Jacob Chappuis. The Maison or Campagne Chappuis, as the Shelleys called it, was hidden from the road by trees and vineyards and was yet only a stone's throw from the lake, where a little private harbor sheltered their boat. To celebrate the occasion, they dined together, went out in the boat, and then chatted long over tea. Byron regaled them with stories of the literary men he had known in London.

Mary Shelley, who was enchanted with Byron from the first meeting in London, later recalled for Moore with a melancholy nostalgia some of the idyllic moments of their moonlight rides upon the water: "The waves were high and inspiriting,—we were all animated by our contest with the elements. 'I will sing you an Albanian song,' cried Lord Byron; 'now, be sentimental and give me all your attention.' It was a strange, wild howl that he gave forth; but such as, he declared, was an exact imitation of the savage Albanian mode,—laughing, the while, at our disappointment, who had expected a wild Eastern melody."

[7] This seems to mean that the rent was one hundred louis per year, and that they could pro-rata it for any period from a week to as long as they wished to stay up to a year. The louis or napoleon was a gold coin worth twenty francs, with a nominal value of $3.86, or something less than an English pound—though it is always difficult to equate these sums in terms of purchasing power; it is generally safe to multiply by three or four any such figures in trying to get at a modern equivalent.

Out of these evenings, and later ones, with the stimulus of the sky and the water and the discussions with Shelley, who, himself an ethereal presence, opened up wide vistas in Byron's mind, came new verses for *Childe Harold*. In the quiet early-morning hours poetry, "the lava of the imagination," flowed from his pen:

> *There breathes a living fragrance from the shore,*
> *Of flowers yet fresh with childhood; on the ear*
> *Drops the light drip of the suspended oar,*
> *Or chirps the grasshopper one good-night carol more. . . .*
> *Then stirs the feeling infinite, so felt*
>   *In solitude, where we are* least *alone. . . .*[n]

In this atmosphere, under the spell of Shelley's eloquence, Byron imbibed something of the Wordsworthian pantheistic feeling. No one had made Wordsworth's philosophy more appealing to Byron than did Shelley, for he too longed to spurn "the clay-cold bonds which round our being cling." [n]

> *When Elements to Elements conform,*
> *And dust is as it should be, shall I not*
> *Feel all I see less dazzling but more warm?*
> *The bodiless thought? the Spirit of each spot?*
> *Of which, even now, I share at times the immortal lot?*
>
> *Are not the mountains, waves, and skies, a part*
>   *Of me and of my Soul, as I of them?* [n]

But Byron usually ended in a basis of tangible reality, however much he might let his fancy play.[8]

On the 3rd or 4th of June the Shelley ménage was established at Montalègre, and at the same time Byron entered into negotia-

---

[8] Byron later told Medwin: "Shelley, when I was in Switzerland, used to dose me with Wordsworth physic even to nausea: and I do remember then reading some things of his with pleasure." (Medwin, II, 40.) Hobhouse, who discounted and scoffed at Shelley's influence on Byron, wrote in the margin of his copy of Moore (II, 25) opposite the statement that Shelley was an "aristocrat by birth and, as I understand, *also in appearance*": "not the least unless to be lean and feeble be aristocratical." When Moore referred to Byron and Shelley as "the two friends," Hobhouse said scornfully: "they never were friends." And on Moore's statement that the opinions of Shelley "were not altogether without some influence on his mind," Hobhouse commented: "quite otherwise."

tions again for the Villa Diodati, with the situation of which he was first taken. On the 6th, Polidori recorded: "With Lord Byron in the calèche to Hentsch, where we got the paper making us masters of Diodati for six months to November 1 for 125 louis." [n]

After the Shelley party left the hotel, Byron, usually accompanied by Polidori, crossed over daily by boat to see them. Mrs. Shelley later told Moore that, though the weather had changed and was become windy and cloudy, with frequent rain squalls, Byron made the crossing every evening, and "as he returned again . . . over the darkened waters, the wind, from far across, bore us his voice singing your Tyrolese Song of Liberty, which I then first heard, and which is to me inextricably linked with his remembrance." [n] With the expectation of taking more extensive excursions on the lake, Byron and Shelley bought a boat for twenty-five louis, a small sailing vessel with a keel, capable of withstanding most of the lake squalls. [n] It was kept in the little harbor below Shelley's house.

On the 10th, Byron and Polidori and the servants got ready for moving, and the whole entourage left Dejean's hotel at three in the afternoon for Diodati. Byron was well pleased with his new home. The little villa was a square structure of gray stone and masonry rising two stories above the basement, with a wrought-iron railing enclosing a balcony that ran around three sides of the *rez-de-chaussée*. The entry was from a tree-sheltered court on the side away from the lake. The great door opened to a long hallway which went through to the balcony.[9] Byron, who, from the days of his boyhood when he had roamed the ruined halls and the park at Newstead, loved expansiveness, never had a house with a nobler view than that from the balcony of the Villa Diodati. [n]

Here too he had a cozy seclusion without feeling shut in. It was only an eight- or ten-minute walk down the slope through the vineyard to Shelley's house, and a few steps farther to the

[9] The first door to the right was that of the dining-room, and the next gave access to the grand salon, a room of ample proportions whose windows opened to the front and side balconies. It was decorated in elegant but simple eighteenth-century style, and was cheered by a great fireplace on rainy nights. Across the hall, on the lake side, was the rather narrow but adequate bedroom used by Byron. (See Polidori: *The Vampyre*, p. ix.)

boat harbor. It was a novelty for Byron to have found agreeable persons untrammeled by the conventions of society, well read and intelligent, with sensitive appreciation, ready to discuss any subject under the sun with speculative intensity. With Hobhouse and Davies he had been able to discuss politics and morals with frankness, and to indulge in Voltairean skepticisms, but there were imaginative realms that were shut to the rationalistic and downright John Cam.

When the weather permitted, Byron and the Shelleys went on the lake in the quiet evening; when it was stormy, they gathered before the fire at Diodati and talked, the conversation ranging from poetry to the appearance of ghosts.

The only discord in the harmony of their lives was created by the vanity and flightiness of the impossible Doctor. Byron wrote later: "I never was much more disgusted with any human production than with the eternal nonsense, and *tracasseries*, and emptiness, and ill humour, and vanity of that young person. . . ." [1]

Quick to take offense, particularly at anything that touched his pride, Polidori, once having lost a sailing-match to Shelley and imagining that he had been treated with contempt, challenged him to a duel. Shelley merely laughed at him, but Byron, thinking the Doctor might take some other means of revenge, warned Polidori: "Recollect, that though Shelley has some scruples about duelling, *I* have none; and shall be, at all times, ready to take his place." [n]

But Byron tolerated Polidori partly because of the merriment his foolishness caused, finding relief for his annoyance by making sly remarks about him such as that "he was exactly the kind of person to whom, if he fell overboard, one would hold out a straw to know if the adage be true that drowning men catch at straws." [n]

Byron had another embarrassment in the presence of Claire, to whom he was afraid to show any particular attention for fear she would take advantage of it. Perhaps for no better reason than to draw his attention, she seems to have made a critical

[1] *LJ*, IV, 140. Letter of June 17, 1817, to Murray. But Byron did at the same time recommend Polidori to Murray, who, he thought, might use his influence to get him a physician's berth in the Admiralty.

observation on his manner of speaking. Mary obviously referred
to Claire when she told Moore of "the half playful rage, into
which she saw him thrown, one day, by a heedless girl, who
remarked that she thought he had a little of the Scotch accent.
'Good God, I hope not!' he exclaimed. 'I'm sure I haven't. I
would rather the whole d——d country was sunk in the sea—I,
the Scotch accent!' " [n]

It may well have been during the time when they were all
forced indoors that Claire induced Byron to renew his intimate
relations with her. He had once confessed that his heart always
alighted on the nearest perch. He excused himself to Augusta
later by saying: "I was not in love nor have any love left for any,
but I could not exactly play the Stoic with a woman who had
scrambled eight hundred miles to unphilosophize me, besides I
had been regaled of late with so many 'two courses and a
desert' (Alas!) of aversion, that I was fain to take a little love
(if pressed particularly) by way of novelty." [n]

But Claire could not see him alone as often as she wished,
partly because Dr. Polidori was too egotistic to realize that he
was de trop. "Pray if you can," she wrote, "send M. Polidori either
to write another dictionary or to the lady he loves. I hope this
last may be his pillow & then he will go to sleep; for I cannot
come at this hour of the night & be seen by him; it is so extremely
suspicious." [n]

Careful as they were, gossips were not slow to circulate stories,
often distorted. Byron told Medwin while at Pisa: "I never led
so moral a life as during my residence in that country; but I
gained no credit by it. . . . there is no story so absurd that they
did not invent at my cost. I was watched by glasses on the
opposite side of the Lake, and by glasses too that must have had
very distorted optics. I was waylaid in my evening drives—I
was accused of corrupting all the grisettes in the Rue Basse. I
believe that they looked upon me as a man-monster, worse than
the piqueur." [n] He ascribed part of the feeling toward him to the
fact that he went so little among the Genevese, since he did
not speak French.

The English, too, who came in droves during the summer,
heard many fantastic stories. Lord Glenbervie, who arrived early

in July, found the hotel at Sécheron full, and went to a lodging, where he confided to his diary: "Among more than sixty English travellers here, there is Lord Byron, who is *cut* by everybody. They tell a strange adventure of his at Dejean's Inn. He is now living at a villa on the Savoy side of the lake with that woman, who it seems proves to be a Mrs. Shelley, wife to the man who keeps the Mount Coffee-house." [n]

Trying to thin himself, for he had grown heavy again from the unrestrained feasting of his last days in England, Byron settled into a spartan regime. Moore, no doubt drawing upon Mary Shelley's memory, says: "His system of diet here was regulated by an abstinence almost incredible. A thin slice of bread, with tea, at breakfast—a light, vegetable dinner, with a bottle or two of Seltzer water, tinged with vin de Grave, and in the evening, a cup of green tea, without milk or sugar, formed the whole of his sustenance. The pangs of hunger he appeased by privately chewing tobacco and smoking cigars." [n]

Polidori said that "he retired to rest at three, got up at two, and employed himself a long time over his toilette; that he never went to sleep without a pair of pistols and a dagger by his side, and that he never eat animal food." [n] He had dinner at five, which he usually preferred taking alone, probably so that his abstemious diet would not be noticed and commented upon.[n]

During the first stormy days at Diodati, Byron remained in the house. On the 14th, Pellegrino Rossi came out from Geneva, and Shelley dropped in during the evening.[n] After dinner the next day, Shelley and the ladies came as usual. Either that same night or the next, which they all spent under Byron's roof, the host suggested that they each write a ghost story, to which they all agreed. "You and I," Byron said to Mary, "will publish ours together." [n]

On the 17th, Polidori recorded that "The ghost-stories are begun by all but me." [n] Shelley started one "founded on the experiences of his early life," but he too soon lost interest in it.[n] What Claire's story was we are not told, but she also failed to go on. Byron apparently outlined the plot of his story to the whole company. Mary thought it "very dramatic & striking." [n] According to Polidori, it was this: "Two friends were to travel from England into Greece; while there, one of them should die, but before his death, should obtain from his friend an oath of secrecy with regard to his decease. Some short time after, the remaining traveller, returning to his native country, should be startled at perceiving his former companion moving about in society, and should be horrified at finding that he made love to his former friend's sister." " Byron began his tale promptly with the others on June 17, but abandoned it after writing only a few pages, which took the travelers to the ruins of Ephesus rather than to Greece and broke off with the death and burial of the one after the ominous promise had been extracted from the other."

Only Mary took the pact to write a ghost story really seriously. She pondered a subject day and night, but the inventive faculty seemed wanting. Then the seminal spark came from one of the nightly discussions at Diodati.[2] "During one of these, various philosophical doctrines were discussed, and among others the nature of the principle of life, and whether there was any probability of its ever being discovered and communicated. . . . Perhaps a corpse would be re-animated; galvinism [sic] had given token of such things: perhaps the component parts of a creature might be manufactured, brought together, and endued with vital warmth. Night waned upon this talk, and even the witching hour had gone by, before we retired to rest." " Mary could not sleep, and there was born in her mind the frightening form of the monster created by Frankenstein.

The interest in the ghost stories was still high at Diodati on the 18th. Polidori said that at twelve o'clock they "really began to talk ghostly." Byron repeated the verses of Coleridge's *Christabel*

[2] Mary later recorded in her journal: ". . . since incapacity and timidity always prevented my mingling in the nightly conversations of Diodati, they were, as it were, entirely tête-à-tête between my Shelley and Albè." (*Mary Shelley's Journal*, p. 184; entry of Oct. 19, 1822.) "Albè" (written variously by the Shelley circle—sometimes without an accent, "Albe," and sometimes with the French accent, "Albé") was the nickname adopted in the Shelley ménage in Switzerland for Byron. Dowden (*Life of Shelley*, II, 13) suggests that it was a shortening of "Albaneser," applied to him after he had imitated the wild Albanian song on the lake, but Forman, Dowden says, believed it was formed from the initials L.B. (Lord Byron).

concerning the witch's breast, "Hideous, deformed, and pale of hue—" in such tones that "Shelley, suddenly shrieking and putting his hands to his head, ran out of the room with a candle." ⁿ Polidori and Byron followed him and found him "leaning against a mantle-piece, with cold drops of perspiration trickling down his face." ⁿ They threw water in his face, and Polidori afterward gave him ether. When he had revived, he said he had been looking at Mary when he "suddenly thought of a woman he had heard of who had eyes instead of nipples, which, taking hold of his mind, horrified him." ⁿ

On June 22, Byron and Shelley embarked in their small open sailboat for the contemplated tour of the lake,ⁿ taking the excuse of Polidori's lameness (he had sprained an ankle) to leave him behind. They arrived two days later at Meillerie, the first goal of their pilgrimage to sites immortalized by Rousseau. There they dined on honey from mountain flowers on the enchanted ground where St.-Preux spent his exile.ⁿ

They left Meillerie in a calm, but "the wind gradually increased in violence," Shelley wrote, "until it blew tremendously; and, as it came from the remotest extremity of the lake, produced waves of a frightful height, and covered the whole surface with a chaos of foam. One of our boatmen [they had two boatmen besides luggage in the shallow craft], who was a dreadfully stupid fellow, persisted in holding the sail at a time when the boat was on the point of being driven under water by the hurricane. . . . The sail was, however, again held, the boat obeyed the helm, and still in imminent peril from the immensity of the waves, we arrived in a few minutes at a sheltered port, in the village of St. Gingoux [St. Gingolph]." ⁿ Byron later corroborated Shelley's story, with a tribute to his companion's courage. "I stripped off my coat—made him strip off his and take hold of an oar, telling him that I thought . . . I could save him [Shelley could not swim at all], if he would not struggle when I took hold of him. . . . We were then about a hundred yards from shore, and the boat in peril. He answered me with the greatest coolness, that 'he had no notion of being saved, and that I would have enough to do to save myself, and begged not to trouble me.' " ⁿ

Shelley passed the evening reading Rousseau's *Nouvelle*

Héloise. Byron had read it often, and knew it almost by heart. The next day being calm, they sailed first to the castle of Chillon. While visiting its towers and torture chamber and the dungeons where political prisoners and heretics had been chained to the columns, Shelley was sunk in the depths of melancholy at this monument of "cold and inhuman tyranny." " Byron was more impressed with the story of an individual prisoner, François Bonivard," a sixteenth-century independent spirit who had thrown in his lot with the patriot conspirators against Duke Charles III of Savoy. He had been confined in the lower dungeon, where the water of the lake could be heard lapping on the wall." Byron got the story in garbled form, possibly from the gendarme who conducted them through the castle, but it was enough to work upon his imagination.

They next sailed for Clarens, and felt themselves immediately on Rousseau's holy ground. From the window of their lodging their landlady pointed out *"le bosquet de Julie,"* and they walked there in the evening, where hay was making under the trees in Julia's wood." As they trod the soil where Rousseau's heroine had been, they were both deeply moved, and Byron suddenly exclaimed: "Thank God, Polidori is not here." "

Byron's impulse again was to find words for the feelings that overpowered him, and he wrote some more stanzas for *Childe Harold.*

> *Clarens! by heavenly feet thy paths are trod,—*
> *Undying Love's, who here ascends a throne*
> *To which the steps are mountains. . . . ."*

But he had already paid a finer tribute to Rousseau in the verses he wrote before leaving Diodati, perhaps while rereading him preparatory to making the tour." He was more than half aware that he was describing himself more closely than the eighteenth-century sentimentalist when he wrote:

> *His love was Passion's essence. . . .*
> *But his was not the love of living dame,*
> *Nor of the dead who rise upon our dreams,*
> *But of ideal Beauty, which became*

In him existence, and o'erflowing teems
Along his burning page, distempered though it seems.[3]

But Rousseau symbolized to Byron more than the passionate self. He had inspired the Revolution and set the libertarian principle loose in the world, a principle that, though set back, would not die.[n]

From Clarens the travelers sailed to near-by Vevey, where Rousseau had conceived the plan of the *Nouvelle Héloise.* They passed on to Ouchy, a village just below Lausanne on the lake. There at the inn (Hôtel de l'Ancre, now d'Angleterre), where the bad weather kept them for two days (June 27 and 28), Byron wrote *The Prisoner of Chillon,* composing rapidly as he did when a subject filled his mind.[n] With dramatic simplicity and deftness in phrasing, he poured out the pathetic story of the Promethean figure of Bonivard, chained to his dungeon pillar and watching his brothers die in their shackles. It became for him as he wrote, and has remained for countless readers since, the embodiment of the "chainless mind" that defies intolerance and tyranny and of the defiant courage of a man willing to suffer for a principle.[n]

But Byron could turn, with that easy mobility of mind and temper observed by all who knew him well, from the solemnity of Bonivard's fate and the sentiment of Rousseau to the irony and wit of Voltaire and Gibbon. On the anniversary of the day (June 27, 1787) that Gibbon wrote the last lines of the last page of his famous *History* in the summerhouse in his garden, Byron and Shelley visited the spot. Later the same day Byron wrote to Murray: ". . . I enclose you a sprig of *Gibbon's Acacia* and some rose-leaves from his garden, which, with part of his house, I have just seen." In the same letter he announced to Murray his completion of 117 stanzas of the new canto of *Childe Harold.*[n]

On the 29th the travelers left Ouchy; they arrived at Montalègre on July 1.[n] Byron was amused, on his return, to find

[3] *Childe Harold,* III, 78. The reference to "ideal Beauty" shows Byron nearer to Shelley than to Rousseau in his conception of love. It may be significant that Shelley (according to Mary's notes) conceived his "Hymn to Intellectual Beauty" while on the tour with Byron around the lake.

that Polidori, who had been frequenting the salons of Geneva, had fallen in love. Moore says: "On the evening of this tender confession they both appeared at Shelley's cottage—Lord Byron, in the highest and most boyish spirits, rubbing his hands as he walked about the room, and in that utter incapacity of retention which was one of his foibles, making jesting allusions to the secret he had just heard. The brow of the doctor darkened as this pleasantry went on, and, at last, he angrily accused Lord Byron of hardness of heart. 'I never,' said he, 'met with a person so unfeeling.' This sally, though the poet had evidently brought it upon himself, annoyed him most deeply. 'Call *me* cold-hearted —*me* insensible!' he exclaimed, with manifest emotion—'as well might you say that glass is not brittle, which has been cast down a precipice, and lies dashed to pieces at the foot!' " [n]

For a few days Byron was busy rearranging and correcting the accumulated stanzas of *Childe Harold,* which had been written on scraps of paper as the inspiration struck him. On the 4th of July he had completed it to his satisfaction.[n] He had decided to end as he began with some lines addressed to his daughter.

> *Yet, though dull Hate as duty should be taught,*
> *I know that thou wilt love me: though my name*
> *Should be shut from thee, as a spell still fraught*
> *With desolation, and a broken claim:*
> *Though the grave closed between us,—'twere the same.*[n]

Byron then turned the manuscript over to Claire for copying. She jumped at the chance (it is not improbable that she first suggested it), for it was her one opportunity and excuse to be at Diodati alone with him. She had finished the fair copy for the printer by July 10,[n] and then started to copy *The Prisoner of Chillon.* But Byron soon grew tired of her constant pleading for his attention. Having just come from the contemplation of an ideal love in the creations of Rousseau, he rebelled against a real love that he did not want. His impatience made him petulant and cruel.

Mme de Staël had returned to her château at Coppet across the lake, and from the second week in July Byron was a frequent visitor there. He enjoyed the society of the Shelleys, but now would gladly have dispensed with their company for the sake of getting Claire out of the way. The Shelley party was planning a tour to Chamouni and Mont Blanc. But Claire wanted to see Byron before she left. A pathetic undated note of hers may have been written about this time: "I would have come to you to-night if I thought I could be of *any use* to you. If you *want* me or any thing of, or belonging to me I am sure Shelley would come and fetch me if you ask him. I am afraid to come dearest for fear of meeting any one. Can you pretext the copying? Tell me any time I shall come & I will because you will have then made your arrangements. Every thing is so awkward. We go so soon. Dearest pray come and see us pray do." "

But Byron had taken the Shelleys into council and urged that she not be allowed to come to Diodati. On July 16 she wrote him: "We go I believe in two days—are you satisfied!— It would make me happy to finish Chillon for you. It is said that you expressed yourself so decisively last Evening that it is impossible to see you at Diodati; If you will trust it down here I will take the *greatest* possible care of it; & finish it in an hour or two. . . . When you had such bad news to announce, was it not a little cruel to behave so harshly all the day." "

Shelley already understood the necessity of getting Claire away from Byron, since remaining near him would only make her unhappy. Writing the next day (July 17) to his friend Thomas Love Peacock, he made a comment on Byron which may well have reference to his eccentric conduct and wild statements to Claire. "Lord Byron," he wrote, "is an exceedingly interesting person, and as such is it not to be regretted that he is a slave to the vilest and most vulgar prejudices, and as mad as the winds?" "

Byron on his side no doubt felt some relief when the Shelley party set off on the 21st for Chamouni on a tour that lasted almost to the end of the month. He divided his time between going to Mme de Staël's, boating alone on the lake, and extracting verses from his distempered brain in the small hours. On his first visit to Coppet (in the second week of July)," "following the servant who had announced his name," according to Polidori, who accompanied him, "he was surprised to meet a lady carried out fainting. . . ." " Of this incident Byron wrote to Murray: "It is true that Mrs. Hervey (she writes novels) fainted at my entrance into Coppet, and then came back again. On her fainting, the Duchesse de Broglie exclaimed, 'This is *too much*—at *sixty-five* years of age!' "" Byron told Medwin later that Mme de Staël had invited him to a family dinner, "and I found the room full of strangers, who had come to stare at me as at some outlandish beast in a rareeshow." He added that they "looked as if his Satanic Majesty had been among them." "

On this same occasion Mme de Staël told him "marvelous and grievous things" of *Glenarvon*, of which he had then seen only the motto, taken from his *Corsair*:

> *He left a name to all succeeding times,*
> *Link'd with one virtue and a thousand crimes.*"

Writing to Murray, he spoke ironically of the "generous moment selected for the publication," and continued: "I have not even a guess at the contents, except from the very vague accounts I have heard, and I know but one thing which a woman can say to the purpose on such occasions, and that she might as well for her own sake keep to herself, which by the way they very rarely can—the old reproach against their admirers of '*Kiss* and *tell*,' bad as it is, is surely somewhat less than—and publish." "

Byron was nevertheless pleased with the society at Coppet, and found Mme de Staël more agreeable at home than she had been in London, though their mutual *franchises* sometimes brought them into verbal combat. Although some English appeared at her dinners and salons, it was mainly a cultivated Continental society that Byron met there. The chatelaine was cordial and invited him oftener than he cared to go, but he did frequently cross the water to her hospitable château in July and August, and more frequently yet after Hobhouse's arrival. It was a much more congenial atmosphere than he had found in the drawing-rooms of Geneva, which were filled with English people. The general conversation was in French, which he understood well enough, though he would not undertake to speak it, but most of the cosmopolitan guests also spoke English. There was besides

M. de Rocca, a young French officer whom Madame had secretly married in 1811 (it was pretty much an open secret by then), the Duchesse de Broglie, her daughter by her first husband, the Swedish Ambassador Baron de Staël Holstein. Though over-shadowed by his brilliant and talkative wife, Rocca was capable of sallies of wit.[n]

Living at the château also was Mme de Staël's great literary friend August Wilhelm von Schlegel, "a presumptuous literato," said Polidori, "contradicting à outrance." [n] Byron agreed with Polidori's judgment of Schlegel, finding him ridiculously vain. He later told Murray: "He took a dislike to me, because I refused to flatter him . . . though Madame de Broglie begged me to do so, 'because he is so fond of it. Voilà les hommes!'" [n]

Among others whom Byron met at Coppet, the Abbé de Brême (or di Breme) was one who, like Pellegrino Rossi, kindled Byron's interest in Italian freedom. Polidori described Di Breme as a "friend of Ugo Foscolo, enthusiastic for Italy, encomiast in all, Grand Almoner of Italy, hater of Austrians." [n]

After the departure of the Shelley party for Chamouni, on the quiet lake alone or undisturbed in the sequestered Diodati, Byron was again possessed by the urge to write. He had sent off on the 20th to Kinnaird, who had requested it, a *Monody on the Death of the Right Hon. R. B. Sheridan*, to be read at Drury Lane Theatre. Sheridan had died on July 7 "in a squalid bed in a house filled with bailiffs his head cover[ed] up his face unwashed his eyes glaring," as Lady Bessborough, Caroline Lamb's mother, who had once been Sheridan's mistress, de-scribed the scene to Hobhouse.[n] But any request performance was a chore for Byron. Despite his fondness for Sheridan, and though he told Lady Blessington: "My feelings were never more excited than while writing the Monody on Sheridan,—every word that I wrote came direct from the heart," [n] he was nevertheless con-strained by the form and the destined purpose of the piece. He labored over the lines, but could come up with nothing better than

> *Sighing that Nature formed but one such man,*
> *And broke the die—in moulding Sheridan!* [n]

He was well aware that it was only a *pièce d'occasion*. He later confessed to Murray: "I did as well as I could; but where I have not my choice I pretend to answer for nothing." [n]

News from England had brought back the whole stream of his past, which now rolled through his mind as a fevered reverie. Here by the Alpine lake he composed "The Dream," giving a capsule history of his life from youthful idealism through disillusionment to sad resignation and melancholy despair. In the dream he pictured himself and the Lady of his love, who was his boy's idealization of Mary Chaworth.[4]

In the same dejected spirit he wrote another dream poem which he called "Darkness," a terrifying vision of man's last days in a dying universe.

> *The bright sun was extinguished, and the stars*
> *Did wander darkling in the eternal space,*
> *Rayless, and pathless, and the icy Earth*
> *Swung blind and blackening in the moonless air. . . .*

All civilization crumbled in the primordial struggle for existence. The altruistic instinct was sunk in every creature but one dog,

> *And he was faithful to a corse, and kept*
> *The birds and beasts and famished men at bay,*
> *Till hunger clung them, or the dropping dead*
> *Lured their lank jaws; himself sought out no food,*
> *But with a piteous and perpetual moan,*
> *And a quick desolate cry, licking the hand*
> *Which answered not with a caress—he died.*

At about the same time Byron wrote some verses on "Prometheus," who had been his defiant hero since as a schoolboy at Harrow he had written a paraphrase of a chorus of the *Prometheus Vinctus* of Æschylus. The theme was filling his mind more

---

[4] Moore (II, 35) said "The Dream" cost Byron "many a tear in writing." Hobhouse, who seldom saw—and could never understand or sympathize with—Byron's sentimental moods, wrote in the margin of his copy of Moore: "not one I believe." What Hobhouse failed to recognize was that the mental image of Mary Chaworth which Byron carried with him and which fostered his romantic dreams of youthful innocence and perfection bore little resemblance to the real Mary, about whose marriage to Jack Musters he could talk with some ribaldry in later years.

and more, and the contemplation of his own baffled existence gave it fire.

> *Titan! to thee the strife was given*
> *Between the suffering and the will,*
> *Which torture where they cannot kill. . . .*
> *Like thee, Man is in part divine,*
> *A troubled stream from a pure source;*
> *And Man in portions can foresee*
> *His own funereal destiny. . . .*

In his solitary musing upon the failure of life to provide the bright dreams of youth with any satisfying reality, Byron turned again to the vision of Augusta, who had never failed him. Here, in the nearest thing to himself, he found the only satisfaction for his craving for sympathy, understanding, and undemanding love. He poured out his overflowing feelings in some new verses to her:

> *Though the day of my Destiny's over,*
> *And the star of my Fate hath declined,*
> *Thy soft heart refused to discover*
> *The faults which so many could find;*
> *Though thy Soul with my grief was acquainted,*
> *It shrunk not to share it with me,*
> *And the Love which my Spirit hath painted*
> *It never hath found but in Thee.*"

But Byron was quite unaware of the dreadful ordeal his sister was undergoing as the prongs of the "Iron Maiden" of Lady Byron and Mrs. Villiers closed upon her. As soon as Augusta had recovered from her confinement, the moral crusade was begun. Mrs. Villiers wrote to her partner in the inquisition: "Did you tell her of his having betrayed her to others or do you think it possible to do this? Could she once be brought to *believe* this fact, I should hope much from it. . . . She is ordered to come to London for the P[rince]ss. Mary's marriage which I am very sorry for—the *tourbillon* of that, & her present exertions to sell the Six mile will give her no time for reflection." "

Lady Byron replied: "I am sorry too on some accounts that A. is going to Town, but may you not do some good by seeing

her, & contribute to dispel her delusions? Except at one period
I have always found her much more collected & prepared to
repel suspicion than he was—and I have always observed the remarkable difference, that his feelings—distinct from practice—
were much more sensitive & correct on all moral questions than
hers. She did not appear to think these transgressions *of consequence*. Her self-condemnation has seemed so exclusively attached to what preceded my marriage, that, in opposition to
every other probability, it *has* led me to doubt a positive renewal
subsequently—but it is not uncommon in such cases for a compromise to be made with conscience when *mischief* has not been
intended." "

Augusta was in a sad predicament indeed. On June 10 she
wrote to Hodgson that she was weak and nervous, "and no wonder, for none can know *how much* I have suffered from this
unhappy business—and, indeed, I have never known a moment's
peace, and begin to despair for the future." " To Annabella she
wrote piteously: "I only wish *every past & present* thought
could be open to you—you would *then* think *less* ill of me than
you do now. . . . Dearest A—— *I have not wronged you. I
have not abused your generosity.*" "

Lady Byron thought she perceived some desire of Augusta to
"atone for the past," and she was now ready to let go with both
barrels. She appealed to Augusta to be "perfectly confidential":
"Dearest Augusta—You will think, perhaps justly, that I erred in
encouraging you myself—but my situation was most extraordinary—I could not, till a late period, *bear to admit things to
myself* sufficiently to act upon them—and resisted what would
have brought absolute conviction to any other person—and you
were to me the kindest friend and comforter. . . . From this
motive I have appeared unconscious of a thousand allusions, as
intelligible to me as to you—To my husband I had another
motive for assuming ignorance, having *had reason* to think that
my life & every hope might depend upon it." "

Augusta was now completely shaken. Although it was a relief
that she had regained the confidence of Annabella, she saw
where it must carry her, and it made her uneasy. On July 11
she went to London," and two days later Hobhouse called on

her at St. James's Palace. She was eager to send some word to Byron, but now she did not know what to tell him. Hobhouse recorded in his diary: "poor thing she did not know what to say—Lady B corresponds with her again on good terms but not so affectionately as before." [n]

Augusta could now only appeal to the one counselor into whose hands she had thrown herself. She wrote to Annabella: ". . . it is still like a *horrid dream* to me my dearest A—— that *I* caused yr sufferings whose whole anxiety was at least to mitigate them. . . . I am perfectly unable to decide *how* to act for the best respecting *him* & his knowledge of what has passed between us. . . . I wish you to reflect on what I had better do— I really *must now* entirely mistrust my own judgment—there are dangers to be apprehended *both* ways—at least I see many from his ignorance." [n]

Annabella was well pleased with the ascendancy she now held over Augusta, but she still must set her right on some things: "It seems to me that you dwell too much on the pain you involuntarily occasioned me, and not enough on the irreparable injury you did *him* by the voluntary sacrifices (for to principles & feelings like yours they must have been *entirely* sacrifices) which you once made to his immediate indulgences." [n]

Annabella assured Mrs. Villiers that she was thoroughly convinced that Augusta's errors toward her were not "of the *heart* but the judgment." [n] Her correspondent in turn reported faithfully every symptom of pain, amendment, or danger in the victim. "Yesterday, for the first time, she dined here . . . & I must say that in my life I never saw any thing equal to her dejection— her absence—her whole mind evidently preoccupied & engrossed —& apparently insensible of being in society." She added a warning or two, however. "I accidentally found yesterday by her question about foreign postage of letters that she was going to write to Ld. B. to-day. . . . Another day she told me she had seen Messrs Hobhouse & Davies together & that they were going to Geneva directly. . . ." [n]

Augusta was in a greater quandary than ever. She saw disastrous consequences in breaking off correspondence with Byron, nor could she change the tone of her letters without arousing his suspicions. Once more she appealed to Annabella: "If I did but know how to contribute to his ULTIMATE good! but Alas! I do not." ⁿ Lady Byron's London coadjutor urged her to hint to Augusta "that the continuation of *your* friendly intercourse with her depends upon the cessation of hers with *him*. . . . Now this I know she has not done—for since my last letter to you I have seen upon her table a thick unsealed letter addressed by her to him." ⁿ

Lady Byron replied: ". . . I am now leading her on to promise that she will never renew a confidential intercourse by letter— or any personal intercourse—I find it necessary to gain step by step, and to disclose my views less abruptly than with some. She is perpetually relapsing into compromises with her con- science. . . ." ⁿ

On July 30, Lady Byron drove her point home vigorously and directly: "Consider all the reasons against any future personal intercourse between you & him by an earlier regard to which evils might have been prevented. . . . Till you feel that he has in reality been your worst friend—indeed, *not* your friend— you cannot altogether think rightly . . . forgive him—desire his welfare—but resign the pernicious view of being his friend more nearly. . . .

"I should not advise you for his sake to restrict your corre- spondence further than by keeping always in view to *rectify* instead of *soothing* or *indulging* his feelings—by avoiding there- fore all phrases or *marks* [Annabella remembered the cryptic crosses in Augusta's letters to him] which may recall wrong ideas to his mind . . . and let me also warn you against the levity & nonsense which he likes for the worst reason, because it prevents him from reflecting seriously. . . ." ⁿ

It is a measure of the abject state of Augusta's mind at the time that she acquiesced in this. The poor child of nature had now begun to doubt the wisdom of her best impulses and to imagine artificial sins that complicated her simple catechism. The streak of spurious piety in her confounded her other surer instincts.

Byron, in the meantime, was concerned only with the publi- cations issuing from England. Mme de Staël had lent him a copy of *Glenarvon,* supplied probably by one of her English friends.ⁿ On July 29 he wrote to Rogers: "I have read *Glenarvon*—

> *'From furious Sappho scarce a milder fate,*
> *—— by her love or libelled by her hate—'"* ⁿ

But his own portrait in the book did not disturb him. He later observed to Moore: "It seems to me, that if the authoress had written the *truth,* and nothing but the truth—the whole truth— the romance would not only have been more *romantic,* but more entertaining. As for the likeness, the picture can't be good—I did not sit long enough." ⁿ

What annoyed him more was an advertisement of a spurious publication of verses attributed to him. It was a Grub Street effusion entitled: *Lord Byron's Farewell to England,* with Three other Poems,—*Ode to St. Helena, to My Daughter on the Morn of her Birth,* and *to the Lily of France.* "I never wrote, nor conceived, a line on any thing of the kind," he complained to Murray; ". . . and as to the 'Lily of *France,*' [symbol of the Bourbons he hated] I should as soon think of celebrating a turnip. . . . I suspect that when the Arab Patriarch wished that his 'Enemy had written a book,' he did not anticipate his own name on the title-page." ⁿ

Byron had also read Benjamin Constant's novel picturing the author's painful liaison with Mme de Staël, so well camouflaged that she could not or would not see herself in it. "Madame de Staël it was who first lent me 'Adolphe,'" Byron later told Lady Blessington. ". . . it is very clever, and very affecting. A friend of hers told me, that she was supposed to be the heroine, and I, with my *aimable franchise,* insinuated as much to her, which rendered her furious. She proved to me how impossible it was that it could be so, which I already knew, and complained of the malice of the world for supposing it possible." ⁿ Reflecting on his own experience, Byron on another occasion told Lady Blessington: "The truest picture of the misery unhallowed *liaisons* produce is the 'Adolphe' of Benjamin Constant. I told Madame de Staël that there was more *morale* in that book than in all she ever wrote; and that it ought always to be given to every young woman who had read 'Corinne,' as an antidote. Poor De Staël!

she came down upon me like an avalanche, whenever I told her any of my amiable truths, sweeping everything before her, with that eloquence that always overwhelmed, but never convinced." [n]

The rainy squalls continued through much of the summer. The conversations at Coppet were almost Byron's sole diversion. Polidori was constantly at parties in Geneva, but the only house Byron cared to visit there was that of Hentsch, his banker. On his invitation Byron even summoned up courage to face the great crowd at the summer festival given by MM. Hentsch and Saladin at Mon Repos on July 30. There were six hundred English in the crowd, but Byron preferred to talk to Charles de Constant. [n]

The Shelley party had returned from Chamouni on July 27. They arrived at the Villa Diodati at nine in the evening and talked until midnight before they returned to their own house. For the next two weeks the boating and the evening discussions at Diodati continued as before. When the weather was favorable, Byron and Shelley usually went out in the boat in the morning or afternoon and sometimes again in the evening. After dinner Shelley and the ladies walked up the hill to Byron's villa.

On August 2, Mary recorded in her journal: "In the evening Lord Byron and he [Shelley] go out in the boat, and, after their return, Shelley and Clare go up to Diodati; I do not, for Lord Byron did not seem to wish it." The next day they were all at Diodati, but "come down early, and talk of our plans," Mary wrote. [n] In these cryptic sentences may be seen a hint that everything was not as it had been. If Shelley and Mary had not known it before, they were aware now of Claire's condition. Shelley was eager to do the best for Claire, and yet by his own code he could not condemn Byron for not wanting to live with her if he was not in love with her. It would be easier to discuss matters if Mary was not there. The Shelleys were already preparing to return to England, and Byron expected to leave shortly for Italy. Shelley was willing to take Claire back to England, but what to do with the child when it came? Claire wrote years afterward to Trelawny: "Before we parted at Geneva he [Byron] talked over with me our situation—he proposed to place the Child when born in Mrs. Leigh's care. To this I objected on the ground that a Child always wanted a parent's care at least till seven years old. . . . He yielded and said it was best it should live with him—he promised faithfully never to give it until seven years of age into a stranger's care. I was to be called the Child's Aunt and in that character I could see it and watch over it without injury to anyone's reputation." "

Byron studiously avoided seeing Claire alone, and when she came to Diodati she was always accompanied by Shelley. He allowed her to do more copying for him, but only at home or when others were present. " He had many distractions and was now little disposed to listen to her sentimentalities. He was continually annoyed by the "tracasseries" of the bumptious "Polly-dolly," as he called the doctor." On August 10, Mary wrote in her journal: "A writ of arrêt comes for Polidori, for having 'cassé ses lunettes et fait tomber son chapeau' of the apothecary who sells bad magnesia."

On August 14, Matthew Gregory ("Monk") Lewis arrived for a visit at Diodati. On the 16th, Byron accompanied Lewis to Ferney to see Voltaire's château." From this time forward Shelley was with them frequently and accompanied them on the water and in masculine evenings at Diodati. Byron pacified the ladies by calling occasionally at Shelley's cottage for an hour. Though he was sometimes annoyed by his guest, Byron was fascinated by Lewis's verbal translation of portions of Goethe's *Faust*. Stored in his retentive memory, it gave him the unconscious framework for his poetic drama of *Manfred*, composed a few weeks later. "

Byron continued his visits to Mme de Staël, who in her frank, not to say tactless, way had reopened the old sore of the separation and had so far worked upon Byron's mind as to persuade him that if he overcame his pride a reconciliation might still be possible. She had precipitated the matter by calling his attention to a newspaper account of his wife's illness." She asked him for some expression of his feelings which she might send to a friend near to Lady Byron. On August 24, Byron wrote the Baroness: "To say that I am merely sorry to hear of Lady B['s] . . . illness is to say nothing, but she has herself deprived me of the right to express more. The separation may have been my fault, but it was her own choice. I tried all means to prevent and would do as much and more to end it—a word would do so, but it does not rest with me to pronounce it. You asked me if I thought that Lady B. was attached to me? To this I can only answer that I love her." [n]

But Byron's concession was more than half owing to Mme de Staël's amiability in his behalf, for he had no real hope that this attempt would be more successful than others.[n] How quickly Byron's moods and feelings could change concerning his wife is indicated by the fact that he had begun a prose tale of the "Marriage of Belphegor," a thinly veiled allegory of his own matrimonial difficulties, and when he heard that Lady Byron was ill he cast it into the fire.[n] And, as always when he was troubled, he turned to his sister. He had written an "Epistle to Augusta"—not the poem beginning "Though the day of my Destiny's over," but a far more intimate one:

> Go where I will, to me thou art the same—
> A loved regret which I would not resign.
> There yet are two things in my destiny,—
> A world to roam through, and a home with thee.[n]

Augusta's letter, which Byron received toward the end of August, was full of alarms and anxieties, though vague enough, for she could not tell her brother how deeply now she was in Annabella's confidence. In his reply Byron charged her with "starting at shadows," and added:

You distress me with—no—it is not *you*. But I have heard that Lady B—— is ill, & I am so sorry—but it's of no use—do not mention her again—but I shall not forget her kindness to you. . . . do not be uneasy—and do not 'hate yourself' if you hate either let it be *me*—but do not—it would kill me; we are the last persons in the world—who ought —or could cease to love one another.

> Ever dearest thine
> +B [n]

John Cam Hobhouse and Scrope Davies arrived finally on August 26. They had passed through Calais to see Scrope's old gambling companion George Brummell, who had recently run away to the Continent owing £50,000.[n] They appeared in time for dinner. Shelley, who, called by business, was reluctantly leaving for England in a few days, spent the evening, and the next day dined with them at Diodati. Hobhouse and Davies went to Ferney on the 28th, and Byron made his farewell call at Shelley's cottage. But Mary and Claire did not meet Byron's cynical guests. Claire went to Diodati for the last time on the 25th, the day before the arrival of his English friends."

Claire was bitterly disappointed that Byron had found no time for her in these last days before her departure and would not even give her a kind word at parting. The pathos of her farewell letter could only make him more determined not to yield again to the softness he had once had the weakness to show her.

She wrote: "Indeed I should have been happier to have seen and kissed you once before I went. . . . Farewell my dearest dear Lord Byron. Now don't laugh or smile in your little proud way for it is very wrong for you to read this merrily which I write in tears. . . . dearest I shall love you to the end of my life & nobody else, think of me as one whose affection you can count on. . . ." "

But Claire was never to hear directly from Byron again. The only communication he grudgingly sent her was through Shelley. Shelley, Mary, and Claire left at nine on the morning of August 29." Byron had entrusted to Shelley the manuscript (Claire's transcription) [5] of the third canto of *Childe Harold, The Prisoner*

[5] Byron's own corrected copy he kept and later sent to England by Scrope Davies. He showed the manuscripts of what he had written to Hobhouse, who on September 1 commented in his diary: ". . . it is very fine in parts but I doubt whether I like it so much as his first cantos—there is an air of mystery & metaphysics about it. . . ." Byron apparently did not show Hobhouse his "Stanzas to Augusta" beginning "Though the day of my Destiny's over." When later he saw them in the *Prisoner of Chillon* volume Hobhouse wrote a satire on them:

> *Dear* Byron *this humbug give over;*
>   *Never talk of decay or decline.*
> *No mortal alive can discover*
>   *The cause of so causeless a whine.* . . .
>
> *Though a poet, you should not abuse us;*
>   *Though a wit, have a truce with your jokes;*
> *Though you govern us all, yet excuse us*
>   *If we think there's enough of this hoax.*
> *Though trusted, no creditors touch thee;*
>   *Though parted, 'tis but from thy wife;*
> *Though wakeful, with Molly to much thee*
>   *'Tis not such a damnable life.*   (*LJ*, IV, 73-4 n.)

of Chillon, and other shorter poems written during the summer. He wrote to Murray: "There is in the volume—an epistle to Mrs. Leigh—on which I should wish her to have her opinion consulted—before the publication; if she objects, of course *omit* it." [n]

The same day the Shelley party left Geneva, Byron, Davies, Hobhouse, and Polidori set out in two carriages with three servants for Chamouni. In the afternoon of August 30 they came into full view of the breath-taking valley and the needles of Mont Blanc. After dinner in the "damned bad & dear inn" (Hôtel d'Angleterre), they made the usual jaunt to see the famous Mer de Glace. [n] Byron recalled later that "in the very eyes of Mont Blanc" he had heard an English woman "exclaim to her party 'did you ever see any thing more *rural?*'—as if it was Highgate, or Hampstead, or Brompton, or Hayes,—'*Rural!*' quotha!—Rocks, pines, torrents, Glaciers, Clouds, and Summits of eternal snow far above them—and '*Rural!*'" [n]

At one of the inns where they had stopped during the tour, Hobhouse later recalled, "the travellers' book was put before us, and Lord Byron, having written his name, pointed out to me the name of Mr. Shelley, with the words atheist and philanthropist written in Greek opposite to it; and observing: 'Do you not think I shall do Shelley a service by scratching this out?' he defaced the words with great care." [n]

Back at Cologny, Byron was disturbed by some of the stories that had been circulated about him in England—stories repeated to him by Hobhouse and Davies. Knowing that many of these had already come to Mrs. Leigh's ears, Hobhouse, possibly at Byron's suggestion, wrote her some reassuring words: ". . . your excellent relative is living with the strictest attention to decorum, and free from all offence, either to God, or man, or woman. . . . A considerable change has taken place in his health; no brandy, no very late hours, no quarts of magnesia, nor deluges of soda water. Neither passion nor perverseness, even the scream has died away. . . ." [n]

On September 5, Scrope Davies left for England, taking Robert Rushton and various manuscripts of Byron's with him. Three days later Byron wrote again to Augusta. Apropos of the strange stories told about him in England, he assured her: ". . . as to all these 'mistresses'—Lord help me—I have had but one. Now don't scold—but what could I do? A foolish girl, in spite of all I could say or do, would come after me, or rather went before for I found her here, and I have had all the plague possible to persuade her to go back again, but at last she went. Now dearest, I do most truly tell thee that I could not help this, that I did all I could to prevent it, and have at last put an end to it."

But the heaviness of his present feelings had other causes: ". . . she—[Lady Byron] or rather the Separation—has broken my heart. I feel as if an Elephant had trodden on it. I am convinced I shall never get over it—but I try. I had enough before I knew her and more than enough, but time & agitation had done something for me; but this last wreck has affected me very differently. If it were *acutely* it would not signify; but it is not that—I breathe lead." [n]

If Byron had known on what terms his sister was then corresponding with his wife, he would have been doubly shocked. On August 5, Augusta had seemed to capitulate in a manner entirely satisfactory to Lady Byron. She wrote to Annabella: "I have considered my dearest A all the reasons you *have* kindly represented against future personal intercourse & others which you have *not* & I perfectly agree with you it is most desirable to avoid it—at the same time I think it wd be very difficult for me & might lead to consequences very injurious to more than me to make any open *declarations* about it. . . . I assure you most solemnly—most truly—I have *long* felt that he has *not* been my friend—but from my heart I forgive him. . . . nothing should induce me to see him again so frequently or in the way I have done . . . but . . . I see difficulties in saying *I will never see you again*. . . ." [n]

Despite her apparent compliance with Lady Byron's wishes, however, Augusta had kept the way open for continued communication with her brother. She was so evasive that Annabella thought it desirable to clinch the matter with an interview and get a full confession. In preparation for this interview she made some memoranda of questions to be asked:

"Do you sorrow most for the sin or for the consequences?—

for the offence towards God—or the injury towards your fellow-creatures?

"Do you sufficiently feel that every *thought* associated with such sin, is sinful, that the heart may be criminal though the actions are innocent? . . .

"Whenever you have any communication with him, question your own heart most scrupulously whether these be simply your objects—whether you are not deceived by the wish of still being dear to him, or by the dread of those consequences from *his* displeasure, which led you to incur God's anger—" [n]

Lady Byron went to London on August 31 and stayed a fortnight. During that time she saw Augusta several times in lengthy interviews. She had now accomplished her purpose. She wrote exultantly to Mrs. Villiers: ". . . I see all I could wish in her towards you—& the humblest sense of her own situation. . . . I have settled with Murray to cut out those lines [the "Epistle to Augusta"?] & give them to *her*—She has shown me of her own accord *his* letters to her—having only suppressed them because of the bitterness towards me—they are *absolute love letters*—and she wants to know how she can stop them—" [n]

Mrs. Villiers added her moral suasion to keep Augusta in line. "I told her," she wrote Lady Byron, ". . . that not a letter—a note—a word should pass between her & him without being submitted to you—that you were her Guardian angel. . . . I am glad she was horror struck with his further treachery [Lady Byron had warned Augusta that Byron had betrayed her secret to several persons]—all this will help to alienate her feelings from him. . . ." [n]

After receiving Mrs. Villiers's letter, Augusta wrote to Annabella: ". . . *I* am the one *much* the most to blame—& *quite* inexcusable— You know—I trust—that I am anxious to make every atonement. . . . When I write to B. it will be as you advise. . . . My Guardian Angel!" [n]

Byron sensed that something or someone had put Augusta in a dither, but he supposed it was some more of the machinations of Caroline Lamb, and did not dream that his letters were shown to Lady Byron. On September 14 he wrote again: "If I understand you rightly, you seem to have been apprehensive—or menaced (like every one else) by that infamous Bedlamite [erased—Caroline Lamb]. . . . You know I suppose that Lady B[n] . . . *has* . . . *been* (*during* or since the separation) in *correspondence with* that self-avowed libeller & strumpet [erased— William Lamb's] wife." [n]

Augusta promptly and obediently sent the letter off to her "Guardian Angel" with apologies for the attacks on her. Lady Byron replied: "Oct. 2. . . . All that is said of CL appears to me nothing but the effect of apprehension—and the design to blacken me by association with her . . . in order to invalidate any future disclosure which he may suspect or know it is in my power to make so as to convince others—the temper of the whole letter is decidedly that of a conscience enraged by anticipating judgment *here* as well as *hereafter*. . . ." [n]

Despite the darkness within his mind and feelings, Byron was outwardly agreeable and sociable and tried his best to entertain his guest. In addition to seeing the Jerseys, who were visiting Geneva, he received a number of other guests at Diodati, including "Conversation" Sharp.[n] On the 7th, Byron was at Mme de Staël's. Among others he met there the lawyer Brougham, who (unknown to him then, for Hobhouse had not yet told him) had been spreading stories against him in London. Hobhouse strongly suspected that Brougham had also put a damper on Mme de Staël's efforts to effect a reconciliation.[n]

Some hint that those negotiations were not going well must have reached Byron about this time, for his sorrow for Lady Byron's illness turned to gall and he wrote some vengeful and bitter "Lines on Hearing that Lady Byron Was Ill," accusing Annabella of "implacability" and designating her "The moral Clytemnestra of thy lord." [n]

Considering the fact that Annabella was now committed to saving Byron's soul through reforming Augusta, the good-natured attempt of Mme de Staël was doomed to failure from the beginning, but her choice of intermediaries was about as tactless as could be imagined, though she was probably quite ignorant of the prejudices involved. One was Lady Romilly, wife of Sir Samuel Romilly, who had kindled Byron's anger and filled him with undying enmity for having advised Lady Noel despite his general retainer for Byron, and the other was Henry Brougham, who was as antithetical to Byron as any Englishman.[n]

Lady Romilly reported to Mme de Staël the failure of her efforts, and Brougham quoted Lady Byron directly: ". . . I may hope that I have saved him additional remorse by the step I took, and whatever pain may be inflicted upon me by the expression of sentiment on his part which though it is impossible for me to trust it is equally impossible for me to hear with indifference, I am not weak enough to be shaken in that resolution."[n]

Byron had left for Italy before these letters arrived, but it is probable that Mme de Staël sent them on to him, completing the corrosion of his feelings in regard to his wife. But during his last days in Switzerland he was still waiting for the outcome of the negotiations with an oppression of spirit which he kept well beneath the surface.

Two young Greeks (brothers), then in Geneva, dined with Byron and Hobhouse at Diodati on September 14, perhaps recommended by some English friend who knew Byron's interest in their homeland. Their visit revived Byron's memories of the East. Though his knowledge of Romaic had become rusty, he could converse with them in Italian, which carried him back to the days when he was learning that language from Nicolo Giraud at Athens. The brothers, Nicolas and Francis Karvellas, were from Zante and had studied at the University of Padua, and, like many intelligent young Greeks, were already enthusiastic about the coming revolution.[n]

Before leaving on a tour of the Bernese Alps with Hobhouse, Byron had finally decided to give Dr. Polidori his *congé*. They parted friends. Byron told Murray later: "I know no great harm of him; but he had an alacrity of getting into scrapes, and was too young and heedless. . . ."[n] Polidori took his dismissal philosophically and was well pleased with Byron's generosity. He left at six on the morning of September 16 for Italy without saying good-by to anyone.[n] Byron later said: "I was sorry when we parted, for I soon get attached to people. . . ."[n]

On the morning of September 17, Byron and Hobhouse started on their tour to the Bernese Oberland. Byron decided to keep a

journal of the trip for his sister. From Ouchy, where they spent
the first night of their journey, he wrote her a letter. Augusta's
assurances that Lady Byron had been very kind to her rankled.
"*Of* her," he wrote his sister, "you are to judge for yourself,
but do not altogether forget that she has destroyed your brother.
. . . I do not think a human being could endure more mental
torture than that woman has directly & indirectly inflicted upon
me—within the present year. . . .

"What a fool I was to marry—and *you* not very wise—my
dear—we might have lived so single and so happy—as old
maids and bachelors; I shall never find any one like you—nor
you (vain as it may seem) like me. We are just formed to pass
our lives together, and therefore—we—at least—I—am by a
crowd of circumstances removed from the only being who could
ever have loved me, or whom I can unmixedly feel attached to." [n]

When they ascended the high Alps, Byron and Hobhouse encountered wonders new to both of them. At the approach of the
summit of Dent Jamant, Byron dismounted from the mule he
was riding. "Arrived at a lake in the very nipple of the bosom
of the Mountain," he recorded. "*H.* went to the highest *pinnacle;*
I did not, but paused within a few yards (at an opening of
the Cliff). In coming down, the Guide tumbled three times; I
fell a laughing, and tumbled too—the descent luckily soft, though
steep and slippery: H. also fell, but nobody hurt. The whole of
the Mountain superb. A Shepherd on a very steep and high cliff
playing upon his *pipe.* . . . The music of the Cows' bells . . .
in the pastures . . . and the Shepherds' shouting to us from
crag to crag, and playing on their reeds where the steeps appeared almost inaccessible, with the surrounding scenery, realized all that I have ever heard or imagined of a pastoral existence . . . this was pure and unmixed—solitary, savage, and
patriarchal: the effect I cannot describe. As we went, they played
the 'Ranz des Vaches' and other airs, by way of farewell. I have
lately repeopled my mind with Nature." [n] On the 22nd, Byron
wrote in his journal: "Arrived at the foot of the Mountain (the
Yung frau, *i.e.* the Maiden); Glaciers; torrents; one of these torrents *nine hundred feet* in height of visible descent. Lodge at
the Curate's. Set out to see the Valley; heard an Avalanche fall,

*❧ LADY FRANCES WEDDERBURN WEBSTER

)◈ LADY BYRON

)◈ ADA BYRON

like thunder; saw Glacier—enormous. Storm came on, thunder, lightning, hail; all in perfection, and beautiful. . . . The torrent is in shape curving over the rock, like the *tail* of a white horse streaming in the wind, such as it might be conceived would be that of the *'pale* horse' on which *Death* is mounted in the Apocalypse." [n]

The high mountains raised Byron's feelings to an unearthly ecstasy. The goal on the 23rd was the ascent of the Wengen Alp. At the summit, he wrote, "On one side, our view comprized the *Yung frau,* with all her glaciers; then the *Dent d'Argent,* shining like truth; then the *little Giant* (the Kleiner Eigher); and the great Giant (the Grosser Eigher), and last, not least, the Wetterhorn. . . . Heard the Avalanches falling every five minutes nearly—as if God was pelting the Devil down from Heaven with snow balls." He closed his journal for the day: "Passed *whole woods of withered pines, all withered;* trunks stripped and barkless, branches lifeless; done by a single winter,—their appearance reminded me of me and my family." [n]

On the 24th they were up at five and set out at seven for Brienz, but as they descended, the glow Byron had felt on the Wengen Alp subsided. In the evening at Brienz "four Swiss Peasant Girls of Oberhasli came and sang the airs of their country; two of the voices beautiful—the tunes also: they sing too that *Tyrolese air* and song which you love, Augusta, because I love it—and I love, because you love it; they are still singing. Dearest, you do not know how I should have liked this, were you with me." [n]

They spent the next night at Thoun, and the following day (the 26th) started home by way of Bern and Fribourg. "Being out of the mountains, my journal must be as flat as my journey," Byron wrote. The event he found most worth recording was that he bought an ugly and bad-tempered shepherd dog named Mutz.[n] At Aubonne on the 28th,[n] Byron finished his journal with a summary for the benefit of his sister: He had seen "some of the noblest views in the world. But in all this—the recollections of bitterness, and more especially of recent and more home desolation, which must accompany me through life, have preyed upon me here; and neither the music of the Shepherd, the crashing of the Avalanche, nor the torrent, the mountain, the Glacier, the Forest, nor the Cloud, have for one moment lightened the weight upon my heart, nor enabled me to lose my own wretched identity. . . ." [n]

The travelers arrived at Diodati on the 29th at four o'clock. Byron was confronted with a mass of correspondence, some with agreeable news and some disturbing. Shelley had delivered the manuscript of *Childe Harold* to Murray on September 11.[n] The publisher, "trembling with auspicious hope," carried it immediately to Gifford, who, though ill, sat up until he had finished every line. "It had actually agitated him into a fever. . . ." [n]

Douglas Kinnaird, whom now and henceforward Byron entrusted with the business arrangements of the sale of his manuscripts, including the setting of the price to the publisher, wrote on the 13th: "Murray proposes 1500 guineas for the two Poems [*Childe Harold* and *The Prisoner of Chillon*]—shall I say satis? He will pay the money down." [n] But, noting the general enthusiasm among those who had seen the poems, in Byron's interest Kinnaird raised the price to £2,000. Grumbling a little, Murray agreed, but wrote to Byron: "Remember I do stipulate for all the original MSS., copies or scraps." [n] And Murray had no cause to regret his bargain.

Among Byron's letters from England was one from the unhappy Claire, who with Mary had gone on to Bath, where, taking the name of Mrs. Clairmont, she had settled down to await the birth of her child. To her pathetic appeals to his good nature and her agonized playfulness, Byron felt that silence was the only answer he could give. But after Shelley had returned from London, bringing news and gossip, the poor girl could not refrain from writing again: "Don't look cross at this letter because perhaps by the same post you expected one from Mrs. Leigh & have not got it.[6] That is not my fault dearest. I am not the

[6] Shelley wrote the same day as Claire (September 29): "I saw Kinnaird, and had a long conversation with him. He informed me that Lady Byron was now in perfect health—that she was living with your sister. I felt great pleasure from this intelligence. I consider the latter part of it as affording a decisive contradiction to the only important calumny that ever was advanced against you. On this ground at least it will become the world hereafter to be silent." (*LBC*, II, 17–18.) Apparently Lady Byron's visits to Augusta at St.

postman. . . . Mary has been musing how to send her message. She says 'my love' is too familiar & so it is changed to 'remembrances.' . . . Kinnaird says you told him I was an Atheist & a Murderer. You see the stupidity of people so be chary of my name. A fine Character I shall have between you all when I'm nothing more than an innocent quiet little woman very fond of Albé." [n]

Shelley was a constant admirer of Byron, and did not hesitate to convey his confidence in his friend's poetic future. "I hope for no more than that you should, from some moment when the clearness of your own mind makes evident to you the 'truth of things,' feel that you are chosen out from all other men to some greater enterprise of thought. . . . *What* it should be, I am not qualified to say. In a more presumptuous mood, I recommended the Revolution of France as a theme involving pictures of all that is best qualified to interest and to instruct mankind. But it is inconsistent with the spirit in which you ought to devote yourself to so great a destiny, that you should make use of any understanding but your own—much less mine." [n]

It was good advice, but Byron could only follow his own bent and proceed in the direction his destiny was carrying him, for he had a kind of perfervid faith that he was in the hands of fate even when he defied it. But first he must free his mind with a poetic catharsis different from anything he had attempted before. All the unhappiness, the sense of guilt, the frustrations, and the dismal broodings which had grown out of his reflection during the summer on his relations with Augusta, his marriage, and the separation, found relief in a poetic drama that had been conceived amid the avalanches in the high Alps and now burned for expression. The accumulation of his sufferings, intensified by the implacable silence of Lady Byron and her refusal to make any response to Mme de Staël's overtures or his own appeal for her forgiveness, reached a climax when on his return from the tour with Hobhouse he heard that Lady Byron had some inten-

James's Palace in September (Augusta left for Six Mile Bottom on September 14) had their effect in stilling the persistent rumors of the incest. This was the reward Augusta received for her complete submission to Annabella's guidance and for showing her all of Byron's letters.

tion of passing the winter on the Continent. He appealed to Augusta to convey his wishes: ". . . I must strongly protest against my daughter's leaving England, to be taken over the Continent at so early a time of life. . . . My whole hope—and prospect of a quiet evening (if I reach it), are wrapt up in that little creature—Ada—and you must forgive my anxiety in all which regards her even to minuteness." [n]

Once more opposition and contest had given "a rebound" to his spirits, and he found an outlet for his "mind diseased" in impassioned contemplation. His conception of Manfred, stimulated first by the passages of Goethe's *Faust* which "Monk" Lewis had translated to him, had something more of the Promethean character than of the Faustian. Byron later told Murray that "it was the *Staubach* [*sic*] and the *Jungfrau,* and something else, much more than Faustus, that made me write *Manfred.* The first Scene, however, and that of Faustus are very similar." [n]

But the real drama was within his mind. And the conflict was both personal and cosmic. From the beginning, it is Byron speaking. When Manfred conjures up the spirits, including that of the star which rules his own destiny, he asks from them, not power or pleasure, or even wisdom, but "Forgetfulness." Upon their further urging that he ask for something they can give, he finally requests to see one of the spirits face to face, and the spirit of his own star of fate appears to him in the form of a beautiful woman. The sight of this ideal form reanimates him, but the figure vanishes and Manfred falls senseless. A voice is heard chanting a witch's incantation:

> *By the cold breast and serpent smile,*
> *By thy unfathomed gulfs of guile,*
> *By that most seeming virtuous eye,*
> *By thy shut soul's hypocrisy . . .*
> *I call upon thee! and compel*
> *Thyself to be thy proper Hell!* [7]

---

[7] *Manfred,* Act I, Scene i. It has been suggested that this "Incantation," which was written earlier in the summer and published separately with *The Prisoner of Chillon and Other Poems,* was originally directed against Lady Byron. Indeed the language of part of it parallels some of Byron's diatribes

Manfred, on a high cliff of the Jungfrau contemplating suicide, yet does not make the plunge, for

> *There is a power upon me which witholds,*
> *And makes it my fatality to live,—*

He envies a soaring eagle and exclaims:

> *Beautiful!*
> *How beautiful is all this visible world!*
> *How glorious in its action and itself!*
> *But we, who name ourselves its sovereigns, we,*
> *Half dust, half deity, alike unfit*
> *To sink or soar, with our mixed essence make*
> *A confllict of its elements, and breathe*
> *The breath of degradation and of pride,*
> *Contending with low wants and lofty will,*
> *Till our Mortality predominates,*
> *And men are—what they name not to themselves,*
> *And trust not to each other.*[n]

Saved by a chamois-hunter from self-destruction, Manfred
puzzles his benefactor with his strange talk and partly reveals
the obsession that haunts him: When the hunter offers him wine,
Manfred sees blood upon the cup's brim,

> *. . . the pure warm stream*
> *Which ran in the veins of my fathers, and in ours*
> *When we were in our youth, and had one heart,*
> *And loved each other as we should not love. . . .*[n]

Wandering out by a cataract, Manfred calls up next the Witch
of the Alps, only to look upon her beauty, nothing more. Asked
what boon he wishes, he replies:

> *Well, though it torture me, 'tis but the same;*
> *My pang shall find a voice. From my youth upwards*
> *My Spirit walked not with the souls of men,*
> *Nor looked upon the earth with human eyes. . . .*

At the urging of the Witch, Manfred confesses that there was
"but One" who shared his sympathy.

---

against his wife in his letters to Augusta. But in another mood he could also
see it as applicable to his alter ego, Manfred.

> *She was like me in lineaments—her eyes—*
> *Her hair—her features—all, to the very tone*
> *Even of her voice, they said were like to mine;*
> *But softened all, and tempered into beauty:*
> *She had the same lone thoughts and wanderings. . . .*
> *Her faults were mine—her virtues were her own—*
> *I loved her, and destroyed her!*

The Witch asks: "With thy hand?" And Manfred replies:

> *Not with my hand, but heart, which broke her heart;*
> *It gazed on mine, and withered.*[n]

The Witch disappears, and on the summit of the Jungfrau Manfred encounters the Destinies and finally Nemesis. And when they mount their clouds, Manfred dares to leave the earth too and to enter the hall of the powerful evil spirit Arimanes.[n] When the spirits bid him bow down and worship, Manfred refuses, and the first Destiny recognizes his equal. Through the power he has gained with them, Manfred conjures Nemesis to call up the phantom of Astarte, the one he has loved. But not Arimanes himself can make her speak to him. Manfred calls on her:

> *Astarte! my belovéd! speak to me. . . .*
>   *Thou lovedst me*
> *Too much, as I loved thee: we were not made*
> *To torture thus each other—though it were*
> *The deadliest sin to love as we have loved.*

But she will not utter one word of comfort or mercy or say she loves him; she utters his name and says "Farewell!" She disappears, and one of the spirits says:

> *He is convulsed—This is to be a mortal*
> *And seek the things beyond mortality.*

And another says:

> *Yet, see, he mastereth himself, and makes*
> *His torture tributary to his will.*
> *Had he been one of us, he would have made*
> *An awful Spirit.*[n]

Byron could not then write the third act, for he did not know how to carry on from there. But the composition had served its chief purpose; he had found the most effective relief for his guilt and his despair. And he had discovered that his real quarrel with life was that he could not transcend the bounds of mortality; the "half deity" did not compensate for the "half dust."

At the same time, to outward appearances, so far as Hobhouse and Mme de Staël could observe, Byron was enjoying an active social life during his last days in Switzerland. He took affectionate leave of Mme de Staël at a family dinner on October 3.[n] Byron felt as warmly toward her as toward any one he had met at Geneva. "She has made Copet as agreeable as society and talent can make any place on earth," he told Murray.[n]

At half past eleven on the morning of October 5, Byron and Hobhouse left Diodati for Milan, after taking a last look at the lake that had for four months been Byron's chief inspiration.[n] Neither had the enthusiasm for the voyage which they had felt on their journey to the Bernese Oberland. Byron really had no aim and no destination. He still thought of going to Greece again, or Dalmatia, but he would first spend some time in Venice.[n]

The proprietor of the villa, a great admirer of Byron's poetry, coming in immediately after his tenant had departed, asked the caretaker if he had preserved the numerous first drafts which Byron had scattered through all the rooms of the house and which M. Diodati considered as so many precious autographs of the poet. The reply he received was: "I should lie to you, Sir, if I didn't tell you that at least two days were occupied in burning all those scraps of paper."[n]

CHAPTER XVII

1816–1817

Milan, Venice, Rome

TRAVELING in Byron's heavy Napoleonic coach, Byron and Hobhouse avoided Geneva and followed the southern side of the lake.[n] Their Italian guide, Angelo Springhetti, conducted them up the Rhone Valley to the Simplon Pass. They found the Simplon Napoleon road equal to its reputation and in some places like a carriage-way through an English park.

On the 10th they descended rapidly toward Lago Maggiore, passing the customs at the little village of Iselle. They soon were in the green vale of Domo d'Ossola. Coming into the inn where they dined, they realized by the stone floors, the dirty, badly locked doors, the painted ceilings, and the nasty necessaries that they were in Italy. They stopped for the night at Ornavasso. Fearing robbery, Hobhouse wrote, "we took great precautions about luggage &c. Berger slept in B's carriage, the dogs were chained under our chaises—our pistols well primed in our rooms and all other warlike preparations made." [n] The next morning they had several frights, but no encounters on the road. Five or six dark characters running after their last carriage turned out to be boatmen seeking a fare. Sending the carriages ahead, they were rowed down Lago Maggiore to Isola Bella, where in the palace they saw the room in which Bonaparte had slept. Landing at Arona, they were escorted by gendarmes to Sesto.

Rising early the next morning (the 12th), they drowsed through the dreary Lombardy plain until within half an hour of

Milan, when they saw the spires of the cathedral but nothing that looked like a city of 130,000 people. Their first impression was not improved by the dirty rooms into which they were ushered in L'Ancien Hôtel de St. Marco." Within a day or two this impression was changed. Byron wrote Murray: "Milan is striking—the cathedral superb. The city altogether reminds me of Seville, but a little inferior." " The pleasant society into which they were immediately thrown increased the charm of Milan for them.

While they were at breakfast on the morning after their arrival, Dr. Polidori called and gave them an account of his journey on foot across the Alps. Byron and Hobhouse proceeded to take a box at the Teatro della Scala, the social center of Milan, and that evening Polidori and Karvellas, one of the Greek brothers they had met in Geneva, called on them there." But they were most delighted by their next visitor, Monsignore Ludovico di Breme, whom Byron had seen at Coppet. Di Breme told them the gossip of the boxes, and, turning to more serious topics, he spoke of Italian literature "as in a deplorable state and limited the poets of the day to Foscolo, Monti, and Pindemonte —but even these he said were only first in the second order and in some sort imitators." " Byron and Hobhouse were delighted with the ballet, and, though the talking in the boxes was never interrupted, they stayed until the closing, well pleased with their new acquaintance.

The following morning Byron, Polidori, and Hobhouse went in a carriage to visit the Ambrosian Library. And in the evening in Di Breme's box at the theater, which he had lighted with candles in their honor, they met his elder brother the Marquis. There they heard something of the discontents in Piedmont and Lombardy.[1] But there seemed no rational hope of bettering the condition of the people, who gave in to the present govern-

---

[1] After the fall of Napoleon, the Congress of Vienna (1815) had divided Italian territory into several small states, none large enough to be a danger. The provinces of Lombardy and Venice were given outright to Austria, and Piedmont, incorporated with the island to the south as the Kingdom of Sardinia, though nominally independent, felt strong Austrian pressures, as did the Church states such as the Romagna.

ment as easily as they had given in to the last, and who had no sympathy for Murat.

Byron and Hobhouse went again on the 15th to the Ambrosian Library. Writing to Murray later that day, Byron said: ". . . it is a fine collection—full of MSS. edited and unedited. . . . For me, in my simple way, I have been most delighted with a correspondence of letters, all original and amatory, between *Lucretia Borgia and Cardinal Bembo,* (preserved there). I have pored over them and a lock of her hair, the prettiest and fairest imaginable—I never saw fairer—and shall go repeatedly to read the epistles over and over. . . ." [n] Hobhouse recorded: "B. tried to get a copy of the letter & was half promised . . . but he failed—he has taken a hair however—which he says he will have this motto for—

And beauty draws us by a single hair." [n]

The letters, Byron wrote to Augusta, were "so pretty & so loving that it makes one wretched not to have been born sooner to have at least seen her. And pray what do you think is one of her *signatures?*—why this + a Cross—which she says 'is to stand for her name &c.' Is not this amusing? I suppose you know that she was a famous beauty, & famous for the use she made of it; & that she was the love of this same Cardinal Bembo (besides a story about her papa Pope Alexander & her brother Cæsar Borgia—which some people don't believe—& others do). . . ." [n]

On October 17, Byron and Hobhouse dined with Di Breme and his brother the Marquis at the latter's palace, the Casa Roma. Hobhouse was impressed by the deference paid to Byron. Breme compared him to Petrarch. Among other guests Hobhouse noted "a Mr. de Beyle, one of Napoleon's secretaries and intendant de la nobilière de la couronne." [n] Hobhouse also observed at dinner "the little Silvio Pellico, author of Francesca da Rimini—I did not hear him say a word." [n] "In the middle of dinner," Hobhouse wrote, "Monsignore [Breme] got up and brought in il Cavaliere Monti and introduced him to B & to me. . . . He is very deaf of his left ear—his face is very expressive & large shaggy eyebrows, a nose rather hooked at the end. . . ." [n]

Mr. Beyle (later known by his pen name, Stendhal) apparently
did not meet Byron that evening, but was a quiet observer in
the background. He noted that when Monti recited the first
lines of his finest poem, the "Mascheroniana," Byron "was in
raptures." [n]

The next morning Colonel Fitzgerald, an Irish soldier of fortune, called and regaled Byron and Hobhouse with tales of
Milan under Napoleon and after. His own history, as they then
learned it, Byron later recounted amusingly to Moore: "Six-and-
twenty years ago, Col. [Fitzgerald], then an ensign, being in
Italy, fell in love with the Marchesa [Castiglione] and she with
him. The lady must be, at least, twenty years his senior. The
war broke out; he returned to England. . . . and *she*—heaven
knows what she did. In the year 1814, the first annunciation of
the Definitive Treaty of Peace (and tyranny) was developed to
the astonished Milanese by the arrival of Col. [Fitzgerald],
who, flinging himself full length at the feet of Mad. [Casti-
glione], murmured forth, in half-forgotten Irish Italian, eternal
vows of indelible constancy. The lady screamed, and exclaimed,
'Who are you?' The Colonel cried, 'What! don't you know me?
I am so and so,' etc., etc., etc.; till, at length, the Marchesa,
mounting from reminiscence to reminiscence, through the lovers
of the intermediate twenty-five years, arrived at last at the recollection of her *povero* sub-lieutenant. She then said, 'Was
there ever such virtue?' (that was her very word) and, being
now a widow, gave him apartments in her palace, reinstated
him in all the rights of wrong, and held him up to the admiring
world as a miracle of incontinent fidelity, and the unshaken
Abdiel of absence." [n]

In the box of Monsignore di Breme at La Scala, Byron was
first introduced formally to Henri Beyle on the evening of October 23. As a close associate of Napoleon on his Russian cam-
paign he had a fascinating interest for both Byron and Hobhouse.

The observant M. Beyle took careful note of some of Byron's
foibles. "Lord Byron always entertained a great horror of cor-
pulency," Beyle recalled. "His antipathy to a full habit of body
might be called a fixed idea. . . . During at least a third part

of the day, Byron was a dandy, expressed a constant dread of augmenting the bulk of his outward man, concealed his right foot as much as possible, and endeavoured to render himself agreeable in female society. His vanity, however, frequently induced him to lose sight of the end, in his attention to the means. Love was sacrificed; an affair of the heart would have interfered with his daily exercise on horseback. . . . In his moments of dandyism, he always pronounced the name of Brummel with a mingled emotion of respect and jealousy."

But Beyle noted too that Byron could rise above such vanities whenever he met a real challenge to his faculties. "When literary subjects were introduced, Byron was exactly the reverse of an academician; his thoughts flowed with greater rapidity than his words, and his expressions were free from all affectation or studied grace." Beyle saw him frequently in the days that followed, and recalled that "After the lapse of a few weeks, Byron seemed to have acquired a taste for the society of Milan. When the performances for the evening were over, we frequently stopped at the door of the theatre to enjoy the sight of the beauties who passed us in review. . . . Many of them had flattered themselves with the idea that Byron would seek an introduction; but whether from pride, timidity, or a remnant of dandyism, which induced him to do exactly the contrary of what was expected, he invariably declined that honour." [n]

Byron's diffidence and his preference for masculine companionship were no doubt caused by the lowness of his spirits at the time and his reluctance to become involved in another love affair. He had memories sufficiently painful of the clinging Claire, and he was always shy in the presence of ladies who were at ease on his own social level. Much as he felt the need for feminine companionship, he knew his own weaknesses well enough to feel that, despite all he might say, he could never take any liaison as lightly as he could wish, and that the trouble likely to ensue was in direct proportion to the social standing of the woman (witness Caroline Lamb).

Outside of the theater, Byron had no lack of masculine companionship. Colonel Finch called frequently, as did Polidori and several of his new Italian friends such as Di Breme. On the 23rd, Hobhouse returned from a sightseeing ramble to find the two Karvellas brothers and Polidori with Byron. And the next day the young Greeks brought two of their countrymen, one a Corfiote and the other "a gentlemanly looking young man" by the name of Schinas who had come all the way from Paris to see Byron."[n] Their enthusiasm for Greece and their nationalist sympathies kindled the desire, always present in Byron, to return to the land where he had been happy.

The famous *improvisatore* Sgricci attracted a large crowd to La Scala on October 25.[n] Though the Milanese were inclined to scoff, Byron was astonished by his fluency, but later told Moore apropos of the actor's dialect: "although I understand Italian . . . I could only carry off a few very common-place mythological images. . . ."[n]

Byron had not heard from Augusta for a month when her letter arrived on October 28. She tried to break the news gently that if he returned to England she could not see him intimately. He had written a note on arriving in Milan and another anxiously on the 26th.[n] Now he wrote once more: "I really do not & cannot understand all the mysteries & alarms in your letters & more particularly in the last. All I know is—that no human power short of destruction—shall prevent me from seeing you when— where—& how—I may please—according to time & circumstance; that you are the only comfort (except the remote possibility of my daughter's being so) left me in prospect in existence, and that I can bear the rest—so that you remain; but anything which is to divide us would drive me quite out of my senses; Miss Milbanke appears in all respects to have been formed for my destruction; I have thus far—as you know—regarded her without feelings of personal bitterness towards her, but if directly or indirectly—but why do I say this?—You know she is the cause of all. . . .

"My health is good, but I have now & then fits of giddiness, & deafness, which make me think like Swift—that I shall be like him & the *withered* tree he saw—which occasioned the reflection and 'die at top' first. My hair is growing grey, & *not* thicker; & my teeth are sometimes *looseish* though still white & sound. Would not one think I was sixty instead of not quite nine & twenty?" [n]

Augusta had been much disturbed by the "Epistle" to herself, which she prevented Murray from publishing, and which she told Lady Byron she wished at the bottom of the sea.[n] She was also embarrassed by certain lines in the Alpine journal he had sent her.

Byron's mind was not made easier by a letter from Claire Clairmont. He had hoped that that account was closed, but she was as infatuated as ever. She had read *Glenarvon* when she wrote on October 6 from Bath: "Some of the speeches are yours I am sure they are: the very impertinent way of looking in a person's face who loves you & telling them you are very tired & wish they'd go. . . . My dearest Albé we have been gone from Geneva these six weeks & not one word of news have we of you. . . . My darling Albé I know what you will say, 'There now I told you it would be so. I advised you not. I did every thing I could to hinder you & now you complain of me.' I don't complain of you dearest nor would not if you were twice as unkind. Sometimes I do feel a little angry that you should make me so very wretched for want of sacrificing a little time to tell me how you are & that you care a little for me. . . ." [n]

After receiving these embarrassing protestations, Byron was more firmly resolved never to write to the foolish girl, by whom one act of kindness would inevitably be interpreted as a partiality for her which he could never feel. Though it always made him unhappy and uncomfortable to give anyone pain, and though he liked to have others think well of him, he knew that silence was the only course, the one that must cause the least unhappiness in the end.

On the evening of the 28th he had gone to Di Breme's box at the opera as usual. Hobhouse was in the pit when Polidori came in with the Italian writer Borsieri. They stood for a while watching the performance. An Austrian officer of the guard came presently and placed himself in front of Polidori so that his grenadier's hat completely blocked the Doctor's view. Polidori asked him to remove it. The officer kept his hat on and replied with an uncivil "You wish it?" and a smile of insult on his face. Polidori, heated, said: "Si, lo voglio." The officer then asked him to step outside. Polidori, thinking he meant for a duel, asked Hobhouse to accompany him. But the officer took him to the guardhouse. There the foolish Doctor argued with the officer, saying that in the theater he was the equal of anybody." Meanwhile the writer Silvio Pellico brought the news to Di Breme's box. Beyle, who was there, has left an account of what then happened: "We instantly ran to the guard-house. . . . The poet Monti had accompanied us, and, to the number of fifteen or twenty, we surrounded the prisoner. Every one spoke at once; Polidori was beside himself with passion, and his face red as a burning coal. Byron, though he too was in a violent rage, was, on the contrary, pale as ashes. . . . Monti's idea was excellent: 'Sortiamo tutti; restino solamente i titolati' ["Let us all go out; let those only remain who are titled personages"]. De Brême remained, with the Marquis de Sartirana, his brother, Count Confalonieri, and Lord Byron. These gentlemen having written their names and titles, the list was handed to the officer on guard, who instantly forgot the insult offered to his fur cap, and allowed Polidori to leave the guard-house." " Polidori, however, was not through with the Austrians. According to his own story, he was released when "the officer took Lord Byron's card, as bail that I would appear to answer for my conduct on the morrow." " The next morning he received a printed order to attend. Accompanied by Di Breme, he went to the police, who presented him with an order to be off for Florence in twenty-four hours. Despite all the efforts of Byron, Hobhouse, Di Breme, and Colonel Fitzgerald, who went to the highest authorities without being able to get the order rescinded, Polidori was forced to leave the next morning."

Byron, though he was concerned for the foolish Doctor, and though he had no liking for the arrogant Austrians, had to admit that Polidori had courted trouble. But the poet had had his first view of the Austrian tyranny, and the ideas he had already imbibed from Pellegrino Rossi and others in Switzerland were confirmed. His contempt for Austrian rule in Italy was now fixed, and was to govern his attitudes and actions henceforth.

On the other side, not only the officer of the guards but also the highest Austrian authorities noted his associations, and from that time his movements were watched with interest by the secret police; and, while the authorities paid polite respect to his English title and his literary fame, they were constantly suspicious.[2]

The Polidori affair, coming fast upon letters from England, had the effect of depressing Byron's spirits still further. Henri Beyle observed: "The morning after Polidori's departure, Byron, in a *tête-à-tête* with me, complained bitterly of persecution." [n]

Beyle noted the quick changes in Byron's moods: "I never observed Byron in a more delightful or unaffected vein of gaiety than on the day when we made an excursion about two miles from Milan, to visit the celebrated echo of *la Simonetta,* which repeats the report of a pistol-shot thirty or forty times." By way of contrast, the next day, at a grand dinner given by Monsignor de Brême, his appearance was lowering as that of Talma in the part of Nero. Byron arrived late, and was obliged to cross a spacious saloon, in which every eye was fixed on him and his club foot." [n]

During their last days in Milan, Byron and Hobhouse went several times to the Teatro Re, the theater of the common people. Byron was inclined at first to look down upon the dialect poetry and drama of the people, but when Silvio Pellico introduced him to Buratti, he took a new view of it. According to Beyle, Pellico once said to Byron: " 'The most delightful of the ten or twelve Italian dialects, unknown beyond the Alps, is the Venetian. The Venetians are the French of Italy.' 'They have, then, some comic poet living?'—'Yes,' replied Pellico; 'a charming poet; but as his comedies are not allowed to be performed, he composes them under the form of satires. The name of this delightful poet is Buratti; and every six months, by the governor's orders, he pays a visit to one of the prisons of Venice.' " [3]

[2] The Austrian police did not apparently seriously interest themselves in Byron's activities until 1819, but his associations with Italians of liberal sympathies were marked.

[3] Galt, p. 247. Pietro Buratti's racy colloquial verse, satirizing Venetian politics and manners, no doubt gave Byron ideas and encouragement for his *Beppo* and *Don Juan.*

Byron asked eagerly for the name of the bookseller who sold Buratti's books, and his friends laughed, for no printer dared to publish his work. They borrowed some manuscript copies for him. This was Byron's first acquaintance with the Venetian dialect, which later was to please him greatly.

Byron took leave of his Italian friends on November 2. The travelers set out at eleven o'clock on the 3rd in Hobhouse's carriage, Byron having engaged Springhetti to take his two carriages with the luggage to Venice. Traveling by Gorgonzola, Coravaggio, Brescia, and Desenzano, they arrived at Verona on the 6th. There they intended to stop for a day or two.

On the 7th, Byron and Hobhouse saw the amphitheater and the supposed tomb of the Capulets. At half past nine the next morning they set off for Vicenza, thirty miles distant through a level, cultivated country, the Alps on the left and a part of the Euganean range on the right. They spent most of the following morning visiting the edifices of Vicenza erected by or to the memory of the great Palladio, who had lived and died in the town. Then continuing their journey, they arrived at the Stella d'Ora Inn in Padua in time for a good dinner with red and white wine of the country.[n]

Byron was now so eager to reach Venice that he could not even wait to see the university or any of the historic sights of the town, to the regret of Hobhouse, who was much more of a sightseer. Following along the Brenta to Mestre the next day (the 10th), they left their carriages and horses at the inn there with a servant and embarked in a pouring rain in a gondola for the island city. For an hour and a half they could see nothing from the hearse-like black box in which they were cabined but stakes in the water. Then suddenly they were among the lights of Venice, and, "peeping through our black casements," Hobhouse wrote, "saw we were gliding by high houses and stone piers— The echo of the oars told us [we] were under a bridge and a boatman cried out to us—'the Rialto'—shortly afterwards we landed under the *Hotel of Great Britain* on the great canal and were shown up a magnificent flight of stairs into rooms whose gilding & painted silks showed they belonged to better people in better times. . . ."[n]

Their first real impression of the city was formed the next day, which they spent under the guidance of their lackey Zanetto, darting down the canals in a graceful gondola and walking through the narrow streets and the great squares. Byron took to Venice immediately. It was a magic world, a theatrical setting for life, with a melancholy background of decayed history that touched a chord of sympathy in him. Zanetto pointed out that from the columns near the lagoon on which the Piazza San Marco faced, one crowned by the lion brought from Les In-valides at Paris and the other by Theodoric and his crocodile, they could see fourteen centuries of architecture.

They learned that the brilliant social life of Venice was no more. Two or three *conversazioni* were all that remained. Only two coffeehouses were open all night. The population had dropped from 130,000 to perhaps less than 100,000 in the few years since 1797. Now all the taxes went to Vienna, and every-thing was more expensive than they had been led to believe, especially to Englishmen. The colorful native costumes had al-most disappeared. And yet Venice was still a fascinating place. They felt it as they crossed the lagoon to the Lido, passing the Palladian church of San Giorgio Maggiore and looking back at the fabulous towers. Byron then got his first glimpse of the Adriatic, and against the distant view of the Alps they saw Venice all golden under the setting sun."

On the 12th, Byron and Hobhouse went in a gondola to call on Colonel Finch, whom they had met in Milan, at his hotel, the Favoretti. There they met the learned Greek Mustoxidthi, about whom they had heard from the Karvellas brothers. Mus-toxidthi, who had translated some of the Greek manuscripts in the Ambrosian Library, took Byron and Hobhouse to the Doge's Palace and introduced them to the custodian of the famous Marciana Library, the old Abbé Morelli. The great salon of the palace, which was formerly the council room in the days of the doges, was now the library. Around the walls were pictures of the doges. Byron was most impressed with that of Marino Faliero, who was beheaded on the stairs in the yard for con-spiracy against the state in 1355."

After breakfast on the 13th, Dr. Francesco Aglietti, a famous physician, editor of a medical journal, and counselor of state of Venice, called on Byron. On entering the room, he said: "Lady Holland has given me an introduction to the first poet of England." [n] His account of Italy was the same as that of all his countrymen: it was fallen forever, and England was partly responsible; the Austrians were governing only for their own good. Byron and Hobhouse then went in a gondola to the island of San Lazzaro to visit the Armenian monastery. Byron was immediately impressed with the courtesy and quiet devotion to learning of the monks who showed them about the establishment, then about a hundred years old. The printing-shop interested them particularly.[4]

Byron had decided to leave the hotel for a private abode, and found one to his taste in the Frezzeria, a small alley-like street just off the Piazza San Marco. The lodgings, for which he was to pay twenty francs a day and to keep for two months [5] were over the shop of a draper by the name of Segati. The shop bore the sign of Il Cervo (The Stag).[6] Not the least of the attractions of his new quarters to Byron was the young dark-eyed wife of the draper. Three days later he wrote to Moore: "It is my intention to remain at Venice during the winter, probably, as it has always been (next to the East) the greenest island of my imagination.[7] It has not disappointed me; though

[4] Hobhouse diary, entry of Nov. 13, 1816. The Armenian Mekhitarist Convent, on the island of San Lazzaro, near the Lido, about two miles from the Piazza San Marco, was founded by Father Peter Mekhitar about 1717. When Byron visited it, there were about forty "frate" and eighteen pupils. (Hobhouse diary.)

[5] Hobhouse diary, entry of Nov. 14, 1816. Hobhouse left at the same time for a lodging at No. 3056 Calle degli Avvocati, near the Campo San Angelo, but he continued to dine at the hotel. From that time forth he saw Byron less frequently.

[6] A scandalous chronicle says that Byron "scattered money in abundance and even reopened the draper's shop of [Pietro] Segatti which had been deserted—the people say that a new sign was posted, that is Al Corno Inglese. . . ." Quoted from the diary of E. A. Cicogna, Museo Correr e Civico, Venezia, 25 Agosto, 1817, in Meneghetti: Lord Byron a Venezia, pp. 85–6. My translation.

[7] Moore (Memoirs, I, 316; entry of Dec. 24, 1819) records that "It is a curious idea of Madame Flahault [the former Miss Mercer Elphinstone], that Lord Byron chose Venice for a residence, because, as nobody walks there, his not having the power is not so remarkable."

its evident decay would, perhaps, have that effect upon others. But I have been familiar with ruins too long to dislike desolation. Besides, I have fallen in love, which, next to falling into the canal, (which would be of no use, as I can swim,) is the best or the worst thing I could do. I have got some extremely good apartments in the house of a 'Merchant of Venice,' who is a good deal occupied with business, and has a wife in her twenty-second year. Marianna (that is her name) is in her appearance altogether like an antelope. She has the large, black, oriental eyes, with that peculiar expression in them which is seen rarely among *Europeans*—even the Italians. . . . I cannot describe the effect of this kind of eye,—at least upon me. Her features are regular, and rather aquiline—mouth small—skin clear and soft, with a kind of hectic colour—forehead remarkably good: her hair is of the dark gloss, curl, and colour of Lady J[ersey]'s: her figure is light and pretty, and she is a famous songstress—scientifically so; her natural voice (in conversation, I mean) is very sweet; and the naïveté of the Venetian dialect is always pleasing in the mouth of a woman." "

So the *"besoin d'aimer"* had returned to him under the mild Italian skies, and it gave a new enchantment to the fabled city which he had been predisposed to like. Within a few days Byron was introduced to the Countess Albrizzi, whose *conversazione* was the center of the literary-social life of Venice.[8] Among her friends she numbered Ippolito Pindemonte, the abbate Morelli (librarian of the Marciana), V. Alfieri, Ugo Foscolo, and the famous sculptor Antonio Canova, who in 1814 had presented his bust of Helen of Troy to her in gratitude for her book on his sculptures (first published in 1809).

To Murray Byron confessed: "Venice pleases me as much as I expected, and I expected much. It is one of those places which I know before I see them, and has always haunted me the most

---

[8] Isabella Teotochi, Countess Albrizzi (1761?–1836), was a native of Corfu. She assured Hobhouse that her family was Athenian, and talked Romaic to him. Greeks were much in favor at her parties. Hobhouse wrote of the Countess Albrizzi that she "has been called . . . the Madame de Staël of Italy—a very poor copy indeed, though she seems a very good natured woman." (Hobhouse diary, entry of Nov. 16, 1816.)

after the East. I like the gloomy gaiety of their gondolas, and the silence of their canals. . . .

"St. Mark's, and indeed Venice, is most alive at night. The theatres are not open till *nine*, and the society is proportionably late. All this is to my taste; but most of your countrymen miss and regret the rattle of hackney coaches, without which they can't sleep. . . . I have got my gondola; I read a little, and luckily could speak Italian (more fluently though than accurately) long ago. I am studying, out of curiosity, the *Venetian* dialect, which is very naïve, and soft, and peculiar, though not at all classical; I go out frequently, and am in very good contentment."

He confessed also that he was in love, "fathomless love," with the black-eyed wife of his landlord. ". . . her great merit is finding out mine—there is nothing so amiable as discernment. Our little arrangement is completed; the usual oaths having been taken, and every thing fulfilled according to the 'understood relations' of such liaisons." [n]

Byron had now fallen into a routine, which he always did easily, and this was one which particularly pleased him. He announced his good fortune to Douglas Kinnaird on November 27. After a few boasting facetiæ, he added more seriously: "I have books—a decent establishment—a fine country—a language which I prefer—most of the amusements and conveniences of life—as much of society as I choose to take—and a handsome woman, who is not a bore—and does not annoy me with looking like a fool, setting up for a sage." If he could only arrange his financial affairs in England, he concluded, "you might consider me as *posthumous*, for I would never willingly dwell in the 'tight little Island.'" [n]

On the 5th, Hobhouse left with his brother and sister (who had arrived in Venice on November 23) for an extended tour of Italy. Writing to Moore the same day, Byron confessed: ". . . I am more pleased than ever with my Venetian, and begin to feel very serious on that point—so much so, that I shall be silent. . . . By way of divertisement, I am studying daily, at an Armenian monastery, the Armenian language. I found that my mind wanted something craggy to break upon; and this—as the

most difficult thing I could discover here for an amusement—
I have chosen to torture me into attention. . . . I try, and shall
go on;—but I answer for nothing, least of all for my intentions
or my success." [n] But he told Murray that his love and his study
should last the winter. "The lady has, luckily for me, been less
obdurate than the language, or, between the two, I should have
lost my remains of sanity." [n]

Byron felt that he had written himself out, for the present.
England and the passions he had felt there were quickly fading,
and he had not adjusted himself enough to his new experiences
to write about them. And he could not write about what he had
not experienced. Speaking of the spurious "Pilgrimage to Jerusalem" which had been published under his name in London, he
told Murray: "How the devil should I write about *Jerusalem,*
never having yet been there?" [n] Moreover, in the past the impulse to write had always been roused by unhappiness and
frustration, and now that he had achieved a kind of calm contentment the compulsion was not strong. On December 17 he
told Kinnaird that the last month had been "one of the pleasant-
est, and withal the *quietest,* in my recollection." [n]

And writing to Augusta the next day, he spoke lightheartedly
and enthusiastically of his new love affair. "She does not plague
me (which is a wonder) and I verily believe we are one of the
happiest—unlawful couples on this side of the Alps. . . . This
adventure came very opportunely to console me . . . I have
been very tranquil, very loving, & have not so much embarrassed
myself with the tortures of the last two years and that virtuous
monster Miss Milbanke, who had nearly driven me out of my
senses—curse her. . . . You can have no idea of my thorough
wretchedness from the day of my parting from you till nearly a
month ago though I struggled against it with some strength.
At present I am better—thank Heaven above—& woman beneath
—and I will be a very good boy." He added in a casual postscript:
"I forgot to tell you—that the *Demoiselle* [Claire Clairmont]—
who returned to England from Geneva—went there to produce
a new baby B., who is now about to make his appearance." [n]

The next day (the 19th) Byron received a letter from Augusta, and, amused and a little piqued at her piety, wrote

again: "Your letter of the 1st is arrived, and you have 'a *hope*' for me, it seems: what '*hope*,' child? my dearest Sis. I remember a methodist preacher who, on perceiving a profane grin on the faces of part of his congregation, exclaimed 'no *hopes* for *them* as *laughs*.' And thus it is with us: we laugh too much for hopes, and so even let them go." [n]

He continued: "The Carnival is to begin in a week, and with it the mummery of masking. . . . And then there is the place of St. Mark, and conversaziones, and various fooleries, besides many *nau:* indeed, every body is *nau* [naughty], so much so that a lady with only *one lover* is not reckoned to have over-stepped the modesty of marriage—that being a regular thing. . . . The husbands of course belong to any body's wives—but their own. . . . That amatory appendage called by us a lover is here denominated variously—sometimes an 'Amoroso' (which is the same thing) and sometimes a Cavaliere Servente [9]—which I need not tell you is a serving Cavalier. I told my fair one, at setting out, that as to the love and the Cavaliership I was quite of accord, but as to the *servitude* it would not suit me at all: so I begged to hear no more about it. . . . The Society here is something like our own, except that the women sit in a semi-circle at one end of the room, and the men stand at the other. . . . To-night I am going to the Countess Albrizzi's one of the *noblesse*." [n]

The same day Byron sent Hobhouse, then at Florence, some more details of his life in Venice. He was, he said, "studious in the day and dissolute in the evening." He was continuing his Armenian lessons. "I have about mastered thirty of the thirty-eight cursed scratches of Mesrob, the maker of alphabets, and some words of one syllable. My lessons are in the Psalms—and Father Pasqual is a very attentive preceptor. By way of requital for his instructions (as I could not offer sordid money to these friars), I have taken upon me the expenses of his Armenian and English grammar, which is now printing. It costs but a thousand francs to print five hundred copies, and being the first published in these joint languages, I think 'I do the state some service.' . . ." [n]

[9] Byron learned later that the correct spelling was *Cavalier Servente*.

The *Grammar*, the printing of which was finished early in the following year, was, according to the title page, "by P. Paschal Aucher and Lord Byron." But Byron's share in it, aside from his paying for the publication, must have been slight, for by his own confession he knew little Armenian when it was published.[n] He no doubt corrected and clarified the English explanations of the grammatical terms, and he wrote a preface glowing with praise of the gentle friars which was rejected by Father Aucher because it contained an attack on the Turks.[n] The intellectual occupation, the unperturbed isolation of the lovely island where he could read undisturbed in the library, walk unobserved by curious eyes through the quiet cloisters, or sit on the terrace in the sight of Venice or alone under the olive trees, all appealed to the contemplative side of his nature. The friars, on their side, became attached to him. Father Aucher remembered him as "a young man quick, sociable, with burning eyes." [n]

Byron had no news yet of the fate of his poems in England. But, however much he may have attempted to put England out of his mind, he was not forgotten there. Murray had published the third canto of *Childe Harold* on November 18,[n] and *The Prisoner of Chillon and Other Poems*, including all the poems written in his dark moods in Switzerland, came out in a thin volume on December 5.[n] Among the most eager to see *Childe Harold* was Caroline Lamb. Inspired by alternate fits of jealousy and curiosity, of frustrated passion and admiration, she wrote diatribes against her former lover and praised his work, begging Murray to let her see it before publication. And she observed shrewdly: ". . . whenever he may speak of *himself* Lord Byron will succeed. . . . What he feels he can describe extravagantly well. . . ." [n]

With the third canto of *Childe Harold*, Byron had captured and captivated his British audience once more. There were not many dissenting voices, critical or general, and the majority of feminine readers succumbed completely. Lady Byron read the poem with the greatest interest. On December 2 she wrote to Lady Anne Barnard: [n] "I am a very incompetent judge of the impression which the last canto of 'Childe Harold' may produce on the minds of indifferent readers. It contains the usual trace of a conscience restlessly awake; though his object has been too long to aggravate its burden, as if it could thus be oppressed into eternal stupor. . . . He is the absolute monarch of words, and uses them, as Bonaparte did lives, for conquest, without more regard to their intrinsic value. . . . His allusions to me in 'Childe Harold' are cruel and cold, but with such a semblance as to make *me* appear so, and to attract all sympathy to himself. It is said in this poem that hatred of him will be taught as a lesson to his child. . . . It is not my duty to give way to hopeless and wholly unrequited affection; but, so long as I live, my chief struggle will probably be not to remember him too kindly." [n]

As for John Murray, he was well pleased with his bargain. Writing to Byron on December 13, he stated that he had sold to the booksellers assembled at a dinner at the Albion Tavern seven thousand copies of the third canto of *Childe Harold* and a like number of *The Prisoner of Chillon*. [n]

Other news from England was more depressing. Claire Clairmont, approaching her confinement, began a letter on October 27 while in the depths of melancholy over her own forlorn condition. She was too dispirited to continue the letter, but she resumed it on November 17. She could not hold to her resolution not to write until she had heard from him, and she could not stifle a complaining note that she knew would offend him. "I love you too much dearest. I would do any thing, suffer any pain or degradation so I might be so very happy as to receive a letter from you. . . . tell me that you *like* me that you will be very pleased to have a little baby of which you will take great care. Make as many jokes on me as you will dearest I shall be so happy to receive *any thing* from you." Claire added that she wished she could call on Ada and "kiss her because she belongs to you," a suggestion that must have given Byron a start. [n]

When Shelley received another letter from Venice on the 19th, Claire knew that her hopes of ever hearing directly from Byron were over. It was a bitter blow to all her wishful thinking, but she tried to put the best face she could on the now incontrovertible facts of her situation. And she continued to write to him. "If you should alter your mind about the Child's name you will let us know for it would be difficult to set out calling it one name & then change it for another." ⁿ Claire had planned to name the child if it were a girl "Alba," the feminine of her favorite name for Byron.

Shelley, though fully cognizant of Byron's feeling concerning Claire, the next day wrote in an attempt to enlist as much sympathy for her as possible. "If you do not like to write to Clare, send me some kind message to her, which I will, to give suspicion his due, throw into the fire as a sacrifice." ⁿ Shelley gave Byron some details of "the tumultuous state of England," saying that the people were in a sullen mood awaiting what Parliament would do.

Writing to Thomas Moore the day before Christmas, Byron made pointed reference to the information contained in Claire's and Shelley's letters concerning the rebellious state of England and the rising of the Nottingham weavers. "Are you not near the Luddites? By the Lord! if there's a row, but I'll be among ye!"

The exuberance of his mood inspired a light-hearted *jeux d'esprit:*

> But the Carnival's coming,
>   Oh Thomas Moore,
> The Carnival's coming,
>   Oh Thomas Moore;
> Masking and mumming,
> Fifing and drumming,
> Guitarring and strumming,
>   Oh Thomas Moore.ⁿ

There was something intriguing to Byron in a society that put so much energy into its gaieties. Everything was subordinated to the coming festival. "The Carnival is commencing," he wrote Murray on the 2nd, "and there is a good deal of fun here and there—besides business; for all the world are making up their intrigues for the season—changing, or going on upon a renewed lease. I am very well off with Marianna, who is not at all a person to tire me; firstly, because I do not tire of a woman *personally,* but because they are generally bores in their disposition; and, secondly, because she is amiable, and has a tact which is not always the portion of the fair creation; and, thirdly, she is very pretty; and, fourthly—but there is no occasion for further specification. I have passed a great deal of my time with her since my arrival at Venice,[n] and never a twenty-four hours without giving and receiving from one to three (and occasionally an extra or so) pretty unequivocal proofs of mutual good contentment."

The frankness of the Italians in love matters amused at the same time that it slightly shocked Byron. The naïve absence of hypocrisy contrasted strongly with the Regency society he had known in England, and at the same time the code of extramarital relations was much stricter. "The general state of morals here is much the same as in the Doges' time," he observed; "a woman is virtuous (according to the code) who limits herself to her husband and one lover; those who have two, three, or more, are a little *wild;* but it is only those who are indiscriminately diffuse, and form a low connection, such as the Princess of Wales with her courier,[1] (who, by the way, is made a knight of Malta,) who are considered as overstepping the modesty of marriage. In Venice, the Nobility have a trick of marrying with dancers or singers: and, truth to say, the women of their own order are by no means handsome; but the general race—the women of the 2^d and other orders, the wives of Advocates, merchants, and proprietors, and untitled gentry, are mostly *bel' sangue,* and it is with these that the more amatory connections are usually formed: there are also instances of stupendous constancy. I know a woman of fifty who never had but one lover, who dying early, she became devout, renouncing all but her husband: she piques herself, as may be presumed, upon this miraculous fidelity, talking of it occasionally with a species of misplaced morality, which is rather amusing." [n]

The distractions of the Carnival did not, however, wean Byron from concern for his publications in England. He mistrusted

---

[1] The Princess of Wales, wife of the Prince Regent and later Queen Caroline of England, had engaged Bartolommeo Bergami at Milan in 1814 as a courier. The rumor was already abroad that she had committed adultery with him, and that was the charge upon which she was tried before the House of Lords in 1820.

Murray: ". . . if he has made alterations or omissions, I shall not pardon him," he wrote Kinnaird. "I suspect him as a *Tory* of softening my M.S.[2] If he has, by the Ass of Balaam! he shall endure my indignation." [n] And he asked Augusta whether Murray had omitted any stanzas in *Childe Harold*. "The number sent was *118* to the 3[d] Canto. You do not mention the concluding *4* to my daughter Ada which I hoped would give *you* pleasure at least. I care not much about opinions at this time of day, and I am certain in my mind that this Canto is the *best* which I have ever written. . . . I never thought that it would be *popular* & should not think well of it if it were, but those for whom it is intended will like it." [n]

At Bath on January 12, Claire Clairmont had given birth to a daughter whom she called Alba. The next day Mary Shelley announced the event to Byron with a casualness which she probably sensed would please him more than the histrionic sentiment Claire had recently forced upon him. "Shelley being in London upon business I take upon myself the task & pleasure of informing you that Clare was safely delivered of a little girl yesterday morning (Sunday, January 12) at four. She sends her affectionate love to you and begs me to say that she is in excellent . . . spirits and as good health as *can be expected.*" Then she quickly turned to other matters. The Shelleys had taken a house at Marlow, about thirty miles from London, "where we dare hope to have the pleasure of your society on your return to England." [n] She signed herself proudly "Mary W. Shelley," for, following the death of Shelley's wife Harriet, Mary had finally become a legal spouse.

On the 17th, Shelley wrote to Byron from London. He had less happy news. He had now to face a Chancery suit instituted to deprive him of his children. But he had the consolation of

---

[2] Byron was aware that many things in the canto would not have set well with Murray's Tory friends: his generally favorable picture of Napoleon, his praise of Rousseau as the father of the French Revolution, the *lèse-majesté* of his account of the sovereigns who had been the allies of the English Tory government during the late war. But he was even more concerned that Murray should not omit the stanzas on his daughter, with their implied criticism of the implacability of Lady Byron and her family.

the friendship of Byron's friend Leigh Hunt, an "excellent man" who listened with sympathy to the story of his persecution."

Byron was concerned with his own affairs. He wrote Kinnaird on the 20th: "I have been up all night at the opera, and at the Ridotto and its masquerade, and the devil knows what; so that my head aches a little—but to business." Creditors were pressing, but he protested: ". . . as to the produce of my *brain*— my MS.—my night-mare is my own *personality,* and by the Lord, as I have earned the sum, so will I expend it upon my own proper pleasures. . . . Since my departure from England, I have not spent (in nine months) within some hundreds of two thousand pounds. . . ."

"You know," he continued, "and I believe saw once, that odd-headed girl, who introduced herself to me shortly before I left England; but you also know that I found her with Shelley and her sister at Geneva. I never loved nor pretended to love her, but a man is a man, and if a girl of eighteen comes prancing to you at all hours, there is but one way—the suite of all this is that she was with *child*—and returned to England to assist in peopling that desolate island. Whether this impregnation took place before I left England or since I do not know; the (carnal) connection had commenced previously to my setting out—but by or about this time she is about to produce—the next question is, is the brat mine? I have reasons to think so, for I know as much as one can know such a thing—that she had *not lived* with S. during the time of our acquaintance—and that she had a good deal of that same with me.

"This comes of 'putting it about' (as Jackson calls it) and be damned to it—and thus people come into the world."

Concerning his present life he added in a postscript: "Venice and I agree very well—in the mornings I study Armenian, and in the evenings I go out sometimes, and indulge in coition always. . . . pray answer my letters, and mention anything or everything except my—*family*—I will say, for the other word makes me unwell." "

Moore had expressed admiration for the new canto of *Childe Harold,* and Byron confessed: "I am glad you like it; it is a fine indistinct piece of poetical desolation, and my favourite. I was half mad during the time of its composition, between metaphysics, mountains, lakes, love unextinguishable, thoughts unutterable, and the nightmare of my own delinquencies. I should, many a good day, have blown my brains out, but for the recollection that it would have given pleasure to my mother-in-law. . . ."

Then he proceeded to regale Moore with a Venetian adventure in which he had been involved but which he recounted with detachment and humor: "A few days ago a gondolier brought me a billet without a subscription, intimating a wish on the part of the writer to meet me. . . . A ten o'clock I was at home and alone (Marianna was gone with her husband to a conversazione), when the door of my apartment opened, and in walked a well-looking and (for an Italian) *bionda* girl of about nineteen, who informed me that she was married to the brother of my *amorosa*, and wished to have some conversation with me. I made a decent reply, and we had some talk in Italian and Romaic (her mother being a Greek of Corfu), when lo! in a very few minutes, in marches, to my very great astonishment, Marianna Segati, *in propriâ personâ*, and after making a most polite courtesy to her sister-in-law and to me, without a single word seizes her said sister-in-law by the hair, and bestows upon her some sixteen slaps, which would have made your ear ache only to hear their echo. I need not describe the screaming which ensued. The luckless visitor took flight. I seized Marianna, who, after several vain efforts to get away in pursuit of the enemy, fairly went into fits in my arms; and, in spite of reasoning, eau de Cologne, vinegar, half a pint of water, and God knows what other waters beside, continued so till past midnight. . . . After about an hour, in comes—who? why, Signor Segati, her lord and husband, and finds me with his wife fainting upon the sofa, and all the apparatus of confusion, dishevelled hair, hats, handkerchiefs, salts, smelling-bottles—and the lady as pale as ashes, without sense or motion. His first question was, 'What is all this?' The lady could not reply—so I did. I told him the explanation was the easiest thing in the world; but in the mean time it would be as well to recover his wife—at least, her senses. . . . I thought the best way would be to let her explain it as she chose (a woman being never at a loss—the devil always sticks by them)—only determining to protect and carry her off, in case of any ferocity on the part of the Signor. I saw that he was quite calm. She went to bed, and next day—how they settled it, I know not, but settle it they did. . . ." [n]

Byron wrote again to Kinnaird on February 3 on business, adding a few lines of his usual badinage. "Tell me of Scrope— is he as full of fierce 'embraces' as when I last saw him? He had made then innumerable conquests, according to his own account; I wish he would marry and beget some Scrooples; it is a pity the dynasty should not be prolonged. I do not know any-one who will leave such a 'gap in Nature.' I hope also that he wins the specie still left among you." [n]

Byron's life was not so entirely given up to dissipations as he implied to his English correspondents, however, for sometime during the Carnival he had finished the poetic drama of *Manfred*, which he had begun before leaving Switzerland. On February 15 he wrote to Murray: "I forgot to mention to you that a kind of Poem in dialogue (in blank verse) or drama, from which 'The Incantation' [published as a separate poem in the *Chillon* volume] is an extract, begun last summer . . . is finished; it is in three acts; but of a very wild, metaphysical, and inexplicable kind. . . . but I have at least rendered it *quite impossible* for the stage, for which my intercourse with D[rury] Lane has given me the greatest contempt." [n]

It is obvious that Byron was a little uneasy about the impression the drama would make among his hardheaded friends in England. He first sent a few extracts and then the first act. [n] It was three weeks before he had copied out and sent the whole of the drama, which he did with some misgiving. "I have really and truly no notion whether it is good or bad," he told Murray; "and as this was not the case with the principal of my former publications, I am, therefore, inclined to rank it but humbly." [3]

The festivities in Venice ended on February 18, but Byron lingered in the city, though he had urgent invitations to join

---

[3] *LJ*, IV, 68–9. Letter of March 9, 1817. Murray finally paid the three hundred guineas Byron had asked for it. Though Gifford had some misgivings, he thought the first act "wonderfully poetical." *Manfred* was published June 16, 1817. (*LJ*, IV, 69 n., 54 n.)

Hobhouse in Rome, for the nightly revels and the literary labor which he managed to sandwich in had left him in a debilitated state. On the 19th he wrote to Augusta: "The Carnival closed last night, and I have been up all night at the masked ball of the Fenice, and am rather tired or so. . . . All the Virtue and Vice in Venice was there. There has been the same sort of thing every night these six weeks—besides Operas, Ridottos, parties, and the Devil knows what. I went out *now* and *then,* but was less dissipated than you would expect." " But writing to Moore some days later he reported that he was still on an "invalid regimen" and that he had found " 'the sword wearing out the scabbard,' though I have just turned the corner of twenty-nine." It took just such a mood of satiation and wearied pleasure to inspire Byron to write one of his finest lyrics, which he sent forthwith to Moore:

> *So we'll go no more a roving*
> *So late into the night,*
> *Though the heart be still as loving,*
> *And the moon be still as bright.*

> *For the Sword outwears its sheath,*
> *And the soul wears out the breast,*
> *And the heart must pause to breathe,*
> *And Love itself have rest.*"

But in his debility there also came upon him a growing dissatisfaction with his present aimless life. An attack in the *Edinburgh Review,* in an article on Coleridge," had brought home to him the precarious state of his literary reputation. Such a blow to his self-esteem undermined his confidence and strengthened his recurring conviction that he and all his contemporaries were on the wrong track when measured by the great model of Pope. He was self-critical enough also to know that his own work failed of the highest polish and imaginative flights even in the genre he had adopted. It was in such moods that the half-formed ambition to try his mettle in a political, or perhaps a military, career surged upward in him.

"If I live ten years longer," he told Moore, "you will see, however, that it is not over with me—I don't mean in literature, for that is nothing; and it may seem odd enough to say, I do not think it my vocation. But you will see that I shall do something or other—the times and fortune permitting. . . . But I doubt whether my constitution will hold out. I have, at intervals, exorcised it most devilishly." [n]

The illness which followed the Carnival did not subside, but grew worse. Cheered by the favorable review of the third canto of *Childe Harold* and *The Prisoner of Chillon* in the *Quarterly Review* (by Walter Scott, though Byron did not know it at the time),[n] he wrote to Murray on March 3 without any evidence of depression of spirits. He announced that the Armenian grammar was published, "but my Armenian studies are suspended for the present, till my head aches a little less." [n] In the meantime, he was under the loving care of his *amorosa*, the draper's wife.

Though he still talked of returning to England in the spring, the thought of his last months in that country were increasingly painful. To Augusta's vague pious hopes (probably for his religious redemption) he replied with quite another subject in mind. "What you 'hope' may be, I do not know, if you mean a reunion between Lady B. and me, it is too late. It is now a year, and I have repeatedly offered to make it up, with what success you know. At present if she would rejoin me to-morrow, *I* would not accept the proposition. I have no spirit of hatred against her, however, I am too sensitive not to feel injuries, but far too proud to be vindictive. She's a fool, and when you have said that, it is the most that can be said for her." [n]

On that subject it was easy for Byron to lose his balance and to become obsessed with the feeling that he was the object of deliberate persecution. After hearing from Hanson, who relayed to him the results of his correspondence with Sir Ralph Noel and Dr. Lushington concerning Ada, he felt compelled to relieve his mind by writing to his "moral Clytemnestra" herself. It was the thought that his daughter might be taken from him that froze up all sympathy for his wife and her relations.[4] He asked her to

---

[4] Byron's fear that efforts were afoot to deprive him of the control of his daughter was not unjustified. On February 3 Dr. Lushington wrote to Hanson to announce that Ada had been made a ward in Chancery. (Murray MSS.)

remember that he had not been the first to begin, "but, being begun, neither shall I be the first to recede. . . . Throughout the whole of this unhappy business, I have done my best to avoid the bitterness, which, however, is yet amongst us; and it would be as well if even you at times recollected, that the man who has been sacrificed in fame, in feelings, in every thing, to the convenience of your family, was he whom you once loved, and who —whatever you may imagine to the contrary—loved you. . . . If you think to reconcile yourself to yourself by accumulating harshness against me, you are again mistaken: you are not happy, nor even tranquil, nor will you ever be so, even to the very moderate degree which is permitted to general humanity." [n]

Byron's life was still without motive and without direction. He had lingered so long in Venice that it was now, he thought, too late to join Hobhouse in Rome. It was not only illness which held him. Added to that was the general inertia which made it difficult for him to break any routine, especially one so pleasant and consoling, and a good-natured compliance with the wishes of Marianna Segati. But the main reason for delaying was his abhorrence of the traveling English. [n]

Despite Marianna's careful nursing, Byron's fever grew worse, and he was confined to his bed for more than two weeks. On March 25 he wrote to Moore again: "I have been very ill with a slow fever, which at last took to flying, and became as quick as need be. But, at length, after a week of half-delirium, burning skin, thirst, hot headach, horrible pulsation, and no sleep, by the blessing of barley water, and refusing to see any physician, I recovered. It is an epidemic of the place, which is annual, and visits strangers." [n]

His plans were still uncertain; he confessed that the most potent cause of his indecision was Marianna Segati. "I am still in love,—which is a dreadful drawback in quitting a place, and I can't stay at Venice much longer. What I shall do on this point I don't know. The girl means to go with me, but I do not like this for her own sake. . . . she has a child; and though, like all the 'children of the sun,' she consults nothing but passion, it is necessary I should think for both; and it is only the virtuous, like

* * * *," who can afford to give up husband and child, and live happy ever after." "

Since Hobhouse and other English acquaintances had left Venice, Byron had retired more and more into the sole society of his inamorata and a few Italian friends. His preoccupation with the Carnival and with Marianna, and later his illness, had interrupted his study of Armenian. He did not know even one "English gentleman" whom he could get to witness a deed Murray had sent him. ". . . this was one reason why I staid here," he wrote Murray, "till the season of the purgation of Rome from these people—which is infected with them at this time—should arrive. Besides, I abhor the nation, and the nation me. . . ."

He had already tired of the formal social life of Venice. He had gone two or three times to the Governor's *conversazioni,* but as he saw there only very plain women and a formal circle, he did not go again. He felt much more comfortable and happy with Marianna, he told Murray with his usual frankness, "because she is very pretty and pleasing, and talks Venetian, which amuses me, and is naïve, and I can besides see her, and make love with her at all or any hours, which is convenient with my temperament. I have seen all their spectacles and sights, but I do not know anything very worthy of observation except that the women *kiss* better than those of any other nation, which is notorious, and is attributed to the worship of images and the early habit of osculation induced thereby." "

Having now completely recovered from the fever, Byron found his intellectual energies burgeoning again. He bought a complete set of Voltaire in ninety-two volumes and amused himself by reading the old scoffer, whom he pronounced "delightful, but dreadfully inaccurate frequently." "

Turning over the subject of Marino Faliero, he told Murray he thought it superior as a story to Otway's *Venice Preserved.* "There is still," he wrote, "in the Doge's Palace, the black veil painted over Falieri's picture, and the staircase whereon he was first crowned Doge, and subsequently decapitated. This was the thing that most struck my imagination in Venice—more than the Rialto, which I visited for the sake of Shylock. . . . But I hate things *all fiction;* and therefore the *Merchant* and *Othello* have no great associations to me. . . . There should always be some foundation of fact for the most airy fabric, and pure invention is but the talent of a liar." [n]

When Byron wrote to Murray on April 9, he was still in Venice and still talking of going to Rome. His indecision made him reckless, and he told Murray that he had contemplated suicide the year before. But now he had some reasons for living: ". . . there are one or two people whom I have to put out of the world, and as many into it, before I can 'depart in peace;' if I do so before, I have not fulfilled my mission. Besides, when I turn thirty, I will turn devout; I feel a great vocation that way in Catholic churches, and when I hear the organ." [n]

Byron had apparently gained the consent of Marianna to make the voyage to Rome by himself on condition that he return to her in Venice within a few weeks. But before he could leave, some English visitors had descended upon him. In a letter to Moore he reported: "My late physician, Dr. Polidori, is here on his way to England, with the present Lord Guilford [n] and the widow of the late earl. Dr. Polidori has, just now, no more patients, because his patients are no more. He had lately three, who are now all dead—one embalmed. . . . Lord Guilford died of an inflammation of the bowels: so they took them out, and sent them (on account of their discrepancies), separately from the carcass, to England. Conceive a man going one way, and his intestines another, and his immortal soul a third!—was there ever such a distribution? One certainly has a soul; but how it came to allow itself to be enclosed in a body is more than I can imagine." [n]

Byron protested that he hated sightseeing, but on April 13 he visited with Polidori the Manfrini Palace, which he had not before taken the trouble to see in all the months he had been in Venice. "You must recollect, however," he wrote Murray, "that I know nothing of painting; and that I detest it, unless it reminds me of something I have seen, or think possible to see. . . . Depend upon it, of all the arts, it is the most artificial and unnatural, and that by which the nonsense of mankind is the most imposed upon. I never yet saw the picture—or the statue—

which came within a league of my conception or expectation; but I have seen many mountains, and Seas, and Rivers, and views, and two or three women, who went as far beyond it,— besides some horses; and a lion (at Veli Pasha's) in the Morea; and a tiger at supper in Exeter 'Change." [n]

When Polidori left for England along with the Guilford party, he carried with him to deliver to Murray for Mrs. Leigh two miniatures of Byron recently painted in Venice. Byron instructed Murray to have Mr. Love the jeweler "set them in plain gold, with my arms complete, and 'Painted by Prepiani—Venice, 1817,' on the back." [n] He also asked that the English painter Holmes be requested to make a copy of each—these to be kept by Murray until Byron's return. At last he could announce to Hobhouse: "On next Thursday (the 17th, I guess) it is my indelible purpose to be upon my way to Rome—by Ferrara. . . ." [n]

Before departing, he had heard from Murray, who had finally received the manuscripts of *Manfred*, and who wrote that both he and Gifford were delighted. But Byron had become more uncertain of it, especially of the third act, which had, he said, the dregs of his fever, during which it was written. He would try to rewrite it, but the impulse was gone, and he was not sure he would succeed.

Once on the road, however, inspiration came to him again. Travel and new sights drew him out of the lethargy into which he had fallen in Venice. But he turned to other themes. He was peculiarly attracted to literary and classical associations. At Padua he went out of his way to visit the habitations of Petrarch, which he found "rather ragged, and somewhat poetical." He crossed "the winding Po" and paused at Ferrara, which filled his mind with a ferment of poetical thoughts. In the first place, it was the scene of his own *Parisina*. And he was fascinated by the tomb of Ariosto and the cell where Tasso had been incarcerated—"all the Girusalemme, all Guarini's original Pastor Fido," &c. &c., letters of Titian to Ariosto, and Tasso's correspondence about his dirty shirts, are all duly displayed." [n]

Here, as at the castle of Chillon, the thought of a sensitive being confined worked powerfully on Byron's imagination, and be-

fore he reached Florence he had committed to paper the burning lines of *The Lament of Tasso.* He saw Tasso as an "eagle-
spirit of a Child of Song," suffering

> *Long years of outrage—calumny—and wrong;*
> *Imputed madness, prisoned solitude. . . .*"

Inevitably as he wrote, Byron identified himself with the unfortunate poet who had been imprisoned in the hospital of Sant'
Anna in the sixteenth century.

> *For I have anguish yet to bear—and how?*
> *I know not that—but in the innate force*
> *Of my own spirit shall be found resource.*"

A pause in Bologna gave him a chance to work on the poem,
and he wrote the last lines while crossing the Apennines to Florence." He had taken his Swiss shepherd dog Mutz along on the
journey, but, far from being useful as a protector, the timorous
animal was routed by a simple pig.

Although he remained only a day in Florence, Byron proceeded to do a little selective sightseeing. ". . . I went to the
two galleries," he wrote Murray, "from which one returns drunk
with beauty. The Venus [de' Medici] is more for admiration
than love; but there are sculpture and painting, which for the
first time at all gave me an idea of what people mean by their
cant, and what Mr. Braham calls 'entusimusy' (*i.e.* enthusiasm)
about those two most artificial of the arts. What struck me most
were, the Mistress of Raphael, a portrait; the mistress of Titian,
a portrait; a Venus of Titian in the Medici gallery—*the* Venus;
Canova's Venus also in the other gallery: Titian's mistress is also
in the other gallery (that is, in the Pitti Palace gallery); the
Parcæ of Michael Angelo, a picture; and the Antinous—the Alexander—and one or two not very decent groupes in marble; the
Genius of Death, a sleeping figure, etc., etc. I also went to the
Medici chapel—fine frippery in great slabs of various expensive
stones, to commemorate fifty rotten and forgotten carcases. . . .
The church of 'Santa Croce' contains much illustrious nothing." "

Byron arrived in Rome a few days later, on April 29, " and
was immediately delighted with it. Hobhouse was still there, and

was able to act as his cicerone, for he had been studying the antiquities diligently for some weeks, gathering anecdotes, observations, and historical lore which he later incorporated into his ponderous *Historical Illustrations of the Fourth Canto of Childe Harold.*[n] For the first week Byron was occupied with the revision and rewriting of the third act of *Manfred,* which had been on his mind during his travels, and which he finished and sent off to Murray by May 5. He offered Murray the drama and *The Lament of Tasso* together for six hundred guineas. "I have this morning seen a live pope and a dead cardinal," he told Murray. "Rome has delighted me beyond every thing, since Athens and Constantinople. But I shall not remain long this visit. . . . I have got my saddle-horses here, and have ridden, and am riding, all about the country."[n]

There is no record of where Byron resided while in Rome, but according to one local tradition it was in the vicinity of the Piazza di Spagna, where Keats later died.[n] Seeing the historic ruins and the environs in the Roman spring brought back to him the pleasant equestrian excursions he and Hobhouse had made in the vicinity of Athens. It was a happy thought to bring his saddle horses along, for he would have been very uncomfortable had he been forced to walk over the hills of Rome. Writing to Murray again on the 9th, he spoke with mounting enthusiasm: "As a *whole, ancient* and *modern,* it beats Greece, Constantinople, every thing—at least that I have ever seen. But I can't describe, because my first impressions are always strong and confused, and my Memory *selects* and reduces them to order, like distance in the landscape, and blends them better, although they may be less distinct."[n]

Overwhelmed as he was by the relics of ancient majesty in Rome, his mind was busy storing impressions from which in a few weeks the fourth canto of *Childe Harold* was distilled. In the three weeks of his sojourn in the Eternal City he saw and his memory recorded an amazing panorama of the living and the dead images which stimulated his mind and senses more than anything he had ever experienced. And they were images which grew in sharpness as they crystallized in his recollections.

Fortunately, the few English he encountered were acquaintances and bearable. On the 11th he dined with Lord Lansdowne, who was on his way north.[n] The only other Englishman he mentioned as having been in Rome while he was there was "that old Blue-*bore* Sotheby, who will give a fine account of Italy, in which he will be greatly assisted by his total ignorance of Italian, and yet this is the translator of Tasso." [n]

Byron was no doubt unaware of the impression he made on an English party at St. Peter's. According to Lord Lovelace, "A friend of Lady Byron's family, Lady Liddell (afterwards the first Lady Ravensworth), who had never seen Lord Byron, suddenly came upon him on the roof of St. Peter's at Rome, while walking with her daughter and friends. In a moment it struck her who it was:

" 'And what came over me I cannot describe, but I felt ready to sink, and stood as if my feet were rooted to the ground, looking at him, as Mr. Blakeney told me, as if I were horror-struck.'

"Lady Liddell was so alarmed at the terrible reprobate that she insisted on her daughter (Maria, afterwards Marchioness of Normanby) keeping her eyes down, saying, 'Don't look at him, he is dangerous to look at.' " [n]

Letters from Murray, Moore, and Augusta diverted Byron's thoughts to England, but gave him no great desire to return there. Murray had written that Southey was in a scrape: someone had published a poem he had composed in full revolutionary fervor in 1794 to embarrass his Tory attacks on Whigs and Radicals in 1817.[n] Though Byron apparently had not yet heard of the gossip Southey had spread about him in England, he was delighted that the Laureate's indiscreet chickens had come home to roost. "I hate all intolerance, but most the intolerance of Apostacy. . . . It is no disgrace to Mr. Southey to have written *Wat Tyler*, and afterwards to have written his birthday or Victory odes (I speak only of their *politics*), but it is something, for which I have no words, for this man to have endeavoured to bring to the stake (for such would he do) men who think as he thought, and for no reason but because they think so still, when he has found it convenient to think otherwise." [n]

To Augusta, who had heard of his illness and was greatly worried, he wrote reassuringly: "I am very well, quite recovered, &

as is always the case after all illness—particularly fever—got
large, ruddy, & robustous to a degree which would please you
—& shock me." He was still unsatisfied with Lady Byron's assurances about Ada, and, once launched on that subject, he easily lost perspective and grew ferocious. "Will you tell my wife
'mine excellent Wife' that she is brewing a Cataract for herself
& me in these foolish equivocations about *Ada,*—a job for lawyers—& more hatred for every body, for which—(God knows),
there is no occasion." [n]

But not even that bitterness, now distant, could disturb for
long the exhilarating pleasure of his Roman sightseeing with
Hobhouse as knowledgeable guide.

Bertel Thorwaldsen, the Danish sculptor, then had a studio in
Rome. Hobhouse, eager to have a bust of his poet friend, had
written the sculptor to ask whether he would let Byron sit to him
while in Rome. He had not received an answer when his friend
arrived, but nevertheless Byron went to the sculptor. As Thorwaldsen told the story, "Byron placed himself opposite me, but at
once began to put on a quite different expression from that usual
to him. 'Will you not sit still?' said I—'you need not assume that
look.' 'That is my expression,' said Byron. 'Indeed?' said I, and
I then represented him as I wished. When the bust was finished,
it was universally admitted to be an excellent likeness. Byron
when he saw the bust, said: 'It is not at all like me; my expression is more unhappy.' He intensely desired to be so exceedingly
miserable. . . ." [n] But Thorwaldsen smiled in telling the story,
for he was a great admirer of Byron. Hobhouse later wrote to Murray: "I would have had a wreath round the brows, but the poet
was afraid of being mistaken for a king or a conqueror. . . ." [5]
Byron was a little embarrassed by the transaction, and he felt
superstitiously that, unlike a painting, there was something of a
"posthumous" character in a bust, but at the same time he took
a sheepish pride in being thus immortalized in marble while still

[5] Smiles, I, 391. Letter of Dec. 7, 1817. On June 20, 1817, Byron wrote to
Hobhouse: ". . . I won't have my head garnished like a Christmas pie with
holly—or a cod's head and fennel, or whatever the damned weed is they
strew round it. I wonder you should want me to be such a. mountebank."
(*LBC*, II, 56.)

alive. The bust was made at Hobhouse's expense, but Byron later paid the cost of its transportation to England.

On May 19, irresistibly drawn by the macabre and the horrific, Byron witnessed, probably with Hobhouse, a public execution. This Roman spectacle he described for Murray with frank and excruciating details: "The day before I left Rome I saw three robbers guillotined. The ceremony—including the *masqued* priests; the half-naked executioners; the bandaged criminals; the black Christ and his banner; the scaffold; the soldiery; the slow procession, and the quick rattle and heavy fall of the axe; the splash of the blood, and the ghastliness of the exposed heads—is altogether more impressive than the vulgar and ungentlemanly dirty 'new drop,' and the dog-like agony of infliction upon the sufferers of the English sentence. Two of these men behaved calmly enough, but the first of the three died with great terror and reluctance, which was very horrible. He would not lie down; then his neck was too large for the aperture, and the priest was obliged to drown his exclamation by still louder exhortations. The head was off before the eye could trace the blow; but from an attempt to draw back the head, notwithstanding it was held forward by the hair, the first head was cut off close to the ears: the other two were taken off more cleanly. . . . The first turned me quite hot and thirsty, and made me shake so that I could hardly hold the opera-glass (I was close, but determined to see, as one should see every thing, once, with attention); the second and third (which shows how dreadfully soon things grow indifferent), I am ashamed to say, had no effect on me as a horror, though I would have saved them if I could." ⁿ

Eager to get back to Venice and Marianna Segati, Byron left Rome on the 20th and traveled rapidly, making few stops. The next day Hobhouse set out for Naples. He wanted Byron to accompany him, but the latter made the excuse that there were too many English in the vicinity.ⁿ

Before leaving Rome, Byron had received a letter from Shelley, who had removed his household, including Claire and Byron's daughter, from Bath to Marlow in Buckinghamshire.ⁿ On March 27, Lord Eldon, the Chancellor, had handed down a decision depriving Shelley of the guardianship of his children by his first marriage, and Byron was fearful that he too might be victim of a decision that would deprive him of the care of his legitimate daughter. Shelley wrote, however, chiefly on behalf of Claire, "and of a little being whom we—in the absence of all right to bestow a *Christian* designation—call Alba, or the Dawn. . . . what are your plans with respect to the little girl? . . . we find it indispensable that Clare should reside with us; and a perpetual danger of discovery that it is hers impends." [n]

Byron's reaction to this news is reflected in his letter to Augusta from Florence on his return from Rome: "I am a little puzzled how to dispose of this new production (which is two or three months old, though I did not receive the accounts till at Rome), but shall probably send for and place it in a Venetian convent, to become a good Catholic, and (it may be) a *Nun*, being a character somewhat wanted in our family.

"They tell me it is very pretty, with blue eyes and *dark* hair; and, although I never was attached nor pretended attachment to the mother, still in case of the eternal war and alienation which I foresee about my legitimate daughter, Ada, it may be as well to have something to repose a hope upon. I must love something in my old age, and probably circumstances will render this poor little creature a great and, perhaps, my only comfort than any offspring from that misguided and artificial woman, who bears and disgraces my name." [n]

Byron returned to Venice on May 28 and found Marianna Segati just recovering from the same fever that had attacked him earlier.[n] His jaunt across Italy and his Roman experience, now ordering itself in his imagination, together with the news he had lately received from his native land had convinced him more than ever that he could not happily return to live in England and had confirmed his resolution not to go back even for business except under dire necessity. Returning to Marianna was more consoling to his spirit and more conducive to his comfort. He was resigned to being an expatriate.

CHAPTER XVIII

1817

La Mira, Venice Again

ON HIS return to Venice, Byron's first concern was so to arrange his business affairs in England that he could pay his debts and live comfortably abroad. Only "absolute and imperious necessity," he told Kinnaird, would bring him back to that country. Byron, who had urged Kinnaird to put pressure on Hanson, now spoke of "the indispensable obligation I feel of disposing of Newstead without further delay, in the course of the present summer, at *any price* which it will bring. . . ." [n]

His anxiety for the sale of his property did not arise from any immediate need, he assured Kinnaird.[n] He had raised £2,500 on promissory notes before he left England.[n] And since then he had sold to Murray the copyrights of the third canto of *Childe Harold, The Prisoner of Chillon,* and other poems for fifteen hundred guineas. Murray subsequently agreed to pay six hundred guineas for *Manfred* and *The Lament of Tasso.*

One of the reasons for Byron's reluctance to return to England and for his present resolution never to live there again was no doubt the equivocal nature of the recent letters of the one person who might have drawn him back. Augusta, who had been such a stanch friend and so loyal a supporter in the bitter months of the separation, had now begun to be frightened at shadows—or was there really some sinister influence undermining her love for him? He wrote: "I have received all your letters I believe, which are full of woes, as usual, megrims & mysteries; but my sympathies remain in suspense, for, for the life of me I can't make out whether your disorder is a broken heart or the

earache—or whether it is *you* that have been ill or the children
—or what your melancholy & mysterious apprehensions tend to,
or refer to, whether to Caroline Lamb's novels—Mrs Clermont's
evidence—Lady Byron's magnanimity—or any other piece of
imposture. . . . I should think all that could affect *you* must
have been over long ago; & as for me—leave me to take care of
myself." ⁿ

And another letter from Augusta exasperated him again; her
innuendoes were more baffling than ever. "What do you mean?"
he wrote, "what is there known? or can be known? which *you &
I* do not know much better? & what concealment can you have
from me? *I* never shrank—and it was on your account principally that I gave way at all—for I thought they would endeavour
to drag you into it—although they had no business with anything previous to my marriage with that infernal fiend, whose
destruction I shall yet see." ⁿ

But Venice still had distractions and charms that turned his
mind from such thoughts. Shortly after his return, Byron met at
last the poet Ippolito Pindemonte, who was a friend of the Countess Albrizzi and who had been recommended to him by several
of the literati in Milan. Byron described him as "a little thin man,
with acute and pleasing features; his address good and gentle;
his appearance altogether very philosophical; his age about sixty,
or more. He is one of their best going. . . . After having been
a little libertine in his youth, he is grown devout, and takes prayers, and talks to himself, to keep off the Devil; but for all that,
he is a very nice little old gentleman." ⁿ

In the same letter to Murray, Byron gave the first intimation
of his intention to leave Venice for the summer. He had taken
a six months' lease on the Villa Foscarini on the left bank of
the Brenta River at La Mira, a village about seven miles inland
from the river's mouth at Fusina on the Venetian lagoon. The
villa, on the dusty road to Padua, was a large boxlike palace considerably altered from the converted convent which had become
the Palladian mansion of the patrician Foscarini family in the
early seventeenth century.ⁿ

The old mansion was spacious though rather empty, but it had
a small English garden that gave shade and was an escape from

the breathless heat of the narrow Venetian streets and the summer effluvia of the canals. Most of the Venetians who could afford it retired to the mainland during the summer, and the
Brenta was lined with the Palladian mansions of the gentry. Marianna Segati also had an excuse for coming to La Mira, for she
had friends living near by. By June 14, Byron was installed in
his great palace."

One of the chief attractions of this *villeggiatura* to Byron was
that he could keep his horses at La Mira and ride at will, for
his happiest memories were associated with horseback rides
through pleasant countrysides from Scotland to Constantinople.
This pleasure compensated for the dullness of the house itself,
which looked out on the placid, canal-like Brenta and the dusty
road.

Freed from the distractions of Venice, his mind turned again
to literary matters, but he had not yet settled his Roman impressions. He was principally concerned with *Manfred,* and was irritated by the fact that Murray had hinted it was a "dear purchase" at three hundred guineas. Murray, no doubt warned by
some of his readers, feared the public reaction to the poem's un-
orthodox and daring speculations and its too obvious identifica-
tion of Astarte with Byron's sister. But Murray knew its value as
a poem, and finally ventured to publish it on June 16.

Byron was anxious about the poem, too, for he had poured his
heart's blood into it. In it he had fought out, though he had arrived at no very satisfying philosophical conclusions, the metaphysical problems which had long been troubling him. They had
been made more acute by his reading of Voltaire while he was
struggling with the final draft of the third act. Striving with the
ingrained feelings of predestination and sin which were the her-
itage of his Calvinistic youth, he sought the assurance of the
superiority of man's reason and will over all supernatural powers. But he could find it only temporarily.

After hearing Manfred's strange defiance of man and gods,
the Abbot concludes (a conclusion of Byron's own alter ego):

This should have been a noble creature: he
Hath all the energy which would have made

A goodly frame of glorious elements,
Had they been wisely mingled; as it is,
It is an awful chaos—Light and Darkness—
And mind and dust—and passions and pure thoughts
Mixed, and contending without end or order,—
All dormant or destructive."

When the spirits come to carry Manfred to his Faustian ending, he does not submit, but defies them:

What I have done is done; I bear within
A torture which could nothing gain from thine:
The Mind which is immortal makes itself
Requital for its good or evil thoughts,—
Is its own origin of ill and end—
And its own place and time. . . ."

Murray's worst fears were realized when, a week after the publication, a review of *Manfred* appeared in a London newspaper, *The Day and New Times*. It contained an outspoken attack on the incest theme of the poem, with a pointed reference to its autobiographical significance. "*Manfred,*" the reviewer wrote, "has exiled himself from society, and what is to be the ground of our compassion for the exile? Simply the commission of one of the most revolting of crimes. He has committed incest! Lord Byron has coloured *Manfred* into his own personal features." " No one, it seems probable, of all Byron's friends in England had the temerity to bring this article to his attention (though it did not escape Lady Byron),[1] and the later reviews in the great quarterlies shied away from the forbidden subject.

In the meantime, in the still hours in the empty palace at La Mira, Byron began to capture the essence of his Roman adventure. On July 1 he wrote to Murray: ". . . I have been working up my impressions into a 4th Canto of *Childe Harold*, of which

[1] *Astarte*, p. 69. Letter of July 6, 1817. When Augusta wrote to Annabella for advice, the latter replied: "You can only speak of *Manfred* . . . with the most decided expressions of your disapprobation. He practically gives you away, and implies you were guilty *after* marriage." Annabella wrote to Mrs. Villiers: ". . . I make no mystery of having known his cruel designs towards her. The kindness I am known to feel for her removes every impression of her having been the accomplice. I did not see the newspaper. What does the Queen think, I wonder?" (Mayne: *Lady Byron*, p. 271.)

I have roughened off about rather better than thirty stanzas, and mean to go on. . . ." " He sent Murray his now famous first stanza as a sample of the new canto. He had started Harold on his Italian pilgrimage, not in Rome, but in Venice, for that was still his "greenest isle." But it was, of course, the mood of the Childe to ponder upon the decayed past of the city.

> *I stood in Venice, on the "Bridge of Sighs";*
> *A palace and a prison on each hand:*
> *I saw from out the wave her structures rise*
>
> *As from the stroke of $\left\{\begin{array}{l} an \\ the \end{array}\right\}$ Enchanter's wand:*
> *A thousand Years their cloudy wings expand*
> *Around me, and a dying Glory smiles*
> *O'er the far times when many a subject land*
> *Looked to the winged Lion's marble piles,*
> *Where Venice sate in state, throned on her Seventy Isles.*

In the same letter Byron announced that "Monk" Lewis had arrived in Venice, and that he was "going up to stay a week with him there—as it is one of his enthusiasms also to like the city." " From Venice he wrote to congratulate Moore on the publication of his "Persian Tale," *Lalla Rookh*, extracts of which Murray had sent him by the post.[2] A reference to Sam Rogers recalled to Byron nostalgic memories of their London gaieties, and he concluded his happy reminiscence with a slight misquotation of Falstaff: "Ah, Master Shallow, we have heard the chimes at midnight." In this mood he added some stanzas to a poem he had begun to Moore just before leaving England the year before:

> *My boat is on the shore,*
> *And my bark is on the sea;*
> *But, before I go, Tom Moore,*
> *Here's a double health to thee!*
>
> *Here's a sigh to those who love me,*
> *And a smile to those who hate;*
> *And whatever sky's above me,*
> *Here's a heart for every fate.*"

[2] *LJ*, IV, 148. Hobhouse wrote in the margin of his copy of Moore: "Nevertheless I have heard him express a very different opinion of Tommy's [Turkish?] tale." Because Moore was his friend, Byron leaned over backward to praise him, reserving his true opinion for Hobhouse.

Then he revealed the reason for his high spirits: "I am just come out from an hour's swim in the Adriatic; and I write to you with a black-eyed Venetian girl before me, reading Boccaccio." [n] Marianna Segati was still his chief consolation, and was apparently always at his call.

But his frequent jaunts to Venice and his rides at La Mira did not interfere with the rapid composition of the new canto, for his mind was now heated with the subject. He announced to Murray on the 15th that the number of completed stanzas had jumped to 104, "and such stanzas! By St. Anthony (who has a church at my elbow, and I like to be neighbourly) some of them are the right thing!" [n] Five days later he gave Murray notice that he had "completed the 4th and *ultimate* Canto of *Childe Harold*. It consists of 126 stanzas, and is consequently the longest of the four." [n] But the poem was not finished yet: Hobhouse, after his arrival at the end of July, suggested more subjects for stanzas on the antiquities he had seen (though Byron had not), and the poem continued to grow, while Hobhouse himself added learned notes.

The composition perhaps did as much as anything to lift Byron's spirits during the summer. The poem turned out to be not only a panorama of his Italian experience and his journey to Rome, but also, as usual, a history of his deepest feelings and his inner conflicts during its creation. With less pretense of distinguishing the Childe from himself than in any of the preceding cantos, Byron carried his readers through the impressions of his journey, through Arqua, where he ruminated on "the bones of Laura's lover," along the "wide and grass-grown streets" of Ferrara, where "Tasso is their glory and their shame," and on to Florence, where the Venus de' Medici "loves in stone, and fills/ The air around with Beauty." Coming to Rome finally in the seventy-eighth stanza, he gave rein to his highest flights of fancy and of rhetoric:

> *Oh, Rome! my Country! City of the Soul!*
> *The orphans of the heart must turn to thee,*
> *Lone Mother of dead Empires! and control*
> *In their shut breasts their petty misery.*

During the first week of his Roman visit Byron had been deep in the revision of the third act of *Manfred*, and his mind had fed on thoughts of alternate unutterable longing and despair while he viewed the mementos of the glorious past of the ancient city. What had touched him most deeply, however, was the site of what was believed to be the valley of Egeria, the scene of his favorite Latin writer Juvenal's story of Numa and the fountain nymph." The immortal longings roused by the image of human love for a nymph, a goddess beyond the limitations of human frailty, now carried him out of himself in the most poignantly personal stanzas of *Childe Harold*:

> *Oh, Love! no habitant of earth thou art—*
> *An unseen Seraph, we believe in thee,—*
> *A faith whose martyrs are the broken heart,—*
> *But never yet hath seen, nor e'er shall see*
> *The naked eye, thy form, as it should be;*
> *The mind hath made thee, as it peopled Heaven. . . .*
>
> *Of its own beauty is the mind diseased,*
> *And fevers into false creation:—where,*
> *Where are the forms the sculptor's soul hath seized?*
> *In him alone. Can Nature show so fair? . . .*
>
> *Our life is a false nature—'tis not in*
> *The harmony of things,—this hard decree,*
> *This uneradicable taint of Sin,*
> *This boundless Upas, this all-blasting tree,*
> *Whose root is Earth—whose leaves and branches be*
> *The skies which rain their plagues on men like dew. . . .*
>
> *Yet let us ponder boldly—'tis a base*
> *Abandonment of reason to resign*
> *Our right of thought—our last and only place*
> *Of refuge; this, at least, shall still be mine. . . ."*

It was characteristic that Byron should have ended his flight on that note: he always returned from his most airy speculations to reason and common sense. Not that he was the happier for it; it was only an innate compulsion that drove him like the other forces beyond his control.

These nightly bouts with poetry—for he wrote best in the early morning hours—constituted his secret life and his greatest pleasure and gave a quiet satisfaction to his days in that felicitous July of his *villeggiatura*. Having purged himself in his nightly vigils, he could spend his days in the leisurely pursuits of a gentleman: rising late, making occasional jaunts to Venice to see Monk Lewis (who was staying on the Grand Canal), crossing in his gondola to the Lido and bathing in the Adriatic, and riding at sunset along the Brenta toward Dolo or paying visits to his neighbors. Then in the evening came two of the greatest pleasures, conversation and love-making. No one who saw him during the day could have guessed that after all became still in the empty palace he would be back again battling with the spirits of ancient Rome and his own aspirations and delinquencies.

Before the end of July, Monk Lewis had come to stay with Byron at La Mira. Despite the fact that he was a bore, Byron liked Lewis. Hobhouse, who had visited most of the important Italian cities on his return from Rome, going as far north as Turin, finally arrived at La Mira from Padua at half past eleven on the morning of July 31. Though it was before his usual rising-time, Byron gave him a hearty welcome.

"I saw my friend well & in spirits," Hobhouse wrote in his diary, "Mr. Matt. Lewis was in the house with him—and part of the same house was occupied by Signora Zagati [sic] of Venice the drapier's lady. . . . Signor Piero her husband visits her on a Saturday & Sunday & attends another lady." Byron, who apparently had not enough furniture in the great house to accommodate Hobhouse with sleeping-quarters while Lewis was there, arranged for him to stay with Marianna's friends near by. Hobhouse's diary continues: "B took me with him to the house of a physician where I am to have a bed—his four daughters & wife chatted with him & asked fondly after Marianna Mrs. Sagati [sic]—whose child is with them—This is a singular state for they seem modest though lively poor things. . . ." [n]

The next evening Byron, Lewis, and Hobhouse, together with Mme Segati, attended a party at a neighboring Jew's house, and the following morning Lewis and Hobhouse accepted an invitation to attend the ceremony of a circumcision in the same house (there is no record in Hobhouse's diary of Byron's attending—perhaps it was too early for him). Hobhouse was shocked to learn that "there was not a girl there who did not know what the child was to lose and more than one joked about the ceremony in my hearing." [n]

Hobhouse was shocked too when he heard that the *parroco* (parish priest) of La Mira "sent Me Zagati a present of figs—This to a woman living in open adultery is too bad even I think." [n]

Hobhouse generally dined with Byron, and afterward frequently rode with him along the Brenta. On August 5, "Hobby" recorded significantly: "passed the evening strolling about on horseback with B. and making assignations." Perhaps Byron was eager to help his friend to form as agreeable a liaison as his own. In the end, however, it was Byron who had another woman on his hands. As he described it some time later for John Murray and his friends, the fateful meeting took place in this wise:

"In the summer of 1817, Hobhouse and myself were sauntering on horseback along the Brenta one evening, when, amongst a group of peasants, we remarked two girls as the prettiest we had seen for some time. About this period, there had been great distress in the country, and I had a little relieved some of the people. Generosity makes a great figure at very little cost in Venetian livres, and mine had probably been exaggerated—as an Englishman's. Whether they remarked us looking at them or no, I know not; but one of them called out to me in Venetian, 'Why do not you, who relieve others, think of us also?' I turned round and answered her—'Cara, tu sei troppo bella e giovane per aver' bisogno del' soccorso mio.' She answered, 'If you saw my hut and my food, you would not say so.' All this passed half jestingly. . . .

"A few evenings after, we met with these two girls again, and they addressed us more seriously, assuring us of the truth of their statement. They were cousins; Margarita married, the other single. As I doubted still of the circumstances, I took the business up in a different light, and made an appointment with them for the next evening. Hobhouse had taken a fancy to the single lady, who was much shorter in stature, but a very pretty girl also. They came attended by a third woman, who was cursedly in the way, and Hobhouse's charmer took fright (I don't mean at Hobhouse, but at not being married—for here no woman will do anything under adultery), and flew off; and mine made some bother—at the propositions, and wished to consider of them. . . . She said that she had no objection to make love with me, as she was married, and all married women did it: but that her husband (a baker) was somewhat ferocious, and would do her a mischief. In short, in a few evenings we arranged our affairs. . . ."

There was a certain animal fierceness and passionate assurance about this girl, Margarita Cogni, that added to the charm of her beauty in Byron's eyes, and that soon gave her an unprecedented hold upon him. He was pleased and amused at her self-confidence and leonine aggressiveness. She was not too much perturbed by his liaison with Marianna or his later affairs with other women, and she openly boasted that he would always come back to her. Byron told Murray frankly that the reasons for her ascendancy "were, firstly, her person—very dark, tall, the Venetian face, very fine black eyes—and certain other qualities which need not be mentioned. She was two and twenty years old, and, never having had children, had not spoilt her figure, nor anything else—which is, I assure you, a great desideration in a hot climate where they grow relaxed and doughy, and flumpity a short time after breeding. She was, besides, a thorough Venetian in her dialect, in her thoughts, in her countenance, in every thing, with all their naïveté and Pantaloon humour. Besides, she could neither read nor write, and could not plague me with letters. . . ."

Signora Segati, Byron continued, "was silly enough one evening at Dolo, accompanied by some of her female friends, to threaten her; for the Gossips of the Villeggiatura had already found out, by the neighing of my horse one evening, that I used to 'ride late in the night' to meet the Fornarina. Margarita threw back her veil (*fazziolo*), and replied in very explicit Venetian, 'You are *not* his *wife*: I am *not* his *wife*: *you* are his *Donna*, and I am his *Donna*: *your* husband is a cuckold, and *mine* is another. For the rest, what *right* have you to reproach me? if he prefers what is mine to what is yours, is it my fault?'" [n]

Hobhouse was restless once more and wanted to travel to the Levant again, but was thwarted by the difficulty of finding safe transportation. In the meantime he settled down to observe Italian morals and politics. He quizzed Byron's mistress, Marianna Segati, and learned "that Cavalieri Serventi are often provided for in the marriage contract with nobles, and that the higher class may change these cavaliers often as they like—whilst those of her set can not have more than one except after a reasonable lapse." [n]

Lewis, who was still at La Mira regaling Byron and his company with stories from Holland House and elsewhere in England, had apparently carried to his host the gossip that the legal advisers of Lady Byron were saying that "their lips were sealed" concerning the cause of the separation. Byron, immediately suspicious that they were trying to imply that he had been responsible directly or indirectly for their silence, gave into Lewis's hands on the eve of the latter's departure for England a formal statement saying: "If their lips are sealed up, they are not sealed up by me, and the greatest favour *they* can confer upon me will be to open them." He expressed a willingness to cancel the separation and bring the matter before "any tribunal which may discuss the business in the most public manner." He asserted in a postscript: "I have been, and am now, utterly ignorant of what description her allegations, charges, or whatever name they may have assumed, are; and am as little aware for what purpose they have been kept back—unless it was to sanction the most infamous calumnies by silence." [n]

Before he left, Lewis read the manuscript of Byron's fourth canto of *Childe Harold*. Hobhouse had then heard only the first stanza, which he pronounced "Very good indeed." [n] But after Lewis's departure, Byron, finding that Hobhouse approved of this canto more than he did of the metaphysical one completed in Switzerland under the influence of his talks with Shelley, shared it with his friend and even added stanzas at his suggestion. Soon Hobhouse was engaged in writing notes on Tasso and later on Roman themes touched on in the poem. Stimulated by his rides at sunset along the Brenta, Byron added more stanzas.

Murray had finally sent copies of *Manfred* and *The Lament of*

Tasso (the latter was published July 17). Byron reprimanded him for giving no news of the public reception of *Manfred*. And in reply to other news sent by Murray, Byron wrote: "I have been very sorry to hear of the death of Me de Stael, not only because she had been very kind to me at Copet, but because now I can never requite her. In a general point of view, she will leave a great gap in Society and literature." ⁿ

Murray's request in another letter that Byron write for him a "civil and delicate declension" of a medical tragedy which Dr. Polidori had submitted to him elicited some rollicking verses from Byron:

> *Dear Doctor,—I have read your play,*
> *Which is a good one in its way,*
> *Purges the eyes, and moves the bowels,*
> *And drenches handkerchiefs like towels. . . .*
> *But—and I grieve to speak it—plays*
> *Are drugs—mere drugs, Sir, nowadays. . . .*
> *There's Byron too, who once did better . . .*
> *So altered since last year his pen is,*
> *I think he's lost his wits at Venice,*
> *Or drained his brains away as stallion*
> *To some dark-eyed and warm Italian. . . ."*

Having heard nothing definite yet on the efforts to sell New-stead, Byron was uneasy because Kinnaird, on whom he had counted to accelerate the business, was leaving for Italy. In the meantime, the August days passed pleasantly at La Mira. The rides to Dolo were interspersed with visits to neighbors along the Brenta. One of these, the Marquis Moncada, a Spaniard who had known Voltaire, was a stimulating conversationalist, and for lighter social pleasures they could spend an evening with the doctor and his four friendly daughters. Byron had his regular *amica*, Marianna, always at hand, and in the late hours the excitement of a rendezvous with the baker's wife, Margarita Cogni.

On weekends Signor Segati appeared regularly, not to disturb his wife's *servente*, but to court another lady near by, and incidentally to bring Byron and his guests the latest gossip from Venice. On Friday the 29th he told two "singular stories" at din-

ner, one of which particularly appealed to Byron for its revelation of the quality of Venetian life and morals. As Hobhouse recorded it in his diary:

"A Turk arrived at the Regina di Ungheria [*sic*] inn at Venice
and lodged there—he asked to speak to the mistress of the inn
a buxom lady of 40 in keeping with certain children & who had
lost her husband many years before at sea—after some prelimi-
naries my hostess went to the Turk who immediately shut the
door & began questioning her about her family & her late husband—She told her loss—when the Turk asked if her husband
had any particular mark about him she said—yes he had a scar
on his shoulder. Something like this said the Turk pulling down
his robe—I am your husband—I have been to Turkey—I have
made a large fortune and I make you three offers—either to quit
your amoroso and come with me—or to stay with your amoroso
or to accept a pension and live alone." " Hobhouse added: "The
lady has not yet given an answer, but Mᵉ Zagati [*sic*] said I'm
sure I would not leave my amoroso for any husband—looking
at B. this is too gross even for me." "

Byron, who had for some time been meditating a composition
of a new kind either in prose or verse which would embody
something of his own observation of Venetian life, had found
just the story to give corporeal substance to his inchoate impressions. On the ride and the moonlight walk, which according to
Hobhouse they took after dinner, Byron must have begun to fit
this story into the setting of his whole Venetian experience, for
in a few days he was at work on a mock-heroic poem that was
to open up a new vein of literary activity in him.

The course of that activity may have been guided accidentally
by the arrival on the scene early in September of William Stewart Rose, who carried magnesia and tooth-powder and certain
books for Byron from John Murray." Byron, in his days of fame
in London, had met Rose in Murray's office." Rose was a friend
and admirer of John Hookham Frere, who had just published a
clever mock-heroic satirical poem in the manner and meter of
Luigi Pulci, the fifteenth-century precursor of Casti " in the use
of the adaptable *ottava rima*." Frere's *Whistlecraft*, an imitation
of Pulci's *Morgante Maggiore*, the mock-heroic romance of

monks and giants, rambled with abandoned colloquial ease over diverse subjects, incidents, and characters. It was a style which had grown out of the temper and talents of Italian writers. Its lack of unity, its disgressions, its epigrammatic wit, its ironic deflation of sentiment emphasized in the punch-lines of the couplets at the ends of the eight-line stanzas, the conversational tone, the unheroic portraits of the characters, and the disarming realism of its interpretation of life made it an ideal medium for Byron's purpose. Perhaps Murray had already sent Byron Frere's book, but it seems more probable that either Rose or the Kinnairds, who arrived in September, brought it along and recommended it to his attention.[⁷]

The frank colloquial undress of Frere's verse must have had a special appeal to Byron, for he was always contemptuous of the canting generalizations and pomposities of English poetry. And he no doubt read with relish Frere's defense of the common vocabulary:

> Preserve with care your noble Parts of speech
> And take it as a maxim to endeavour
> To talk as your good mothers us'd to teach,
> And then these lines of mine may last for ever;
> And don't confound the language of the nation
> With long-tail'd words in osity and ation.[⁸]

Once having found the form, Byron went to work with enthusiasm, taking Segati's anecdote of the tolerant Turk as the bare bones of a story upon which to hang the amusing pageantry of Venetian life and morals as he had seen them during his months of residence in that fabulous island city. With one stroke he freed himself from the fetters of British propriety and the *Childe Harold* manner, and something of the careless and relaxed realism of his letters invaded his verse.

The beauty of this style of writing was that it was as leisurely as the country; whatever struck the fancy—description, cynical comment, sentiment, digressions of all kinds—was savored to the full as in a letter, and the story could wait. Having described the Carnival setting, Byron turned to the women who made the occasion so exciting.

> *Shakespeare described the sex in Desdemona*
> *As very fair, but yet suspect in fame,*
> *And to this day from Venice to Verona*
> *Such matters may be probably the same,*
> *Except that since those times was never known a*
> *Husband whom mere suspicion could inflame*
> *To suffocate a wife no more than twenty,*
> *Because she had a "Cavalier Servente."*

Then it seemed fit to describe the gondola, so convenient for assignations:

> *It glides along the water looking blackly,*
> *Just like a coffin clapt in a canoe,*
> *Where none can make out what you say or do. . . .*
> *But not to them do woeful things belong,*
> *For sometimes they contain a deal of fun,*
> *Like mourning coaches when the funeral's done."*

It was not until the twenty-first stanza that he introduced his heroine, Laura, who no doubt was a composite of Marianna Segati and other Italian women he had observed, with perhaps a dash of his new *amica*, the "Fornarina," the baker's wife.

> *She was a married woman; 'tis convenient,*
> *Because in Christian countries 'tis a rule*
> *To view their little slips with eyes more lenient. . . ."*

After her merchant husband sailed away Laura

> *. . . thought it prudent to connect her*
> *With a vice-husband, chiefly to protect her."*

And this gave Byron a chance to comment on the easygoing Italian acceptance of the extramarital relationship, and led naturally to a disgression on the charms of married ladies, who

> *. . . should preserve the preference*
> *In tête à tête or general conversation . . .*
> *Because they know the world, and are at ease,*
> *And being natural, naturally please.*

> *'Tis true, your budding Miss is very charming,*
> *But shy and awkward at first coming out. . . .*
> *The Nursery still lisps out in all they utter—*
> *Besides, they always smell of bread and butter."*

Freed at last from the inhibitions of England and the conventions of English modes of writing by this new genre, Byron felt that he owed a tribute to the Italian life and sunshine which contributed to his sense of emancipation.

> With all its sinful doings, I must say,
>   That Italy's a pleasant place to me,
> Who love to see the Sun shine every day. . . .
>
> I love the language, that soft bastard Latin,
>   Which melts like kisses from a female mouth,
> And sounds as if it should be writ on satin,
>   With syllables which breathe of the sweet South,
> And gentle liquids gliding all so pat in,
>   That not a single accent seems uncouth,
> Like our harsh northern whistling, grunting guttural,
> Which we're obliged to hiss, and spit, and sputter all.[n]

And the inevitable comparison with England followed, not without revealing in playful malice some of his deep-seated grudges against that island.

> "England! with all thy faults I love thee still,"
>   I said at Calais, and have not forgot it;
> I like to speak and lucubrate my fill;
>   I like the government (but that is not it);
> I like the freedom of the press and quill;
>   I like the Habeas Corpus (when we've got it) . . .
>
> I like the taxes, when they're not too many;
>   I like a seacoal fire, when not too dear;
> I like a beef-steak, too, as well as any;
>   Have no objection to a pot of beer;
> I like the weather,—when it is not rainy,
>   That is, I like two months of every year.
> And so God save the Regent, Church, and King!
> Which means that I like all and every thing. . . .
>
> Our cloudy climate, and our chilly women,
>   All these I can forgive, and those forget,
> And greatly venerate our recent glories,
>   And wish they were not owing to the Tories.[n]

With the same tongue-in-cheek banter, he recalled in the fiftieth stanza that he had not got on with the story. And so he proceeded for a time to detail the ups and downs of Laura's relations with her *amoroso*.

But, on the whole, they were a happy pair
  As happy as unlawful love could make them;
The gentleman was fond, the lady fair,
  Their chains so slight, 'twas not worth while to break them. . . ."

But soon another digression on the education of "mussul-women" gave Byron a chance for a sly gibe at the "Princess of Parallelograms," the mathematical Annabella.

They stare not on the stars from out their attics,
  Nor deal (thank God for that!) in Mathematics."

But once Byron took hold of the story, he brought it rapidly in the last few stanzas to its ironic and yet perfectly natural conclusion: Laura and the Count invited the husband in to talk the matter over; she put the husband in the wrong, but took him back quite calmly, while he and the Count remained good friends.

By October 10, Byron had finished his new poem," if such a poem could ever be said to be finished—as with *Childe Harold,* he added more stanzas later. On the 23rd he wrote Murray: "Mr. Whistlecraft has no greater admirer than myself. I have written a story in 89 stanzas," in imitation of him, called *Beppo* (the short name for Giuseppe, that is, the *Joe* of the Italian Joseph,) which I shall throw you into the balance of the 4th Canto to help you round to your money; but you perhaps had better publish it anonymously; but this we will see to by and bye." "

In the meantime Byron had been adding stanzas to *Childe Harold,* apparently shifting from the humorous poem to the serious one without strain upon his creative powers. Murray, who had been made cautious by the reaction to *Manfred,* had offered only fifteen hundred guineas for the new canto, a figure which Byron thought niggardly considering the sale of the third canto. He wrote with firmness to Murray on September 4: ". . . I won't take it. I ask two thousand five hundred guineas for it, which you will either give or not, as you think proper. It concludes the poem, and consists of 144 stanzas." The notes are numerous, and chiefly written by Mr. Hobhouse, whose researches have been indefatigable; and who, I will venture to say, has more real knowledge of Rome and its environs than any Englishman who has been there since Gibbon." " What galled him was that Murray had paid more for poems of writers who, he was sure, had less ability and popular appeal, and he cited the three thousand guineas Longman had paid Moore for *Lalla Rookh.*

But even as he labored to persuade Murray of the value of *Childe Harold,* the recurrent conviction came over him that he and all the modern poets had taken the wrong road. He wrote the publisher: "I am the more confirmed in this by having lately gone over some of our classics, particularly *Pope* . . . and I was really astonished . . . at the ineffable distance in point of sense, harmony, effect, and even *Imagination,* passion, and *Invention,* between the little Queen Anne's man, and us of the Lower Empire. . . . if I had to begin again, I would model myself accordingly." "

It is curious that Byron should have spoken thus at the very moment when he had discovered his own most original bent in *Beppo,* but he had not confidence enough yet in that vein and considered the new poem only a *jeu d'esprit* such as he had written in many a letter to Murray or Moore. He was thinking then rather of his own poems in the romantic style.

As usual, Byron's literary activities did not interfere with an active social life. William Stewart Rose had gone on his travels, but Byron had other English visitors during the autumn, and he had at last made the acquaintance of Richard Belgrave Hoppner, who had been British Consul in Venice since 1814. Byron had eschewed the Consul's society during his first months in the island city, preferring to cultivate that of the Countess Albrizzi and her circle of Italians and Greeks and to spend the rest of his time with the dark-eyed Marianna or the Armenians on San Lazzaro. He was shy of Englishmen, particularly those with official connections, who might be supposed to send frequent reports back to England. But sometime during the summer or early autumn he had met Hoppner and had been immediately captivated by his graciousness and his eagerness to be of service." The Consul was the second son of the famous portrait-painter John Hoppner, R.A. He himself had studied painting, was an amateur of the arts, and dabbled in literature. He had married a Swiss woman, whom Shelley later described as having "hazel eyes and sweet looks." " The Hoppners were no doubt proud of the friendship of the poet, and paid him the greatest deference, going out of their way to befriend him. Soon Byron was lending books to Hoppner, and the latter was handling a good deal of Byron's business for him, particularly when he was absent from Venice. Byron later said that Hoppner was "a good listener, and his remarks were acute and original; he is beside a thoroughly good man, and I know he was in earnest when he gave me his opinions." "

On Hoppner's invitation, Hobhouse and Byron set out in the latter's carriage at five thirty on the morning of September 11 to pay a visit to the Consul at his summer house at Este in the Euganean Hills between Padua and Ferrara. But they did not reach their destination. Since the only horses left by the Austrian troops could hardly crawl, they turned aside to visit the village and house of Petrarch at Arqua."

Not long after his attempted visit to Hoppner's villa at Este, Byron had, without seeing it, leased the house from the Consul for a two-year period." Perhaps the quietness of the village at Arqua had persuaded him. The Euganean Hills in the background would be preferable to the dusty road along the stagnant Brenta, and he could find more tranquillity there for a *villeggiatura* than in the empty palace in such easy proximity to Venice. It may be, too, that he wanted a place where he could, if he wished, escape from the too closely attached Marianna, whose friends at La Mira kept a watch on his movements. Fond of her as he was, there are indications that she was the cause of some vexations to him. On September 6, Hobhouse had recorded that "M⁰ Zagati [*sic*] in a jealous fit came after her husband from Venice at night—was stopped by thieves—thought nothing of it & on overtaking him flung a pair of scissors at him—she told this herself to us—she is so vindictive." She had found out that her husband had been maintaining some woman, Hobhouse continued. "She has cost B. about 500£ he says." [n] And not long after this, Hobhouse, then in Venice with Byron, wrote: "Find B in great tribulation and jealous about Mᵉ Z. [*sic*] to whom somebody, so she says, has been sending a billet doux." [n]

Hobhouse was still Byron's most trusted confidant. One evening at La Mira, Byron confessed his present feelings concerning Annabella. "B. talked to me about family affairs tonight," Hobhouse wrote in his diary on September 14; "he does not care about his wife now—that is certain." [3]

On the 17th, Byron and Hobhouse went to Venice to spend some days with Douglas Kinnaird and his brother when they should arrive. Hobhouse put up at the Gran Bretagna, and Byron went as usual to his rooms at the Segatis'. On the 19th, the Kinnairds arrived and sent for Byron, who saw them often during the next week. Byron took them to the Manfrini Palace to see his favorite Giorgione portrait, but mainly left Hobhouse to act as guide, joining them in the evening for dinner at the Pellegrino or another inn and taking them to the ballet afterward. One evening they spent at Byron's rooms, where they were entertained by Marianna's singing. But on the 27th, Byron returned to La Mira, leaving the Kinnairds to spend their last few days in Venice with Hobhouse. [n] They left on October 1, and Hobhouse remained several days, working diligently in the public library and the Apollo Library on his historical notes for the fourth canto of *Childe Harold*, and did not return to take up quarters with Byron again until the 14th.

For the next month the two friends lived a quiet country life filled with literary labors and pleasant diversions. There were some discomforts in the great drafty palace, but there were compensations in the evening rides in fine weather and in the conversations by the fire. On the 19th, a Mr. Joy and a Mr. Gregson from Oxford called with an introduction from Scrope

[3] This does not mean, however, that Byron had ceased to think of his wife, and in certain moods to imagine that he was still attached to her and that she had been cruelly unresponsive to his affection. An ever renewing spring of remorse mingling with the idealization of a lost past troubled his recurring recollections of her through the rest of his life.

Davies and were given a hearty welcome. And the following morning they had another visitor, an American whom Byron had seen last in London in the early days of his married life in Piccadilly Terrace. George Ticknor, who had spent the intervening months traveling in France and Germany, where he had studied at the University of Göttingen, was on his way home. Byron was particularly happy to get news of Goethe, with whom Ticknor had had several conversations at Weimar (much of their talk, indeed, was about Byron). Byron, Ticknor wrote in his journal, looked "exactly as he did in London two years and a half ago. In conversation he was more lively and various, and came nearer to what a stranger might expect from him, but still he did not attain it; for I have never heard him make one extraordinary or original observation, though I have heard him make many that were singular and extravagant. . . .

"His residence in Italy, he said, had given him great pleasure; and spoke of the comparatively small value of his travels in Greece, which, he said, contained not the sixth part of its attractions. Mr. Hobhouse had already told me of a plan formed by himself and Lord Byron to go to the United States, about a year hence. . . . Hobhouse, who is a true politician, talked only of seeing a people whose character and institutions are still in the freshness of youth; while Lord Byron, who has nothing of this but the prejudices and passions of a partisan, was evidently thinking only of seeing our Indians and our forests; of standing in the spray of Niagara; even of climbing the Andes, and ascending the Oronoco. They are now in all respects so different that I hardly think they will ever undertake the expedition. . . ." [n]

Byron was probably not in the best humor with either Goethe or Ticknor, for the latter had told Hobhouse, so Byron reported it to Murray, "that *Manfred* was taken from Goethe's *Faust*." Byron added impatiently: "The devil may take both the Faustuses, German and English,—I have taken neither." [n]

On November 1, Byron and Hobhouse made their long-delayed journey to Este to see the house that Byron had leased from Hoppner, starting at a quarter past six in Byron's carriage. They were not disappointed in the villa or its location. Hobhouse reported it "a beautiful place on a green knoll. . . ."

❧ *CLAIRE CLAIRMONT*

"LORD BYRON SHAKING THE DUST OF ENGLAND FROM HIS SHOES," BY MAX BEERBOHM

But Byron was destined never to live there. He and Hobhouse stayed a pleasant hour and then returned to La Mira, jogging along with four horses, "after a lovely agreeable day." "

As long as the weather would permit, Byron lingered on at La Mira, reluctant to leave the tranquillity of his *villeggiatura*. But in November the nights were chill in the drafty rooms of the old palace. On the 12th, Byron and Hobhouse spent their last evening at La Mira. And on the 13th they removed to Venice, where Hobhouse took up his abode in a house opposite Byron's in the Frezzeria.

Byron was now busy putting the final touches on the fourth canto of *Childe Harold*, which Hobhouse, who had resolved to return to England in a few weeks, would carry with him. In Venice they settled down to a new winter routine. Hobhouse rose early and worked on his notes, and then the two went in Byron's gondola to the Lido to feel the Adriatic breezes and watch the sunset on the lagoon on their return. Or they walked in the public gardens. In the evening they drank brandy and water in Byron's rooms or went to the San Benedetto Theatre to see one of Goldoni's plays." But the high point of the day was the gondola ride to the Lido. On the 21st, Byron's horses, and hay for them, arrived from La Mira and were ferried to the Lido.[4] From then on, the pleasure of their excursion was increased by a gallop along the sands of several miles each day.

Up to this point Byron, not having heard from Hanson, did not know whether any attempts were being made to sell Newstead. His only news was from Augusta, who wrote in such cryptic terms that he could not understand her. "If you see Augusta," he wrote to Kinnaird, "give my love to her, and tell her that I do not write because I really and truly do not understand one single word of her letters. . . . there is so much paraphrase, parenthesis, initials, dashes, hints—and what Lord Ogleby calls 'Mr. Sterling's damned crinkum crankum,' that,

---

[4] Hobhouse diary. Byron's horses on the Lido became a byword in the city. When Henry Matthews, brother of Byron's Cambridge friend, visited Venice in 1819, he recorded: "There are only eight horses in Venice: four are of brass, over the gate of the cathedral; and the other four are alive in Lord Byron's stable." (Matthews: *Diary of an Invalid*, 5th ed., Paris, 1836, p. 199.)

sunburn me! if I know what the meaning or no meaning is, and am obliged to study Armenian as a relief." [n]

But by December 10 he had received news of the sale of the Newstead estate to his Harrow schoolmate Major [afterward Colonel] Thomas Wildman for £94,500.[5] The first step, Byron wrote to Hanson, would be the liquidation of his debts, which he then proceeded to outline, as well as he could remember them. Besides the minority debts to moneylenders and more recent borrowings, he still owed Baxter the coachmaker £500 for the Napoleonic coach made for him just before he left England, and he was embarrassed by a letter from the Duchess of Devonshire concerning the still unpaid half-year's rent of the Piccadilly Terrace house." [n]

The prospect of clearing his obligations and having a fixed income after all the years of anxiety was a considerable relief and made him feel easier about incurring other responsibilities. He had finally written to Shelley that he was willing to undertake the care of his daughter by Claire, and had asked that she be sent under proper care to Italy. Shelley had written in July that they were considerably embarrassed to explain the presence of the child and had suggested that she might be put in the charge of two respectable young ladies at Marlow if Byron could make no immediate provision for her.

He wrote again in September after receiving Byron's commission to say that he expected to spend the winter in Pisa for his health's sake and that he would in that case bring Alba himself." [n] In weekly expectation of leaving England, Shelley did

---

[5] Hobhouse recorded the fact in his diary of Dec. 10, 1817. In addition to the purchase money, Colonel Wildman eventually spent upward of £100,-000 in repairing and improving the Abbey and the grounds (by 1832 he had spent £80,000 and the work was still going on—see Irving: *Newstead Abbey*, p. 60). Hobhouse wrote in his diary on Dec. 28, 1818, that Wildman was "the son of an attorney, with £10,000 a year. . . ." (Broughton, II, 108.) In 1860, Wildman sold the Abbey to William Frederick Webb, a friend of David Livingstone, the African traveler, and on Webb's death it was occupied by his descendants until it was purchased in 1930 by Sir Julien Cahn and by him presented to the Corporation of Nottingham to be used as a city park and museum. The Abbey now houses the valuable Roe-Byron library. (*The Roe-Byron Collection*, p. 20.)

not write again until December 17, when he reported that it seemed improbable he could leave soon for the Continent and asked Byron to make arrangements for his daughter's transportation. Claire had contemplated christening the child after herself, but, Shelley said, "she delays this *important ceremony* until I hear whether you have a predilection for any other name." [n]

After receiving this letter, Byron wrote to Douglas Kinnaird: "Shelley (from *Marlow*) has written to me about my daughter, (the last bastard one), who, it seems, is a great beauty. . . . will you think of some plan for remitting her here, or placing her in England? I shall acknowledge and breed her myself, giving her the name of Biron (to distinguish her from little Legitimacy), and mean to christen her Allegra, which is a Venetian name." [n]

During the last weeks of Hobhouse's stay in Venice, Byron led a more social life than he ordinarily cared for. He was developing a friendly feeling for Hoppner, the British Consul, as a sophisticated Englishman who had lived abroad enough to be a man of the world and who showed him deference without being obsequious or too curious about his private life. And toward the end of November the Countess Albrizzi returned from Paris, and Hobhouse and Byron attended some of her *conversazioni* again, where everyone sat in a circle and the conversation was generally dull.

The chill December days did not deter Byron from his daily gallop on the Lido sands. Riding always raised his spirits, and crossing the lagoon in the goldola with the towers of Venice making a fairyland in the mists of sunset primed him for dinner at the Pellegrino or at Hoppner's and an hour or so at the Albrizzi's, or conversation at home with Hobhouse. Byron and Hobhouse often went to the theater or the opera, mostly to see comedies or farces at the San Benedetto. On the 20th they were at the San Lucca and heard Sgricci, the *improvisatore*, again. On the 29th, Byron and his friend were in the Hoppners' box at the San Moïse and heard "gazza ladra made an opera by Rossini." [n] But toward the end of the year they spent more and more evenings in Byron's rooms going over the fourth canto and the notes to *Childe Harold*. Occasionally, however, Byron was otherwise occupied, for he still had Marianna to console his leisure hours. Hobhouse wrote significantly in his diary: "went to B. found him engaged in the old way." [n]

The two friends ushered in the new year in Byron's rooms, and one evening before Hobhouse left, Byron showed him the manuscript of a novel which he had begun—"he adumbrates himself Don Julian." [6] And they spent some time in plotting an epic for Byron to write, one of the subjects proposed by Hobhouse being the fall of the Goths in Italy.

On January 7, Hobhouse took his last ride with Byron on the Lido. In closing his diary for the day he wrote: "passed the evening with Byron, who put the last hand to his Childe Harold, and took leave of my dear friend, for so I think him, at twelve o'clock—a little before my going he told me he was originally a man of a great deal of feeling, but it had been absorbed—I believe the first part of what he said literally—god bless him." [n] The next morning Hobby left for England, carrying Byron's manuscript with him.

[6] Hobhouse diary, entry of Jan. 4, 1818. This story, which Byron later gave to Moore (in 1821 it had grown to nearly a hundred pages) was a transparent recounting of the separation with a Spanish setting, Lady Byron appearing as Donna Josepha. Moore quoted only three paragraphs of it (Moore, II, 522–3).

CHAPTER XIX

1818–1819

Venice, Palazzo Mocenigo, *Don Juan*

THE CARNIVAL began in January just after Hobhouse left Venice. Byron participated in it more wholeheartedly than he had the previous winter when he was amused by the spectacle but was still something of an observer. Then he had been too absorbed in the charms of Marianna Segati to do much philandering at the ridottos or masquerades. But now, though he still had his rooms at the draper's house in the Frezzeria, some of the *tracasseries* of this black-eyed girl—her jealousies and tantrums, as well as her inclination to make him jealous—were beginning to wear out the freshness of the liaison. According to Moore, what disillusioned him was the fact that she sold some jewels he had given her." Though he bought them back and presented them to her a second time, this was not the sort of thing that Byron easily forgot or forgave.

Relaxed and free as he now felt from obligations, Byron deliberately sought solace in the Carnival's adventures. Perhaps he wanted to break with Marianna because she was taking the affair too much *au sérieux,* or because he feared that he himself was doing so. Though he missed Hobhouse, a certain restraint fell from him with the departure of his balanced and sensible friend.

The Carnival had a special fascination for him because of its good-natured camaraderie and the romantic mystery stimulated by the masks. He later wrote nostalgically of it in a prose fragment:

"It is at this periodical Saturnalia . . . that all ranks are jostled, and mingled, and delighted, and all this without fear, observance, or offence. . . . There is a Masque, and recollect that it is a female, at every turn. . . . Curiosity is always excited, sometimes Passion, and occasionally Pleasure. If you do not always recognise, you are generally recognised. . . . Life becomes for the moment a drama without the fiction." [n]

Byron was already in a gay Carnival mood when he wrote to Murray, on January 8, a verse epistle full of wit and ribaldry:

> My dear Mr. Murray,
> You're in a damned hurry
>   To set up this ultimate Canto;
> But (if they don't rob us)
> You'll see Mr. Hobhouse
>   Will bring it safe in his portmanteau. [n]

And he concluded wickedly:

> Now, I'll put out my taper
> (I've finished my paper
> For these stanzas you see on the brink stand)
> Theres a whore on my right
> For I rhyme best at Night
> When a C——t is tied close to my Inkstand.
>
> It was Mahomet's notion
> That comical motion
> Increased his "devotion in prayer"—
> If that tenet holds good
> In a prophet it should
> In a poet be equally fair.
>
> For, in rhyme or in love
> (Which both come from above)
> I'll stand with our "Tommy" or "Sammy"
> But the Sopha and lady
> Are both of them ready
> And so, here's "good night to you damnee!" [n]

In the midst of the masking and the foolery, however, Byron found time to finish copying *Beppo*, which he sent off to Murray on January 19. *"Print alone, without name,"* he wrote; "alter nothing; get a scholar to see that the *Italian phrases* are correctly published, (your printing, by the way, always makes me ill with its eternal blunders, which are incessant), and God speed you." [n]

He wrote again on the 27th: "It is the height of the Carnival, and I am in the *estrum* and agonies of a new intrigue with I don't exactly know whom or what, except that she is insatiate of love, and won't take money, and has light hair and blue eyes, which are not common here, and that I met her at the Masque, and that when her mask is off, I am as wise as ever. I shall make what I can of the remainder of my youth, and confess that, like Augustus, I would rather die *standing."* [n]

Byron drew closer to Hoppner after Hobhouse left, and the Consul joined him on his daily gallop. During the Carnival, and for some time after its close, Byron continued his attendance at the Countess Albrizzi's *conversazioni,* which had been less dull of late because there were some new and not unpleasant faces there. He was sufficiently diverted to spare his friends any melancholy comment on the passing of his thirtieth birthday (January 22), which, had he been in another mood, might have aroused most bitter reflections. In his letter to Hobhouse the next day his observations were more objective than usual on such anniversaries. He had been to Mme Albrizzi's, he said, where he had met Count Rizzo [1] "and a lot of the learned (besides the prettiest girl I ever saw, half Greek, half French, a foreigner from Padua, for the Carnival)." [n] That same evening he met there another pretty young girl, a bride of three days from Ravenna, the Countess Teresa Guiccioli. He offered her his arm to go in to see the famous bust of Helen of Troy by Canova, but she was so weary from two days of traveling and so confused by her new status (she and her aging husband were on their honeymoon trip to Venice) that she scarcely noticed her escort and had to be told the next day that she

---

[1] Count Francesco Rizzo-Patarol, "a well-known Venetian gossip" (Origo, p. 92 n.), had met Byron and Hobhouse in 1817, and is frequently mentioned in Hobhouse's diary. Meneghetti (p. 97) calls him a *"viveur veneziano"* (sensualist, debauchee).

had met the famous English poet Lord Byron. And apparently she made little impression on him; [n] he was well occupied elsewhere and was not looking for new conquests. He had told Hobhouse: "I miss you damnably; there is no bad fun at the Ridottos, &c., this Carnival. I have lately (as a resource to supply your loss) taken again to the natives." [n]

In fact, Byron had been rather too "thoroughgoing" with some of the natives, for by the middle of February, just after the Carnival had ended, he had acquired, to his chagrin, the ancient disease of the votaries of Venus, which had not troubled him since his voyage home from Greece in 1811, when it had alternated with hemorrhoids and a tertian fever in tormenting his passage through "the gut of Gibraltar." In a letter to Hobhouse on February 23 he reported that Petritini, the Venetian censor, whom Hoppner and others had described as a great liar, had told him the truth in this respect—namely, that "Elena da Mosta, a Gentil Donna, was clapt, and she has clapt me; to be sure it was gratis, the first gonorrhea I have not paid for." [n]

But, though he was discommoded for a while, the illness scarcely interrupted his social pleasures, and within a week he was going to the opera and to *conversazioni*. Byron also found time to write some lines on the birth of Hoppner's son, [n] and, having heard a story that the gossipy Rogers was spreading about him, he wrote in a truculent mood to Murray: "He cannot say that I have not been a sincere and a warm friend to him, till the black drop of his liver oozed through, too palpably to be overlooked. Now, if I once catch him at any of his jugglery with me or mine, let him look to it. . . ." [n]

In the heat of his indignation at Rogers's scandalmongering, Byron dashed off some of the most caustic lines he ever penned:

QUESTION

Nose and Chin that make a knocker,
Wrinkles that would puzzle Cocker. . . .
Skin all sallow, flesh all sodden,
Form the Devil would frighten G—d in. . . .
Vampire, Ghost, or Goul, what is it?
I would walk ten miles to miss it.

ANSWER

. . .

That's the Bard, and Beau, and Banker. . . .
Mark that (as he masks the bilious)
Air so softly supercilious,
Chastened bow, and mock humility,
Almost sickened to Servility. . . .
You're his friend—for that he hates you,
First obliges, and then baits you. . . ."

But when Byron received a cordial letter from Rogers a short time after, his rancor subsided and he replied with an equal cordiality and an unreserve that showed no wariness. He kept the poem by him, however, for possible future use.

Byron's illness had temporarily stopped his daily rides, but he had at the same time extended his social activities. There were oratorios by Haydn and Handel at the San Benedetto, and sometime during the early months of the year he had become a regular attendant at the *conversazioni* of the Countess Marina Querini Benzoni, an aging beauty who refused to relinquish the gaieties of her youth and the illusion that at sixty she had the same charm that had captivated Venice and made her the toast of the canals.

According to the chroniclers of the time, Marina had joined with the young Ugo Foscolo in dancing clumsily about a liberty tree in the piazza in a spontaneous fête inspired by the French Revolution. She was dressed in an Athenian petticoat open along the flanks, with a vest which left her breast free, and a little cap on her disheveled short hair. She had also turned the head of Lamberti, who made her the heroine of the popular ballad *"La Biondina in Gondoletta."* "

The Cavalier Giuseppe Rangone had given up a diplomatic career to serve her, and remained her *cavalier servente* for thirty years, finally marrying her when he was nearing seventy. Though she had grown unseemly plump with advancing years ("like a gigantic sausage," says Meneghetti), Rangone "still considered her as a divinity" at the time Byron met her. When Byron one morning asked the cavalier how his mistress was, he replied with the one glowing word *"Rugiadosa"* ("Dewy")."

Despite her devotion to Beppe, as she called him, the Countess
Benzoni could not restrain herself from making amorous advances to the handsome young English poet. Whether, as the
scandalous chroniclers aver, she one day presented herself quite
nude before him, or whether she wooed him by subtler means, it
is certain that she did show a marked delight in his company.
The Cavalier Mengaldo later recorded in his diary: "*Mad. Benzon se rende ridicule par ses transports envers lord Byron.*" [n]
But she was good-natured and unaffectedly kind. Her *conversazioni* were more informal than those of the Albrizzi. In fact,
Meneghetti says that in passing from the Albrizzi salon to that
of the Benzoni, Byron took a backward step from the ideals
of his own life.[n] But Byron kept a detachment in his social
contacts which permitted him to maintain his own equilibrium,
and he never surrendered himself completely to any mode of
life or point of view not dictated by his inner urges and his
critical intelligence.

Stendhal later wrote that "the most brilliant salons of Paris
are quite insipid and *dry* compared to the society of Madame
Benzoni." [n] Byron enjoyed that society because he could be at
ease, but he had not given up his attendance upon the Albrizzi.[n]
It is true that he was a little annoyed that the Countess Albrizzi
wished to include a character sketch of him in a new edition of
her *Ritratti*, a portrait gallery of memories of famous men she had
known.[n] She threw out hints several times that she had written
one, and finally asked if he would like to see it, whereupon he
told her rather bluntly that he did not think she knew him well
enough to draw his portrait.[n] The "character" which she published after his death, however, was on the whole quite flattering
and often astute.

She wrote of his lameness: "His figure left nothing to be
desired, particularly by those who found rather a grace than
a defect in a certain light and gentle undulation of the person
when he entered a room, and of which you hardly felt tempted
to inquire the cause. Indeed it was scarcely perceptible,—the
clothes he wore were so long."

She observed in him "a constant, and almost infantine timidity . . . a sentiment which had the appearance of modesty."

Aware that in company all eyes were fixed on him, "he necessarily found himself in the situation of an actor obliged to sustain a character, and to render an account, not to others (for about them he gave himself no concern), but to himself, of his every action and word. . . .

"No one ever heard him utter a word of French, although he was perfectly conversant with that language. He hated the nation and its modern literature; in like manner, he held the modern Italian literature in contempt. . . ." [2]

It is not surprising that Byron turned to the natives after Hobhouse departed, for they were less inclined to obtrude into his private life. But he soon found that the Italians, at least their literary men, were curious in another realm where he was quite as touchy—namely, with regard to his poetry. Being rather disdainful of the modern Italian writers, he was loath to stand comparison with them. Having heard that an Italian translation of *Manfred* was being contemplated, he wrote to Hoppner in a great state of perturbation:

"As I did not write *to* the Italians, nor *for* the Italians, nor *of* the Italians, (except in a poem not yet published, where I have said all the good I know or do not know of them, and none of the harm,) I confess I wish that they would let me alone. . . ." [n]

When he learned that the most the translator could hope to make by his labor was two hundred francs, Byron offered him that sum to give up the project, but the Italian held out for more, whereupon Byron, according to Moore, "intimated to him pretty plainly" that "should the publication be persisted in, he would horsewhip him the very first time they met." [n] The translator then accepted the two hundred francs and signed an agreement never to translate any other of Byron's works.

Byron had an uneasy feeling among the literary men he met at the salon of the Countess Albrizzi, who was most assiduous in collecting men of letters. It was perhaps one reason for his gradual withdrawal from her *conversazioni*. He had been dis-

[2] Moore, II, 255–7; *LJ*, IV, 437–41. Writing to Rogers on March 3, 1818, Byron said: "I can read French with great pleasure and facility, though I neither speak nor write it." (*LJ*, IV, 209.)

appointed in Pindemonte and many others he encountered there. It seems likely that he had his eye as much on the Italian as on English writers when he wrote in *Beppo:*

> *One hates an author that's all author—fellows*
> *In foolscap uniforms turned up with ink,*
> *So very anxious, clever, fine, and jealous,*
> *One don't know what to say to them, or think. . . .*[n]

Pietro Giordani was an exception. Byron may have liked him because he was a good listener. At any rate, Giordani catered to Byron's whims and they got along swimmingly. At first Byron refused to be introduced to him and, according to Giordani, finally gave way only on condition that the conversation should not be "about his works, about poetry, or worst of all about the Romantics, whom he abominates! I kept the pact and our conversations were then so long and so intimate that the numerous assembly was surprised and amused." They spoke of politics in Italy and England, of Byron's travels, and even of his personal affairs. Byron showed Giordani Marianna Segati's portrait, and spoke to him of Annabella. "He exhorted me to settle in Venice, so that we could see each other often." [n] But Giordani left Venice, and they never corresponded.

Byron soon plunged with more recklessness than ever into new affairs with Venetian women. The middle- or lower-class Italian woman delighted him most—her flashing eyes, her frank abandonment to passion, her peasant humor. To indulge in promiscuous sensual pleasures with these women was for him a kind of revenge upon the cold and mathematical Annabella. Moore, prompted probably by the Countess Guiccioli, who in her apology for Byron took that view of his dissipations at Venice,[n] was only partly right in assuming that the failure of Mme de Staël's attempts at mediation with Lady Byron and his consequent desperation were the chief causes of his extravagances.[n] For it is apparent that he had a manifest delight in physical pleasures of a nature that to some of his friends, even to Hobhouse, seemed coarse or gross. His slightly sadistic love of boxing and his friendship with "Gentleman" Jackson and the fencing-master Henry Angelo and their pothouse cronies were perhaps remotely related to his penchant for the "fine animals" among the Italian women. But, whatever he may have said afterward in detailing these affairs to his friends in England, most of his liaisons and even his most casual encounters were lightened in his own mind at the time by a certain romantic aura.

Byron told Lady Blessington that the Italian women "are natural, frank, and good-natured, and have none of the affectation, petitesse, jealousy and malice, that characterize our more polished countrywomen. This gives a raciness to their ideas as well as manners, that to me is peculiarly pleasing; and I feel with an Italian woman as if she was a full-grown child, possessing the buoyancy and playfulness of infancy with the deep feeling of womanhood. . . ." [n]

The woman who had the strongest hold upon him at this time, for her liveliness as well as her voluptuousness and beauty, was Margarita [3] Cogni, the baker's wife. This girl, whom he had met in August during one of his rides along the Brenta, would not give him up when he returned to Venice. According to the Countess Guiccioli, she persuaded her husband to take a *"four"* (an oven) in the city so that she could be near Byron." [n] In describing the affair to Murray later, Byron wrote:

"I never had any regular *liaison* with her, but whenever she came I never allowed any other connection to interfere with her; and as she found herself out to be a favourite, she came pretty often. But she had inordinate Self-love, and was not tolerant of other women. . . . At the *Cavalchina,* the masqued ball on the last night of the Carnival, where all the World goes, she snatched off the mask of Madame Contarini, a lady noble by birth, and decent in conduct, for no other reason, but because she happened to be leaning on my arm." [n] When Byron reproached her, she had a ready answer. "I represented to her that she was a lady of high birth, '*una dama,*' etc." She replied: *"Se Ella è dama, mi (io) son' Veneziana"*—"If she is a lady, I am a Venetian." [n]

He described Margarita as about five feet ten inches tall

[3] This is Byron's usual spelling of the name. The commoner Italian form would be Margherita.

with a fine figure, "fit to breed gladiators from." ⁿ He had already grown tired of his first *amica,* and he soon gave Marianna her *congé.*⁴ It was probably his break with La Segati that hastened his search for another habitation. He liked expansive houses, and only his attachment to Marianna could have held him so long in his narrow quarters in the Frezzeria. Measured in English pounds, palaces were cheap in Venice. On March 25, after announcing to Hobhouse that his liaison with the Segati had ended, he added: "I have taken a Palazzo on the Grand Canal for two years. . . ." ⁿ But he failed to reach an agreement with the landlord, Count Gritti, and finally settled for a palazzo of the Mocenigo family, into which he moved sometime before the first of June.

The Palazzo Mocenigo, which he took on a three-year lease for forty-eight hundred francs (two hundred louis) a year, ⁿ was a massive gray building, relic of the days of the merchant princes, facing to the north just beyond the first sharp turn of the S-shaped canal, within sight of the Rialto Bridge and only a few hundred yards from the Piazza San Marco. The third palace, the one Byron occupied (they presented a solid face to the Grand Canal), was built after 1600. It had three floors above the damp and chilly ground floor, which opened out to the gondola landing. On the second of these upper floors was a great high-ceilinged drawing-room. Stone balconies overlooked the canal from each of the center floors. Dozens of rooms large and small made it possible for him to house a considerable number of servants and to entertain guests in a way that had been impossible in his smaller quarters in Venice.

There was an additional reason, however, for his taking larger quarters. He must make provisions for the accommodation of his illegitimate daughter, who was being brought out from England by the Shelleys. Though he tried to hide his paternal feelings under a cynical bravado, he was already beginning to display some impatience to see the child. He had confessed to Moore, while condoling him on the loss of his daughter: ". . . I am

---

⁴ On March 25, Byron wrote Hobhouse: ". . . my old 'relazione' is over, but I have got several new ones (and a Clap, which is nearly well at present)." (Unprinted passage, Murray MSS.; Hobhouse proofs.)

quite wrapped up in my own children. Besides my little legitimate, I have made unto myself an *il*-legitimate since (to say
nothing of one before),[5] and I look forward to one of these as
the pillar of my old age. . . . I have a great love for my little
Ada, though perhaps she may torture me like * * * * *
[Moore no doubt omitted here some bitter words about Ada's
mother]." [n]

A few weeks later he wrote again facetiously to Hobhouse:
"A clerk can bring the papers [legal papers to be signed in
connection with the sale of Newstead] (and, by-the-bye, my
shild by Clare, at the same time. Pray desire Shelley to pack
it carefully), with *tooth-powder, red only;* magnesia, soda-pow-
ders, tooth-brushes, diachylon plaster, and any new novels good
for anything." [n] In the meantime Byron was confirmed still more
in his resolve never to write directly to the child's mother by
a long, reproachful, and pathetically sentimental letter which
she sent on the anniversary of Allegra's birth, January 12. She
wrote wishfully, to reinforce her resolution to send her daughter
to him, and perhaps also consciously to appeal to his sympathies:
"I have observed one thing in you which I like; it is this: let a
person depend on you, let them be utterly weak & defenceless,
having no protector but yourself and you infallibly grow fond
of that person. How kind & gentle you are to Children! How
good-tempered & considerate towards your servants, how ac-
commodating even to your dogs! And all this because you are
sole master & lord; because there is no disputing your power
you become merciful & just. . . ."

At the same time she could not conceal her misgivings at
the thought of consigning the child to his care. "Poor little
angel! in your great house, left perhaps to servants while you
are drowning sense & feeling in wine & striving all you can to
ruin the natural goodness of your nature who will there be to
watch her. She is peculiarly delicate—her indigestions are frequent & dangerous if neglected. . . ." But she ended on a
pleasanter note: "What news shall I tell you? Mary has just
published her first work a novel called Frankenstein or, the

[5] A reference probably to his child by the chambermaid Lucy at Newstead
(see Chapter VI, pp. 165–6).

Modern Prometheus. It is a most wonderful performance full of genius & the fiction is of so continued and extraordinary a kind as no one would imagine could have been written by so young a person." [n]

The determined effort of this girl to get a hold upon his sympathy only strengthened Byron's resolution to get the child out of her hands without seeing the mother.

On March 11 the Shelleys left for Italy, taking with them Claire and Byron's daughter, together with an English maid and Elise, a Swiss nurse whom they had brought from Geneva in 1816.[6] Two days before their departure, on the 9th, Claire took the child and the two Shelley babies to the parish church of St. Giles-in-the-Fields, where her daughter was baptized "Clara Allegra Byron, born of Rt. Hon. George Gordon Lord Byron ye reputed Father by Clara Mary Jane Clairmont." [n] She thus joined her own name to the one Byron had chosen and made record of their relationship.

The Shelley party arrived at Milan on April 4 and remained there in the hope that Byron would come to meet them, but he would not stir from Venice. In the meantime the Shelleys were seeking a summer place on the Lake of Como. Not having heard from Byron, Shelley wrote again on April 13 to inform him that the "little girl has arrived here in excellent health and spirits, with eyes as blue as the sky over our heads." And with Claire's interests at heart, perhaps at her prompting, he added an invitation for Byron to visit them.[n]

Byron had no desire to renew on the shores of Lake Como the liaison which had discolored his memories of the lake of Geneva. He wrote rather sharply to Shelley, seeing Claire's schemes prompting him, and asked that he send the child on to Venice with a nurse; he was sending a messenger from Venice to conduct her.[7] Shelley felt constrained to defend himself and Claire.

[6] Claire Clairmont described Elise as "a very superior Swiss woman of about thirty, a mother herself." (Dowden, II, 190 n.) There is no record of her last name at this time. Later in Italy she married Paolo Foggi, for a time a servant of the Shelleys.

[7] Byron's letter has not been preserved, and its contents and tone may be reconstructed only from Shelley's reply. Byron's messenger was Francis

"You write as if from the instant of its departure all future intercourse were to cease between Clare and her child. This I cannot think you ought to have expected, or even to have desired. . . . I know the arguments present in your mind on this subject; but surely, rank and reputation, and prudence are as nothing in comparison to a mother's claims."

One aspect of his appeal, however, showed insufficient knowledge of either Byron or Claire. He said he had hoped Byron would accept his invitation. "Clare's pain would then have been mitigated by the prospect of seeing her child with you, and she would have been reassured of the fears which your letter has just confirmed, by the idea of a repetition of the visit. . . . You can stop when you please; and you are not so infirm of purpose that soothing words, and gentle conduct need betray you in essential matters further than you mean to go." [n]

It was always Shelley's weakness to assume that human nature was more amenable to reason than experience justified, and that the emotions can be put under rational control. Such advice could be given by a man who had seen no potential source of unhappiness in inviting his deserted wife to come and live as a friend with him and his mistress.[n] But Byron knew more of the world and of himself, as well as of Claire.

Claire wrote in her diary on April 21: "Letter from Albè. Nothing but discomfort. . . ." [n] Shelley, who had heard some account from a Venetian at the post office in Milan of Byron's dissipations and promiscuities in Venice,[n] urged Claire not to

---

Merryweather (Francesco in the legal documents from which most of the information about him comes). Byron had apparently come to know him through the recommendation of his valet Fletcher sometime during his first year in Venice. Byron purchased from this Englishman, who had a shop at the bridge of the Bereteri, a considerable quantity of produce, for which he paid 3,530 lire. Toward the end of 1817, Merryweather became entangled in difficulties with the authorities for having violated the laws governing the importation of large quantities of tobacco, and Byron, always generous in coming to the aid of tradesmen and especially of his countrymen abroad, loaned him 600 lire on December 12, 1817, to pay his fine. Byron also paid him generously for his services as a messenger to Milan. Later, on July 11, Byron, incensed by some unexplained "ingratitude" of Merryweather, brought legal action against him for the repayment of the 600 lire (with legal interest). (Olschki: *"Lord Byron a Venezia, Episodi e Documenti Inediti,"* pp. 442–5.)

part with Allegra on Byron's terms." But another letter from Byron in reply to Shelley's, couched in somewhat milder tones and promising that she should see her child again soon," softened Claire toward him, and she sent Allegra off with Elise and Byron's messenger on April 28." She took the occasion to send another letter to Byron: "Dearest and best I entreat you to think how wretched & lone I feel now she is gone and to write word that she is well the darling bird. . . . I have one favour to beg of you. Send me the smallest quantity of your own dearest hair that I may put with some of Allegra's in a locket. . . . My dearest Lord Byron best of human beings you are the father of my little girl and I cannot forget you." "

Poor Claire made it only too clear that she was still in love with Byron, and she was too blinded by her own feelings to realize what an impression this desperate pleading for a crumb of kindness would make. If she had convinced him that she was solely interested in the welfare of the little girl and was indifferent to him, he could much more easily have treated her with common courtesy and fairness. The knowledge that she was attempting to use Allegra as a wedge to force herself into his affections made it impossible for him ever to treat her with real kindness. Her attempt to play upon what she had observed and experienced of his weakness—his generosity and kindness to those dependent upon him—turned to hatred and cruelty any benevolent feelings he might have had toward her. He had not sought her favors in the first place, and he had not deceived her. He had never told her that he loved her, and had urged her against the liaison upon which she was determined. And now she tried by all the wiles of sentiment and sympathy to make him feel remorse for having wronged her. It was maddening, but his only recourse was silence.

When Allegra and her nurse arrived in Venice at the end of April or the first of May, Byron had not yet moved into his palace, and it is probable that the Hoppners kept her. As soon as he was established in the Palazzo Mocenigo, he brought his child there. The poor Swiss nurse, Elise, was probably more confused in that great mansion than was the child. She could speak with neither the English nor the Italian servants, and she no doubt gave an unfavorable report of the coming and going of Byron's mistresses and of his irregular hours. Claire had counted on Elise to keep her informed about Allegra, and the fact that she could not read the nurse's handwriting was a sufficient excuse to write to Byron again.

Byron had a growing fondness for his daughter, and his attachment was increased by the fact that she did not seem to resemble her mother. After Allegra had been with him three months, he wrote to Augusta: ". . . she is very pretty, remarkably intelligent, and a great favourite with every body; but, what is remarkable, much more like Lady Byron than her mother—so much so as to stupefy the learned Fletcher and astonish me. . . . she has very blue eyes, and that singular forehead, fair curly hair, and a devil of a Spirit—but that is Papa's." [n]

During the spring of 1818 the publication of *Beppo* and the fourth canto of *Childe Harold* in England increased Byron's literary reputation, while at the same time the former tended to confirm the stories that were steadily drifting back to London concerning his wild escapades in Venice (his own letters to his friends had been the basis of a good many of them). Murray published *Beppo* anonymously on February 28. On the 24th, Hobhouse had found the poem the topic of conversation already at Devonshire House. Caroline Lamb was shrewd enough, however, to guess the authorship.

In more solemn quarters the poem failed to amuse. Lady Byron wrote to her friend Emily Milner on March 19: "Beppo is just imported but not perused. The greater the levity of Lord Byron's Compositions, the more I imagine him to suffer from the turbid state of his mind. It was always so in his manners. I am told from credible authority that he is translating his own works into Italian and is living with a Venetian wife whose jealousy is extravagant, and probably contributes to his amusement while it flatters his vanity. . . ." [n]

But the good humor of the satire won over most of the critics. Jeffrey in the *Edinburgh Review* praised the poem and compared it to the lighter pieces of Prior, Peter Pindar, and Moore. [n] Byron, however, had been doing some reading in the Italian writers of mock-heroic verse and felt that they were the real precursors in the vein he had adopted from Frere. On receiving the news from Murray that Croker had divined the authorship, he replied: "Croker's is a good guess; but the style is not English, it is Italian;—Berni ⁿ is the original of *all*. Whistlecraft was *my* immediate *model!* Rose's *Animali* I never saw till a few days ago, —they are excellent."ⁿ But (as I said above) Berni is the father of that kind of writing. . . .

"If you think it will do *you* or the work, or works, any good, you may, or may not, put my name to it; *but first consult the knowing ones.* It will, at any rate, show them that I can write cheerfully, and repel the charge of monotony and mannerism." ⁿ

It was not because of the "monotony and mannerism" of the poem that Murray delayed the publication of the fourth canto of *Childe Harold,* however, but for other reasons. Hobhouse had delivered the manuscript to the publisher on February 4. Murray, he reported, "was in raptures," ⁿ but was not so enthusiastic about the lengthy notes which Hobhouse had concocted. Piqued at the slight to the learned commentaries on which he had put so much work, Hobby was inclined to withdraw them altogether. Byron protested:

"You have vexed me mightily about *your notes,* on which I depended seriously, and was quite anxious, though you thought the contrary. However, you must do as you like—only recollect that I protest against withholding the notes, and look upon myself as an ill-used gentleman." ⁿ Both Hobhouse and Gifford had read the proofs, and Byron accepted most of Gifford's suggestions for verbal improvements. But opposite Hobhouse's comment: "Recollect you have Nemesis again," he wrote: "I know it—and if I had her ten times I would not alter once. She is my particular belief and acquaintance, and I won't blaspheme against her for anybody." ⁿ

As it turned out, however, Hobhouse got into more trouble with his notes than Byron with his poem. Murray had finally consented to publish Hobhouse's contributions, and the fourth canto together with the notes appeared on April 28. About a month before that, on March 23, Hobhouse had met at a dinner in London the eloquent red-haired Italian patriot and exile Ugo Foscolo, whose autobiographical novel, *Le Ultime Lettere di*

Jacopo Ortis,[8] Hobhouse and Byron had read appreciatively. He was immediately taken with Foscolo's knowledge and eloquence, and as the Italian was about to publish a work on Dante, he gave him a puff in the notes to *Childe Harold*.[n]

Shortly after their first meeting, it occurred to Hobhouse that he might enlist the talents of Foscolo for the notes on the present state of Italian literature which both Byron and he had wished to incorporate but which neither felt capable of tackling. Hobhouse offered to pay the Italian exile, who was in financial distress, a substantial sum to write an extensive essay on the literature of his country for the *Historical Illustrations of the Fourth Canto of Childe Harold*, which Hobhouse now planned to publish separately from *Childe Harold*. Foscolo wrote the essay, but stipulated that the secret of his authorship should be kept. This unfortunate collaboration continued to plague Hobhouse, as did Foscolo himself with his appeals for money and his sensitivity.[n]

It was no consolation to Hobhouse that when Byron finally saw the *Illustrations*, it was Foscolo's work alone that he praised. In September Byron wrote: "I saw the other day by accident, your 'Historical, &c.' The essay is *perfect*, and not exceeded by Johnson's Poets, which I think the type of perfection." [n] Moreover, when Hobhouse became embroiled with Di Breme and other Italian literary men who were offended by Foscolo's essay, Byron took a devilish delight in passing on their letters. Apropos of Di Breme, he wrote Hobhouse: "Row him, I say, he gives you devilish bitter words, and I long to see you by the ears, that I do." [n]

Disinclined as Byron was to become involved in the literary controversies of the Italian coteries, he by no means eschewed Italian society. If he thought of the Albrizzi as the De Staël of Venice, the Countess Benzoni was to him "a kind of Venetian (late) Lady Melbourne." [n] And he had always felt relaxed with Lady Melbourne, news of whose death on April 6, 1818, had been a blow to him.

---

[8] This *Werther*-like novel appealed to Byron not only for its expression of the melancholy disappointments of love, but also for the Italian patriotism of the hero, who, like the author, had hailed Napoleon as a liberator and was bitterly disillusioned when he handed Venice over to the Austrians.

He had been thinking much about his old friend lately. And after her death he told Murray: "The time is past in which I could feel for the dead,—or I should feel for the death of Lady Melbourne, the best, and kindest, and ablest female I ever knew —old or young." ⁿ

Byron continued to find pleasure in the society of Hoppner and the select English and foreign guests who frequented his hospitable home. When Byron had recuperated from the Carnival, he and the Consul resumed their daily rides on the Lido. They were later joined by Alexander Scott, a young English bachelor of independent means, who lived at Venice.ⁿ

Byron dined with Hoppner often while W. S. Rose was in Venice, and at the Consul's on March 27 he met an interesting soldier who had been in the Napoleonic wars, the Cavalier Angelo Mengaldo.ⁿ An excellent swimmer, Mengaldo had once escaped from the enemy by swimming across the Danube. He was reserved, studious, and sensitively introspective. He, like Byron, had lived isolated from family life, and had suffered the tortures of an unhappy love. He had formed a hopeless attachment for Carolina, daughter of the noted Dr. Aglietti, and in his desperation had engaged in various philandering ventures which he tried to romanticize. He was a year older than Byron. His devotion to the memory of the fallen Napoleon, his republican sympathies, his interest in poetry, and his own literary ambitions all drew him to the English poet. But his self-consuming ego, too much like that of Byron, was a recurrent cause of friction between them.

For all that, Mengaldo did not cultivate Byron's acquaintance less assiduously. The latter's flirtation with Carolina Aglietti, which had driven the Cavalier to distraction shortly after he met Byron,ⁿ was a passing one, and perhaps did not extend beyond the conversation of an evening; he had plenty of other women to occupy him.

One evening at the Benzoni's, the conversation had turned on swimming, and Byron had not failed to vaunt his prowess in crossing the Tagus at Lisbon and the Hellespont. Mengaldo likewise was not silent concerning his swimming of the Danube and the Beresina under enemy fire. Before the evening ended they had agreed to enter into a swimming competition as soon as summer had warmed the water of the lagoon."

Byron had kept in natatorial practice. Even while he was at La Mira he had made frequent trips to Venice mainly for the purpose of taking a gondola to the Lido to swim in the Adriatic. After he was installed in the Palazzo Mocenigo, he often swam in the Grand Canal itself. The Countess Albrizzi recorded that he was once seen, "on leaving a palace situated on the Grand Canal, instead of entering his own gondola, to throw himself into the water dressed as he was and swim to his lodging. At night, in order to avoid the peril, which he had incurred on the preceding occasion, of being wounded by the thick oars of the gondoliers who were conducting their own gentlemen home in their fast pleasure-boats, so intolerant was he of every obstacle that he was seen to cross the same canal swimming with his right hand and holding up in his left a torch in order to light his way." "

The swimming contest with Mengaldo took place in June. In fact, there were two attempts; the first, on the 15th, seems to have been a practice or preliminary bout. On June 25, Byron reported to Hobhouse: "Since my last I have had another *swim* against Mingaldo, whom both Scott and I beat hollow, leaving him breathless and five hundred yards behindhand, before we got from Lido to the entrance of the Grand Canal. . . . I was in the sea from half-past four till a quarter-past eight without touching or resting. . . . [Scott] got as far as the Rialto, swimming well; the Italian miles behind and knocked up, hallooing for the boat." He added in a postscript: *"The wind and tide were both with me."* [9]

This was a triumph which, like his swimming of the Hellespont, Byron did not soon forget. Mengaldo apparently was not aware at the time of having acquitted himself too badly, for, though tired, he made a few visits in the evening and received

[9] *LBC*, II, 84–5. Byron could not refrain from boasting to Hobhouse that his feat was so much the more remarkable in that he had been debilitated by love-making. He wrote: "I could not be much fatigued, having had a *piece* in the fore-noon, and taking another in the evening at ten of the clock." (B.M., Add. 42093; Hobhouse proofs—unpublished sentence in letter of June 25, 1818.)

congratulations for his display of swimming skill, and, meeting Byron and Scott the same evening, he recorded having had from them "a new proof of friendship." [n] It was only later, when he discovered that Mengaldo was allowing his imagination to color the event in his own favor, that Byron spoke of him with some asperity.

Through the spring and summer Byron continued his escapades with Venetian women. One who pleased him particularly was an opera singer. Byron wrote Hobhouse with waggish glee on May 19: "Tell Ld Kinnaird that the lady to whom Vendiamini would *not* introduce him . . . within the last ten days has become as far as a Cappriccio—Roba mia. . . . She is the prettiest Bacchante in the world—and a piece to perish *in*. The Segati and I have been off these two months, or rather three. I have a world of other harlotry, besides an offer of the daughter of the Arlechino of St. Luke's theatre—so that my hands are full. . . . With regard to Arpalice Taruscelli (the madcap above mentioned) recollect there is no *liaison* only *fuff-fuff* and passades." [n]

However lightly Byron may have spoken of the affair, he cannot have treated the girl badly, for she continued to have a warm feeling of gratitude toward him for many years after.

Byron, once established in the Palazzo Mocenigo, began to live expansively and freely, as he loved most to do. Before long he had fourteen servants,[n] to whom he was so graciously lenient that they took advantage of him. Of all these, William Fletcher, who had been with him since before his first voyage abroad in 1809, and who continued to serve him as valet to the end of his life, was his only English servant and the one he indulged the most, though he loved to make sport of Fletcher's illiterate letters and his other foibles.

In the first exuberance of his residence at the Palazzo Mocenigo, Byron wrote Hobhouse a mock account of his own death as he supposed Fletcher might have written it.

"Sir,—With great grief I inform you of the death of my late dear Master, my Lord, who died this morning at ten of the Clock of a rapid decline and slow fever, caused by anxiety, sea-bathing, women, and riding in the Sun against my advice. . . .

"I saved in his service as you know several hundred pounds.

God knows how, for I don't, nor my late master neither; and if my wage was not always paid to the day, still it was or is to be paid sometime and somehow. You, Sir, who are his executioner won't see a poor Servant wronged of his little all. . . . His nine whores are already provided for, and the other servants; but what is to become of me?" [n]

Though Byron was detained in the city during the summer, waiting for the dilatory Hanson to bring the Newstead papers, when he would have preferred being in the country, the delight of his new quarters somewhat mitigated the chagrin. His mind stimulated by conversation or love-making, he generally finished off the night by writing. He concluded a long letter to Moore on June 1: "Good night or rather, morning. It is four, and the dawn gleams over the Grand Canal, and unshadows the Rialto. I must to bed; up all night—but, as George Philpot says, 'it's life, though, damme it's life!'" [n]

Except late at night, however, the Palazzo Mocenigo was not very quiet. Byron had always had a fondness for animals; it was not merely to be singular that he had kept a bear at Cambridge and a parrot in his rooms at the Albany. Now that he had plenty of room, he indulged his fancy by adding to his menagerie. Some time after he had been installed in his palace, he reported to Douglas Kinnaird: "I have got two monkeys, a fox, and two new mastiffs, Matz [Mutz] is still in high old age. The monkeys are charming." [n] These animals were kept on the ground floor where Byron could stop to watch them or play with them on his way to his gondola.

Despite some minor thievery and petty quarrels, Byron's servants were, for the most part, exceptionally devoted to him. Among his most faithful was Giovanni Battista Falcieri, commonly known as Tita, whom Byron took into his service as gondolier after he moved into the Palazzo Mocenigo. He belonged to a celebrated family of gondoliers in Venice, his father and brother being in the service of the Mocenigo family. Though he was of a kindly disposition and followed his master as faithfully as a dog (he later accompanied Byron to Ravenna and Pisa, and was with him in Greece when he died), his prodigious black beard gave him an unmerited reputation of ferocity and

probably accounted for the legend that he had stabbed two or
three people."

Through the spring and summer Byron's irritation grew at
what he considered neglect by his friends in England. Murray did
not reply to his letters and had given him no satisfactory account of the reception and sale of his poems. Newstead was sold,
apparently, but the bargain could not be closed until the papers
were signed, and Hanson was procrastinating as usual. And when
Byron wrote to Hobhouse and Kinnaird, both of whom were
becoming increasingly engrossed in English politics, he got no
answer. When Hanson's son Charles finally wrote that they were
sending a messenger to Geneva with the papers, Byron lost his
temper. "I was paralysed yesterday," he wrote Hobhouse on
April 17, ". . . by a letter from young Spooney, containing the
news of a messenger for *Geneva,* and desiring me to repair
there!!! . . . I need hardly add that the messenger should be
directed to go on to Venice—if not, he may go to Hell." "

His indignation overflowed into almost every letter he sent to
England for the next two months. The savagery of his mood
and his disgust with all things English did not make him respond
favorably to Murray's plea that he spare Sotheby because he
was an "amiable man." He still believed Sotheby the author of
the anonymous letter he had received at Rome concerning *The
Prisoner of Chillon,* "telling me that out of ten things eight were
good for nothing." " Even after Sotheby's denial, Byron would
not relent or consent to modify the satire on him in *Beppo.*

He was still inclined to savage plain speaking about his English contemporaries when he wrote to Moore on June 1. Something Moore had told him of Hunt touched the springs of an
irritation he had hitherto suppressed in the knowledge that Hunt
had paid him considerable deference and befriended him at the
time of the separation: "He is a good man, with some poetical
elements in his chaos; but spoilt by the Christ-Church Hospital [1]
and a Sunday newspaper,—to say nothing of the Surrey gaol,

[1] Hunt got his early education at the famous charity school of Christ's
Hospital, where he followed Lamb and Coleridge. Byron no doubt associated
the "Bluecoat" boys with the so-called "Cockney School" of poetry.

which conceited him into a martyr. But he is a good man. When I saw *Rimini* in MS., I told him that I deemed it good poetry at bottom, disfigured only by a strange style. His answer was, that his style was a system, or *upon system*, or some such cant; and, when a man talks of system, his case is hopeless. . . ." [n]

Byron was vexed with Murray on several accounts. Worst of all was Murray's "horrid stillness" concerning the reception of his "Poeshie" by the English public, a silence which made him fear the worst. On June 28 he wrote Murray threatening to give his future work to Longman. [n] Two days later he wrote again: "I will wait ten days longer; if by that time I do not hear from you, you will then receive the last letter to be addressed to you from me." [n]

Characteristically, however, all Byron's malice melted when he finally heard from Murray. A thousand guineas deposited to his account eased his mind, [n] but he was still anxious about the Newstead sale. On July 10 he asked Murray to have Hobhouse and Kinnaird "expedite" Hanson and then turned to literary matters (he had forgotten all about his threat to take his work to another publisher):

"Your projected editions for November had better be postponed, as I have some things in project, or preparation, that may be of use to you, though not very important in themselves. I have completed an Ode on Venice; [n] and have two Stories, one serious and one ludicrous (*à la Beppo*), not yet finished, and in no hurry to be so." [n] This seems to be Byron's first hint that he was already at work on *Don Juan*, the first canto of which he finished in September. [n] The success of *Beppo* encouraged him to continue mining so rich a vein, and he had been studying the Italian models of the mock-heroic style. He had also essayed something in prose, which had several times tempted him, but in this as in his verse he was determined to leave fiction for reality.

"I think of writing (for your full edition) some memoirs of my life, to prefix to them, upon the same model (though far enough, I fear, from reaching it) as that of Gifford, Hume, etc.; and this without any intention of making disclosures or remarks upon living people, which would be unpleasant to them: but I think it might be done, and well done. However, this is to be considered." [2]

If Byron had any regrets for the sale of Newstead, they were now buried in his determination not to return to England. He had written feelingly to Hanson protesting against its sale when he was in Greece in 1811, saying that if it was sold he would remain abroad. It may be surmised that part of his anxiety to conclude the bargain with Major Wildman stemmed from the pain of parting with a property that held so many memories of his youth, and which he had early associated with the pride of his ancestry and dreams of an expansive baronial life. Augusta, who still had sentimental recollections of Newstead, and had always protested against his intention to sell it, now felt herself so cut off from her brother that she did not remonstrate with him.

The sale of the Abbey revived memories also in one who had never up to this time seen it—in Lady Byron herself. Byron would no doubt have been gratified had he known that indirectly he had stirred what he considered the hard and unrelenting soul of Annabella. Murray had sent her an advance copy of the last canto of *Childe Harold*. Despite the fact that she knew that the imprecation, supposedly spoken in the Colosseum, was aimed at her, and despite all her resolutions to be indifferent, she was touched by it. She read the lines:

> But there is that within me that shall tire
> Torture and Time, and breathe when I expire. . . ."

And she wrote: "The passage was probably intended to make a great impression on *me*." In fact, it did. A few days later she

[2] *LJ*, IV, 246. Letter of July 10, 1818. This was the beginning of the famous "Memoirs," which Byron gave later to Moore, which Moore sold to Murray, and which were finally burned in Murray's office after Byron's death. On August 26, Byron wrote: "You may go on with your edition, without calculating on the Memoir, which I shall not publish at present. . . . I shall keep it among my papers. . . . The Memoir is already above forty-four sheets of very large, long paper, and will be about fifty or sixty; but I wish to go on leisurely. . . . it is full of many passions and prejudices, of which it has been impossible for me to keep clear:—I have not the patience." (*LJ*, IV, 251.)

was "well, but very *weak.* . . . The new canto is beautiful indeed." Her distress was increased by letters from the Montgomerys, who had seen Byron in Venice and reported him, with malicious delight, "Extremely fat . . . bloated and heavy"; "His face is much more like a full moon than ever *yours* was." Restless and unhappy, she fled from Kirkby and paid a visit to the Abbey, from which Byron had proposed to her in the days when he had filled all her life with romantic dreams."

Annabella spent the greater part of the summer at Seaham, steeping herself again in poignant memories. She could not escape the force of *Childe Harold.* That last canto haunted her. She wrote in her secret book: ". . . may not each of the children of passion at least, feel that he understands the nature of the confession so much more intimately than the colder multitude, that to him it is really private? It conveys a mystical sense—so I have felt." "

Cut off as he felt himself from England and his English friends, Byron took his pleasures as they came, and they came in droves of dark-eyed beauties eager for his attentions, some of them for gain, for he had a reputation for generosity, but more for the singular attraction of his person, which, despite his growing obesity, still appealed strongly to women of all sorts. Moreover, he showed a peculiar deference to the sex; there was a subtle, almost womanly gentleness in his manner, of which his cynical letters to his English friends gave no inkling. J. Cordy Jeaffreson observed shrewdly: "Less harm would have come to him from the creatures, who composed the vagrant harem of the Palazzo Mocenigo, had he possessed the cynical hardness and spiritual grossness to think of them as animals, differing from the brutes only in shape and speech. . . . However dissolute she might be, the woman he regarded with passion became for a moment the object of an affection that was no less tender than transient." "

What Byron was inclined to be rather callous about, however, was the jealousy engendered in his harem. The Fornarina was unrestrainedly ferocious in her handling of any rival who came in her way, but Byron rather admired the leonine directness of her prowess. Other intriguers caused him more trouble. He wrote to Murray in August:

"Tell young Hammond that his *Dama*—the Countess S^a [3] fell into my hands after his departure, that the consequence was a violent quarrel between her and the Taruscelli, who, finding us out, has been playing the devil . . . and, by means of espionage and anonymous letters, doing a world of mischief. . . ." [n]

It was the éclat of these scandals which reverberated through the canals and caused this *"stravagante"* English lord to be talked of even by the gondoliers. English visitors were still consumed with a morbid eagerness to see him. Hoppner recalled that some of them "under pretext of seeing his house . . . contrived to obtain admittance through the cupidity of his servants, and with the most barefaced impudence forced their way even into his bedroom, in the hopes of seeing him." [n]

It is no great wonder, then, that he avoided the English when he met them in an occasional Venetian *conversazione*. He was aware, for one thing, of the sort of stories they carried back to England. A typical account is one recorded in Lord Glenbervie's diary in the autumn of 1818. Glenbervie had met at dinner a Mrs. and Miss Leycester. They had been to Venice, "and confirm the multiplied anecdotes of Lord Byron's metamorphoses into a fat, fat-headed, middle-aged man, slovenly to the extreme, unkempt, with long, untied locks that hang down on his shoulders,[4] shabbily dressed . . . when they were presented to him, as his country-folk direct from England, not uttering a word, but immediately flinging himself into an armchair with his back to them and the greatest part of the company." [n]

Aside from the irritations caused by English visitors, however, Byron was well contented with his life in Venice. Writing to Wedderburn Webster at the end of the summer, he expressed general satisfaction with his situation. The sale of Newstead

[3] Possibly the Countess Santa. In a letter to Hobhouse and Kinnaird written on January 19, 1819, Byron mentions "the Santa" as one of the many women he has had in Venice during the past year. (Murray MSS.; Hobhouse proofs.)

[4] The portrait drawing by George Henry Harlow, dated by Byron "A[gost]o 6, 1818," shows him with his hair, curly and unkempt, hanging down over his open collar. At about the same time Harlow made a drawing of Margarita Cogni, which, after the painter's death in 1819, Murray bought from his effects as a specimen of the Italian beauties, paying a good price for it because Byron's autograph was on it. (*LJ*, IV, 327-8.)

would make him independent, far more so than if he had remained in England. "There is (as is usually said) a great advantage in getting the water between a man and his embarrassments. . . . In the two years I have been at Venice I have spent
about *five* thousand pounds, and I need not have spent a *third*
of this, had it not been that I have a passion for women which
is expensive in its variety every where, but less so in Venice
than in other cities. . . . more than half was laid out in the
Sex;—to be sure I have had plenty for the money, that's certain
—I think at least two hundred of one sort or another—perhaps
more, for I have not lately kept the recount." [5]

Comfortable as Byron was in his palace, he realized that it
was hardly the place to bring up a daughter. Elise, the Swiss
nurse of the little Allegra, had sent several disquieting reports
to the child's mother, who had accompanied the Shelleys to the
Bagni di Lucca. She may have told Claire something of the
quarreling servants and mistresses at the Palazzo Mocenigo. It
is possible too that Elise herself became involved in some of
the quarrels and neglected her charge. At any rate, in the early
days of August, whether at the suggestion of the Consul and
his wife or by Byron's own request it is not clear, Allegra and
her nurse were taken in by the Hoppners. The proposal was
perhaps prompted by friendship for Byron, or an offer of money,
or both, for the Consul later wrote that Allegra "was not by
any means an amiable child, nor was Mrs Hoppner or I particularly fond of her. . . ." [n]

It was, however, probably the news that Allegra was no longer
living under her father's roof, but had been sent among strangers,
that upset her mother particularly. She received a letter from
Elise on August 14 and another on the 16th, and on the 17th
she and Shelley left suddenly for Venice. [n] They arrived at midnight on August 22. The first plan was for Claire to remain at
Padua while Shelley negotiated with Byron. But her impatience

[5] *LJ*, IV, 254–6. Letter of Sept. 8, 1818. The part of this last sentence beginning "I think at least two hundred," which was omitted in *LJ*, is supplied
here from the original letter in the Murray MSS. Not all Byron's "charity"
was bestowed on women, however. Hoppner recalled that Byron "sent fifty
louis-d'or to a poor printer whose house had been burnt to the ground, and
all his property destroyed." (Moore, II, 265–6.)

to get firsthand news of Allegra and the intolerable thought of waiting in a strange city alone caused her to venture into Venice with Shelley.

They went directly to the Hoppners', where they saw Allegra "so grown you would hardly know her," Shelley wrote Mary; "she is pale and has lost a good deal of her liveliness, but is as beautiful as ever, though more mild. The account they gave of Albè unfortunately corresponds too justly with most of what we have heard, though doubtless with some exaggeration." It was agreed that Claire's presence in Venice should be kept from Byron.

At three in the afternoon Shelley ventured to call on Byron at the Palazzo Mocenigo. ". . . he was delighted to see me," he reported to Mary, "and our first conversation of course consisted in the object of my visit. The success of this is yet doubtful, though certainly the spirit in which he receives the request, and the anxiety he shows to satisfy us and Clare, is very unexpected."[n]

Despite the fact that Shelley would have preferred to return to Claire, Byron insisted on taking him to the Lido in his gondola, where they rode their horses along the sands while talking. Byron was in an excellent mood. Shelley always stimulated him to the height of his powers. Though Byron loved to twit him on his atheistic views and his transcendental notions, Shelley too was delighted with the conversation and the ride, and later made a poetic record of it in *Julian and Maddalo*. In the preface he spoke of Count Maddalo (Byron) as "a person of the most consummate genius, and capable, if he would direct his energies to such an end, of becoming the redeemer of his degraded country. But it is his weakness to be proud. . . . in social life no human being can be more gentle, patient, and unassuming than Maddalo. He is cheerful, frank, and witty. His more serious conversation is a sort of intoxication; men are held by it as by a spell." [n]

As they crossed the lagoon on their return to Venice, the sun's last rays empurpled the backdrop of the magic isles and the distant peaks of the Euganean Hills. Maddalo (Byron) commanded the gondoliers to stop rowing and pointed out to Julian

⫷ PERCY BYSSHE SHELLEY

)❧ *MARY SHELLEY*

(Shelley) a madhouse and its belfry tower, which pealed out at that hour to call the madmen to Vespers. To Julian's indignant objection to making madmen pray, Maddalo replied:

"And this must be the emblem and the sign
Of what should be eternal and divine!—
And like that black and dreary bell, the soul,
Hung in a heaven-illumined tower, must toll
Our thoughts and our desires to meet below
Round the rent heart and pray—as madmen do. . . ." [n]

When they returned to Byron's palace, the conversation continued until the small hours of Monday morning. Claire had been waiting for Shelley since three o'clock Sunday afternoon. But he had an optimistic report when he wrote to Mary at five in the morning on his return. Byron had generously offered Shelley and his family the use of his villa at Este, where Allegra could visit her mother.[n] Shelley urged Mary to come immediately to Este, where he and Claire and Allegra would meet her.[n] Meanwhile, the Hoppners took care of Claire and concealed from Byron the knowledge of her presence in Venice. The next day Shelley called on Byron again. While waiting for his host, he played with Allegra, who, it seems, Byron had sent for, not knowing that Shelley had already seen her at the Hoppners'.[n]

When Byron entered, the conversation returned to the discussion of the day before on free will and destiny, and Julian maintained stoutly:

                              "it is our will
That thus enchains us to permitted ill—
We might be otherwise—we might be all
We dream of happy, high, majestical. . . ."
"Ay, if we were not weak—and we aspire
How vainly to be strong!" said Maddalo:
"You talk Utopia." [n]

Meanwhile, during the first three weeks of September, Byron was absorbed in the writing of the first canto of a new poem which he had started in July. On September 19 he wrote to Moore:

"I have finished the first canto (a long one, of about 180

octaves) of a poem in the style and manner of *Beppo*, encouraged by the good success of the same. It is called *Don Juan*, and is meant to be a little quietly facetious upon every thing. But I doubt whether it is not—at least, as far as it has yet gone —too free for these very modest days. However, I shall try the experiment, anonymously; and if it don't take, it will be discontinued. It is dedicated to Southey in good, simple, savage verse, upon the Laureat's politics, and the way he got them." [n]

Byron had great plans already for his new poem, and he wrote both the first canto and the dedication *con amore* and with more seriousness of intention than he was willing to acknowledge until he saw how it would go with the public. There was a certain defiance in his choosing the legendary devil's disciple and heartless rake Don Juan for the hero of his mock-heroic epic, and he found additional sport and ironic force in reversing his protagonist's traditional character and making him an innocent creature of circumstances with a well-meaning naïveté akin to that of Candide.[6]

Byron's accumulated observations of the farcical freedoms of Italian manners and his own contacts with the frailties of Venetian women gave him ample background for the rollicking bedroom comedy that is the climactic episode of the first canto, but what he wrote with the most exquisite relish was the description of Don Juan's mother, Donna Inez, a transparent portrait of Lady Byron.

The old festering sore was not healed, and it frequently generated poison in his system and ruined his pleasure. Boasting to Moore of his leonine Venetian mistress, with "a face like Faustina's, and the figure of a Juno—tall and energetic as a Pythoness, with eyes flashing, and her dark hair streaming in the moonlight—one of those women who may be made any thing," he wrote, "I am sure if I put a poniard into the hand of this one, she would plunge it where I told her,—and into *me*, if I offended her. I like this kind of animal, and am sure that I should have preferred Medea to any woman that ever breathed." [n]
But at this point he was reminded again of that other cruel

[6] Byron was familiar with the Don Juan legend; and he could have seen Mozart's *Don Giovanni* in Venice.

woman of Greek mythology, Clytemnestra, to whom he had compared his implacable wife, and in bitterness he wrote: "I could have forgiven the dagger or the bowl,—any thing, but the deliberate desolation piled upon me, when I stood alone upon my hearth, with my household gods shivered around me.* * " Do you suppose I have forgotten it? It has comparatively swallowed up in me every other feeling, and I am only a spectator upon earth, till a tenfold opportunity offers." "

Though the whole portrait of Annabella as Donna Inez is painted in the spirit of amusing caricature, the barb of bitterness is detectable in it:

> *Her favourite science was the mathematical,*
> *Her noblest virtue was her magnanimity. . . ."*

Her learning and her prim perfection were themes of several stanzas:

> *Her thoughts were theorems, her words a problem,*
> *As if she deemed that mystery would ennoble 'em. . . .*
> *Some women use their tongues—she looked a lecture,*
>   *Each eye a sermon, and her brow a homily. . . .*
> *To others' share let "female errors fall,"*
> *For she had not even one—the worst of all."*

But since "perfection is/ Insipid in this naughty world of ours," her husband, Don Jose, "like a lineal son of Eve,/ Went plucking various fruit without her leave." " This part of the satire reached a climax in the couplet:

> *But—Oh! ye lords of ladies intellectual,*
> *Inform us truly, have they not hen-pecked you all?* "

When Donna Inez took charge of Juan's education, however, she became in Byron's mind a combination of his mother and Lady Byron. She decided that he should be "quite a paragon," but the problem was to keep his breeding "strictly moral."

> *He learned the arts of riding, fencing, gunnery,*
> *And how to scale a fortress—or a nunnery. . . .*
> *Arts, sciences—no branch was made a mystery*
> *To Juan's eyes, excepting natural history.*

His classic studies made a little puzzle,
  Because of filthy loves of gods and goddesses,
Who in the earlier ages raised a bustle,
  But never put on pantaloons or bodices. . . ."

This description of the early training of Juan prepared for the scene of the innocent seduction of the sixteen-year-old boy by Donna Julia, married and twenty-three—one of the most amusing and realistic seduction scenes in literature. And there was a half-serious puritan remorse—a curious and not infrequent alloy of his libertine cynicism—in his exclamation:

Oh Plato! Plato! you have paved the way,
  With your confounded fantasies, to more
Immoral conduct by the fancied sway
  Your system feigns o'er the controlless core
Of human hearts, than all the long array
  Of poets and romancers:—You're a bore,
A charlatan, a coxcomb—and have been,
At best, no better than a go-between."

As for Julia,

A little still she strove, and much repented,
  And whispering "I will ne'er consent"—consented."

The dedication of the poem was an afterthought, but motivated by as lively an animus as that which had put barbs in his satire on his wife. Sometime during the late summer Byron had learned, perhaps from an English visitor,[7] that Robert Southey, the Laureate, had been spreading stories about him. Always sensitive and suspicious about what was being said of him in England, he was still hot with indignation when he wrote to Hobhouse some weeks later:

"The son of a bitch on his return from Switzerland, two years ago, said that Shelley and I 'had formed a League of Incest, and practised our precepts with, &c.' He lied like a rascal, for they *were not sisters,* one being Godwin's daughter by Mary Wollstonecraft, and the other the daughter of the present Mrs. G. by a *former* husband. . . . He lied in another sense, for there

---

[7] It is not impossible that Shelley, who was also involved in the scandal spread by Southey, brought the gossip with him from England.

was no promiscuous intercourse, my commerce being limited to the carnal knowledge of the Miss C. I had nothing to do with the offspring of Mary Wollstonecraft; which Mary was a former love of Southey's, which might have taught him to respect the fame of her daughter." [n]

The dedication itself was no less bitter because it was phrased in a clever and humorous rhyme. He referred familiarly to "Bob Southey," the Poet Laureate, as an "Epic Renegade," and his irritation with Coleridge, who, he heard, had spread Southey's story, caused him to lump all the "Lakers" together, as turn-coats who had gone back to Toryism:

> *And Coleridge, too, has lately taken wing,*
> * But like a hawk encumbered with his hood,—*
> *Explaining Metaphysics to the nation—*
> *I wish he would explain his Explanation. . . .*
> *And Wordsworth, in a rather long "Excursion,"*
> * (I think the quarto holds five hundred pages),*
> *Has given a sample from the vasty version*
> * Of his new system to perplex the sages. . . .*
> *And he who understands it would be able*
> *To add a story to the Tower of Babel.*

Still he conceded:

> *You're shabby fellows—true—but poets still,*
> *And duly seated on the Immortal Hill.*[n]

But he was not so indulgent to the apostate apologist for kings and tyrants, Southey, the "Tory, ultra-Julian." [n] He was to be classed with "the intellectual eunuch Castlereagh," the "vulgarest tool that Tyranny could want." [n] He was happy to make "Southey" rhyme with "mouthy," [n] and as alternate rhymes to the ones on Castlereagh he wrote:

> *Would he [Milton] subside into a hackney Laureate—*
> *A scribbling, self-sold, soul-hired, scorned Iscariot?*

And he added a note: "I doubt if 'Laureate' and 'Iscariot' be good rhymes, but must say, as Ben Jonson did to Sylvester, who challenged him to rhyme with—

> *'I, John Sylvester,*
> *Lay with your sister.'*

Jonson answered—'I, Ben Jonson, lay with your wife.' Sylvester answered,—'That is not rhyme.'—'No,' said Ben Jonson; 'but it is *true.*' " "

Byron had just finished the first canto of *Don Juan* when the Shelleys returned hastily to Venice. Percy and Mary arrived on September 24 to seek medical aid for their daughter Clara, but the child died almost immediately on their arrival, and the Hoppners took the parents to their home and tried to distract them." Shelley called on Byron the next day and heard him read the fourth canto of *Childe Harold,* and before they left on the 29th Mary accompanied Shelley to the Palazzo Mocenigo, where she saw the Fornarina, and also read the fourth canto. The evening before their departure Byron called on them at the Hoppners'." During his stay Shelley had also heard the first canto of *Don Juan,* which delighted him. Byron had been most gracious and charming. Shelley described him as "the liveliest and happiest looking man I ever met." " Mary, who was always fascinated by him, carried back to Este not only his promise to allow Allegra to extend her visit with her mother, but also two of Byron's manuscripts (*Mazeppa* and the *Ode on Venice*) which Mary had agreed to copy."

At about this time Byron's difficulties with the ungovernable Fornarina reached their climax. He later recounted the history of the affair in a long letter to Murray:

"At last she quarrelled with her husband, and one evening ran away to my house. I told her this would not do: she said she would lie in the street, but not go back to him; that he beat her (the gentle tigress), spent her money, and scandalously neglected his Oven. As it was Midnight I let her stay, and next day there was no moving her at all. Her husband came, roaring and crying, and entreating her to come back:—*not* she! He then applied to the Police, and they applied to me: I told them and her husband to *take* her. . . . She went before the Commissary, but was obliged to return with that *becco ettico* ('consumptive cuckold'), as she called the poor man, who had a Ptisick. In a few days she ran away again. After a precious piece of work, she fixed herself in my house, really and truly without my consent, but, owing to my indolence, and not being able to keep my countenance; for if I began in a rage, she always finished by making me laugh with some Venetian pantaloonery or another; and the Gipsy knew this well enough, as well as her other powers of persuasion, and exerted them with the usual tact and success of all She-things—high and low, they are all alike for that.

"Madame Benzone also took her under her protection, and then her head turned. She was always in extremes, either crying or laughing; and so fierce when angered, that she was the terror of men, women, and children—for she had the strength of an Amazon, with the temper of Medea. She was a fine animal, but quite untameable. *I* was the only person that could at all keep her in any order, and when she saw me really angry (which they tell me is rather a savage sight), she subsided. But she had a thousand fooleries: in her *fazziolo,* the dress of the lower orders, she looked beautiful; but, alas! she longed for a hat and feathers, and all I could say or do (and I said much) could not prevent this travestie. I put the first into the fire; but I got tired of burning them, before she did of buying them, so that she made herself a figure—for they did not at all become her. . . . In the mean time, she beat the women and stopped my letters . . . [she] actually studied her Alphabet, on purpose (as she declared) to open all letters addressed to me and read their contents. I must not omit to do justice to her housekeeping qualities: after she came into my house as *donna di governo,* the expences were reduced to less than half. . . . That she had a sufficient regard for me in her wild way, I had many reasons to believe. I will mention one. In the autumn, one day, going to the Lido with my Gondoliers, we were overtaken by a heavy Squall, and the Gondola put in peril—hats blown away, boat filling, oar lost, tumbling sea, thunder, rain in torrents, night coming, and wind encreasing. On our return, after a tight struggle, I found her on the open steps of the Mocenigo palace, on the Grand Canal, with her great black eyes flashing through her tears, and the long dark hair, which was streaming drenched with rain over her brows and breast. . . . On seeing me safe, she did not wait to greet me, as might be expected, but calling out to me—*Ah! can' della Madonna, xe esto il tempo per andar' al'*

Lido? (Ah! Dog of the Virgin, is this a time to go to Lido?) ran into the house, and solaced herself with scolding the boatmen for not foreseeing the *'temporale.'* I was told by the servants that she had only been prevented from coming in a boat to look after me, by the refusal of all the Gondoliers of the Canal to put out into the harbour in such a moment. . . . Her joy at seeing me again was moderately mixed with ferocity, and gave me the idea of a tigress over her recovered Cubs.

"But her reign drew near a close. She became quite ungovernable. . . . I told her quietly that she must return home, (she had acquired a sufficient provision for herself and mother, etc., in my service,) and She refused to quit the house. I was firm, and she went, threatening knives and revenge. . . . The next day, while I was at dinner, she walked in, (having broke open a glass door that led from the hall below to the staircase, by way of prologue,) and, advancing strait up to the table, snatched the knife from my hand, cutting me slightly in the thumb in the operation. . . . I then called my boatmen, and desired them to get the Gondola ready, and conduct her to her own house again. . . . I resumed my dinner.

"We heard a great noise: I went out, and met them on the staircase, carrying her up stairs. She had thrown herself into the Canal. . . . I had her sent home quietly after her recovery. . . . She made many attempts to return, but no more violent ones. . . . I forgot to mention that she was very devout, and would cross herself if she heard the prayer-time strike—sometimes when that ceremony did not appear to be much in unison with what she was then about.

"She was quick in reply; as, for instance—One day when she had made me very angry with beating somebody or other, I called her a *Cow* (*Cow*, in Italian, is a sad affront and tantamount to the feminine of dog in English). I called her *'Vacca.'* She turned round, curtesied, and answered, *'Vacca tua, 'Celenza'* (*i.e. Eccelenza*). *'Your* Cow, please your Excellency.' In short, she was, as I said before, a very fine Animal, of considerable beauty and energy, with many good and several amusing qualities, but wild as a witch and fierce as a demon. She used to boast publicly of her ascendancy over me, contrasting it with that of other women, and assigning for it sundry reasons, physical and moral, which did more credit to her person than her modesty." [n]

On October 12, Shelley and Mary arrived in Venice once more for a more extended visit and dined with the Hoppners, who regaled them with various choice bits of gossip concerning Byron's way of life and his scandalous affairs with women. During their stay, Mary read *Beppo* and probably connected it with Byron's own Venetian escapades. [n] Shelley spent a number of evenings with Byron, [n] no doubt discussing the future of Allegra, about Byron's care of whom he was beginning to worry. Nevertheless, he felt obliged to return her to her father according to the agreement, and on the 24th he left for Este, returning with her on the 29th. [n] He and Mary then made their farewells and left on the 31st to prepare for their journey to Rome, leaving Allegra with some uneasiness with the Hoppners.

The rumors current in Venice and the tales of the Hoppners had disturbed Shelley considerably, and his conversations with Byron during this last visit had not reassured him. ". . . L.[ord] B.[yron] is familiar with the lowest sort of these women," he wrote Peacock, "the people his gondolieri pick up in the streets. He allows fathers and mothers to bargain with him for their daughters. . . . He says he disapproves, but he endures. He is not yet an Italian and is heartily and deeply discontented with himself; and contemplating in the distorted mirror of his own thoughts the nature and the destiny of man, what can he behold but objects of contempt and despair? But that he is a great poet, I think the address to ocean proves. And he has a certain degree of candour while you talk to him, but unfortunately it does not outlast your departure." [n]

Byron's annoyance at Hanson was again reaching the fever point. The attorney had not gone even to Geneva in the spring when he had asked Byron to meet him there to sign the Newstead sale papers. Byron had several times urged Hanson to send a clerk with the papers, but to no avail. Hobhouse wrote on August 17: "I have presented myself to Chancery-Lane so often as to be a nuisance and an eye-sore to his retainers below-stairs. . . . I anticipate the combing down he will get from you, although, to be sure, I must say that in propriâ personâ you are a mighty mitigable devil, and do not at all answer to the Jupiter of your own distant storm." ⁿ

But so far as Hanson was concerned, Byron was not appeased. The attorney, before leaving England on October 12, had again blandly asked Byron to meet him at Geneva. And Byron again exploded. But when he learned that Hanson was finally setting out, he wrote him at Geneva in exasperated but somewhat more moderate terms. The party, consisting of Hanson, his son Newton, and a Mr. Townsend representing the purchaser, Major Wildman, arrived at the Grande Bretagne hotel in Venice on November 11. According to Newton Hanson's account, when they reached the Palazzo Mocenigo they ran the gantlet of Byron's menagerie and "proceeded up a flight of massive marble staircases, through a lofty billiard-room, and then through a bedroom, to an apartment, to the door of which his lordship advanced and cordially greeted my father. At their meeting, I could not help observing a nervous sensitiveness in his lordship, which produced a silence for some minutes. It was broken by his lordship observing, 'Well, Hanson! I never thought you would have ventured so far. I rather expected you would have sent Charles.'

"Lord Byron, as, I suppose, in common with all poets, was remarkable for evincing, on any sudden emotion of the mind, a strong burst of deep feeling. On this occasion his eyes were suffused with tears."

Newton Hanson was probably only partly right in his interpretation of Byron's sensitiveness and silence and the eventual overflowing of his emotion. When Fletcher had first called at their hotel, he had asked for some books which Byron had expected them to bring. But Hanson had brought only one of the three packages Murray had sent him, and it contained not a single book.

It was no doubt the emotion of anger that Byron was trying to control on their first meeting, and the upsurge of tears came when the anger passed and he was overcome with a flood of memories of his association with the Hansons from his boyhood

—an emotion that made it impossible for him not to soften at an actual meeting. But he did not cease to be annoyed.

The Hansons saw Byron at his worst physically. For some months he had been easygoing and self-indulgent. "Lord Byron could not have been more than 30," Newton observed, "but he looked 40. His face had become pale, bloated, and sallow. He had grown very fat, his shoulders broad and round, and the knuckles of his hands were lost in fat."

According to his son, Hanson—quite unaware of Byron's feeling on the subject—had come to Venice himself rather than send someone, in the hope that he might effect a reconciliation between Lord and Lady Byron. He was soon made aware of the futility of such a hope, however. Newton says: "The third day after our arrival, Lord B. received a letter from Mr. Murray, which contained the news of the melancholy death of Sir Samuel Romilly. He came down in his gondola to our hotel to communicate the sad event to my father. The cause was alleged to be grief at the recent death of Lady Romilly. Lord B.'s remark was, 'How strange it is that one man will die for the loss of his partner, while another would die if they were compelled to live together!' This was said so pointedly that my father never again referred to the delicate subject of his domestic affairs." [n]

The death of Romilly brought back to Byron with a surprising bitterness all the frustrations and wounded feelings of the separation proceedings, as any event recalling that time of agony seemed capable of doing through the rest of his life. With a complete abandonment of reason and judgment, he wrote a letter to Lady Byron for Hanson to carry back to England:

"Sir Samuel Romilly has cut his throat for the loss of his wife. It is now nearly three years since he became, in the face of his compact (by a retainer—previous, and, I believe, general), the advocate of the measures and the Approver of the proceedings, which deprived me of mine. . . . This Man little thought, when he was lacerating my heart according to law, while he was poisoning my life at it's sources . . . that a domestic affliction would lay him in the earth, with the meanest of malefactors. . . ." [n]

A month later he could speak of Romilly to Hobhouse with no abatement of bitterness: "I never would have forgiven him living, and will not affect to pity him dead—I hate him still; as much as one can dislike dust." "

On November 17, Byron signed a codicil to his will, witnessed by Newton Hanson and Fletcher, leaving £5,000 to his natural daughter, Allegra." Hanson carried with him, when he left on November 19, a letter from Byron to Major Wildman, wishing him every happiness at Newstead, and a sealed and private letter from Byron to Hobhouse and Kinnaird, to whom jointly he entrusted all his business affairs. Byron had come to distrust, if not Hanson's honesty, at least his business methods, particularly as Hanson had never itemized his own bill. He came to the heart of the matter with clarity and succinctness:

"Of the principal of the purchase money, I request and direct that the superflux (after claims and settlements) be applied to the payment of my debts, in such portion and manner as may seem best.

"The settled part I wish to be invested either in mortgage or other security—provided the *security* be such as may deserve the *name*. The interest accruing since last April on Major Wildman's purchase money—amounting to about two thousand eight hundred pounds or thereabouts, according to the statement made to me—I request to be transmitted to me in letters of credit and circular notes—as being income which I wish to employ in my personal expenses. Of the principal—I devote all, as far as the surplus goes, to the creditors, and I hope that you Hobhouse—and you Kinnaird will understand me, and see that it is properly applied." "

Douglas Kinnaird took over immediately, and wrote Byron at once concerning his financial situation. The letter clarifies many details that have been foggy in Byron biography: "You are to receive £94.500 of which £66.200 is to be paid over to Mr. Bland & myself in order to be laid out in Government Security or real security, & the interest arising therefrom, together with about £200 per an. from Sʳ R. Noel to be paid to your annual use— The remaining £28.300 I shall conceive it to be the duty of Hobhouse & myself to apply to the payment of your debts—

which by the account transmitted to me appear to amount to about £34.162 leaving a deficiency of funds amounting to about £5860— But the *lawyer's* Bill is *stated* in this to amount to no less a sum than between nine and ten thousand Pounds— It is my decided opinion that not one farthing of this should be paid till the whole Bill up to the date of it's delivery is given in by Mr & the Messrs Hanson— The whole amount of any debts from which any deduction by way of compromise can be expected is so small that I do not lead you to count upon any relief from any item but that of the *lawyer—*" You may *rely* on the most unremitting attention to your interest on my part. Hobhouse, feeling himself incompetent to speak decisively on matters of business—proposes to call in his Father as part of himself. . . . It is my own advice to you, anticipating the probability that Hanson will be anxious to finger the money, under the pretence of his paying your debts, that you write a letter to Hobhouse & myself desiring that the whole surplus, namely the £28.300 be placed to the credit of a *separate account* in your name in this House, & that Hobhouse's & my joint drafts be given for the disbursement of it & payment of your debts— This appears to me to answer the triple purpose, of preventing Hanson from paying himself, of guaranteeing to you that the debts *are* paid, & keeping an authentic record in our books, should any thing happen to Hob or myself, of how any sum was applied, & of keeping in our (i.e., the House's) custody the receipts & documents. . . . You will receive this day a letter of credit for £2000." "

On December 28, Hobhouse and his father met with Hanson at a dinner at Kinnaird's to settle Byron's financial affairs. Hanson read his note proposing a pro-rata payment of Byron's simple contract debts, but stating that his own bill, amounting to nearly £12,000, was not to be docked. Hobhouse and Kinnaird, as Byron's agents, vetoed the proposal. As there would be about £4,000 left over to pay, they decided that Hanson should wait for his money. Byron would get the interest (£3,300) from the £66,200 put in trust for Lady Byron, besides £3,000 in interest from April on the purchase money of Newstead."

In the meantime Byron had sent a cargo of poetry to England by Lord Lauderdale, who had visited him in Venice early in November, and he was eager to get his friends' opinion of it. It contained the first canto of *Don Juan*, then consisting of "two hundred *Octaves*." He also sent the fair copy of *Mazeppa* made by Mary Shelley and the *Ode on Venice*, composed some time before, but he was most concerned about the first poem. He wrote Hobhouse:

"As one of the poems is as free as La Fontaine; and bitter in politics, too; the damned cant and Toryism of the day may make Murray pause; in that case you will take any bookseller who *bids best*. When I say *free*, I mean that freedom which Ariosto, Boiardo, and Voltaire—Pulci, Berni, all the best Italian and French—as well as Pope and Prior amongst the English—permitted themselves; but no improper words, nor *phrases;* merely some situations which are taken from life. . . . mind and make me a proper paction with Murray, or others. I submit the matter to you and Doug., and you may show the MS. to Frere, and William Rose, and Moore, and whoever you please." "

When Byron heard that Hobhouse was seeking election to Parliament from Westminster, to fill the seat left vacant by the death of Romilly, with a knowledge of his friend's abilities and a nostalgic thought of his own once strong but diverted political ambitions, he wrote enthusiastically to Kinnaird: "You may depend upon it, that Hobhouse has talents very much beyond his *present rate*, and even beyond his own opinion. He is too *fidgetty*, but he has the elements of greatness, if he can but keep his nerves in order." "

While awaiting the verdict of Murray and his friends in England on the first canto of *Don Juan*, Byron began, on December 13, a second canto, plunging with immense gusto into the narrative of Juan's voyage and shipwreck on Haidée's isle, drawing freely from his own varied experiences for his savory comments on women, love, and human frailties. Engrossed in its composition, Byron ended the year pleasantly enough. On Christmas Day he attended a party at the Hoppners', a birthday fête for Mrs. Hoppner, where he saw the Countess Albrizzi, Dr. Aglietti, the Russian Consul Naranzi, Count Rizzo-Patarol, and Mengaldo, who had just returned from the country. Byron had become more friendly with Mengaldo in September after Alexander Scott, his most intimate English companion, had left Venice temporarily. Characteristically, Byron easily overlooked the vanities and foibles of the Cavalier and genially accepted the companionship and homage the latter was eager to bestow. During the Carnival of 1819 Mengaldo noted a greater intimacy in his relations with the poet. On January 10, during a performance of *Elizabetta*, Byron made to Mengaldo *"la recit très-interessant de son mariage et de ses amours."*[n]

In the meantime, the first canto of *Don Juan* had arrived in England and made an immediate stir among Byron's friends. As soon as Lord Lauderdale arrived with Byron's manuscripts, Hobhouse breakfasted with Scrope Davies to read and talk them over. "I have my doubts about Don Juan," Hobhouse wrote in his diary, "the blasphemies & facetiæ and the domestica facta overpower even the great genius it displays—of Mazeppa & the ode I do not think much."[n] Of all those who read it, Kinnaird was the only one who did not let caution weigh more than his appreciation of the poem's value in his judgment. He wrote: "Don Juan is exquisite." But he added: "It must be *cut* for the *Syphilis*."[n]

Cutting, however, did not meet Byron's views, though he was willing to make some concessions. He wrote a joint letter to his friends: ". . . you may omit the stanzas on Castlereagh, indeed it is better, and the two *'Bobs'* at the end of the 3rd stanza of the dedication, which will leave 'high' and 'a dry' good rhymes without any *'double* (or Single) Entendre,' but no more.[8] I appeal, not 'to Philip fasting,' but to Alexander drunk; I appeal to Murray at his ledger, to the people, in short, Don Juan shall be

---

[8] Byron referred to the *double-entendre* in the lines of the dedication referring to Southey:

> And then you overstrain yourself, or so,
>   And tumble downward like the flying fish
> Gasping on deck, because you soar too high, Bob,
> And fall, for lack of moisture quite a-dry, Bob!

The term "a dry bob" was well known in the Regency slang of Byron's day. Partridge's *Dictionary of Slang and Unconventional Language* gives the definition: "Coition without (male) emission."

an entire horse, or none. If the objection be to the indecency, the Age which applauds the 'Bath Guide,' [9] and Little's poems,[1] and reads Fielding and Smollett still, may bear with that. If to the poetry, I will take my chance. I will not give way to all the Cant of Christendom." "

Hobhouse's first opinion of Byron's new poem was confirmed by Frere, with whom he had a long conversation about *Don Juan*. On January 5, after a meeting of the conclave, Hobhouse wrote Byron a long letter, which he showed to Murray, Kinnaird, and Davies before sending." He was as temperate and persuasive as he knew how to be.

"The first time I read your 'Don Juan,' " he wrote, "our friend Scrope Davies was in the room, and we mutually communicated with each other from time to time on the papers before us. Every now and then on reading over the poem, both the one and the other exclaimed, *'It will be impossible to publish this.'* I need not say that these exclamations were accompanied with notes of admiration at the genius, wit, poetry, satire, and so forth. . . ."

In outlining Frere's objections to publication of the poem, Hobhouse added: "Mr. Frere is one of your warmest admirers, and the greatest part of his arguments were drawn from the admitted acknowledgment that you had, and deserved to have, by far the greatest reputation of any poet of the day. The objections were, you may easily imagine, drawn from the sarcasms against the lady of Seaham, from the licentiousness, and in some cases downright indecency of many stanzas, and of the whole turn of the poem; from the flings at religion, and from the slashing right and left at other worthy writers of the day. . . . Frere particularly observed that the world had now given up the foolish notion that you were to be identified with your sombre heroes, and had acknowledged with what great success and

[9] Christopher Anstey's *New Bath Guide, or Memoirs of the B—r—d Family, in a Series of Poetical Epistles,* which first appeared in 1766, was notorious for the eighteenth-century freedom of its language and descriptions of moral lapses. Smollett was said to have drawn largely from it for his *Humphrey Clinker*.

[1] Moore's amorous poems, which Byron read avidly while a schoolboy at Harrow, were first published under the pseudonym of Thomas Little.

good keeping you had portrayed a grand imaginary being.[2] But the same admiration cannot be bestowed upon, and will not be due to the Rake Juan. . . . All the idle stories about your Venetian life will be more than confirmed. They will be exaggerated. . . .

"Lastly, the satire. Both Scrope and myself agreed that the attack on Castlereagh was much better than that on Southey (which, by the way, has the phrase *'dry-Bob!!'*), but we both agreed that you could not publish it unless you were over here ready to fight him. . . . Neither Southey, Wordsworth, nor Coleridge have any character except with their own crazy proselytes, some fifty perhaps in number: so what harm can you do them, and what good can you do the world by your criticism?"

Hobhouse admitted that he did not know how amputation would save the poem, "more particularly as the objectionable parts are in point of wit, humour, and poetry, the very best beyond all doubt of the whole poem. This consideration, therefore, makes me sum up with strenuously advising a total suppression of 'Don Juan.'. . . I should tell you that Douglas Kinnaird has now changed his opinion and coincides with Frere, S.B.D., and myself."[n]

It was the feeling of Byron's friends that he had been out of England so long that he was unaware of the growing moral temper of the bulk of the reading public, a development which was in part a general reaction to the profligacy of the court under the Regent and to the moral laxness of the upper classes that Byron had chiefly known during his years of fame in London.[3] Moore concurred in that view when he returned to

---

[2] To Hobhouse's objection that the poem was too close to the facts, Byron replied that the motto from Horace, "domestica facta," merely meant *"common life"* and that "the *Julian* adventure [the bedroom farce with Donna Julia] detailed was none of mine; but one of an acquaintance of mine (*Parolini* by name), which happened some years ago at Bassano, with the Prefect's wife when he was a boy; and was the subject of a long case, ending in a divorce or separation of the parties during the Italian Viceroyalty." (*LBC*, II, 101.)

[3] The demand for Victorian reticences in literature began much before the reign of Queen Victoria in England. The rise of Grundyism and other characteristic mid-century mores is well discussed in Maurice J. Quinlan's *Victorian Prelude* (New York, 1941). E. D. H. Johnson, in *"Don Juan* in

London the end of January and read the manuscript.[4]

Byron's first reaction to the objections of his English friends was to acquiesce in their judgment, though under protest. But he still wanted fifty copies for private distribution. To Murray he stipulated: "*Print Don Juan entire,* omitting, of course, the lines on Castlereagh, as I am not on the spot to meet him." In a postscript he added: ". . . it is idle to detail my arguments in favour of my own Self-love and 'Poeshie;' but I *protest.* If the poem has poetry, it would stand; if not, fall: the rest is 'leather and prunella,' and has never yet affected any human production 'pro or con.' Dullness is the only annihilator in such cases." [n]

But he had not given up the poem, and continued to send corrections and additions to Murray, whose interest might be aroused in a potential *succès de scandale* and who therefore might be susceptible to his propaganda for *Don Juan,* "which my cursed puritanical committee have protested against publishing; but we will circumvent them on that point in the end. . . . I say all this to them as to you; that is, for *you* to say to *them,* for I will have nothing underhand. If they had told me the poetry was bad, I would have acquiesced; but they say the contrary, and then talk to me about morality—the first time I ever heard the word from any body who was not a rascal that used it for a purpose. I maintain that it is the most moral of poems; but if people won't discover the moral, that is their fault, not mine." [n]

Through most of the Carnival of 1819, Byron had entered into every variety of the pleasures of the season with complete abandon. He had continued his intimacy with Mengaldo. During January and the early days of February they were together almost daily, and the Cavalier viewed the opera from Byron's box at the Fenice, or they went together to the San Benedetto or the San Luca, and to the Ridotto afterward. But on the 4th,

England," pp. 135-53, has emphasized how completely Byron misjudged the moral standards of his middle-class readers in his accusations in *Don Juan* of British hypocrisy and cant. Johnson maintains that the poem's freedom in discussing sex, love, and religion genuinely shocked the majority of readers of the puritan middle class—a class with whose views and moral caliber Byron was little acquainted.

[4] Moore was nevertheless carried away by the poetry, passion, wit, and intellectual vigor of the poem as he read later cantos. (See Moore, II, 189.)

Alexander Scott had returned to Venice, and Mengaldo sensed immediately that Byron found the Englishman a more congenial companion than himself.

Under the circumstances, it was easy for Mengaldo, who was half Bohemian and half moralist, to take a moral view of Byron's dissipations. He himself indulged freely in amours with various disreputable countesses and actresses, but always sentimentalized them to himself and felt remorse for his backsliding. Byron's more frank avowal of his pleasures, his failure to deceive himself concerning their nature, and his systematic pursuit of women who attracted him, by methods which had become almost scientific in their thoroughgoing design, now shocked Mengaldo. Probably to have a retreat for his intrigues which would be undisturbed by the tigress Margarita Cogni, Byron had taken a "Casino" at Santa Maria Zobenigo (Santa Maria del Giglio), not far from the Piazza San Marco." After riding with Byron on the Lido on the 12th, Mengaldo recorded with a sense of shocked moral sensibility: *"Au retour dans son* CASINO: *je fus effrayé de son orrible systhème."* " And later he wrote sadly: *"L'amitié de Lord Byron pour moi s'allentis: mes sermons n'etaient pas de son goût."* "

Byron was in no mood to be lectured by Mengaldo. He was annoyed that Lord Lauderdale had carried gossip about his amours to London. But if his friends wanted the facts they could have them:

"Which 'piece' does he mean? Since last year I have run the gauntlet [*sic*]; is it the Tarruscelli, the Da Mosti, the Spineda, the Lotti, the Rizzato, the Eleanora, the Carlotta, the Giulietta, the Alvisi, the Zambieri, the Eleanora de Bezzi (who was the King of Naples' Gioaschino's mistress, at least, one of them), the Theresina of Mazzurati, the Glettenheim and her sister, the Luigia & her mother, the Fornaretta, the Santa, the Caligara, the Portiera Vedora, the Bolognese figurante, the Tentora and her sister, cum multis aliis? Some of them are countesses, and some of them cobblers' wives; some noble, some middling, some low, & all whores; which does the damned old 'Ladro and porco fottuto' mean? I have had them all and thrice as many to boot since 1817."

And Byron's postscript indicated that he was not inclined to change his way of life: "Whatever brain-money you get on my account from Murray, pray remit me. I will never consent to pay away what I *earn*, that is *mine*, & what I get by my brains I will spend on *my* b——cks as long as I have a tester or a t * * * *remaining.*" ⁿ

Perhaps partly to cover up the wound to his authorship, Byron in bowing temporarily to the judgment of his friends in the matter of publication had turned the discussion upon money matters. To Kinnaird he wrote:

"I have received a very clever letter from Hobhouse against the publication of Don Juan in which I understand you have acquiesced (you be damned). I acquiesce too, but reluctantly.

"This acquiescence is some thousands of pounds out of my pocket, the very thought of which brings tears into my eyes. I have imbibed such a love for money, that I keep some Sequins in a drawer, to count and cry over them once a week; ⁵ and if it was not for a turn for women (which I hope will be soon worn out), I think in time that I should be able, not only to clear off, but to accumulate. . . . This comes of consulting friends. I will see you all damned before I consult you again. What do you mean now by giving advice when you are asked for it?" ⁿ

But before the Carnival was ended, he had decided that he would not be bullied by timid friends; he would trust his own judgment. "Tell Hobhouse that 'Don Juan' must be published—" he wrote Kinnaird on February 22, "the loss of the copyright would break my heart. All that he says may be very fine, & very true; but my 'regard for my fee' is the ruling passion, and I must have it." ⁿ By March 6 he had taken firm resolution. He

⁵ There is further evidence that most of what Byron wrote in *Don Juan* was not far from the fact. In the 216th stanza of the first canto he had written:

> *So for a good old-gentlemanly vice,*
> *I think I must take up with avarice.*

On his visit to Byron in October 1819 Moore observed Byron's "hoarding-box," adding: "His own ascetic style of living enabled him, as far as himself was concerned, to gratify this taste for economy in no ordinary degree. . . ." (Moore, II, 268.)

wrote to Douglas Kinnaird as more amenable to his proposals than Hobhouse:

"After mature consideration I have determined to have Don Juan published (*anonymously*); and I venture to request you will bargain with Mr. Murray for that, for Mazeppa, and for the Ode, and for a *second* canto of two hundred and six stanzas, which I have begun to copy out—(it is finished), and will send at leisure. You will get what you think a fitting price. . . . The poem has merit, you all say. Very well; leave the rest to the chances, and recollect that nothing would console me for the omission of the monies. . . . when the public leaves off reading what I write, the booksellers will tell us. . . ." [n]

Byron was not altogether without justification in his concern about money matters, for, despite the sale of Newstead, he was not yet in the clear. Some thousands of pounds of debts were still to be paid. The purchase money and interest, which had been deposited with Kinnaird by February 16, amounted to £ 97,554. 3s. 1d. Of this sum, Kinnaird and Bland, as trustees of the settlement on Lady Byron, had invested £ 66,200 in three-per-cent government consols.[n]

Kinnaird had protested against paying Hanson even a penny on account until he had his whole bill, but Byron, having given his promise while Hanson was in Venice, instructed his banker to pay £ 5,000 on account, at the same time scolding the attorney for not presenting his bill. And he expressed to Kinnaird his fear of the Funds, an unreasoning fear, based partly on his vague distrust of the Tory government and his expectation of some kind of violent overthrow of the regime as a result of the widespread misery and discontent which Shelley and others had reported to him and which he had sensed from Hobhouse's accounts of the political temper in England. Despite the reassurances of his banker, he reiterated his opposition to the Funds until it became almost an obsession. On March 9 he wrote to Kinnaird: "I shall never rest while my property is in the English funds; do, for God sake, let it be invested in *land* or *mortgage*, although at a present loss." [n]

His suspiciousness was quite as unreasoning in another quarter.

Failure to hear from Murray had caused him to discount what Hobhouse had told him of the publisher's willingness, even eagerness to print *Don Juan*. But though he was willing enough to publish the poem, Murray hoped to persuade Byron to cut out all the "indelicacies," and so urged him in a flattering letter.[n] Byron's response was eloquent and trenchant. He had found his own true genius in the rambling satire of *Don Juan*, and he was not to be diverted from it by the flattery of a bookseller or the moral squeamishness of friends. "You sha'n't make *Canticles* of my Cantos," he protested. "The poem will please, if it is lively; if it is stupid, it will fail; but I will have none of your damned cutting and slashing. If you please, you may publish *anonymously;* it will perhaps be better; but I will battle my way against them all, like a Porcupine." [n]

Murray had written that Foscolo was "deploring that a man of your genius will not occupy some six or eight years in the composition of a work and subject worthy of you." [n] "I'll try no such thing," Byron retorted; "I hate tasks. And then 'seven or eight years!' God send us all well this day three months, let alone years. . . . And works, too!—is *Childe Harold* nothing? You have so many 'divine' poems, is it nothing to have written a *Human* one? without any of your worn-out machinery. Why, man, I could have spun the thoughts of the four cantos of that poem into twenty, had I wanted to book-make, and its passion into as many modern tragedies. Since you want *length*, you shall have enough of *Juan*, for I'll make 50 cantos." [n]

Kinnaird, reporting that Hobhouse had lost the Westminster election by the active campaigning of Caroline Lamb for her brother-in-law George Lamb, hinted that Byron might injure him by the publication of *Don Juan*.[n]

But in consoling Hobhouse for his ill-success, Byron turned the matter off with ribaldry:

"With the Burdettites divided, and the Whigs and Tories united, what else could be expected? If I had guessed at your opponent, I would have made one among you, Certes, and have f——d Caroline Lamb out of her 'two hundred votes,' although at the expense of a t * * * *.

"I think I could have neutralized her zeal, with a little management—but alas! who would have thought of that Cuckoldy family's *standing* for a *member*." [n]

Despite the bravado of his letters to his cronies in England, Byron had reached a kind of impasse in his personal life. The pleasures of Venice, though he could not quite admit it to himself yet, had begun to pall on him. Burning the candle to the end of the wick during the Carnival had affected adversely his health and spirits. At the beginning of April he wrote Murray: ". . . about the beginning of the year I was in a state of great exhaustion, attended by such debility of Stomach that nothing remained upon it; and I was obliged to reform my 'way of life.' . . . " [n]

One step in his reform had been the final dismissal of Margarita Cogni, "the gentle tigress." And he had lost most of his zest for adding to the count of his women. Nevertheless, he had sometime in the winter, perhaps during the Carnival when the masking facilitated new intrigues, formed for novelty's sake a clandestine acquaintance with an unmarried girl of eighteen. The great fondness for youthful innocence which had clung to him from his earliest days, which had made him idealize Margaret Parker and Lady Oxford's eleven-year-old daughter, Lady Charlotte Harley, perhaps prompted his first impulse to find satisfaction in the company of someone less blasé than the sophisticated married women who had been his main diversion during the past year. To what extent he had recaptured in this new affair the romance of early love which he wearily longed for may partly be inferred from the cynical tone of his correspondence concerning it. His libertine habits, combined with a wide experience of the weaknesses of women, militated against his maintaining the romantic bloom of this liaison for very long, even though it was stimulated by the need for secrecy and the necessity of climbing a balcony to keep his rendezvous. But it was more as Don Juan than as Romeo that he reported the event. His first reference to the girl was in a postscript to a letter to Hobhouse early in April, and then it was a casual remark at the end of an account of an elephant that had gone berserk, "for want of a She, it being his rutting month." He continued:

"Last month I had a business about a Venetian girl who wanted to marry me. . . . I was very honest, and gave her no hopes, but there was a scene, I having been found at her window at Midnight. . . ." [n]

Byron later told Murray that she was the daughter of a Venetian noble, that she was eighteen, and that her name was Angelina. "She is a very dear friend of mine, and I have undergone some trouble on her account, for last winter the truculent tyrant her flinty-hearted father, having been informed by an infernal German, Countess Vorsperg (their next neighbor), of our meetings, they sent a priest to me, and a Commissary of police, and they locked the Girl up, and gave her prayers and bread and water, and our connection was cut off for some time. . . ." [6]

He afterward told Medwin that he was indifferent to the outcome of the affair, and did not care whether the police officer had come to shoot or to marry him again. "I was disgusted and tired with the life I led at Venice, and was glad to turn my back on it." [n]

He had already summed up at the end of the first canto of *Don Juan* the mood that was settling more heavily upon him since the turn of the year:

> *But now at thirty years my hair is grey—*
> *(I wonder what it will be like at forty?*
> *I thought of a peruke the other day—)*
> *My heart is not much greener; and, in short, I*
> *Have squandered my whole summer while 't was May. . . .*
> *No more—no more—Oh! never more, my heart,*
> *Canst thou be my sole world, my universe!* [n]

[6] *LJ*, IV, 302–3. Letter of May 18, 1819. Teresa Guiccioli, in her manuscript "*Vie de Lord Byron en Italie*" (1st series, pp. 130–5), gave an idyllic picture of this episode, perhaps as Byron told it to her, showing him to have been motivated by the most altruistic desire to help the young girl save her innocence. Either Byron or Teresa distorted the picture somewhat, as may be seen from Byron's letters to his friends in England. If he did finally give the girl up, it was because he was wearied to satiety with love-making rather than because he was overcome with virtue, as Teresa would have her readers believe.

While his mind had never been more acute or his creative powers more active, he was physically and emotionally weary. The sword had at length, he felt, indeed worn out its sheath. It was in this indifferent humor that he accompanied his friend Alexander Scott to the Countess Benzoni's on an evening in the first days of April. They entered about midnight and sat on a sofa facing the door of the grand salon, where guests were beginning to arrive after the theater. Scarcely had they taken their place when the door opened again and there appeared in it a petite girl with rich auburn curls falling down to beautifully molded shoulders.[7] Her bust and arms were plump and full but well-shaped, and her complexion was fair and radiantly fresh. A critical observer might have noted that her legs were rather short and her lower figure too ample, but one who looked into her voluptuous and yet naïve face would have judged her rather by her handsome nose, mouth, and chin, and particularly by the melting softness of her large eyes.[8]

If Byron had looked closely, he might have remembered that he had seen her before, for it was the young Countess Guiccioli, whom he had escorted to view Canova's "Helen" at the Countess Albrizzi's the year before. She was nineteen, and had been married only a little over a year. Her husband, Count Alessandro Guiccioli, now fifty-eight,[9] who had exercised his strong will over

[7] Most of the details of this meeting between Byron and the Countess Teresa Guiccioli come from Teresa's manuscript *"Vie de Lord Byron en Italie"* (now in the Biblioteca Classense, Ravenna). Teresa's loquacious account is colored by the romantic haze of memory, but is more circumstantial and probably more reliable than the one she gave to Moore (II, 206–7). Teresa does not give the precise date of the meeting, but it must have been the 2nd or 3rd of April, for she says it was an evening *"dans les premier d'avril,"* and Byron spoke as if he had known her at least two or three days when he wrote to Hobhouse on April 6.

[8] This composite portrait of Teresa at the time Byron met her is based partly on the drawing by John Hayter (1818) and partly on contemporary accounts (brought together by Iris Origo in *The Last Attachment*, p. 12). Captain Gronow, who met her after Byron's death but when she was still young, said that "though handsome, she gave one more the idea of a healthy, rosy, jolly-looking milkmaid, than a heroine of romance." (Gronow: *Reminiscences*, I, 311.)

[9] Guiccioli was born in 1761 and was therefore fifty-seven when he married

two other wives before her, had insisted that she come to this *conversazione*, though she was weary (they had arrived only the night before in Venice) and saddened by the recent loss of her elder sister and her mother. She had with reluctance acceded to his desire to go to the theater, which, she said, "for him was a necessity," and she had protested with tears in her eyes against prolonging the evening by going to a party where she would be among strangers. She consented out of "pure obedience" and with the promise from her husband that they would remain only a few minutes."

But as soon as she entered, Teresa saw the Grecian beauty of Byron's face, and as their eyes met she felt an irresistible attraction to him. The rough waters of the lagoon and the late hour (it was now nearly one o'clock) had thinned the circle of habitual visitors, and the Countess Benzoni, wanting to furnish entertainment for her young guest, approached Byron and asked him to meet her. But he refused. "You know very well," he said, "that I do not want to make any new acquaintances with women; if they are ugly because they are ugly—and if they are beautiful because they are beautiful." " Alexander Scott, who was seated by his side, in vain urged him to make an exception for this young woman, "in a salon where beauty is not common." Still he refused. But finally, "subjugated by the gracious insistence of Mme. Benzon he rose—evidently from pure complaisance—and advanced toward the young lady preceded by the mistress of the salon." " The Countess Benzoni presented him as "Peer of England and its greatest poet," which, Teresa recalled, "brought to the lips of Lord Byron one of those charming smiles that Coleridge admired so much—and which he called *the Gate of Heaven*." " The mysterious effect upon her of his look, she said, was to continue and develop "in that ineffable smile, in the extraordinary melody of his voice, in his beauty."

Byron seated himself beside her, and the conversation was

Teresa Gamba in 1818. Teresa later said she was married at sixteen, but Iris Origo conjectures, from the birth dates of her brothers and sisters—no record of her own birth is extant—that she was born in 1800, and was therefore eighteen when she married and nineteen at the time of her meeting with Byron at the Countess Benzoni's. (Origo, p. 493.)

soon established by Teresa's reminding him of the circumstances of their meeting the year before when she had not even noticed him in the agitations of the first days of her marriage. What had happened in the meantime, though she did not tell him so then, had done much to disillusion her with her marriage and her husband. But her bright eyes shone at this "celestial apparition whom it seemed to her she had already seen and loved before, having seen him in her imagination." [n]

When she told him that she came from Ravenna, he replied that it was a city he wished to visit on account of the tomb of Dante and of Francesca da Rimini. Dante then became the subject of their conversation, for, thanks to the intelligent guidance of the Abbess of the Convent of Santa Chiara at Faenza, where she had gone to school, Teresa knew more of classical Italian literature than most young girls of her age. Her true love for the great Italian poets of the past captivated Byron immediately. It was a theme he was not accustomed to hear from such pretty Italian lips at a *conversazione*. She spoke of Dante and Petrarch with enthusiasm and assurance. Recalling that evening years later, she wrote: "But already the subject of the conversation had become an accessory—already the important thing was to converse—was the development of that mysterious sympathy which grew with each word from the one and the other—and that had already rendered them insensible to what was happening around them—" When her husband came to tell her banteringly that the five minutes had slipped by long ago, "She rose as if she were coming out of a dream—and in crossing again the threshold of this Palace she was no longer as tranquil as she had been on entering. These mysterious sympathies shake the soul too much and frighten one." [n]

Though Byron, with greater experience of these emotions, was not at the moment to the same extent shaken in his soul, he was a believer in fate, and might not have disagreed later with her statement that "the effect of this meeting was the seal of the destiny of their hearts." [n]

CHAPTER XX

1819

Ravenna, Bologna, La Mira Again

WHEN Byron left the Benzoni's that April evening after his meeting with the Countess Guiccioli, he too was less tranquil than when he entered the salon. But he was exhilarated by the thought of a conquest somewhat different from his recent ones, rather than buoyed up by any such angelic visions as had agitated the bosom of Teresa. Teresa's attractiveness coupled with good breeding and a naïve intellectual enthusiasm free from all the affectations of the "blue stocking" or the sophisticated "literary lady" had pleased Byron first of all. Then her deference toward him as a poet and as a man was a subtle flattery more stirring than the passionate attachment of the "fine animals" he had consorted with in the past months.

All Byron's resolutions not to make new feminine acquaintances evaporated, and before they parted he had asked to see her privately. It was not difficult to arrange. Byron had the technique for such affairs well in hand, and Teresa, once the motive was glossed over with justifying sentiment, was not without her own devices of deceit. Teresa gave an account of the progress of the affair in her "Confession" to her husband, that strange document apparently extracted from her after Byron's death. After speaking of her first meeting with Byron at the Benzoni's, she said: "I then felt attracted to him by an irresistible force. He became aware of it, and asked to see me alone the next day. I was so imprudent as to agree, on condition that he would respect my honour: he promised and we settled on the hour after dinner, in which you [Count Guiccioli] took your rest. At that time an old boatman appeared with a note, in an unknown gondola, and took me to Mylord's gondola, where he was waiting, and together we went to a *casino* of his. I was strong enough to resist at that first encounter, but was so imprudent as to repeat it the next day, when my strength gave way—for B. was not a man to confine himself to sentiment. And, the first step taken, there was no further obstacle in the following days." [n]

In Teresa's roseate reconstruction, in her later years, of the circumstances of these first days of their meeting, however, she was considerably more vague, confining herself to descriptions of gondola rides and sunsets, of conversations at the theater and afterward at the Countess Benzoni's.[1]

Teresa would have been shocked at the realistic terms in which Byron phrased the characteristics of his quandary to his friends. A few days after his first meeting with Teresa, he wrote to Hobhouse: "I must write again in a few days, it being now past four in the morning; it is Passion week, & rather dull. I am dull too, for I have fallen in love with a Romagnuola Countess from Ravenna, who is nineteen years old, and has a Count of fifty— whom She seems disposed to qualify, the first year of marriage being just over. . . . and I have hopes, Sir,—hopes. . . . She is pretty, but has no tact; answers aloud, when she should whisper—talks of age to old ladies who want to pass for young; and this blessed night horrified a correct company at the Benzona's, by calling out to me '*mio Byron*' in an audible key, during a dead Silence of pause in the other prattlers, who stared and whispered their respective Serventi. . . .

"What shall I do? I am in love, and tired of promiscuous concubinage, and have now an opportunity of settling for life." [n]

What troubled Byron most in the relationship was that Teresa, despite her indiscretions, very evidently wanted him to become her devoted *cavalier servente*. Despite his tolerance and his in-

---

[1] This account, in Teresa's manuscript "*Vie de Lord Byron en Italie*," which is so delicately balanced between her desire to let the world know that Byron really loved her and her wish to portray the whole beautiful friendship as Platonic and proper, makes rather curious reading.

clination to defend the Italian manners against the more hypo-
critic English, Byron still could not help feeling as an Englishman
that the office was little better than that of a high-class *gigolo*.
The fact that he frequently preferred to use the colloquial and
slightly cynical term *cicisbeo* ("pretty chick") indicated that he
thought the position more than a little silly. He had ridiculed
the custom good-humoredly in *Beppo,* and though he realized
that the Italians took it seriously as a useful and necessary adjunct
to marriages of convenience, he could not but smirk at the fan-
and shawl-carrying traditions of the cult. Its most distasteful
feature in his eyes was the moral pretense that the relationship
was Platonic and honorable, and the demand that the *servente*
display a certain chivalric formality to preserve the fiction of the
descent of the custom from the traditions of "courtly love." The
gentleman was accepted in society as the *amico* or "friend" not
only of the wife but also of the husband, and the lady was
known as his *dama* or *amica,* while the association was called
an *amicizia* or *relazione.* Since it was a "friendship," the husband was not supposed to be jealous.

The code of *serventismo* was even stricter than that of marriage. The improper conduct of a *dama* and her *amico* was more
likely to shock polite society than the mere cuckolding of a husband. It was not long before fans were fluttering and tongues
wagging at the theater and in the salons where Byron and
Teresa appeared. And Teresa was too happy to care. Byron, on
his side, was persuasive, and he was "not a man to confine himself to sentiment," or to live long on mere "hopes." His private
meetings with Teresa, soon known to everyone but her husband,
were facilitated by a most faithful and understanding confidante,
a governess in Count Guiccioli's household by the name of Fanny
Silvestrini,[2] with whom Teresa took long rides in a gondola on
the pretext of studying French."

When they met daily on the lagoon, as Teresa tries to imply
they did quite by chance, "their gondolas came along side each
other, and then they could speak freely, narrate the sadnesses

[2] Fanny, who was a convenient go-between when the lovers were separated,
was at the time the mistress of Count Guiccioli's steward, Lega Zambelli,
who subsequently passed into Byron's service. (Origo, p. 40.)

of their souls and augment thus their sympathy and strengthen
the bonds of their hearts." [n] They often went as far as the Lido
or to other islands to view the flamboyant Venetian sunsets.
Soon, Teresa recalled, that existence seemed natural to her and
became necessary. If Byron was sometimes "preoccupied and
melancholy," she attributed it to his reflections on the sense of
duty and his superior knowledge of "the human heart." As for
herself, "she gave up her soul entire, or her heart carried it
away. . . . This Venice appeared to her now the abode of light
—of life—the earthly paradise." [n]

The ten days of their bliss came to an end when the Count's
pressing affairs called him back to Ravenna. But the lovers had
accomplished much in that time. It seems apparent that Byron
had tried at first to consider this as just another liaison, and he
was somewhat surprised and shaken by the seriousness it had
early assumed, not only on her side but also on his. The fact that
she was of a noble family, was cultured without being pretentious,
and had, despite her flair for sentiment, a sense of humor not
unlike his own, completed his subjugation. That she had
cuckolded the Count did not surprise Byron so much as that he
himself had been drawn so seriously under her spell. Part of the
melancholy preoccupation that Teresa observed could have re-
sulted from his uneasy feeling that he might not be able to hold
himself to the demands of so unreserved a love, particularly in
the opera-buffa setting of cicisbeism.

Then there was the husband. Though Teresa assured him that
the Count was not jealous, and though the code of serventismo
gave him rights and a respectable standing as an amico, Byron
was not inclined to love by any code but his own, and Count
Guiccioli was something of an enigma. Reputed to be the richest
man in the Romagna, he was also one of the most cultivated.
He had been a friend of Alfieri and was a principal supporter of
the theater in Ravenna, having restored it largely with his own
money." [n] He was, according to his grandson, a handsome man,
"vigorous, rich, intelligent, agreeable in conversation, skilled in
seduction, of fine manners and illustrious family." [n] But he was
also reputed to be somewhat wily and opportunistic, and he was
certainly a man of strong will and determination. Both in politics

and in matrimony he had been shrewd and calculating. During the French occupation of the Romagna, he had realistically preferred putting himself at the head of the canaille to losing his head to them, as he cynically expressed it.[n] With the fall of Napoleon and the coming of the Papal regime, he did not lose his composure, but proceeded to make himself agreeable to the Cardinal Legate and the Papal court. But there lingered a suspicion of his harboring Jacobinical sympathies, particularly since by his third marriage he had allied himself with one of the most ardent of the aristocratic "patriots." Teresa's father, Count Ruggero Gamba Ghiselli, and her brother Pietro were among the stanchest supporters of libertarian principles in Ravenna, and soon became leaders in the revolutionary society of the Carbonari.

Perhaps the authorities wronged Count Guiccioli in their suspicions, for he had too much at stake to be other than favorable to established authority. Besides his palace in Ravenna, he had properties in several provincial towns. The foundation of his fortune had been a calculated marriage with the Contessa Placidia Zinanni, who (according to the Vice Legate's acid report on the Count to the Austrian police) "made up for the disparity of her age—much greater than that of the Cavaliere— and for her physical imperfections, by a very large dowry." [n] One of Guiccioli's housemaids, Angelica Galliani, bore him six illegitimate children, and when his wife protested, he sent the wife, not the mistress, away to a lonely country house, from which she returned only in time to make her will in his favor before she died under circumstances that caused "poison" and "murder" to be whispered by his enemies.

Then he married Angelica, and it was said that with the help of Cardinal Malvasia, to whom he presented a ring, he legitimized some of his children.[n] But on the night his second wife died in 1817, he went to the theater as usual.[n] Before the year was out Count Guiccioli was searching for another wife. This time he sought youth and beauty. Teresa Gamba had recently come from the convent school at Faenza. She was innocent, but smart and pretty.[n] One evening in the home of his old friend Count Gamba she was brought out for his inspection. According to the Count's grandson, it was not a romantic meet-

ing. There was little light in the room, and the aging suitor—
there was nearly forty years difference in their ages—who was
shortsighted, took a candle in hand and walked around her to
see her better, "as if he were engaged in buying a piece of
furniture." [n]

The "furniture" pleased him, for he accepted with her the
comparatively modest dowry of forty-five hundred scudi (Count
Gamba was not wealthy). [n] For the first few months of her marriage—this is probably something she did not tell Byron, although her letters, preserved in the Guiccioli archives, recount
the story—she seemed ecstatically happy and in love with her
husband. But there came a change. Before the year ended she
had become disillusioned.

As soon as she began to see her husband with realistic eyes,
she was ready to welcome an *amico*. She might, indeed, have
succumbed to something less than the "celestial apparition"
which Byron presented to her vision. Once she had given herself, she had no reserve and little discretion. Byron, who was
slightly embarrassed by her flouting of customs for his sake, was
even more proud of his conquest, and could not help boasting to
Kinnaird:

"I have fallen in love . . . with a Romagnuola Countess from
Ravenna, the Spouse of a year of Count Guiccioli, who is sixty—
the Girl twenty. He has eighty thousand ducats of rent, and has
had two wives before. But he is sixty. He is the first of Ravenna
Nobles, but he is sixty. She is fair as Sunrise, and warm as
Noon, we had but ten days to manage all our little matters in
beginning, middle and end; & we managed them; and I have
done my duty with the proper consummation. . . . She is a sort
of an Italian Caroline Lamb, except that She is much prettier,
and not so savage. But she has the same red-hot head, the same
noble disdain of public opinion, with the superstructure of all
that Italy can add to such natural dispositions." [n]

Count Guiccioli's sudden announcement that they must leave
Venice the day after the morrow put Teresa in such a state that
she hurried to the theater with a friend, ahead of her husband,
and, finding Byron in the corridor, went into his box with him,
which in itself was a flouting of custom, for it was always the

duty of the *amico* to visit his lady in her box, and usually in the presence of the husband. There, seated facing him in full view of all the Venetian gossips, she told him of her chagrin. The opera, Rossini's *Otello,* had begun. "It was in the midst of that atmosphere of passionate melody and harmony," Teresa recalled, that she announced to him that she must leave Venice." The following day they had only a chance for some whispered exchanges as Byron handed her into the gondola. It was night, and the Countess, now quiet beside a husband who in her eyes had become doubly dull, felt that "her spirit did not follow her," " but remained behind in Venice.

If not so sentimental, Byron was quite as disconsolate. The worst of it was that he could not communicate with her for some time, for the Count had taken her to one of his properties at the mouth of the Po, and they were to move on from there to another country estate before reaching Ravenna. Teresa had given him the name of an obliging priest, Don Gaspare Perelli, to whom he could in confidence address his letters to her at Ravenna, and she had left the faithful Fanny Silvestrini behind in Venice to receive her own letters to her lover, and to give her news of him. Fanny went to the post office every day to look for letters, but it was not until the 18th that a letter arrived from Cà Zen on the Po.

Teresa, alone in the flat marshy land without flowers or trees, was glad for the absence of her husband on his business, for she could dream of Byron and write him long letters which she took to the neighboring town of Loreo to post." In sweet sadness she wrote in the best style of Santa Chiara, and it is a measure of Byron's infatuation that he was not critical, but only grateful to receive her letter. He replied (and this is the first of his letters which she preserved) in a clear hand as if he had copied it out carefully after making a rough draft in this unfamiliar language, for he wrote in a fluent but somewhat rhetorical Italian, quite unlike his usual English letters: "My dearest Love: Your dearest letter came today and gave me my first moment of happiness since your departure. . . . Perhaps if I loved you less it would not cost me so much to express my thoughts, but now I have to overcome the double difficulty of expressing an unbearable suffering in a language foreign to me. . . .

"You vowed to be true to me and I will make no vows to you; let us see which of us will be the more faithful. . . . This however I promise you: You sometimes tell me that I have been your *first* real love—and I assure you that you shall be my last Passion. I may well hope not to fall in love again, now that everything has become indifferent to me. Before I knew you—I felt an interest in many women, but never in one only. Now I love *you*, there is no other woman in the world for me." [n]

Still lovesick as an adolescent in the first throes of the passion, or at least self-intoxicated to the same degree with the sweet melancholy of separation and longing, Byron wrote again on the 25th: "My Teresa, where are you? Everything here reminds me of you—everything is the same, but you are not here, and I still am. In separation the one who goes away suffers less than the one who stays behind. . . . When I go to the Conversazione, I give myself up to Tedium, too happy to suffer ennui rather than grief. . . . I hear, without the slightest emotion, the opening of that door which I used to watch with so much anxiety when I was there before you, hoping to see you come in. I will not speak of *much dearer* places still, for *there* I shall not go—*until* you return."

He continued: "For some years I have been trying systematically to avoid strong passions, having suffered too much from the tyranny of Love. *Never to feel admiration*—and to enjoy myself without giving too much importance to the enjoyment in itself—to feel indifference towards human affairs—contempt for many, but hatred for none,—this was the basis of my philosophy. I did not mean to love any more, nor did I hope to receive Love. You have put to flight all my resolutions—now I am all yours. . . . You have been mine—and, whatever the outcome—I am, and eternally shall be, entirely yours. I kiss you a thousand and a thousand times. . . ." [n]

From Cà Zen the Guicciolis had moved on, in the meantime, to another property of the Count, an old abbey among the marshes, where Teresa developed a fever that grew worse. The

doctor ordered her back to Ravenna, but during the forty-mile
jaunt over bad roads she had a miscarriage and arrived in a state
which made it necessary for her to take to her bed. As soon as
she was able to write, she passed the news on to Fanny, who
told Byron. When Byron wrote again, he was disturbed by the
fact that Teresa had not mentioned having received two previous
letters he had addressed to Perelli, and that she had been rather
vague about her illness. It is apparent that Byron was a little
put out by Teresa's lack of caution, and her subsequent letters
did not reassure him. But Fanny felt certain that Byron's reluctance to move until he had greater assurances of safety in
their liaison was caused by no cooling of his passion, for "he has
been so full of you that he has not allowed himself any diversion,
for all Byron's diversions are proclaimed by the whole of Venice;
but now no one hears any more talk about him. . . ." [n]

Despite Byron's undoubted fervor, however, the passing of
time, the equivocal situation in Ravenna, and the dissuasion
of his English friends (Hoppner and Scott apparently thought
he was making a fool of himself and tried to magnify the embarrassments and dangers of his going to Ravenna) caused him
to postpone indefinitely his leaving. And inevitably in the frustration of the delay other thoughts came to him, disturbing
thoughts that he could not control. In the first days after Teresa's
departure, while she was at Cà Zen, he began some "Stanzas to
the Po," [n] which were a franker outpouring of his feelings than
could have pleased the lady to whom they were addressed:

> River, that rollest by the ancient walls,
>   Where dwells the Lady of my love, when she
> Walks by thy brink, and there perchance recalls
>   A faint and fleeting memory of me . . .
>
> But that which keepeth us apart is not
>   Distance, nor depth of wave, nor space of earth,
> But the distraction of a various lot,
>   As various as the climates of our birth. [n]

During the first half of May these disquieting reflections in
creased with further delays, which in his sensitiveness he as-

cribed to her unwillingness to give him clear instructions. In the meantime he had received a warning from Hobhouse in reply to his first letter announcing the new liaison. "Don't you go after that terra firma lady," Hobhouse wrote; "they are very vixens, in those parts especially, and I recollect when I was at Ferrara seeing or hearing of two women in the hospital who had stabbed one another in the ——, and all *per gelosia!*" [n]

But Byron replied with his usual frankness and some bravado: "The adventure is so far past preventing—that we had consummated our unlawful union with the proper rites four days and daily, previously to *her* leaving Venice. She was with child too, previous to this ingrafting, and to our connection, but miscarried at Pomposa on the road to R[avenn]a, on her return, and is now on her recovery.[3] For anything I know, the affair may terminate in some such way as you hint at, for they are liberal with the knife in R[avenn]a and the Cavalier Conte G., her respected Lord, is shrewdly suspected of two assassinations already. . . . be that as it may, everything is to be risked for a woman one likes. . . ." [n]

Amid these uncertainties, held in the vise of this new passion, Byron turned involuntarily back to the one satisfactory love of his life. With uninhibited fervor he poured out to Augusta his deepest longings for a renewal of what he knew in his inmost mind could never be restored.

"My dearest Love—" he wrote, ". . . I have never ceased nor can cease to feel for a moment that perfect & boundless attachment which bound & binds me to you—which renders me utterly incapable of *real* love for any other human being—for what could they be to me after *you?* My own x x x x [n] we may have been very wrong—but I repent of nothing except that cursed marriage—& your refusing to continue to love me as you had loved me—I can neither forget nor *quite forgive* you for that precious piece of reformation.—but I can never be other than

[3] Byron later wrote to Lord Kinnaird: "I can't tell whether I was the involuntary cause of the miscarriage, but certes I was not the father of the fœtus, for she was three months advanced before our first passade, and whether the Count was the parent or not I can't imagine; perhaps he might; they are but a year married, and she miscarried once before." (*B-SP*, II, 456. Letter of May 26, 1819.)

I have been—and whenever I love anything it is because it reminds me in some way or other of yourself. . . .[4] It is heart-
breaking to think of our long Separation—and I am sure more
than punishment enough for all our sins—Dante is more humane
in his 'Hell' for he places his unfortunate lovers (Francesca of
Rimini & Paolo whose case fell a good deal short of *ours*—
though sufficiently naughty) in company—and though they suffer—it is at least together. . . . you may have seen me harsh
& exasperated with all things around me; grieved & tortured
with *your new resolution,*—& the soon after persecution of that
infamous fiend who drove me from my Country & conspired
against my life—by endeavouring to deprive me of all that could
render it precious—but remember that even then *you* were the
sole object that cost me a tear? and *what tears!* do you remember
our parting? . . . They say absence destroys weak passions—&
confirms strong ones—Alas! *mine* for you is the union of all passions & of all affections—Has strengthened itself but will destroy me. . . ."[n]

It was easy too for Byron in his present frustrated mood to
slip back into his libertine habits of the past months. The fact
that he could do so in the face of his sincere passion for Teresa
added to his self-dissatisfaction and made him wonder the more
whether he could commit himself to one woman forever. The
very night that he wrote to Augusta he had an adventure with
the young daughter of a nobleman, Angelina, about whom he
had written to Kinnaird some weeks earlier, before he met Teresa. He could look at the affair with a detached amusement; he
felt himself no more than physically and technically unfaithful
to either Augusta or Teresa, and that from habit had become
scarcely important. The next day he wrote to Murray:

[4] The Marchesa Origo emphasizes the fact that Teresa reminded Byron
in many ways of Augusta. "To both Augusta and Teresa he showed the
same half-humorous, half-mocking tenderness; with both of them he found
the release from self-consciousness that brought him gaiety and peace. For
Byron did not want women to understand him: Annabella had understood
him, and what had that led to?" (Origo, p. 13.) Byron later wrote to
Augusta about Teresa: "She has a good deal of *us* too. I mean that turn for
ridicule like Aunt Sophy and you and I & all the B's." (*Astarte,* p. 308.
Letter of Oct. 5, 1821.)

"In going, about an hour and a half ago, to a rendezvous with a Venetian girl (unmarried and the daughter of one of their nobles), I tumbled into the Grand Canal, and, not choosing to miss my appointment by the delays of changing, I have been perched in a balcony with my wet clothes on ever since, till this minute that on my return I have slipped into my dressing-gown." The connection had been cut off for some time by Angelina's "flinty-hearted father," "but the father hath lately been laid up, and the brother is at Milan, and the mother falls asleep, and the Servants are naturally on the wrong side of the question, and there is no Moon at Midnight just now, so that we have lately been able to recommence." [n]

While he was waiting for Teresa's instructions, Byron was annoyed by seeing in *Galignani's Messenger*, a newspaper published in English in Paris and circulated widely on the Continent, an announcement of a tale called *The Vampyre*, with his name attached to that of the author, Dr. Polidori, his erstwhile physician, who had taken a ghost-story idea which Byron had projected at Diodati and written a story of his own on the subject. With it, as advertised by Galignani, was a wholly spurious "Account of Lord Byron's Residence in the Island of Mityline." Byron asked the editor of the *Messenger* for a contradiction: "If the book is clever, it would be base to deprive the real writer, whoever he may be, of his honours; and if stupid, I desire the responsibility of nobody's dullness but my own." [n]

Byron was further irritated by a remark about the second canto of *Don Juan* in a letter from Hobhouse: "I hope it is more decenter than the first, else were we all shamed." [n] "Mr. Hobhouse is at it again about indelicacy," he wrote to Murray. "There is *no indelicacy*; if he wants *that*, let him read Swift, his great Idol. . . ." [n]

And, writing to Murray again after receiving his plea to avoid "approximations to indelicacy," [n] Byron finally abandoned any pretense that there was no indelicacy in the poem, saying: "this reminds me of George Lamb's quarrel at Cambridge with Scrope Davies. 'Sir,' said George, 'he *hinted* at my *illegitimacy*.' 'Yes,' said Scrope, 'I called him a damned adulterous bastard'; the approximation and the hint are not unlike." [n]

Byron was eager enough to see Teresa again, but he was not as devoid of amusement in Venice as Fanny Silvestrini wished her friend in Ravenna to think. Apparently he kept up his intrigue with Angelina or some "other harlotry," to use his own expression, until very near the time of his departure, for on the 25th he confessed to Murray:

"I write to you in the agonies of a *Sirocco* which annihilates me—and I have been fool enough to do four things since dinner, which are as well omitted in very hot weather: 1stly—to take a woman—" 2ndly to play at billiards from ten till twelve, under the influence of lighted lamps that doubled the heat—3rdly to go afterwards into a red-hot Conversazione of the Countess Benzon's—and 4thly, to begin this letter at three in the morning.— But being begun, it must be finished." [n]

Nevertheless on the 26th he announced to Lord Kinnaird, who was still traveling in Italy, that he was leaving on Saturday (the 29th). His intention was to stop at Bologna going and returning and to remain only a few days at Ravenna. ". . . I am really very much in love," he confessed, "yet I see no great use in not adopting a little caution; we had already terminated the *Essential* part of the business four continuous days previous to her setting out from V. (the whole affair was of a week) so that there is nothing very new before us." [n]

Just before he left, Fanny, aware of Byron's uneasiness, wrote Teresa pleadingly: "Control yourself, for Mercy's sake, before your husband and the whole of Ravenna. Do not let Love betray you. . . ." [n]

Fanny could afford to be ardent in her efforts to make things run smoothly for the lovers, for she had been liberally rewarded by Byron for her faithful service as a female Pandarus. She confessed naïvely to Teresa that "Mylord has shown me such signs of his generosity and his good heart that I have been astounded and shall always be grateful." [n]

At best, traveling was onerous to Byron. It was the first of June before he actually left Venice. He had sent his horses from the Lido to La Mira sometime before. Though he expected to be back within a month, many arrangements had to be made. Allegra was left with the Hoppners, and Hoppner's clerk Richard

Edgecombe, who had for some time looked after Byron's business affairs, was left in charge of the Palazzo Mocenigo and all the servants and the menagerie, which was constantly growing (Byron had only a few days before leaving ordered Murray to send out to him along with toothbrushes, powder, magnesia, and Macassar oil, "a Bulldog, a terrier, and two Newfoundland dogs").[n] Dorville, secretary to the Consul, was to check the accounts of Edgecombe, and Hoppner himself promised to keep a watch on Byron's affairs in Venice and to forward his letters.[n]

It was in a very mixed mood that Byron quitted the island city for this adventure to which he was drawn by the mingled weakness and fidelity of his nature. Before leaving, he wrote out a new draft of the poem he had begun in April, the "Stanzas to the Po." He finished it the next day at Padua. The last lines now expressed the conflict in his emotions:

> My heart is all meridian, were it not
>   I had not suffered now, nor should I be
> Despite old tortures ne'er to be forgot
>   The slave again—Oh! Love! at least of thee!
> 'Tis vain to struggle, I have struggled long
>   To love again no more as once I loved,
> Oh! Time! why leave this ~~worst of~~ earliest Passions strong?
>   To tear a heart which pants to be unmoved? [n]

From Padua, Byron wrote to Hoppner on June 2: "I am just setting off for Ferrara. . . . I am proceeding in no very good humour, for La G[uiccioli]'s instructions are rather calculated to produce an *éclat*—and perhaps a scene—than any decent iniquity. . . . Now to go to cuckold a Papal Count, who, like Candide, has already been 'the death of two men one of whom was a priest,' in his own house is rather too much for my modesty, when there are several other places at least as good for the purpose. . . . The Charmer forgets that a man may be whistled anywhere *before*, but that *after*—a Journey in an Italian June is a Conscription, and therefore she should have been less liberal in Venice, or less exigent at Ravenna. If I was not the most constant of men, I should now be swimming from the Lido, instead of smoking in the dust of Padua." [n]

But Byron was in his own way the most constant of men. An inner compulsion kept him from backing down once he had committed himself. It was indeed disturbing to find how strong that "earliest passion" ("worst of passions"?) still was. But he moved on to Ferrara the next day. There Count Mosti, to whom he had sent a letter of introduction which Mengaldo had given him, called on him. Byron attended the Count's *conversazione* and was much pleased with him and his family and the company. "Whenever I meet with any thing agreeable in this world," he wrote Hoppner, "it surprises me so much, and pleases me so much (when my passions are not interested one way or the other), that I go on wondering for a week to come. I feel, too, in great admiration of the Cardinal Legate's red stockings." [n]

But what pleased him more than anything else in Ferrara was the Certosa cemetery, where he saw two epitaphs that threw him back into the old *Childe Harold* mood:

> "*Martini Luigi*
> *Implora pace;*

and

> "*Lucrezia Picini*
> *Implora eterna quiete.*"

"That was all," he wrote Hoppner; "but it appears to me that these two and three words comprise and compress all that can be said on the subject,—and then, in Italian, they are absolute music." [n]

On the 5th, Byron pushed on through the stifling June heat to Bologna and put up at the ancient Pellegrino inn,[n] where he was chagrined to find no letter from Teresa. His intention had been either to go on to Ravenna for a brief visit and then perhaps return to Bologna when the Guicciolis should be there, or to remain in Bologna until they should come. Now he suddenly changed his plans and wrote Hoppner to have preparations made for his return. He wrote that he would be back by the 11th or sooner. But still he lingered, hoping for a letter.

After "picture-gazing" the next morning "at the famous Domenichino and Guido, both of which are superlative," he went to the beautiful cemetery beyond the walls, and, though he found no epitaphs to please him so much as those at Ferrara, he did find "an original of a *Custode,* who reminded me of the grave-digger in Hamlet." "

Still having had no word from Teresa, Byron suddenly gave in to curiosity and anxiety and headed for Ravenna. On June 8 he wrote to Hoppner: "I changed my mind this morning, and decided to go on." " The suspense was too much. A single hair in the balance of impulses and emotions drew him on. Armed with introductions, he could enter the town in the character of a famous poet coming to see the tomb of Dante, and then he might without compromising himself or her discover what was to be done about the Guiccioli business.

The journey over the flat Romagna plain in his heavy Napoleonic carriage took him two days. It was Thursday the 10th when he pulled up at the Porta Sisi, halted by the colorful procession of the festival of Corpus Domini (Corpus Christi), which filled the streets." Byron's enormous carriage itself was an object of curiosity to the crowd that surrounded it. And it happened that one of Teresa's close friends,[5] observing the handsome occupant and knowing something of Teresa's secret, carried the news to her immediately, saying that "never had she seen a man of such beauty." Teresa "did not doubt for an instant that it was Lord Byron." " She was at that moment writing a letter begging him not to come to Ravenna because she had had a relapse and it would be difficult for him to see her."

Byron, still knowing nothing of her condition, finally got passage, after the procession had re-entered the church, to the mean little hotel with the grand name of Albergo Imperiale in the Via di Porta Sisi, only a few steps from the piazza of St. Francis and the tomb of Dante."

He had, Teresa says in her *"Vie de Lord Byron,"* a letter of introduction to Count Alborghetti, "a man of intelligence and Chief of the government of the Lower Romagna in the absence of the Prince Legate." " In order to orient himself and to get some information, he sent off this letter at once, and in return he

[5] The friend, it appears, was Signora Geltrude Vicari, Byron's interest in whom later caused some fits of jealousy in Teresa.

received an invitation to the Count's box at the theater that evening. In the meantime he wrote a note to Teresa announcing his arrival and sent it by a messenger to Perelli."

In the Count's loge, his host, on arriving, asked Byron whether he had any acquaintances in Ravenna.

"'Yes,' replied Byron, 'I am very friendly with Count and Countess Guiccioli.' 'But alas,' replied Alborghetti, 'you will not be able to see the young lady, as they say she is at death's door.' At this sudden and unexpected news, given so abruptly, Byron lost his head—and, unable to control his emotion, replied that if the lady should die, he hoped he would not survive her. Count Alborghetti, who had believed that Byron was attracted to Ravenna by literary interests . . . gaped round-eyed at the emotion of the young Lord. . . . Fortunately, Count Guiccioli, who had caught sight of Lord Byron, then called on him in the box and calmed him by giving him better news." "

After the theater, repentant for having doubted her love and loyalty, Byron wrote again to Teresa, this time without reserve. He knew now why she had not written, and he was caught up again in the web of this passion which was stronger than ever:

"My sweetest Soul—believe that I live for you alone—and do not doubt me. I shall stay here until I know what your wishes really are: and even if you cannot arrange to see me I shall not go away. I beseech you to command me as entirely and eternally yours. I would sacrifice all my hopes for this world and all that we believe we may find in the other—to see you happy. I cannot think of the state of your health without sorrow and tears. Alas, my Treasure! How much we endured—and shall still have to endure! And you so young—so beautiful—so good— you have had to suffer through my fault—what a thought!

"I kiss you a thousand thousand thousand times with all my soul." "

At Count Guiccioli's invitation (prompted by Teresa, no doubt), Byron went to see her the next day. The Count called for him at the hour of the evening promenade and conducted him to her sickbed. The lovers were both extremely agitated, but the circumstances of the meeting were such that they could say little. The emotional phrases of the letter he wrote after he had returned to his hotel give some indication of the state of his mind: "You are so surrounded. . . . It is impossible for me to live long in this state of torment—I am writing to you in tears— and I am not a man who cries easily. When I cry my tears come from the heart, and are of blood." [n]

The first week of his sojourn in Ravenna was trying for Byron. Though he saw her often, as long as Teresa was in bed he had no opportunity for private interviews with her. On her side, she showed a marked improvement as soon as he arrived, and her spirits began to revive. Teresa naïvely believed that the fre- quency of his visits (such being customary in Italy) would cause no astonishment. [n] Byron was not so innocent, but he did not care so long as it brought no harm to Teresa.

Byron was so absorbed in his love that he paid little attention to the local nobility and gentry to whom he had letters, and who called on him and were exceedingly attentive. Having run through the things that might have interested him in the sleepy little town—he cared little for sightseeing even with agreeable companions—he spent hours brooding in his stuffy room at the Imperiale and wrote long impassioned letters to Teresa. The frustration of this situation was almost too much for him. He would have preferred an elopement, "a romance in the Anglo fashion."

In fact, on the 14th, after she had told him that their courier Perelli had left for the country with her uncle, he suspected that they had been betrayed and he suggested a drastic remedy, knowing, however, that she was too tied to convention to agree to such a step. "If trouble arises," he wrote her, "there is only one adequate remedy, that is, to go away together—and for this a great Love is necessary—and some courage. Have you enough?

"I can already anticipate your answer. It will be long and divinely written—but it will end in a negative.

"I kiss you from my heart ten million times." [n]

Teresa treasured this letter as a "masterpiece of passion, of devotion, and of generosity." [n] But Byron was right; her answer was in the negative.

The tension lessened considerably, however, when Teresa was able to leave her bed and go for a ride in the country. On the

15th the doctor thought she was strong enough to take a carriage ride the next day, and she invited Byron to share this first outing she had been able to take since her return to Ravenna. They drove to the forest of umbrella pines that reached from a short distance outside the city to the sea and as far south as Rimini. When they arrived in the forest, the sun was setting in an aureole of gold and opal. "Everything on the earth," Teresa recalled, "was green and fresh from the dews of the morning and the evening. The nightingales were singing—the crickets were sending up their cries of pleasure at the return of coolness. Lord Byron was under the charm of these phenomena of nature. He seemed happy and melancholy at the same time. . . . And when they heard from afar the bells of the city it was impossible not to recall the verses of Dante which begin the 8th Canto of the *Purgatory*." [n]

It was then, Teresa says, that Byron's *Prophecy of Dante* had its origin. Since he had written of Tasso, she said, she would be very happy if he would write something on Italy's greatest poet. "Your desires are my commands," he replied and the next day began the poem, which he dedicated to her. [n] It was finished within the month. Had Teresa been able to read and understand it fully—she knew very little English then—she might have been startled by its defiant and melancholy tone. It was not a simple eulogy of Dante the poet, but was intended as a political appeal using Dante as a symbol of liberty and of principles unshaken by exile and persecution—an appeal to the new Italy to throw off the Bourbon yoke. [n] Interwoven with this theme, as in the *Lament of Tasso*, however, are many of Byron's personal moods and quandaries.

The air of the forest, and especially the chance to have some privacy with Byron, improved Teresa's health, and she seemed to be growing steadily stronger. He generally called twice a day, in the afternoon and again in the evening, and when she could she went riding with him in the forest. One day he saw on her table a copy of Dante's *Inferno*, and they read together what was already a favorite passage of Byron's, and what seemed to parallel their own situation so closely, the episode of Paolo and Francesca. Teresa asked him if it had been translated into English. He replied: *"Non tradotto, ma tradito"*—not translated but betrayed—and he set about making a translation of his own."

But even when they had moments to themselves, Byron was still uncomfortable in the situation, chafing under the necessity of visiting her in the Count's palace while her relatives and friends were about and might come in at any minute. He was unsure of himself in this society. It was a strange, unwelcome feeling for Byron to know that he could not call the plays in a love affair. Not since he had been rebuffed by Mary Chaworth had he felt such insecurity (always excepting the frustration caused by Annabella during the separation). Although he knew that Teresa loved him, he was confused and slightly irritated by the fact that she was determined to make him conform to the conventions of *serventismo*—and it was a condition of that creed that the lady should stay with her husband, not abandon him for the lover. Byron apparently brought up the subject of an elopement again during their first private interview, and she put him off with references to his "duties."

But in a letter of June 20 to Hoppner, Byron made it clear enough that their misunderstandings had been dissolved in a resumption of the relations that had started in Venice—under conditions of danger that made the adventure all the more piquant. Teresa had silenced the doubts of her lover by finding a way to cuckold her husband in his own house. "*She* manages very well—though the local[e] is inconvenient—(no *bolts* and be d——d to them) and we run great risks (were it not at sleeping hours—after dinner) and *no* place but the great Saloon of his own palace—so that if I come away with a Stiletto in my gizzard some fine afternoon—I shall not be astonished—I can't make *him* out at all—he visits me frequently—and takes me out (like Whittington, the Lord Mayor) in a coach and *six* horses. The fact appears to be, that he is completely *governed* by her—for that matter so am I. . . . By the aid of a Priest—a Chambermaid—a young Negro-boy, and a female friend—we are enabled to carry on our unlawful loves. . . .""

It is not then strange that Byron did not at first cultivate the acquaintance of the Ravennese. Even after the Countess began to improve, he went out very seldom except to the Palazzo Guiccioli, though a number of the Ravenna gentry would gladly have shared his society. By the end of June, Byron's saddle horses had arrived, and when he was not with the Guiccioli he preferred communing with the shades of Boccaccio and Dryden in the solitude of the Pineta to frequenting the drawing-rooms of Ravenna. By that time, however, the Cardinal Legate, Alessandro Malvasia, who had been absent when Byron arrived, had returned to Ravenna, and Count Alborghetti, who must have seen the poet several times since that memorable meeting in the theater, was eager for his new friend to meet the Cardinal.

Giuseppe Alborghetti, Secretary General of the Government of the Lower Romagna, was destined to play an important role in Byron's life in Ravenna. As a lay official second in command under the Cardinal Legate, he was in a position of great power and influence. His taste for poetry and his knowledge of English probably drew him first to Byron, who, however, was too much occupied with Teresa just after his arrival to pay much attention even to the chief of the government of the Lower Romagna."

But Byron did accept the Count's invitation to meet the Cardinal," whom he found agreeable. On July 5 he wrote to Lord Kinnaird: "I have been exchanging visits with the Cardinal Legate who called on me to day. He is a fine old fellow, Malvasia by name, and has been rather loose in his youth, without being much tighter in his age. He and I took very kindly to each other." " After the first introduction, the Cardinal was well enough pleased with Byron's conversation to arrange a special party for him, but was amazed and angered when Byron sent a lame excuse and did not appear.

Despite the habitual flippancy of Byron's remarks to his English friends, it is apparent that he was deeply concerned about the health of his *amica*. According to Teresa, it was "impossible to describe the anxiety he showed,—the delicate attentions that he paid me. For a long time he had perpetually medical books in his hands; and not trusting my physicians, he obtained permission from Count Guiccioli to send for a very clever physician, a friend of his, in whom he placed great confidence." " This was Dr. Aglietti of Venice, professor and head of the medical school, who came to Ravenna to see her on Byron's invitation, though ordinarily, Teresa says, he would not "absent himself from Venice for a sovereign." [n]

Byron's anxiety had increased when he wrote to Hoppner on the 2nd: "I greatly fear that the Guiccioli is going into a consumption. . . . Thus it is with every thing and every body for whom I feel any thing like a real attachment. . . . I never even could keep alive a dog that I liked or that liked me." Her cough and fever continued, and yet she would not relinquish any of their love trysts for the sake of her health. Byron observed with his usual frankness: "She bears up *gallantly* in every sense of the word, but I sometimes fear that our *daily* interviews may not [sic] tend to weaken her (I am sure they *don't strengthen me*) but it is not for me to hint this. . . ." [6] But he added with feeling in a postscript: "If any thing happens to my present *Amica*, I have done with the passion for ever—it is my *last* love. As to libertinism, I have sickened myself of that, as was natural in the way I went on, and I have at least derived that advantage from vice, to *love* in the better sense of the word. *This* will be my last adventure—I can hope no more to inspire attachment, and I trust never again to feel it." [n]

This was not a mere rhetorical or histrionic gesture, for Byron realized that he, like Childe Harold, had, both physically and emotionally, grown old beyond his years, that he had lived through all the experiences of life, and yet was driven by habit to seek constantly new sensations to quicken his jaded emotions. The same day that he wrote to Hoppner he confessed to Wedderburn Webster, who had written him a despondent letter: "Mine has not been the most regular, nor the most tranquil, of lives. At thirty I feel there is no more to look forward to. With regard to the imputed 'Corpulence'—my size is certainly increased con-

---

[6] This sentence, omitted by Prothero, is here supplied from a quotation from the letter in the Sotheby Catalogue for Dec. 10–14, 1917. Byron had written to Murray on June 29: ". . . I fear that neither the medical remedies— nor some recent steps *of our own to repair at least the miscarriage*—have done her any great good. . . ." But he added more seriously: "In losing her, I should lose a being who has run great risks on my account, and whom I have every reason to love. . . . I do not know what I *should* do if she died, but I ought to blow my brains out—and I hope that I should." (*LJ*, IV, 320–1; the first sentence here quoted is from the original letter in the Murray MSS.)

siderably; but I am not aware that it amounts to that 'Stupendous' degree which you enquire after. . . . my hair is half grey, and the Crow's-foot has been rather lavish of its indelible steps. My hair, though not gone, seems going, and my teeth remain by way of courtesy; but I suppose they will follow, having been too good to last. I have now been as candid as anything but a too faithful Mirror can be." "

The Guiccioli affair had roused Byron in large part because it had rather surprisingly demonstrated to him that he could still mingle sentiment with passion and that he was not too blasé to respond to a genuine attachment. And yet a remnant of self-distrust manifested itself in a cynical disbelief in the constancy of Teresa. To Lord Kinnaird he wrote on July 5: "I doubt her liking anything for very long, except one thing, and I presume she will soon arrive at varying even that, in which case I should be at liberty to repass the Po. . . ."

It may have been in self-defense, then, that he flirted tentatively with her friend Geltrude (or Gertrude) Vicari. He confided in Lord Kinnaird: "La Geltruda is gone to Bologna, after pinching her left thigh. . . . I was never permitted to set eyes on her *not no more*." "

In the meantime, however, Teresa's health showed a marked improvement shortly after Dr. Aglietti arrived on July 4. He prescribed only a few leeches and some Peruvian bark, which Byron sent for to Venice, but he established in her confidence and the will to get well. The bookish Doctor believed much more in the curative power of the mind and of nature than of pills or plasters. He openly stated that he did not believe in medicine," and he had an intuitive insight into what are now called the psychosomatic causes of illness. Teresa herself came to realize that her ailment had emotional causes, and she later ascribed her cure largely to the presence of Byron and his solicitous attentions. Byron reported to Scott on the 7th: "The G. is better—and will get well with prudence.—Our amatory business goes on *well* and *daily*." "

But the tranquillity of the delicately balanced relations between Byron and his *amica* was soon disturbed by two letters. One was to Teresa from her brother Pietro, who had heard gossip about Byron in Rome and wrote apprehensively about this

seductive English lord and poet, fearing that with her intellectual education she would see him as a Petrarch and herself as a
Laura. "Well, you must know that this man, whom you described
to me in your last letter as an angel upon Earth, is the husband
of a young woman full of innocence and affection like yourself;
and, not satisfied with having abandoned her to give himself up
to a life of disorder, he keeps her shut up in a Castle, of which
many dark mysterious tales are told. It is even said that, in spite
of his rank, he has been a Pirate during his journeys in the
East." "

Though Teresa did not believe the stories about her lover, she
was distressed. She showed the letter to Byron, who was amused
but at the same time annoyed, and she wrote seriously to Pietro
defending her liaison: "I have had constant proofs of the extreme goodness of his Heart! Tears of mental or physical suffering make him almost ill—the dread of treading on an ant makes
him go out of his way—a scene at a play, a sad story or a melodious tune bring tears to his eyes." "

Byron was much more upset, however, by a letter he received
a few days later from Hoppner, the British Consul in Venice, who,
along with Alexander Scott and Mengaldo, was a little piqued
that Byron should have quitted their society for a serious attachment to a woman whom they believed fickle and unworthy of
him. It is probable that Hoppner and his rather prim Swiss wife
genuinely believed that they were doing their friend a service
by warning him against this entanglement. Hoppner deliberately
hit at a very tender spot by suggesting that Teresa intended to
entangle Byron in her net merely from vanity and then make
him a laughingstock."

Byron was naturally angry at Hoppner and did not reply, but
he felt called on to defend his vanity to Alexander Scott: "I
never supposed that the G. was to be a despairing shepherdess
—nor did I search very nicely into her motives—all I know is
that *she* sought me—and that I have *had her—there and here
and everywhere*—so that if there is any fool-making on the occasion I humbly suspect that *two* can play at that. . . . What
does H. mean by '*when she is sure of me*'? how '*sure*'? When a
man has been for some time in the habit of *keying* a female—

methinks it is his own fault if the being 'left in the lurch' greatly incommodes him, because the woman can never forget that she has been 'under his paunch.' . . ."

He freely admitted his attachment: "You will think me a damned fool—but when she was supposed in danger—I was really and truly on the point of poisoning myself—and I have got the drug still in my drawer." "

The letter as a whole does not show the best sides of Byron's character, but, as the Marchesa Origo remarks, what it "does *not* show, is indifference to Teresa." " And Teresa sensed this.

Teresa, for her part, lost her head much less than Byron over the accusations against her. She wrote a letter of calm dignity and assurance to Scott, urging him to "give counsels of patience to those who are condemning me for future errors. . . . What a wretch I should consider myself if I feared that, one day, so great a man would blush to have loved me!" "

Despite these distressing episodes, Teresa's health improved remarkably and constantly while she basked in the assurance of Byron's love. And in her joyous confidence she could sometimes be fickle and cause her *amico* the exquisite torture of jealousy. At best, passion was always coupled with pain in Byron's experience, and now the venom of Hoppner's letter heightened his sensitivity to imagined slights, even though he knew that Teresa loved him. She had only to talk with someone else at the theater and he was in agony. By himself in his wretched hotel room, his imagination heated, he wrote:

"I have noticed that every time I turned my head toward the stage you turned your eyes to look at that man—and this, after all that had happened today! But do not fear, tomorrow evening I shall leave the field clear to him. I have no strength to bear a fresh torment every day—you have made me despicable in my own eyes—and perhaps soon in those of others. . . . Let me go —it is better to die from the pain of separation, than from that of betrayal—my life now is a constant agony." "

Teresa's sufficient comment on this letter was written years later when she was sorting over the precious letters and notes of the lover she never forgot: "*Billet de jalousie* magnifique—passionné—sublime mais *très injuste. Il ne me connaissait encore*

que depuis trop peu!!!" [n] When she saw him alone she could easily allay his doubts and suspicions, but the equivocal situation
which forced him to make love in the palace of the Count who
befriended him and to dodge relatives and friends made him
peculiarly prone to see slights where none was intended.

But greater tranquillity came to Byron as his *amica* grew
stronger and he was able to see her alone more often, particularly
during their rides in the Pineta. He had easily made a conquest
of Count Guiccioli's elder son Ferdinando, not too well treated
by his father. When Teresa was not able to go out, the boy, then
about fourteen, sometimes accompanied Byron on his canters
through the forest. And by the middle of July, when Teresa could
drive out again, she and Byron often took him along, thus satisfying the proprieties without obliging the Count to disturb his
siesta by trailing along in his coach and six horses. But they
found most pleasure, when Teresa was strong enough, in mounting on horseback for their ride among the pines.

Teresa recalled it as a wholly idyllic experience. But such quiet
pleasure was boring to the wayward heart of Byron after a time.
And since he had never trained that untamed heart to restrain
its impulses, his thoughts traced a backward course that was
often to puzzle and sometimes to disturb Teresa. It took only a
letter from Holstein enclosing a paper discussing the Byron separation to cause him to pause and pen a curious objective letter
to Annabella.[n] Teresa wrote him at a later time apropos of his
recurrent return to sentimental thoughts of his wife: "The human
heart is very complicated—and I fear I shall never be able to
understand it." [n]

But fonder memories were roused when he heard again from
Augusta. He wrote: "I do not like at all this pain in your side
and always think of your mother's constitution—you must always be to me the first consideration in the World.—Shall I come
to *you?*—or would a warm climate do you good?—if so say the
word—and I will provide you & your whole family (including
that precious luggage your Husband) with the means of making
an agreeable journey—you need not fear about *me*—I am much
altered—and should be little trouble to you—nor would I give
you more of my company than you like. . . .

"I write from Ravenna—I came here on account of a Countess Guiccioli. . . . She is pretty—a great Coquette—extremely vain—excessively affected—clever enough—without the smallest principle—with a good deal of imagination and some passion;— She had set her heart on carrying me off from Venice out of vanity—and succeeded—and having made herself the subject of general conversation has greatly contributed to her recovery. . . .[7]

"She is an Equestrian too—but a bore in her rides—for she can't guide her horse—and he runs after mine—and tries to bite him—and then she begins screaming in a high hat and Sky-blue riding habit—making a most absurd figure—and embarrassing me and both our grooms—who have the devil's own work to keep her from tumbling—or having her cloathes torn off by the trees and thickets of the Pine forest.—I fell a little in love with her intimate friend—a certain Geltruda—(that is Gertrude) who is very young & seems very well disposed to be perfidious— but alas!—*her* husband is jealous—and the G. also detected me in an illicit squeezing of hands, the consequence of which was that the friend was whisked off to Bologna for a few days—and since her return I have never been able to see her but twice . . . But I have a Priest who befriends me—and the Gertrude says a good deal with her great black eyes, so that perhaps—but Alas! I mean to give up these things altogether." [n]

It is a mistake, however, to judge Byron's feelings for Teresa solely by his detached and sometimes caustic letters, which were always for him a kind of release for the uninhibited ego and no adequate measure of his capacity for affection and devotion. He could see quite as well as Hoppner and Scott, in the devastatingly clear light which filled his mind in the early morning hours when he did his writing, that Teresa was slightly ridiculous and

[7] Byron enclosed a copy of a printed broadsheet with a sonnet addressed by Teresa to her cousin, the Countess Teresa Cavalli, on her marriage with Count Francesco Sassi. He marked several lines in which she mentioned her spouse, who, she said, satisfied all her desires and to whom she was "before God eternally linked in faithfulness." Opposite Teresa's statement "And thus cemented in its vows my heart which is of adamant does not yield to any force" he wrote: "150 volte" ("150 times").

vain, but he was equally sincere when he assured her that he loved her and that her wish was his command.

By the end of July, Byron finally decided to cut his ties with Venice entirely. Despite the fact that he knew he had good friends there, the gossip retailed him by Hoppner and Scott had caused a revulsion of feeling toward all its inhabitants.

In his new resolution to leave Venice for good, Byron was perplexed with the problem of what to do with Allegra. He had a certain fondness for her, and would have been glad to have her with him, but he also felt the responsibility for her welfare and knew that with the uncertainty of his plans and the irregularity of his life he could not give her a proper environment, especially as she grew older. In May, at the time Byron was planning his visit to Teresa in Ravenna, a Mrs. Vavassour, a wealthy childless widow from the north of England, having seen Allegra at the Hoppners', was much taken with her and offered to adopt her provided Byron would relinquish all parental authority." Mrs. Hoppner promptly wrote to Claire of the proposal, and Claire dashed off a letter to Byron urging him not to make any decision hastily.

Byron declined to give up parental authority over his child, but apparently he still thought of the possibility of Mrs. Vavassour taking charge of her education." As summer came on, the Hoppners were concerned for Allegra's health and proposed that she be sent to Switzerland, but Byron demurred. Possibly at the Hoppners' suggestion, Elise, the Swiss nurse who had brought her to Venice, was dismissed sometime after the Shelleys left, and Allegra had been entrusted to a maid of Mrs. Hoppner's choice. The Consul's wife wrote to Mary Shelley in the winter that the child *"est devenue tranquille et sérieuse comme une petite vieille, ce qui nous peine beaucoup."* "

When the Hoppners departed, they left Allegra with Mrs. Martens, the wife of the Danish Consul, at La Mira, "a change of air being absolutely necessary for her, until you decide what is to be done with her." " But Byron's decisions still depended very much upon his *dama,* despite what he might say, and she was, however little he liked it, dependent upon the movements of her husband the Count. In the meantime the tranquillity of the rides in the pine forest was disturbed by letters from England which irritated Byron anew. Murray was apparently stalling on the publication of *Don Juan* until he could get Byron to consent to more excisions of matter that he thought might damage his reputation or react against the sale. But, having given up the attack on Castlereagh and the caustic dedication to Southey, Byron would yield no more. "You ask me to spare Romilly—" he wrote, "ask the worms." [n]

Douglas Kinnaird had got Murray to consent to pay five hundred guineas for *Mazeppa* and fifteen hundred guineas for the first two cantos of *Don Juan,* with the *Ode on Venice* thrown in.[n] *Mazeppa* and the *Ode* were published June 28, 1819. On July 15, Murray, with considerable trepidation, sent out to the booksellers the quarto edition of the two cantos of *Don Juan* with only the printer's name on the title page.[n]

Murray's fears concerning the reception of the poem were not groundless. Gifford, who was well disposed toward Byron, wrote to the publisher: "How goes on, or rather how goes off, the Don? I read the second canto this morning, and lost all patience at seeing so much beauty so wantonly and perversely disfigured." [n] And a week after the poem appeared Kinnaird wrote to Hobhouse: "Don Juan has, as far as I can learn, *failed*—I think the quarto edition has disgusted people, & has announced a pretension it never was meant to put forth." [n]

Strangely enough, however, the satire on Lady Byron as Donna Inez, which Hobhouse and Augusta and everyone else feared would mortally wound the sensitive Annabella, made, apparently, a very light impression in that quarter. Perhaps Augusta's dire forebodings had made Annabella expect something much worse, or she may only have been stoically pretending that it did not affect her. She saw it soon after its publication and reported that "the impression was not so disagreeable as I expected." She continued:

"In the first place I am very much relieved to find that there is not anything which I can be expected to notice. As for myself, I do not think that my sins are in the pharisaical or pedantic line, and I am very sure that he does not think they are, but

avails himself of the prejudices which some may entertain
against me, to give a plausible colouring to his accusations. I
must however confess that the quizzing in one or two passages
was so good as to make me smile at myself. . . ." [n]

But other matters were again absorbing Byron's attention in
Ravenna. On an evening in July, Teresa had just sent her lover
a jocular note when her husband walked in and handed her some
verses which he had received in an anonymous communication
which said they were being sung by the boys in the street. [n] The
verses were in the form of a satirical sonnet directed at the
Count:

> Of Lord enamoured, all the world knows,
> The wife her falcon has a Cuckoo made,
> While still in ignorance the old bird goes
> That low he now should hang his horned head. [n]

After some hesitation, Teresa showed Byron the verses. He
"was extremely agitated." [n] But she quieted him with the assurance that the Count had only disdain for the anonymous sonnet.
Though the Count remained polite and apparently friendly, this
episode made Byron feel the more wary and the more insecure
in his position. Was the Count really so innocent, or so forgiving,
or was he merely biding his time for a more exquisite revenge?
But while the Count was generally disliked, Byron was already
popular, both among the patricians, though he saw little of them,
and among the ordinary people, for his generosity and his willingness to relieve distress were well known. And he had taken a
seat at the theater, of which he became a regular patron.

But now a new blow struck the lovers. Since Teresa's health
had so much improved, she could no longer refuse to accompany
her husband on his projected journey to his property in Bologna.
Whether this was a calculated design of the Count to separate
them or to escape from the buffoons of Ravenna, Byron could
not tell. As usual, the Count's announcement came suddenly.
The separation was not to be long, for the lovers planned to meet
in Bologna, but to them it seemed forever.

Teresa apparently reproached Byron for having departed so
suddenly when he got the astounding news. He replied: "I kissed

your hand and hurried away, so as not to show my suffering, which would only too clearly have revealed the whole, whole truth! I vow that I love you a thousand times more than when I knew you in V[enice]. You know it—you feel it. *Think*, my love, of *those* moments—delicious—dangerous. . . . The hall! Those rooms! The open doors! The servants so curious and so near— Ferdinando—the visitors! how many obstacles! But all overcome —it has been the real triumph of Love—a hundred times Victor." "

Before going to Bologna, the Guicciolis spent a couple of days at a summer residence of the Count at Forlì, a transformed abbey. Piqued by the discovery that she had concealed the loss of a ring he had given her, Byron wrote Teresa:

"Farewell, my dearest *Evil*—farewell, my torment—farewell, my *all* (but *not all mine!*) I kiss you more often than I have ever kissed you—and this (if Memory does not deceive me) should be a fine number of times, counting from the beginning. Meanwhile,—you can be sure of me—of my love—and of your power." "

The Guicciolis left for Bologna on Monday the 9th," Byron following the day after. Starting at three on the morning of August 10, Byron must have arrived in Bologna by nightfall. He took the same rooms again at the Pellegrino. The next evening he accompanied the Guicciolis to the Arena del Sole Theatre to see the tragic actress Mme Pelzet in Alfieri's *Mirra*." The play, based upon a theme of incest, the love of a young girl for her father (suggested by Ovid's *Metamorphoses*, lib. x, wherein Myrrha became the mother of Adonis by her father), affected Byron profoundly. He wrote about it to Murray the next day:

". . . the two last acts . . . threw me into convulsions. I do not mean by that word a lady's hysterics, but the agony of reluctant tears, and the choaking shudder, which I do not often undergo for fiction. . . . The worst was, that the 'dama,' in whose box I was, went off in the same way, I really believe more from fright than any other sympathy—at least with the players: but she has been ill, and I have been ill, and we are all languid and pathetic this morning, with great expenditure of Sal Volatile." "

Then, in answer to Murray's account of the English reaction to *Don Juan,* he wrote with an exasperated eloquence born of confidence in the creation of his brain. "You are right, Gifford is right, Crabbe is right, Hobhouse is right—you are all right, and I am all wrong; but do, pray, let me have that pleasure. Cut me up root and branch; quarter me in the *Quarterly;* send round my *disjecti membra poetæ,* like those of the Levite's Concubine; make me, if you will, a spectacle to men and angels; but don't ask me to alter, for I can't:—I am obstinate and lazy—and there's the truth.

"But nevertheless, I will answer your friend C[ohen]," who objects to the quick succession of fun and gravity, as if in that case the gravity did not (in intention, at least) heighten the fun. His metaphor is, that 'we are never scorched and drenched at the same time.' Blessings on his experience! . . . Did he never play at Cricket, or walk a mile in hot weather? Did he never spill a dish of tea over his testicles in handing a cup to his charmer, to the great shame of his nankeen breeches? Did he never swim in the sea at Noonday with the Sun in his eyes and on his head, which all the foam of Ocean could not cool? Did he never draw his foot out of a tub of too hot water, damning his eyes and his valet's? Did he never inject for a Gonorrhea? or make water through an ulcerated Urethra? Was he ever in a Turkish bath, that marble paradise of sherbet and Sodomy?"

Murray had asked him for the plan of *Don Juan* in future cantos. He replied: "I *have* no plan—I *had* no plan; but I had or have materials; though if, like Tony Lumpkin, I am 'to be snubbed so when I am in spirits,' the poem will be naught, and the poet turn serious again. If it don't take, I will leave it off where it is, with all due respect to the Public; but if continued, it must be in my own way. . . . Why, Man, the Soul of such writing is its licence; at least the *liberty* of that *licence,* if one likes—*not* that one should abuse it. . . . But a truce to these reflections. You are too earnest and eager about a work never intended to be serious. Do you suppose that I could have any intention but to giggle and make giggle?" "

After the unhappy experience at the theater, Teresa went out very little, but spent most of her time in the Palazzo Savioli in

Via Galliera, a massive palace with a high-ceilinged and elabo-
rately decorated gallery and a many-windowed loggia." There
Byron joined her, and they spent the evenings, when the Count
went to the theater or to *conversazioni*, under the cool trees or
by the fountain in the garden. The calculating Count was willing
enough to be tolerant of his wife's *cavalier servente*. Perhaps
the fires of passion had burned out in him and he was not
really jealous. Perhaps he even liked Byron. At least he felt
that the English lord could be useful to him, and soon after
his arrival in Bologna he broached a wish which Byron, always
obliging, was willing enough to attempt to fulfill. On August
12, Byron wrote to Murray:

"Will you get a favour done for me? *You* can, by your Government friends, Croker, Canning, or my old Schoolfellow Peel,
and I can't. Here it is. Will you ask them to appoint (*without
salary or emolument*) a noble Italian (whom I will name afterwards) Consul or Vice-Consul for Ravenna? . . . I know that
in the Levant you make consuls and Vice-Consuls, perpetually,
of foreigners. This man is a Patrician, and has twelve thousand
a year. His motive is a British protection in case of new In-
vasions." [n]

Count Guiccioli was aware that his equivocal politics as well
as his wealth were watched by the Austrians and by others,
and that it would be valuable to have powerful foreign support
in the event that political uprisings upset the *status quo*. Byron
did not know, however, that his own movements were being
watched by the Austrian police. From the time that he first
set foot in Italy, and especially since his attempt to rescue Dr.
Polidori from the police in Milan, he had been under suspicion
as a liberal, a freethinker, and a friend of a number of suspect
Italian writers (his friendship with Pellegrino Rossi was made
much of). And now that there was known to be plotting against
the government in the Romagna, his visit there was watched
with particular care. While he was still in Ravenna, directives
had gone out from the assistant to the Director-General of Police
in Rome to the Director of Police at Bologna suggesting that his
correspondence with Count Rangone be watched and he himself be observed "to gain information concerning his attitude

towards political questions." ⁿ And on his return to Bologna, police spies watched him constantly, noting his movements, his rising- and retiring-hours, his visitors and his visits to others, and generally reporting extremely garbled information to headquarters.

In order to have greater privacy and more room, soon after his arrival Byron had taken the Palazzo Merendoni in the Via Galliera, only a few doors from the Guicciolis' palace.ⁿ He was already planning to have his daughter Allegra sent on from Venice. On August 21 the police spies reported that he was still at the Pellegrino waiting until the Casa Merendoni was ready for his occupancy. The report added: *"Byron is a man of letters, and his literary merit will attract to him the most distinguished men of learning in Bologna. This class of men has no love for the Government."* ⁿ

On the 22nd the police spy informed his superior that Byron had that day sent a messenger to the police to demand a passport for a servant to carry a pressing letter to Venice.ⁿ That that letter was not concerned with treasonable business we now know, for it is still extant. It was addressed to Alexander Scott, urging him to send Allegra with a governess and accompanied by the clerk Edgecombe.

In the intervals of love-making—which never in itself completely satisfied Byron's active spirit—he began to think of England or of carving out a fresh career in some new world like South America, which region was increasingly to occupy him as the milieu of his dream of escape. He wrote to Hobhouse on the 20th:

"My time has been passed viciously and agreeably; at thirty-one so few years, months, days hours or minutes remain, that 'Carpe *diem*' is not enough. I have been obliged to crop even the seconds, for who can trust to *to-morrow? to-morrow* quotha? *to-hour, to-minute.* I can not repent me (I try very often) so much of anything I have done, as of anything I have left undone. Alas! I have been but idle, and have the prospect of an early decay, without having seized every available instant of our pleasurable years."

News that Douglas Kinnaird had been elected to Parliament

from Bishop's Castle turned Byron's thoughts tentatively again
to a political career, or perhaps even something more military
and daring, if the battle for reform in England turned to revolution. He wrote Hobhouse that he had two notions: ". . . one
to visit England in the Spring, the other to go to South America.
Europe is grown decrepit; besides, it is all the same thing over
again; those fellows are fresh as their world, and fierce as their
earthquakes. . . .

"I would embark (with Fletcher as a breeding beast of
burthen) and possess myself of the pinnacle of the Andes, or
a spacious plain of unbounded extent in an eligible earthquake
situation." [n]

On the 22nd, Teresa was obliged to leave for several days with
her husband to visit some of his properties between Bologna and
Ferrara, and Byron had more time for his melancholy reflections
and self-questioning. As he wandered about disconsolately in
the garden filled with the memories of his love (Teresa had left
him the key to the Palazzo Savioli and had given orders that
he was to be given freedom of the garden), Byron became
almost physically ill with the conflict of emotions. "I am so
bilious," he wrote Hobhouse, "that I nearly lose my head, and so
nervous that I cry for nothing; at least to day I burst into tears,
all alone by myself, over a cistern of Gold fishes, which are not
pathetic animals. . . . I have had no particular cause of griefs,
except the usual accompaniments of all unlawful passions. I
have to do with a woman rendered perfectly disinterested by
her situation in life, and young and amiable and pretty. . . .
But I feel—and I feel it bitterly—that a man should not consume
his life at the side and on the bosom of a woman, and a stranger;
that even the recompense, and it is much, is not enough, and
that this Cicisbean existence is to be condemned. But I have
neither the strength of mind to break my chain, nor the insensibility which would deaden its weight." [n]

Love such as Byron had for Teresa exerted a kind of oppressive
compulsion, as much pain as pleasure, and bound him to a
fidelity that weathered all the revolts of the free male ego and
all reasoned analysis. Teresa herself had wisely kept his passion
tied to conceptions of youthful romance. It had been his habit

since she left to go daily to the Palazzo Savioli at the usual
hours of his visiting her and to wander through her rooms. One
of her favorite books was a fat little volume of Mme de Staël's
Corinne, in small print and bound in purple plush. Byron used
to twit her about her fondness for this sentimental novel, but
now he grew sentimental himself when he saw it. He carried
it out into the garden, where he wrote on the margin of the
index page: *ⁿ*

"My dear Teresa,—I have read this book in your garden;—
my love, you were absent, or else I could not have read it.
It is a favourite book of yours, and the writer was a friend
of mine. You will not understand these English words, and
others will not understand them—which is the reason I have not
scrawled them in Italian. But you will recognise the handwriting of him who passionately loved you, and you will divine
that, over a book which was yours, he could only think of love.
In that word, beautiful in all languages, but most so in yours—
Amor mio—is comprised my existence here and hereafter. . . .
my destiny rests with you, and you are a woman, seventeen
years of age [*sic*], and two out of a convent. I wish that you
had stayed there, with all my heart,—or at least, that I had
never met you in your married state.

"But all this is too late. I love you, and you love me,—at
least, you *say so,* and *act* as if you *did* so, which last is a
great consolation in all events. But *I* more than love you, and
cannot cease to love you.

"Think of me, sometimes, when the Alps and the ocean divide
us,—but they never will, unless you *wish* it." *ⁿ*

Allegra arrived before the end of August. "She is English,"
Byron wrote to Augusta, "but speaks nothing but Venetian. 'Bon
di, papa' &c &c she is very droll, and has a good deal of the
Byron—can't articulate the letter *r* at all—frowns and pouts
quite in our way—blue eyes—light hair growing *darker* daily   √
—and a dimple in her chin—a scowl on the brow—white skin
—sweet voice—and a particular liking of Music—and of her own
way in every thing—is not that B. all over?" *ⁿ*

After the return of the Guicciolis, Byron regained some of
his tranquillity. At Teresa's suggestion, Count Guiccioli readily

consented to invite him to move his furniture into a vacant apartment on the ground floor of their palace." The police spies, who observed every movement of the dangerous English lord and questioned his servants, were quick to note these changes."

The afternoons and evenings in the garden of the Guiccioli palace were now pleasant enough. Byron could watch his daughter playing by the fountain, attracting the admiration of Teresa as well as of the visitors and servants. And the private meetings with Teresa had now become easier, thanks to the complaisance of Count Guiccioli, who for his own particular reasons seemed to be amazingly agreeable to his wife's *amico*. Teresa later admitted that the facility with which he agreed to let Byron take an apartment in his palace might have been thought due to imprudence by those who did not know the Count, who was "a man different from others—eccentric—seeing things from a point of view peculiar to himself and very often even indulgent and almost generous." " Moreover, she said, as a man of intellect and wit Byron pleased him and he was flattered by the attention paid him by this famous man of letters. But, according to her statement to the Sacra Rota Tribunal in 1841, Guiccioli had deeper schemes. When Byron took the apartment in the Guiccioli palace, the Count seized the opportunity to make an unusual request: to lend him a considerable sum of money. Byron promised it, but, having been warned by his banker, Insom, that Guiccioli was not acting in good faith, he finally refused, giving the excuse that his banker had not sufficient funds at his disposal."

The Count then lost his temper and blamed the failure of his scheme on Teresa. She, however, had her recourse. She had another relapse and found that she needed Dr. Aglietti's care and must return to Venice. Teresa described these events with tact in the *"Vie,"* saying: "Lord Byron was returning there also. The Countess, encouraged by the conduct, so little jealous, of the Count, proposed to him that she make the voyage at the same time as Lord Byron—and the Count saw nothing inconvenient in that." " But in her "Confession" to her husband she gave what was probably the more truthful story:

"You suggested another travelling companion, but I insisted

)❧ *THE VILLA DIODATI*

)► *MARGARITA COGNI*

on having Byron, to whom you added my maid and the oldest
servant of our household, and I promised to stay in the apartment
that you ordered Lega, then your steward, to prepare for me." [n]
The alert Director of Police in Bologna reported to Rome on
September 15 that Byron and the Countess had left for Venice
on the 12th.[n]

When Sir Charles and Lady Morgan, then gathering material
for her book on Italy ("on the liberal side"), arrived in Bologna
the day after Byron's departure, the gossip on this extraordinary
event was still stirring the town.[n] Strangely enough, the police
spies had begun to connect the name of Byron with that of
Lady Morgan, and to see her and all other liberal English as
associated in a gigantic plot fostered by what they called the
Società Romantica, which they easily confused with the individual practices and creeds of romantic writers.[8]

In the meantime the ruthless conspirator was traveling toward Venice by easy stages in his Napoleonic carriage, from
which the green paint was beginning to chip. It was laden with
his traveling bed and his books as well as his servants and his
blue-eyed daughter, and it followed in the dust of Count
Guiccioli's coach-and-six, which carried Teresa and her maid
and the old manservant. Their activities were not political but
amatory, not calculated but spontaneous. Teresa remembered
this trip as one of the happiest of her life. At last she was really
alone with her lover. "They made their halts together—they
stopped at the same hotels," she recalled with pleasure.[n]

The second day of their voyage they were among the
Euganean Hills, and they turned off the road to visit at Arqua
the home and grave of Petrarch, Teresa's favorite Italian poet.
When the road became impracticable for the postilions, they
continued on foot. In that romantic setting, with Teresa on his
arm, Byron did not complain, though walking any distance was

[8] There was apparently a secret society, with aims and purposes not essentially different from that of the Carboneria, which bore the name of
Società Romantica, derived from Roma Antica. There is no evidence, however, that Byron or any others of the English in Italy were members. That
Byron was spoken of as a romantic writer was sufficient to cause the confusion.

always painful to him and just then he was suffering from corns." To Teresa it was all *couleur de rose.*

Though Byron preferred Dante to Petrarch, and would, Teresa said, have subscribed to the opinion of Sismondi, who said: "I am tired of this veil always lowered," yet he did not want to destroy her illusions and listened with pleasure while she recited Petrarch's verses." In the visitor's album in the Italian poet's house, "She wrote her name with emotion—and then Lord Byron receiving the pen from her wrote his beside hers, saying that the two names would never be separated." " After drinking some water from the fountain, they descended the hill again to their carriages. Byron gave his arm to the Countess, and they advanced in solemn silence."

At the inn in Padua where they stopped for the night Teresa was amazed at the reception given Byron by the host. She finally drew from her *amico* the fact that the innkeeper owed his prosperity to Byron, who the previous year had rescued him from financial embarrassment. Even Byron was overcome by the man's gratitude, and could scarcely control his tears when they were served a sumptuous meal and serenaded from an adjoining room."

The next day, which was to be the last of their idyllic journey, was agitated at the beginning by a visit to Byron of the Countess Benzoni and her *cavalier servente,* "Beppe" Rangone, who feared that Byron was getting into a serious scrape." Byron later told Teresa that "they expressed their anxiety on my account because of the character of the Count who passed at Venice for a being so jealous, so capable of everything, and so crafty, that he deserved to be called by the poet Monti "a *Brunello.*" [9]

Both Byron and his *amica* saw now what their situation would be in a Venice already seething with gossip. Teresa was even more completely aware than Byron to what extent they had violated Italian conventions, but she could not think of giving up her lover, and on the impulse of the moment proposed that they escape together to the ends of the world. It was Byron

[9] *"Vie,"* p. 247. In Ariosto's *Orlando Furioso* (Canto III, stanza 60) "Brunello," a misshapen dwarf, who is a leader in the Saracen army, to whom the king gave a talismanic ring, is described as "so practiced and so sly."

who counseled prudence, from motives which, while honest, were as mixed as most human motives and probably would not have been entirely pleasing to Teresa."

They made a leisurely journey, stopping for several hours at Byron's summer villa at La Mira, which, with its plane trees, its cool shade in the English garden filled with flowers, and the view from the windows of the boats on the Brenta and the summer villas, quite enchanted Teresa. In the cool of the evening they went on to Venice by gondola."

Teresa had a truly audacious confidence that her husband's complaisance would be unlimited, for she wrote him a most amazing letter the next day (the 15th): "This morning Aglietti came, and having examined me, ordered me no drugs, but instead advised another journey and change of air. Your affairs, I feel sure, would not allow you to come with me, so Byron having offered to take me with him to the lakes of Garda and Como—a journey suitable to the season, and which he is now thinking of taking, not being much pleased with Venice,— I ask for your permission, and await its speedy arrival with the greatest anxiety. . . .

"Byron greets you and charges me to tell you that the English friend to whom he wrote about the Vice Consulate, etc., has answered him that he will send in a petition at once and do everything possible to obtain it." "

Teresa did not say what house she was in, allowing the Count to suppose that she had gone according to agreement to the Palazzo Malipiero, "on one of the small canals in Venice, disagreeable on account of their exhalations." But two days later Lega Zambelli, the Count's steward, reported that she was living in Byron's palace."

Before Teresa received the Count's reply, she had gone to La Mira. Byron had left Allegra there. The villa was spacious, and, according to Teresa's delicate account in the "Vie," she took Fanny Silvestrini along as a companion, as well as her servants, and Byron, "who came only occasionally, lived in a completely separate wing of the building." " But it is evident that the arrangements were not quite so innocent. If Fanny accompanied her for appearances' sake, she was back in Venice by the 20th (perhaps the very day of the move to La Mira), assiduously looking after the post and other affairs of the lovers in the city, for on that day she wrote to Teresa:

"The Cavaliere has written to Lega, asking him to keep him *informed* about his wife. He asks him [Lega] to give more detailed news of you, which he is awaiting impatiently. In answer Lega will write to him in the most appropriate manner." [n] There is little doubt that Lega wrote that answer under the eye of Fanny, for she was his mistress and could bear witness to him of Lord Byron's generosity.

It is evident also that Byron spent most if not all of his time at La Mira while Teresa was there. After a few days Fanny wrote delightedly: "So now La Mira has become for you the enchanted abode of Armida." [n]

At last the lovers were together under one roof, alone and without danger of interruption. They rode along the Brenta or sat in the shade of the trees in the English garden. Byron regaled Teresa with a description of the lakes and mountains and the Alpine scenery he had known, for the dream of escape which they had briefly contemplated at Padua still haunted them. But when the Count's reply came to Teresa's request to travel to the lakes with Byron, his easy compliance left Byron more puzzled than ever as to his motives, though Teresa was willing to ascribe his concessions to mere "indifference" and "eccentricity." [n]

By the time the reply arrived, Teresa was so happy at La Mira that she was in no hurry to see the lakes. Moreover, she was suffering from two ailments which made her unwilling to move and might have embarrassed the love-making of a less ingenuous child of nature. After she had been a week at La Mira she wrote to break the news to her husband. ". . . I am not in Venice but at La Mira, a delightful place, where I have come by Aglietti's advice . . . I am going on looking after myself under the direction of Aglietti and also of the surgeon Campana, having had much inconvenience in the last few days from piles, from which I am not yet quite recovered. He has, however, reassured me on the point which interested me most, the supposed *prolapsus uteri,* so that I am much more at ease. Byron, who overwhelms me with kindness, greets you cordially." "

If the reactions of Count Guiccioli to his wife's situation were difficult to divine, those of her father, Count Ruggero Gamba, were clear enough. As soon as he heard from his daughter that she was at La Mira with Byron, he hastened to Ravenna from his country house at Filetto and protested with vehemence to his son-in-law for having allowed his wife to return to Venice "accompanied by a man like Lord Byron—too gifted, too seductive not to trouble the heart of a young woman and not to excite the observation of the public." " The Count promised to go for her as soon as practical. In the meantime, Count Gamba wrote to his daughter, expressing his entire confidence in her but warning her of the dangers she was facing of being condemned in the eyes of the world."

And so Teresa promised her father—not to leave Byron, nor to return to her husband's apartment in the city, but—to remain at La Mira awaiting the arrival of her husband, and to renounce the excursion to the lakes with Byron."

While they were at La Mira, Byron told Teresa his version of the whole story of his marriage and separation, no doubt softening certain harshnesses in it, and forever after she believed that she knew all that was to be known about it and that Byron was the victim of malignant people and circumstances. He swore his ignorance then and always of the real causes of the separation, and he spoke of his repeated efforts to find out, to provoke an open trial."

Foreseeing that Teresa would not have the courage to defy the conventions of her world and the entreaties of her family, or that if a showdown came he would counsel her against any rash step for her own sake, Byron was already thinking of an escape that would enable him to begin life anew. He wrote seriously to Hobhouse on October 3:

"My South American project, of which I believe I spoke to you . . . was this . . . advantageous offers were—or are to be held out to settlers in the Venezuela territory. My affairs in England are nearly settled or in prospect of settlement; in Italy

I have no debts, and I could leave it when I choose. The Anglo-Americans are a little too coarse for me, and their climate too cold, and I should prefer the others. I could soon grapple with the Spanish language. Ellice or others would get me letters to Bolivar and his government . . . with some capital, I might be suffered as a landholder there, or at least a tenant, and if possible, and legal—a Citizen. . . .

"I should go there with my natural daughter, Allegra,—now nearly three years old, and with me here,—and pitch my tent for good and all.

"I am not tired of Italy, but a man must be a Cicisbeo and a Singer in duets, and a connoisseur of Operas—or nothing—here. I have made some progress in all these accomplishments, but I can't say that I don't feel the degradation. Better be an unskilful Planter, an awkward settler,—better be a hunter, or anything, than a flatterer of fiddlers, and fan carrier of a woman. I like women—God he knows—but the more their system here developes upon me, the worse it seems, after Turkey too; here the *polygamy* is all on the female side. I have been an intriguer, a husband, a whoremonger, and now I am a Cavalier Servente—by the holy! it is a strange sensation."

In recent months he had considered the idea of returning to England, but he conceived it possible only if by some heroic gesture he could justify his return and again recapture his own self-esteem and the admiration of his countrymen. To take part with Kinnaird and Hobhouse and others in a reform movement by peaceful means was hardly enough. He had spoken a number of times of coming over to take a leading role in a revolution, though this was mostly bravado. Soberer thinking brought home to him the fact that with his foreign experience behind him he could not re-establish himself in England. He told Hobhouse: "I had a house and lands, and a wife and child, and a name there—once—but all these things are transmuted or sequestered. Of the last, and best, ten years of my life, nearly six have been passed out of it. I feel no love for the soil after the treatment I received before leaving it for the last time, but I do not hate it enough to wish to take part in its calamities, as on either side harm must be done before good can accrue; revolutions are not to be made with rosewater. My taste for revolution is abated, with my other passions." "

For the present, however, La Mira was a pleasant place to Byron, and to Teresa it was an "earthly paradise" as long as her father could be kept calm and her husband placated. Byron had gone back to his old regime of rising about two in the afternoon, having a light breakfast, and then sitting in the garden, reading or talking or playing with Allegra, riding with Teresa at sunset along the Brenta, conversing or love-making in the evening. But he was most awake in the early hours of the morning when he sat writing new verses of *Don Juan,* for, despite the reports that had come from England concerning the first two cantos, he knew that in it he had found his forte. Taking up again the story of Juan and Haidée on the Ægean island, he easily found in their situation much of his own. He wrote rapidly, for he had only to pour out what was in his mind. Self-expression was always the motive which drove him most furiously to write, and his greatest happiness came from that relief. Sometimes he wrote while Teresa was chattering by his side, for, she said, "he worked better while he saw her and heard her speak." " Occasionally he translated selected portions to her. But she could not have been flattered by some of the lines that expressed his nearest thoughts and feelings. He was perhaps thinking of his own marriage, and possibly also of Teresa's, but more likely of what might happen to their own relationship should they elope or settle into something as fixed as marriage, when he wrote:

> *'Tis melancholy, and a fearful sign*
> *Of human frailty, folly, also crime,*
> *That Love and Marriage rarely can combine,*
> *Although they both are born in the same clime;*
> *Marriage from Love, like vinegar from wine—*
> *A sad, sour, sober beverage—by Time*
> *Is sharpened from its high celestial flavour*
> *Down to a very homely household savour.*"

Then came this irreverence to Teresa's adored poet of Arqua:

> *Think you, if Laura had been Petrarch's wife,*
> *He would have written sonnets all his life?* "

He had written some three or four hundred lines when the routine of La Mira was interrupted by the arrival of Thomas Moore on his long-promised visit to Venice. He drove up to Byron's door about two o'clock in the afternoon of October 7, from Padua.[n] Byron was delighted and in high spirits, for to see Moore was to revive memories of some of his happiest bachelor years in London. Moore noted: "He had grown fatter both in person and face, and the latter had most suffered by the change, —having lost, by the enlargement of the features, some of that refined and spiritualized look that had, in other times, distinguished it. The addition of whiskers, too, which he had not long before been induced to adopt,[1] from hearing that some one had said he had a 'faccia di musico,' as well as the length to which his hair grew down on his neck, and the rather foreign air of his coat and cap,—all combined to produce that dissimilarity to his former self I had observed in him. He was still, however, eminently handsome; and, in exchange for whatever his features might have lost of their high, romantic character, they had become more fitted for the expression of that arch, waggish wisdom, that Epicurean play of humor, which he had shown to be equally inherent in his various and prodigally gifted nature. . . ."[n]

Byron speedily finished his breakfast and prepared to accompany Moore to Venice. Before they left, Byron called in the Countess Guiccioli and introduced her to his friend. On this first meeting, Moore found her "not very pretty,"[n] but he granted her "intelligence and amiableness."[n] At Fusina, Byron bustled about to facilitate Moore's passing of the customs inspection, and seemed to Moore to be handicapped by his lame foot much less than he had remembered. Byron, on seeing Moore, no longer saw Venice, but filled his mind and his conversation with the London of his memory. "All that had ever happened, of gay or ridiculous, during our London life together,—" Moore recalled, "his scrapes and my lecturings,—our joint adventures with the Bores and Blues . . . was passed rapidly in review between us," with a continual flow of humor and hilarity on Byron's part.[n]

Since Byron could not spend the night in Venice, feeling that

[1] There is no extant portrait of Byron with "whiskers," though a drawing by D'Auria (reproduced, Origo, opposite p. 404) shows him with a mustache.

he must return to the Guiccioli, Moore was more than willing to
go to the Gran Bretagna Hotel, but Byron insisted that he stay
at the Palazzo Mocenigo. As they groped their way through the
dark hall on the ground floor, Byron cried out: "Keep clear of
the dog," and a little later: "Take care, or that monkey will
fly at you." [n] At nine o'clock, promising to return again the
next day, Byron departed for La Mira, leaving Moore in the
hands of Alexander Scott.

Byron went to Venice the next evening as he had promised,
and joined Moore and Scott at dinner at Pellegrino's. Moore
records that it was at this time that Byron was developing his
miserly habits, which he exaggerated playfully in conversation
and in letters to his friends. [n]

The chief subject of Byron's conversation when he was alone
with Moore was his marriage, and particularly the reaction to it
in England. "He was most anxious to know the worst that had
been alleged of his conduct," Moore wrote. "To all this he
listened with patience, and answered with the most unhesitat-
ing frankness, laughing to scorn the tales of unmanly outrage
related of him, but, at the same time, acknowledging that there
had been in his conduct but too much to blame and regret. . . ."
What haunted Byron, Moore said, was the feeling that there had
been engendered in England such a "fixed hostility" to himself
that it would continue to persecute his memory after his death. [n]

On the 10th, Moore's last full day in Venice, Byron arrived as
usual for dinner and told him, "with all the glee of a schoolboy who had just been granted a holiday, that, as this was my
last evening, the Contessa had given him leave to 'make a night
of it,' and that accordingly he would not only accompany me
to the opera, but that we should sup together at some café
(as in the old times) afterwards." [n] Byron had brought along his
manuscript, and before dinner read Moore what he had written
of the third canto of *Don Juan,* some two or three hundred lines,
beginning with the satire on Wellington. [n]

After dinner Byron took Moore in his gondola to see the night
views of Venice at their grandest, and he himself momentarily
fell into his guest's poetic mood and "his voice, habitually so
cheerful, sunk into a tone of mournful sweetness." But "some

quick turn of ridicule soon carried him off into a totally different vein." At three, Byron dropped him at the door of the Palazzo Mocenigo and headed back to La Mira.

Invited to stop at La Mira for dinner the next day on his way to Padua, Moore arrived at three. Byron met him, and passing through the hall they saw Allegra, who had just returned from her walk with the nursery maid. Moore spoke to the child and made some remark on her beauty. Byron, perhaps to pass off his embarrassment, asked: "Have you any notion— but I suppose *you* have—of what they call the parental feeling? For myself, I have not the least." But Moore was aware that Byron felt more pride in the child than he would allow him to see.

Before dinner Byron left the room and returned with a little white leather bag. He held it up and said: "Look here—this would be worth something to Murray, though *you*, I dare say, would not give sixpence for it." "What is it?" Moore asked. "My Life and Adventures," he answered. "It is not a thing that can be published during my lifetime, but you may have it, if you like—there, do whatever you please with it." " This was the manuscript of the Memoirs that Byron had begun in Venice when the oppression of past events had driven him to find expression for his own frank interpretation of his life in England.

Shortly after Moore's departure, Byron described the transaction to Murray, and added: "The *Life* is *Memoranda,* and not *Confessions*. I have left out all my *loves* (except in a general way), and many other of the most important things (because I must not compromise other people), so that it is like the play of Hamlet—'the part of Hamlet omitted by particular desire.' But you will find many opinions, and some fun, with a detailed account of my marriage and its consequences, as true as a party concerned can make such accounts, for I suppose we are all prejudiced." "

Moore's visit had opened old memories and made Byron more restless in his present situation. He fretted when no mail arrived from England. By the end of October he had not even seen a printed copy of *Don Juan,* which was published the middle of July. Refusing to have anything more to do with the Venetians, whom he considered rascals and gossip-mongers, he was even glad for the return of Hoppner from Switzerland and was willing to forget his anger of the summer.

Partly from boredom and partly from the feeling, always intolerable to him, that he was being cheated, he became deeply involved in exposing the peculations and dishonesties of his agent Edgecombe, and dragged Hoppner in as mediator. His new penny-pinching proclivities no doubt entered into his concern for his accounts, but, as in the affair of Merryweather, it was the principle of the thing, the affront to his self-esteem, that roused his ire, rather than the money involved, for he would gladly have disbursed more than the amount lost to a worthy man. He wrote to Hoppner: "He [Edgecombe] charged for a comb *eighteen* francs—the real price was *eight*." "

A few days later he complained: "I should be glad of an explanation from him *why* Merryweather has not been arrested, the cause having been decided six months ago. I suspect *Collusion* between Mr. E. and Merryweather, and Castelli the Advocate." ²

Although he had no encouragement from Murray, Byron proceeded with the third canto of *Don Juan*. He wrote Hoppner: "There has been an eleventh commandment to the women not to read it—and what is still more extraordinary they seem not to have broken it. But that can be of little import to them poor things—for the reading or non-reading a book—will never keep down a single petticoat;—but it is of import to Murray—who will be in scandal for his aiding as publisher." "

But underneath the jocular boasting and the ribaldry of his tone in a letter to Kinnaird about the same time, there is evidence of his unshaken confidence in the merits of the poem as an expression of the rigors of real life. He wrote: "As to 'Don Juan,' confess, confess—you dog and be candid—that it

² *LJ*, IV, 365. Letter of Oct. 28, 1819. The judge gave a decision against Merryweather on August 11, 1818, but Merryweather appealed the case and it dragged on until February 15, 1819, when the decision went against Merryweather's appeal. As the months dragged on and still Merryweather did not pay, pleading "unfortunate vicissitudes," Byron sought to have him arrested and put in jail, but the magistrates were in no great haste to imprison the poor man for debt. (Olschki, pp. 443–6.)

is the sublime of *that there* sort of writing—it may be bawdy but is it not good English? It may be profligate but is it not *life,* is it not *the thing?* Could any man have written it who has not lived in the world?—and tooled in a post-chaise?—in a hackney coach?—in a gondola?—against a wall?—in a court carriage?—in a vis-à-vis?—on a table?—and under it? I have written about a hundred stanzas of a third canto, but it is damned modest; the outcry has frightened me. I had such projects for the Don, but Cant is [so] much stronger than C * * * now-a-days, that the benefit of experience in a man who had well weighed the worth of both monosyllables, must be lost to despairing posterity." "

As for present matters, he could be just as cavalier. He told Kinnaird: "I have been faithful to my honest liaison with Countess Guiccioli, and I can assure you that *She* has never cost me, directly or indirectly, a sixpence. Indeed the circumstances of herself and family render this no merit. I never offered her but one present—a broach of brilliants—and she sent it back to me with her *own hair* in it (I shall *not* say of *what part,* but *that* is an Italian custom). . . . I have not had a whore this half year, confining myself to the strictest adultery." "

His ennui grew deeper as the period of his independent life with his mistress drew to an end, and, as usual, he tried to cover his chagrin with facetiousness and nonchalance, particularly in his communications with Hoppner, whose attitude toward the liaison put him on the defense. Replying to a letter from Hoppner telling him of another fantastically distorted story of his abduction of the Countess, he wrote: " '*Convent*'—and '*carry off*' quotha!—and '*girl*'—I should like to know *who* has been carried off—except poor dear *me.* I have been more ravished myself than any body since the Trojan war. . . ."

But he could not keep long from the subject that concerned him most nearly, though he tried to pass it off with seeming indifference: "Count G[uiccioli] comes to Venice next week and I am requested to consign his wife to him, which shall be done— with all her linen.

"What you say of the long evenings at the Mira, or Venice, reminds me of what *Curran* said to Moore—'so—I hear—you

have married a pretty woman—and a very good creature too—
an excellent creature—pray—um—*how do you pass your evenings?*' it is a devil of a question that, and perhaps as easy to
answer with a wife as with a mistress; but surely they are longer
than the nights." ⁿ

When Byron went to Venice a day or two after, he was seized
with a violent fever, a consequence of his severe chilling in a
sudden rainstorm on the 28th, and took to his bed in the
Palazzo Mocenigo. Teresa, recovered from her own ailments,
hastened in to tend him. According to her story in the *"Vie,"*
she watched constantly at his side.

While he was still ill and feverish, Count Guiccioli arrived
according to schedule on All Saints Day,ⁿ descending at the
gondola landing of the Palazzo Mocenigo with his son and several
servants. That he should stay at Byron's palace was apparently
his own idea, seconded by old Count Gamba. It would be the
surest means to allay gossip in Venice, to show that all was
amicable between them, and that the Count trusted his wife's
friend.ⁿ

Within the palace, however, all was not so tranquil as it
seemed. As soon as Byron was well enough to receive him, the
Count called on him privately and with his usual courtesy explained that he would welcome him back to Ravenna, but that
because of the gossip an obstacle had arisen in the person of
Count Gamba, who was alarmed by what was said of his
daughter's too great intimacy with a stranger. He did not wish
to embroil himself with the Gambas and so had promised to
beg Byron to abstain from returning to Ravenna. And he asked
Byron to say nothing of this to the Countess. Byron did not
know what to reply, and so kept his sentiments to himself.[3]

The fact seems to be that the Count felt he could manage
Byron much better than he could his wife. To bring her to
reason, as he had his former wives, he had prepared twenty-five
maxims to govern her conduct when she returned to him. To
him they seemed quite simple and reasonable. But his "In-

[3] *"Vie,"* pp. 318–20. This is Teresa's story. It seems, however, that in the
end it was Byron who wanted to withdraw, while the Count thought that
too extreme a measure. See Chapter XXI, p. 833 n.

dispensable Rules," which were intended to govern her conduct from rising to retiring through every minute activity of the day, were quite unacceptable to the independent Teresa. Some of them were particularly galling:

"Let her busy herself at once with those household matters which are within her competence . . . let her offer suggestions and ask for advice, but not give orders. . . .

"After our drive together, in the early part of the evening, reading aloud as before dinner, then together to the theatre, then conversation and to supper and bed together." [n]

Teresa had tasted freedom long enough to know how to reply:

"To get up whenever I like.

"Of my toilette I will not speak.

"In domestic matters to be absolute mistress of all that is within a Lady's province. . . .

"To dine together as usual, but to spend the time of your rest as I please, even if it were in pulling the donkey's tail. . . .

"But all this would not be enough to live together peacefully, etc.,—if you should refuse to grant me the following:

"A horse with everything necessary for riding.

"*To receive, without discrimination, any visitor who may come. . . .*" [n]

These were the lines on which the first battle was fought, while Byron abstained from open participation. Teresa was adamant. If she went back to Ravenna, her *amico* should accompany her. The Count was equally obstinate. Then something happened that affected the Count and roused him more than all the ribaldry of street songs ridiculing his cuckoldry, more than any concern for the gossip that was current. He intercepted a letter of Count Gamba to Teresa, "giving her some prudent advice to smooth the husband; & this," Byron wrote later to Hobhouse, "blew up the whole affair, besides some awkward evidence about sleeping together, and doors locked—which like a Goose had been locked, and then afterwards forgotten to be re-opened; so that he knocked his horns against the door of his own drawing-room." [n]

For several days the battle raged in Byron's house, while his emotions were "scorched and drenched" until he wished only for peace and escape. When it was all over, he could write with the calm of exhaustion of the whole affair. He reported to Kinnaird on November 16: "[Count Guiccioli] found his wife considerably improved in health, but hating him so cordially, that they quarreled violently. He had said nothing before, but at last, on finding this to be the case, he gave her the alternative, *him,* or *me.* She decided instantly for *me,* not being allowed to have both, and the lover generally having the preference. . . . At twenty I should have taken her away, at thirty, with the experience of *ten such years!* I sacrificed myself only; and counselled, and persuaded her with the greatest difficulty, to return with her husband to Ravenna, not absolutely denying that I might come there again; else she refused to go." [n]

Apparently there were some terrible scenes at the last. In writing to Hobhouse, Byron continued the account: "He [Guiccioli] actually came to *me,* crying about it, and I told him, 'if you abandon your wife I will take her undoubtedly; it is my duty, it is also my inclination in case of such extremity; but if, as you say, you are really disposed to live with, & like her as before, I will not only not carry further disturbance into your family, but even repass the Alps; for I have no hesitation in saying that Italy will be now to me insupportable.'

"After ten days of such things during which I had (& have still) the tertian ague, She agreed to go back to him; [n] but *I* feel so wretched and low, and lonely, that I will leave the country, reluctantly indeed, but I will do it; for, otherwise, if I formed a new *liaison* she would cut the figure of a woman *planted,* and I never will willingly hurt her Self-love." [n]

Left in the great palace that now seemed empty and desolate, Byron thought again, though with little enthusiasm, of returning to England. "But I shall quit Italy," he wrote Kinnaird just after Teresa departed with her husband. "I have done my duty, but the country has become sad to me; I feel alone in it; and as I left England on account of my own wife, I now quit Italy for the wife of another." [n]

One reason for his lack of taste for the journey was that he had pledged himself before he ever returned to meet in a duel on the sands of Calais the man whom he considered above all others his mortal enemy—the man who had calumniated him on his leaving and had interfered to prevent the reconciliation with his wife initiated by Mme de Staël—Henry Brougham.

On the 17th, Byron wrote Kinnaird to say that Allegra and her nurse had also fallen ill, and that he therefore could not set a day for his departure.[n] In the meantime, he had to soothe Teresa. He had not yet had the heart to tell her that he was not coming back, but was leaving for England. The increasing melancholy of his letters and the fact that he said nothing of coming drew from her quite frantic letters. On November 25, Dr. Aglietti pronounced Allegra well enough to travel,[n] and Byron felt that he must now break the news to Teresa. The faithful Fanny Silvestrini had already warned her of his promise to Count Guiccioli not to return to Ravenna. Teresa felt that she had been betrayed, and it was to her reproaches that he must pen his farewell: "I go *to save you,* and to leave a country which, without you, has become insupportable. . . . Farewell!—in that one word is comprised the death of my happiness."[n]

But he wrote in a different tone to Augusta. He and all his family had had the fever, he said. "I cured myself without bark, but all the others are taking it like trees. I have also had another hot crater, in the shape of a scene with Count Guiccioli who quarrelled with his wife, who refused to go back to him, and wanted to stay with me—and elope—and be as good as married. . . . You must not dislike *her,* for she was a great admirer of *you,* and used to collect and seal up all *your letters* to me as they came that they might not be lost. . . .

"All this—and my fever—have made me low and ill; but the moment Allegra is better we shall set off over the Tyrolese Alps. . . . As to the Countess G. if I had been single and could have married her by getting her divorced, she would probably have been of the party; but this being out of the question— though *she* was as 'all for love or the world well lost'—I, who know what 'love' and 'the world' both are, persuaded her to keep her station in society."[n]

Before this letter arrived in England, Augusta had learned

from Hobhouse of Byron's intention to return. Her agitation was evident in her reply: " ". . . with *humble* submission to *wiser* opinions I can't but think that the less that is said of this return the better—Let him *come* & *go* (if possible) like other people! —or else he may share the fate of his odious DON. . . . *Burn this immediately.*" "

She felt the need of "wiser opinions" before she could reply to her brother, and she sent off Byron's second note to Annabella, throwing the burden of decision upon her. With a seriousness and an alarm that would have made the easygoing and easily managed Byron laugh, Annabella replied: "I have, throughout our confidential communication, strongly pointed out to you the pernicious effects that must result from B's associating with you, unless the circumstances were wholly changed, and the proofs of his reformation unequivocal. . . . It can scarcely be doubted, from the whole series of his correspondence, that you are his principal object in England." "

Fortunately, Byron knew nothing of the to-do that was being made in these quarters concerning his return, and at the time he was thinking more of Ravenna than of London. Having made the decision to cut the tie, he could not deny to himself that there was a certain relief in being free once more from the strongest passions, and, he told himself, perhaps it was better that it should have ended before love could be killed by habit. While the preparations were going forward for his departure, he found time to compose some stanzas which for him expressed the quintessence of the experience:

> *When lovers parted*
> *Feel broken-hearted,*
> *And, all hopes thwarted,*
>   *Expect to die;*
> *A few years older,*
> *Ah! how much colder*
> *They might behold her*
>   *For whom they sigh. . . .*
> *You'll find it torture*
> *Though sharper, shorter,*
> *To wean, and not wear out your joys.*"

He had not written these stanzas for Teresa, and it was just as well that he did not show them to her. But it would be wrong to suppose that their separation did not affect him as ruefully as it did her, though he did not express his feelings in the style of *Corinne*. As soon as the fever had subsided, he plunged again into *Don Juan*. Regardless of what was thought of it in England, he knew it was his most honest production and superior to most of the work of the century in its expression of the realities of life. Taking up again the theme of the ideal and natural love of Juan and Haidée, he continued:

> And these [joys] were not of the vain kind which cloys
> For theirs were buoyant spirits, never bound
>   By the mere senses; and that which destroys
> Most love—possession—unto them appeared
> A thing which each endearment more endeared.[n]

In a few days (and nights) he had added more than a hundred stanzas to the canto, but Murray's next letter blew cold air upon all his hopes and plans for the poem. The first two cantos had been pirated, and Murray said he was applying to the Chancellor, Lord Eldon, for an injunction against the pirating publisher. But now Byron's apprehensions were not for the poem. He replied: "Eldon will decide against you, were it only that my name is in the record. You will also recollect that if the publication is pronounced against, on the grounds you mention, as *indecent and blasphemous*, that *I* lose all right in my daughter's *guardianship* and *education*—in short, all paternal authority, and every thing concerning her, except the pleasure I may have chanced to have had in begetting her. It was so decided in Shelley's case, because he had written *Queen Mab*, etc., etc." [n] And he offered to refund Murray's payment for the copyright.[4]

Byron was several times on the point of leaving, but something always held him up. On December 7 he wrote a farewell letter

---

[4] Despite Byron's fears, however, Murray won his case and secured the copyright, possibly because his counsel, Sharon Turner, himself read the poem with care and was able to convince the Chancellor that there was nothing seditious or indecent in its language. (*LJ*, IV, 380 n.; Smiles, I, 405–8)

to Hoppner in a melancholy tone, asking the Consul to oversee his business affairs. Fanny had already written to break the shock to Teresa, trying to persuade her that her lover was "going to England for you, only for you . . . and this is your great triumph." " But Byron did not leave the Palazzo Mocenigo. Three days later he wrote to Kinnaird: "The Winter has set in hard, and my daughter not being well re-established, I have put off my intended voyage, till the Spring, or perhaps to the Greek Calends." "

In the delicate balance of motive and will it is not unlikely that inertia played as great a part as inclination in the decision to remain. As Fanny reported it to Teresa: "He was ready dressed for the journey, his gloves and cap on, and even his little cane in his hand. Nothing was now waited for but his coming down stairs,—his boxes being already all on board the gondola. At this moment, my lord, by way of pretext, declares, that if it should strike one o'clock before every thing was in order (his arms being the only thing not yet quite ready), he would not go that day. The hour strikes and he remains!" Fanny added by way of interpretation: "It is evident he has not the heart to go."

According to Moore, who probably was depending on Teresa's account, "The very next day's tidings from Ravenna decided his fate. . . ." " The decisive letter, however, was not from Teresa, but from her father. As usual, the psychosomatic illnesses of Teresa were useful to her in a crisis. As Byron later told Moore: "After her arrival at Ravenna, the Guiccioli fell ill again too; and at last, her father (who had, all along, opposed the *liaison* most violently till now) wrote to me to say that she was in such a state that *he* begged me to come and see her,—and that her husband had acquiesced, in consequence of her relapse, and that *he* (her father) would guarantee all this, and that there would be no further scenes in consequence between them, and that I should not be compromised in any way." "

With a mingling of relief and resignation Byron wrote to Teresa: "F * * * [anny] will already have told you, *with her accustomed sublimity*, that Love has gained the victory. I could not summon up resolution enough to leave the country where you are, without, at least, once more seeing you. On *yourself,* perhaps, it will depend, whether I ever again shall leave you." "

Byron sent this letter by courier so as not to prolong her suffering, Teresa said." And she recuperated rapidly when the cause of the illness was removed. Perhaps for that reason Byron did not feel required to leave immediately for Ravenna. It was a good ten days before he started. He had to make new arrangements and provisions for his numerous entourage, and there was Allegra to care for and get properly prepared for the voyage. But he was on his way about the 21st. On the 23rd he wrote to Augusta from Bologna, enclosing all his long hair: "You will see that it was not so very long. I curtailed it yesterday, my head and hair being weakly after my tertian." " He arrived in Ravenna on Christmas Eve, and was joyously welcomed by a smiling Teresa and her father and friends in the gala atmosphere of the holiday season. All was well, for her *amico* had come home.

CHAPTER XXI

1820

Ravenna—the Guiccioli Separation

BYRON, who hardly knew what to expect on his return to Ravenna, was at first delighted, a little flattered, and somewhat embarrassed by his reception. He was overwhelmed with attentions by everyone, but he knew on what terms he had come back, for it was evident that Teresa now considered him her acknowledged *cavalier servente*. And she was proud of her triumph, not so much over her husband and her father as over Byron himself. She had rightly sensed that it was his resistance to this regularizing of their relationship which was more responsible than the attitude of Count Guiccioli for the unhappy struggle in Venice and for the interlude when he had tried to break his chains.[1]

Still Byron did not know what Count Guiccioli really thought. The Count's welcome was suave and polite as ever, though he was aloof, inscrutable, and shrewd, if not sinister. But there was

---

[1] Though Byron would not acknowledge it at the time—perhaps even to himself—and though he maintained that it was Count Guiccioli who was intransigent, who had forced Teresa to make a choice between them—he himself had been the one to hold out for "all or nothing." At the time of a later quarrel he revealed something which he had not told before. "All this would already be over," he wrote Teresa when, made unhappy by some action of hers, he was again trying to break away, "if that man [Guiccioli] had allowed me to leave in December of last year. He not only *wished* me to come—but he said to me with his own lips that I ought not to go away—this being too far-fetched a remedy." (Origo, p. 149.) It is apparent that Guiccioli even then was willing to bow to Teresa's wishes if Byron would accept the conventional pattern of serventism.

no reserve in the welcome of the other Ravennese, including Teresa's father. The night after Byron's arrival there was a grand reception and ball at the home of her uncle, the Marchese Cavalli, to which Teresa's *amico* received a special invitation. "The G.'s object," Byron wrote to Hoppner, "appeared to be to parade her foreign lover as much as possible, and, faith, if she seemed to glory in the Scandal, it was not for me to be ashamed of it." [n]

And so Byron settled down to a pleasant routine of social activities such as he had not indulged in for some time. After the New Year the Carnival was to begin, and he found himself the center of attention in the provincial town. But within a week or two old wounds and old pangs troubled him again. The turn of the year was always a melancholy time for him. He recalled that five years before, he had been on his way to be married. On New Year's Eve he wrote a nostalgic letter to Lady Byron. He had two ostensible reasons for writing. One was to ask her again for a portrait of Ada, copy or original, "something to remind me of what is yours and mine." The other was to ask her to read and comment on the Memoirs which he had sent to England by Moore. He wrote: ". . . the part you occupy . . . is long and minute, and I could wish you to see, read and mark any part or parts that do not appear to coincide with the truth. . . . You will find nothing to flatter you, nothing to lead you to the most remote supposition that we could ever have been, or be happy together."

But he could not resist making some other remarks not pertinent to these purposes: "This time five years . . . I was on my way to our funeral marriage. . . . That I think of you is but too obvious, for three hours have not passed, since in society where I ought not to think of you . . . the principal person concerned said to me—'tu pensi di tua moglie' ["you are thinking of your wife"]—it was so right a conjecture that I started and answered why do you think so? The answer was—'because you are so serious—and she is the woman whom I believe tu ami piu ed ami sempre' ["you love most and love always"]. . . ." [n]

When this letter reached Lady Byron at Kirkby Mallory, she drafted a reply, following her first impulse, declining to peruse the Memoirs, and sent it off to her advisers, Colonel Doyle and

Dr. Lushington in London. Dr. Lushington strongly advised her not to enter into any direct correspondence with her husband, and suggested that she communicate with him only through Augusta as theretofore. Byron should be made *"aware* of the *extent* of the *information* you possess, and be made to believe that the consequence of commencing an attack which would lead necessarily from one thing to another, would be the ultimate disclosure of everything." [n]

Lady Byron, however, had grave objections of her own to this procedure, and after some weeks of discussion it was finally decided that she should send a direct refusal to read the manuscript with a veiled threat of the measures she would be forced to if the Memoirs were made public. She wrote: "I consider the publication or circulation of such a composition at any time as prejudicial to Ada's future happiness. For my own sake I have no reason to shrink from publicity, but notwithstanding the injuries which I have suffered, I should lament some of the *consequences."* [n]

Since news had come to Byron of hunger riots and other disturbances in England, he had urged Kinnaird with greater vehemence to transfer his investments to something safer. Kinnaird had suggested an Irish mortgage, and Byron now wrote Augusta to get Annabella's consent to the transfer (as was necessary under the terms of the separation settlement).

But in Ravenna he had even more immediate and distressing preoccupations. Within a week of his arrival, frictions and misunderstandings began to arise between Byron and Teresa. They were no longer under the same roof. In that situation Byron chafed as he had on his first visit during the previous summer when he had been forced to see her among her family and friends. Moreover, he was uncomfortable in the miserable Albergo Imperiale, and he was increasingly ill at ease in his role of *cavalier servente.*

Not being able to see Teresa privately every day, he began to imagine slights, lack of candor, and even familiarities with her husband and friends in his presence designed to torment him. The Count, too, was a continual puzzle, alternately courteous and morose and aloof, and Byron, with a chip on his shoulder,

was ever ready to take offense if he imagined discourtesy was
intended. He had thought before that he understood these people,
but now he felt again a stranger in a strange land, incapable
of fathoming the Italian character. Unable to stand uncertainties
and impatient of any dissimulation, he wrote Teresa long letters
baring his feelings. Two of these Teresa later enclosed in a folder
with her own explanation:

> Two very unjust notes, caused by
> 1. my having taken and kept in my service a maid who, he had been
> told, was not respectable, and whom Count G. wished to keep near me
> to spy on me.
> 2. my having received and conversed in a familiar manner with an old
> family friend (aged 60) Count R * * * who had always treated me as
> a daughter, and
> 3. my having suggested that a woman friend [Geltrude Vicari, with
> whom Byron confessed to Augusta he had fallen "a little in love" the
> previous summer and who seemed "very well disposed to be perfid-
> ious"], who had been dear to me in the past, was rather flighty, and
> above all, that she had tender feelings for him."

Byron's first letter, dated January 3, 1820, expressed puzzle-
ment at her conduct and tried to make her understand why he
had been upset. And he continued: "If you can reconcile your
code as a lady with your defence of the aforesaid woman who
is now in your service; if you can reconcile your love for me
with the liberties you have permitted to another man in my
presence; and your most sincere (or most affected) friendship
with the Vicari with the way in which you spoke of her to me
tonight—I shall admit that you are a lady of great gifts—but
no longer my friend." "

Teresa was always able to bring him out of these moods, however, for he was easily managed by any woman who loved him
and used her feminine persuasions. Still, the irritation of these
quarrels was disturbing his equanimity when he wrote Hoppner
on January 10: "I have not decided any thing about remaining
at Ravenna. I may stay a day, a week, a year, all my life. . . .
My attachment has neither the blindness of the beginning, nor
the microscopic accuracy of the close to such *liaisons;* but 'time
and the hour' must decide upon what I do." "

And what he did in the meantime was what Teresa wished, though he sulked frequently under the rules of *serventismo* and was quick to take umbrage when his ignorance of the finer points of the social customs made him suspicious of some slight—particularly from the Count. His temper was the worse for his being deprived of his daily ride. The weather continued bad and he was shut in the Albergo Imperiale except when he went to see Teresa or took her to the frequent balls and assemblies of the Carnival season.

Byron's furniture was on the way from Bologna, but he had as yet no place to put it, for he found great difficulty in getting a suitable house in Ravenna. The large houses, such as he would have wished for his entourage and his menagerie, were all occupied by the aristocratic families, and the others were too small and cramped.

It was at this point that Count Guiccioli, not unlikely prompted by Teresa, though the Count himself seems to have had some private motives of his own beyond mere hospitality, offered to rent the upper floor of his palace to Byron. The Guicciolis themselves occupied only the ground floor of the capacious Palazzo Osio, while the upper floor had been left entirely empty.[2] Teresa said that Byron finally accepted the offer, "after some hesitation, and probably even encouraged and urged by the Countess." And she added: "Certainly the offer might appear strange. It was so, indeed, but people were accustomed to consider the Count *an eccentric*, and after a few days they stopped talking about it." ⁿ But this was hardly the whole truth.[3]

What the Count's motives were it is difficult to fathom, even after weighing all the later evidence. His grandson believed that he wanted incontestable evidence of the guilt of his wife and Byron, and thought he could spy on them in his own house better,ⁿ but the matter seems to be somewhat more complicated.

[2] The arsenal-like heavy stone building, which surrounded a court leading back to stables, fronts on one of the narrow streets of the town, not far from the Basilica of San Vitale. When I visited Ravenna in 1948 it was used as a military headquarters for the district.

[3] The Marchesa Origo (p. 146) comments: "But Teresa can hardly have believed this herself—or expected us to believe it. They went on talking—and have indeed been doing so ever since."

Byron's hesitancy to accept was motivated by several considerations beyond the thought of the equivocal situation and the gossip it would cause. One was his growing distrust of Teresa's candor, and a suspicion at times that she was siding with her husband, or at least making too great an effort to persuade her lover to placate the Count's whims. The sticking-point was Byron's resolution not to enter Count Guiccioli's house so long as the suspected maid was there. Byron was so tenacious that Teresa finally dismissed her. But the Count, having learned that it was by Byron's advice, became obstinate and insisted that she be kept, and, according to Teresa, "expressed his will as master of the house, in a manner wounding both to Lord Byron and the Countess." [n]

For some days Byron would not enter the Palazzo Guiccioli, but he continued to write to and to argue with his *amica*. On January 31 he pleaded: "The other evening I gave you my *word of honour* not to go into any house where that woman is—and in my country this counts for more than an oath. As to the rest—everyone is master in his own house, and no one more than A[lessandro]." [n]

More than a little vexed by the bonds of his *serventismo*, Byron wrote cavalierly to Hoppner, who, he knew, would relish a cynical view of Italian society, and who had not ceased to wish Byron well out of his liaison in Ravenna. "I am drilling very hard to learn how to double a shawl, and should succeed to admiration if I did not always double it the wrong side out. . . . it is a dreadfully moral place, for you must not look at any body's wife except your neighbour's,—if you go to the next door but one, you are scolded, and presumed to be perfidious." [n]

But the next day he wrote in quite a different tone to Teresa. Even while he maintained that he would hold firm to his resolution not "to go into a house where someone lives whom I deem to be evil in every way; especially when it is a case (as recently it has been) of my occupying part of the same house," he was already weakening. [n] Teresa had won again, as she always did. Shortly after this he capitulated, though it was painful and extremely trying to his self-esteem. In a few days, despite his pride, he had accepted the offer on the Count's own terms as the price of regaining an opportunity for intimacy with Teresa. She later confessed in a statement to her lawyers: "The world talked a great deal and my father was upset, but Guiccioli found it to his own advantage. . . ." [n]

The moving that was always a burden to Byron was not made easier by the fact that he had acquired more servants and a constantly increasing menagerie of queer beasts. He still could not part with any of his pets. He wrote to Hoppner: "Why did Lega give away the goat? a blockhead—I must have him again." [n] And he readily accepted Murray's offer to send him some English bulldogs. [n]

As soon as he was settled in the Palazzo Guiccioli, with its spacious rooms, and had his horses in the stables (the weather had become milder in February, and he could ride once more), Byron's temper improved and he relaxed in an expansive atmosphere of pleasant living. The fact that his *amica* was now more accessible also decreased his emotional tension, even though their meetings had to be arranged to coincide with Guiccioli's absence or his naps. Byron soon acquired as his confidential agent one of the Negro pages employed by Guiccioli. This one, from East Africa, was faithful to Teresa; another, who came from the coast of Guinea, played Guiccioli's game, and no doubt reported everything he saw to his master. Both wore "rich oriental costumes, with pistols and daggers in their belts." [n] The East African carried Teresa's messages and Byron's replies and watched the stairs in a kind of operatic setting.

It seems, too, that the Count, having gained his point, was himself more good-natured toward his lodger. Apparently he had sent away, at least temporarily, the maid whose presence had offended the English milord. [n]

Within two or three weeks Byron felt at home again. What was more important than anything else to him was habit. The Carnival having ended, he subsided into the routine he liked best, late rising, rides in the forest, the evening with Teresa at the theater or at home, the early morning hours devoted to the exhilarating release of writing. On February 19 he sent off the third and fourth cantos of *Don Juan*, and on the 21st announced to Murray that he had finished his translation of Pulci's *Morgante*

Maggiore. He had previously told Murray that he had some doubt whether the new cantos of *Don Juan* "ought to be published, for they have not the Spirit of the first: the outcry has not frightened but it has *hurt* me, and I have not written *con amore* this time." "

In the meantime, reverberations from the first two cantos were still being heard. Harriette Wilson, the famous courtesan of the Regency, who had seen Byron at a ball in 1814 and had never forgotten him, ran across a copy of the poem in Paris and "at exactly 20 minutes past 12 o'clock at night" sat down to reprimand him for his wickedness: "Dear *Adorable* Lord Byron, *don't* make a mere *coarse* old libertine of yourself. . . . What harm did the Commandments (no matter by whom composed, whether god or mortal) ever do you or anybody else, and what catchpenny ballad writer could not make a parody on them? When you don't feel quite up to a spirit of benevolence . . . throw away your pen, my love, and take a little *calomel*." "

There was keen interest in *Don Juan* in another quarter also. Needless to say, all the women who had known Byron, both those who had been intimate with him and those who had not, read the poem with avidity. Claire Clairmont, then in Florence, noted in her diary on January 3, 1820: "Read Don Juan." She conceived the idea of writing a satire on it to expose Byron's character, and thenceforth she entered in her diary "Hints for Don Juan." The first of these appeared in her journal of February 1, after she had moved to Pisa with the Shelleys: "Hints for Don J—which appears to me a soliloquy upon his own ill-luck— ungraceful & selfish—like a beggar hawking his own sores about and which create disgust instead of pity." "

Later, in the summer of 1820, Caroline Lamb went to a masquerade at Almack's dressed as *Don Juan. The Morning Chronicle* gave a paragraph to her performance the next day (August 1): "Lady Caroline Lamb appeared, for the first time, in the character of *Don Giovanni,* but unfortunately there were too many *Devils* provided for the climax." [4]

Murray was not sorry for such publicity for his volumes. He

[4] *LJ,* V, 69 n. The "Devils" may have been pages dressed for the part by Caroline Lamb herself.

was, despite his timidity, aware that Byron's work always sold, and he had asked him for "a volume of manners, etc., on Italy." Byron replied: "I have lived in their houses and in the heart of their families, sometimes merely as 'amico di casa,' and sometimes as 'Amico di cuore' of the Dama, and in neither case do I feel myself authorized in making a book of them. . . . I know not how to make you comprehend a people, who are at once temperate and profligate, serious in their character and buffoons in their amusements. . . . Their Conversazioni are not Society at all. They go to the theatre to talk, and into company to hold their tongues. . . . they transfer marriage to adultery, and strike the not out of that commandment. The reason is, that they marry for their parents, and love for themselves. They exact fidelity from a lover as a debt of honour, while they pay the husband as a tradesman, that is, not at all. . . . If I wrote a quarto, I don't know that I could do more than amplify what I have here noted." [n]

As for returning to England, he had little taste for it now, what with Hobhouse in jail, and the reform movement, which he once had had glorious dreams of leading, dragged in the mud of an unwashed canaille whose heroes were the demagogues "Orator" Hunt and Cobbett. The arrest of Hobhouse, which he had first heard about in January,[5] had somehow brought to a focus the strange contradictions of Byron's liberal sympathies balanced against his aristocratic pride. This paradox, so frequently noted in him, is partly resolved by a recognition of his eighteenth-century conception of liberalism as a revolt against tyranny which might go even so far as republicanism, but which always envisioned an aristocratic or gentlemanly leadership. This concept involved distrust of the mob and lack of sympathy for democratic or proletarian, or even middle-class, control or participation in government. But beyond any philosophical considerations was the pride of birth, heightened by the social insecurity that often troubled him, and even more by the prejudices of his public-school

[5] Byron had read in Galignani's Messenger that Hobhouse had been arrested for writing a pamphlet that had been voted a breach of privilege by the House of Commons, but it was some time before he received an authentic account from Hobhouse himself.

and college training which stressed the importance of breeding and class and which had been stamped upon his subconscious mind too indelibly ever to be erased, however detached a view of the English character he may have acquired through his residence abroad.[6]

From Newgate, where he had ample leisure for writing, Hobhouse sent Byron the whole story. He had written a pamphlet called *A Trifling Mistake* in reply to his political opponent Lord Erskine's *A Defence of the Whigs*. In it was a phrase formed as a question, which a member took to be a recommendation that "the people . . . pull the members of the House of Commons out by the ears." The whole House "took fire or fright," and Hobhouse, having revealed his name as the author to spare the printer, who had been called to the bar of Parliament, was promptly (December 13, 1819), in his absence, "without citing, hearing, or seeing," voted to be in contempt of the House and committed to Newgate.[7]

But Byron was not so much wrought up by the arbitrary actions of Parliament as by Hobhouse's low company among the Westminster Reformers, which he considered the real cause of his being in a "filthy puddle." He had already heard of the death of George III (January 29, 1820), which caused only faint nostalgia for a time when he might have participated in the pageantry of the funeral. He wrote to Murray: "By the king's death Mr. H[obhouse], I hear, will stand for Westminster: I shall be glad to hear of his standing any where except in the pillory, which, from the company he must have lately kept (I alway except Burdett, and Douglas K., and the genteel part of the reformers), was perhaps to be apprehended. . . . I am out of all patience

[6] Byron often spoke sympathetically of the frame-breakers or other insurrectionists among the people, but he always envisioned himself and others of his class as men on horseback leading and directing a rebellion which would lead to a new government by gentlemen of liberal sympathies. Since this was the general view of intellectuals through most of the nineteenth century (*vide* Carlyle, Tennyson, Ruskin, Arnold), Byron's anti-democratic sentiments should in fairness be judged in the perspective of the age in which he lived. The idea that the lower classes might be capable of participating in government did not gain much currency until the late nineteenth century.

to see my friends sacrifice themselves for a pack of blackguards, who disgust one with their Cause, although I have always been a friend to and a Voter for reform. . . . If we must have a tyrant, let him at least be a gentleman who has been bred to the business, and let us fall by the axe and not by the butcher's cleaver." [n]

And he took much the same tone to Hobhouse himself, tincturing his admonitions with a little pleasant banter, but he added: "However, if this be but a prologue to a seat for Westminster I shall less regret your previous ordeal. . . . Seriously; I did not 'laugh' as you supposed I would; no more did Fletcher; but we looked both as grave as if we had got to have been your bail. . . ." [n]

Byron found an additional reason for not returning to England in the news Hobhouse had sent of the final debacle of their friend Scrope Davies, who had escaped to Bruges, as Brummell before him had gone to Calais, hopelessly in debt. He had confessed to Hobhouse and Kinnaird before he left that he owed £12,000, "and every one of his friends in for something." [7] Byron wrote:

"So Scrope is gone—down-*diddled*—as Doug. K. writes it. . . . Gone to Bruges where he will get tipsy with Dutch beer and shoot himself the first foggy morning. Brummel at Calais; Scrope at Bruges, Buonaparte at St. Helena, you in your new apartments, and I at Ravenna, only think! so many great men! There has been nothing like it since Themistocles at Magnesia, and Marius at Carthage." [n]

Another circumstance had made him even more cynical in his views of "the tight little island." R. C. Dallas, often a recipient of Byron's copyrights and generosity before he left England, had asked for more money and then reproached *him* for ingratitude. Byron told Murray: "This comes of doing people good. At one time or another (including copy-rights) this person has had

---

[7] Hobhouse proofs, letter of Jan. 18, 1820. Hobhouse says that Scrope still retained his Kings College, Cambridge, Fellowship, the stipend of which was forwarded regularly to him. He spent his last days in Paris. According to Captain Gronow, "He daily sat himself down on a bench in the garden of the Tuileries, where he received those whose acquaintance he desired, and then returned to his study, where he wrote notes upon the men of his day, which have unfortunately disappeared. . . ." (Gronow: *Reminiscences*, II, 95.)

about fourteen hundred pounds of my money, and he writes what he calls a posthumous work about me, and a scrubby letter accusing me of treating him ill, when I never did any such thing." [n]

In Ravenna, having succumbed to the customs of the country, Byron felt a greater ease than he had ever known in Whig society in England. He could ask Sgricci,[8] the *improvisatore*, then engaged at the local theater, the proper translation of a word in Pulci, and he could check it with the Florentine bride of Count Gabriel Rasponi as well as with Teresa. He was on friendly terms with Count Alborghetti, the Secretary General of the Lower Romagna, who took him immediately to see the new Legate, Cardinal Antonio Rusconi, on his arrival.

He ended his letter to Hobhouse on March 3 with a slightly sheepish and cynical boasting of his accomplishments in Ravenna society. "I have settled into regular *serventismo,* and find it the happiest state of all. . . ." [n] To Teresa, Byron was faithful and devoted. He found her quite as delightful a creature as ever, but, disillusioned by certain aspects of her character, he had lost the hope that had filled his imagination during the first months of their liaison of finding in her the perfect companion of mind and spirit. Though occasionally from habit he used the language of his earlier passion, there is growing evidence in his letters and notes to her that he now accepted her as a fascinating but sometimes wayward and fickle child.

Teresa bore the brunt of Byron's annoyance with her husband for not giving him a receipt for the two hundred scudi Byron had contributed to engage Mme Pasta for the theater.[n] Teresa tried to make peace between them, but succeeded only in offending Byron and irritating her husband. The result was that Byron and the Count were embroiled without reserve, and from "apparent friends" became "open enemies." It was perhaps her part in this

---

[8] "Sgricci is here improvising away with great success," Byron wrote Hobhouse on March 3; "he is also a celebrated Sodomite, a character by no means so much respected in Italy as it should be; but they laugh instead of burning, and the women talk of it as a pity in a man of talent, but with greater tolerance than could be expected, and only express their hopes that he may yet be converted to adultery." (From the original letter, Murray MSS.; Hobhouse proofs.)

꘎꘎ *BYRON, 1817*

THE PALAZZO MOCENIGO, VENICE

BYRON'S SUMMER PALACE AT LA MIRA

quarrel over the receipt that brought the lovers almost to a break, for Teresa "did not want to think too evil of the Count," ⁿ and Byron spoke his mind freely.

Though the incident left its scar, Byron's temper was soon smoothed, and in the mild days of the Italian spring he settled again into his pleasant course. He continued to take pride in his daughter, who was thriving and being spoiled by Teresa and the servants. But to Hoppner he wrote: "Allegra is prettier I think, but obstinate as a Mule, and as ravenous as a Vulture. Health good to judge by the complexion, temper tolerable, but for vanity and pertinacity. She thinks herself handsome, and will do as she pleases. . . ." ⁿ

In spite of moving and quarrels Byron had managed to continue his literary labors. Before the end of February he had sent Murray the two cantos of *Don Juan,* and during March he finished and sent the translation of the first canto of the *Morgante Maggiore* (which he asked the publisher to show to Frere, Rose, Hobhouse, Merivale, and Foscolo); the *Prophecy of Dante;* a translation of Dante's episode of Francesca da Rimini; and "Some Observations upon an Article in *Blackwood's Magazine,*" a long reply to the personal attack upon him that had appeared the previous summer and had rankled ever since. He began these "Observations" on March 15, and wrote rapidly, as he always did when the subject compelled him.

His first concern was to refute the accusation that all his fictional characters were himself, and in doing so he skirted some dangerous territory. He took particular umbrage at a reference to his "selfish and polluted exile." ⁿ It was the word "selfish" which galled Byron, who knew that one of his greatest weaknesses was his generosity, which had impoverished him in England and had accounted for a large part of his expenditure abroad. After denying that he had satirized Lady Byron in *Don Juan,* he turned to the separation, reiterating his grievances against the public outcry which had banished him without a trial.

And his contempt for the Lake Poets led him to a favorite theme: the superiority of Pope and Dryden to all the lesser poets of his own day. He apologized for his own failure to follow Pope on the ground that his literary efforts were not serious attempts in poetry. "Could I have anticipated the degree of attention which has been accorded me, assuredly I would have studied more to deserve it. . . . almost all I have written has been mere passion . . . my *indifference* was a kind of passion, the result of experience, and not the philosophy of nature. Writing grows a habit, like a woman's gallantry. . . ." [n]

Byron aimed a parting shot at John Keats, "a tadpole of the Lakes," who in a poem "entitled *Sleep and Poetry* (an ominous title,)" had dared to say it was easy to imitate Pope by following "wretched rule and compass vile." [9]

Before he had finished this long "screed," he took time out to compose a ballad accusing Hobhouse of deserting the Whigs and consorting with the mob. He had completed the verses on March 23 and enclosed them in a letter to Murray, saying: "Pray give *Hobhouse* the enclosed song, and tell him I know he will never forgive me, but I could not help it." [n] The song itself was sufficiently provoking to Hobhouse, but the manner in which it was conveyed was even more so. He was hurt most by Byron's perverse determination to ignore the real issues involved in his arrest and the sacrifices he had made for the principles of liberty and constitutional government. Moreover, it showed that Byron persisted in believing, in spite of all that Hobhouse had told him, that the Whigs were still the liberal party in England, whereas they had sided with the Tories whenever it was necessary to beat the Westminster Reformers. But the ballad was written with a fun-loving gusto which Hobhouse in another situation might have enjoyed:

> *How came you in Hob's pound to cool,*
> *My boy Hobbie O?*
> *Because I bade the people pull*
> *The House into the Lobby O. . . .*
>
> *When to the mob you make a speech,*
> *My boy Hobbie O,*

[9] *LJ*, IV, 493. It was perhaps as well that these "Observations" were not published in Byron's lifetime. Murray wisely held them back, and they were not published until 1833 in Murray's seventeen-volume edition of Byron's works (XV, 57–98).

> *How do you keep without their reach*
> *The watch within your fobby O?*
>
> *But never mind such petty things,*
> *My boy Hobbie O;*
> *God save the people—damn all Kings,*
> *So let us crown the Mobby O!*

He signed the poem "Infidus Scurra," a term they had commonly applied to Scrope Davies.

Before Hobhouse received the ballad, he had been released from prison and elected to a seat in Parliament (on the day Byron wrote the satire), but it struck him very hard, especially as Murray had circulated it freely among his friends before sending him a clerk's copy, and a mutilated copy had already been published in the Tory *Morning Post* before Murray condescended to send it on to him."

Hobhouse recorded sadly in his diary on April 16: "I am exceedingly unwilling to record this proof of the bad nature of my friend—he thought me in prison—he knew me attacked by all parties & pens—he resolved to give his kick too. . . . for a man to give way to such a mere pruriency & itch of writing against one who has stood by him in all his battles & never refused a single friendly office—is a melancholy proof of want of feeling & I fear of principle." "

Byron's bantering but kindly letter of March 29 arrived a few days later, and Hobhouse's resolution to cut his friendship melted. He wrote in his diary on the 20th: "I have had a letter from Byron in which he talks of the song I think half ashamed—& very friendly & kind poor fellow in every respect. . . . wrote to Byron telling him he is a shabby fellow and leaving him to chew that phrase without any other comment." "

The post from England always seemed to bring Byron disturbing and irritating news. It is not surprising that Teresa trembled when it arrived. At the beginning of April, Byron received his wife's curt and threatening reply to his offer to let her view the Memoirs. He wrote immediately: "My offer was an honest one, and surely could be only construed as such even by the most malignant Casuistry. I *could* answer you; but it is too late, and it is not worth while." [n]

And shortly after, contradictory reports on the Irish mortgage came from Hanson and Kinnaird. After repeated requests by Byron to get his money out of the government Funds, Kinnaird had proposed taking a six-per-cent mortgage on the Irish property of Lord Blessington.[n] But now Hanson had objected that if he sold out of the Funds he would lose £8,000, and that in Ireland six per cent really meant five. When Byron's financial advisers disagreed, he felt helpless to make a decision. Shortly afterward Byron had word that the Funds were going up in value, and he gave his written consent to the Irish mortgage,[n] but the trustees waited in anticipation of further increase in the Funds, and the matter dragged on for months.

As the spring wore on, Byron became increasingly absorbed in Italian affairs, even while he viewed them with detachment. He enclosed for Murray's amusement the circular for the Cardinal Legate's *conversazione* of April 9. "The Cardinal himself is a very good-natured little fellow, Bishop of Imola and Legate here,— a devout believer in all the doctrines of the Church. He has kept his housekeeper these forty years, for his carnal recreation; but is reckoned a pious man, and a moral liver." [n]

But the social life of the provincial town was already losing its novelty and had begun to bore Byron, except as a topic to enliven his letters. Other interests absorbed his attention. He had told Moore in 1817 that he did not consider literature his vocation. "But you will see that I shall do something or other—the times and fortune permitting. . . ." [n] And now in Ravenna, by the middle of April, time and fortune were thrusting that something in his way, and he was beginning to realize it. Despite the alarmed reports of the police spies who had watched him through the latter half of 1819, he had been little aware of Italian politics or of insurrectionary movements either during his first residence in Ravenna or for the first three months of his return to the Romagna. It may have been his conversations with Count Ruggero Gamba, Teresa's father, an ardent Italian patriot and liberal, which first drew his attention to the growing strength of organizations like the Carbonari.

"We are in expectation of a *row* here in a short time," he wrote Douglas Kinnaird on April 14. "The Spanish business has set all Italy a constitutioning,[1] and they won't get it without some *fechting*, as we Scottish say. . . . You can have no idea of the ferment in men's minds, from the Alps to Otranto. . . . if matters wax serious, I should not like to sit twirling my thumbs, but perhaps 'take service,' like Dugald Dalgetty and his horse, on the savage side of the question." [n]

And he elaborated his views in much the same vein to Murray two days later: ". . . I shall think it by far the most interesting spectacle and moment in existence, to see the Italians send the Barbarians of all nations back to their own dens. I have lived long enough among them to feel more for them as a nation than for any other people in existence; but they want Union, and they want principle; and I doubt their success. However, they will try, probably; and if they do, it will be a good cause." [n]

This new feeling must have caused a gradual souring of Byron's relations with the Cardinal, that devout believer in the doctrines of the Church whose temporal power was being fortified and supported by the Austrians. Byron had soon discovered that, although support for the autocratic political power of Church and State centered around the Archbishop's palace, there was much political division among churchmen themselves, and that then, as in later times of political upheaval in Italy, many laymen, who never questioned the spiritual authority of the Church and who paid due respect to the priesthood, openly or secretly rebelled against the dictatorial political authority of churchmen. In Ravenna this was peculiarly true of a large number of the aristocratic older families, including Count Gamba and his friends and relations, whom Byron met most intimately.

On the 23rd he informed Murray: "Last night they have overwritten all the city walls with 'Up with the Republic!' and 'death to the Pope!' etc., etc. This would be nothing in London, where the walls are privileged. . . . But here it is a different

[1] On March 9, 1820, Ferdinand VII of Spain was forced to take an oath of fidelity to a free constitution which had been written in 1812 and abolished by him in 1814. The successful popular rising encouraged the leaders of Italian insurrectionist movements and secret societies.

thing; they are not used to such fierce political inscriptions, and the police is all on the alert, and the Cardinal glares pale through all his purple." "

By the end of April, Byron had settled down comfortably into his palace, feeling as much at home as he had at La Mira or the Palazzo Mocenigo. The best thing perhaps was to ignore Count Guiccioli. For the rest of Ravenna accepted Byron quite easily as Teresa's *cavalier servente*.

Murray's lack of warmth for *Don Juan* had dulled Byron's enthusiasm for writing. "I have quite lost all personal interest about anything except money to supply my own indolent expences," he wrote Hobhouse; "and when I rouse up to appear to take an interest about anything, it is a temporary irritation like Galvanism upon Mutton." " And, as he revealed to Murray later, there were other obstacles to his progress on the tragedy of *Marino Faliero*—a drama of his own that divided his attention. "I never wrote nor copied *an entire Scene of that play,* without being obliged to *break* off—to *break* a commandment, to obey a woman's, and to forget God's. . . . The Lady always apologized for the interruption; but you know the answer a man must make when and while he can. It happened to be the only hour I had in the four and twenty for composition, or reading, and I was obliged to divide even it. Such are the defined duties of a *Cavalier' Servente* or *Cavalier' Schiavo*." "

In his uncertain situation, Byron was distracted also by consideration for the care and education of his daughter. She was past three years old, and he was aware that she had not had the proper attention and training. During the spring Claire had bombarded him, through the Hoppners, with a number of letters which he had mostly ignored, but when she threatened a visit to her daughter he was forced to give some attention to her demands. Claire had noted with irony in her diary on January 8: "A letter from Madame Hoppner—The Hero is gone to Ravenna." " This move had at once filled her with alarm, which was augmented by the gossipy reports on Byron's life which she received at intervals from the Hoppners. On January 23, Elise, the Swiss nurse who had first gone to Venice with Allegra, called on her and the Shelleys and no doubt added to the gossip."

From Pisa on February 20, Claire wrote a letter to Byron,[n] and, getting no reply, she wrote again on March 16, asking him to send Allegra to the Shelleys for a visit, since it was inconvenient for her or Shelley to come to Ravenna.[n] Still hearing nothing, she wrote a determined letter on April 23. This time she made a proposal that was alarming to Byron:

"I have therefore no resource ignorant as I am of all that passes in your mind but to set out to fetch her. . . . Though I can scarcely believe it possible you will refuse my just request yet I beg you to remember that I did not part with her at Milan until I had received your formal & explicit declaration that I should see my child at proper intervals. Nearly two years have now elapsed since I had that pleasure and no time can be more proper than the period of our visit to the Baths of Lucca so favourable to the health of every one." [n]

Before Byron received that letter, however, the Hoppners had forwarded to him belatedly her first request that he send Allegra to the Shelleys at Pisa. He replied with asperity: "About Allegra, I can only say to Claire—that I so totally disapprove of the mode of Children's treatment in their family, that I should look upon the Child as going into a hospital. Is it not so? Have they *reared* one? Her health here has hitherto been *excellent,* and her temper not bad; she is sometimes vain and obstinate, but always clean and cheerful, and as, in a year or two, I shall either send her to England, or put her in a Convent for education, these defects will be remedied as far as they can in human nature. But the Child shall not quit me again to perish of Starvation, and green fruit, or be taught to believe that there is no Deity. Whenever there is convenience of vicinity and access, her Mother can always have her with her; otherwise no. It was so stipulated from the beginning." [n]

When this reply was relayed to Claire by Mrs. Hoppner, she recorded laconically in her diary: "A letter from Mad. Hoppner concerning green fruit and god—strange jumble. . . ." [n] Claire continued her importunities through the month of May. But Byron became less and less inclined to entrust his daughter at her now impressionable age to what he considered erratic care and influences. On May 19, Claire wrote in her diary: "A Brutal

letter from Albè. . . ." " This was no doubt a letter which Byron
had written to Shelley to complain of Claire's annoying persistence. Shelley replied very sensibly: "I wish you had not expressed
yourself so harshly in your letter about Clare—because of necessity
she was obliged to read it. . . . What letters she writes to you I
know not; perhaps they are very provoking; but at all events it is
better to forgive the weak. I do not say—I do not think—that
your resolutions are unwise; only express them mildly—and pray
don't *quote me*." "

By the middle of May, Byron's relations with Teresa and her
husband had reached a crisis. From the somewhat scanty and
not altogether explicit evidence it is possible to reconstruct the
main elements of the story, though Count Guiccioli's motives,
particularly for turning on Byron and his wife at this moment,
after all his months of acquiescence or tolerance, are clouded
in obscurity. After the affair of Byron's payment to the theater
for which the Count refused to give a receipt, and the violent
quarrel which ensued on the 3rd of March, Guiccioli no longer
took pains to conceal his resentment. Byron had had some warning also that the Count was searching for evidence against him
when on April 2 he received an agitated note from Teresa saying
that a servant had told her that early that morning before she was
up her husband had broken open her writing-desk and gone
through all the letters in it. Fortunately, it contained no compromising ones from Byron." Teresa professed to believe that
the breaking-point came when Guiccioli was urged and perhaps
taunted by some of his cronies among the ecclesiastical party,
who, suspicious of Byron's politics, wanted to get him out of
Ravenna. She blamed particularly a young prelate (afterward
cardinal), Monsignor Pietro Marini, who had come to Ravenna
with Cardinal Malvasia and was co-founder with him of the
literary academy known as the Malvasiana." Hating Byron for
his liberal sentiments and his popularity with the people, Marini,
according to Teresa, stirred up the Count's passions against him,
"by insinuating that he ought not to have taken as a lodger a
man so seductive as Lord Byron but that at the least he should
not tolerate the intimacy of this Lord with the Countess. . . ." "

Whatever the motive Teresa says that the Count returned

one evening "in a state of extreme irritation—and having found Lord Byron as usual chatting quietly with the Countess he went straight up to him and told him that his visits which he had formerly desired were now displeasing to him and asked him to be so good as to stop them. Lord Byron had enough control over himself to listen with sufficient coolness to such words— and after having replied with a noble pride a few words which signified that he had regard for his age and his house he went up the stairs to his own apartment. The scenes which took place after his departure wounded and frightened the young woman to such a point by their violence that she called to her the following morning the Count her father and after she had confided to him all that had passed, she declared it was impossible for her to live any longer with the Count and asked his permission to return under his protection." ⁿ

But Byron, always more circumstantial and certainly more frank and unembarrassed in his accounts of his amours, intimated that the Count had encountered something more than a mere quiet conversation between the lovers when he arrived on the scene. Byron wrote Murray a few days later that the trouble arose "on account of our having been taken together *quasi* in the fact, and, what is worse, that she did not *deny* it." ²

The climax did not come as a complete surprise either to Teresa or to Byron, for there had been indications of the Count's displeasure and of his spying. Lulled by the failure of the Count to take any action, however, they continued to ignore the warnings and to carry on their affairs as openly as need be, while Teresa thought she was sufficiently placating her husband when she read to him and allowed him certain conjugal familiarities. Once the storm broke, Byron's first impulse was to withdraw and "sacrifice" himself rather than compromise her or embarrass her relations. But Teresa only wept and accused him of not loving her. He replied:

"*Of my love be assured*—but I cannot understand how a love

---

² *LJ*, V, 28. Letter of May 20, 1820. On May 15, Byron had written to Harriette Wilson that he was in a "scrape" which might end seriously that very evening, the aggrieved person, "a rich noble and old," having had "a fit of discovery against his moiety." (*Harriette Wilson's Memoirs*, p. 614.)

can be *true* that sacrifices the beloved object. With me you would be unhappy and compromised in the eyes of the world; with your husband you would be, if not happy, at least respectable and respected. So I see no alternative except a separation, which sooner or later would in any case have to come." [n]

The Marchesa Origo acutely observes at this point: "I do not think we need see in all this only the last efforts of a reluctant lover to free himself [as Hoppner, Moore, and others liked to think]. Byron's conventionality was genuine, and he probably believed every word of these remarks. If he had played for so many years the rebel's part, it was because society, to his mind, had not been kind to him. But he never questioned—as Shelley did—the essential validity of the social laws." [n] In writing to Moore, he referred to himself and Teresa with genuine candor as "those who are in the wrong." [n] He had been revolted in his earliest years by the violence of his mother, and he had a native distaste for women who made scenes, like Caroline Lamb. But, more than this, he had a sharp and sensitive revulsion peculiar to fastidious libertines against the outward show of unconventionality in women. Add to this the remnant of Calvinism which clung to him to the end of his life and kept alive in him a deep-seated sense of sin.

For a few days Byron urged caution on Teresa, for they did not know what the Count's game was or what might be expected. After the violent scenes belowstairs following his blunt statement to Byron, however, Teresa was frightened for her lover as well as for herself. How much did the Count know, and how would he use his knowledge? Teresa wanted Byron's counsel. He wrote: "My love + What do you want me to reply? He has known—or ought to have known, all these things for many months—there is a mystery here that I do not understand, and prefer not to understand. Is it only now that he knows of your infidelity? [3] What can he have thought—that we are made of stone—or that I am *more* or *less* than a man? I know of one remedy only—what I have already suggested, *my departure.*" [n]

Teresa was all for leaving the Count immediately and seeking

[3] Teresa later tried to erase this and change it to "is suspicious of your fidelity." (Origo, p. 177 n.)

a separation, but Byron counseled her to "Speak to Papa." He continued: "If the matter ends with your separation from him—(which I do not wish—though, on the other hand, it would not surprise me) we shall make our decision,—and I shall do all that should be done in the circumstances." " But at the same time he reminded her that he was not free to make her an "honest woman" if she did leave her husband.

After a few days of tension, however, when nothing happened, Teresa and Byron relaxed their precautions and she made regular visits to him in his own apartment. And while they posted trusty servants as guards, Guiccioli, who now felt that he must gather evidence seriously against them, paid servants and workmen to watch and to make written statements and sign affidavits of what they saw. His purpose apparently was to justify himself for having winked at the infidelity of his wife for so long, and to have ample evidence to counter any plea from the other side that he should return his wife's dowry or make her an allowance. He later gathered the statements of eighteen of his servants and sent them to the Pope after Count Gamba had applied for a separation for his daughter."

According to the statement of one of the servants, Teresa "made use of the theatre hours to join Mylord in his rooms, taking care to be warned of her husband's return by one of her own footmen, Luigi Morelli, who used to stand on guard outside the house door." " Realizing how far the Count might go in his search for evidence, Byron asked Teresa to return his letters and other incriminating objects for safekeeping, and in her excited state, smarting under his apparent eagerness to leave her, Teresa easily misunderstood his purpose and was offended.

Within a very few days, however, Byron had accepted the necessity of the separation and no longer counseled Teresa to remain with her husband. But, while Teresa believed his resolution not to desert her was brought about by the description she gave of her anguish and his recognition of the character of the Count, there seems little doubt that it was also powerfully fortified by the attitudes of Count Gamba and his Ravenna friends. On May 20, Byron wrote to Murray: ". . . the Italian public are on our side, particularly the women,—and the men also, because they say that *he* had no business to take the business up now after a year of toleration. The law is against him, because he slept with his wife after her admission. All her relations (who are numerous, high in rank, and powerful) are furious *against him* for his conduct, and his not wishing to be cuckolded at *three*score, when every one else is at ONE." [n]

Guiccioli not only tried to get Byron to leave, but also, apparently, again attempted to extract money from him. This, like everything else connected with the spicy scandal, was common gossip in Ravenna, and soon reached the chronicles of Francesco Rangone in Bologna.[n] Even after he had told Byron that he did not want to see him in his house any more, Count Guiccioli continued for some time to seek daily conferences with his wife's lover. This conduct was so strange, Teresa says in the *"Vie,"* that "Ld. Byron as well as the general public suspected some hidden motive—and he kept himself on guard." [n]

Teresa thought one of these interviews so critical in rousing Byron's determination not to yield to the Count and so consequential to her own subsequent relationship with her lover that she later divided his notes and letters of this period into packets *"avant"* and *"après"* the interview.[n] In one of the latter Byron reported to her:

"He [Guiccioli] proposed that I should *go away* (saying that this is the *general desire* and opinion—and that his friend Marini is surprised that I should stay to cause trouble in the life of a family) or else that I should use my influence over you to persuade you to detach yourself from *me* and to love *him*—and also that I should attach myself, as soon as possible, to *another*.

"As to separation—he says that he does not want it—not being disposed to 'lose the woman'—to disgust his relations—and above all, to *pay* an allowance. He does not want to cut the figure, he says, of a 'complacent cuckold'—and he charges me to persuade you that true love is *conjugal* love." [n]

In the meantime Teresa had followed Byron's advice to "Speak to Papa," and had told him such a tale of her husband's strange conduct, tyrannies, and unnatural behavior as to rouse his anger at his son-in-law and to give him complete confidence in the rightness of his daughter's cause. There are dark hints in some of Teresa's later statements that suggest her husband was capable of perverted sensualities mounting to violence when his will was thwarted,[4] and he seems to have had a peculiar hold on Teresa despite her rebellion against him. How much she told her father it is impossible to know—perhaps more than she ever told Byron, for it overcame any restraints or consideration for proprieties which that conventional old gentleman may have had, and instead of telling her to dismiss her lover (for it seems incredible he could any longer be convinced, even with the indulgence he always showed his daughter, that her relation with Byron was only Platonic) and go back to her husband, he deliberately sought a duel with his son-in-law."

If Byron was governed to a large extent in his acquiescence to Teresa's wish that he remain by the fact that her father and relatives turned against Guiccioli, Count Gamba was no less influenced in his actions, so contrary to the ordinary proprieties, by a genuine liking and respect for Byron, not altogether influenced by Teresa's prepossessions in his favor. It seems that he had already come under the spell of the young English lord and would have much preferred him as a son-in-law to the scheming old man who had been unkind to his daughter. Moreover, Byron had consulted him in everything and had offered to act as he thought best for Teresa's reputation, happiness, and station in life. His fondness for Byron was no doubt also increased by their essential agreement in politics, for old Gamba still retained his revolutionary principles and hated the Austrian oligarchy as much as Byron did.

Count Gamba soon took the resolution to apply in his own name to the Pope for a separation of his daughter from this unnatural husband. His appeal was brief and direct: "In the short space of one year the Cavaliere has behaved so strangely and heaped so many insults upon his unhappy bride, that it has become wholly impossible for her to live any longer with so exact-

[4] After Teresa had returned to her husband, in 1826, following Byron's death, she found him so violent in his conduct that she soon applied for a second separation, his behavior having been "of so vile a nature" that she could not speak of it except to her lawyer, or to a priest in confession. (Origo, pp. 29–30.)

ing a Husband, and she is obliged, in the opinion of the whole
city, to seek a complete separation.

"In this state of affairs the petitioner humbly appeals to Your
Holiness, beseeching that the Cav. Guiccioli may be ordered to
pay a suitable allowance to his wife (the aforesaid daughter) in
accordance with the position of her husband, in order that she
may live suitably, as befits her birth and position." [n] For more
intimate details, he probably relied on his messenger, Teresa's
maternal grandmother, Cecilia Machirelli Giordani, a personal
friend of Pius VII.[n]

Byron had told Moore that all the world, "including priests
and cardinals," were implicated in the quarrel, and soon it
touched him more nearly. He had suspected from the beginning
that the clerical party, knowing his politics, would like to seize
the occasion to get him out of the Romagna, though they did
not dare to attack an English lord directly. One way of annoying
Byron was to attack or pick quarrels with his Italian servants, of
whom he had accumulated a considerable number. Some of them
he had brought from Venice, and others he had taken on in
Ravenna.[n] Two of his most trusted ones had come under the
watchful eye of the authorities. Lega Zambelli, once in the employ of Guiccioli, had accompanied him from Venice as his secretary. Soon after his arrival, the Archbishop of Ravenna, Antonio Codronchi, had thought Lega a sufficiently subversive
character to report his presence to the Papal Secretary of State,
Cardinal Consalvi.[n]

In a letter of June 9 to Moore, Byron reported another vexation: ". . . I have incurred a quarrel with the Pope's carabiniers,
or *gens d'armerie*, who have petitioned the Cardinal against my
liveries, as resembling too nearly their own lousy uniform. . . .

"I have sent a trenchant reply . . . and I have directed my
ragamuffins, six in number, who are tolerably savage, to defend
themselves, in case of aggression. . . ." [n]

In these squabbles Byron was fortunate in having a friend in
the inner sanctum of the Cardinal Legate, the Secretary General
Count Alborghetti, who—perhaps for pecuniary gain, for he already knew Byron's generosity, but also because of personal
admiration and attachment—had become his informant and in-

termediary. That Alborghetti used what influence he had with the Cardinal in the separation business in behalf of Byron and Teresa seems evident. Count Guiccioli accused the Secretary General of being the chief instrument for bringing about a decision unfavorable to him, referring to him as "a Minister who has a reputation for venality and who was always attached in a particular manner to Byron." "

Through May and June, Byron continued his daily round of activity on the second floor of the Palazzo Guiccioli, playing with his menagerie, riding in the forest, seeing Teresa clandestinely while Morelli and the Negro boy watched the stairs, and writing late into the night. He found time to write to Hoppner concerning the Merryweather case. No longer trusting Castelli, he left it to the Consul to push the matter. He had ceased to care about the money and merely wanted the rascal to be punished for his ingratitude. "If Merryweather's *in*—let him out—if *out*—put him in—for a week merely for a lesson—and lecture him in *your best style.* . . ." " When his adversary was finally imprisoned on June 7 and held for a short time, Byron was satisfied." And now he decided to give up the Palazzo Mocenigo, and he ordered Hoppner to sell his gondola."

During the time the separation was pending, Byron was deeply disturbed by what he thought to be Teresa's weakness in acquiescing to the wishes of her husband, with whom her father had counseled her to stay until she had the legal right to leave. Byron could not understand how, if she loved her *amico* as she said she did, she could be so compliant; was there something deeper than he could fathom in the Count's hold over her? In one of his notes before his remarkable interview with the Count, he had written to Teresa: "If, after suffering the insult of his requiring separate rooms—owing to his mad folly—you go back to yielding to his false blandishments and dotardly caresses, it is you who will be to blame, and your weakness of character will be more confirmed than ever." "

But as usual Teresa was able to reassure him by means that she knew best how to employ, and when her family had definitely embarked on the request for a separation, Byron felt that since she was giving up her station in society for his sake, he must stand by her to the end. He did not then, however, see what the end would be. He wrote her with resignation and loyalty, but one statement in his letter impressed Teresa more than anything he had written her before. It was the thing she had never been sure about. She wrote on the letter, preserved among her Byron treasures: *"Promesse!!!! d'être mon Époux!!"* In that treasured letter he wrote: ". . . as that man has persecuted you in words and deeds for injuries to which no one has *contributed,* and which no one has protected—more than he—now I can hesitate no longer.—He may abandon you—but I *never. . . .* my love—my duty—my honour—all these and everything should make me forever what I am *now,* your lover friend and (when circumstances permit) your *husband."* ⁿ

No answer had come yet to Count Gamba's petition, and the matter remained in suspense well into July. Byron was already planning an escape if the decision went against a separation. He wrote to Hobhouse on July 6: "When the *Pope* has decided on Madame Guiccioli's business . . . I will tell you whether I can come to England (viâ Switzerland) or not. . . . I can't settle anything till I know the result. . . ." ⁿ

But that very day the Pope had written his decree granting Teresa her separation from Count Guiccioli because it was "no longer possible for her to live in peace and safety with her husband." ⁿ The decree was sent by the Pope direct to Countess Cecilia Giordani at Pesaro, who forwarded it to Ravenna, so that the official news did not reach Teresa until July 14.ⁿ Byron (and Teresa), however, knew the substance of it two days earlier, very likely through Count Alborghetti. Byron wrote to Moore on July 13: ". . . the Pope has pronounced *their separation.* The decree came yesterday from Babylon. . . . He [Guiccioli] swore that he thought our intercourse was purely amicable, and that *I* was more partial to him than to her, till melancholy testimony proved the contrary. . . .

"Now he says that he encouraged my return to Ravenna, to see *'in quanti piedi di acqua siamo'* [how many feet of water we are in], and he has found enough to drown him in. . . . She returns to her father's house, and I can only see her under great restrictions—such is the custom of the country. The relations behave very well:—I offered any settlement, but they refused to accept it. . . ." " Teresa was to have an allowance from Count Guiccioli, to be paid to the Legate for her, of one hundred scudi a month.[5]

In sending the news to his daughter, Count Gamba fixed an hour the following afternoon when she should meet him in her carriage outside the walls of the city and be taken to his country house at Filetto, about fifteen miles southwest of Ravenna. The Cardinal had agreed not to apprise Count Guiccioli of the Pope's decision until after she had departed, "to avoid violence or scandal." " During this last day in the Palazzo Guiccioli, Teresa was "full of fears and anguish," and the Count "full of suspicions." " One cause of her agitation was the realization that she must part from Byron, at least for some time. They were together now in the same palace for the last time, and she must carry on normal conversation with her husband. The Count must have known that something was in the wind, for he had given orders that none of the servants should put horses to a carriage that day without his permission. One of them, however (perhaps Morelli, who, with Teresa's maid, accompanied her), disobeyed the orders, and she set off at four o'clock." Teresa does not say whether she had an opportunity for a farewell visit with Byron, who, she says, "was the occasion rather than the cause" of the separation." But she does record that in those hectic days after the news arrived he was "very much tormented." " For both of them it was the end of a chapter. Byron had been transformed from a *cavalier servente*, not into the husband she had dreamed of, but into something much more anomalous: the lover of a "respectable and noble Lady separated from her husband."

[5] Byron told Kinnaird that this would be worth about £1,000 a year in England. (*B-SP*, II, 520. Letter of July 20, 1820.)

CHAPTER XXII

1820

Ravenna—Filetto—Politics

BYRON seems to have been aware from the time Teresa left
that the stipulations of the separation decree requiring her
to live under the parental roof would place serious restrictions on
their meeting as freely as they had done before. Count Gamba,
though friendly enough to Byron, was not eager to jeopardize
his daughter's allowance by encouraging the visits of the man
whom Guiccioli was still trying to prove guilty of cuckolding
him. Though Byron professed himself willing to provide for her
so that she could be independent of Guiccioli's allowance, both
Teresa and her father were too proud to accept his well-meant
generosity.

Count Guiccioli in his apartments on the ground floor of the
palace was as enigmatic as ever, and common report hinted at
the possibility of some sly violence on his part, toward either
Byron or Teresa. Though Byron was closer to whatever danger
there might be and had provoked the Count by refusing to leave
the palace where he had established himself at some trouble and
expense,[n] he was more concerned about Teresa and warned her
not to go out alone. After his evening ride on the day of her departure (July 15), he sent her his cook Valeriano to act as a
bodyguard along with Luigi Morelli, who had accompanied her.
He wrote: "I am expecting your news and *superior orders.*—I
will do what you wish—but I hope that in the end *we may be
happy.*—Of my love you cannot doubt—let yours continue.—
Remember me to Count G[amba] your father. . . .

"P.S. It is said that A[lessandro] cuts a poor figure. Write to me in the finest style of Santa Chiara. Very naughty O. ++++ +++ Be very careful!!" [n]

This tone of affectionate solicitude mingled with teasing, and sometimes scolding, which henceforth characterized his letters, reveals how much Byron had come to consider his relationship with Teresa a calm domestic one. There is no longer any of the emotional anguish of the days when they were living under the same roof in the Palazzo Guiccioli, and when he felt that she catered too much to her husband's wishes. In all but a few respects he considered himself and wrote as if he were in fact, if not in name, a fond husband. Passion had not died, for she always attracted him strongly as a woman, but his indulgent tenderness did not stand in the way of an open-eyed appraisal of her faults and affectations.

According to Teresa, they did not meet again for more than a month and a half. (Actually it was only a month.) [n] In the meantime the letters flew back and forth, carried by the faithful Perelli or by a servant, and sometimes by "Papa" himself, who apparently called on Byron when he went to Ravenna. Very soon after Teresa left, Byron began searching for a summer house near Filetto where he could place Allegra and her nurse, and from which he could make an easy and unobtrusive journey to the Casa Gamba. But it was almost the middle of August before he found one suitable. It was Teresa who was impatient; Byron found sufficient occupation in Ravenna. He no longer went to the theater or the assemblies, but *Marino Faliero* and his English correspondence filled his days and nights, and his only recreation was the daily ride.

It is not a little surprising how Byron got through so much literary work and correspondence in his most distracting times of love and revolution, emotional crises and *serventismo*. But emotional tension seemed to spur his creative powers. In the letter in which he announced to Moore the exciting news of the Pope's decision he showed equal concern for his literary productions. "M.[urray]," he wrote, "has shuffled, and almost insinuated that my last productions are *dull*. Dull, sir!—damme, dull! I believe he is right." [n]

In announcing the completion of *Marino Faliero* to Murray a few days later, he made a great point of the historical accuracy of his drama.ⁿ He had been captivated by the theme as one in which he could embody an imaginative concept of the historic past of the decaying city. "Everything about Venice is," he wrote in the Preface, "or was, extraordinary—her aspect is like a dream, and her history is like a romance." ⁿ

Murray's failure to commit himself about publication of the new cantos of *Don Juan* roused Byron's ire. On June 22 he wrote Hobhouse that the continued silence of the "high minded Moray" had brought him to a decision. He ordered the manuscript placed in the hands of Moore's publisher, Longman, or any other who would take it. "To Mr. Murray say thus—I have no *personal* difference with him, & shall continue an acquaintance and correspondence while he chooses; but as publisher, *that* leaf of his ledger will close for ever." But, as usual, it required only a friendly and enthusiastic letter from Murray to calm his suspicions, and he not only ceased to talk of Longman, but by the middle of August had copied and sent all five acts of the tragedy.ⁿ

Another matter in England that began to absorb his interest more and more was the trial of Queen Caroline, instigated by George IV and his Tory ministers to deprive her of her rights and privileges as Queen and secure a divorce on the grounds of her misconduct while abroad. When she returned to London on June 6 to assume her role as Queen after the death of George III, she was enthusiastically received by the populace, and after a Bill of Pains and Penalties was proposed against her in Parliament on July 5, liberal sentiment rallied to her and made her trial a popular cause against the King and ministers. Leading her legal defense was Byron's arch-enemy Henry Brougham, but, despite this, partly in response to the appeals of Hobhouse and Kinnaird and partly because he remembered with gratitude the kindnesses she had shown him when he visited her with Lady Oxford and others in 1813, Byron soon entered into her defense also and even talked of going to England to vote for her in Parliament. The fact that he did not seriously believe in her innocence of the principal charge, that of having had an intrigue with her Italian courier Bartolommeo Bergami, did not lessen his efforts to find witnesses for her and to discredit those who had been brought to England to testify against her.

Count Guiccioli did not take the Pope's decision calmly or without protest, but he was not meditating any violence toward either Byron or Teresa. Two days after he had received the news of the separation decree, he wrote a long letter to his lawyer, Vincenzo Taglioni, in Rome, asking him to try to get the decision revoked or modified." The Count seemed so firmly convinced that he would succeed that he was in no mood to take any rash measures of revenge.

In the meantime, Teresa, at Filetto, impatient to see her lover, had been making inquiries about country houses near her that might be available for him. Byron was feeling the deprivation of love-making as keenly as did Teresa. It had become an agreeable part of his life. In that one respect she remained entirely satisfactory, for in her embraces he could even recapture something of the ideal vision, or at least still the critical mind. He took a kind of roguish pleasure in hinting at the physical aspects of their love which she camouflaged in sentiment. He wrote: *"This separation from you inconveniences me greatly—you understand,"* underscoring the words. And in a postscript he added: "Yes, my Duck—I have understood you—with all your +++ poor child! I hope that we shall fulfil all these wishes of ours very soon—have a little more patience." "

It seems that Ruggero Gamba had brought his son Pietro to see the dangerous, seductive, and heartless English lord, for Byron wrote: "I like your little brother very much—he shows character and talent—Big eyebrows! and a stature which he has enriched, I think, at your expense—at least in those. . . . do you understand me? His head is a little too hot for revolutions—he must not be too rash." "

Pietro had just returned from his studies in Rome with an earnest and youthful enthusiasm for the ideals of liberty which were everywhere stirring in Italy. Byron's own interest in the Italian cause no doubt combined with the fascination of his appearance and personality to make Pietro succumb immediately to his friendly advances. Youthful charm such as Pietro's (he was scarcely a year younger than Teresa) " always had a strong appeal for Byron. Pietro's naïveté, his sincerity and loyalty, his idealism, and even his impracticality, at which Byron laughed (but which also sometimes exasperated him), combined with boyish good spirits and a sense of humor more lively than his sister's, struck a responsive chord in Byron, and they were soon fast friends.

Pietro had brought fresh news of the abortive and somewhat ridiculous revolution against the Bourbon tyranny in Naples. The fact that it was temporarily successful in forcing a constitution upon the weak and frightened Ferdinand I, King of Naples by grace of the Holy Alliance and Austrian power, served, however, greatly to encourage the secret societies who were plotting insurrection throughout Italy.

Byron had told Moore on July 13: "There is a revolution at Naples. If so, it will probably leave a card at Ravenna in its way to Lombardy." " But as more news came through he saw how much the Neapolitan revolution was worth. He wrote to Murray on the 22nd: "The Neapolitans are not worth a curse, and will be beaten if it comes to fighting: the rest of Italy, I think, might stand. The Cardinal is at his wits' end; it is true that he had not far to go. . . . Here there are as yet but the sparks of the volcano; but the ground is hot, and the air sultry. Three assassinations last week here and at Faenza—an anti-liberal priest, a factor, and a trooper last night,—I heard the pistol-shot that brought him down within a short distance of my own door." "

Through the Gambas, father and son, Byron was during the summer and autumn initiated into the inner meetings of some of the secret societies then forming in the Romagna. Their romantic names," their night meetings in a guarded room or in the forest, the passwords and cabalistic rituals and organization half attracted Byron and half aroused his contempt for their impracticality. But his sympathy for the cause made him bear with the melodrama of their organizations, though he was, especially later, openly critical of their grand talk and little action."

According to Primo Uccellini, who as a schoolboy had been initiated into the Carboneria in 1818, in Ravenna it "was divided into three branches: the first was given the name of *Protettrice*

(Protectress), because it controlled the others; the second that of *Speranza* (Hope) because it was composed chiefly of young students; and the third, because it included a mixture of all sorts of people, mostly workmen, and was the most prepared for action, was named *Turba* (Mob)." "

This last was the one to which Byron later attached himself, and in which he became a kind of honorary "*Capo*" or chief. It also went under the name of "*Mericani*" (Americans), or "*Cacciatore Americani*" (American Hunters). It seems strange that Byron, who had so recently ridiculed Hobhouse for allying himself with the mob among the English reformers, should have joined this particular group and been proud of it. But it may have appealed to him because, unlike the others, it was not given to mysteries and talk and was prepared to do something practical if need be. Then, too, the mob seemed more picturesque in a foreign land, and the Continental deference paid to him as a leader (and later a provider of arms) made him feel that even revolutionaries here recognized the leadership of gentlemen.

But what drew him most confidently into the movement was the fact that all his best friends, the enlightened aristocracy of Ravenna, were moving spirits in the Carboneria, among the most active and enthusiastic being Ruggero and Pietro Gamba and the old Count's nephew the Marchese Antonio Cavalli." Pietro and Antonio were constantly under the watchful eye of the police, and it was not long before Byron's connection with the Carboneria was brought to the attention of the Cardinal himself. There can be little wonder that Byron's activities and sympathies were known to the authorities, for he had been free enough in writing of them to his friends in England, and he was not unaware that his letters were opened.

During the greater part of August, however, Byron's attention was drawn from politics by personal matters. Allegra had become ill again in the heat of Ravenna, and he continued his desperate search for a house where she could have country air. He had had difficulty in getting a nurse for Allegra, for no one wanted to take service in Guiccioli's house. Teresa sent some toys to Allegra, but at the same time she could not help giving way to a fit of jealousy, for her lively imagination made her suspect that Byron's delays in coming to see her must be caused by his interest in some other woman.

Byron gave Teresa some solid reasons why he could not yet come. Lega, he said, was preparing the villa,[1] but he did not want to risk calling on her until his household was established there because he did not want to give an advantage to the Count, "who would at once run to the Cardinal with a thousand lies and some *truths*——" [n] Byron had nearly come to blows with one of Guiccioli's spies who had followed him during his ride in the forest the day before.

A rumor was circulated in August that Byron had arrived in London. The stir that it caused pleased Hobhouse, for he had always tried to convince Byron that the feeling against him in England which he believed had caused his exile was all a myth of his friend's own making.[2] Hobhouse wrote Byron: "The queen somehow or other heard you were coming over—The poor creature was very much affected at this mark of recollection of her former attentions—She said several very handsome and true things of you." [n]

The rumor of Byron's arrival had been touched off by an item in the *Morning Chronicle*, August 18, 1820,[n] the editor, Perry, as usual not taking the trouble to verify the report. Caroline Lamb wrote eagerly to Murray to inquire "if he [Byron] is grown fat, if he is no uglier than he used to be, if he is good-humoured or cross-grained, putting his brows down. . . ." [n]

---

[1] Byron wrote Teresa on August 3 that he had taken the Villa Spreti. (Origo, p. 207.) Guiccioli's spies referred to Byron's house in the country near the Gambas' as Villa Bacinetta.

[2] Opposite Moore's statement in his life of Byron (II, 1) that Byron betook himself "to an exile which had not even the dignity of appearing voluntary," Hobhouse wrote: "There was not the slightest necessity even in appearance for his going abroad." Sir Harold Nicolson has called to my attention an entry in an old minute book of the Travellers Club in London which tends to confirm Hobhouse's conviction. On June 1, 1820, the Committee decided to extend another three months the invitation to membership to those on the original list, which included the name of Lord Byron. The original Committee, as listed for me by the Secretary of the Club, Mr. R. P. McDouall, included some of the most eminent men of the day, among them Lord Aberdeen, whom Byron had satirized in *English Bards and Scotch Reviewers*.

Leigh Hunt, probably having seen the note in the *Morning Chronicle*, wrote with a magnificent complacence to Shelley on August 23: "Lord Byron, they say, came to town on Saturday, with a packet for the Queen. I know not whether he will send to me, and I delay going to him; so between both, perhaps, neither will be done." [n]

The news reached Augusta through Murray, but she knew her brother too well to believe that he would come to London incognito.[n] She might not have looked upon Byron's arrival with such disapproval as she had the previous December, for the Leighs were, as usual, in serious financial difficulties. Someone had purchased the bond the Colonel had signed as nominal security for the £3,000 Byron had given Augusta in 1814 to extricate her husband from creditors. On August 10, Byron wrote to reassure her, and he repeated his assurances on the 19th:

My dearest Augusta—
I always loved you better than any earthly existence, and I always shall unless I go mad. And if I did *not* so love you—still I would not persecute or oppress any one wittingly—especially for debts, of which I know the *agony by experience*. Of Col. Leigh's bond, I really have forgotten all particulars, except that it was *not* of *my wishing*. . . . I would *not take the money* if he had it.[n]

Having the pretext of his daughter in the country to justify his visits, Byron now began to make occasional trips to Filetto. Teresa says the villa he had taken for Allegra was only six miles from Ravenna,[n] so that when there he must have been at least nine miles from the Villa Gamba, but in the country he supposed, probably rashly, that he was not under the surveillance of Guiccioli's spies. They seemed well aware of his movements, however, and described for their employer with considerable detail Byron's first visit to Teresa on Wednesday, August 16.[n]

The Villa Gamba lay in a flat but fertile plain on the opposite side of Ravenna from the Pineta and the Adriatic. The marshy land was drained by canals, and the meandering river Montone flowed close by the comfortable country house of the Gambas, a spacious family mansion dating from the late seventeenth century. Byron delighted in the genial life he saw and participated in there. His pleasant visits to Filetto during the summer and autumn gave him the feeling that he had truly found a family life such as he had never known before. He came increasingly to like the whole Gamba clan, their well-bred manners, their warm-hearted affection toward one another which was easily extended to him. Teresa says that he formed a great fondness for her little sisters. He "caressed them affectionately, and said that he liked *le beau sang* of the family; he felt as if he had become part of it." " But he liked the men of the family as much, if not more. He respected old Ruggero, and Pietro became his stanch friend and companion.

Great informality and naturalness reigned at the Villa Gamba, which, primarily a summer house, was designed for intimate ease. The windows and doors of the bedrooms on the second floor opened on an interior balcony which looked down on a high-ceilinged great hall or salon. One visitor to Teresa a few years later was slightly shocked by the unembarrassed ease with which the occupants of these rooms conversed from their beds when the windows and doors were open on hot nights." From the salon, stone steps, spreading fanwise toward the bottom, led to a wide lawn framed by old olive trees.³ On fine days in the summer, much of the family life was spent on the lawn or in the shade of these trees.

Replying to some pleasantries of Moore concerning the life he was living in Italy, Byron wrote at the end of August: "I verily believe that nor you, nor any man of poetical temperament, can avoid a strong passion of some kind. It is the poetry of life. What should I have known or written, had I been a quiet, mercantile politician, or a lord in waiting? A man must travel, and turmoil, or there is no existence. Besides, I only meant to be a Cavalier Servente, and had no idea it would turn out a romance, in the Anglo fashion. . . . Now, I have lived in the heart of their houses, in parts of Italy freshest and least influenced by strangers,— have seen and become (*pars magna fui*) a portion of their hopes,

³ These steps and some of the foundation were about all that was left of the Villa Gamba when I visited it in 1948. It had been used as headquarters by the Germans in 1944 before they retreated north over the Romagna plain.

and fears, and passions, and am almost inoculated into a family. This is to see men and things as they are." [n]

Except for occasional visits to Filetto, Byron remained in the Palazzo Guiccioli, going his own way and maintaining a contemptuous disregard for his landlord. Only once was he roused to address a complaint to him. Piqued by Guiccioli's statement that Byron was thirty-six (he was then thirty-two) in a letter to Pietro Gamba, in which Guiccioli told his brother-in-law his side of the story, Byron wrote with a curt politeness: "If I, in drawing up a memorandum of *your history*, were to make you out a man of *seventy*, adding one seventh to your age, you would not assuredly be pleased, and I will certainly not bear this injustice—" [n]

Byron was developing a peculiar sensitivity to references to his age, for he responded rather sharply to Moore's letter, received shortly after, congratulating him "upon arriving at what Dante calls the *mezzo cammin* [halfway point] of life, the age of thirty-three." [n] "D——n your *mezzo cammin*," he wrote— "you should say 'the prime of life,' a much more consolatory phrase. Besides, it is not correct." [n]

While the August heat still persisted, Byron was thrown into consternation, as he amusingly described his feelings to Teresa, by a threatened visitation from Fanny Silvestrini, who was probably longing for her lover Lega Zambelli. Byron had listened to her rhetorical blandishments willingly enough when she was his only means of communicating with or getting news of Teresa, but after their return to Ravenna both lovers were glad to neglect her, and Byron found her a bore. He had written to Teresa on July 26: "Lega tells me that Fanny has produced another bastard—a boy—whom I believe she is to present to the Venice hospital. . . ." [n] And now that Teresa announced Fanny's intention to come to Ravenna, Byron wrote: "No—no—no. Write,—send—stop her—deliver me—otherwise I don't know what will become of me—I said it—I foresaw it—she is coming. If she really comes—I shall turn monk at once, and the Church will gain . . . what she has lost in losing Lega. . . ." [n]

To amuse her in the country when they could not be together, Byron sent Teresa a number of books to read, mostly in French.

The book that touched her to the quick, however, was one that came too close to describing her own situation for comfort. What wounded her was that Byron could not have sent it if he had not been callous to her feelings, or insensitive to the parallel she must see between the unhappy liaison pictured in the novel and their own position. Perhaps he was both, for he had at times the sensitive person's insensitivity to the wounds he could inflict by the barbs of some unpalatable truth. The book was Benjamin Constant's novel *Adolphe,* which pictured the tortures of the unequal love affair of Constant and Mme de Staël. Byron told Lady Blessington later that it was "the truest picture of the misery unhallowed *liaisons* produce." [n]

Teresa's Santa Chiara style did not prevent her from rising to a dignified melancholy on this occasion. "Byron—why did you send me this book? This was not the moment—*indeed perhaps the moment will never come again for me!*—To be able to endure and enjoy that story one must be more remote from the condition of Eleonore *than I am*—and to give it to one's mistress to read, one must be *either very near to* the state of Adolphe, or very far away from it! Either you, my Byron, did not know this book (terrifying mirror of the truth) or you are not yet acquainted with your friend's heart—or you are aware in yourself of a greater or lesser strength than I think you have." [n]

Byron refused to take seriously her concern over *Adolphe.* Perhaps on discovering the depth of her sensitivity he thought the best remedy was to pretend ignorance of any close parallel with her situation. He wrote:

"My Love +++ The circumstances of Adolphe are very different. Ellenore was not married, she was many years older than Adolphe—she was not amiable—etc., etc.—Don't think any more about things so dissimilar in every way." [n]

Despite the gossip, Byron continued to make frequent trips to Filetto, though as discreetly as he could, and usually when the whole family was at home. Teresa describes in the "*Vie*" one idyllic day early in September [n] when Byron arrived by invitation to view with them an eclipse of the sun. He had, she said, a great love for astronomical studies, "considering them a puissant means of ameliorating humanity morally and intellectually

—of humiliating their pride—of consoling afflictions." He arrived at the moment when Teresa and the whole company, "armed with optical instruments and with smoked glasses, were observing the heavenly bodies whose meeting was already beginning to envelope the earth in shadow. Lord Byron seated himself among them, not wishing to disturb by his arrival the silence with which they were following the movements of the astral bodies." They watched with a "solemn and almost religious silence." [n]

But as soon as the sun was unveiled again, they regained speech and Byron "associated himself in the gaiety of the company," for they had made an outdoor festival of the occasion. He took part in a game of bowls and also in his favorite sport of shooting, but he refused to participate when the targets were live birds. [n]

On his arrival in town, he was stirred up by the mail from England and by the news, which he first saw in the *Milan Gazette*, that he had *"arrived* in London about the Queen's Business." [n] He wrote immediately asking Murray to contradict the rumor. Further news in letters from England made him chafe still more. "My Sister tells me," he wrote Murray, "that you sent to her to enquire where I was, believing in my arrival *'driving a curricle,'* etc., etc., into palace yard: do you think me a coxcomb or a madman, to be capable of such an exhibition? My Sister knew me better, and told you that *could not* be true: you might as well have thought me entering on 'a pale horse,' like Death in the Revelations." [n]

Byron's chief concern now was to hear more of what had been said of his tragedy. Murray had told him only what Gifford remarked on reading the first act, and that was "very consolatory." [n] Byron's opinion of contemporary poetry in England had not been enhanced by the perusal of Wordsworth's *Peter Bell*, which Murray had sent him earlier in the year. On the margins of the first page he had begun a burlesquing parody of it. [n] And a few weeks later, after reprimanding Murray for not sending Scott's *Monastery* in a packet of books, he wrote: "Instead of this, here are Johnny Keats's *p-ss a bed* poetry, and three novels by God knows whom. . . ." [n] His prejudice against Keats was not lessened by the new volume (*Lamia, Isabella, The Eve of St. Agnes, and other Poems*); indeed, it seems that he cast it aside without reading it.

He dug up a satire he had written earlier on another English poet and sent it off to Murray—his "Question and Answer" ridiculing not the poetry, but the personality of Samuel Rogers. He was a little fearful that Murray would be too free in showing it, but he wanted some of his particular friends to see it and could not resist taking the chance.

"Is it like?" he wrote, "if not, it has no merit. Does he deserve it? if not, burn it. He wrote to M[oore] (so M. says) the other day, saying on some occasion, 'what a fortunate fellow you are! surely you were born with a rose in your lips, and a Nightingale singing on the bed-top.' M. sent me this extract as an instance of the old Serpent's sentimental twaddle. I replied, that I believed that 'he (the twaddler) was born with a Nettle in his *, and a Carrion Crow croaking on the bolster,' a parody somewhat *un*-delicate; but such trash puts one stupid, besides the Cant of it in a fellow who hates every body." "

In his renewed disgust with English literary productions, Byron asked Murray again to get from Hobhouse and set up in type the *Hints from Horace*, which he had written in Athens in 1811. It was his *Baviad and Mæviad*, and his *Dunciad* against the little wits of the time. "I have a notion that, with some omissions of names and passages, it will do; and I could put my late observations *for* Pope " among the notes, with the date of 1820, and so on. . . . I wrote better then than now; but that comes from my having fallen into the atrocious bad taste of the times— partly. It has been kept too, *nine years;* nobody keeps their piece nine years now-a-days, except Douglas K.; he kept his nine years and then restored her to the public." "

Through the summer Byron had been annoyed by cajoling and threatening letters from Claire concerning Allegra. Finally he appealed to Shelley, who had maintained a constant friendly feeling toward him: "I should prefer hearing from you—as I must decline all correspondence with Claire who merely tries to be as irrational and provoking as she can be—all which shall not alter my regards to the Child—however much it contributes to confirm my opinion of the mother." [4]

Shelley replied calmly and with perfect candor: "That her disappointment should vex her, and her vexation make her write absurdly, is all in the natural order of things. But, poor thing, she is very unhappy and in bad health, and she ought to be treated with as much indulgence as possible. The weak and the foolish are in this respect like kings; they can do no wrong." [n]

In the meantime, Hoppner, who like his wife had a great penchant for gossip, had hinted at some unspeakable misdeeds of Shelley, but Byron came to his brother poet's defense. On September 10 he wrote: "I regret that you have such a bad opinion of Shiloh [a nickname they had adopted for Shelley]; you used to have a good one. Surely he has talent and honour, but is crazy

---

[4] Bodleian MS. Shelley C1. Letter of Aug. 25, 1820. A number of oblique references in Claire's diary (in the summer and autumn of 1820) to Byron's egotism and cruelty show that she was obsessed with the subject. After Byron declined to correspond with her, her bitterness against him grew pathological. She continued her "Hints for Don Juan," and her dreams were disturbed by visions of her daughter. And on November 8 she wrote four pages of suggestions for "Caricatures for Albé." Among them was one called: "Lord Byron's receipt for writing pathetic History." " 'First prepare a small colony, then dispatch the Mother, by worrying and cruelty, to her grave; afterwards to neglect and ill-treat the children—to have as many and as dirty mistresses as can be found; from their embraces to catch horrible diseases, thus a tolerable quantity of discontent and remorse being prepared, give it vent on paper, and to remember particularly to rail against learned women. This is my infallible receipt by which I have made so much money.' "

Then she listed three more to be called "Lord Byron's Morning, Noon and Night. The first he looking at the sky, a sun brightly shining—saying: 'Come I feel quite bold and cheerful—there is no God.'

"The second towards evening, a grey tint spread over the face of Nature, the sun behind a cloud—a shower of rain falling—a dinner table in the distance covered with a profusion of dishes, he says—'What a change I feel in me after dinner; where we see design we suppose a designer; I'll be, I am a Deist.'

"The third—evening—candles just lighted, all dark without the windows (a cup of green tea on the table): and trees agitated much by wind beating against the panes, also thunder and lightning. He says 'God bless me, suppose there should be a God—it is well to stand in his good graces. I'll say my prayers to-night, and write to Murray to put in a touch concerning the blowing of the last Trump.' " (Grylls: *Claire Clairmont*, pp. 125–6.)

against religion and morality. . . . If Clare thinks that she shall ever interfere with the child's morals or education, she mistakes; she never shall. The girl shall be a Christian and a married woman, if possible. As to seeing her, she may see her— under proper restrictions; but she is not to throw every thing into confusion with her Bedlam behaviour. To express it delicately, I think Madame Clare is a damned bitch. What think you?" [n]

Hoppner immediately seized the opportunity offered by Byron's disgust with Claire to relay to him, with the relish of moral superiority and in the slightly sycophantic tone which he generally adopted in writing to Byron, the noisome details of a piece of gossip which he had had from a very questionable source. Elise, the Swiss maid who had brought Allegra to Venice, had gone back to the Shelleys and shortly after had married their Italian servant Paolo Foggi. When Foggi was dismissed for misconduct, he, abetted by his wife, spread scandalous stories concerning the Shelley household and tried to blackmail Shelley.[n] Elise passed through Venice at the end of the summer and gave her moral countrywoman Mrs. Hoppner an earful of the scandal, which, without investigation or any attempt to get the other side of the story, Hoppner passed on to Byron on September 16:

"You must know then that at the time the Shelleys were here Clare was with child by Shelley. . . . they proceeded from here to Naples, where one night Shelley was called up to see Clara who was very ill. His wife, naturally thought it very strange that he should be sent for; but although she was not aware of the nature of the connexion between them, she had had sufficient proof of Shelley's indifference, and of Clara's hatred for her. . . . A Mid-wife was sent for, and the worthy pair, who had made no preparation for the reception of the unfortunate being she was bringing into the world, bribed the woman to carry it to the Pietà, where the child was taken half an hour after its birth, being obliged likewise to purchase the physician's silence with a considerable sum." [n]

Byron, preoccupied with other matters, replied briefly to this long moral tale. Although he was aware of the questionable char-

acter of the evidence, he was willing to believe tentatively from
his knowledge of the defiance of conventions in that family and
from his general cynical view of weak human nature that such a
thing could have happened. But, remembering how Claire had
once worked upon his own weaknesses and persuaded him
against his better judgment to accede to her wishes, he was far
from condemning Shelley as smugly as Hoppner had done.

"The Shiloh story is true no doubt," he wrote, "though Elise
is but a sort of *Queen's evidence*. You remember how eager she
was to return to them, and then she goes away and abuses them.
Of the facts, however, there can be little doubt; it is just like
them. You may be sure that I keep your counsel." [5] And he enclosed Shelley's letter.

During September and October, Byron's interests were divided between the local political scene and its relation to the
larger cause of Italian freedom on the one hand and the trial of
the Queen as it was reported to him by his friends in England
on the other. Having decided that he could not go to England,
as Hobhouse had been urging him to do, he was gathering evidence to confute the Italian witnesses imported by the government to testify against the Queen. His first move was to get
Count Gamba to write to his relatives the Machirellis in Pesaro,
where the Queen had resided for some time." And on the 22nd,
Hoppner, who knew of Byron's interest in the case, sent him
some confidential evidence on the unreliability of the witnesses
against the Queen."

In view of Hobhouse's attempts to persuade him that it was
his duty to come to England at this time, Byron was rather glad
to learn that only two days' absence of a Peer during the earlier
part of the trial precluded voting. Hobhouse wrote: "I never see
her [the Queen] without her sending some civil message to you.

[5] *LJ*, V, 86. Letter of Oct. 1, 1820. A new hypothesis, supported by rather
convincing though not conclusive evidence, has recently been advanced by
Ursula Orange ("Elise, Nursemaid to the Shelleys.") The theory that Elise
was the mother by Shelley of the child born in Naples December 27, 1818,
and named Elena Adelaide Shelley (see White: *Shelley*, II, 71–83) accounts
for several important details of the scandal, such as Elise's hurried marriage
to Paolo Foggi, his attempt to blackmail Shelley, and the stories she told the
Hoppners about Shelley and Claire.

It is, indeed, a pity you are not here to do an act of justice to this unfortunate woman." [n]

A little shamefaced that he had not been able to do something more active in the cause, Byron fell back on facetiousness and apologies in his letters to Hobhouse and Kinnaird. "I have not come to England," he wrote Kinnaird, "not feeling myself pious enough to decide whether the Queen fell or no." [n]

The secret societies of the Romagna had been in a ferment, expecting great things since the uprising at Naples in the summer. They were optimistically hoping for help from the Neapolitans if they rose, but the Austrians were on the Po, keeping a watchful eye on events. On August 31, Byron had written to Murray:

"We are here going to fight a little, next month, if the Huns don't cross the Po, and probably if they do: I can't say more now. . . . Depend upon it, there will be savage work, if once they begin here. The French courage proceeds from vanity, the German from phlegm, the Turkish from fanaticism and opium, the Spanish from pride, the English from coolness, the Dutch from obstinacy, the Russian from insensibility, but the *Italian* from *anger;* so you'll see that they will spare nothing." [n]

In fact, a rising had already been planned at a meeting of the Carbonari in Cesena, where the restless and impatient Vincenzo Gallina of Ravenna had stirred up the delegates to a concerted action throughout the Romagna to begin on September 3 or 4. [n] But spies and counterspies were everywhere, and some must have been among the Carbonari, for the plans were known immediately to the police and to the Cardinal, and Byron was suspected of furnishing supplies and money to the insurgents. Cardinal Rusconi had ample information to justify the arrest of dozens of the conspirators, but he feared that in the present state of unrest he could not assemble the witnesses to convict them. The Cardinal had expressed his anxiety in a letter to Cardinal Spina at Bologna, adding:

"And also suspected of complicity in this bold plot is the well known Lord Byron, who for some time has been living in this city: on this subject I have given information to his Eminence the Cardinal Secretary of State [Consalvi], but up to now the superior government has taken no measure against him." [n]

Among those suspected, the Cardinal no doubt reckoned Vincenzo Gallina and Pietro Gamba, who, at a meeting at Filetto, which was called after news came that Bologna had defected and Faenza was weakening, argued that it was too late to retreat, that the government knew their plans, and that they would be arrested whether they went ahead or not. Whether Byron was present and whether he took the side of his young friend who was so "hot for revolution" or counseled waiting, one can only guess. But at a subsequent meeting where Gallina pleaded for violent action, Count Ruggero Gamba was among the prudent whose counsel prevailed, and the plan was given up. [n]

Though Byron spoke with vigor and violence in his letters to England, it is probable that he realized that the withdrawal of Bologna left them no choice and that he was on the side of "Papa" and prudence. Some arrests were made, some of the conspirators fled, but the Gambas and Byron stood their ground and, for the time being, were not molested. One reason Byron explained to Kinnaird: "The fact is the Government is weak, for a Government, and the Constitutionals strong for such, but what will be the issue is doubtful. My *voice* was, like that of Sempronius, somewhat warlike, but the autumnal rains have damped a deal of military ardour. In the meantime both sides embody and pay bands of assassins, or *brigands* as they call them, at about ninepence a head per diem, so you may suppose that I could soon whistle a hundred or two lads to my back when I want them." [n]

After the party alfresco early in September when they watched the eclipse, it seems that Byron did not go to Filetto again until October 4. Perhaps in the current state of unrest he thought it better to remain in the Palazzo Guiccioli. On the 14th he excused himself on the ground that he had letters to write, but he promised to come the following Monday (the 18th). Allegra had come in from the country for a day, but still had some fever. And he reported that Ferdinando, Count Guiccioli's eldest son, was very ill. [n]

That night or the following day Ferdinando died, and Teresa, to whom Lega had sent a messenger with the news, wrote a letter of condolence to her husband, adding at the end a warning to him not to go to Milan," for she knew that in the present temper of the revolutionaries, Guiccioli, formerly known as a liberal, who had taken no part in the recent plottings and who was generally disliked, might be the victim of some hotheaded reprisals. When Byron heard of her letter he flared up in anger and sent a cutting rebuke to her by Pietro. For two weeks he did not go to see her or write, until she sent him a placating letter and some roses. In the Palazzo Guiccioli a vast melancholy settled upon him.

Byron could not remain angry after receiving Teresa's letter, but the melancholy did not leave him. Perhaps it was the weather and the season and his thoughts turning back upon him, but he recognized it as a "disease" which he had only temporarily driven away by the activities and excitement of the past months. And he could not refrain from a rather weary reprimand to Teresa in his reply: "You cannot need my letters so long as you are (or were) in correspondence with your husband—nor can you be in any hurry for my presence—since you have been to Ravenna without telling me to come and see you. . . . This season kills me with sadness every year. You know my last year's melancholy—and when I have that disease of the Spirit—it is better for others that I should keep away." "

In October, Byron received a print of Ada's picture and news of the death of the faithful old servant of the Abbey, Joe Murray. His thoughts returning to England and Newstead, he unburdened himself to Augusta. The playfulness mingled with bitterness had become a habit in his letters to her, but perhaps it was also an aftermath of his melancholy. Recalling that his daughter was nearly five years old and that he had been almost that long out of England, he asked: "And *you?* What have *your* 'five years' done?—made your house like a Lying-in Hospital;—there never was such a creature, except a rabbit, for increase and multiplication.[6] In short we are five years older in

[6] On February 15 of the following year Hobhouse wrote to Byron: "Mrs. Leigh is looking very well, and is very well; seven children have not spoilt her appearance at all." (Murray MSS.; Hobhouse proofs.)

fact, and I at least *ten* in appearance. The Lady B——, I suppose, retains her old starch obstinacy, with a deeper dash of Sternness from the dint of time, and the effort it has cost her to be 'magnanimous,' as they called her mischief-making."

He closed with good-natured banter: "I have got a flourishing family, (besides my daughter Allegra); here are two Cats, six dogs, a badger, a falcon, a tame Crow, and a Monkey. The fox died, and a Civet Cat ran away. With the exception of an occasional civil war about provisions, they agree to admiration, and do not make more noise than a well-behaved Nursery." ⁿ

Byron's news from London convinced him of the untrustworthiness of the Neapolitans, whom he had considered joining after the fiasco in the Romagna, perhaps indeed half persuaded by the ardor of the young Pietro. He could not have been reassured by the news that was seeping through from Naples itself. The Congress at Troppau, composed of the great European powers, agreed on a secret protocol affirming the right of collective "Europe" to suppress dangerous internal revolutions. England and France did not go along with the general principle, but remained neutral and acquiesced in the special right of Austria to protect her interests in Italy by crushing the Neapolitan revolution. In consequence, King Ferdinand was invited to attend the adjourned meeting of the Congress at Laibach the following spring.

In ignorance of what was happening behind the scenes, however, the Romagnuola patriots continued to hope much from the revolution in Naples, and Byron, though his native skepticism and good sense restrained his ardor somewhat, was inclined to view the *fait accompli* in Naples as an encouragement to the rest of Italy.

Writing to Teresa on the 11th to say that he could not come because the rains had made the roads impracticable, Byron sent her "a very bad translation in French" of his works which he had just received from Paris." He was half flattered and half chagrined by this evidence of his popularity in France. But seeing his sentiments in French was a little embarrassing. His single comment to Murray was: "The French translation of us !!! *Oime!*

Oime!" " A few days later he wrote to Moore: "Only think of being *traduced* into a foreign language in such an abominable travesty! It is useless to rail, but one can't help it." "

He had not imagined what impression his poems would make on Teresa when she read them for the first time in a language she could understand. The poems of the separation, "Fare Thee Well" and the "Sketch from Private Life," bitterly attacking Mrs. Clermont, gave her a very different idea of his feeling toward his wife and of his unforgiving hatred of those who advised her, than she had acquired from his tale told under the trees at La Mira. She was more shaken in her conception of his character than she had been when he sent her Constant's novel *Adolphe.* She wrote: "The experience of a year and a half did not tell me as much about you as reading *two of your pages.* I must however confess to you that this increase of light on the subject is to your disadvantage; I do not mean as to your genius, for that must be adored in silence, but as to *morals.* . . . you have written one thing that, in my opinion, might give the impression that in some moments of your life you showed a certain weakness of character. It is your *Farewell,* and the *Sketch from Private Life* that make me think so. In these there is more than talent, tenderness and Love; more than was proper towards a woman who had offended you; and besides it is completely in contradiction with all that you have told me about your feelings for your wife." If the sentiment expressed in his "Fare Thee Well" was sincere, she said, "I cannot understand how the proudest, the coldest, of Englishwomen could refrain from coming to throw herself into your arms and beg for mutual forgiveness." "

What struck Byron most in this was not that Teresa had discovered the lack of candor in his account of the separation, or that she had seen a side of his character that he would have preferred to conceal from her, but that she agreed with Mme de Staël, who had said much the same thing after seeing his farewell poem to Annabella.

Teresa had already seen the French translation of *Don Juan,* for Byron wrote to Murray on the same day that he penned his reply to her: "What do you think a very pretty Italian lady said to me the other day? . . . '*I would rather have the fame of *Childe Harold for* THREE YEARS *than an* IMMORTALITY *of Don Juan!*' The truth is that *it is* TOO TRUE, and the women hate every thing which strips off the tinsel of *Sentiment;* and they are right, as it would rob them of their weapons." "

If Teresa agreed so far with English opinion, perhaps it was something more than mere hypocrisy that had caused the outcry against the poem. But what made Byron pause was the fear that if he put his name to the poem, he would lose the guardian rights to his daughter Ada, "on the plea of its containing the *parody.* . . . Now I prefer my child to a poem at any time," he had told Murray a few days before."

Nevertheless, his feeling that it was the medium for his most sincere expression and would in the end find its readers soon won out once more. Amid the autumnal rains, in the stimulating uncertainty of political events, Byron was keyed to composition. In the intervals of his visits to Filetto, which were not too frequent now that the weather had turned bad, he spent many hours at his desk in the Palazzo Guiccioli. On October 14 he wrote, on the strength of Goethe's not altogether unqualified praise of him in the review of *Manfred,* a dedication of *Marino Faliero* to the German poet, "by far the first literary Character which has existed in Europe since the death of Voltaire." [7] And on the 16th the spirit moved him to begin a fifth canto of *Don Juan.* He wrote rapidly, as he usually did when the *estro* was on him, carrying Juan from the slave market into the Sultan's palace, where he was taken for a girl and led by a eunuch into the harem. Writing for his own pleasure with enormous gusto, he had completed 149 stanzas and was copying them out by December 9. As usual, he lavished his best efforts and his most lively wit on the digressions which reflected the mood of the moment. In defiance of the moral critics of his earlier cantos, and of Teresa's strictures on the poem for its ridicule of sentiment, he began:

> *When amatory poets sing their loves*
> *In liquid lines mellifluously bland,*

[7] *LJ,* V, 103. When Murray published *Marino Faliero* in April of the following year, the dedication did not appear. Byron had no doubt come to feel that it was too frivolous.

And pair their rhymes as Venus yokes her doves,
  They little think what mischief is in hand; . . .
Even Petrarch's self, if judged with due severity,
Is the Platonic pimp of all posterity.

I therefore do denounce all amorous writing,
  Except in such a way as not to attract. . . ."

And for sheer devilry he could not resist putting in two stanzas he knew would make his English friends wince. One was a pointed reference to the Queen and her courier Bergami. Referring to "the calumniated queen Semiramis," he wrote:

That injured Queen, by chroniclers so coarse,
  Has been accused (I doubt not by conspiracy)
Of an improper friendship for her horse
  (Love, like Religion, sometimes runs to heresy):
This monstrous tale had probably its source
  (For such exaggerations here and there I see)
In writing "Courser" by mistake for "Courier:"
I wish the case could come before a jury here."

This Byron himself suppressed at Hobhouse's request." The other, the penultimate stanza of the canto, he was furious at Murray for omitting in the first edition:

Thus in the East they are extremely strict,
  And wedlock and a padlock mean the same:
Excepting only when the former's picked
  It ne'er can be replaced in proper frame;
Spoilt, as a pipe of claret is when pricked:
  But then their own polygamy's to blame;
Why don't they knead two virtuous souls for life
Into that moral centaur, man and wife?"

Thrown back among his memories in the loneliness of Ravenna, Byron began a continuation of his Memoirs. By the 5th of November he had completed "twelve more sheets." " And on December 9 he was ready to send Moore three packets, "containing, in all, 18 more sheets of Memoranda, which, I fear, will cost you more in postage than they will ever produce by being printed in the next century. Instead of waiting so long, if you could make any thing of them *now* in the way of *reversion*, (that is, after *my* death,) I should be very glad,—as, with all due regard to your progeny, I prefer you to your grandchildren. Would not Longman or Murray advance you a certain sum *now*, pledging themselves *not* to have them published till after *my* decease, think you?—and what say you?" [8]

Moore was still living in Paris to keep out of the way of his creditors, and Byron was eager to help him. He was also not unwilling that Murray should have the Memoirs to pass around among his friends in England. Moore in the meantime was making excellent social capital of the Memoirs. He apparently showed them to almost everyone he met in Paris. [9]

The last numbers of the *Quarterly Review* and the *Edinburgh*

[8] *LJ*, V, 131. There is a hint as to what this continuation of the Memoirs contained in a diary entry of Moore, Jan. 5, 1821: "I see that Byron in his continuation says, that I advised him to go into the details of his loves more fully; but, if I recollect right, it was only his adventures in the East I alluded to, as in recounting these there could be but little harm done to any one. He showed me once, I recollect, a letter of Lord Sligo's, relating the adventure by which the Giaour was suggested, and with which he seemed to intimate that he himself was connected." (Moore: *Memoirs*, I, 353.) Moore took up the matter of the "reversion" with Murray, who had in the meantime been prodded by Byron, and on July 27, 1821, recorded: "Received also a letter from Murray, consenting to give me two thousand guineas for Lord Byron's 'Memoirs,' on condition that, in case of survivorship, I should consent to be the editor." (Moore: *Memoirs*, I, 380.)

[9] On his return home on May 25, Moore "found that Lord Kinnaird had been to bring back Lord B.'s 'Memoirs,' and Bessy had asked him to dinner." (Moore: *Memoirs*, I, 326.) On the 27th, "Williams came to write out the Memoirs, and dined with us." (Moore: *Memoirs*, I, 327.) Douglas Kinnaird wrote Byron (Feb. 20, 1821) after a visit to Paris: "I read with the greatest interest & pleasure your memoir at Paris—It is excellent—your [*sic*] curse & swear occasionally in the second part." (Murray MSS. Unpublished letter.)

It cannot be said with certainty how many people read the Memoirs. It is possible to establish the names of about two dozen persons to whom Moore showed them, in Paris and after he returned to London. There was a large English colony in Paris while he was there, and many English people were passing through. On July 2 he collected the manuscript from Lady Mildmay (Moore: *Memoirs*, I, 375), and on the 5th gave it to Lady Holland. (Moore: *Memoirs*, I, 377.) While he was in Paris, Moore employed a man by the name of Williams, another named Dumoulin, and possibly a third, to copy the Memoirs. (Moore: *Memoirs*, I, 325, 333, 362.) It is known that one copy was burned with the original in 1824. Whether the other copies were completed and what became of them no one knows.

Review, which Murray had sent Byron, contained articles that stirred up his ire. The article in the *Quarterly* on Pope, based on the recently published *Observations, Anecdotes and Characters of Books and Men* by Joseph Spence, quoted a passage from William Lisle Bowles's *Invariable Principles of Poetry* (1819) in which Bowles described his correction of a line in *English Bards and Scotch Reviewers.*[n] "Mr. Bowles shall be answered," Byron told Murray. But what concerned him more was the attack of Bowles on Pope. "They support Pope, I see, in the *Quarterly,*" he wrote. "Let them continue to do so: it is a Sin, and a Shame, and a *damnation* to think that *Pope!!* should require it—but he does. Those miserable mountebanks of the day, the poets, disgrace themselves and deny God, in running down Pope, the most *faultless* of Poets, and almost of men."[n]

The article in the *Edinburgh* incensed him even more. That it should praise the milk-and-water poetry of Keats, who had had the insolence to attack Pope, was too much for him. He wrote Murray:

"The *Edinburgh* praises Jack Keats or Ketch,[1] or whatever his names are: why, his is the Onanism of Poetry. . . ."[n] And he recurred to the subject in his next letter: "Mr. Keats, whose poetry you enquire after, appears to me what I have already said: such writing is sort of mental masturbation—he is always f—gg—g his *Imagination.* I don't mean he is *indecent,* but viciously soliciting his own ideas into a state, which is neither poetry nor any thing else but a Bedlam vision produced by raw pork and opium."[n]

Murray, prompted by some of his literary advisers, and also by Hobhouse, who always had a weather eye out to Byron's reputation in England, had suggested that he might want to make some revisions in the new cantos of *Don Juan,* and particularly in the *Hints from Horace,* before publication.[n] But Byron, who never had any relish for cold-blooded revisions, was in no mood for such journeywork now, and, strangely enough for one who so admired the polish of Pope, he made a virtue of the romantic dogma that literary work was best when it came hot from the creative fire. He replied: "I am like the tyger

[1] Jack Ketch was a notorious executioner of the days of Charles II.

(in poesy), if I miss my first Spring, I go growling back to my Jungle. There is no second. I can't correct; I can't, and I won't." [2]

Despite the surface calm that had settled over the Romagna since the abortive *coup* of September, there was a seething unrest among the people, Byron's popularity with whom was greatly resented by the government and the more rabid of the clerical party. He was aware that by indirect means they were scheming to get him out of Ravenna.

On October 17 he informed Hobhouse: "They sent an order from Rome to disarm my Servants. The best of it is that they were *not armed!*" [n] When the order came, the local police were too timid to enforce it, and replied to Cardinal Consalvi: "The operation is difficult, because they do not generally carry arms except when their master is with them." After some weeks of correspondence with Rome, the Ravenna police agreed "confidentially to warn Lord Byron that it did not look well for his servants to accompany him fully armed." [n]

In the continued state of tension, Byron took a kind of boyish pleasure in playing up the danger he faced to his friends in England. On November 5 he wrote to Moore: "If 'honour should come unlooked for' to any of your acquaintance, make a Melody of it. . . . In case you should not think him worth it, here is a Chant for you instead—

> *When a man hath no freedom to fight for at home,*
> *Let him combat for that of his neighbours;*
> *Let him think of glories of Greece and of Rome,*
> *And get knock'd on the head for his labours." [n]*

Knowing himself useful to the Carbonari, and feeling himself in this heroic position on the eve of great events which he might have a part in shaping, Byron was not a little piqued with a letter from Hobhouse taunting him with laziness and with being

---

[2] *LJ*, V, 120. Letter of Nov. 18, 1820. The evidence of Byron's manuscripts, however, indicates that he did a good deal of verbal revision, most of it before he had copied the final draft, and, though he sometimes added lines or stanzas after his poems had gone to the printer, he had little interest in making author's corrections in the proof, or in revising anything that had once been printed. Most of his revisions in the several editions of *English Bards* were additions or subtractions of lines, not verbal improvements.

so immersed in his sensual pleasure that he would not come home
to do his duty by the Queen.

Though he complained to Murray, in replying to Hobhouse
himself, Byron, after defending his capabilities of abstention and
activity, in the end paid a handsome compliment to his old
friend. "Yours is now a more active life, I admit. . . . We will
divide the parts between us of '*player* and poet,' as you have
taken up the former one with great success . . . . you *happen
to have great talent,* more, *I* think, than you yourself or others
have yet given you credit for; and you are besides sure to train
on, because you have strong powers of application. . . ." " In
this tribute to Hobhouse, Byron was really offering, not without
a passing regret, his own excuses for not having made a name
for himself in Parliament as he had once dreamed of doing.

Since Byron constantly postponed his visits to Filetto, Teresa
grew restive in the country, and apparently by the middle of
November had persuaded her father to take her back to his town
house in Ravenna. In the meantime she refused to accept the
counsels of prudence of her father and of Byron himself. In reply
to one of her outbursts of impatience, Byron wrote on November
22: "My Love, + But what then can be done? . . . If I
did not love you—if I *wished to get rid of you without blame*—
and also with the best excuse for myself—the most certain way
would be to *visit you*—and to commit such imprudences in the
face of the world and of the priests—who make up the *world*
here." "

Byron was indeed well aware of the dangers to Teresa in the
situation, for it seems from the evidence of later correspondence
that Count Alborghetti's service to him had extended to sending
or showing him copies of letters from the Cardinal's own mail
pouch on subjects which touched him closely. In revealing plans
of the government and of the movement of Austrian troops,
Alborghetti was—for money, favors, or friendship (perhaps a
combination of all three)—running close to treason to the government he served. The information Byron relayed to Kinnaird
on November 22, the day of his last letter to Teresa directed to
Filetto, could have come only from someone who had access
to the Cardinal's mail. He wrote: "If the Scoundrels of Troppau

decide on a Massacre (as is probable) the Barbarians will march in by one frontier, and the Neapolitans by the other. They have *both asked* permission of his Holiness so to do, which is equivalent to asking a man's permission to give him a kick on the a—e; if he grants it, it is a sign he can't return it."

He had inside information, too, on what more closely concerned himself and Teresa. "I come in for my share of the *vigorous* system of the day. . . . They try to fix squabbles upon my servants, to involve me in scrapes (no difficult matter), and lastly they (the governing party) menace to shut Madame Guiccioli up in a *Convent*." One of the stipulations of the separation decree was that Teresa should live respectably under her father's roof. Byron, however, was as unwilling to bow to Italian social customs in this as Teresa herself. Later in his letter to Kinnaird, his indignation rose to the fever pitch:

"If they should succeed in putting this poor Girl into a convent for doing that with me which all the other Countesses of Italy have done with everybody for these 1000 years, of course I would accede to a retreat on my part, rather than a prison on hers, for the former only is what they *really* want." [n]

As the threat to Teresa's freedom blew over, or the menace was abandoned for the time being, it may be assumed that Alborghetti was this time successful in some rather delicate diplomatic maneuvers with the Cardinal. The next day (November 23) Byron wrote to Alborghetti to thank him for the news (garnered, no doubt, from the Cardinal's express dispatches just received) that Queen Caroline had been acquitted. [n]

When, a few days later, he received news that the Queen had gone in state to St. Paul's to offer thanks for her acquittal, and along with it a moralizing letter from Augusta commenting on this shocking procedure and Hobhouse's connection with it, the prospect of such double hypocrisy caused Byron to reply to his sister with a brutal frankness: "Hobhouse cares about as much for the Queen as he does for St. Paul's. One ought to be glad however of anything which makes either of them go to Church. I am also delighted to see *you* grown so *moral*. It is edifying." [n]

At eight o'clock on the evening of December 9, as Byron

was preparing to go out to visit the Countess Guiccioli (who had now moved back to Ravenna with her father), he heard a shot. Running down with the bravest of his servants, Tita, he found the commandant of the troops, Luigi Dal Pinto,[n] expiring on the ground with five wounds. Later that night he opened his letter to Moore to add an account of this exciting event:

"As nobody could, or would, do any thing but howl and pray, and as no one would stir a finger to move him, for fear of consequences, I lost my patience—made my servant and a couple of the mob take up the body—sent off two soldiers to the guard—despatched Diego to the Cardinal with the news, and had the commandant carried upstairs into my own quarter. But it was too late, he was gone—not at all disfigured—bled inwardly—not above an ounce or two came out.

"I had him partly stripped—made the surgeon examine him, and examined him myself. He had been shot by cut balls or slugs. I felt one of the slugs, which had gone through him, all but the skin. Everybody conjectures why he was killed, but no one knows how. The gun was close by him—an old gun, half filed down.

"He only said, O Dio! and Gesu! two or three times, and appeared to have suffered very little. Poor fellow! he was a brave officer, but had made himself much disliked by the people. I knew him personally, and had met with him often at conversazioni and elsewhere."

And so the corpse remained on Fletcher's bed through the night, while the town was in great confusion. Byron added in a postscript: "The lieutenant on duty by the body is smoking his pipe with great composure.—A queer people this."[n]

Byron, for that matter, was a queer revolutionary. Individual humanity was always stepping in to blur the vision which partisan zealots must see before them. If he could use his influence with both sides to avoid unnecessary violence and savagery, he would do so. In fact, his humanity to the commandant almost jeopardized his standing with the leaders of the Carbonari, and might indeed have done so had it not been for the equal humanity and understanding of the Gambas.

Byron might also have been suspected of consorting with the

enemy in his odd friendship with Count Alborghetti, who, as Secretary General of the Lower Romagna, must have been allied in the popular mind with the oppressive government, whatever his liberal professions. In the exchange of information with the Count, however, Byron never let out anything that could not safely be passed along to the Cardinal, and he never compromised his friends of the Carbonari.

Byron had written several times during the year to Lady Byron, usually with the excuse of appealing to her to urge the trustees of the marriage settlement to sell out of the Funds before it was too late. And latterly, since the uncertainties and dangers of his situation had been impressed upon him by the events of the past few months, he had repeated the request made in his farewell letter of Easter Sunday, 1816, that she be kind to Augusta. Annabella was moved to write him once more, and her carefully worded note was her last letter to her husband: "The past shall not prevent me from befriending Augusta Leigh & her Children in any future circumstances which may call for my assistance—I promise to do so.—She knows nothing of this—" [n]

Byron received this note just before the end of the year, and replied in haste on December 28: "I acknowledge your note which is on the whole satisfactory—the style a little harsh—but that was to be expected. . . . As to Augusta—she knows as little of my request, as of your answer—Whatever She is or may have been—*you* have never had reason to complain of her—on the contrary—you are not aware of the obligations under which you have been to her.—Her life & mine—and yours & mine—were two things perfectly distinct from each other—when one ceased the other began—and now both are closed. . . . She and two others were the only things I ever really loved—I may say it now,—for we are young no longer.——" [n]

As the year ended, Byron had settled down to a pleasant routine interrupted only by the excitement of political events, which for him was stimulating rather than distracting. He paid frequent visits to Teresa in the Gambas' town house. There seem to have been no further threats to put her in a convent. Perhaps Byron's humanity to the commandant had made the authorities less eager to persecute him through her. She seems also to have convinced her grandparents as well as her father that her relation with Byron was merely Platonic. In fact, as a friend of the family he called almost every evening, and, though Teresa had her own apartment in her father's house, as befitted a "respectable married lady" living apart from her husband, he seems to have spent as much time in conversation with Pietro and her father as with her, and to have enjoyed it as much. Political matters were, as they believed, coming to a crisis again. If life in Italy became impossible, there was always the dream of an escape. He had not yet given up the idea of a return to England. Having no relish for going back during the Queen's trial to find the cause he must espouse defended by Brougham and Lushington, he had several times intimated that he might return in the spring. But it was only a wishful dream. Basically, he knew that he could not go back: he himself had changed too much. Writing to Hodgson on December 22, he found it difficult to establish a common ground for communication, and he fell back on a rather perfunctory recital of his daily routine, and inquiries after old friends."

It would have been necessary, above all, to have some purpose for returning. He thought he had found it in a plan for a periodical which he and Moore might edit and largely write. His imagination kindled by the prospect, he wrote Moore on Christmas day: "I have been thinking of a project for you and me, in case we both get to London again [Moore was still in Paris] . . . to set up jointly a *newspaper*—nothing more nor less—weekly, or so, with some improvement or modifications upon the plan of the present scoundrels, who degrade that department,—but a *newspaper*, which we will edite in due form, and, nevertheless, with some attention. . . .

"Why, man, if we were to take to this in good earnest, your debts would be paid off in a twelvemonth, and, by dint of a little diligence and practice, I doubt not that we could distance the common-place blackguards who have so long disgraced common sense and the common reader. . . . We will modify it into as literary and classical a concern as you please, only let us put out our powers upon it, and it will most likely succeed. But you must *live* in London, and I also, to bring it to bear, and *we must keep it a secret* . . . and, in any case, we should have some fun, composing, correcting, supposing, inspecting, and supping together over our lucubrations." As an afterthought he considered a "middle plan between a *Spectator* and a newspaper." How remote he was from English thinking on the subject, however, is indicated by one of the names he suggested for the paper: ". . . we will call it *Gli* or *I Carbonari*, if it so please you—or any other name full of 'pastime and prodigality,' which you may prefer." [n]

On December 28, Byron finally sent Kinnaird the fifth canto of *Don Juan*, consisting of 155 octave stanzas with notes.[n] *Don Juan* was, after all, as his best critical sense told him, the one thing that he could most effectively "put out his powers upon."

CHAPTER XXIII

1821

Ravenna—Exile of the Gambas

THE NEW year began with bad weather again, and revolutionary excitement had risen to the fever pitch once more with the Austrians poised for the invasion of Naples. In the midst of alarms and rumors, which served to drive away boredom and to stimulate his imaginative faculties, Byron found the usual outlet for his energies in writing. Reiterating to Moore on January 2 his earnestness in the scheme for a newspaper, he wrote: "I feel exactly as you do about our 'art,'[1] but it comes over me in a kind of rage every now and then, like ❋ ❋ ❋ ❋," and then, if I don't write to empty my mind, I go mad. As to that regular, uninterrupted love of writing, which you describe in your friend, I do not understand it. I feel it as a torture, which I must get rid of, but never as a pleasure. On the contrary, I think composition a great pain."[n]

Thinking perhaps that the coming events would be sufficiently interesting to be worth recording, and not having an incentive or a subject at the moment for poetry, he began a journal, the first he had kept since his tour of the Bernese Alps in 1816. The first day's entry (January 4) set the pattern for the kaleidoscopic chronicle of thoughts and events set down in a prose that was sometimes staccato and sometimes consciously dramatic.

"This morning I gat me up late, as usual—weather bad—bad

---

[1] Moore had written that, unlike Lord John Russell, who found a pleasure in writing, he always felt about his art "as the French husband did when he found a man making love to his (the Frenchman's) wife: 'Comment, Monsieur,—sans y être *obligé!*'" (*LJ*, V, 215 n.)

as England—worse. The snow of last week melting to the
sirocco of to-day, so that there were two damned things at once.
Could not even get to ride on horseback in the forest. Stayed
at home all the morning—looked at the fire—wondered when the
post would come. Post came at the Ave Maria, instead of half-
past one o'clock, as it ought. . . . I was out of spirits—read the
papers. . . . Wrote five letters in about half an hour, short and
savage, to all my rascally correspondents. . . . Carriage at 8 or
so—went to visit La Contessa G.—found her playing on the
piano-forte—talked till ten, when the Count, her father, and the
no less Count, her brother, came in from the theatre. . . . Came
home at eleven, or rather before. . . . Read a Life of Leonardo
da Vinci . . . ruminated—wrote this much, and will go to
bed." [n]

One of his "savage" letters was to Murray, saying that he had
written him at least ten letters without having a reply. And
partly in defense of *Marino Faliero* he gave the publisher the
benefit of his cogitations on the drama. If the modern writer
wishes to write a great tragedy he must write "naturally and
regularly, and producing *regular* tragedies, like the *Greeks;* but
not in *imitation,*—merely the outline of their conduct, adapted
to our own times and circumstances. . . ." [n]

A few days later he had found a theme ideally suited to his
purpose for "regular" drama. Again he chose a historical subject with close parallels in the world he knew, and a protagonist
who bore a more striking resemblance to himself than did the
Doge of Venice. Sardanapalus, the Assyrian king, effeminate,
slothful, immersed in luxury and debauchery, spurred to take
up arms against those plotting his overthrow, was sufficiently
vague in the records of Diodorus and Ctesias so that Byron
could mold his character and motives as he wished. [n]

Practically the only social life Byron indulged in now was
his evening visit to Teresa and her family. Because of Teresa's
precarious position, they did not venture to the theater or to
balls or the Carnival festivities as they had the previous winter
when he was her accepted *cavalier servente.* When the weather
permitted, Byron took his daily ride about four o'clock, sometimes alone, but often with Pietro Gamba.

Despite the fact that he liked a routine, the sameness of his life and the suppression of the revolutionary activity he had expected led to the boredom reflected in his journal of January 6:

"What is the reason that I have been, all my lifetime, more or less *ennuyé?* and that, if any thing, I am rather less so now than I was at twenty, as far as my recollection serves? I do not know how to answer this, but presume that it is constitutional, —as well as the waking in low spirits, which I have invariably done for many years. Temperance and exercise, which I have practised at times, and for a long time together vigorously and violently, made little or no difference. Violent passions did;— when under their immediate influence—it is odd, but—I was in agitated, but *not* in depressed, spirits.

"A dose of salts has the effect of a temporary inebriation, like light champagne, upon me. But wine and spirits make me sullen and savage to ferocity—silent, however, and retiring, and not quarrelsome, if not spoken to. Swimming also raises my spirits, —but in general they are low, and get daily lower. . . . But I feel a something, which makes me think that, if I ever reach near to old age, like Swift, 'I shall die at top' first." [n]

But the next day brought some excitement that temporarily dispelled his ennui. The evening of the 7th he attended a *conversazione* where he saw some of Teresa's friends. Pietro took him aside to say that the patriots of Forlì had sent word that the government was about to strike and that the Cardinal had ordered a number of arrests. Byron's advice was "Fight for it, rather than be taken in detail." And he offered his house as a refuge for the Liberals in case of need. Exhilarated, he wrote in his journal before retiring:

"It wants half an hour of midnight, and rains. . . . If the row don't happen *now*, it must soon. . . . Expect to hear the drum and the musquetry momently (for they swear to resist, and are right,)—but I hear nothing, as yet, save the plash of the rain and the gusts of the wind at intervals." [n]

When news came some time later that Naples would resist the Austrians, Byron composed an address to the Neapolitan insurgents, offering to contribute to their cause a thousand louis and his own services as a volunteer "without any other motive

than that of sharing the destiny of a brave nation. . . ." " But this
"noble letter," as Teresa called it, never reached its destination,
for Byron entrusted it to a Neapolitan named Giuseppe Gigante,
who said he was a representative of General Pepe. When Gigante
was arrested at Pesaro, he swallowed some of the documents he
carried, perhaps including Byron's letter to the insurgents." On
the 10th, Alborghetti, whom Byron already suspected of being
a "trimmer" and of trying to please both sides, sent word that
the Pope, the King of Turin, and the Duke of Tuscany had all
been invited to the Congress at Laibach, but that the Pope and
his Secretary of State, Consalvi, would be represented only by
proxy."

The humid weather continued and the roads were impassable,
and Byron was thrown back again on reading and his literary
pursuits. On the 13th he sketched the outline and the dramatis
personæ for his intended tragedy of *Sardanapalus*. When he discussed his projected plot with Teresa that evening, he maintained that love should not be the central theme of tragedy.
And he took her plea for "a noble passion" lightly. But he recorded in his diary on returning home: "I must put more love
into *Sardanapalus* than I intended." " Teresa recalled with pride:
"The sublime love of Myrrha was conceived that evening." " The
next day he wrote the opening lines, a transparent revelation of
his own conflict.

> *He must be roused. In his effeminate heart*
> *There is a careless courage which Corruption*
> *Has not all quenched, and latent energies,*
> *Repressed by circumstance, but not destroyed—*
> *Steeped, but not drowned, in deep voluptuousness.*"

Exhilarated by the possibility of exciting action soon, and
settled in the habitual daily round that contributed most to his
creative vigor, he wrote rapidly several scenes of the tragedy.
But his nerves were so overstimulated that on the evening of the
18th when Lega came in with a letter about an unpaid bill at
Venice, he "flew into a paroxysm of rage" that almost made him
faint."

His temper was made increasingly short by the persistent reports that, despite his protests, *Marino Faliero* was to be put

on the stage in London. Much as Byron had once longed for fame in the theater, he had seen too much of the "insolence" of audiences at Drury Lane to trust his self-esteem to their mercies. And he would not hear of inferior actors attempting it. To Murray he wrote: ". . . the play is *not for acting:* Kemble or Kean could *read* it, but where are they? Do not let me be sacrificed in such a manner. . . ." [n]

But seeing persistent rumors in the foreign papers of the imminent performance of the drama, he wrote frantically again on the 20th, enclosing a letter to the Lord Chamberlain asking for an injunction against the performance. He also requested Murray to ask Lord Holland and other friends to intercede to stop it. He added: "God help me! at this distance, I am treated like a corpse or a fool by the few people whom I thought that I could rely upon; and I *was* a fool to think any better of them than of the rest of mankind." [n]

The action that might have drawn him out of his melancholy seemed as far removed as ever, or as little likely to come to anything but defeat and retreat or banishment. On the 23rd, after returning from the Gambas', he recorded: "The Carbonari seem to have no plan—nothing fixed among themselves, how, when, or what to do. In that case, they will make nothing of this project, so often postponed, and never put in action." [n] The best he could do in the circumstances was to make preparations for a removal in case of necessity, for he was determined to accompany Teresa and her father if they were obliged to retire.

In the meantime the Carnival was in full swing. ". . . the Germans are on the Po," Byron wrote, "the Barbarians at the gate . . . and lo! they dance and sing and make merry. . . ." [n] What seemed a greater frivolity to Byron was that the Gambas, father and son, and other leaders of the Carbonari had gone on a shooting expedition.

In his disconsolate mood, from time to time he thought of escape. On the 25th he received a letter from Lord Sidney Osborne, stepson of Augusta's mother,[2] then state secretary of

---

[2] Sidney Osborne (1789–1861) was the son by the second wife of the fifth Duke of Leeds, from whom Augusta's mother ran away when she eloped with Byron's father.

the Ionian Islands, inviting him to go to Corfu. He wrote in his diary: "Why not?—perhaps I may, next spring." " And, writing to Hoppner a few days later, he asked: "Could not you and I contrive to meet somewhere this spring? I should be *solus.*" " But he knew that if it came to the test and Teresa wished him to stay, he could not leave.

Queer speculations ran through his mind and were confided to his diary: "Scrawled this additional page of life's log-book," he wrote on the 25th. "One day more is over of it and of me:— but 'which is best, life or death, the gods only know,' as Socrates said to his judges, on the breaking up of the tribunal. . . . It has been said that the immortality of the soul is a *grand peut-être*—but still it is a *grand* one. Every body clings to it—the stupidest, and dullest, and wickedest of human bipeds is still persuaded that he is immortal." "

Thinking back over the events of the year 1820, Byron concluded that it had been an unfortunate one for him. He had lost the Rochdale lawsuit (what the long issue of the appeal would be he did not know, but since it had dragged on for fifteen years he could not be hopeful). The Irish mortgage had been finally rejected by the trustees of the settlement. Brooding on it, he wrote to Lady Byron: "Yours has been a bitter connection to me in every sense, it would have been better for me never to have been born than to have ever seen you. This sounds harsh, but is it not true? and recollect that I do not mean that you were my *intentional* evil Genius but an Instrument for my destruction —and you yourself have suffered too (poor thing) in the agency, as the lightning perishes in the instant with the Oak which it strikes." "

And among the misfortunes of the year he counted the fact that the Countess Guiccioli, "in despite of all I said and did to prevent it, *would* separate from her husband." "

He could not get on with the drama he had started, but he was already planning more ambitious literary projects: ". . . Cain, a metaphysical subject, something in the style of Manfred, but in five *acts*, perhaps, with the chorus; Francesca of Rimini, in five acts"; and a tragedy based on the life of Tiberius."

He jotted down some random thoughts growing out of his

present contemplations: "Why, at the very height of desire and human pleasure,—worldly, social, amorous, ambitious, or even avaricious,—does there mingle a certain sense of doubt and sorrow. . . . I allow sixteen minutes, though I never counted them, to any given or supposed possession." [n]

To pass the time, Byron read again the pamphlets and periodicals Murray had sent him on the dispute about Pope in which Bowles and Campbell had become involved. The defense of Pope was something that had been much in his mind since he had written his "Observations" on the article in *Blackwood's.* In returning the proof of a part of the *Hints from Horace,* which Murray had set up at his request, he asked that the part of the "Observations" referring to Pope be included as a note under the first mention of that poet's name. [n] Byron had been eager to join the fray, but the imminence of a real battle had restrained him from indulging in the literary one. Now as the time dragged on and he stuck close to the house waiting for word from the leaders, he turned the subject of Bowles's reply to Campbell over in his mind and found it the kind of controversy he could dig into when he could not concentrate sufficiently for poetic composition. On the 7th he began his *Letter to ✻ ✻ ✻ ✻ ✻ ✻ ✻ ✻ ✻ ✻ [John Murray], on the Rev. W. L. Bowles' Strictures on the Life and Writings of Pope.*

This was Byron's chance to assail English hypocrisy, and he seized it with zest: "The truth is, that in these days the grand *'primum mobile'* of England is *cant;* cant political, cant poetical, cant religious, cant moral; but always *cant,* multiplied through all the varieties of life. It is the fashion, and while it lasts will be too powerful for those who can only exist by taking the tone of the time. I say *cant,* because it is a thing of words, without the smallest influence upon human actions; the English being no wiser, no better, and much poorer and more divided amongst themselves, as well as far less moral, than they were before the prevalence of this verbal decorum." [n]

Byron then turned his attack upon Bowles's *Invariable Principles.* Bowles had stated categorically: *"Works of Nature,* speaking of those *more* beautiful and sublime, are *more* sublime and beautiful than works of Art; therefore more poetical." [n] "Art is *not* inferior to nature for poetical purposes," Byron declared. "Away, then, with this cant about nature, and 'invariable principles of poetry!' A great artist will make a block of stone as sublime as a mountain, and a good poet can imbue a pack of cards with more poetry than inhabits the forests of America." "

Byron would not presume to place his idol as high in the poetical scale as Shakespeare and Milton. But he considered Pope ". . . the moral poet of all civilization; and as such, let us hope that he will one day be the national poet of mankind. He is the only poet that never shocks; the only poet whose *faultlessness* has been made his reproach." "

Byron completed the letter (which ran to fifty-five pages in the first edition) four days after he had begun it.[3] In the meantime, on February 9 news came that the Austrians had crossed the Po before the expected date and had thus frustrated the plan of the Carbonari for a concerted uprising, leaving them with no plan but to harass the march of the troops toward Naples. Byron saw no reason for despair, for he still expected strong opposition from the Neapolitans to which the Carbonari in the north would lend their strength in the rear of the advancing armies."

On the eve of what he believed would soon develop into bloody insurrection in which he would inevitably be deeply involved, he had begun to consider making some provision for Allegra. He concluded a letter to Hoppner on the 10th: "Allegra is well—but not well disposed—her disposition is perverse to a degree—I am going to place her in a Convent for education." "

In this period of waiting, an event occurred which brought home to Byron how thoughtlessly unreliable his friends were and in what peril he might be plunged in case of real trouble. On February 16 he wrote in his diary: ". . . the rising is prevented by the Barbarians marching a week sooner than appointed; and an *order* is issued, and in force, by the Government, 'that all persons having arms concealed, etc., etc., shall be liable to, etc., etc.'—and what do my friends, the patriots, do two

---

[3] *LJ*, V, 201. Byron sent the letter to Murray on February 13, 1821, and it was published in a pamphlet volume soon after Murray received it, in March; a second edition appeared, with a postscript, before the year was out.

days afterwards? Why, they throw back upon my hands, and into my house, these very arms (without a word of warning previously) with which I had furnished them at their own request, and at my own peril and expense." It is not surprising that after returning from his usual evening visit Byron "Beat the crow for stealing the falcon's victuals." [n]

Despite his feeling that he could make a solid reputation in literature only in dramas following the pure classical models, and despite his recent interest in Pope that had caused him to exhume and polish his *Hints from Horace,* Byron was still drawn by a sure instinct back to *Don Juan.* He wrote Murray:

"The 5th. is so far from being the last of *D.J.,* that it is hardly the beginning. I meant to take him the tour of Europe, with a proper mixture of siege, battle, and adventure, and to make him finish as *Anacharsis Cloots* [4] in the French revolution. To how many cantos this may extend, I know not, nor whether (even if I live) I shall complete it; but this was my notion: I meant to have made him a *Cavalier Servente* in Italy, and a cause for a divorce in England, and a. Sentimental 'Werther-faced man' in Germany, so as to show the different ridicules of the society in each of those countries, and to have displayed him gradually *gâté* and *blasé* as he grew older, as is natural. But I had not quite fixed whether to make him end in Hell, or in an unhappy marriage, not knowing which would be the severest. The Spanish tradition says Hell: but it is probably only an Allegory of the other state. You are now in possession of my notions on the subject." [n]

Still full of hope and the "*poetry* of politics," Byron recorded in his diary on the 19th: "Came home *solus*—very high wind— lightning—moonshine—solitary stragglers muffled in cloaks— women in masks—white houses—clouds hurrying over the sky, like spilt milk blown out of the pail—altogether very poetical. It is still blowing hard—the tiles flying, and the house rocking—

---

[4] Jean Baptiste Cloots, better known as Anacharsis, was a Prussian baron born at Clèves who took an active part in the French Revolution. He described himself as *l'orateur du genre humain.* Falling under the suspicion of Robespierre, he was executed in March 1794. (See Elizabeth F. Boyd: *Byron's Don Juan,* pp. 39–41.)

rain splashing—lightning flashing—quite a fine Swiss Alpine evening, and the sea roaring in the distance." [n]

Up to this point Byron had continued to be optimistic, but in a few days the news came of the defection of the Neapolitans and the collapse of the revolution in that province. On the 24th he recorded wearily in his diary: "The *plan* has missed—the Chiefs are betrayed, military, as well as civil—and the Neapolitans not only have *not* moved, but have declared to the P. government, and to the Barbarians, that they know nothing of the matter!!!

"Thus the world goes; and thus the Italians are always lost for lack of union among themselves." [n]

The next day he had little heart to record anything beyond the fact that he had a headache. It is significant that in his disillusionment Byron did not blame his friends among the leaders of the Carbonari. Part of his capacity for friendship rested upon his wide tolerance of human frailties and his ability to look with a half-cynical, half-humorous eye upon the slightly less than noble characters of those to whom he was attached. Speaking of the Italians in a letter to Moore a few weeks later, he said: "As a very pretty woman said to me a few nights ago, with the tears in her eyes, as she sat at the harpsichord, 'Alas! the Italians must now return to making operas.' I fear *that* and maccaroni are their forte, and 'motley their only wear.' However, there are some high spirits among them still." [n]

Still uncertain about the future and anticipating political turbulence, Byron put his daughter Allegra in the convent of Bagnacavallo on March 1. The Capuchin nuns of the convent—or monastery, to use the common Italian term—of S. Giovanni Battista in Bagnacavallo, some dozen miles from Ravenna on the road to Bologna, had recently established a school for girls from seven to eighteen which was then drawing children from the best families of the region. [n] Byron learned of it either through the Gambas or from his Ravenna banker, Pellegrino Ghigi, who the year before had taken his own daughter there. It was, in fact, Ghigi who brought Allegra to the convent, which Byron, lazily relying on the recommendations of others, never took the trouble to inspect at first hand. [n] Lega had paid the seventy scudi re-

quired for the first half-year's tuition on March 1." Apparently
Allegra arrived the same day, for on the 2nd the brother of one
of the nuns wrote reassuringly to Byron: "Last night she slept
quietly, and this morning I have found her more cheerful and
lively than ever. She has already chosen her favourite playmate,
among the many who are here, and with her she is enjoying
herself—always, however, under the eyes of the Mother Superior
and of my Sister." "

Byron's putting his daughter in a convent did much to reconcile
Teresa's conservative grandparents, who had been shocked by
her liaison with this infidel, and thereafter she found little difficulty in convincing them that her relation with Byron "confined
itself to the outward tokens of the purest friendship." " The old
Count and Countess visited Allegra in the convent, and no doubt
gave a good account of her.

Byron had apparently reported the removal of Allegra to the
convent to the Shelleys, who passed his letter on to Claire, then in
Florence. In the succeeding days she wrote to Byron several
times, and on the 24th sent him a long letter of protest." She
continued her attempt to shame him into withdrawing Allegra
and placing her in an English boarding-school chosen by his
own friends, and she appealed to the advice of Mrs. Hoppner,
who she knew was equally opposed to a Catholic education for
Byron's daughter. But in sending her letter on to Hoppner,
Byron wrote across the top: "The moral part of the letter
upon the Italians, etc., comes with an excellent grace from the
writer now living with a *man* and his *wife*—and having planted
a child in the R. Foundling, etc. With regard to the rest of the
letter, you know as well as any one how far it is or is not
correct." "

This was, of course, a reference to Hoppner's own story picked
up from Elise the previous summer. In his letter to Hoppner
(April 3) Byron wrote: "You know (perhaps more than I do)
that to allow the child to be with her mother and with them
and their principles would be like absolute insanity if not worse;
that even her health would not be attended to properly and to
say nothing of the indecorum. . . . You recollect also the pretty
story you told me of what occurred at Naples, which I see no

reason to doubt in the main points, though Elise might not relate all accurately. . . .

"It is also fit that I should add that I by no means intended, nor intend, to give a *natural* child an *English* education, because with the disadvantages of her birth, her after settlement would be doubly difficult. Abroad, with a fair foreign education and a portion of five or six thousand pounds, she might and may marry very respectably. In England such a dowry would be a pittance, while elsewhere it is a fortune. It is, besides, my wish that she should be a Roman Catholic, which I look upon as the best religion, as it is assuredly the oldest of the various branches of Christianity." [n]

Having put his daughter in what he believed to be good care, and having freed himself from the irritations of daily contact with the spoiled child, he could be solicitous for her and even at times a little sentimental about her. She had taken with her some beautiful dolls (possibly the gift of Teresa and her friends) with dresses of fine material. And Byron sent his peer's gown, the one he had used when he first entered the House of Lords, to be made into dresses for his daughter. [n]

Byron had written to Shelley again protesting the unfairness of Claire's attacks upon him. On April 16, Shelley replied that he and Mary agreed that Byron's conduct toward Allegra had been "irreproachable," and that in the circumstances placing her in a convent was necessary. He concluded the letter with the announcement of the death of a poet who in his view had had great but unused powers: "Young Keats, whose 'Hyperion' showed so great a promise, died lately at Rome from the consequences of breaking a blood-vessel, in paroxysms of despair at the contemptuous attack on his book in the *Quarterly Review*." [n]

Probably because of what he had written recently on Keats in the "Observations" on the *Blackwood's* article, which he now intended as a note to *Hints from Horace*, the last paragraph of Shelley's letter was a considerable shock to Byron. He replied: "I did not think criticism had been so killing. Though I differ from you essentially in your estimate of his performances, I so much abhor all unnecessary pain, that I would rather he had been seated on the highest peak of Parnassus than have perished in such a manner. Poor fellow! though with such inordinate self-love he would probably have not been very happy. I read the review of *Endymion* in the *Quarterly*. It was severe,—but surely not so severe as many reviews in that and other journals upon others." [n]

In the meantime, news of the fiasco of the Neapolitans, who melted before the approaching Austrian army, had reached Ravenna. Byron had contemplated returning to England in the spring if no patriotic action held him in Italy. But now in his disappointment he had no relish for the return. Murray had still made no commitment concerning the publication of his manuscripts. Kinnaird could offer nothing more palatable than the suggestion that he pay one of his most pressing creditors, to which Byron replied: "But as to my parting at this present with a thousand guineas—I wonder if you take me for an Atheist, to make me so unchristian a proposition." [n]

Murray's quick acceptance and printing of the reply to Bowles had encouraged Byron to press the publisher to make some bargain with Moore. He wrote Murray: "As you say my *prose* is good, why don't you treat with *Moore* for the reversion of the *Memoirs?—conditionally, recollect;* not to be published before decease. *He* has the permission to dispose of them, and I advised him to do so." [n] He had told Moore a few months before: ". . . a man always *looks dead* after his Life has appeared, and I should certes not survive the appearance of mine." [n]

In the meantime he had written a sheet or two more of the Memoirs and offered to send this and the journal he had kept in January and February to Moore at the first safe opportunity.[n] And on the first of May he began again some desultory jottings which he called "My Dictionary."

Early in May, Byron became absorbed again in the controversy with Bowles over Pope. On the 8th he sent Murray some additional notes to be added to his second letter, begun in March after he had read Bowles's personal attack on Octavius Graham Gilchrist, a reviewer who had entered the lists on the side of Pope.[n] His second letter was mainly a defense of Gilchrist against the acrimony of Bowles. But Byron was also concerned about further aspersions on Pope's character and references to his licentiousness in his relations with Martha Blount and Mary Wortley Montagu. In the additional notes he took occasion to include a few slighting remarks about not only the "Lakers" but the "Cockneys," who had launched attacks on Pope from the superior ground of their "systems." Among the latter he mentioned Leigh Hunt. "When he was writing his *Rimini,* I was not the last to discover its beauties, long before it was published. Even then I remonstrated against its vulgarisms; which are the more extraordinary, because the author is any thing but a vulgar man. Mr. Hunt's answer was, [']that he wrote them upon principle; they made part of his *system!!'* I then said no more. When a man talks of his system, it is like a woman's talking of her *virtue.* I let them talk on." [n]

On May 10, Byron received from Murray a good-humored letter which Bowles had written him concerning his first *Letter* on Pope. No doubt Bowles wished to placate so powerful and popular a writer as Byron. The overture was, at least for the time being, successful. Byron wrote to Murray: "Of course, after the new tone of Mr. B., you will *not* publish my *defence of Gilchrist:* it would be brutal to do so after his urbanity, for it is rather too rough, like his own attack upon G." [n]

Early in the month, Byron received from Hoppner, who was as strongly opposed to a convent education as Claire herself, a suavely flattering letter proposing to take Allegra to Switzerland when he and his wife left for their summer vacation, and place her in the family of a Protestant clergyman there. This would obviate Claire's objections and would not interfere with his plan to establish his daughter on the Continent.

Hoppner's flattering diplomacy succeeded well enough, for Byron did not take umbrage, but answered reasonably: "If I had but known your notion about Switzerland before, I should have adopted it at once. As it is, I shall let the child remain in her convent, where she seems healthy and happy, for the present. . . ." [n]

Murray had informed Byron on March 20 that he was publishing *Marino Faliero* at last, along with the *Prophecy of Dante,* [n] but Byron heard nothing more of it until he read in a Milan paper on May 14 that the drama had been represented in a

London theater and universally condemned. He expressed his vexation to Murray, upbraiding him for not extracting a promise from the managers before publication not to act it."

Murray had done what he could to stop the representation, but could not prevail against the eagerness and enterprise of Elliston, the actor-manager of Drury Lane Theatre. Murray put out a handbill saying that the performance was in defiance of the injunction of the Lord Chancellor, applied for "at the earnest desire of the noble author." But the tragedy went on. Though the receipts were only £147 and the audience unenthusiastic, it was not "hissed off the stage." "

That Byron was seriously agitated during the time he believed the tragedy was "unanimously hissed" is indicated in his letters to Murray and Kinnaird. He wrote Murray on the 19th that he had been kept for four days in that belief, and added: "Suppose that I had burst a blood vessel, like John Keats, or blown [out] my brains in a fit of rage,—neither of which would have been unlikely a few years ago. At present I am, luckily, calmer than I used to be, and yet I would not pass those four days over again for—I know not what." "

It seemed strange that the government had made no move against the Liberals, whose leaders were well known to the spies of the Austrian police, but the authorities were biding their time, following the debacle of the revolutionary plans. Byron told Hoppner: "They believed, and still believe here, or affect to believe it, that the whole plan and project of rising was settled by me, and the *means* furnished, etc., etc. All this was more fomented by the barbarian agents, who are numerous here. . . ." "

The likelihood of any heroic action having passed, Byron turned again to the drama that expressed most fully his dissatisfaction with the life of slothful self-indulgence. But as the play unfolded under his rapid hand, Sardanapalus became not an indolent wallower in voluptuousness, but a contemplative character whose inaction was due partly to his humanitarian hatred of war and violence and partly to his contempt for the ends of worldly ambition and the lust for power. His indulgence in sensuous pleasures, as Byron conceived his own, was only an escape from worse and more ignoble passions. The absorbing interest he had in this historical drama of a dead past, the thing that had kept him at it for hours at a stretch at white heat, was generated by the fact that it was, like almost everything he wrote *con amore*, the apologia for his own life, the escape from his own self-criticism.

News of the outbreak in March of the Greek war for independence, which reached him in May, might at an earlier period have fired his mind with hopes enlivened by his nostalgia for the land so closely associated with the fondest recollections of his youth. But now, his dreams of a free Italy blasted, he scarcely had the heart to blow upon a new spark: "The Greeks! what think you?" he wrote to Moore on June 4. "They are my old acquaintances— but what to think I know not. Let us hope howsomever." [n]

Despite Murray's neglect and the fact that a number of manuscripts he had sent to London were still unpublished, Byron began on June 12 a new tragedy based on Venetian history. *The Two Foscari*, the story of a fifteenth-century doge and his son, was based on his reading of Daru and Sismondi.[n] As in *Marino Faliero*, he prided himself on his faithfulness to history and to the backgrounds of Venetian life. He beguiled the tedium of his life by writing, and act followed act with remarkable rapidity. Byron finished the tragedy on July 9, less than a month after he had begun it.[n]

Beneath the calm surface of life in Ravenna there were seething hatreds and resentments among both the Liberals and the more fanatic clericals. Byron was fortunate that his charities and sympathies for the common people had made him popular in Ravenna, and he had at least the outward respect of the Cardinal and the devoted friendship of the Secretary General. Byron, cynical as he might be concerning the motives of Alborghetti, realized his value and was generous in rewarding him for services performed. It was in reference to Byron's munificence that the Secretary wrote him on June 17: "What must I say of your kindness and generosity? Or how can I say enough? You act like the Lord, whose rewards are of a hundred for one. The duties of society and friendship prescribed the little service, that I made you; and I am confounded in seeing at what a high rate you have put it. I then devote my-self to your service for ever. . . ." [n]

In a few days Alborghetti had an opportunity to show proof
not only of his gratitude, but also of his most delicate tact, again
as intermediary between Byron and the Cardinal. Byron's Italian
servant Tita, [5] with the ferocious-looking beard, who had been his
gondolier in Venice, got into a heated argument with an officer
named Pistocchi. Though they drew knives and pistols, they did
not come to actual blows. The servant was arrested, and Byron
took the matter to Alborghetti, offering to let the Cardinal deal
with the man as he thought just, thinking that he would be sent
home with a reprimand. But the Secretary apprised him of a
contemplated punishment much more severe.

Byron's reply (June 22) was immediate and indignant though
courteous: "If the man is to be conducted to the *frontier*—and
lose his bread also,—with a stain upon his character—I beg leave
to submit respectfully to the *Cardinal* that I cannot dismiss him
from my service. . . . the Sr. Pistocchi has no more right to
carry arms at *night & out* of *uniform* than the lowest Citizen
off duty.—If one is to be punished *both* should be punished." [n]

The matter dragged on, the Cardinal remaining adamant in
his decision. In the meantime Byron, who was always indulgent
and loyal to his servants, had written an appeal direct to the
Cardinal in terms so forthright as to cause some uneasiness to the
more timid Alborghetti, who was accustomed to a more deferen-
tial style in addresses to His Eminence. Byron's patience was
growing thin when he wrote again to the Secretary on June 28:

"It appears to me that there must be some *clerical* intrigue of
the low priests about the Cardinal to render all this nonsense
necessary about a squabble in the Street of *words only* between a
Soldier and a Servant. . . . If they think to get *rid* of *me*—they
shant—for as I am conscious of no fault—I will yield to no oppression; but will go at my own good time when it suits my inclination
and affairs. . . . I wrote to the Cardinal in the only style that it
became me to use.—I am not conscious of being wanting in respect to his age and station—in other points I used the freedom
of Statement due to my own rank—and the circumstances of the
business." [n]

[5] Byron does not name the servant, but Teresa in the "*Vie*" (p. 386) says
that Tita was arrested for having fought with an officer.

The affair was pending for three weeks, during which much else distracted Byron. In a packet from Murray he had received a pamphlet entitled *Letter to the Right Hon. Lord Byron,* by "John Bull." The anonymous author (recently proved to be John Gibson Lockhart, son-in-law of Sir Walter Scott and later editor of the *Quarterly Review*),[n] starting from Byron's statement in his letter on Bowles that "the great *primum mobile* of the present age is *cant,*" took the author of *Don Juan* to task for wasting his energies on "Billy Bowles," and, in a cocky and blustering style which did not conceal his real admiration for Byron, accused him of being the prince of humbugs, and most completely so in belittling his own merit as a poet in comparison with that of Pope.

But after clearing away this peccadillo, he turned to advice that so closely matched Byron's own conception of his forte as to be eminently agreeable: "Stick to Don Juan: it is the only sincere thing you have ever written. . . . Don Juan . . . [is] out of all sight the best of your works; it is by far the most spirited, the most straight-forward, the most interesting, and the most poetical; and every body thinks as I do of it, although they have not the heart to say so." [n]

John Bull continued: ". . . I think the great charm of its style is, that it is not much like the style of any other poem in the world. . . . Your Don Juan again, is written strongly, lasciviously, fiercely, laughingly—every body sees in a moment, that nobody could have written it but a man of the first order both in genius and in dissipation;—a real master of all his tools—a profligate, pernicious, irresistible, charming Devil—and, accordingly, the Don sells, and will sell to the end of time, whether our good friend Mr. John Murray honours it with his *imprimatur* or doth not so honour it." [n]

After reading such a panegyric, Byron could bear without malice the reprimand, following the usual line of English criticism, for his satire on Lady Byron in the first canto of *Don Juan.* And he must have been especially pleased by the encouragement, of which he had had very little from his friends in England, to go on with his efforts in the drama.

In a letter to Murray on June 29, Byron wrote: "I have just read

'John Bull's letter:' it is diabolically *well* written, and full of fun and ferocity. I must forgive the dog, whoever he is. I suspect three people: one is *Hobhouse,* the other Mr. Peacock (a very clever fellow), and lastly Israeli. . . . There is something too of the author of the *Sketch-book* [Washington Irving] in the Style. Find him out." [6]

He had thought of Washington Irving because a friend of that genial American had just sought him out in Ravenna. He wrote Moore on the 5th of July: "I have had a friend of your Mr. Irving's—a very pretty lad—a Mr. Coolidge, of Boston—only somewhat too full of poesy and 'entusymusy.' I was very civil to him during his few hours' stay, and talked with him much of Irving, whose writings are my delight. But I suspect that he did not take quite so much to me, from his having expected to meet a misanthropical gentleman, in wolf-skin breeches, and answering in fierce monosyllables, instead of a man of this world. I can never get people to understand that poetry is the expression of *excited passion,* and that there is no such thing as a life of passion any more than a continuous earthquake, or an eternal fever. Besides, who would ever *shave* themselves in such a state?" [7]

Nevertheless, Byron was pleased with the young American's hero-worship. Some months later he recorded in his "Detached Thoughts": "I confess I was more flattered by this young enthusiasm of a solitary trans-atlantic traveller, than if they had decreed me a Statue in the Paris Pantheon . . . because it was *single, un-political,* and was without motive or ostentation—the pure and warm feeling of a boy for the poet he admired." [8]

Byron was still interested in *Don Juan* and had extensive plans for its continuation, but at the very moment when the encouraging words of "John Bull" might have spurred him to resume it, he bowed to the earnest desire of Teresa that he should give it up. She had been made uneasy about it when she read the first two cantos in a French translation some months before, but what made her more insistent was an article in the Milan *Gazzetta,*

---

[6] *LJ,* V, 315–17. Thanks to John Wilson Croker (the only one who was in the secret), who "lied like a gentleman" and thus protected the young Lockhart (then only twenty-six), the authorship was concealed for over a hundred years. See Strout, pp. 50–6.

quoting some attacks on Byron's morals from certain English papers and reviews." At first he only laughed at her, but she "only knew that *he* was being attacked, tormented, calumniated," " and held to her purpose. His arguments were futile.

He finally succumbed to her entreaties and told her: "Very well, I promise you not to write any more of the *Don Juan* until you yourself authorize it." " After telling Murray of the promise wrested from him, Byron continued: "The reason . . . arises from the wish of all women to exalt the *sentiment* of the passions, and to keep up the illusion which is their empire. Now *Don Juan* strips off this illusion, and laughs at that and most other things." "

On July 10 a crisis arrived in the fortunes of the Gambas. As Pietro was returning from the theater that night he was arrested and conducted to the frontier to be cast into perpetual exile as a leader in the plots against the state." Teresa had been warned in time to destroy any compromising papers before his rooms were searched the next morning, but his activities as a leader of the Carboneria were well known to the government. Though it occurred after long suspense, his arrest had been inevitable. That he was not, like so many others, cast into a dungeon and subjected to interrogations may have been indirectly owing to Byron and his influence with Count Alborghetti, but more probably, as Byron gradually came to realize, Pietro's banishment, and that of his father, Ruggero (who it seemed for a while might be spared as the head of a family and one who had not been an actual leader among the Carbonari), were part of a deeper design to get rid of Byron himself. Though the authorities were timorous about attacking Byron directly, they felt certain that if her father were exiled, Teresa, who was required to live in his house and under his protection by the separation decree, would accompany or follow him, and that then Byron would also leave the Romagna. But when Count Ruggero was ordered to leave the state within twenty-four hours, Teresa was so upset at the idea of leaving Byron in Ravenna, where she imagined his life in danger, that she persuaded her father to let her remain in their town house while he went to Filetto to arrange his affairs for their departure. She wanted time to see Byron again and to get his assistance and advice. The thought of leaving him was intolerable, though she had not had the courage to ask her father for permission to remain in Ravenna when he left the Romagna.

Byron hurried to her and was easily persuaded to write a letter to her father pointing out the wisdom of allowing Teresa to remain until he and Pietro were sure that they would be given asylum in Tuscany. The letter was successful. Count Gamba gave his consent, and Teresa reported with relief to Byron: "I breathe again. . . . Now I am only left with the pain of uncertainty about my father's and my brother's fate—Pierino's especially. But what a compensation to be able to stay here—where you are! This evening we shall see each other again." [n]

Pietro and his father went to Bologna and then to Florence, where they were permitted to remain. Reluctant to leave Ravenna, where he had put down deeper roots than he realized, Byron needed little urging from Teresa to try every expedient (though he must have felt that it was useless) to have the exiles recalled. On July 15 he sent an earnest appeal to the Duchess of Devonshire, who had long been a resident of Rome, and who he knew had the ear of Cardinal Consalvi, Papal Secretary of State. The tide of reprisals had swept over the heads of the more humane of the local governors. Count Alborghetti could be of little use to him here. [n]

But the Duchess had left Rome for Spa and did not receive Byron's letter until the middle of the next month, and, though she pronounced herself happy to forward an appeal from "the author of *Childe Harold*" and assured him of the "justice, goodness, and benevolence in the present Government of Rome" and the "truth and frankness" of the regime of Consalvi, nothing came of her efforts. [n]

At this point Alborghetti announced with satisfaction the triumph of his diplomacy and the release of Byron's servant. He was no doubt the more happy in his success in that he had been helpless to halt the exile of the Gambas. Perhaps the Cardinal felt that, having accomplished his main purpose, he could afford to be generous in this small matter, for Teresa must surely follow her father, and Byron would follow her.

But the Cardinal was no doubt chagrined to find that Teresa remained alone in Ravenna and that Byron apparently had no intention of leaving. And Count Guiccioli saw his opportunity to force his wife to return to him or face the threat of being shut up in a convent for violating the terms of the separation.[7] In this he was no doubt encouraged by the reactionary priests then in power. As soon as Count Alborghetti heard of this new move, he sent a family friend of the Gambas, Count Rampi of Faenza—"a wise, prudent, and influential man," Teresa called him—to warn her of the danger. Teresa was hysterical again.

In her agitated state, she believed that the whole thing was a plot devised by Alborghetti to get her out of Ravenna and that Guiccioli had not really applied to Rome, but Count Rampi urged her to go and so did her uncle, the Marchese Cavalli.[n] Byron too believed that Alborghetti had the facts, and strongly advised her to leave immediately.[n] Byron was resolved to leave, too, but his cumbersome household could not be set in motion in a moment.

The next day (July 23), perhaps after Teresa had tearfully promised to go if she could have a twenty-four-hour respite ("Do not oppose this determination, my friend," she wrote. "One more day in the same place as you, is worth a century to me"),[n] Byron calmed her by promising to take her whole family to Switzerland as soon as arrangements could be made.

Finally, on July 25, probably early in the morning, Teresa tore herself from Byron and made her escape from Ravenna. But at Bologna, though the Costa family was waiting for her and ready to take her on to Florence immediately, she lost her head entirely and refused to go on, appealing to Byron to let her return or to meet her at Bagnacavallo. When Teresa was with Byron she knew instinctively that this kind of hysterical behavior failed to touch his sympathies and might, as she said, lose him to her forever, but her vivid romantic imagination pictured all kinds of harm which might come to him as a cover for her real fears— that he would be able to get along without her, that he would

---

[7] Teresa would have liked the world to believe later that she was at Filetto after her father departed and that she wrote to Byron from there, but she had remained in Ravenna and had seen Byron constantly until she left for Bologna and Florence. Count Guiccioli had a strong case, for her violation of the separation decree was obvious.

expend his ardor on some other woman if she was not there to watch him. Byron must have felt that he had another Caroline Lamb on his hands—and he tried to show her how mad her proposal was, while at the same time he soothed her excited apprehensions. Immediately on receiving her letter he wrote: "I love you and shall love you as I have always loved you— but I cannot encourage such fatal madness as your return here would be, the day after your departure." In a postscript he added mischievously as to a wayward, lovable child: "Little gossip [8]— get into a good humour—things will go better than you think." [n]

But when he learned three days later (the 29th) that Teresa had not left Bologna, he wrote in exasperation: "Once again I *urge* you to continue your journey, for every reason. With your father you are safe—and besides—you are doing your duty as a daughter. . . . If you believe that you are safe from the attempts already made (and that would be made again) to put you away in a convent so long as you remain in the *Papal States—you are mistaken.*" [n]

But every urging of Byron convinced Teresa's diseased imagination that he did not want her and that he was trying to get rid of her, and she continued to write him reproachful letters from Bologna. It was not until August 2 that she calmed herself sufficiently to cross the Apennines and join her father and brother in Florence. After the stormy scenes of the past fortnight, Byron settled down with a feeling of relief to think of other matters which concerned him and to enjoy a brief respite from the strains of an emotional relationship which had governed his life for more than two years, and which, despite the conjugal aspects it had assumed since the Guiccioli separation, had never quite contributed to his peace of mind.

The summer wore on and Byron remained in Ravenna, partly in the forlorn hope that he could have the exiles pardoned and recalled, but more because it took a major effort to break an established routine. In the meantime he did what he could to

[8] When Byron wanted to tease Teresa he called her *pettegola*, "little gossip." She later erased this undignified epithet and changed it to *piccinina*, "little one" (a diminutive endearment), in several of his letters. (See Origo, p. 471.)

help the families of the unfortunates who had been torn from their homes. Gamba had left all his younger children in Ravenna, including a baby born just before Byron met Teresa, and the families of other refugees were in a still more pitiable plight.

The news of the death of Napoleon, which in other times and in other moods might have stirred him to write, now only increased his feeling of desolation. "Why don't you write on Napoleon?" he asked Moore. "I have no spirits, nor *estro* to do so. His overthrow, from the beginning, was a blow on the head to me. Since that period, we have been the slaves of fools." Thinking rather wistfully of another possible escape from the present upset in his plans and hopes, he concluded: "Is there no chance of your return to England, and of our Journal? . . . If you went to England, I would do so still." [n]

But he had promises to keep, and, though he might guard in the inner recesses of his mind certain weary longings for freedom from that harrowing "earliest passion" which he could never take as lightly as his own words sometimes seemed to indicate, he had a stronger impulse to please those who loved and trusted him. In spite of the "heart that pants to be unmoved," he would go to Teresa—but in his own good time.

Meanwhile Byron had begun another drama. No sooner had he sent off to Murray the manuscript of *The Two Foscari* than he started, on July 16, a poetic exposition of a subject that had long absorbed his interest. It was not historical but metaphysical and concerned itself with the grandest and broadest considerations of evil and death and sin and immortality. He called it *Cain*, but though he borrowed much Biblical phraseology, his purpose was not to dramatize the Bible story but to make it a springboard for a leap into the furthest realms of speculation his mind could encompass. Since his earliest reading of the Bible, under the tutelage of a Scotch Presbyterian nurse and Calvinistic tutors, he had been fascinated by questions of predestination, fate, free will, and the problem of the responsibility for evil. And in his first rationalistic reactions against the dogmas he had been taught in youth he did not avoid theological subjects, but rather welcomed disputations with his pious friends such as Dallas and Hodgson.

When he had pondered the drama in January while he was still composing the first act of *Sardanapalus*, he conceived of it in terms of "a metaphysical subject, something in the style of *Manfred*." [n] But the mood that first suggested it was not that of *Manfred*. The key to it was his question: "Why, at the very height of desire and human pleasure,—worldly, social, amorous, ambitious, or even avaricious,—does there mingle a certain sense of doubt and sorrow. . . ?" [n]

Manfred was mainly inspired by remorse and dissatisfaction with events in the past which had made him wretched. But when, in the words of Manfred, Byron complained that we are "half dust, half deity," he expressed the ultimate of his revolt against the conditions of life itself. Nothing real in the human and tangible world could ever satisfy one who aspired to the freedom of spirit and the omniscience and omnipotence of deity. In *Cain* he went one step further toward the bleakness of despair. For when Lucifer had taken Cain on a voyage through the spirit world and shown him things

> *Beyond all power of my born faculties,*
> *Although inferior still to my desires*
> *And my conceptions,* [n]

he came to the bitter conclusion that even deities may not be happy. All knowledge does not bring all happiness. Nothing remained for him but a kind of desperate stoicism—a reliance on his own unconquerable will and a fortitude born of recognition of the hopelessness of aspiration.

Despite his protestation in the Preface that Lucifer's words were those of the character and not of the author and were necessary for the dramatic development, and that it was difficult "to make him talk like a clergyman upon the same subjects," Byron did make him voice some of his own speculations and stand as an alter ego to Cain, who is a compound of intellectual rebel and rationalistic skeptic of the Age of Reason. Through him he spoke his admiration of

> *Souls who dare use their immortality—*
> *Souls who dare look the Omnipotent tyrant in*

His everlasting face, and tell him that
His evil is not good! [n]

The fact that he knew he was daring, if not the Omnipotent, at least the pious British public, is indicated in some sentences which he wrote in his Preface but deleted before publication: "I am prepared to be accused of Manicheism, or some other hard name ending in *ism,* which makes a formidable figure and awful sound in the eyes and ears of those who would be as much puzzled to explain the terms so bandied about, as the liberal and pious indulgers in such epithets." [n]

When or whether the poem would ever be published he did not know, and at the moment cared not too much. Murray's reluctance to publish *Don Juan* made it doubtful that he would welcome this new iconoclastic piece which ventured on much more dangerous ground. Though he was out of humor with Murray, it was more for his delays and evasion of direct commitments than for any hard terms. When Douglas Kinnaird indicated that he had spoken rather curtly to this "Tradesman," Byron defended the publisher. "I believe M[urray] to be a good man, with a personal regard for me. But a bargain is in its very essence a *hostile* transaction. . . . I contend that a bargain, even between brethren, is a declaration of war. . . . I have no doubt that he would lend or give freely what he would refuse for value received in MSS. So do not think too hardly of him. . . . It is different with me. A publisher becomes identified almost with his authors, and can say anything, or hear anything." [n] And, though he continued to twit and to scold Murray, Byron's letters to his publisher were in the main the frankest and most friendly as well as the most interesting of all his letters from Italy.

Byron was now waiting for a long-delayed visit from Shelley, who had sent some verses he had composed shortly after he heard the news of Keats's death, his *Adonais,* which he had had printed at Pisa. After receiving the poem, Byron wrote to Murray: "Are you aware that Shelley has written an elegy on Keats, and accuses the *Quarterly* of killing him? . . . You know very well that I did not approve of Keats's poetry, or principles of poetry, or of his abuse of Pope; but, as he is dead, omit *all* that is said *about him* in any *MSS.* of mine, or publication. His *Hyperion* is a fine monument, and will keep his name." [9]

In response to a letter he received on August 2, announcing the exile of the Gambas and Teresa and Byron's own imminent departure, Shelley hastened his promised visit to Ravenna. Eager to see for himself what Allegra's situation was and what provision could be made for her if Byron left for Switzerland or elsewhere, he started out on the 3rd[n] and remained the first night at Leghorn, where Claire then was. He spent the 4th (his birthday) rowing with her on the bay,[n] but he left without telling her where he was bound, for he knew that she might insist on accompanying him.

Shelley arrived in Ravenna at ten o'clock the night of the 6th, and he and Byron sat up until five in the morning talking. They had not seen each other since Shelley's visit to the Palazzo Mocenigo in the autumn of 1818. Shelley reported to Mary: "He has in fact completely recovered his health, and lives a life totally the reverse of that which he led at Venice." Besides giving Shelley a graphic picture of the redemptive influence of Teresa on his life, Byron apparently tried, unsuccessfully, to impress him with the poetic principles of Pope.

Turning to another subject of their conversation, Shelley continued: "Allegra, he says, is grown very beautiful; but he complains that her temper is violent and imperious. He has no intention of leaving her in Italy, indeed the thing is too improper in itself not to carry condemnation along with it. Contessa Guiccioli he says is very fond of her; indeed I cannot see why

---

[9] *LJ*, V, 331. Letter of July 30, 1821. During Shelley's lifetime Byron adhered to his resolve not to publish anything against Keats. On November 11, 1821, he wrote a manuscript note on the passage attacking Keats in his reply to *Blackwood's Magazine:* "My indignation at Mr. Keats's depreciation of Pope has hardly permitted me to do justice to his own genius, which, malgré all the fantastic fopperies of his style, was undoubtedly of great promise. His fragment of *Hyperion* seems actually inspired by the Titans, and is as sublime as Æschylus." (*LJ*, IV, 491 n.) But after Shelley's death Byron permitted himself to insert in the eleventh canto of *Don Juan* a barbed reference to Keats, tempered, however, with good-humored praise and pity, which concluded:

'Tis strange the mind, that very fiery particle,
    Should let itself be snuffed out by an article.
                    (*Don Juan*, XI, 60.)

she should not take care of it, [*sic*] if she is to live as his ostensible mistress."

Shelley ended his letter with an agitated recital of what Byron had told him in the small hours of the morning—the lurid gossip which the Hoppners had gleaned from Elise Foggi concerning Shelley and Claire. Why did Byron pass this scandalous tale on to Shelley on the first night of his arrival? Was it because he could not resist the temptation to see what Shelley would say to it, or because he had an irresistible impulse to stir up mischief? Or was it that, as always when he was with Shelley, he was compelled to respect his integrity, and thought he owed it to him to reveal the gossip that had been spread about him? Perhaps a little of all. It may have been the discussion of Claire which induced him to show Shelley Hoppner's letter of the previous September with all the details about the child by Claire which Elise said they had put away in a foundling hospital. After summarizing the letter Shelley concluded:

"As to what Reviews and the world says, I do not care a jot. . . . but that I have committed such unutterable crimes as destroying or abandoning a child, and that my own—imagine my despair of good, imagine how it is possible that one of so weak and sensitive a nature as mine can run further the gauntlet through this hellish society of men. *You* should write to the Hoppners a letter refuting the charge . . . stating the grounds and proofs of your belief. . . . If you will send the letter to me here, I will forward it to the Hoppners. Lord Byron is not up, I do not know the Hoppners' address, and I am anxious not to lose a post." ⁿ

Pending a reply and an opportunity to visit Allegra at the convent, Shelley remained at the Palazzo Guiccioli and saw something of the ancient city. With Tita as an escort, he went in Byron's carriage to see San Vitale, the tomb of Theodoric, and the church of Sant' Appollinare. Byron was delighted to have Shelley with him and reluctant to let him go. Having spent nearly two years in the little provincial town rarely visited by Englishmen, and never by any who could converse with him as Shelley did, he tried to make the most of his friend's visit. Shelley reported to Mary on the 10th: "We ride out in the evening through the pine forests which divide this city from the sea. Our way of life is this, and I have accommodated myself to it without much difficulty. L.B. gets up at two, breakfasts—we talk read etc., until six; then we ride, and dine at eight, and after dinner sit talking till four or five in the morning. I get up at 12. . . ." " Shelley spent the interval until Byron's rising visiting the monuments or writing letters.

The question of Byron's future with Teresa and the Gambas was still undecided, and he took advantage of Shelley's knowledge of Tuscany to discuss possible residences there. He had not yet heard from Hentsch about a house on the Lake of Geneva, and Shelley, eager to have him near by, discouraged that project. In the meantime, Byron tried to quiet the impatience of both Teresa and her brother. Pietro's mind was fixed on the idea of going to Switzerland, which, according to Teresa, he considered "the only country left in Europe where we could still breathe the air of independence." " But discussion with Shelley caused Byron to reverse his opinion, not a very difficult matter once he had been reminded of the strait-laced gossiping Genevese and the spying English tourists. Shelley had been so eloquent against the Swiss scheme that Byron enlisted him to write his reasons to Teresa, who had so far been deaf to his own entreaties.

In the meantime, Byron and Shelley continued their literary discussions far into the night and all night. Shelley was awed by Byron's power in the new cantos of *Don Juan.* He told his friend Peacock, to whom in 1818 he had written his disapproval of *Childe Harold* and his horror at the dissipations of Byron in Venice: " "He lives with one woman . . . and is in every respect an altered man. He has written three more cantos of 'Don Juan.' I have yet only heard the fifth, and I think that every word of it is pregnant with immortality." "

While Shelley was with him, Byron received the news from Murray that the publisher had finally made Moore the handsome offer of two thousand guineas for the Memoirs. The condition of Murray's offer had been that Moore should edit the Memoirs if he survived Byron, but in his enthusiasm Byron now even toyed with the idea of publication in his lifetime."

On hearing of Byron's generosity to Moore, Shelley thought of a much more needy poet in whose behalf he wished to solicit Byron's interest, but he was shy of broaching the subject. He told Mary: "I wish I had been in time to have interceded for a part of it for poor Hunt.—I have spoken to him of Hunt, but not with a direct view of demanding a contribution; and though I am sure that if asked it would not be refused—yet there is something in me that makes it impossible." [n]

Shelley found life in Byron's palace pleasant and amusing enough for a time, though the regime was a little strenuous for his delicate constitution. While wandering about the palace, he had seen more of Byron's astonishing menagerie: "Lord B.'s establishment consists," he wrote to Peacock, "besides servants, of ten horses, eight enormous dogs, three monkeys, five cats, an eagle, a crow, and a falcon; and all these, except the horses, walk about the house, which every now and then resounds with their unarbitrated quarrels, as if they were the masters of it." And after he had sealed his letter he noted: "I find that my enumeration of the animals in this Circean Palace was defective, and that in a material point. I have just met on the grand staircase five peacocks, two guinea hens, and an Egyptian crane." [n]

The next day Shelley reported to Mary the surprising news that Byron had decided to come to Pisa, and asked her to look out for a "large and magnificent" house for him. [n]

His host had kept him occupied so thoroughly that it was the 14th before Shelley found an opportunity to go to Bagnacavallo. The next day he reported to Mary on his visit to Allegra at the convent. He had spent three hours with her. ". . . she has a contemplative seriousness which mixed with her excessive vivacity which has not yet deserted her has a very peculiar effect in a child. She is under very strict discipline as may be observed from the immediate obedience she accords to the will of her attendants. This seems contrary to her nature, but I do not think it has been obtained at the expense of much severity. Her hair, scarcely darker than it was, is beautifully profuse, hangs in large curls on her neck. . . . At first she was very shy, but after a little caressing and especially after I had given her a gold chain which I had bought at Ravenna for her she grew more familiar. . . .

"Her predominant foible seems the love of distinction and vanity, and this is a plant which produces good or evil according to the gardener's skill. I then asked—what I should say to papa? 'Che venga farmi un visitino e che porta seco la *mammina*,'[1] a message which you may conjecture that I was too discreet to deliver. . . . I suppose she is well treated, as far as temper is concerned." " But he doubted that her intellect was much cultivated.

Back in Ravenna, Shelley found Byron eager now to get an establishment in Pisa. Shelley's chief concern, however, was for Allegra. He continued: "On my arrival before the Swiss scheme had been abandoned, I had succeeded in persuading L.B. to take her with him, and had given him such information as to the interior construction of convents as to shake his faith in the purity of these receptacles. This was all settled, and now, on the change of his plans to Tuscany, I wish to hold him to the same determination of taking her with him." "

Teresa's reply to Shelley had arrived on the 15th. She was willing enough to give up Switzerland if Byron would only come to her, and she begged Shelley not to leave Ravenna without Byron. Shelley could not wait for Byron to uproot himself and get under way, but his sense of chivalry was aroused. He felt, however, that Byron was sufficiently eager now to require no prodding. But still Byron was reluctant to let his guest depart.

Shelley lingered two more days in Ravenna. On the 16th he received a long and agonized letter from Mary to Mrs. Hoppner showing how impossible the accusations and calumnies of Elise were. In the first place, Claire was timid and could not be harsh, and "Shelley is as incapable of cruelty as the softest woman. To those who know him his humanity is almost as a proverb. . . . Repair, I conjure you, the evil you have done by retracting your confidence in one so vile as Elise, and by writing to me that you now reject as false every circumstance of her infamous tale." She added in a postscript:

---

[1] "That he come to pay me a little visit and that he bring with him little *mama*." It is possible that Allegra thought of Teresa as "little *mama*"; she was less than two years old when she last saw her real mother, and it is most unlikely that Byron would have kept that memory alive in her.

"I send this letter to Shelley at Ravenna, that he may see it. For although I ought, the subject is too odious to me to copy it. I wish also that Lord Byron should see it. He gave no credit to the tale, but it is as well that he should see how entirely fabulous it is." "

On receiving this letter, Shelley wrote to Mary: "I have not recopied your letter; such a measure would necessarily destroy its authenticity; but have given it to Lord Byron, who has engaged to send it with his own comments to the Hoppners." They, he continued, "had exacted from Lord Byron that these accusations should be concealed from *me*. Lord Byron is not a man to keep a secret good or bad—but in openly confessing that he has not done so he must observe a certain delicacy, and therefore he wishes to send the letter himself, and indeed this adds weight to your representations." [2]

Shelley reported that Byron would set out the moment he

[2] Shelley: *Works*, Julian ed., X, 313–14. Letter of [Aug. 16, 1821]. Whether Byron ever sent Mary's letter on to Mrs. Hoppner is a question which has been violently debated by biographers of Shelley and Byron since Dowden's first publication of it. (See Dowden, II, 429; *LJ*, V, 74 n.; Angeli: *Shelley and His Friends in Italy*, p. 220; *LBC*, II, 192–4.) Unless more concrete evidence presents itself, which now seems unlikely, this matter must remain one of the unsolved problems of Byron biography. Any speculation on it must be based on the facts of Byron's known temperament and proclivities. The pertinent facts are that he was outspoken to a fault to his friends, that he was loyal to them, even when he saw their weaknesses as human beings, and that he would not spare himself when convinced that he had unwittingly misjudged someone. As Shelley indicated in his letter to Mary, Byron was considerably embarrassed by the fact that he had been induced by Hoppner to promise not to reveal Elise's gossip to Shelley. How could he clear Shelley's reputation with the Hoppners without admitting that he had broken his promise? One way would be not to send the letter on, but to give Hoppner the evidence furnished him by Shelley and Mary of the flimsiness of the story told by Elise without indicating that he had betrayed a confidence. That he did something of the sort (if, indeed he did not confess everything and send Mary's letter) and that Hoppner was not wholly convinced by his argument is suggested by a paragraph in Hoppner's letter to him of September 27:

"I trouble you at present merely to enquire whether you received my letter of the Saturday before last. It contained some details of the [Shiloes (partially erased)] which I should be sorry were to travel about the world, or to fall into any other hands but yours." (*LBC*, II, 194.)

It is unfortunate that the letter Hoppner refers to is not extant, for it might could find a house in Pisa. "One thing—" he told Mary, "with Lord Byron and the people we know at Pisa we should have a security and protection which seems to be more questionable at Florence. . . . What think you of remaining at Pisa? The Williams's would probably be induced to stay there if we did— Hunt would certainly stay at least this winter near us, should he emigrate at all; Lord Byron and his Italian friends would remain quietly there, and Lord Byron has certainly a great regard for us —the regard of such a man is worth—*some* of the tribute we must pay to the base passions of humanity in any intercourse with those within its circle; he is better worth it than those on whom we bestow it from mere custom." [n]

At this point, Shelley told Mary, he would have preferred to desert all human society and take her and their child to a solitary island in the sea, but, he concluded:

"The other side of the alternative (for a medium ought not to be adopted) is to form for ourselves a society of our own class, as much as possible in intellect, or in feelings; and to connect ourselves with the interests of that society. Our roots never struck so deeply as at Pisa, and the transplanted tree flourishes not." [n]

Before Shelley left, Byron had received another epistle from Teresa pleading desperately again for him to join her. And when Shelley left Ravenna on August 18 or 19, he carried with him a reassuring letter from Byron for Teresa and one for her brother.

Teresa was somewhat tranquilized when she had seen Shelley, who called on her twice before he left Florence for Pisa. "My Byron," she wrote, "I am aware how great a sacrifice this move will be to you. How shall I be able to show you my gratitude? I have only affection to give to you, and that cannot be increased. I am very sorry to see that you are so reluctant to leave Ravenna, and have such forebodings for the future—but what else can be done?" [n] Teresa was much taken with Shelley. She commissioned him to find a house for her father and his family in Pisa, a task which Shelley set himself to immediately.

---

solve the riddle. There is reason to believe that Byron thenceforward accepted Shelley's and Mary's statement of the facts, for he never again, in any extant letters, referred to the scandal against Shelley and Claire.

Within a day or two, Shelley had found a residence for the Gambas, and one for Byron: a commodious old sixteenth-century palace on the Lungarno which was for lease. The Casa Lanfranchi, so called from the patrician family which had long owned it, was then in the possession of a Mme Felichi." It had been restored by the architect A. Gherardesca at the beginning of the nineteenth century." It faced on the street that followed the right bank of the Arno, and behind it was a small but pleasant garden surrounded by high walls.

After Shelley's departure, Byron's will to move, never very strong, weakened considerably. He wrote Teresa on the 24th that he was coming as soon as arrangements were completed, but added: "I do not deny that I am leaving very unwillingly—foreseeing very serious evils for you all—and *especially for you.* I will say no more—you will see." [3]

In the expectation of Byron's imminent arrival, the Gambas moved to Pisa on September 1 and took lodgings in the Casa Finocchietti on the Lungarno, and on the 23rd moved to the house of the brothers Parrà, also on the Lungarno. They had been given temporary passports in Florence, and instructions were issued to the authorities in Pisa to watch their movements. According to the spy Bandelloni, who reported on their activities to the government of Tuscany, they were joined soon by several friends from Ravenna and Faenza who had been active among the Carbonari. The Gambas went out very little."

Soon after he had found a house for Byron, Shelley wrote to Leigh Hunt inviting him on behalf of Byron to come to Italy and join in the editorship of a literary periodical. Byron had first mentioned the possibility of bringing Hunt to Italy when Shelley visited him in Venice in 1818.[4] Hoping that Byron would be as

[3] Origo, p. 279. Byron had a notion that his following Teresa to a strange town would make their liaison much more conspicuous than it had been in Ravenna, where they were both known and liked, and that it would be injurious to her reputation.

[4] Shelley wrote to Hunt on December 22, 1818, from Naples, after his visit to Byron at Venice: "We talked a good deal about you, and among other things he said that he wished you would come to Italy, and bade me tell you that he would lend you the money for the journey (£ 400 or £ 500) if you were prevented by that consideration. Pray could you not make it in some

generous to Hunt as he had been to Moore, Shelley probably recalled the earlier suggestion to his host. He reported to Hunt on
August 26:

"He [Byron] proposes that you should come out and go
shares with him and me in a periodical work, to be conducted
here; in which each of the contracting parties should publish all
their original compositions, and share the profits. . . . There
can be no doubt that the profits of any scheme in which you and
Lord Byron engage, must from various, yet co-operating reasons,
be very great. As for myself, I am, for the present, only a sort of
link between you and him, until you can know each other, and
effectuate the arrangements; since (to entrust you with a secret
which, for your sake, I withhold from Lord Byron) nothing
would induce me to share in the profits, and still less, in the
borrowed splendour of such a partnership."

At the same time he confessed that he had not been able to
bring himself to ask Byron for a remittance for Hunt's journey,
"because there are men, however excellent, from whom we
would never receive an obligation, in the worldly sense of the
word; and I am as jealous for my friend as for myself." " But
Shelley need not have been so concerned for Hunt's delicacy in
this regard, for he was, as Shelley already knew, notoriously
cavalier in money matters, particularly concerning the honor he
conferred on his friends by accepting their money without intending to repay it."

Shelley concluded: "Lord Byron is reformed, as far as gallantry goes. . . . I trust greatly to his intercourse with you for
his creed to become as pure as he thinks his conduct is. He has
many generous and exalted qualities, but the canker of aristocracy wants to be cut out. . . ." "

As soon as he had heard again from Ravenna, Shelley settled
for the Casa Lanfranchi and reported to Byron that he had
signed the contract on Byron's behalf. The rental was four hundred crowns a year." He gave Byron instructions for bypassing
Florence, where Claire, who was still at Leghorn, was expected

---

way even profitable to visit this astonishing country?" (Shelley: *Works*,
Julian ed., X, 10–11.) Apparently the idea of a jointly edited periodical was
not then discussed.

to return soon. Shelley had finally had to break the news to her that Byron was coming to Pisa.

Once the house was secured, however, Byron found that there were a thousand things to be done before he left Ravenna, and it was two months before he actually got under way. In his letters to Teresa he blamed Lega for malingering and delaying, but there is little reason to believe that anything beyond the steward's natural ineptness together with the complications of moving a household so ponderous as Byron's was responsible for the delay. Having found the Ravennese carriers' charges exorbitant, Byron had asked Shelley to send eight wagons from Pisa. On September 14, Shelley wrote that, through some confusion, Pietro had also sent eight wagons, and sixteen would have arrived had he not intercepted the second caravan at Florence." But the wagons did not reach Ravenna until the 17th. On the 15th the permit for entering Tuscany had expired, and Lega had to write for a renewal."

In the meantime, Byron was not idle in Ravenna. He had written a tour de force which he called "The Blues," a satire on the English "bluestockings," or pretentious literary ladies he had known in his years of fame in London. But he had sent that off to Murray the day after Shelley arrived." And now he returned to *Cain* and finished it by September 9."

After a long delay, Murray had at last offered him one thousand guineas for the two tragedies, *Sardanapalus* and *The Two Foscari,* and another thousand for cantos three, four, and five of *Don Juan*." Byron was incensed at this debasing of his literary coinage. "These matters must be arranged with Mr. Douglas K[innaird]," he wrote. "He is my trustee, and a man of honour. To him you can state all your mercantile reasons, which you might not like to state to me personally, such as 'heavy season' —'flat public'—'don't go off'—'Lordship writes too much'— 'won't take advice'—'declining popularity'—'deductions for the trade'—'make very little'—'generally lose by him'—'pirated edition'—'foreign edition'—'severe criticisms,' etc., with other hints and howls for an oration, which I leave Douglas, who is an orator, to answer." "

Though he continued to resent Murray's carelessness, Byron

could not be permanently angry with him. On September 4 he
wrote him in a grumpy but half friendly tone, his wrath having
"subsided into sullenness." In reading over the newly printed
cantos, he was impressed, he told Murray, with the conviction
that *Don Juan* was the best thing he had written, and he regretted having promised Teresa to abandon it.[n] But he had other
things he could turn his hand to. He had not yet finished with
the Pope controversy. Octavius Gilchrist had sent him three of
his own pamphlets attacking Bowles, and in acknowledging
them Byron warmed to the subject once more. He said that he
had written an answer to Bowles's attack on Gilchrist, which
Bowles's "mild reply" had caused him to suppress. And he took
issue a little touchily with Gilchrist's statement that *Don Juan*
and *Beppo* were more indecent than Pope's *Imitation from
Horace*: "firstly they are *not so* indecent by any means—as for
example,

> '*And if a tight young girl will serve the turn
> In arrant pride continues still to* churn.' "[n]

And in the next place, he added, "it was rather hard in an *ally*
to bring in an 'odious comparison' at the expence of his auxiliary.
However this is a trifle, and if Pope's moral reputation can be
still further elevated at the expence of mine, I will yield it as
freely—as I have always admired him sincerely. . . ."[n]

Byron had informed Kinnaird on September 4 that he intended to dedicate *The Two Foscari* to Sir Walter Scott, *Sardanapalus* to Goethe, and subsequent editions of *Marino Faliero*
to Kinnaird himself, who had given him more encouragement
for his dramas than had his other English friends.[n] But on sending the manuscript of *Cain* to Murray on the 10th, he requested
that the dedication to Scott be transferred to this drama, perhaps because, knowing its explosive potentialities, he counted
on Scott's approval to make it more palatable to the critics and
the public.[n] As he sent it off he grew increasingly anxious about
its reception, and he urged Murray to let him know Gifford's
opinion.

On September 16, Byron wrote a heated and what he knew
would be considered a seditious satire on George IV and on the

servility of the oppressed Irish people who had welcomed and entertained him before the Queen was cold in her grave. He had been roused by the running account in the *Morning Chronicle* of the death and funeral procession of the Queen over against a column describing the festive reception of the King in Dublin.[n] Knowing it could not be published, he sent a copy to Moore the next day, requesting him later to have twenty copies printed to pass around to friends.[n] He had signed it facetiously with the initials of Bowles, adding "written with a view to a Bishoprick." [n] He entitled the poem "To the Irish Avatar."

In the meantime the wagons had arrived from Pisa and the whole household was upset. "I am in all the sweat, dust, and blasphemy of an universal packing of all my things, furniture, etc., for Pisa, whither I go for the winter," he wrote Moore on the 19th.

"It is awful work, this love," he continued, "and prevents a man's projects of good or glory. I wanted to go to Greece lately (as every thing seems up here) with her brother, who is a very fine, brave fellow (I have seen him put to the proof), and wild about liberty. But the tears of a woman who has left her husband for a man, and the weakness of one's own heart, are paramount to these projects, and I can hardly indulge them." [n]

Whether depressed by the failure of Gifford, whose praises he had sought above all others, to applaud him, or whether cast down by the whole clamor of English criticism, Byron sat down on September 24 to compose a strange letter to Murray, asking him to send no new English publications except those of "Walter Scott, Crabbe, Moore, Campbell, Rogers, Gifford, Joanna Baillie, *Irving* (the American), Hogg, Wilson (*Isle of Palms* Man), or *any* special *single* work of fancy which is thought to be of considerable merit"; and "*no periodical works* whatsoever. . . . You will say, 'to what tends all this?' I will answer THAT;—to keep my mind *free and unbiassed* by all paltry and personal irritabilities of praise or censure. . . . When I was in Switzerland and Greece, I was out of the way of hearing either, and *how I wrote there!*" [n]

In the meantime the packing, sweating, and swearing had gone on until there were scarcely beds left to sleep on in the

Palazzo Guiccioli, but Byron lingered on and continued his writing. He told Moore on October 1: "I am setting off for Pisa, if a slight incipient intermittent fever do not prevent me." And in a postscript, following his evening ride, he wrote:

"Since I came back, I feel better, though I stayed out too late for this malaria season, under the thin crescent of a very young moon, and got off my horse to walk in an avenue with a Signora for an hour. . . . But it was not in a romantic mood, as I should have been once; and yet it was a *new* woman, (that is, new to me,) and, of course, expected to be made love to. But I merely made a few common-place speeches. I feel, as your poor friend Curran said, before his death, 'a mountain of lead upon my heart,' which I believe to be constitutional, and that nothing will remove it but the same remedy." ⁿ

Yet in the midst of his depression he had been at work upon one of the most rollicking and high-spirited satires he had ever attempted—as a single sustained literary expression of irony and wit, the masterpiece of his whole writing career. It had been long in brewing, but now in these last days in Ravenna, while his household was being torn from under him and he was reluctantly being uprooted from his routine, his mind bubbled up into the rarest distillation of his satiric genius. Since he had seen in the spring Southey's laureate tribute to George III called A *Vision of Judgment,* he had been mulling over a mock-heroic reply, and in September, in the interregnum between a settled life and he knew not what, he had taken it up again. He announced it first to Moore in his letter of October 1.ⁿ It had grown to eight sheets and 106 stanzas before he sent it to Murray on the 4th. He realized that it would be touchy business for the publisher, and he offered him a way out: "It may happen that you will be afraid to publish it: in that case, find me a publisher, assuring him that, if he gets into a scrape, I will give up *my name* or person." ⁿ

Byron's animosity toward Southey had been growing with the years. And the resentment was returned in full measure by the Laureate. Following the suppression of his dedication to Southey in *Don Juan,* Byron had returned to the attack in the third canto of that poem with some cutting gibes on the Laureate's turncoat propensities; in his "Observations" on the article in *Blackwood's*; and in a "Preface" written about the same time."

None of these diatribes had as yet been published when Southey came to write his preface to *A Vision of Judgment,* but he had sufficient reason for personal rancor against Byron. Without mentioning him by name, Southey left no doubt that he was pointing to Byron in his remarks about the "Satanic" writers of his time. After referring to the "moral purity" of the literature in England for the past half-century, he continued:

"The publication of a lascivious book is one of the worst offences that can be committed against the well-being of society. . . . The school which they have set up may properly be called the Satanic School; for though their productions breathe the spirit of Belial in their lascivious parts, and the spirit of Moloch in those loathsome images of atrocities and horrors which they delight to represent, they are more especially characterized by a satanic spirit of pride and audacious impiety, which still betrays the wretched feeling of hopelessness wherewith it is allied." "

Southey's *Vision* with this preface did not appear until April 11, 1821. When Byron read it, he made a skillful counterattack in a long note added to the appendix of his drama of *The Two Foscari,* on which he was working in June and July.

Having purged himself of the "wormwood and verdigrease," as Shelley called it, of his first reactions to Southey's attack, Byron, in this period of contemplative leisure before he left Ravenna, caught a brilliant glimpse of the whole episode in its ludicrous proportions and poured out the octaves with inspired zeal. He called the poem *The Vision of Judgment.* Southey's own solemn hexameters dealing serious rewards and punishments, and particularly pronouncing heavenly judgment on the mad old King, furnished material for Byron's satiric hand. He had fun enough with the realistic picture of the arrival of George at the celestial gate and the hot debate for his soul between the Archangel Michael and Satan before the "host of witnesses."

But he rose to superb heights of comic situation and ironic humor when Southey was dragged in by the devil Asmodeus, who complained:

> *"Confound the renegado! I have sprained*
> *My left wing, he's so heavy; one would think*
> *Some of his works about his neck were chained."*

Once Michael asked him what he had to say, Southey loosed a spate of words that frightened angels and devils alike. When Michael blew his trumpet to still the tumult of protest that had arisen, Southey entered into his defense.

> *He said—(I only give the heads)—he said,*
> *He meant no harm in scribbling; 'twas his way*
> *Upon all topics; 'twas, besides, his bread,*
> *Of which he buttered both sides. . . .*
> *He had written praises of a Regicide;*
> *He had written praises of all kings whatever;*
> *He had written for republics far and wide,*
> *And then against them bitterer than ever;*
> *For pantisocracy he once had cried*
> *Aloud, a scheme less moral than 'twas clever;*
> *Then grew a hearty anti-jacobin—*
> *Had turned his coat—and would have turned his skin.*

Southey tried to read his *Vision* to the assembly, but Saint Peter at the fifth line knocked the poet down, and he fell into his lake:

> *He first sank to the bottom—like his works,*
> *But soon rose to the surface—like himself;*
> *For all corrupted things are buoyed like corks. . . .*

In the confusion King George slipped into heaven,

> *And when the tumult dwindled to a calm,*
> *I left him practising the hundredth psalm."*

Byron had no sooner finished this robust satire than he sank again into one of his intermittent fits of melancholy. He blamed it partly on the ague that attacked him at this season, he told Moore, but he added: "What I find worse, and cannot get rid of, is the growing depression of my spirits, without sufficient cause." [n]

As always in his melancholy moods, his thoughts turned with nostalgia to Augusta. Except for some short notes, he had not written her since the momentous events of the summer, and he now recapitulated the story of Teresa's separation and exile.

"So you see that I have closed as papa *begun*, and *you* will probably never see me again as long as you live. Indeed you don't deserve it—for having behaved so *coldly—when I was ready to have sacrificed every thing for you—and after* $\begin{bmatrix} you\ had \\ having \end{bmatrix}$ *taken the farther . . . always* [in the manuscript, according to Lord Lovelace, the words in italics were erased and partly illegible]. It is nearly three years that this 'liaison' has lasted. . . . I can say that, without being so *furiously* in love as at first, I am more attached to her than I thought it possible to be to any woman after three years—(*except one & who was she can* YOU *guess?*) [n] and have not the least wish nor prospect of separation from her. . . . If Lady B. would but please to die, and the Countess G.'s husband (for Catholics can't marry though divorced), we should probably have to marry—though I would rather *not*—thinking it the way to hate each other—for all people whatsoever." [n]

Byron was still so reluctant to leave Ravenna that he eagerly seized the excuse of a rumor that the exiles were to be expelled from Tuscany to delay further his departure. [n] Although this rumor was unfounded, other steps had been taken to bring the insurgents to their knees. The Pope had issued an Encyclical against the Carbonari on September 13, threatening with excommunication all who despite this warning remained in the secret revolutionary society. [n] Those who had thought they could reconcile their politics and their religion were now forced to decide one way or the other. The move was successful in divorcing from the Carbonari many good Catholics who had believed that their patriotic zeal was reconcilable with their faith.

A number of exiles were now permitted on petition to return, but only at the cost of bribery and abject penitence. This settled the matter for the Gambas and put an end to Byron's constant hope that they could be recalled with honor to their native city. Neither the fiery Pietro nor his honorable father would bow to such servility."

But even after this strongest reason for delaying had been removed, Byron found further excuses for putting off the dreaded day when he must uproot himself. The bulk of the furniture was gone, but he lingered in the empty palace with his thoughts. When the weather permitted, he went riding daily, as usual, and swam in the Adriatic, and he continued writing and waiting for the English post.

When the first load of Byron's possessions arrived at the Casa Lanfranchi, officials of the city and of the Tuscan government, as well as the spies in the employ of the Austrians, were convinced at last that he was really coming, and some rather fantastic speculations concerning the motives and purposes of this dangerous Englishman were put in the records. The President of the "Buon Governo" wrote to the Grand Duke immediately to warn him against this *Signore Inglese*, "who unites birth, a certain pecuniary fortune, literary fame, and a great determination to favor innovations in states." [5]

The spies would have been confirmed in their fear of Byron's dangerous radicalism had they read the letter he wrote to Hobhouse on October 12. "Your infamous Government will drive all honest men into the necessity of reversing it," he wrote apropos of Hobhouse's remark that they were on the point of a change of government. "I certainly lean towards a republic. All history and experience is in it's favour, even the French; for they butchered thousands of Citizens at first, yet *more* were killed in any one of the great battles, than ever perished by a democratical proscription.

"America is a Model of force, and freedom, and moderation, with all the coarseness and rudeness of it's people." [n]

[5] Archivio di Stato, Firenze, Segretaria di Finanze, No. 6 del Protocollo 40 dell' anno 1821. The document is dated Oct. 4, 1821, and is signed "Aurelio Puccini Presidente del B[uon] Gov[erno]." (From a copy in the Nelson Gay papers, Keats-Shelley Memorial, Rome.) On October 11 one of the Ravenna spies wrote that it was said that Pietro Gamba would give his hand in betrothal to Byron's daughter. (From a copy of a letter dated Oct. 11, 1821, Nelson Gay papers, Keats-Shelley Memorial, Rome.)

But, while he knew that returning to England was out of the question at the time, his mind returned there more and more, for in this blind alley of his life Byron could not with great pleasure look forward. He sought solace in recollections of the happiest days of his life, which, for the most part, were certain moments of his childhood in Aberdeen, of his schooldays at Harrow, of his companionships at Cambridge, and his life in London before his marriage.

To record these memories he began another notebook on October 15, not a diary, but random reminiscences of his vanished youth which he called "Detached Thoughts." As he meditated in the late night in the empty palace, his thoughts frequently went deeper into his own subconscious than he had at first intended in these rambling notes written to supplement the Memoirs for Moore and Murray:

"No man would live his life over again, is an old and true saying, which all can resolve for themselves. At the same time, there are probably *moments* in most men's lives, which they would live over the rest of life to *regain?*" " In another note he observed: "I have written my memoirs, but omitted *all* the really *consequential* and *important* parts, from deference to the dead, to the living, and to those who must be both.

"I sometimes think that I should have written the *whole* as a *lesson*, but it might have proved a *lesson* to be *learnt* rather than *avoided;* for passion is a whirlpool, which is not to be viewed nearly without attraction from its Vortex.

"I must not go on with these reflections, or I shall be letting out some secret or other to paralyze posterity." "

As he was unable to escape from his past, so he was unable to throw off the depression that settled on him in the lonely contemplation of that past. And looking into the future opened a metaphysical problem that continually troubled him. "Of the Immortality of the Soul," he wrote, "it appears to me that there can be little doubt, if we attend for a moment to the action of Mind. It is in perpetual activity. I used to doubt of it, but reflection has taught me better. . . . How far our future life will be individual, or, rather, how far it will at all resemble our *present* existence, is another question; but that the *Mind* is *eternal,* seems as probable as that the body is not so. . . . It is useless to tell me *not* to *reason*, but to *believe*. You might as well tell a man not to wake but *sleep*. . . . Man is born *passionate* of body, but with an innate though secret tendency to the love of Good in his Mainspring of Mind. But God help us all! It is at present a sad jar of atoms. . . . I have often been inclined to Materialism in philosophy but could never bear its introduction into *Christianity*, which appears to me essentially founded upon the *Soul*. . . . I own my partiality for *Spirit*." "

But these reminiscences and speculations scarcely satisfied his need for creative activity. He must turn to some more ambitious project. He had written to Hobhouse to send him the manuscript of the first act of a drama called *Werner*, founded on a German tale by Harriet Lee, which he had begun years before. While waiting and fretting for news of his latest manuscripts and for proofs, his temper was shortened by a letter from his publisher mentioning neither but suggesting that the errors in the last printing of *Don Juan* were in the manuscript, and that he could trust to Murray's honor for a fair payment. "As to 'honour,' " he replied, "I will trust no man's honour in affairs of barter. . . . All men are intrinsical rascals, and I am only sorry that, not being a dog, I can't bite them." "

Byron's impatience with Murray was matched by Teresa's with her lover, for she saw his every delay as deliberate. On the 19th he announced that Lega was leaving certainly the next day, to be accompanied by the grooms and two carriages. And he laid the blame for the delays on the shoulders of the steward.

All poor Teresa knew was that it was nearly two months since he had first announced his intention of coming, and he had not yet set any specific time for his leaving Ravenna. Shelley, who was waiting eagerly for Byron's arrival, wrote on the 21st: "When may we expect you? The Countess G. is very patient, though sometimes she seems apprehensive that you will *never* leave Ravenna." " He reported that Byron's house was ready and his furniture arranged, and gave him the news that Leigh Hunt was planning to come out in November by sea.[6] If Byron's spir-

---

[6] Shortly after Hunt received Shelley's letter, written on his return from Ravenna, telling him of Byron's suggestion for a joint publication, he ar-

its were cast down by the reception of *Don Juan* in England, Shelley's enthusiasm should have revived them. Commenting on the last three cantos, which Byron had sent him, he wrote: "Nothing has ever been written like it in English, nor, if I may venture to prophesy, will there be; without carrying upon it the mark of a secondary and borrowed light." "

But Shelley was now concerned, largely for Claire's sake, with the future provisions for Allegra. He had not extracted a full promise from Byron, during his Ravenna visit, that he would bring his daughter with him. And as early as the 1st of October Byron had indicated that he would not, for the present, remove Allegra from the convent. Claire, still at Leghorn, wrote in her diary on October 3: "Letter from Shelley that Allegra is not coming." "

The news that Byron was leaving Ravenna reached the convent at Bagnacavallo, and the Mother Superior, Marianna Fabbri, wrote him on September 28 expressing regret at his reported departure and inviting him to visit his daughter in the convent before he left. On the opposite side of the nun's letter Allegra wrote in a large, carefully lined, copybook hand, and in an Italian that may have been supervised by the Mother Superior:

My dear Papa—

It being fair-time I should so much like a visit from my Papa, as I have many desires to satisfy; will you not please your Allegrina who loves you so? "

Byron may have been glad that his daughter had thought of him, but in sending her letter on to some correspondent, possibly Hoppner, he pronounced it ". . . sincere enough but not very flattering—for she wants to see me because it 'is the fair' to get some paternal gingerbread—I suppose." "

There is no record of a reply to his daughter or to the Mother

---

ranged to leave with his family, but the vessel they planned to embark on did not leave Blackwall until November 15. They were beaten up and down the Channel by bad weather and finally debarked at Dartmouth. Owing to the ill-health of Mrs. Hunt, they went to Plymouth and did not resume their voyage in another vessel until May 13, 1822. The account of the voyage and its delays is given in Hunt's *Autobiography*.

Superior. Perhaps he left it to Lega or to his banker, Pellegrino Ghigi, who had first made the arrangements and had conducted Allegra to the convent, to convey his excuses and regrets, or he may have intended to call at the convent before he left, but in the confusion of leaving let the opportunity pass. It is more likely, however, that he knew himself a stranger to his daughter and that he did not relish sentimental scenes of parting or exposing his embarrassments with her to the nuns.

Still Byron's feet dragged in making the final move. On the 23rd he wrote to Teresa announcing that Lega had left the previous Saturday, adding: "my departure is settled for next Saturday—that is in four days . . . I hope you will be pleased." [n] Perhaps he would not have set so early a date had he not promised to meet Samuel Rogers in Bologna on his way. When Murray had told him in September that Rogers was on his travels and intended to visit Italy, he replied: "I hope that we shall not have Mr. Rogers here: there is a mean minuteness in his mind and tittle-tattle that I dislike, ever since I *found him out* (which was but slowly); besides he is not a good man: why don't he go to bed? What does he do travelling?" [n]

But when Rogers wrote from Venice that he might visit him at Ravenna, Byron recalled the hospitable friend of London days. In his reply he suggested that they might meet in Bologna and cross the Apennines together. [n]

At last on October 29 [n] in the dark morning Byron's heavy Napoleonic carriage rattled through the silent streets of the medieval town that he had entered in the triumph of his *serventismo* nearly two years before. He was still reluctant to leave, and his departure was regretted by more than Count Alborghetti. Teresa later wrote to Moore: "Many families (in Ravenna principally) owed to him the few prosperous days they ever enjoyed. His arrival in that town was spoken of as a piece of public good fortune, and his departure as a public calamity. . . ." [n]

In the care of Pellegrino Ghigi, his long-suffering banker, to whom Byron delegated all the unpleasant tasks he himself wished to avoid, he left "a Goat with a broken leg, an ugly peasant Dog, a Bird of the heron type which would eat only fish [the Egyptian crane?], a Badger on a chain, and two ugly old

Monkeys," " and his daughter Allegra in the convent at Bagnacavallo.

Later that afternoon, as the carriage was rolling along the
road between Imola and Bologna, Byron was waked from his
drowsiness by a familiar face in an approaching vehicle. In it
was Lord Clare, his favorite at Harrow, whom he had not seen
for seven or eight years. Immediately the past rolled up before
him: "This meeting annihilated for a moment all the years between the present time and the days of *Harrow*. It was a new
and inexplicable feeling, like rising from the grave, to me. Clare,
too, was much agitated—*more* in appearance than even myself;
for I could feel his heart beat to his fingers' ends, unless, indeed,
it was the pulse of my own which made me think so. . . . We
were obliged to part for our different journeys—he for Rome, I
for Pisa; but with the promise to meet again in Spring. We were
but five minutes together, and in the public road; but I hardly
recollect an hour of my existence which could be weighed
against them." "

If Byron was not so much affected by his meeting with Rogers,
the latter seemed to be, for one of his most sentimental descriptions in his poem *Italy* is that which recounts the arrival of Byron at the Pellegrino Inn at Bologna. And Rogers recalled with
equal nostalgia this journey across the Apennines, filled with
sunshine and conversation. He remembered particularly the
procession along the ridges of Byron's "motley household," including the bewhiskered Tita and the bulldog Moretto. But in
later years Rogers said that when he and Byron were traveling
together in Italy, "if there was any scenery particularly well
worth seeing, he generally contrived that we should pass
through it in the dark." "

The traveling poets arrived in Florence on the 30th, putting
up at a "little inn *vis-à-vis* Sneyder's." [7] The next day, he accompanied Rogers to Santa Croce, where he stood unimpressed be-

---

[7] Clayden, I, 321. Rogers recalled: "At this time we generally had a regular
quarrel every night; and he would abuse me through thick and thin, raking
up all the stories he had heard which he thought most likely to mortify me.
. . . But the next morning he would shake me kindly by both hands; and
we were excellent friends again." (Rogers: *Table-Talk*, p. 241.)

fore the tombs of Machiavelli, Michelangelo, and others, but, coming to that of Galileo, said: "I have a pleasure in looking upon that monument; he was *one of us*," meaning one of the nobility."

This was the first time in months that Byron had been the object of the curious observation of his countrymen and women, and he liked it no better than he had in Venice. He had not seen a dozen Englishmen or any English women in his almost two years of isolation in Ravenna. But Florence was full of English, Rogers wrote his sister, and every morning he saw English carriages at the door of the inn. On the morning of November 1, Byron started on the final leg of his journey to Pisa. Rogers wrote his sister: "I wish you had seen him set off, every window of the inn was open to see him." "

Just beyond Empoli, some thirty miles from Florence, Byron's caravan passed the public coach from Pisa. In it was a dark-haired girl who peered out at him without being seen. Claire Clairmont was on her way back to Florence." Oblivious to the apparition he had just passed, Byron was inspirited by the mild Tuscan air and imminent approach to the welcoming arms of Teresa. He composed as he jogged along through the valley of the Arno some stanzas of a lyric:

> *Oh! talk not to me of a name great in story;*
> *The days of our Youth are the days of our Glory. . . .*
> *Oh! Fame! if I e'er took delight in thy praises,*
> *'Twas less for the sake of thy high-sounding phrases,*
> *Than to see the bright eyes of the dear One discover*
> *She thought that I was not unworthy to love her."*

There is no record of Byron's reception in Pisa, but it was no doubt a warm one. It was the moment for which Teresa had waited despairingly more than two months. And his arrival was no less welcome to the warmhearted Pietro and his father, and to Shelley, who had been gathering about him a little society congenial in intellect and feelings, which was soon to become a part of Byron's circle in a new routine quite as pleasant as any he had enjoyed at Ravenna.

NOTES

Notes to Chapter XIII

P.477, l.6 LBC, I, 268. Letter of Sept. 18, 1814.

p.477, l.19 LBC, I, 270. Letter of Sept. 23, 1814.

p.477, l.25 LBC, I, 277. Letter of Oct. 7, 1814.

p.478, l.13 Mayne: *Lady Byron*, pp. 443–4. Letter of Sept. [19], 1814.

p.478, l.20 Ibid., p. 444. Letter of Sept. 20, 1814.

p.478, l.24 Ibid., p. 114.

p.479, l.2 Ibid., pp. 445–6. Letter of Sept. 22, 1814.

p.479, l.23 LJ, III, 139–40. Letter of Sept. 20, 1814.

p.479, l.37 LJ, III, 148n. Letter of "Tuesday" [Oct. 4?, 1814].

p.480, l.10 In his *"Epistle to Augusta"* (stanza 10) Byron reminded his sister of "our own dear Lake,/By the old Hall which may be mine no more."

p.480, l.18 Irving: *Abbotsford and Newstead Abbey*, p. 68. That part of the tree containing their names was later cut out and is now preserved at Newstead Abbey. Brecknock (*Byron*, p. 257) says the names were carved on Sept. 20, 1814.

p.480, l.20 On the 20th, Byron wrote to Annabella: "I proceed on my way to London tomorrow." (Mayne: *Lady Byron*, p. 444.) And he told Moore the same. (*LJ*, III, 139.) Since he did not arrive in London until the night of the 23rd, however, it is possible that he escorted Augusta and her children back to Six Mile Bottom, though his dislike for traveling with children may argue against that speculation.

p.480, l.27 LBC, I, 268–9. Letter of Sept. 23, 1814.

p.480, l.32 LBC, I, 275. Letter of Oct. 5, 1814.

p.480, l.33 LBC, I, 276. P.S. to letter of Oct. 5, 1814.

p.481, l.6 "To Lord Byron," p. 64.

p.481, l.14 Ibid., p. 67.

p.481, l.20 Ibid., p. 68.

p.481, l.22 Ibid., p. 67.

p.481, l.25 Ibid., p. 68n.

p.481, l.29 Murray MSS. Part of this letter is in *"To Lord Byron,"* pp. 68–9.

p.482, l.5 LBC, I, 276. Letter of Oct. 7, 1814.

p.482, l.23 Byron told Annabella: "My debts are reduced very much within the last three years, and a few thousand pounds will cover the rest —considerably above half have been already paid." (Mayne: *Lady Byron*, p. 453. Letter of Oct. 3, 1814.)

p.482, l.28 Foster, pp. 353–4, 367.

p.483, l.9 LBC, I, 271. Letter of Sept. 28, 1814.

p.483, l.18 Byron wrote to John Cowell (who as a boy was present when the bets were made) on Oct. 22: ". . . the bet, or rather forfeit, was one hundred to [Lieutenant Hawkins?], and fifty to Hay (nothing to Kelly), for a guinea received from each of the two former. I shall feel much obliged by your setting me right if I am incorrect in this statement in any way, and have reasons for wishing you to recollect as much as possible of what passed, and state it to Hodgson." (*LJ*, III, 160.) Hay later insisted that the sum was 100 guineas, and received that sum from Byron. (Murray MSS., letters of Hay of Dec. 24, 1814, Jan. 18, and Jan. 30, 1815; Byron to Hay, Jan. 26, 1815, *LJ*, III, 173.) After the marriage took place, Byron was reminded by the Hon. Francis Stanhope (letter of Jan. 19, 1815, Murray MSS.) that he (Stanhope) held a statement: "Lord Byron has taken three guineas of me at the New Inn Brighton Aug. 3, 1808 to return 300 when he marries." When Byron objected, Stanhope wrote again, saying that he would leave the matter with those who were present, Hawkins of the Guards and, he believed, Hobhouse. (Letter of Jan. 22, 1815, Murray MSS.) Whether this debt was ever acknowledged or paid is not known.

p.484, l.5 Mayne: *Lady Byron*, p. 447. Letter of Sept. 26, 1814.

p.484, l.26 Ibid., pp. 448–9. Letter of Sept. 26, 1814.

p.485, l.8 Ibid., p. 470. Letter of Oct. 22, 1814.

p.485, l.15 LJ, III, 161. Letter of Oct. 24, 1814.

p.485, l.19 LJ, III, 162. Letter of Oct. 25, 1814.

p.485, l.32 LBC, I, 282–3.

p.486, l.3 Murray MSS.

p.488, l.9 Eliza's narrative, Gamba papers, Biblioteca Classense, Ravenna.

p.488, l.12 Unpublished letter of Oct. 29, 1814, to Hanson, Murray MSS.

p.488, l.15 Mayne: *Lady Byron*, p. 472. Letter of Oct. 27, 1814.

p.488, l.26 Ibid., p. 466. Letter of Oct. 18, 1814.

p.489, l.11 LBC, I, 286–7. Letter of Oct. 31, 1814.

p.490, l.3 Mayne: *Lady Byron*, p. 122.

p.490, l.14 LBC, I, 287. Letter of Nov. 4, 1814.

p.490, l.32 Mayne: *Lady Byron*, pp. 122–3. Lady Byron included those words in some verses she wrote three years later, thinking back upon that walk by the sea.

p.491, l.3 LBC, I, 287. Letter of Nov. 4, 1814.

p.491, l.6 Mayne: *Lady Byron*, p. 123.

p.491, l.13 LBC, I, 287–8. Letter of Nov. 4, 1814.

p.491, l.23 LBC, I, 288. Letter of Nov. 6, 1814.

p.492, l.8 Mayne: *Lady Byron*, pp. 123–4. Miss Mayne does not say from what documents she extracted the quotations in this paragraph, but they probably came from some of Lady Byron's narratives, of which she wrote a great many in later years. Miss Mayne saw these when she was examining the Lovelace papers, which I have not been able to see.

p.492, l.14 Mayne: *Lady Byron*, p. 123. Lady Byron told this same story to Mrs. Stowe and to her friend the Rev. Frederick Robertson, generally considered a more reliable witness.

p.492, l.17 LBC, I, 290. Letter of Nov. 13, 1814.

p.493, l.4 *LBC*, I, 289–90. Letter of Nov. 13, 1814.

p.493, l.29 Mayne: *Lady Byron*, p. 126.

p.494, l.2 Ibid., pp. 127–8. Letter of [Nov. 16, 1814].

p.494, l.6 Ibid., p. 128. Letter of [Nov. 17, 1814].

p.494, l.10 Ibid., pp. 128–9. Letter of [Nov. 18, 1814].

p.494, l.23 Unpublished letter of Nov. 19, 1814. Murray MSS.

p.494, l.35 Hodgson, I, 290–1.

p.495, l.23 Broughton, I, 168. Diary, Nov. 23, 1814.

p.495, l.26 Mayne: *Lady Byron*, p. 132. Letter of Nov. 23, 1814.

p.495, l.32 Broughton, I, 173; diary, Nov. 26, Dec. 2, 1814. Mayne: *Lady Byron*, p. 135. Letter of Nov. 28, 1814.

p.496, l.3 Mayne: *Lady Byron*, p. 134. Letter of Nov. 26, 1814.

p.496, l.8 Ibid., p. 136. Letter of [Nov. 29?, 1814].

p.496, l.13 Ibid., p. 137. Letter of Dec. 2, 1814.

p.496, l.20 Ibid. Letter of Dec. 3, 1814.

p.496, l.26 Ibid., p. 138. Letter of Dec. 4, 1814.

p.496, l.32 Ibid., pp. 138–9. Letter of Dec. 5, 1814.

p.497, l.8 These and subsequent quotations from Eliza's story are from her manuscript narrative.

p.500, l.12 Manuscript narrative of Eliza.

p.500, l.16 Mayne: *Lady Byron*, p. 146. Letter of Dec. 16, 1814.

p.500, l.24 Ibid., p. 140. Letter of Dec. 7, 1814.

p.500, l.29 Ibid. No date given, but probably Dec. [14–15?] 1814.

p.500, l.34 Ibid., p. 144. Letter of Dec. 12, 1814.

p.501, l.19 Ibid., pp. 146–7. Letter of Dec. 16, 1814.

p.501, l.26 Ibid., p. 148. Letter of Dec. 18, 1814.

p.502, l.3 Ibid., p. 150. Letter of Dec. 22, 1814.

p.502, l.16 Ibid., p. 151. Letter of Dec. 23, 1814.

p.502, l.27 Broughton, I, 191. Diary, Dec. 24, 1814.

p.502, l.36 Mayne: *Lady Byron*, p. 153.

p.503, l.5 Broughton, I, 191.

p.503, l.17 Broughton, II, 195.

p.503, l.24 Broughton, I, 191.

p.503, l.29 Hobhouse diary, Dec. 29, 1814, Berg Collection, New York Public Library. This passage was omitted from the diary entry as given in Broughton.

p.504, l.27 This and subsequent quotations from the Hobhouse diary are from the original manuscript, Berg Collection, New York Public Library. In the *Recollections*, the description of the journey to Seaham and of the wedding is considerably garbled, with some changes and omissions.

p.505, l.26 Miss Mayne saw this wedding dress at Ockham Park, where it was preserved by Lady Lovelace, the widow of Annabella's grandson. (Mayne: *Lady Byron*, p. 157n.)

p.505, l.34 Medwin reported that Byron told him: "Lady Byron (Byrn, he pronounced it) was the only unconcerned person present; Lady Noel, her mother, cried; I trembled like a leaf, made the wrong responses, and after the ceremony called her Miss Millbank." (Medwin, I, 38–9.) At another point Medwin quoted him as saying that he had "a horror of matrimony, from the sight of domestic broils: this feeling came over me very strongly at my wedding. . . . At the last moment I would have retreated, if I could have done so." (Medwin, I, 59.) Medwin also recorded Byron's saying that the fortune-teller, Mrs. Williams, had predicted that twenty-seven was to be a dangerous age for him. (Medwin, I, 38.)

p.506, l.4 Maurois, p. 227.

p.506, l.9 Mayne: *Lady Byron*, p. 152. From a statement made in 1816, after the separation, by Lady Milbanke (then Lady Noel).

Notes to Chapter XIV

P.508, l.5 Mayne: *Lady Byron*, p. 160.

p.508, l.10 Ibid. Again apparently from Lady Byron's narrative in the Lovelace papers.

p.508, l.13 Ibid.

p.508, l.16 Ibid., p. 161.

p.508, l.29 Medwin, I, 40. Medwin's account adds to the confusion. He quotes Byron as saying: "After the ordeal [the marriage ceremony] was over, we set off for a countryseat of Sir Ralph's; and I was surprised at the arrangements for the journey, and somewhat out of humour to find a lady's-maid stuck between me and my bride. It was rather too early to assume the husband; so I was forced to submit, but it was not with a very good grace. Put yourself in a similar situation, and tell me if I had not some reason to be in the sulks." (Medwin, I, 39–40.) But Mrs. Clermont did not accompany the pair to Halnaby, and Mrs. Minns, according to her own story told years later, had gone ahead to prepare Halnaby for the honeymooners. A reporter for the *Newcastle Daily Chronicle* interviewed Mrs. Minns in 1869; the interview is summarized and quoted in the *Quarterly Review*, Vol. CXXVII (Oct. 1869), pp. 411–12n. The only servant to accompany the newlyweds, according to this account, was the faithful Fletcher, who rode outside with the coachman. In a review of Medwin in the *Westminster Review* (Vol. III [Jan. 1825], p. 24) Hobhouse says: "There was nobody in the carriage that conveyed lord and lady Byron from Seaham to Halnaby on the day of their marriage, besides his lordship and his wife." Of course, what Byron told Medwin could have occurred on the return journey.

p.509, l.11 Lord Lindsay's letter to *The* (London) *Times*, Sept. 7, 1869. Reprinted in Stowe: *Lady Byron Vindicated*, p. 305.

p.509, l.13 Medwin, I, 40.

p.509, l.21 Harriet Martineau, p. 285.

p.509, l.28 Quoted in *Quarterly Review*, Vol. CXXVII (Oct. 1869), p. 412n.

p.510, l.2 Pope-Hennessy, p. 71. This and other details of the setting at Halnaby, Dame Una got from a visit to the scene and from local tradition.

p.510, l.7 Hobhouse diary, May 15, 1824.

p.510, l.10 Pope-Hennessy, p. 72.

p.510, l.15 LBC, I, 293. Letter of Jan. 7, 1815, to Lady Melbourne.

p.510, l.21 Mayne: *Lady Byron*, p. 161. Apparently from Lady Byron's journal.

p.510, l.29 Stanley T. Williams: *The Life of Washington Irving*, I, 455, note 75. Irving, who was allowed to read Byron's Memoirs (later burned), recalled this incident as there recorded. Samuel Rogers (*Table-Talk*, p. 236), who also gave the Memoirs as his source, perhaps garbled or dramatized the story. He said that Byron "could not help exclaiming, in a voice so loud that he wakened Lady B., 'Good God, I am surely in hell!' "

p.510, l.31 Broughton, II, 281. Hobhouse recorded that Byron's oppression lasted during the first week of his honeymoon, and that "her Ladyship appeared always dismayed when she spoke of her residence at Halnaby."

p.511, l.8 Mayne: *Lady Byron*, pp. 161–2.

p.511, l.14 *Astarte*, p. 63n. (Lady Byron's Narrative Q.)

p.511, l.16 Mayne: *Lady Byron*, p. 162.

p.511, l.29 Ibid., p. 163.

p.511, l.37 LBC, I, 292. Letter of Jan. 3, 1815.

p.512, l.8 LBC, I, 293–4.

p.512, l.11 LJ, III, 169. Letter of Jan. 10, 1815, to Moore.

p.512, l.27 LJ, III, 168–9.

p.513, l.4 Mayne: *Lady Byron*, p. 165.

p.513, l.13 Fox, pp. 203–4.

p.513, l.27 Mayne: *Lady Byron*, p. 162.

p.513, l.30 Astarte, p. 54n.

p.513, l.32 Mayne: *Lady Byron*, p. 164.

p.514, l.11 Ibid., p. 166.

p.514, l.12 Ibid., p. 169.

p.514, l.14 Ibid., p. 166.

p.514, l.27 Ibid., p. 164.

p.515, l.3 See *Quarterly Review*, Vol. CXXVII (Oct. 1869), p. 412n.

p.515, l.6 Mayne: *Lady Byron*, p. 164. See *Quarterly Review*, Vol. CXXVII (Oct. 1869), p. 412n.

p.515, l.16 Mayne: *Lady Byron*, p. 167.

p.515, l.38 "The True Story of Lady Byron's Life," in Stowe: *Lady Byron Vindicated*, p. 302.

p.516, l.8 Maurois, p. 229.

p.516, l.13 Maurois, p. 227.

p.516, l.19 Mayne: *Lady Byron*, p. 167.

p.516, l.31 Maurois, p. 227. Maurois has presumably paraphrased the account of these events from Lady Byron's journal.

p.517, l.15 LJ, III, 172. Letter of Jan. 19, 1815. In an unpublished letter of Feb. 14 to Henry Drury, Byron said: "I am now at my 'father-in-law sir Jacob's['] (see 'Mayor of Garrot'). . . ." Trinity College MS. R. Z. 40a. The reference is to a loquacious character in Samuel Foote's *Mayor of Garratt*.

p.517, l.22 Maurois, p. 230.

p.517, l.28 Mayne: *Lady Byron*, p. 166.

p.518, l.3 Mayne (*Lady Byron*, p. 1) says Annabella was born May 17, 1792.

p.518, l.9 LBC, I, 295.

p.518, l.29 LJ, III, 175–6. Letter of Feb. 2, 1815.

p.518, l.37 LBC, I, 296. Letter of Jan. 26, 1815.

p.519, l.5 Maurois, p. 231. Maurois fails to give his source, but supposedly this incident is garnered from Lady Byron's journal.

p.519, l.8 Browne: "Voyage from Leghorn to Cephalonia with Lord Byron, in 1823, to the Seat of War in Greece," pp. 60–1.

p.519, l.24 Mayne: *Lady Byron*, p. 172.

p.519, l.31 Bland-Burges papers, p. 339. Quoted in *LJ*, III, 172n.

p.519, l.35 LBC, I, 300.

p.520, l.2 LBC, I, 298. Letter of Jan. 31, 1815.

p.520, l.16 LBC, I, 301–2.

p.520, l.25 Mayne: *Lady Byron*, p. 172.

p.520, l.35 Hodgson, II, 7–8. In the *Memoir* the letter is dated Dec. 15, but it must have been Feb. 15, 1815.

p.521, l.2 Mayne: *Lady Byron*, p. 171.

p.521, l.11 Blessington, p. 92.

p.521, l.18 Byron had borrowed that sum from Sawbridge through Hanson before going abroad in 1809.

p.521, l.24 Byron must have accumulated considerable additional indebtedness or, what is more likely, he miscalculated the amount when he wrote Annabella on Oct. 3, 1814, that a few thousand pounds would cover his yet unpaid debts.

p.521, l.34 Letter of Jan. 26, 1815, to Hobhouse. Murray MSS.; Hobhouse proofs. Except for the first sentence, all the portion here quoted is unpublished.

p.522, l.5 Letters of Tuesday [Jan. 31, 1815] and Monday, Feb. 13, 1815, from Hobhouse to Byron, Hobhouse proofs; and letter of Byron to Hobhouse, Feb. 24, 1815, Hobhouse proofs.

p.522, l.17 LJ, III, 179. It was perhaps while his thoughts were once more dwelling on Greece that Byron began to write *The Siege of Corinth*. He told Coleridge in October that it was begun in January. (*LJ*, III, 229.)

p.522, l.25 LJ, III, 182.

p.522, l.38 Unpublished letter, Hobhouse proofs. Byron had first suggested the possibility of his coming to town alone to settle his business affairs in a letter of Feb. 11 to Hobhouse.

p.523, l.2 Mayne: *Lady Byron*, p. 173. This is probably gleaned from the Lovelace papers.

p.523, l.5 Hobhouse wrote on March 8 that he had rented the house for £700 per annum. The rental year began on March 13. (Murray MSS.; Foster, p. 401.)

p.523, l.12 LJ, III, 186.

p.523, l.15 Maurois, p. 231. From Lady Byron's journal?

p.523, l.22 Mayne: *Lady Byron*, p. 173. From Lady Byron's journal?

p.523, l.27 Maurois, p. 232. From Lady Byron's journal?

p.523, l.33 Mayne: *Lady Byron*, p. 173.

p.523, l.35 Ibid., p. 174.

p.524, l.3 Ibid.

p.524, l.29 Ibid., p. 176.

p.525, l.1 Ibid.

p.525, l.8 Ibid.

p.525, l.9 Maurois, p. 232. This detail is not given by Miss Mayne.

p.525, l.17 Mayne: *Lady Byron*, p. 179.

p.525, l.20 Ibid., p. 177.

p.525, l.27 Ibid., p. 176.

p.525, l.30 Ibid., p. 178.

p.525, l.34 Maurois, p. 233. These are details not in Mayne, possibly paraphrased from Lady Byron's journal.

p.525, l.37 Mayne: *Lady Byron*, p. 178.

p.526, l.10 Hodgson, II, 13–15.

p.526, l.15 Mayne: *Lady Byron*, p. 177.

p.526, l.18 Ibid., p. 176.

p.526, l.22 Maurois (p. 234) mentions this circumstance, whether derived from Lady Byron's statements in her narratives or from conjecture is not clear. Miss Mayne makes no reference to Byron's drinking as a contributing cause of his wild talk at Six Mile Bottom.

p.526, l.26 Mayne: *Lady Byron*, p. 178.

p.526, l.33 Broughton, I, 208–24.

p.526, l.37 Broughton, I, 226.

p.527, l.2 Broughton, I, 227.

p.527, l.8 LJ, III, 187–8.

p.527, l.18 Mayne: *Lady Byron*, p. 178.

p.527, l.29 Ibid., pp. 180–1.

p.527, l.33 From the original MS. of the Hobhouse diary, Berg Collection, New York Public Library. Entry for April 1, 1815, which is inaccurately printed in Broughton, I, 229.

p.528, l.15 Griggs, pp. 1085–8.

p.528, l.18 LJ, III, 190–1. Letter of March 31, 1815. James Dykes Campbell (*Samuel Taylor Coleridge*, p. 188) says that Byron interceded with the managers of Drury Lane to get Coleridge's *Remorse* on the stage in 1812, but there is no evidence of this and every indication that this was the first direct communication between the poets.

p.528, l.21 LJ, III, 192–3.

p.529, l.2 Mayne: *Lady Byron*, p. 181.

p.529, l.14 Smiles, I, 267.

p.529, l.21 Smiles, I, 267–8.

p.529, l.31 Moore, I, 616. Hobhouse wrote in the margin of his copy of Moore after ". . . see you retreat upon the Catholic faith": "as he said he was [inclined?]."

p.530, l.2 Moore, I, 616.

p.530, l.7 Moore, I, 618.

p.530, l.31 Mayne: *Lady Byron*, p. 183.

p.531, l.11 Unpublished letter, Murray MSS.

p.531, l.18 Phillips, p. 78.

p.531, l.26 Slater, p. 86.

p.531, l.32 "To Lord Byron," p. 66. Letter to Murray, not dated but indicated in the Murray MSS. as having been received Aug. 19, 1814 [1815?].

p.532, l.3 L'Estrange, p. 24.

p.532, l.9 Hogg, p. 104. Letter of April 10, 1815.

p.532, l.15 Mayne: *Lady Byron*, p. 181.

p.532, l.24 Byron told Medwin (I, 104–5): "I became a member of Drury-lane Committee, at the request of my friend Douglas Kinnaird, who made over to me a share of 500 *l.* for the purpose of qualifying me to vote."

p.533, l.5 Erdman: "Lord Byron as Rinaldo," p. 194.

p.533, l.8 Ibid.

p.533, l.23 Ticknor, I, 58–9.

p.534, l.8 Ticknor, I, 60.

p.534, l.13 Ticknor, I, 62.

p.534, l.21 Ticknor, I, 66–8.

p.534, l.27 The approximate date of Augusta's departure can be established by her letter to Hobhouse of July 5, 1815, in which she says: "I returned home ten days ago, after more than two months séjour in Piccadilly. . . ." (Broughton, II, 357.)

p.535, l.3 *Astarte*, p. 1n. From narrative by Lady Byron dated March 1817.

p.535, l.11 Hunt: *Autobiography*, p. 253.

p.535, l.17 Hunt: *Lord Byron*, I, 6.

p.535, l.20 Ibid., I, 7.

p.535, l.25 This MS. is now in the Ashley Library in the British Museum. (Ashley 906.) It is described (though misdated 1811) in Wise's *Bibliography* (II, 63–4).

p.535, l.36 *LJ*, III, 210n. The letter is dated only "Tuesday Evening." Since it mentions Moore's proposed visit to the Byrons when they should have removed to Seaham (the invitation was extended by Byron in his letter of July 7, 1815, to Moore), it was possibly written in mid-July. Prothero has conjectured August.

p.536, l.21 Undated letter, Murray MSS. Part of this letter was published in "*To Lord Byron*," pp. 68–9.

p.537, l.6 Byron paid tribute to Frederick Howard in the third canto of *Childe Harold* (stanza 29).

p.537, l.8 Captain Ben Hobhouse was killed at Quatre Bras and not at Waterloo. John Cam heard about it first from English soldiers who had arrived at Paris in July.

p.537, l.12 *LJ*, III, 208–9.

p.537, l.16 *LJ*, III, 302. Letter of Jan. 28, [1816].

p.537, l.26 *LJ*, III, 209n. This was apparently intended for some newspaper, but was not published in Byron's lifetime.

p.538, l.13 Mayne: *Lady Byron*, p. 184.

p.538, l.26 *LJ*, III, 210n. Prothero's conjectured date of August for this letter is probably based on the fact that the will was actually signed and witnessed on July 29, 1815, but Byron had "made" the will before it was legally drawn up by Hanson and it is likely that he discussed its provisions with Annabella before the actual signing.

p.538, l.32 *LJ*, III, 210–11.

p.539, l.9 *LJ*, III, 210–11n.

p.539, l.19 *LJ*, III, 208.

p.539, l.27 From the entry of July 28, 1815, Hobhouse diary MS. in

Berg Collection, New York Public Library. The passage is incomplete and garbled in Broughton, I, 322.

p.539, l.35 Broughton, II, 201.

p.540, l.10 Hobhouse diary, Berg Collection, New York Public Library.

p.540, l.13 Hobhouse diary, Berg Collection, New York Public Library.

p.540, l.24 Mayne: *Lady Byron,* p. 187.

p.541, l.5 Ibid., p. 188.

p.541, l.20 Ibid., pp. 189–90.

p.542, l.6 LJ, V, 442–3.

p.542, l.8 Medwin, I, 168.

p.542, l.9 LJ, III, 424.

p.542, l.12 Fanny Kelly made her debut at the age of seven at Drury Lane, Jan. 16, 1798, in *Bluebeard.* (*LJ,* III, 223n.)

p.542, l.18 LJ, III, 217n.

p.542, l.29 LJ, V, 442. "Detached Thoughts."

p.543, l.2 B-SP, I, 317. Letter of Oct. 18, 1815.

p.543, l.14 LJ, III, 233. Letter of Oct. 28, 1815.

p.543, l.30 Mayne: *Lady Byron,* p. 190.

p.544, l.14 Ibid. Miss Mayne gives no dates for these events and conversations; perhaps none were given in the narrative of Lady Byron.

p.544, l.24 Ibid., pp. 193–4.

p.544, l.28 Unpublished letter, Murray MSS.

p.544, l.38 LJ, III, 238–9. In *LJ* the date is given as "September–October 30, 1815," but the correct date must be Sept. 30, for this is obviously a reply to Hunt's letter of Sept. 28, and Hunt had written again before Byron's letter of Oct. 7, which follows this.

p.545, l.6 LJ, III, 225–6.

p.545, l.10 The original MS. in Byron's hand is dated Jan. 31, 1815, and Byron said he had written most of it before Walter Scott recited him in June [properly May?] the passage from *Christabel* which influenced some of his lines, but he did not have it ready for Murray until the beginning of November, when he suggested that it be published unobtrusively with his other collected poems. (See *Poetry,* III, 443, 448; *LJ,* III, 246.)

p.545, l.19 LJ, III, 242–3.

p.545, l.30 Mayne: *Lady Byron,* p. 194. Miss Mayne does not give the date, but says it was written a week after Annabella had copied out the passage from Hunt's *Rimini,* which Byron had finished reading on Oct. 22 and which he had returned to Hunt before Oct. 30 when the latter thanked him for his marginal comments.

p.545, l.35 In October, Byron's cousin George Anson Byron had sent reports from Newstead of preparations for the sale by the auctioneer Farebrother, who had listed all the furniture and had demanded the key to the wine cellar, which then contained 794 bottles of light wine, port, and Madeira. (Letters of Oct. 4, 10, 13, and 23, 1815, Murray MSS.)

p.546, l.20 Mayne: *Lady Byron,* pp. 194–5.

p.547, l.8 Blessington, p. 42.

p.547, l.9 Blessington, p. 212.

p.547, l.13 Blessington, p. 115.

p.547, l.17 Moore, II, 223n.

p.547, l.23 Blessington, p. 173.

p.547, l.27 Blessington, p. 92.

p.547, l.34 Smiles, I, 286.

p.548, l.3 From the original MS. of the Hobhouse diary, Berg Collection, New York Public Library.

p.548, l.10 Mayne: *Lady Byron*, p. 196.

p.548, l.16 Ibid., p. 191.

p.548, l.21 Ibid., p. 190.

p.548, l.26 Smiles, I, 353.

p.549, l.20 "To Lord Byron," p. 180.

p.549, l.37 Ibid., p. 181.

p.550, l.9 Ibid., pp. 182–3.

p.550, l.19 Ibid., pp. 184–5.

p.550, l.28 B-SP, II, 664n.

p.550, l.35 Unpublished portion of postscript to letter of Aug. 23, 1821. Murray MSS.; Hobhouse proofs.

p.551, l.9 Mayne: *Lady Byron*, p. 196.

p.551, l.21 Lord Lindsay's letter to *The Times*, in Stowe, p. 306.

p.551, l.29 Smiles, I, 353–4. Letter of "December, 1815."

p.551, l.34 *LJ*, III, 251. Letter of Jan. 2, 1816. (Jan. 3 in *LJ*, but Jan. 2 in original letter, Murray MSS.)

p.552, l.1 Unpublished letter of Nov. 19, 1815. From the MS. in the Yale University Library.

p.552, l.11 *Astarte*, p. 209.

p.552, l.20 *Astarte*, p. 322. Miss Mayne, however, says—on what authority is not stated—that Mrs. Clermont was, "at Byron's own suggestion," staying at the house. (Mayne: *Lady Byron*, p. 197.)

p.552, l.27 Mayne: *Lady Byron*, pp. 196–7. In *Astarte* (p. 63) the source of this is given as "Lady Byron's Statement, G."

p.552, l.30 Hobhouse diary, from the original MS., Berg Collection, New York Public Library.

p.553, l.8 Mayne: *Lady Byron*, p. 197.

p.553, l.11 Samuel Haywood, Serjeant-at-law.

p.553, l.16 Fox, p. 97.

p.553, l.26 Broughton, II, 279.

p.553, l.29 Miss Mayne (*Lady Byron*, p. 198) says that "Annabella told this to Lady Anne Barnard."

p.553, l.35 Broughton, II, 280.

p.553, l.37 Augusta wrote to Hodgson on Dec. 11 (*LJ*, III, 291): "The event happened at one o'clock yesterday, and both Mother and Daughter have been, and are, as well as possible in every respect."

p.554, l.3 Quoted in Lord Lindsay's letter to *The Times*, Sept. 7, 1869. (In Stowe, p. 306.)

p.554, l.6 *LJ*, III, 291–2.

p.555, l.7 *Childe Harold*, III, 118.

p.555, l.16 Broughton, II, 201–2.

p.555, l.23 *Astarte*, p. 39.

p.555, l.35 Mayne: *Lady Byron*, p. 198. Miss Mayne has presumably paraphrased this incident from Lady Byron's journal or one of her later narratives. Mrs. Stowe (*Lady Byron Vindicated*, pp. 292–3) tells the same story with a slight variation, not mentioning the earlier expressed hope that Lady Noel would die.

p.556, l.5 Moore, I, 653n.

p.556, l.14 From a "Memorandum" of a conversation with Lord Broughton (Hobhouse) sent to John Murray by Lord Lindsay in 1869. (Murray MSS.)

p.556, l.26 Smiles, I, 354. Letter of Jan. 2, 1816. Date corrected from MS.

p.557, l.1 Astarte, p. 164.

p.557, l.4 Astarte, p. 39. It was then, according to Maurois, that "he spoke of his intention of installing an actress in the house." (Maurois, p. 244.)

p.557, l.8 Astarte, p. 39.

p.557, l.10 LJ, III, 292.

p.557, l.19 A line from Coleridge's *Christabel*.

p.557, l.21 LJ, III, 252–4.

p.557, l.27 Mayne: *Lady Byron*, p. 200. No dates are given for these fragments from Annabella's letters, but the letters must have been written early in January 1816.

p.558, l.11 Astarte, p. 39. There is no way of knowing whether Lord Lovelace included here the whole of the letter. As it is printed, there is no salutation or closing or even signature.

p.558, l.17 Broughton, II, 215.

p.558, l.21 Astarte, pp. 39–40.

p.558, l.32 Moore, II, 815. Hobhouse's comment opposite this last sentence in his copy of Moore was: "Mr. le Mann gives a totally different account of this."

p.560, l.5 Broughton, II, 250–1.

p.560, l.8 LJ, III, 293.

p.560, l.16 Broughton, II, 252.

p.560, l.21 LJ, III, 293.

p.560, l.30 Broughton, II, 253.

p.561, l.16 Broughton, II, 255.

p.561, l.22 Broughton, II, 215–16.

p.561, l.27 Fox, p. 102. From unsent letter of Annabella in the Lovelace papers, written July 6, 1816.

p.562, l.4 Stowe, p. 294. Mrs. Stowe gives the impression that this was on the day of her departure, but, judging from her own account, it must have been the day before.

p.562, l.14 Mayne: *Lady Byron*, p. 202.

Notes to Chapter XV

P.563, l.18 Fox, p. 98. From the Lovelace papers. The reference to "the abominable trade of versifying" Hobhouse took to be an indication that Lady Byron associated her husband's periods of "bargaining with the Muses" with "those in which his health and temperament seemed more painfully affected than at other intervals." (Broughton, II, 239.) But Fox (p. 98), who thought she was merely following the doctor's advice to write on "light and soothing topics," suggested that she was merely using playfully a phrase which Byron had invented.

p.563, l.19 In Annabella's published letter dated Jan. 16 she says they arrived "last night," but Fletcher's wife, who accompanied her, said in her later "deposition" that they "reached Woburn the first night, and arrived at Kirkby Mallory about six o'clock the next evening." (Broughton, II, 264.)

p.564, l.10 Fox, pp. 98-9.

p.564, l.30 LJ, III, 295.

p.564, l.34 LJ, III, 295-6.

p.565, l.6 Fox, p. 100.

p.565, l.8 Lady Byron's "Remarks on Mr. Moore's Life of Lord Byron," Moore, II, 815.

p.565, l.14 Fox, p. 101.

p.566, l.5 LJ, III, 296-7.

p.566, l.13 Fox, p. 104. From Annabella's unsent letter of July 6, 1816 (correspondent not given).

p.566, l.22 LJ, III, 297.

p.566, l.28 LJ, III, 298.

p.566, l.30 LJ, III, 298. Letter of Jan. 19, 1816.

p.567, l.3 LJ, III, 298-9.

p.567, l.9 He told Hobhouse that it was his intention to break up his establishment at Piccadilly. (Broughton, II, 202.)

p.567, l.19 Hobhouse diary. From the MS., Berg Collection, New York Public Library.

p.567, l.22 Broughton, II, 202.

p.567, l.27 Hobhouse's *The Substance of Some Letters Written by an Englishman Resident at Paris during the Last Reign of the Emperor Napoleon* was finally published by Ridgeway, after being turned down at the last minute by John Murray, probably at the instigation of his Tory advisers, in the summer of 1816. (Joyce, pp. 91-2.)

p.567, l.35 Clayden, I, 211. Letter of Friday [Jan. 19, 1816].

p.568, l.1 Smiles, I, 355.

p.568, l.5 LJ, III, 255-6. Letter of Jan. 20, 1816.

p.568, l.16 LJ, III, 257. Letter of Jan. 22, 1816.

p.568, l.22 LJ, III, 259. Letter of Jan. 29, 1816.

p.569, l.2 Fox, pp. 107-8.

p.569, l.6 Fox, p. 104.

p.569, l.15 Fox, pp. 105-6.

p.569, l.23 Fox, p. 108. Letter of Selina Doyle to Lady Byron, Jan. 26, 1816.

p.569, l.31 *Astarte*, p. 41. Presumably from Lady Byron's narratives.

p.570, l.6 Broughton, II, 207.

p.570, l.21 Fox, p. 105.

p.570, l.29 Fox, p. 106.

p.570, l.36 Fox, p. 109. Letter of Jan. 25, 1816.

p.571, l.6 LJ, III, 300-1. Letter of Jan. 25, 1816.

*p.571, l.*9 Mayne: *Lady Byron*, 207.

*p.571, l.*14 Broughton, II, 264.

*p.571, l.*17 Mayne: *Lady Byron*, p. 208.

*p.571, l.*22 Fox, p. 109.

*p.571, l.*26 Broughton, II, 217.

*p.571, l.*38 Broughton, II, 209–10.

*p.572, l.*28 Broughton, II, 211–13.

*p.572, l.*34 *Astarte*, pp. 322–3.

*p.573, l.*3 LJ, III, 302. Letter of Feb. 3, 1816.

*p.573, l.*13 Mayne: *Lady Byron*, p. 210; Broughton, II, 216. Letter of Feb. 3, 1816.

*p.573, l.*16 LJ, III, 303. Letter of Feb. 4, 1816.

*p.573, l.*25 Broughton, II, 217.

*p.573, l.*29 Hobhouse diary, entry for Feb. 5, 1816. From the MS., Berg Collection, New York Public Library.

*p.573, l.*36 Broughton, II, 219.

*p.574, l.*6 LBC, I, 307. Letter of Feb. 5, 1816.

*p.574, l.*21 Broughton, II, 220.

*p.574, l.*33 Broughton, II, 235–6. Letter of Feb. 7, 1816.

*p.575, l.*2 Broughton, II, 223. Letter of Feb. 6, 1816.

*p.575, l.*10 Broughton, II, 237–8. Letter of Feb. 7, 1816.

*p.575, l.*21 Mayne: *Lady Byron*, p. 212.

*p.575, l.*30 Broughton, II, 230. Letter of Feb. 7, 1816.

*p.576, l.*9 Hobhouse diary, entry of Feb. 9, 1816. From the MS., Berg Collection, New York Public Library.

*p.576, l.*12 Byron eventually, probably sometime before he left England in April, did accept payment from Murray for the poems, which were published together in a thin volume.

*p.576, l.*17 Hobhouse diary, entry of Feb. 9, 1816. From the MS., Berg Collection, New York Public Library.

*p.576, l.*25 Broughton, II, 242. Letter of Feb. 11, 1816.

*p.576, l.*29 LJ, III, 303–4. Letter of Feb. 7, 1816.

*p.576, l.*34 LJ, III, 306–7. No date is given, but it was probably written Feb. 11 or 12, 1816.

*p.577, l.*24 Hobhouse diary, entry of Feb. 12, 1816. From the MS., Berg Collection, New York Public Library.

*p.578, l.*7 LJ, III, 309.

*p.578, l.*9 Broughton, II, 259.

*p.578, l.*25 LJ, III, 310. Letter of Feb. 13, 1816.

*p.579, l.*3 LJ, III, 313. Letter of Feb. 15, 1816.

*p.579, l.*11 Hobhouse diary, entry of Feb. 16, 1816. From the MS., Berg Collection, New York Public Library.

*p.579, l.*23 Broughton, II, 258.

*p.580, l.*4 Fox, pp. 109–10.

*p.580, l.*12 Broughton, II, 272–3.

*p.581, l.*2 LJ, III, 262. Letter of Feb. 16, 1816.

*p.581, l.*19 First published in *Poems*, 1816. He told Lady Hardy (June 10, 1823—Gore, p. 52): "She, poor thing, has made a sad affair of it altogether. I had the melancholy task of prophesying as much many years ago in some lines of which the three or four first stanzas only were printed, and of course without names or allusions and with a *false* date."

p.581, l.27 Gore, p. 52. This concluding stanza is in quite a different tone and may have been written later. It was not printed with the poem in 1816.

p.581, l.32 Moore, II, 816.

p.582, l.10 Fox, p. 59. Quoted from the Lovelace papers.

p.583, l.15 Broughton, II, 285-6. No date is given, but it must be Feb. 23, the day after Lady Byron's interview with Lushington. Byron's reply, dated the 23rd, was probably written the same day.

p.583, l.20 Ilchester, p. 277.

p.583, l.28 Broughton, II, 287. The date given by Hobhouse for this note is "March," but in his diary of Feb. 29 he mentioned Byron's having received it.

p.583, l.32 Hobhouse diary, entry of Feb. 29, 1816. From the MS., Berg Collection, New York Public Library.

p.583, l.37 Hobhouse was a little offended by Hunt's audacity in his dedication, but when he met him at Byron's on April 3 he found him "a very agreeable man—one and thirty—and very unassuming notwithstanding his dedication to Rimini beginning 'My dear Byron.'" (Hobhouse diary, entry of April 3. From the MS., Berg Collection, New York Public Library.)

p.584, l.3 LJ, III, 265.

p.584, l.9 Lushington's memoranda on the financial settlement after talking with Hanson gave Byron some cause for concern. He stated that Lady Byron's fortune of £ 20,000 yielded £ 1,000 yearly interest; that, according to Hanson's statement to Hoar at the time of the marriage, the rents from the Newstead estates amounted to £ 3,200 a year. (This was an exaggeration, for collections were so irregular and so much was sunk into repairs that the residue was scarce £ 1,500.) Hanson had also given Lushington an exaggerated picture of the value of other property, including Rochdale, which had cost Byron money and never yielded a farthing. According to Lushington's summary:

"By the marriage settlement, £ 300 per an. was secured to Lady B. as pin-money, and £ 2000 per an. for jointure. The Newstead Estate is security for the jointure, and the pin-money is to be paid by the Trustees who receive Lady B's marriage portion.

"£ 3000 per an. is also secured to a son (if any) upon the Newstead Estate, and there are certain provisions for raising portions for younger children. . . .

"Lady Byron will be satisfied with £ 200 per an. in addition to her pin-money, during the life of Lady Noel, and at her decease one half of the Noel property. . . .

"Under this arrangement Lord B. will claim immediately a pecuniary profit of £ 500 per an. in consequence of his marriage with Lady B., and be relieved from all expence of maintaining her.

"At the death of Lady Noel he will be benefited to the amount of from £ 3500 to 4000 per an." (LJ, III, 319.)

p.584, l.11 Hobhouse diary, entry of March 1. From the MS., Berg Collection, New York Public Library.

p.584, l.17 Hobhouse diary, entry of March 5, 1816. From the MS., Berg Collection, New York Public Library.

p.584, l.23 The interview between Annabella and Augusta took place on March 5. (Broughton, II, 296.)

p.584, l.30 Broughton, II, 290.

p.584, l.33 Broughton, II, 260.

p.585, l.6 Hobhouse diary, entry of March 6, 1816. From the MS., Berg Collection, New York Public Library.

p.586, l.3 Unpublished letter, Murray MSS.

p.586, l.16 LJ, III, 271. Letter of March 6, 1816. It was after this seizure that Byron decided to put the books up for auction.

p.586, l.18 Moore, I, 646.

p.586, l.24 LJ, III, 272. Letter of March 8, 1816.

p.586, l.33 One rumor, hinting at some irregular sexual approach, persisted through the nineteenth century. The gossip that was spread at the time furnished the basis of two items of "curiosa," to use a book-dealers' euphemism, one called *Don Leon* and another (a sequel) *Leon to Annabella*, copies of which are still extant in some public and private libraries. The poems seem to be the product of someone who was no amateur and who knew many of the facts of Byron's life astonishingly well. G. Wilson Knight ("Who Wrote 'Don Leon'?" pp. 67–79) conjectures that the poem was written about 1833, and from internal evidence ascribes the authorship to George Colman the Younger, whom Byron knew during his years of fame and whom he thought even superior to Sheridan in wit. *Don Leon* contains (Knight's summary, pp. 67–8): ". . . a powerful attack on the prevailing laws, which included the death-penalty, against homosexual practices . . . a supposedly autobiographical account of Byron's youthful anxieties regarding his own instincts and the passionate friendships to which they led him . . . an intimate description, supposedly by Byron, of an irregular relation with his wife during her pregnancy, leading on to the second poem, *Leon to Annabella*, which tells the story of the marriage break. . . ."

p.587, l.4 Wilmot apparently had just been let into the secret of the further confessions of Annabella to Dr. Lushington.

p.588, l.4 Hobhouse diary, entry of March 8, 1816. From the MS., Berg Collection, New York Public Library.

p.588, l.13 Broughton, II, 302–4.

p.588, l.14 Hobhouse (diary entry of March 9, 1816) said "he as it appeared to me assented," but when Hanson afterward urged him to make no commitment on the Kirkby property, Byron almost came to blows with Wilmot, who understood that general assent had been given to the proposition concerning the division of the property. Byron maintained, however, that he had agreed to the proposal only as a point to be arbitrated.

p.588, l.21 Fox, p. 112.

p.589, l.7 Fox, p. 113.

p.589, l.34 *Astarte*, p. 47.

p.590, l.3 *Astarte*, p. 203. Letter of May 12, 1816.

p.590, l.17 *Astarte*, pp. 55–6.

p.590, l.28 Hobhouse diary, entry of March 13, 1816. From the MS., Berg Collection, New York Public Library.

p.590, l.30 *Astarte*, pp. 48–9.

p.590, l.34 Hobhouse, after consultation with Hanson, Lushington, and others, worked out with Colonel Doyle the statement of the questions to be arbitrated, which were referred to Sir Samuel Shepherd, who delivered his award on March 27, 1816. He decided that Byron "should *now* bind himself, on the event of Lady Noel's death, to appoint an Arbitrator who, together with an Arbitrator then to be appointed by Lady Byron, should decide whether any and what portion of that Estate should be secured to the sole and separate Use of Lady Byron during the life of Lord Byron." (*LJ*, III, 323–5.)

p.590, l.35 Hobhouse diary, entry of March 22, 1816. From the MS., Berg Collection, New York Public Library.

p.591, l.2 *LJ*, III, 271, 275.

p.591, l.11 *LJ*, III, 270. Letter of March 1, 1816.

p.591, l.28 *LJ*, III, 429. There is no date on this letter, which was signed "E. Trefusis, 21, Noley Place, Mary le Bonne," but since in an early letter she mentioned Shelley's *Alastor*, which was published in March 1816, it is probable that she made her first overtures to him in that month.

p.591, l.35 *LJ*, III, 430.

p.592, l.3 *LJ*, III, 430.

p.593, l.3 Claire Clairmont's journal, Sept. 17, 1814. Quoted in White, I, 366.

p.593, l.34 *LJ*, III, 431–3.

p.594, l.8 *LJ*, III, 434–5.

p.594, l.17 *LBC*, I, 111. Letter of Nov. 26, 1812.

p.594, l.24 *LJ*, III, 436. Short note dated "Saturday Morning."

p.595, l.23 The first draft of the poem was dated March 18.

p.595, l.27 Broughton, II, 316.

p.595, l.38 Hobhouse diary, entry of March 28. From the MS., Berg Collection, New York Public Library. Byron was further incensed by the attitude of Lady Byron's friends toward Augusta.

p.596, l.29 From the original manuscript, Murray MSS. (With some inaccuracies in "*To Lord Byron*," p. 71.)

p.597, l.9 Hunt: *Lord Byron*, I, 7–8.

p.597, l.14 Ibid., I, 8–9.

p.597, l.15 "On the Star of 'The Legion of Honour,'" published anonymously as "From the French" in *The Examiner* of April 7, 1816.

p.597, l.16 Hobhouse diary.

p.598, l.8 Medwin, II, 17–18.

p.598, l.21 Murray's biographer (Smiles, I, 361–2) says the books were sold "by Mr. Evans at his house, 26, Pall Mall, on the 5th of April, and the following day." And Byron's letter to Murray of April 6, 1816 (*LJ*, III, 279–80), seems to indicate that the sale was completed on that date. But Hobhouse wrote distinctly in his diary under date of Monday, April 8: "This day I went to the sale of Lord Byron's books and bought 34 £ worth. . . ."

p.598, l.23 Hobhouse diary, entry of April 8, 1816.

p.598, l.26 Ibid.

p.598, l.29 *Astarte*, p. 50.

p.598, l.34 Moore, I, 665.

p.599, l.7 Hazlitt: *Conversations of James Northcote*, No. 15. The gossip was paraphrased from Northcote by Hazlitt.

p.599, l.17 Hobhouse diary, entry of April 9, 1816.

p.599, l.23 Broughton, II, 324.

p.599, l.28 Entry of April 13, 1816.

p.599, l.31 Hobhouse diary, entry of April 14, 1816.

p.600, l.12 These "Stanzas to Augusta," apparently the last poetic composition of Byron before he left England, are not to be confused with those of the same title written in Switzerland, beginning "Though the day of my Destiny's over," which carried a more frank love theme.

p.600, l.17 A copy of this poem is endorsed by Murray: "Given to me (and I believe composed by Ld. B.), Friday, April 12, 1816." (*Poetry*, III, 545n.)

p.601, l.4 *LJ*, III, 282. Letter of April 15, 1816.

p.601, l.13 Blessington, p. 191.

p.601, l.29 *Astarte*, pp. 51–2. Letter of April [14,] 1816.

p.601, l.33 Hobhouse diary, entry of April 15, 1816.

p.603, l.6 Pryse Gordon: *Personal Memoirs*, II, 328.

p.603, l.8 Unpublished letter, April 16, 1816, Yale University Library.

p.603, l.18 Murray MSS. (Published with some omissions and inaccuracies in "To Lord Byron," p. 209.)

p.604, l.6 Murray MSS. (Published, with some variations, in Grylls: *Claire Clairmont*, pp. 60–1.)

p.605, l.5 Murray MSS. (Part in "To Lord Byron," p. 208.)

p.605, l.24 *LJ*, III, 435–6.

p.605, l.38 Hobhouse diary, entry of April 21, 1816.

p.606, l.7 Unpublished letter of April 22, 1816, Morgan Library.

p.606, l.14 Hobhouse diary, entry of April 22, 1816.

p.606, l.19 *A Catalogue of Music Composed by Mr. Nathan*, published after the first edition of the *Hebrew Melodies*, lists "The Fair Haidee" (from the first *Childe Harold* volume), "My Life, I love You" ("Maid of Athens"), "Thou Art Not False," and several others, eleven in all, including well-known lyrical passages from *Lara*, *The Bride of Abydos*, and *The Giaour*. (Slater, p. 87.)

p.606, l.26 Nathan, p. 87.

p.607, l.2 Grylls: *Claire Clairmont*, p. 61.

p.607, l.11 Murray MSS. (Published, with some variations, in Grylls: *Claire Clairmont*, p. 61.)

p.607, l.20 *LJ*, III, 284n. Byron sent Rushton back home from Geneva with Scrope Davies. Only Fletcher, of the servants who left England with him, accompanied him to Italy.

p.607, l.25 Hobhouse diary, entry of April 23, 1816.

p.607, l.27 Polidori: *Diary*, p. 26.

p.607, l.28 Hobhouse diary, entry of April 23, 1816.

p.607, l.34 Hobhouse diary, entry of April 24, 1816. Byron told Hanson the seizure was for "the half year's rent." (*LJ*, III, 283.)

p.608, l.4 Hobhouse diary, entry of April 24, 1816.

p.608, l.10 Astarte, p. 53. Paraphrased from letter of Dr. Lushington to Lady Byron, May 6, 1816.

p.608, l.17 Hobhouse diary, entry of April 25, 1816.

p.608, l.18 Astarte, p. 53.

Notes to Chapter XVI

P.609, l.12 Childe Harold, III, 5.

p.610, l.4 LBC, II, 2–3. The letter is dated "Ostend, April 27th, 1816," but Byron's statement, "We got in last night very well," suggests that it was really the 26th, since they left Dover on the morning of the 25th.

p.610, l.9 Polidori: *Diary*, pp. 32–3.

p.610, l.11 Polidori: *Diary*, p. 34.

p.610, l.15 Ibid., 36–7.

p.610, l.22 LJ, III, 332. Letter dated "Bruxelles, May 1st, 1816."

p.610, l.29 LJ, III, 377. Letter of Oct. 15, 1816.

p.610, l.34 LBC, II, 5. Letter of May 1, 1816.

p.611, l.8 Pryse Gordon: *Personal Memoirs*, II, 319–20.

p.611, l.14 Polidori's account in his diary (p. 62) strangely fails to mention Pryse Gordon as having been one of the party during the trip to Waterloo.

p.611, l.22 Pryse Gordon: *Personal Memoirs*, II, 322–3.

p.611, l.27 Polidori: *Diary*, p. 213. Letter of May 11, 1816, from Koblenz.

p.611, l.34 Pryse Gordon: *Personal Memoirs*, II, 325. The verses were those which later appeared as stanzas 17 and 18 of the third canto of *Childe Harold*.

p.612, l.6 Childe Harold, III, 6.

p.612, l.12 Childe Harold, III, 13.

p.612, l.27 Childe Harold, III, 21, 28.

p.613, l.5 Childe Harold, III, 42.

p.613, l.11 Polidori: *Diary*, p. 72.

p.613, l.28 Hobhouse diary, entry of April 26, 1816.

p.614, l.11 Hobhouse diary, entry of April 27, 1816.

p.614, l.22 Morgan, II, 201–2.

p.615, l.6 Torrens, I, 112.

p.615, l.16 Morgan, II, 202.

p.615, l.22 Frampton, p. 287. Letter of C. Lemon to Lady H. Frampton, June 28, 1816.

p.615, l.28 Hobhouse diary, entry of May 10, 1816.

p.616, l.10 "To Lord Byron," p. 77.

p.616, l.25 Astarte, p. 54.

p.617, l.29 Astarte, p. 199. Letter of May 6, 1816.

p.617, l.36 Frederick Leigh was born by the second week in May. (*Astarte*, p. 204.)

p.618, l.6 Broughton, II, 363. Letter of May 21, 1816.

p.618, l.25 Murray MSS. (Part of this letter is in *"To Lord Byron,"* pp. 210–12.)

p.618, l.32 Polidori: *Diary*, p. 75.

p.619, l.1 Ibid., pp. 77–8.

p.619, l.4 Ibid., pp. 78–9. They saw in the collection of Professor Wallraf, joint founder of the famous Wallraf-Richartz Museum in Cologne, works by Poussin, Claude Lorraine, Tintoretto, Rembrandt, Teniers, and Albrecht Dürer.

p.619, l.11 Unpublished portion of letter of May 16, 1816. Murray MSS.; Hobhouse proofs.

p.619, l.17 Polidori (*Diary*, p. 87, entry of May 13, 1816) wrote: "This below is what L[ord] B[yron] wrote to Mrs. L[eigh] some days ago: written May 11 on Rhine-banks." These are the lines (*Childe Harold*, III, four stanzas following stanza 55, which is obviously addressed to Augusta) which Byron enclosed in his letter of May 11, 1816, from Coblenz. (See Augusta's letter to Hobhouse, May 21, 1816, Broughton, II, 363.)

p.619, l.27 Williams, p. 122. Williams's journal entry of Jan. 2, 1822. Moore (II, 30) and Medwin (II, 64) give variant versions of this episode.

p.619, l.32 *LBC*, II, 7. Letter of May 16, 1816.

p.619, l.37 Polidori: *Diary*, pp. 88–90.

p.620, l.5 *Childe Harold*, III, note 14 (13 in later editions). The bones, like other relics collected by Byron abroad, were sent to his publisher and still remain in the Murrays' Byron collection.

p.620, l.11 *Childe Harold*, III, 68.

p.620, l.20 Polidori: *Diary*, p. 97.

p.620, l.38 Murray MSS. (Published, with slight variation, in Grylls: *Claire Clairmont*, p. 64.)

p.621, l.14 Polidori: *Diary*, p. 98.

p.621, l.25 Murray MSS. (In Grylls: *Claire Clairmont*, p. 64.)

p.621, l.31 This must be the meaning, although Polidori's phrasing (*Diary*, p. 99) is cryptic: "Went into boat, rowed across to Diodati; cannot have it for three years; English family. Crossed again; I went; L[ord] B[yron] back."

p.622, l.1 Moore, II, 22–3.

p.622, l.12 Polidori: *Diary*, p. 101.

p.622, l.17 Ibid., p. 104; Engel, p. 15.

p.622, l.27 Engel, p. 15. Hentsch's property, Mon Repos, is now a city park of Geneva.

p.623, l.12 Polidori: *Diary*, p. 110.

p.623, l.16 Häusermann: "Shelley's House at Geneva," pp. 183–9. Häusermann based his study on Genevese State Archives and local tradition at Montalègre.

p.623, l.32 Moore, II, 23–4. Moore does not name his informant, but it is obviously Mary Shelley, "a person who was of these parties," for he saw her and corresponded with her while he was writing his life of Byron.

p.624, l.11 *Childe Harold*, III, 86, 90.

p.624, l.16 *Childe Harold*, III, 73.

p.624, l.23 *Childe Harold*, III, 74–5.

p.625, l.4 Polidori: *Diary*, p. 120.

p.625, l.13 Moore, II, 27

p.625, l.16 Moore, II, 31. On the 7th, Polidori wrote in his diary: "went in boat with L[ord] B[yron]; agreed with boatman for English boat." (*Diary*, p. 120.) Byron wrote to Hobhouse on June 23: "At the present writing I am on my way on a water-tour round the Lake Leman, and am thus far proceeded in a pretty open boat which I bought and navigate—it is an English one, and was brought lately from Bordeaux." (*LBC*, II, 11.) Chapuisat (*L'Auberge de Sécheron*, opposite p. 136) shows a picture of the "Chaloupe de Lord Byron," from a design by Albert Hentsch. It looks low to the water, and has two main sails on separate masts, besides small ones fore and aft.

p.625, l.30 According to local tradition, Byron composed part of *Childe Harold* and other poems on the balcony with the lake and the mountains before him. Another tradition is that he used to write under an apple tree in the garden.

p.626, l.25 Moore, II, 30. Moore's informant was Mary Shelley.

p.626, l.31 Moore, II, 29.

p.627, l.7 Moore, I, 24. Moore identifies his informant as Mary Shelley in *Prose and Verse*, p. 431.

p.627, l.17 *Astarte*, p. 267. Letter of Sept. 8, 1816.

p.627, l.24 Murray MSS. Undated note.

p.627, l.34 Medwin, I, 11.

p.628, l.7 Glenbervie, II, 160. Entry of July 3, 1816.

p.628, l.17 Moore, II, 30n.

p.628, l.21 Polidori: *The Vampyre*, pp. ix–x.

p.628, l.23 Moore, II, 30.

p.628, l.26 Polidori: *Diary*, p. 122.

p.628, l.31 Moore, II, 31.

p.628, l.33 Polidori: *Diary*, p. 125.

p.628, l.34 Mary Shelley: *Frankenstein*, 1831 ed., Preface.

p.628, l.37 *The Letters of Mary W. Shelley*, I, 68. Letter of April 27, [1819].

p.629, l.7 *LJ*, IV, 287n.

p.629, l.12 The fragment was published at the end of *Mazeppa* in 1819.

p.629, l.24 Mary Shelley: *Frankenstein*, 1831 ed., Preface.

p.630, l.4 Polidori: *Diary*, pp. 127–8.

p.630, l.6 Polidori: *The Vampyre*, p. xv.

p.630, l.10 Polidori: *Diary*, p. 128. Byron, writing to Murray on May 15, 1819, said Shelley "certainly had the fit of phantasy which Polidori describes [*The Vampyre*, p. xv], though *not exactly* as he describes it." (*LJ*, IV, 297.)

p.630, l.12 There is some confusion about the date of their departure and return. Shelley, who gave a day-by-day account of the journey in a letter dated July 12, 1816, published with the *History of a Six Weeks' Tour*, says that they left Montalègre on June 23. But this letter, written for publication some time later, seems to be in error in the date, for Byron's letter of June 23 is from Evian, their second night's stop. And Polidori in his diary of June 22 wrote: "L[ord] B[yron] and Shelley went to Vevay."

p.630, l.17 Shelley: *History of a Six Weeks' Tour,* letter of July 12, 1816.

p.630, l.29 Ibid.

p.630, l.37 *LJ,* IV, 296–7. Letter of May 15, 1819, to Murray.

p.631, l.6 Shelley: *History of a Six Weeks' Tour,* letter of July 12, 1816.

p.631, l.8 Byron spelled the name Bonnivard, a form used by later chroniclers, but without authority in Bonivard's day.

p.631, l.11 The fifth column is said to be the one to which Bonivard was chained. Byron's name is carved on the southern side of the third column.

p.631, l.19 Shelley: *History of a Six Weeks' Tour,* letter of July 12, 1816.

p.631, l.21 Moore, II, 33.

p.631, l.27 *Childe Harold,* III, 100.

p.631, l.30 This is a conjecture based partly on the fact that there is nothing topical in these verses compared with those on Clarens, and that Byron mentioned on June 23 at Evian having written 111 stanzas and told Murray on the 27th, writing from Ouchy, that he had written 117, which would just account for those concerning Clarens.

p.632, l.6 See *Childe Harold,* III, 81–3.

p.632, l.13 Moore, II, 33. It is probable that Byron revised and corrected and perhaps even added to the poem before he later turned it over to Claire to copy some time after his return to Diodati.

p.632, l.20 When he published the poem, Byron admitted that he was not fully acquainted with Bonivard's history when he wrote it, but instead of revising it to conform to the facts of biography, he appended an account of Bonivard's life furnished by Victor de Bonstetten. (Unpublished letter of Byron, dated "Diodati, July 30, 1816," without the name of the addressee but very likely written to Bonstetten, in the University of Texas Library.) Actually, the details supplied by Bonstetten were from a not quite accurate account by the Swiss naturalist Jean Senebier (1786), which Bonstetten apparently did not make clear to Byron that he had copied out. Bonivard was confined in the dungeon at Chillon only four years (1532–6). There is no authority for Byron's story of Bonivard's brothers dying in chains by his side, nor of his hair turning gray while he was in prison. (See Amstel, pp. 821–9.)

p.632, l.32 *LJ,* III, 334. Byron made contact with another "free spirit" at Lausanne. He later wrote Rogers: "I have a French copy of *Vathek* which I bought at Lausanne." (*LJ,* IV, 209. Letter of March 3, 1818.)

p.632, l.34 The date of the return is again left uncertain because of the discrepancy of contemporary accounts. Polidori's diary, which ought to be most trustworthy as written at the time, records their arrival on July 1. (*Diary,* p. 135.) The probability seems to be that they left Ouchy on *Sunday* the 30th and arrived the evening of July 1.

p.633, l.14 Moore, II, 33.

p.633, l.18 At the end of Claire's fair copy is written: "End of Canto Third. Byron. July 4, 1816, Diodati." (*Poetry,* II, 289n.)

p.633, l.25 *Childe Harold,* III, 117.

p.633, l.30 See *Poetry,* II, 214.

p.634, l.13 Murray MSS. (Part of this is in *"To Lord Byron,"* p. 213.)

p.634, l.22 Murray MSS. Part of this is in *"To Lord Byron,"* p. 214, where the date is given as Aug. 26—probably from internal evidence:

Claire mentions her imminent departure and the Shelley party actually left for England on Aug. 29—but Claire has clearly written "Monday, July 16, 1816" at the top of the letter. (The 16th was a Tuesday, so she may have mistaken either the day of the week or the day of the month.) It seems obvious that the departure she speaks of was to Chamouni, not to England.

p.634, l.31 Peck, I, 464. Yet on the 22nd from Chamouni Shelley wrote to Byron: "I wish the wonders and graces of these 'palaces of Nature' would induce you to visit them whilst we, who so much value your society, remain yet near them. . . ." (*LBC*, II, 14–15.)

p.634, l.37 On July 22, Byron told Murray that he had been at Coppet "ten days ago." (*LJ*, III, 338–9.)

p.635, l.2 Polidori: *The Vampyre*, p. xiii.

p.635, l.6 *LJ*, IV, 300–1. Letter of May 15, 1819.

p.635, l.10 Medwin, I, 12.

p.635, l.15 Caroline Lamb slightly altered this final couplet of *The Corsair*, which read, as Byron published it:

> He left a Corsair's name to other times,
> Linked with one virtue, and a thousand crimes.

p.635, l.23 *LJ*, III, 339. Letter of July 22, 1816.

p.636, l.6 A bon mot of Rocca in his conversation with Byron was variously reported by diarists of the time. As H. W. Häusermann has pointed out (*The Genevese Background*, p. 57), the most accurate account is no doubt that given by Mme de Staël herself in a letter of Sept. 8, 1816, to Dr. Marcet: *"Lord Byron se plaignit de Genève l'autre jour et Rocca lui dit très spirituellement 'croyez-moi, mylord, n'allez pas dans cette caverne d'honnêtes gens.'"* (Byron had been abusing the Genevese as dull, tiresome, stupid people whose strict religion and morality made them troublesome.)

p.636, l.9 Polidori: *Diary*, p. 146.

p.636, l.13 *LJ*, V, 337. Letter of Aug. 4, 1821.

p.636, l.18 Polidori: *Diary*, p. 147.

p.636, l.28 Hobhouse diary, entry of June 18, 1816. Berg Collection, New York Public Library.

p.636, l.32 Blessington, p. 134.

p.636, l.38 The "Monody" was spoken by Mrs. Davison at Drury Lane on the opening night, Sept. 7, and published in a thin volume by Murray on Sept. 9, 1816. Byron had wanted Miss Somerville to speak the lines. (*B-SP*, I, 340–1. Letter of July 20, 1816.)

p.637, l.3 *LJ*, III, 366. Letter of Sept. 29, 1816.

p.638, l.24 The manuscript is dated "July 24, 1816."

p.638, l.35 *Astarte*, p. 218. Letter of June 19, 1816.

p.639, l.12 *Astarte*, p. 220. Letter of June 28, 1816.

p.639, l.17 Hodgson, II, 35. The last part of the sentence, omitted in the Hodgson *Memoir*, is supplied in *Astarte*, p. 61.

p.639, l.21 *Astarte*, pp. 223–4. Letter of July 3, 1816.

p.639, l.34 *Astarte*, pp. 230–2. Letter of July 11, 1816.

p.639, l.38 *Astarte*, p. 60.

p.640, l.5 Hobhouse diary, entry of July 13, 1816.

p.640, l.15 Astarte, pp. 233–4. Letter of July 15, 1816.
p.640, l.22 Astarte, p. 236. Letter of July 17, 1816.
p.640, l.25 Astarte, p. 237. Letter of July 17, 1816.
p.640, l.35 Astarte, pp. 239–40. Letter of July 18, 1816.
p.641, l.3 Astarte, p. 243. Letter of July 23, 1816.
p.641, l.8 Astarte, p. 244. Letter of July 27, 1816.
p.641, l.14 Astarte, p. 245. Letter of July 28, 1816.
p.641, l.30 Astarte, pp. 246–8.

p.642, l.2 Byron told Moore (*LJ*, IV, 11–12; letter of Nov. 17, 1816): "Madame de Staël lent it [*Glenarvon*] me to read from Copet last autumn." But from his earlier letter to Rogers it appears that he had it in July.

p.642, l.4 LJ, III, 342. From Pope's *Imitations of Horace*, Satire 1, lines 83–4.

p.642, l.10 LJ, IV, 12. Letter of Nov. 17, 1816.

p.642, l.21 LJ, III, 337–8. Letter of July 22, 1816. Murray, in Byron's behalf, brought suit for an injunction, and the case of "Lord Byron *v.* James Johnston" was argued in the Court of Chancery on Nov. 28, 1816. Byron's lawyer said "it was not the wish of his Noble Client that the defendant should be restrained from publishing his rhymes; all he wished was, that he should be prohibited from selling them as his, the plaintiff's, poetry, for it was neither grammar nor poetry that he was vending." (*LJ*, IV, 19–20n. Quoted from the account in the *Morning Chronicle*, Nov. 30, 1816.)

p.642, l.31 Blessington, pp. 24–5.

p.643, l.3 Blessington, p. 84.

p.643, l.12 Chapuisat, p. 143.

p.643, l.26 Mary Shelley's Journal, pp. 55–7.

p.644, l.6 Grylls: *Claire Clairmont*, p. 262. Letter of about 1870.

p.644, l.10 Claire copied all the shorter poems Byron had written in July with the exception of the "Sonnet on Chillon" and the "Sonnet to Lake Leman," which are in Byron's own hand in the 119-page quarto manuscript volume containing Claire's transcriptions of the poems written at Diodati. (*Poetry*, II, 214.) On Aug. 14, Mary recorded in her journal: "Shelley goes up there [to Diodati], and Clare goes up to copy." (*Mary Shelley's Journal*, p. 57.)

p.644, l.13 LBC, II, 12. Letter of June 23, 1816.

p.644, l.19 Mary Shelley's Journal, p. 57.

p.644, l.26 LJ, V, 37. Letter of June 7, 1820.

p.644, l.32 Byron told Lady Blessington that he wrote his lines on Lady Byron's illness after reading an account of it in a newspaper. (Blessington, p. 48.) Mary Shelley wrote in her *Journal* (p. 61) on Aug. 23: "Shelley goes up to Diodati, and then in the boat with Lord Byron, who has heard bad news of Lady Byron, and is in bad spirits concerning it."

p.645, l.4 Les Dernières Années de Lord Byron, par l'auteur de Robert Emmett [Comtesse d'Haussonville], Paris, 1874, p. 95. (Quoted in Escarpit, p. 240.)

p.645, l.7 LJ, III, 343. Byron was forever after grateful to Mme de Staël for her sympathetic interest in his domestic tragedy. According to Medwin, he said: "I believe Madame de Staël did her utmost to bring about a reconciliation between us. She was the best creature in the world." (Medwin, II, 24.)

p.645, l.12 Moore, II, 36.

p.645, l.19 First published in Moore, I, 38–41.

p.645, l.32 Astarte, p. 265.

p.645, l.36 Broughton, II, 1.

p.646, l.5 Hobhouse diary, entries of Aug. 27 and 28, 1816; *Mary Shelley's Journal*, p. 61.

p.646, l.17 Murray MSS. No date.

p.646, l.21 Mary Shelley's Journal, p. 61.

p.647, l.5 LJ, III, 346. Letter of Aug. 28, 1816.

p.647, l.12 Hobhouse diary, entry of Aug. 30, 1816.

p.647, l.17 LJ, III, 352.

p.647, l.24 Broughton, II, 9. The inscription in Shelley's hand, *"dimokratikos philanthropotatos kai atheos"* (democrat, lover of mankind, and atheist), still remained in the album at the Hôtel de Londres in Chamouni (not the Hôtel d'Angleterre, at which Hobhouse says Byron's party stopped) for some years to shock Southey and other English travelers. The fact seems to be that Shelley so inscribed his name in several inns along the route. It may have been the one at Sallanche that Byron effaced. (See White, I, 456, 714.)

p.647, l.35 LJ, III, 347–8n. Letter of Sept. 9, 1816.

p.648, l.16 Astarte, pp. 266–7. Letter of Sept. 8, 1816.

p.648, l.31 Astarte, pp. 249–50.

p.649, l.10 Astarte, pp. 253–4.

p.649, l.20 Astarte, p. 257. (Undated, but endorsed by Mrs. Villiers "Septr. 1816.")

p.649, l.28 Astarte, pp. 259–60. Letter dated "Sunday" [Sept. 15, 1816].

p.649, l.33 Astarte, pp. 261–2. Letter of Sept. 17, 1816.

p.650, l.5 Astarte, pp. 268–9.

p.650, l.14 Astarte, p. 270.

p.650, l.19 Hobhouse diary, entries of Sept. 12, 14.

p.650, l.24 Hobhouse diary, entry of Sept. 11; Medwin, I, 176–7.

p.650, l.30 Byron did not publish this poem, nor is there any indication that he intended to publish it. It first appeared in the *New Monthly Magazine*, Vol. XXXV (Aug. 1832), pp. 142–3.

p.651, l.2 Escarpit, pp. 240–1.

p.651, l.10 Escarpit, p. 241. It was Moore's opinion that the failure of this attempt, "after the violence he had done his own pride in the overture, was what first infused any mixture of resentment or bitterness into the feelings hitherto entertained by him throughout these painful differences." (Moore, II, 34.)

p.651, l.27 Hobhouse recorded the visit thus: "Two Carvellas Greeks dined here—one a physician the other student in law. . . . they were from the islands." (Hobhouse diary, entry of Sept. 14, 1816.) Mr. H. B. Forster, late of the British Council in Patras, discovered an unpublished letter of Byron to Nicolas Karvellas (written from Genoa to Karvellas in Pisa in 1823) in the public library of Zante and published it together with an account of the Karvellas brothers in *Symposium*, Autumn 1951, No. 3 (Published by the British Academy, Patras). (Republished in *Keats-Shelley Journal*, Vol. II [1953], pp. 73–7.)

p.651, l.32 LJ, III, 379. Letter of Nov. 1, 1816.

p.651, l.35 Polidori: *Diary*, p. 152.

p.651, l.36 Medwin, I, 123.

p.652, l.15 Astarte, pp. 271–3. Letter of Sept. 17, 1816.

p.652, l.34 LJ, III, 354–5. According to Hobhouse, they ascended the Dent de Jaman and spent the night at the small village of Montboven.

p.653, l.6 LJ, III, 357–8. Hobhouse identifies the 900-foot waterfall as the Staubbach.

p.653, l.18 LJ, III, 359–60.

p.653, l.27 LJ, III, 361.

p.653, l.33 LJ, III, 362.

p.653, l.33 Byron skipped a day in his dating, calling the 27th and 28th the 28th and 29th, as is apparent from Hobhouse's diary and the fact that Byron dated two letters from Diodati on Sept. 29.

p.654, l.4 LJ, III, 364.

p.654, l.8 LBC, II, 16. Letter of Sept. 11, 1816.

p.654, l.11 Smiles, I, 365.

p.654, l.17 Murray MSS.

p.654, l.21 Smiles, I, 367. Letter of Sept. 20, 1816.

p.655, l.7 Murray MSS. The greater part of this is printed in "*To Lord Byron*," pp. 219–22, but the date of the letter is given as Sept. 27, whereas in the MS. it is clearly written "Sunday, Sept. 29th, 1816." It is probable that Byron did not receive this before he left Switzerland.

p.655, l.19 LBC, II, 19.

p.656, l.7 Astarte, pp. 273–4. Letter of Oct. 1, 1816.

p.656, l.17 LJ, V, 37. Letter of June 7, 1820.

p.657, l.17 Manfred, Act I, Scene ii.

p.657, l.25 Manfred, Act II, Scene i.

p.658, l.10 Manfred, Act II, Scene ii.

p.658, l.14 Byron perhaps borrowed this spirit of evil from the Aherman of *Vathek*, adopting and modifying the spelling of the Greek and Latin writers who used the form Arimanius. (See *Poetry*, IV, 112n.)

p.658, l.34 Manfred, Act II, Scene iv.

p.659, l.10 Hobhouse diary, entry of Oct. 3, 1816.

p.659, l.13 LJ, III, 369. Letter of Sept. 30, 1816.

p.659, l.16 Hobhouse diary, entry of Oct. 5, 1816.

p.659, l.21 LJ, III, 368. Letter of Sept. 30, 1816.

p.659, l.29 Fatio, p. 60. Fatio quoted this episode from the account of Vernes-Prescott in his *Causeries d'un Octogénaire*.

Notes to Chapter XVII

P.660, l.3 Hobhouse diary, entry of Oct. 6, 1816. Most of the details of the trip given here are from the Hobhouse diary; the manuscript gives a much fuller account than is included in Broughton.

p.660, l.16 Hobhouse diary, entry of Oct. 10, 1816.

p.661, l.4 Hobhouse diary, entry of Oct. 12, 1816.

p.661, l.7 LJ, III, 375. Letter of Oct. 15, 1816.

p.661, l.15 In Broughton (II, 40) the name is spelled Carnuff, but in the manuscript the name can be made out as Carvellas.

p.661, l.22 Hobhouse diary, entry of Oct. 13, 1816.

p.662, l.11 LJ, III, 376. Letter of Oct. 15, 1816.

p.662, l.15 Hobhouse diary, entry of Oct 15, 1816.

p.662, l.25 Astarte, p. 275. Letter of Oct. 15, 1816.

p.662, l.31 Hobhouse diary, entry of Oct 17, 1816.

p.662, l.33 On Oct. 21 the poet Monti called on Byron and Hobhouse, bringing with him Silvio Pellico. (Broughton, II, 51.) And the next evening Hobhouse recorded: "B & I translated part of Francesca da Rimini till late." For further details of Byron's interest in Pellico, see Beatrice Corrigan: "Pellico's 'Francesca da Rimini': The First English Translation," *Italica*, Vol. XXXI, No. 4 (Dec. 1954), pp. 215–24.

p.662, l.37 Hobhouse diary, entry of Oct. 17, 1816.

p.663, l.5 Countess Guiccioli: *My Recollections of Lord Byron*, p. 203.

p.663, l.29 LJ, IV, 26–7. Letter of Dec. 24, 1816.

p.664, l.24 Galt, pp. 241–3.

p.665, l.7 Hobhouse diary, entries of Oct. 23 and 24, 1816.

p.665, l.11 Hobhouse diary, entry of Oct. 25, 1816.

p.665, l.15 LJ, III, 384. Letter of Nov. 6, 1816.

p.665, l.20 Astarte, pp. 276–7.

p.666, l.3 Astarte, pp. 277–8. Letter of Oct. 28, 1816.

p.666, l.6 Fox, p. 88.

p.666, l.23 Murray MSS. (Part in *"To Lord Byron,"* pp. 222–3.)

p.667, l.6 Polidori (*Diary*, pp 186–7) gives a detailed account of the affair, which is generally corroborated in Hobhouse's diary.

p.667, l.21 Galt, pp. 243–4.

p.667, l.25 Polidori: *Diary*, p. 187.

p.667, l.31 Hobhouse diary, entry of Oct. 29, 1816.

p.668, l.10 Galt, p. 244.

p.668, l.15 Hobhouse records a journey to the echo of Simonetta on Oct. 23, with Byron but does not mention M. Beyle as having been along.

p.668, l.20 Galt, p. 246.

p.669, l.21 Hobhouse diary, entries of Nov. 7, 8, and 9, 1816.

p.669, l.38 Hobhouse diary, entry of Nov. 10, 1816. Lady Dorchester has misdated the entry describing Byron's first arrival in Venice, putting Nov. 11 instead of 10; she has also misdated the entries of the following few days in the diary, putting each forward one day through the 13th. (Broughton, II, 58–61.)

p.670, l.24 Hobhouse diary, entry of Nov. 11, 1816.

p.670, l.37 Hobhouse diary, entry of Nov. 12, 1816.

p.671, l.4 Hobhouse diary, entry of Nov. 13, 1816.

p.672, l.19 LJ, IV, 7–8. Letter of Nov. 17, 1816.

p.673, l.18 LJ, IV, 14–16. Letter of Nov. 25, 1816.

p.673, l.30 LBC, II, 24.

p.674, l.4 LJ, IV, 9–10. Letter of Dec. 5, 1816.

p.674, l.7 LJ, IV, 19. Letter of Dec. 4, 1816.

p.674, l.15 LJ, IV, 22. Letter of Dec. 9, 1816.

p.674, l.20 LBC, II, 25.

p.674, l.36 Astarte, pp. 279–80.

p.675, l.6 B-SP, II, 378. Letter of Dec. 19, 1816.

p.675, l.24 B-SP, II, 378–9.

p.675, l.37 LBC, II, 26. Letter of Dec. 19, 1816.

p.676, l.5 See Gregor, pp. 316–20.

p.676, l.9 LJ, IV, 43–5.

p.676, l.16 Father Paschal: "Autobiographical Diary," quoted in a brochure, *Armenian Album on Byron*, published at S. Lazzaro, 1937.

p.676, l.20 Poetry, II, 213.

p.676, l.23 Poetry, IV, 3.

p.676, l.30 "To Lord Byron," pp. 78–9. Letter of Oct. 13, 1816.

p.676, l.36 The date of the letter, which was first published by Lord Lindsay in *The Times*, Sept. 7, 1869, is given by Lord Lovelace from a draft in Lady Byron's hand. (*Astarte*, p. 343n.)

p.677, l.11 Stowe, pp. 307–9. First printed in Lord Lindsay's letter to *The Times*, Sept. 7, 1869.

p.677, l.16 Smiles, I, 369.

p.677, l.32 Murray MSS. (Part of this letter is in "To Lord Byron," pp. 224–5.)

p.678, l.2 Murray MSS. (Part of this is in "To Lord Byron," p. 226.)

p.678, l.9 LBC, II, 20. Letter of Nov. 20, 1816.

p.678, l.28 LJ, IV, 30–1. Letter of Dec. 24, 1816.

p.679, l.4 The passage from here to the end of the sentence was omitted by Moore, and is here quoted from the MS. letter in the Murray collection.

p.679, l.31 LJ, IV, 39–41. Letter of Jan. 2, 1817.

p.680, l.4 B-SP, II, 391. Letter of Jan. 12, 1817.

p.680, l.12 Astarte, pp. 280–1. Letter of Jan. 13, 1817.

p.680, l.26 Letters of Mary W Shelley, I, 18. Letter of Jan. 13, 1817.

p.681, l.2 LBC, II, 29–31.

p.681, l.12 LBC, II, 32–3.

p.681, l.35 Murray MSS.; Hobhouse proofs. Letter of Jan. 20, 1817. This part of the letter was omitted in *LBC*.

p.683, l.4 LJ, IV, 49–52. Letter of Jan. 28, 1817.

p.683, l.12 LBC, II, 35. Letter of Feb. 3, 1817.

p.683, l.24 LJ, IV, 54–5.

p.683, l.27 LJ, IV, 57, 59. Letters of Feb. 25 and 28, 1817.

p.684, l.9 LJ, IV, 55–6.

p.684, l.23 LJ, IV, 60. Letter of Feb. 28, 1817.

p.684, l.26 Edinburgh Review, Vol. XXVII (Sept. 1816), pp. 58–67.

p.685, l.5 LJ, IV, 62–3. Letter of Feb. 28, 1817.

p.685, l.10 Quarterly Review, Vol. XVI (Oct. 1816), pp. 172–208. Murray had induced Scott to write the review. (Smiles, I, 374.)

p.685, l.13 LJ, IV, 65.

p.685, l.26 Astarte, p. 283. Letter of Feb. 25, 1817.

p.686, l.13 LJ, IV, 66–8. Letter of March 5, 1817.

p.686, l.21 LBC, II, 38.

p.686, l.30 LJ, IV, 78–9.

p.687, l.1 The asterisks indicate Moore's omission of the name.

p.687, l.2 LJ, IV, 81. Letter of March 25, 1817.

p.687, l.25 LJ, IV, 83–7. Letter of March 25, 1817.

p.687, l.30 B-SP, II, 403–4. Letter of March 31, 1817, to Hobhouse.

p.688, l.3 LJ, IV, 92–3. Letter of April 2, 1817.

p.688, l.12 LJ, IV, 98–9.

p.688, l.18 Frederic North, youngest son of George III's prime minister, became Earl of Guilford on the death of his elder brother in Pisa in Jan. 1817.

p.688, l.28 LJ, IV, 101–2. Letter of April 11, 1817.

p.689, l.5 LJ, IV, 107. Letter of April 14, 1817.

p.689, l.11 LJ, IV, 105. Letter of April 14, 1817. It was one of the Prepiani miniatures which Teresa Guiccioli later pronounced her favorite portrait of Byron.

p.689, l.15 LBC, II, 44–5. Letter of April 14, 1817.

p.689, l.33 The poetic drama *Pastor fido* of Giovanni Battista Guarini, contemporary of Tasso, was much admired by both Byron and Shelley. First published in 1590, it had gone into twenty editions by 1602.

p.689, l.35 LBC, II, 49. Letter of April 22, 1817.

p.690, l.5 The Lament of Tasso, lines 3–4.

p.690, l.11 The Lament of Tasso, lines 44–6.

p.690, l.14 Byron dated the manuscript, at the end of the 247th and final line, "The Apennines, April 20, 1817." (*Poetry*, IV, 152.)

p.690, l.34 LJ, IV, 112–14. Letter of April 26, 1817.

p.690, l.35 The statement in Broughton (II, 71n.) that Byron was at Rome "from May 5, 1817, to May 28, 1817," is obviously erroneous. He was at Foligno on April 26, and, eager as he was to get to Rome, it could not have taken him more than three days to reach his destination. On May 5 he told Murray that he had been there "some days." The matter seems to be settled by a letter of Hobhouse, then Lord Broughton, to Earl Stanhope, May 3, 1856: "Lord Byron came to Rome on the 29th of April, 1817, and left it on the 20th of May, 1817." (*LJ*, IV, 122n.) He must have departed shortly before Hobhouse left for Naples on May 21, for he was writing to his sister from Florence on May 27, and on the 30th he wrote to Murray from Venice.

p.691, l.5 Published in 1818.

p.691, l.14 LJ, IV, 115–16. Letter of May 5, 1817.

p.691, l.17 Two letters from W. C. Cartwright to Sir Rennel Rodd, now in the Keats-Shelley Memorial, Rome, give some authority to this tradition. On May 2, 1911, Cartwright wrote: "A great many years ago the sculptor Gibson one day in passing through the Piazza di Spagna pointed to the Balcony of the House the ground floor of which is now occupied by *Spithoever's Bookshop* [now succeeded by the Libraria Bocca] saying he had seen on it Lord Byron . . . the late Mr. Haase—owner of the Bookshop and—I think—of the house, was cognizant of this incident—*from Gibson* himself." Cartwright was born in 1826; Gibson lived 1790–1866. Cartwright continued: "I have repeatedly conversed with Mr. Haase on the matter. He told me he had ascertained that two *ladies*—at the time covered by Byron's presence in Rome—kept rooms which were let out to strangers visiting

Rome." For copies of the letters I am indebted to Signora Cacciatore, curator of the Keats-Shelley Memorial, and for information about Cartwright and Gibson to Professor Mario Praz.

p.691, l.29 LJ, IV, 119. Letter of May 9, 1817. Byron did, however, incorporate one impression of the immediate scene in the last act of *Manfred:* his description of the Colosseum at night in Act IV, Scene iv.

p.692, l.2 LJ, IV, 122. Letter of May 12, 1817, to Moore.

p.692, l.6 LJ, IV, 125. Letter of May 30, 1817.

p.692, l.20 Astarte, pp. 16–17.

p.692, l.26 Smiles, I, 383–4.

p.692, l.36 LJ, IV, 117–18. Letter of May 9, 1817.

p.693, l.9 Astarte, pp. 283–4. Letter of May 10, 1817.

p.693, l.26 Elze, p. 221.

p.694, l.28 LJ, IV, 125–6. Letter of May 30, 1817.

p.694, l.33 LJ, IV, 125.

p.694, l.36 Mary Shelley came to London on Jan. 26, 1817, to join her husband, who was concerned about the case before the Chancellor; Claire followed on Feb. 18 and joined the Shelleys at Marlow a month later. (*Mary Shelley's Journal*, pp. 75, 77, 78.)

p.695, l.8 LBC, II, 52–3. Letter of April 23, 1817.

p.695, l.24 LJ, IV, 124. Letter of May 27, 1817. (The words after "comfort" were omitted in *LJ* and are here supplied from proof sheets at John Murray's.)

p.695, l.27 LJ, IV, 124, letter of May 30, 1817; *LJ*, IV, 130, letter of June 4, 1817.

Notes to Chapter XVIII

P.696, l.8 Murray MSS.; Hobhouse proofs. Letter of May 30, 1817. Quoted from a sentence omitted from the letter as published in *LBC*.

p.696, l.10 Byron did not know very well what his accumulated debts had run up to in the years since his foolish minority. On July 3 he wrote Kinnaird that there was "a sum of six thousand pounds to a Mr. Sawbridge, an annuity (six thousand *principal* that is), and a bond to three thousand more to Mr. Claughton—this is all (I believe) except the Israelites." (Murray MSS.; Hobhouse proofs.) And on July 8 he told Hobhouse that Hanson was wrong in stating that the principal of the "Jewish annuities" was £9,000, "because altogether they did not amount to much more originally, and six thousand pounds have been paid off, which were originally guaranteed by Scrope Davies, to whom I reimbursed the money which he himself discharged a few years ago.

"Since I came of age I raised only one sum, between two and three thousand pounds principal, and subsequently another of six or seven *hundred pounds;* and of these, I paid off just before leaving England most of the interest, and *one principal* sum of *six hundred pounds,* reducing the annuity thereof, of which Mr. H. has the restored papers. . . . There were some others for which a Mrs. Massingberd (since dead) was security, but for these time can be taken, because they cannot come upon the legality of the transaction, being during minority. . . ." (Murray MSS.; Hobhouse proofs.)

p.696, l.11 LJ, IV, 179n.

p.697, l.7 Astarte, p. 285. Letter of June 3, 1817.

p.697, l.16 Astarte, p. 288. Letter of June 19, 1817.

p.697, l.27 LJ, IV, 127–9. Letter of June 4, 1817, to John Murray.

p.697, l.36 The house had passed into the hands of a certain Ferrighi, a Jew of Noventa Vicentina, from whom Byron rented it. (Meneghetti, p. 28.) While the house was traditionally known as the Villa Foscarini, according to Byron's Venetian bankers, Siri and Willhalm, the actual address was "alla Mira, Casa Trabucco N? 160, sulla Brenta." (Broughton Correspondence, Vol. I, B.M. Add. 36456, folio 419. Letter of July 12, 1817, Siri and Willhalm to Hobhouse.)

p.698, l.7 LJ, IV, 134. Letter of June 14, 1817, to Murray.

p.699, l.6 Manfred, Act III, Scene i.

p.699, l.14 Manfred, Act III, Scene iv.

p.699, l.23 I am indebted for a copy of a cutting of this review to Professor Willis W. Pratt of the University of Texas, whose letter concerning this rare and interesting item was published in the *Times Literary Supplement*, May 10, 1934.

P.700, l.2 LJ, IV, 141–2. Byron wrote the following endorsement on the original draft of the poem (including then 130 stanzas):

> "Venice and La Mira on the Brenta,
> Copied, August, 1817.
> Begun, June 26. Finished, July 29th"

But he kept adding stanzas through the autumn, and when the poem was published, April 28, 1818, it had grown to 186 stanzas. (*LJ*, IV, 141–2n.; *Poetry*, II, 315.)

p.700, l.18 LJ, IV, 142.

p.700, l.34 Byron told Moore: "This should have been written fifteen moons ago—the first stanza was." (*LJ*, IV, 149.) Byron sent five stanzas to Moore.

p.701, l.3 LJ, IV, 148–9. Letter of July 10, 1817.

p.701, l.12 LJ, IV, 153. Letter of July 15, 1817.

p.701, l.15 LJ, IV, 153. Letter of July 20, 1817.

p.702, l.8 See Juvenal: *Satire*, I, 3.

p.702, l.31 Childe Harold, IV, 121–2, 126–7.

p.703, l.34 Hobhouse diary, entry of July 31, 1817. Only a small portion of this entry is included in Broughton. (II, 74.)

p.704, l.5 Hobhouse diary, entry of Aug. 2, 1817.

p.704, l.9 Hobhouse diary, entry of Aug. 3, 1817.

p.705, l.38 B-SP, II, 472–4. Letter of Aug. 1, 1819.

p.706, l.9 Hobhouse diary, entry of Aug. 6, 1817.

p.706, l.27 LJ, III, 329. Miss Mayne (*Lady Byron*, p. 274.) says: "Lewis had reported one of Brougham's indiscretions, and Byron 'in a state of the greatest agitation' had drawn up the paper. Some considerable time afterwards Augusta wrote to Annabella of the incident, reported to her by Hobhouse. Byron had 'called upon Hobhouse to prove that he [Byron] had done everything to induce you to come *into Court!!*' Hobhouse had tried to persuade him not to give the paper to Lewis . . . '*in vain,* and an hour after it was gone B. expressed regret he had written and given it.' "

p.706, l.30 Broughton, II, 77.

p.707, l.7 LJ, IV, 156. Letter of Aug. 12, 1817.

p.707, l.22 B-SP, II, 415–16. Letter of Aug. 21, 1817.

p.708, l.16 There is another contemporary account of this incident, differing somewhat from Segati's as recorded by Hobhouse, in the diary of a Venetian by the name of Emanuele Cicogna (the MS. is now in the Museo Correr in Venice) under the date of Aug. 25, 1817. (Meneghetti, p. 96.) In this account the lady was married to the proprietor of the inn when her husband returned. But Segati's version of the story, which had the woman living with her *"amoroso,"* suited Byron's purposes much better and accorded much more with what he had observed of Italian society. It did not matter too much that he learned, apparently after he had finished the mock-heroic version of the episode in *Beppo,* that the story was not true.

p.708, l.19 Hobhouse diary, entry of Aug. 29, 1817. This episode from the diary I have already published in a letter to *The Spectator,* No. 6251 (April 16, 1948), p. 468.

p.708, l.32 LJ, IV, 164. Letter of Sept. 4, 1817.

p.708, l.33 Byron may also have met him in the House of Lords, where he was for some years reading-clerk. Rose had already published a translation of the French medieval poem *Amadis de Gaule* and a ballad in archiac form of his own called *Rufus; or, The Red King.* He had traveled extensively on the Continent since 1814 and was as enthusiastic over the Italian language (which he knew well), Italian literature, manners, and character as Byron himself. He had translated and published anonymously the previous year the Abate Giambattista Casti's *Animali Parlanti.* His extremely free translation, which he called the *Court and Parliament of Beasts,* became a thinly veiled burlesque satire on English manners and politics disguised as an animal fable set in India. Byron had already read the *Animali Parlanti,* possibly in the Italian. (Pryse Gordon: *Personal Memoirs,* II, 328.)

p.708, l.36 Giovanni Battista Casti (1721–1803), inspired by the inquiring minds of the French Revolution, ridiculed the absurdities of various political systems. Byron had already read and admired his *Novelle Galanti,* Boccaccian tales in *ottava rima.*

p.708, l.37 R. D. Waller in the introduction to his edition of Frere's *The Monks and the Giants* gives an excellent survey of Frere's (and Byron's) predecessors, Pulci, Berni, Casti, in the use of the *ottava rima* for mock-heroic purposes. Elizabeth F. Boyd also has some illuminating comment on Byron's borrowings from these sources in her *Byron's Don Juan,* Chapter IV.

p.709, l.12 The fact, which I think has never been stressed before, that Rose arrived at La Mira just before Byron began the composition of *Beppo,* and that Byron never before then mentioned to Murray or anyone else Frere's *Whistlecraft,* which he henceforth praised frequently, suggests that it was Rose who first introduced it to him. E. H. Coleridge in his introduction to *Beppo* says only that *Whistlecraft* "must have reached him in the summer of 1817." (*Poetry,* IV, 155–6.) It is possible also, however, that Byron first learned of Frere's work from Lord Kinnaird, who with his brother Douglas arrived in Venice on Sept. 19. Byron's first mention of *Whistlecraft* was in his letter of Oct. 12 to Murray.

p.709, l.23 Frere: *Whistlecraft*, I, 6.

p.710, l.16 *Beppo*, stanzas 17, 19, 20.

p.710, l.23 *Beppo*, stanza 24.

p.710, l.26 *Beppo*, stanza 29.

p.710, l.37 *Beppo*, stanzas 38–9.

p.711, l.15 *Beppo*, stanzas 41, 44.

p.711, l.36 *Beppo*, stanzas 47–9.

p.712, l.8 *Beppo*, stanza 54.

p.712, l.13 *Beppo*, stanza 78.

p.712, l.20 Hobhouse apparently saw *Beppo* when he visited Byron at La Mira (Hobhouse had moved to Venice then) on Oct. 8. The next day he wrote in his diary: "B has imitated Frere's imitation in a description of Venice and done it well." But the holograph MS. is dated in Byron's hand "October 10, 1817." (*Poetry*, IV, 159.)

p.712, l.24 The poem had grown to 99 stanzas before it was published.

p.712, l.29 LJ, IV, 176.

p.713, l.3 The progress of the poem is indicated in Byron's letters to Murray during the summer and autumn: July 1, 30 stanzas; July 9, 56; July 15, 98; July 20, 126; Aug. 7, 130; Aug. 21, 133; Sept. 4, 144; Sept. 15, 150; Nov. 15, 167. Before it was finally published it had grown to 186. Murray eventually paid Byron 2,500 guineas for the fourth canto of *Childe Harold* when it was published. (Smiles, I, 392–3. Letter of Murray to Byron, June 16, 1818.)

p.713, l.7 LJ, IV, 164–5.

p.713, l.21 LJ, IV, 169. Letter of Sept. 15, 1817.

p.714, l.4 A number of Hoppner's letters to Byron are preserved at John Murray's; the earliest of these is dated Sept. 5, 1817.

p.714, l.8 Dowden, II, 227.

p.714, l.16 Blessington, p. 87.

p.714, l.23 LJ, IV, 166–7. Letter of Sept. 12, 1817.

p.714, l.26 LJ, IV, 175–6. Letter of Oct. 12, 1817.

p.715, l.3 Hobhouse diary, entry of Sept. 6, 1817.

p.715, l.6 Hobhouse diary, entry of Sept. 26, 1817.

p.715, l.24 Hobhouse diary, entries of Sept. 24, 27, and 30, 1817.

p.716, l.28 Ticknor, I, 165; journal entry of Oct. 20, 1817.

p.716, l.33 LJ, IV, 177. Letter of Oct. 23, 1817.

p.717, l.3 Hobhouse diary, entry of Nov. 1, 1817. The house, for which, according to Hobhouse, Byron had agreed to pay 42 louis a year, was called the Villa Berlinguis, perhaps from its recent owner, but it was commonly known as "I Cappuccini."

p.717, l.20 On the 14th they saw Goldoni's "*Il Maldicente*," which Hobhouse pronounced a ludicrous comedy well acted by Vestris. (Diary.) On the 19th they saw Goldoni's harlequin play, "*La Vedova-scalt[r]a.*"

p.718, l.2 LBC, II, 61. Letter of Nov. 19, 1817.

p.718, l.13 LJ, IV, 178–80. Letter of Nov. 3, 1817, Byron to the Duchess of Devonshire.

p.718, l.27 LBC, II, 59. Letter of Sept. 24, 1817.

p.719, l.6 LBC, II, 62. Letter of Dec. 17, 1817.

p.719, l.13 LBC, II, 65. Letter of Jan 13, 1818. The name of Allegra, Teresa says in the *"Vie"* (p. 123, 1st series), Byron took from *"une dame juive qui s'appellait Allegra."* This was probably the name of one of the girls in the Jewish family who were his neighbors at La Mira.

p.719, l.35 Hobhouse diary.

p.720, l.3 Hobhouse diary, entry of Dec. 7, 1817.

p.720, l.16 Hobhouse diary, entry of Jan. 7, 1818.

Notes to Chapter XIX

P.721, l.12 Moore, II, 179.

p.722, l.7 LJ, VI, 440.

p.722, l.15 LJ, IV, 190.

p.722, l.34 These last three stanzas are printed here from the MS. (Ashley, B2777.)

p.723, l.5 LJ, IV, 193-4.

p.723, l.13 LJ, IV, 195. The words in the last sentence after "youth" are here supplied from the Murray MSS.

p.723, l.27 LBC, II, 66. Letter of Jan. 23, 1818.

p.724, l.2 "Vie," pp. 44-6.

p.724, l.6 LBC, II, 66-7.

p.724, l.18 Unpublished letter, Murray MSS.; Hobhouse proofs.

p.724, l.22 Hoppner was so proud of the lines that he had them printed in ten languages. (Moore, II, 164n.) They were, however, mere doggerel.

p.724, l.28 LJ, IV, 202-3. Letter of Feb. 20, 1818.

p.725, l.8 Byron finally sent off the verses to Murray in 1820, to be shown to friends but not to be published. They were first published in *Fraser's Magazine*, Vol. VII (Jan. 1833), pp. 82-4. (See *Poetry*, IV, 538-42.)

p.725, l.29 Most of these details were gathered by Meneghetti from contemporary diaries, the last from Malamanni's *Isabella Teotochi Albrizzi, i suoi amici, il suo tempo.* (Meneghetti, pp. 133-4.)

p.725, l.37 "Vie," pp. 36, 27; Origo, p. 38.

p.726, l.8 Meneghetti, p. 133.

p.726, l.13 Meneghetti, p. 134.

p.726, l.20 Stendhal, pp. 393-4. (My translation.)

p.726, l.21 The Marchesa Origo has accepted apparently at its face value Teresa Guiccioli's statement in the *"Vie"* (p. 33) that early in 1818 Byron had withdrawn entirely from the society of the Countess Albrizzi (Origo, p. 37), but he still mentions having been at her *conversazioni* in his letters as late as March, and in October 1819.

p.726, l.25 The first sixteen portraits appeared at Brescia in 1807. The "character" of Byron was published as No. 23 of the *Ritratti* in the fourth edition (Pisa, 1826). (*LJ*, IV, 14-15n.)

p.726, l.28 Moore, II, 254.

p.727, l.23 LJ, IV, 205. Letter of Feb. 28, 1818.

p.727, *l.29* Moore, II, 165n.

p.728, *l.7* *Beppo*, stanza 75.

p.728, *l.20* Origo, p. 37. Born in 1774 in Piacenza, Pietro Giordani became a Benedictine monk in 1797, but withdrew in disgust in 1800 and became a violent anti-clerical. His career and interests followed a pattern which would obviously have struck a rapport with Byron. In 1807 he had written a panegyric to Napoleon; from 1808 to 1815 he had been a secretary of the Academy of Belli Arti of Bologna; in 1810 he wrote a eulogy to Canova, whose ardent friend he became. He boasted of having discovered Giacomo Leopardi, whose friend and mentor he became when Leopardi was still a boy. (See Origo: *Leopardi*, Chapter V.)

p.728, *l.30* "*Vie*," 1 ser., p. 120ff.

p.728, *l.33* Moore, II, 180–1; Moore: *Memoirs*, II, 689.

p.729, *l.14* Blessington, pp. 105–6.

p.729, *l.22* "*Vie*," 1 ser., p. 124.

p.729, *l.31* *LJ*, IV, 330–1. Letter of Aug. 1, 1819.

p.729, *l.35* *LJ*, IV, 337. Letter of Aug. 9, 1819.

p.730, *l.1* *LJ*, IV, 215. Letter of March 16, 1818.

p.730, *l.10* *LBC*, II, 71.

p.730, *l.15* Unpublished letter, June 3, 1818, B.M.; Hobhouse proofs. John Murray (*LBC*, II, 82) estimates the 200 louis to have been worth about £190.

p.731, *l.7* *LJ*, IV, 196. Letter of Feb. 2, 1818.

p.731, *l.14* *LBC*, II, 71. Letter of March 25, 1818.

p.732, *l.4* Murray MSS. (Part of this letter is in "*To Lord Byron*," pp. 230–3.)

p.732, *l.15* The entry in the Register Book of Baptisms is given in *LJ*, IV, 123n.

p.732, *l.26* *LBC*, II, 71–2.

p.733, *l.15* *LBC*, II, 72–4. Letter of April 22, 1818.

p.733, *l.21* Shelley: *Works*, Julian ed., IX, 95–7. Letter of Aug. 13, 1814.

p.733, *l.24* Ashley 2819.

p.733, *l.26* On April 24 Claire wrote in her diary: "Shelley has a curious *rencontre* at the post-office with a Venetian, and hears no agreeable news of Albè." (Dowden, II, 199.)

p.734, *l.1* Shelley: *Works*, Julian ed., X, 366.

p.734, *l.3* Again the letter has not survived, but the nature of its contents can be surmised from Claire's and Shelley's replies.

p.734, *l.5* *Mary Shelley's Journal*, p. 97.

p.734, *l.12* Murray MSS. (Part of this letter is in "*To Lord Byron*," pp. 236–7.)

p.734, *l.14* *LJ*, IV, 250. Letter of Aug. 3, 1818.

p.735, *l.33* From the original letter in the Library of the University of Texas.

p.735, *l.36* *Edinburgh Review*, Vol. XXIX (Feb. 1818), pp. 302–10.

p.736, *l.4* Francesco Berni (1497–1536) achieved his fame for witty burlesque verse with his recasting of Boiardo's *Orlando Innamorato*.

p.736, *l.6* Byron had, however, for some time known the *Animali Parlanti* of Casti.

p.736, l.11 LJ, IV, 217–18. Letter of March 25, 1818.

p.736, l.16 Broughton, II, 92.

p.736, l.25 LBC, II, 67. Letter of March 3, 1818.

p.736, l.31 LBC, II, 70n.

p.737, l.4 Broughton, II, 95.

p.737, l.16 Hobhouse to Foscolo, March [24–27?] 1818. E. R. Vincent: *Byron, Hobhouse, and Foscolo*, p. 10. Vincent has given a full account from unpublished letters and passages in Hobhouse's diary of this curious collaboration. Most of the details of the episode given here are taken from his book.

p.737, l.21 LBC, II, 88. Letter of Sept. 30, 1818.

p.737, l.27 LBC, II, 86. Letter of Aug. 3, 1818.

p.737, l.32 LBC, II, 82. Letter of May 19, 1818, to Hobhouse.

p.738, l.5 LJ, IV, 228. Letter of April 23, 1818.

p.738, l.11 Austin Gray (*Teresa, or Her Demon Lover*, p. 40) says Scott "served as secretary to the consulate." But Byron wrote to Hobhouse on June 25: "The Scott I mention is not the Vice-Consul, but a traveller who lives much at Venice, like My*sen*." (*LBC*, II, 84.)

p.738, l.15 Mengaldo had met Hoppner at Este in Aug. 1817. (Meneghetti, p. 105.)

p.738, l.31 Meneghetti, pp. 107–8.

p.739, l.2 Meneghetti, pp. 119–20.

p.739, l.17 Albrizzi: *Ritratti*, No. XXIII, quoted, LJ, IV, 440. (My translation from the Italian; this part was not translated by Moore.)

p.740, l.3 Meneghetti, p. 122.

p.740, l.18 B.M. Add. 42093; Hobhouse proofs. (Parts of this letter omitted in LBC, II, 81–2.)

p.740, l.24 LJ, IV, 255. Letter of Sept. 8, 1818.

p.741, l.6 LJ, IV, 234–5. Letter dated June 1818.

p.741, l.16 LJ, IV, 239–40.

p.741, l.25 LBC, II, 106. Letter of March 6, 1819.

p.742, l.2 LJ, IV, 403n.

p.742, l.17 LBC, II, 77–8.

p.742, l.25 LJ, IV, 216. Letter of March 25, 1818.

p.743, l.5 LJ, IV, 237.

p.743, l.10 LJ, IV, 244.

p.743, l.13 LJ, IV, 244. Letter of June 30, 1818.

p.743, l.16 Douglas Kinnaird to Byron, June 26, 1818, Murray MSS.

p.743, l.24 The *Ode on Venice* was not published until the following year (June 28, 1819) with *Mazeppa*.

p.743, l.26 LJ, IV, 245.

p.743, l.28 On April 23 he had written Murray: "If *Beppo* pleases, you shall have more in a year or two in the same mood." (*LJ*, IV, 231.) Apparently the *estro* struck him sooner than he expected. But if he began *Don Juan* in July, as seems possible, he set it aside and did not really get under way until Sept. E. H. Coleridge says (*Poetry*, VI, xv): "Canto I. was written in September, 1818." But in a note to the poem Coleridge wrote: "Begun at Venice, September 6; finished November 1, 1818." (*Poetry*, VI, 11n.)

p.744, l.27 *Childe Harold*, IV, 137.

p.745, l.8 Mayne: *Lady Byron*, p. 277.

p.745, l.16 *Astarte*, pp. 23–4. From Lady Byron's journal of Sept. 14, 1818.

p.745, l.32 Jeaffreson, p. 264.

p.746, l.5 LJ, IV, 250. Letter of Aug. 3, 1818.

p.746, l.13 Moore, II, 264.

p.746, l.26 Glenbervie, II, 329. Entry of Oct. 13, 1818.

p.747, l.26 Origo: *Allegra*, p. 39.

p.747, l.31 *Mary Shelley's Journal*, p. 104.

p.748, l.18 Shelley: *Works*, Julian ed., IX, 326–7. Letter dated "Sunday Night. 5 o'clock in the morning" [actually Monday morning, Aug. 24, 1818].

p.748, l.34 *Julian and Maddalo*, Preface.

p.749, l.9 Ibid., lines 121–6.

p.749, l.16 The letter was torn at this point and the further conversation at Byron's palace is not preserved, but later in the letter Shelley wrote: "Pray come instantly to Este. . . ." (Shelley: *Works*, Julian ed., IX, 329.)

p.749, l.17 Mary arrived at Este on Sept. 5, 1818, where presumably Shelley met her. (*Mary Shelley's Journal*, p. 105.)

p.749, l.22 Most Shelley biographers have assumed that Shelley in *Julian and Maddalo* departed from the literal chronicling of the events—that he had played with Allegra at the Hoppners' and later called on Byron—but it seems altogether likely that Byron, supposing Shelley had not yet seen the child (to confess as much might have betrayed the presence of Claire), requested Elise to bring her to the Palazzo Mocenigo.

p.749, l.32 *Julian and Maddalo*, lines 170–3, 177–9.

p.750, l.8 LJ, IV, 260.

p.750, l.35 LJ, IV, 262. Letter of Sept. 19, 1818.

p.751, l.5 The asterisks indicate an omission by Moore when he first published the letter, probably something still more caustic about Lady Byron or her advisers.

p.751, l.8 LJ, IV, 262–3.

p.751, l.13 *Don Juan*, I, 12.

p.751, l.21 *Don Juan*, I, 13, 15–16.

p.751, l.24 *Don Juan*, I, 18.

p.751, l.27 *Don Juan*, I, 22.

p.752, l.4 *Don Juan*, I, 38–9, 41.

p.752, l.18 *Don Juan*, I, 116.

p.752, l.21 *Don Juan*, I, 117.

p.753, l.5 Murray MSS.; Hobhouse proofs. Letter of Nov. 11, 1818. Only part of this is printed in *LBC* (II, 89).

p.753, l.24 *Don Juan*, Dedication, 2, 4, 6.

p.753, l.26 Ibid., 17.

p.753, l.28 *Don Juan*, Dedication, 11, 12.

p.753, l.29 *Don Juan*, I, 205.

p.754, l.3 *Poetry*, VI, 7n.

p.754, l.9 *Mary Shelley's Journal*, p. 105; Shelley: *Works*, Julian ed., IX, 333.

p.754, l.14 *Mary Shelley's Journal*, p. 105.

p.754, l.17 Shelley: *Works,* Julian ed., IX, 334.

p.754, l.21 The Letters of Mary W. Shelley, I, 58–9.

p.757, l.3 LJ, IV, 331–6. Letter of Aug. 1, 1819.

p.757, l.9 Mary Shelley's Journal, p. 106.

p.757, l.10 Ibid., pp. 106, 108. Mary specifically mentions that Shelley spent the evening with Byron on Oct. 13, 21, and 22.

p.757, l.14 Ibid., p. 108.

p.757, l.30 Shelley: *Works,* Julian ed., X, 12. Letter of Dec. [22,] 1818.

p.758, l.3 Murray MSS.; Hobhouse proofs.

p.759, l.22 LJ, IV, 266–7n.

p.759, l.37 LJ, IV, 268–9. Letter of Nov. 18, 1818. It is difficult to know whether this letter was actually delivered to Lady Byron. Prothero printed it from a rough draft in the Murray MSS.

p.760, l.4 LBC, II, 96. Letter of Dec. 12, 1818.

p.760, l.7 Moore, II, 823.

p.760, l.29 Murray MSS.; Hobhouse proofs. This unpublished letter is dated Nov. 18, 1818.

p.761, l.10 Hanson had tried to persuade Byron to force upon some of his creditors a compromise payment. (*LJ*, IV, 269.)

p.761, l.27 Murray MSS. Letter of Dec. 22, 1818.

p.761, l.37 Broughton, II, 107–8.

p.762, l.18 LBC, II, 89–91. Letter of Nov. 11, 1818.

p.762, l.27 LBC, II, 94. Letter of Dec. 9, 1818.

p.763, l.9 Meneghetti, p. 154.

p.763, l.17 Hobhouse diary. Entry of Dec. 27, 1818. The word "facetiæ" is wrongly given as "bawdry" in Broughton (II, 107).

p.763, l.21 Murray MSS. Letter of Dec. 29, 1818.

p.764, l.5 B-SP, II, 439. Letter of Jan. 19, 1819.

p.764, l.10 Broughton, II, 110. Diary entry of Jan. 8, 1819.

p.765, l.21 Murray MSS.; Hobhouse proofs. Letter of Jan. 5, 1819.

p.766, l.11 LJ, IV, 277. Letter of Jan. 25, 1819.

p.766, l.24 LJ, IV, 279. Letter of Feb. 1, 1819.

p.767, l.16 Origo, p. 494, note 27.

p.767, l.19 Meneghetti, p. 132.

p.767, l.21 Meneghetti, p. 158.

p.768, l.6 Murray MSS.; Hobhouse proofs. Letter of Jan. 19, 1819. (Printed with some omissions in *B-SP,* II, 439–40.)

p.768, l.23 Murray MSS.; Hobhouse proofs. Letter of Jan. 27, 1819. (Printed with some variations in *LBC,* II, 103–4.)

p.768, l.30 LBC, II, 104.

p.769, l.12 Murray MSS.; Hobhouse proofs. Letter of March 6, 1819. (Printed with omissions in *LBC,* II, 104–5.)

p.769, l.20 Murray MSS. Letter of Kinnaird to Byron, Feb. 16, 1819.

p.769, l.36 Murray MSS.; Hobhouse proofs. Unpublished letter of March 9, 1819.

p.770, l.6 LJ, IV, 282–3n. Letter of March 19, 1819.

p.770, l.14 LJ, IV, 283. Letter of April 6, 1819.

p.770, l.17 LJ, IV, 283n. Letter of March 19, 1819.

p.770, l.26 LJ, IV, 284. Letter of April 6, 1819.

p.770, l.30 Murray MSS. Letter of Kinnaird to Byron, March 19, 1819.

p.771, l.2 Murray MSS.; Hobhouse proofs. Letter of April 6, 1819. (Printed with omissions in *B-SP*, II, 441.)

p.771, l.12 *LJ*, IV, 285. Letter of April 6, 1819.

p.772, l.4 *B-SP*, II, 442–3. There is no date on this fragment of a letter, but the F.P.O. (London) postmark is April 20, 1819.

p.772, l.19 Medwin, I, 85.

p.772, l.29 *Don Juan*, I, 213, 215.

p.774, l.10 "*Vie*," pp. 39–40.

p.774, l.20 "*Vie*," pp. 41–2. Here as elsewhere in quotations of the "*Vie*" I am giving a free translation of Teresa's not too perfect French.

p.774, l.26 "*Vie*," p. 43.

p.774, l.30 "*Vie*," pp. 43–4. Teresa is quoting from a conversation attributed to Coleridge in Gillman's reminiscences of Coleridge.

p.775, l.8 "*Vie*," p. 47.

p.775, l.30 "*Vie*," pp. 50–1.

p.775, l.35 "*Vie*," p. 41.

Notes to Chapter XX

P.777, l.9 Origo, p. 40. This is the Marchesa Origo's translation of a portion of the Italian document, which exists only in the Elliot papers, a copy of which is in the Keats-Shelley Memorial in Rome. (See Origo, pp. 480–1.)

p.777, l.31 *LBC*, II, 106–7. Letter of April 6, 1819.

p.778, l.32 Origo, p. 40. Teresa confessed to Moore that she met Byron daily during her stay in Venice, but made no reference to private meetings. (Moore, II, 207.)

p.779, l.2 "*Vie*," p. 61.

p.779, l.10 "*Vie*," pp. 64–5.

p.779, l.34 Origo, p. 24.

p.779, l.36 *I Guiccioli*, I, 18.

p.780, l.4 Ibid., I, 3.

p.780, l.22 Origo, p. 25.

p.780, l.31 Origo, p. 27.

p.780, l.32 Origo, pp. 27–8.

p.780, l.36 Origo, p. 493, note 3 of Prologue.

p.781, l.5 *I Guiccioli*, I, 22.

p.781, l.8 Origo, p. 23.

p.781, l.33 *B-SP*, II, 444–5. Letter of April 24, 1819.

p.782, l.6 "*Vie*," pp. 67–8.

p.782, l.10 "*Vie*," p. 70.

p.782, l.27 "*Vie*," p. 77.

p.783, l.10 Origo, pp. 44–5. Letter of April 22, 1819. This and subsequent letters from Byron to Teresa in Italian I give in the translation of the Marchesa Origo. The Italian text is printed in the Appendix of her *The Last Attachment*.

p.783, l.34 Origo, pp. 47–8.

p.784, l.15 Origo, p. 55. Letter of May 11, 1819.

p.784, l.25 That the stanzas were begun in April while Teresa was at the Guiccioli estate at the mouth of the Po seems evident from the context, though the manuscripts were dated "June" and "June 2," the latter date being in all probability the one on which the final draft was written. For a further discussion of this see my article "Lord Byron and Count Alborghetti," pp. 977–8.

p.784, l.34 *Poetry*, IV, 545–7.

p.785, l.7 Murray MSS.; Hobhouse proofs. Letter of April 27, 1819.

p.785, l.19 Murray MSS.; Hobhouse proofs. Letter of May 17, 1819. Parts of this paragraph were quoted in Origo, pp. 26–7; and more in my article "Lord Byron and Count Alborghetti," p. 977.

p.785, l.29 The note in *Astarte* says there was in the manuscript here a "short name of three or four letters obliterated," no doubt one of Byron's pet names for Augusta.

p.786, l.18 *Astarte*, pp. 81–3. Letter of May 17, 1819.

p.787, l.12 *LJ*, IV, 301–2. Letter of May 18, 1819.

p.787, l.25 *LJ*, IV, 288. Letter of April 27, 1819.

p.787, l.28 Murray MSS.; Hobhouse proofs. Letter of May 3 [1819].

p.787, l.31 *LJ*, IV, 295. Letter of May 15, 1819.

p.787, l.33 Smiles, I, 402. Letter of May 3, 1819.

p.787, l.38 *LJ*, IV, 304–5. Letter of May 20, 1819.

p.788, l.10 This phrase, omitted by Prothero, is supplied here from the Murray MSS.

p.788, l.14 *LJ*, IV, 306. Corrected from Murray MSS.

p.788, l.23 B-SP, II, 455–6.

p.788, l.27 Origo, p. 60. Letter of May 28, 1819.

p.788, l.33 Origo, p. 61. In the manuscript letter Teresa later tried to obliterate the word "me," probably to prevent the world from knowing that Byron had paid Fanny as a go-between in their love affair.

p.789, l.7 *LJ*, IV, 306. Letter of May 25, 1819.

p.789, l.9 This arrangement is discussed later in Byron's letters to Hoppner.

p.789, l.23 There are at least two extant manuscripts of this poem. One, in the Morgan Library, follows fairly closely the text as first given by Medwin and followed by Moore. The other, copied by Byron in a neat hand, is in the Berg Collection of the New York Public Library. The lines given here are from this copy. They differ considerably from those in the Medwin version. On June 8, 1820, Byron wrote to Hobhouse: "You say the Po verses are fine; I thought so little of them, that they lay by me a year uncopied, but they were written in *red-hot* earnest and that makes them good." (Quoted from an unpublished letter in the Murray MSS., in my article "Lord Byron and Count Alborghetti," p. 978n.)

p.789, l.37 *LJ*, IV, 307–8.

p.790, l.13 *LJ*, IV, 309. Letter of June 6, 1819.

p.790, l.25 *LJ*, IV, 310.

p.790, l.27 The Pellegrino was in via Vetturini, 86 (now via Ugo Bassi,

7). Byron occupied room number 5 on the first floor. (Cantoni: *La Prima Dimora di Lord Byron a Bologna*, p. 20.)

p.791, l.4 LJ, IV, 313. Letter of June 7, 1819, to Murray. According to Cantoni (*La Prima Dimora di Lord Byron a Bologna*, p. 23n.), the *custode* was Germano Sibaud, who had five children. The third, Matilde, a beautiful girl of twelve, was particularly noticed by Byron on his second sojourn in Bologna.

p.791, l.8 LJ, IV, 310–11n.

p.791, l.18 These details are given in Teresa's "*Vie*," pp. 113–15.

p.791, l.24 "*Vie*," p. 115.

p.791, l.26 "*Vie*," pp. 116–20.

p.791, l.31 Pasolini: *Ravenna e le sue Grandi Memorie*, p. 252. The hotel, the best the provincial town afforded at the time, was at No. 295, but now other buildings have replaced it near the square. The picture of it reproduced by Count Pasolini shows a plain two-story building with narrow windows.

p.791, l.35 "*Vie*," p. 120.

p.792, l.3 Origo, pp. 64–6.

p.792, l.16 Origo, p. 65. This is the Marchesa Origo's translation of Teresa's account in the "*Vie*," pp. 121–3.

p.792, l.32 Origo, p. 66.

p.793, l.5 Origo, p. 67.

p.793, l.12 "*Vie*," p. 133.

p.793, l.33 Origo, pp. 69–70.

p.793, l.35 "*Vie*," p. 133.

p.794, l.15 "*Vie*," pp. 137–40.

p.794, l.20 "*Vie*," p. 141.

p.794, l.27 The Austrian authorities noted well the character of the poem when it was published in Italian in 1822. The Royal Commissioner at Volterra wrote to the Buongoverno at Florence: "The work is certainly not written in the spirit of our Government or of any Italian Government. It seems to me intended to rouse still further the animosities of a populace already sufficiently excited. Lord Byron makes Dante his spokesman, and the prophet of democratic independence, as if this were the salvation of Italy. . . ." (Felice Tribolati: *Saggi Critici e biografici*, Pisa, 1891, pp. 158–9; quoted *LJ*, VI, 402.)

p.795, l.2 "*Vie*," p. 146.

p.795, l.35 B-SP, II, 459–60. Corrected from Murray MSS.

p.796, l.18 Some details of the career of Alborghetti are given in Moroni's *Dizionario Storico-Ecclesiastico*. Alborghetti's own poetic pretensions probably accounted in part for the eager interest he took in Byron.

p.796, l.20 Cardinal Malvasia was sent to Ravenna in 1816 as the first "*Legato apostoloca*" on the re-establishment of the Papal States after the Napoleonic occupation. Besides being a lover of parties, he was a celebrated scholar and founder of the literary academy called after him "Le Malvasiana," to which most of the well-known Italian poets and scholars of the day belonged.

p.796, l.25 B-SP, II, 461.

p.796, l.36 Moore, II, 221.

p.797, l.2 "Vie," pp. 146–7.

p.797, l.20 LJ, IV, 325–6.

p.798, l.7 LJ, IV, 323–4.

p.798, l.21 B-SP, II, 461.

p.798, l.28 Origo, p. 79.

p.798, l.34 From the MS. letter, Morgan Library.

p.799, l.10 Origo, p. 86.

p.799, l.18 Origo, p. 87.

p.799, l.29 Origo, p. 90. Letter of July 9, 1819.

p.800, l.7 Origo, pp. 90–2. Letter of July 12, 1819. (Some words are here supplied from the MS. in the Morgan Library.)

p.800, l.10 Origo, p. 90.

p.800, l.16 Origo, p. 94.

p.800, l.34 Origo, pp. 76–7. Undated letter.

p.801, l.1 Origo, p. 76.

p.801, l.25 Astarte, pp. 291–3. Letter of July 20, 1819. Byron did not post the letter until Aug. 31 from Bologna, with a short postscript.

p.801, l.28 Origo, p. 30.

p.802, l.24 B-SP, II, 464–6. Letter of July 26, 1819. (I have made some corrections from the MS. letter in the Morgan Library.)

p.803, l.17 Dowden, II, 328–9. Dowden got the information from Mrs. Hoppner's letter to Claire.

p.803, l.23 LJ, IV, 325.

p.803, l.31 Dowden, II, 328.

p.803, l.35 Hoppner to Byron, July 9, 1819, Morgan Library.

p.804, l.9 LJ, IV, 319. Letter of June 29, 1819.

p.804, l.12 Smiles, I, 403.

p. 804, l.16 The date of publication is given in *Poetry,* VI, xv.

p.804, l.21 Smiles, I, 404.

p.804, l.25 Letter of July 21, 1819, Hobhouse papers.

p.805, l.4 Mayne: *Lady Byron,* p. 283. (Miss Mayne gives neither the date nor the addressee of the letter, but in Lady Byron's *Lady Noel Byron and the Leighs,* pp. 68–9, the letter is given somewhat more fully as of July 18, 1819, to Mrs. Villiers.)

p.805, l.9 "Vie," pp. 167–8.

p.805, l.15 Origo, p. 497. The original sonnet in the Ravennese dialect is in Cantoni: *La Prima Dimora di Lord Byron a Bologna,* pp. 36–7.

p.805, l.17 "Vie," p. 177.

p.806, l.9 Origo, p. 99.

p.806, l.19 Origo, pp. 101–2.

p.806, l.20 "Vie," p. 190.

p.806, l.25 "Vie," pp. 192–3. Although neither Byron nor Teresa says so, it may be assumed that the Count was also present, for he had been a friend of Alfieri and was an ardent theatergoer.

p.806, l.38 LJ, IV, 339–41. Letter of Aug. 12, 1819.

p.807, l.11 Francis Cohen, who later took the name of Palgrave, was well versed in Italian and later translated for Byron a passage from the *Cronica di Sanuto* which was included, as one of the historical sources, in the Appendix of *Marino Faliero.*

p.807, l.36 LJ, IV, 341–3. Letter of Aug. 12, 1819. Some omissions in the letter supplied from the MS., Ashley 4743.

p.808, l.2 The Palazzo Savioli, so-called from its former owner (Count Lodovico di Gio. Andrea Savioli), who in the eighteenth century had enlarged and improved it, was purchased by Count Guiccioli in 1807 for 96,-533 lire. It was then No. 567 via Galliera. The number was later changed to 40 and it became a girls' school. It still stands, somewhat battered by the fighting in the Second World War. Its history and some pictures of the interior are given in Cantoni: *Byron e La Guiccioli a Bologna*, pp. 6–15.

p.808, l.21 LJ, IV, 343–4.

p.809, l.1 LJ, IV, 459. Police report dated July 25, 1819.

p.809, l.8 The Palazzo Merendoni was at No. 574 via Galliera (now No. 26). Rebuilt in the eighteenth century by the Counts Merendoni, it had come into the possession of Byron's Bologna banker, Cristoforo Insom, when Byron rented it. It was unfurnished, and he furnished only a few rooms at the back near the garden. (Cantoni: *Byron e La Guiccioli a Bologna*, p. 7n.)

p.809, l.15 LJ, IV, 455.

p.809, l.18 LJ, IV, 455.

p.810, l.12 LBC, II, 121–2.

p.810, l.33 LBC, II, 123. Letter of Aug. 23, 1819.

p.811, l.8 Origo, pp. 112–13. The volume was among Teresa's Byron "relics" when she died.

p.811, l.28 LJ, IV, 350. The note is dated Aug. 25, 1819.

p.811, l.36 Astarte, pp. 294–5.

p.812, l.2 "Vie," p. 209.

p.812, l.4 LJ, IV, 457.

p.812, l.17 "Vie," p. 210.

p.812, l.27 Origo, p. 115.

p.812, l.36 "Vie," pp. 218–19.

p.813, l.3 Origo, pp. 115–16.

p.813, l.6 LJ, IV, 458. There is some confusion about the date of their departure, for Teresa says it was the 15th ("Vie," p. 219) and Prothero published a letter of Byron to Murray, dated "Bologna, Sept. 17, 1819," but Byron's "2" sometimes resembles a "7." The police report is probably correct, since the journey took three days and Teresa wrote a letter to her husband from Venice on the 15th saying that she had arrived the night before.

p.813, l.10 Morgan, II, 116. Letter of Oct. 28, 1819, to Lady Clarke.

p.813, l.26 "Vie," p. 219.

p.814, l.2 Letter of Aug. 9, 1819, to Alexander Scott, Morgan Library.

p.814, l.7 "Vie," pp. 222–3.

p.814, l.10 "Vie," p. 225.

p.814, l.13 "Vie," pp. 227–34.

p.814, l.21 "Vie," pp. 241–3.

p.814, l.25 Origo, p. 118.

p.815, l.3 LBC, II, 126. Letter of Nov. 16, 1819, to Kinnaird.

p.815, l.9 "Vie," pp. 248–50.

p.815, l.24 Origo, p. 119. This is the Marchesa Origo's translation of the Italian letter, which is published in *I Guiccioli*, I, 28.

p.815, l.30 Origo, pp. 118–19.

p.815, l.36 "Vie," p. 253.

p.816, l.7 Origo, p. 120.

p.816, l.14 Origo, p. 121.

p.816, l.25 "Vie," p. 258.

p.817, l.2 Origo, p. 122. The Italian original of this letter (with omissions indicated) is published under date of Sept. 27, 1819, in *I Guiccioli*, I, 29.

p.817, l.11 "Vie," p. 260.

p.817, l.15 "Vie," p. 264.

p.817, l.19 Byron had already made some plans for this journey. On Sept. 23 the Vice-Consul, Dorville, wrote him: "[Do you] still intend pursuing your excursion to the Lakes?" (Murray MSS.)

p.817, l.27 "Vie," pp. 293–5.

p.819, l.2 LJ, IV, 355–8. Letter of Oct. 3, 1819.

p.819, l.20 "Vie," p. 305. According to Teresa, Byron was also working at this time on a translation of the burlesque chivalric romance of Pulci, the *Morgante Maggiore*. ("Vie," pp. 306–9.)

p.819, l.34 Don Juan, III, 5.

p.819, l.37 Don Juan, III, 8.

p.820, l.5 Moore gives the date as Oct. 8 in his life of Byron, but it is the 7th in Moore's *Memoirs* (I, 289), and other dates in the diary agree with this.

p.820, l.21 Moore, II, 248.

p.820, l.25 Moore: *Memoirs*, I, 290. Diary entry of Oct. 7, 1819.

p.820, l.26 Moore, II, 249.

p.820, l.35 Moore, II, 250.

p.821, l.6 Moore, II, 251.

p.821, l.13 Moore, II, 268; Moore: *Memoirs*, I, 291. Diary entry of Oct. 9, 1819.

p.821, l.24 Moore, II, 259–60.

p.821, l.31 Moore, II, 269.

p.821, l.34 Moore, II, 270; Moore: *Memoirs*, I, 291.

p.822, l.20 Moore, II, 272–3.

p.822, l.33 LJ, IV, 368–9. Letter of Oct. 29, 1819.

p.823, l.14 LJ, IV, 363. Letter of Oct. 25, 1819.

p.823, l.27 B-SP, II, 493. Letter of Oct. 29, 1819. Corrected from Murray MSS.

p.824, l.12 B-SP, II, 491. Letter of Oct. 26, 1819. (Corrected and omissions supplied from the MS. letter, B.M.; Hobhouse proofs.)

p.824, l.21 B-SP, II, 490. (Corrected and omissions supplied from the MS. letter, B.M.; Hobhouse proofs.)

p.825, l.5 LJ, IV, 370–2. Letter of Oct. 29, 1819.

p.825, l.13 I Guiccioli, I, 32.

p.825, l.19 Origo, p. 130.

p.826, l.10 Origo, pp. 132–3. The whole Italian text of the rules is given in *I Guiccioli*, I, 33–6.

p.825, l.23 Origo, p. 135. The complete Italian text of Teresa's reply is given in *I Guiccioli*, I, 36.

p.826, l.37 LBC, II, 129. Letter of Nov. 20, 1819.

p.827, l.14 LBC, II, 126–7.

p.827, l.25 But the Director of Police of Venice reported to the Governor on Nov. 19: "He [Guiccioli] came post haste from Ravenna the 6 November, to take back with him his strayed wife, and with her returned to his native city the 10th of the same month."

p.827, l.29 *LBC*, II, 129. Letter of Nov. 20, 1819.

p.827, l.36 *LBC*, II, 127. Letter of Nov. 16, 1819.

p.828, l.7 Murray MSS.; Hobhouse proofs.

p.828, l.12 Origo, p. 137.

p.828, l.20 Origo, p. 137. Translated by the Marchesa Origo from the Italian text printed by Moore (II, 289).

p.828, l.37 *Astarte*, pp. 295–7. Letter of Nov. 28, 1819.

p.829, l.2 The letter is headed merely "Dear Sir," but the context seems to indicate it is addressed to Hobhouse, to whom Byron had written of his intention to return on Nov. 20, and who shared Augusta's fears concerning *Don Juan.*

p.829, l.6 Murray MSS. Original letter in Augusta's hand.

p.829, l.17 *Astarte*, p. 92. Letter of Dec. 23, 1819.

p.829, l.38 The manuscript was dated "December 1, 1819." Three years later he showed the verses to Lady Blessington in Genoa, but they were first published in the *New Monthly Magazine* in 1832 (Vol. XXXV, pp. 310–12).

p.830, l.15 *Don Juan*, IV, 16.

p.830, l.30 *LJ*, IV, 380. Letter of Dec. 4, 1819.

p.831, l.5 Origo, p. 141. The letter is dated Nov. 6, but the contents show that it must have been Dec. 6, for it was then that Byron was on the point of leaving.

p.831, l.9 *LBC*, II, 131. Letter of Dec. 10, 1819.

p.831, l.23 Moore, II, 289–90. Moore gives neither the date nor the sender of the letter, but both can be made out from the context and the circumstances. It must have been written the 8th or 9th, for by the 10th Byron had made his decision not to leave Italy.

p.831, l.33 *LJ*, IV, 396. Letter of Jan. 2, 1820.

p.832, l.1 Moore, II, 290.

p.832, l.3 "*Vie*," pp. 344–5.

p.832, l.12 *LJ*, IV, 389–90.

Notes to Chapter XXI

P.834, l.7 *LJ*, IV, 393. Letter of Dec. 31, 1819.

p.834, l.35 *Astarte*, pp. 298–9. Letter of Dec. 31, 1819; finished Jan. 1, 1820.

p.835, l.8 *Astarte*, p. 104. Letter of Jan. 27, 1820, from Colonel Doyle to Lady Byron.

p.835, l.18 *Astarte*, p. 108. Letter of March 10, 1820. This letter was first published with Moore's diaries in 1853, together with Byron's reply. (Moore: *Memoirs*, I, 324–5.)

p.836, l.19 Origo, p. 150.

p.836, l.29 Origo, p. 152.

p.836, l.38 LJ, IV, 398. Date corrected from MS., Huntington Library.

p.837, l.26 Origo, p. 146.

p.837, l.32 I Guiccioli, I, 41.

p.838, l.13 Origo, p. 150.

p.838, l.20 Origo, p. 156.

p.838, l.29 LJ, IV, 400. Letter of Jan. 31, 1820.

p.838, l.35 Origo, p. 158.

p.839, l.4 Origo, p. 146.

p.839, l.9 LJ, IV, 401. Letter of Jan. 31, 1820.

p.839, l.11 LJ, IV, 405–6. Letter of Feb. 21, 1820.

p.839, l.24 I Guiccioli, I, 68.

p.839, l.30 Origo, p. 159. On Feb. 6, 1820, Teresa wrote Francesco Rangone that she had just dismissed a chambermaid and asked him to try to find a suitable one in Bologna. (Cantoni: *Byron e la Guiccioli a Bologna*, p. 37.)

p.840, l.5 LJ, IV, 402. Letter of Feb. 7, 1820.

p.840, l.17 "To Lord Byron," pp. 159–60.

p.840, l.29 From the MS. diary, Ashley 2819.

p.841, l.17 LJ, IV, 407–9. Letter of Feb. 21, 1820.

p.842, l.17 Letter of Jan. 18, 1820, Hobhouse proofs.

p.843, l.5 LJ, IV, 410. Letter of Feb. 21, 1820.

p.843, l.12 B-SP, II, 503–4. Letter of March 3, 1820.

p.843, l.25 B-SP, II, 504. Letter of March 3, 1820.

p.844, l.4 LJ, IV, 414. Letter of March 1, 1820.

p.844, l.17 B-SP, II, 505.

p.844, l.28 "Vie," pp. 371–4.

p.845, l.2 "Vie," p. 374.

p.845, l.12 B-SP, II, 510. Letter of March 31, 1820.

p.845, l.28 Blackwood's Edinburgh Magazine, Vol. V (Aug. 1819), pp. 512–18.

p.846, l.6 LJ, IV, 488.

p.846, l.16 LJ, IV, 422.

p.847, l.15 A garbled version of the ballad appeared in the *Morning Post*, April 15, 1820. It was first published in its entirety in *Murray's Magazine*, March 1887, pp. 292–3.

p.847, l.23 Here quoted from the MS. diary; the passage is incomplete, badly garbled, and changed in Broughton, II, 123–4.

p.847, l.30 Hobhouse diary.

p.848, l.2 LJ, V, 1–2. Letter of April 3, 1820.

p.848, l.7 LJ, V, 3.

p.848, l.12 His joint note to Hanson and Kinnaird is dated May 20, 1820. (Murray MSS.; Hobhouse proofs.)

p.848, l.22 LJ, V, 6. Letter of April 9, 1820.

p.848, l.28 LJ, IV, 62. Letter of Feb. 28, 1817.

p.849, l.8 LBC, II, 141.

p.849, l.16 LJ, V, 10. Letter of April 16, 1820.

p.850, l.3 LJ, V, 18–19.

p.850, l.14 B-SP, II, 515–17. Letter of June 8, 1820.

p.850, l.24 LJ, V, 90–1. Letter of Oct. 8, 1820.

p.850, l.34 Ashley 2819.

p.850, l.38 Claire Clairmont's diary, Ashley 2819.

p.851, l.1 This letter seems not to be extant, but it is mentioned in Claire's diary of that date.

p.851, l.4 "To Lord Byron," p. 244.

p.851, l.15 Murray MSS. This letter, with some errors and omissions, is in "To Lord Byron," pp. 245–6.

p.851, l.31 LJ, V, 14–15. Letter of April 22, 1820, to Hoppner. Byron's reference to "Starvation, and green fruit" is of course directed at Shelley's vegetarianism.

p.851, l.34 Claire Clairmont's diary, April 30, 1820. Ashley 2819.

p.852, l.1 Ashley 2819.

p.852, l.9 LBC, II, 149. Letter of May 26, 1820.

p.852, l.25 "Vie," pp. 376–8. The edges of the MS. at this point are mouse-eaten, so that some words of Teresa's letter are missing, but the gist of it can be made out.

p.852, l.32 Origo, p. 170.

p.852, l.37 "Vie," pp. 386–7.

p.853, l.15 "Vie," pp. 387–9.

p.854, l.5 Origo, p. 176.

p.854, l.13 Origo, p. 174.

p.854, l.15 LJ, V, 32. Letter of May 24, 1820.

p.854, l.35 Origo, p. 177. This, like most of the notes of Byron to Teresa of this period, is undated.

p.855, l.5 Origo, p. 178.

p.855, l.20 Origo, p. 172.

p.855, l.25 Origo, p. 173.

p.856, l.6 LJ, V, 28.

p.856, l.11 Origo, p. 180. According to Rangone's *Cronaca*, Guiccioli tried to borrow an additional 4,000 scudi from Byron.

p.856, l.16 "Vie," p. 407.

p.856, l.21 Origo, p. 174.

p.856, l.33 Origo, p. 181.

p.856, l.12 LJ, V, 35. Letter of June 1, 1820, to Moore.

p.858, l.7 Origo, p. 172. Translated from the document in the Secret Archives of the Vatican.

p.858, l.10 "Vie," p. 406.

p.858, l.20 The names and vital statistics of Byron's household are listed in the book "*Stati d'anime*" of the parish of Sant' Eufemia in Ravenna: "*Lord Byron anni 40* [sic]; *Allegrina sua figlia anni 5* [sic]; *Lega Zambelli segretario ex frate anni 50; Fletcher famigliare anni 22* [sic]; *Tita famigliare anni 22; Gaetano Forestieri coniugato, famigliare anni 26; Pasquale anni 22; Agostino anni 30; Valeriano fu Battista Nanni anni 31; Vincenzo famigliare anni 35; Giuseppe di nazione ebreo anni 22.*" (Borgese, p. 159.) The names are accurate enough, but the ages given seem to be wild guesses.

p.858, l.26 On Feb. 5, Archbishop Codronchi wrote that Lega, who came from Brisighella in the diocese of Faenza, had been for seven years a messenger or runner of the civil court in Forlì, and that, "forgetting entirely his priestly character, he abandoned the ecclesiastical garb giving himself up to a life completely secular, and now comes here in quality of secretary with Milord Biron, an Englishman, who seems inclined to fix his residence in Ravenna. The arrival of this Priest . . . has not failed to excite talk prejudicial to the Ecclesiastical order." (Pasolini Archives, Ravenna, Vol. 40, Pag. 3605. I am indebted to the Marchesa Origo for a copy of this letter.)

p.858, l.33 LJ, V, 42–3.

p.859, l.7 From an unpublished letter, July 18, 1820, Count Guiccioli to his attorney Taglioni, complaining of the separation decree. University of Texas Library.

p.859, l.18 From an unpublished postscript of Byron's letter of May 25, 1820, Clark Library, University of California, Los Angeles.

p.859, l.19 Castelli interceded at the court "at the instance of the most honorable Peer of England, etc.," and the same day, June 7, that the imprisonment was ordered and executed, Merryweather was released. (Olschki, p. 446.) Just what Merryweather's ingratitude consisted of, there is no clear evidence.

p.859, l.21 LJ, V, 44. Letter of June 12, 1820.

p.859, l.34 Origo, p. 179.

p.860, l.13 Origo, pp. 185–6. Undated.

p.860, l.20 LBC, II, 152.

p.860, l.24 Origo, p. 188.

p.860, l.26 Teresa says that the Pope sent the decree first to Countess Cecilia and that her son Edoardo sent news of it by express to his brother-in-law, Count Gamba. ("*Vie*," p. 416.) But the document itself must have gone to Cardinal Rusconi, who relayed it (together with a letter of his own to Teresa, dated July 14) to her father. ("*Vie*," p. 413.)

p.861, l.2 LJ, V, 49–50.

p.861, l.11 "*Vie*," p. 414 bis.

p.861, l.13 "*Vie*," p. 415.

p.861, l.21 "*Vie*," pp. 420–1.

p.861, l.23 "*Vie*," p. 421.

p.861, l.25 "*Vie*," p. 416.

Notes to Chapter XXII

P.862, l.18 According to Federico della Torre, in a letter of June 24, 1820, to Francesco Rangone, even before the separation decree came Guiccioli had tried unsuccessfully to dislodge Byron. Della Torre wrote: "Yesterday Guiccioli gave notice to Lord Byron to leave his apartment vacant by the end of the month." (Cantoni: *Lord Byron e la Guiccioli a Bologna*, p. 34.) Byron's reply was to take the courier who brought Guiccioli's message into his own employ.

p.863, l.3 Origo, p. 193.

p.863, l.17 "*Vie*," p. 431. Byron made his first visit to Teresa at Filetto on Aug. 16. (Origo, p. 210.)

p.863, l.38 LJ, V, 51. Letter of July 13, 1820.

p.864, l.3 Byron's chief source for the story was the Latin chronicle of Venice by Marino Sanuto, first published by Muratori in 1733, which he had had translated to go in the appendix.

p.864, l.7 Marino Faliero, first edition, Preface, p. ix.

p.864, l.16 Murray MSS.; Hobhouse proofs. Unpublished except for the postscript.

p.864, l.20 Byron sent the first act on July 24. Three acts had been sent by Aug. 7, the fourth was sent on Aug. 12, and the fifth went on Aug. 17. (*LJ*, V, 62–5.)

p.865, l.9 Unpublished letter, July 18, 1820, University of Texas Library. The sworn statements of eighteen servants who had acted as his spies were sent a week later, July 25, 1820. (Origo, p. 503.)

p.865, l.25 Origo, p. 198. Letter of July 26, 1820.

p.865, l.32 Origo, p. 198. Letter of July 29, 1820.

p.866, l.1 According to Primo Uccellini's *Dizionario Storico di Ravenna e di altri luoghi di Romagna* (Ravenna, 1855), Pietro Gamba was born in 1800. This would have made him nineteen or twenty when Byron met him (according to when his birthday came). Teresa was twenty at this time (Count Guiccioli gave that as her age in his letter of July 18, 1820, to his lawyer Taglioni). It is possible that she was born early in 1800 and Pietro late in the same year.

p.866, l.17 LJ, V, 51.

p.866, l.26 LJ, V, 57.

p.866, l.30 Origo (p. 203) lists a considerable number, some of them suggesting direct links with the Freemasons. She says that by the spring of 1820 these secret organizations were said to have enrolled 15,000 members in the Romagna. (Origo, p. 204.)

p.866, l.35 Origo, pp. 205–6.

p.867, l.5 Uccellini: *Memorie di un vecchio Carbonaro ravegnano*, pp. 6–7. According to Giovanna Foà (*Lord Byron, Poetà e Carbonaro*, p. 183) one of the Carboneria societies in Ravenna was called the Società degli Amici del Dovere (Society of the Friends of Duty), consisting of very mixed elements.

p.867, l.24 Origo, p. 203.

p.868, l.9 Origo, p. 209. Letter of Aug. 8, 1820.

p.868, l.20 Murray MSS.; Hobhouse proofs. Letter of Aug. 31, 1820.

p.868, l.22 LJ, V, 72 n.

p.868, l.26 Smiles, I, 411.

p.869, l.6 Hunt: *Correspondence*, I, 157.

p.869, l.9 LJ, V, 77. Letter of Sept. 21, 1820.

p.869, l.22 Astarte, p. 300.

p.869, l.26 "Vie," p. 461.

p.869, l.31 Elliot papers, Keats-Shelley Memorial, Rome.

p.870, l.8 Origo, p. 199.

p.870, l.19 Young Lord Fitzharris recorded his impressions of this unconventionality when he visited Teresa at Filetto in 1829. Malmesbury, I, 32.

p.871, l.2 LJ, V, 70–1. Letter of Aug. 31, 1820.

p.871, l.12 Origo, p. 212. Letter of Aug. 21, 1820.

p.871, l.17 Moore, II, 341n.

p.871, l.19 LJ, V, 70. Letter of Aug. 31, 1820.

p.871, l.30 Origo, p. 198.

p.871, l.35 Origo, p. 213. Letter of Aug. 24, 1820.

p.872, l.12 Blessington, p. 84.

p.872, l.23 Origo, p. 214. Letter of Aug. 26, 1820.

p.872, l.31 Origo, p. 215.

p.872, l.35 In the *"Vie"* (p. 468) Teresa says it was Sept. 10, but her letter of Sept. 7 indicates that it must have been that day or the day before.

p.873, l.9 *"Vie,"* pp. 468–70 bis.

p.873, l.15 *"Vie,"* pp. 470 bis–471 bis bis.

p.873, l.19 Origo, p. 218. Letter of Sept. 9, 1820, to Teresa.

p.873, l.27 LJ, V, 77. Letter of Sept. 21, 1820.

p.873, l.31 LJ, V, 75. Letter of Sept. 11, 1820.

p.873, l.34 Byron wrote four stanzas of an "Epilogue," imitating the silliness of Wordsworth's "Prologue":

> There's something in a Stupid Ass
> And something in a heavy Dunce;
> But never since I went to School
> I heard or saw so damned a fool
> As William Wordsworth is for once.

Facsimile published in the Catalogue of Samuel T. Freeman & Co., Dec. 10, 1928; *Poetry*, VII, 63–4. In a letter to Kinnaird of Aug. 31, 1820, Byron said his own play was "at least as good as Mr. Turdsworth's Peter Bell." (Murray MSS.)

p.873, l.38 LJ, V, 93. Letter of Oct. 12, 1820.

p.874, l.19 LJ, V, 80. Letter of Sept. 28, 1820.

p.874, l.26 Byron refers to his defense of Pope in the "Observations on an Article in *Blackwood's Magazine*," which Murray was still holding in manuscript.

p.874, l.31 LJ, V, 77–8. Letter of Sept. 23, 1820.

p.875, l.8 LJ, V, 497. Letter of Sept. 17, 1820.

p.876, l.8 LJ, V, 73–5.

p.876, l.19 Dowden, II, 251, 325–6; *Letters of Mary W. Shelley*, I, 108. Letter of June 18, 1820.

p.876, l.36 LBC, II, 181.

p.877, l.23 LBC, II, 152–3. Count Gamba did actually get one of his relatives to go to England. Byron recommended him to Hobhouse.

p.877, l.26 This letter was first printed from a copy in Vol. 98 of the Liverpool papers in the British Museum (Add. MS. 38287, ff. 256–7) in a letter by C. S. B. Buckland to the *Times Literary Supplement*, Jan. 22, 1925, p. 56.

p.878, l.2 Murray MSS.; Hobhouse proofs. Letter of Nov. 6, 1820.

p.878, l.7 LBC, II, 157. Letter of Oct. 1, 1820.

p.878, l.21 LJ, V, 68–9.

p.878, l.25 The story of the plot is given in the interrogation of Count Giacomo Laderchi by the Austrian police, recorded in Pierantoni: *I Carbonari dello Stato Pontificio*, p. 11. (See Origo, pp. 222, 224, 504 note 39.)

p.879, l.1 F. A. Gualtierio, I, 264 (my translation from a copy furnished me by the Marchesa Origo.)

p.879, l.12 Pierantoni: *I Carbonari dello Stato Pontificio*, p. 11. (Origo, pp. 223–4.)

p.879, l.27 LBC, II, 156–7. Letter of Oct. 1, 1820.

p.879, l.36 Origo, p. 219.

p.880, l.2 Origo, p. 220. Letter of Sept. 15, 1820.

p.880, l.23 Origo, p. 221. Letter of Sept. 28, 1820.

p.881, l.10 B-SP, II, 528–30. The letter is dated only October, but Lord Lovelace says it was written about Oct. 20, 1820. (*Astarte*, p. 110.) A line has been cut out at the end of the letter.

p.881, l.34 Origo, pp. 228–9. This was no doubt the first half-dozen volumes (or perhaps more) of the first French translation of Byron's works: *Œuvres de lord Byron, traduites de l'anglais* (par Amédée Pichot et Eusèbe de Salle), 10 vol. in-12, Paris, 1819–21. It was published without the names of the translators. (See Estève: *Byron et le Romantisme Français*, "Appendice Bibliographique," pp. 526–7.

p.882, l.1 LJ, V, 96. Letter of Oct. 12, 1820.

p.882, l.3 LJ, V, 105. Letter of Oct. 17, 1820.

p.882, l.28 Origo, pp. 229–30. This letter is dated Oct. 10, 1820, but either it or Byron's to which it is a reply and which is dated Oct. 11 must be misdated.

p.883, l.4 LJ, V, 96–7. Letter of Oct. 12, 1820.

p.883, l.11 LJ, V, 92. Letter of Oct. 8, 1820.

p.884, l.6 Don Juan, V, 1–2.

p.884, l.18 Don Juan, V, 61.

p.884, l.19 Murray MSS.; Hobhouse proofs. Letter of June 19, 1821, Hobhouse to Byron.

p.884, l.29 Don Juan, V, 158.

p.884, l.32 LJ, V, 113.

p.886, l.7 Quarterly Review, Vol. XXIII (July 1820), pp. 400–34. The reference to Byron is on p. 425.

p.886, l.14 LJ, V, 108–9. Letter of Nov. 4, 1820.

p.886, l.20 Wise, II, 18. Wise has supplied the omissions in the letter as printed in LJ (V, 109; letter of Nov. 4, 1820.)

p.886, l.27 From the manuscript letter, Ashley 5161. Letter of Nov. 9, 1820. Omissions in LJ (V, 117) and Wise (II, 19).

p.886, l.32 Murray MSS.; Hobhouse proofs, Aug. 31, 1820.

p.887, l.11 LBC, II, 159.

p.887, l.17 Origo, p. 232. From the Vatican Archives, Segretaria di Stato, Sezione Interni.

p.887, l.27 LJ, V, 111.

p.888, l.11 LBC, II, 162. Letter of Nov. 9, 1820.

p.888, l.26 Origo, pp. 234–5.

p.889, l.20 LBC, II, 163–4. Letter of Nov. 22, 1820.

p.889, l.27 Marchand: "Lord Byron and Count Alborghetti," pp. 988–9.

p.889, l.37 Astarte, p. 301. This is a fragment printed from a half-burned sheet.

p.890, l.4 The Commandant's name is given in an edict of Cardinal Rusconi, issued Jan. 22, 1821, offering a reward of 1,000 scudi for information leading to the conviction of the assassin. (From a printed copy of the edict, Keats-Shelley Memorial, Rome.)

p.890, l.29 LJ, V, 134–5. Letter of Dec. 9, 1820.
p.891, l.20 Astarte, pp. 110–11. Letter of Dec. 10, 1820.
p.891, l.32 Astarte, pp. 111–13.
p.892, l.20 LJ, V, 140–2.
p.893, l.10 LJ, V, 143–5.
p.893, l.12 LJ, V, 145. Letter of Dec. 28, 1820, to Murray. Begun on Oct. 16, 1820, the first draft of the new canto was completed Nov. 20, but a few stanzas were added and some deleted before the canto was published Aug. 8, 1821, along with cantos III and IV.

Notes to Chapter XXIII

P.894, l.9 Moore's indication that he had omitted some word or words.
p.894, l.14 LJ, V, 214–15.
p.895, l.14 LJ, V, 147–51.
p.895, l.22 LJ, V, 217–18.
p.895, l.31 Byron derived the major facts of the story from Diodorus Siculus: *Bibliothecæ Historicæ*, lib. II, 78 ff. (ed. of 1604). Diodorus had drawn from the *Persica* of Ctesias, private physician at the court of Artaxerxes Mnemon (B.C. 405–359). Whether Sardanapalus was a fictitious or a historical character is not certainly known.
p.896, l.20 LJ, V, 155–6.
p.896, l.34 LJ, V, 157–8.
p.897, l.1 LJ, V, 596.
p.897, l.6 "Vie," p. 578. Teresa kept a copy of the letter—it may be that it was she who gave it the nobility of Santa Chiara's rhetoric.
p.897, l.12 Marchand: "Lord Byron and Count Alborghetti," p. 993. Letter of Alborghetti to Byron, Jan. 10, 1821.
p.897, l.21 LJ, V, 172–3. Diary entry of Jan. 13, 1821.
p.897, l.22 "Vie," p. 526. The name of Myrrha was probably derived not from Byron's reading of ancient history but from the *Mirra* of Alfieri. He later told Murray: "It has been my object to be as simple and severe as Alfieri." (*LJ*, V, 323. Letter of July 14, 1821.)
p.897, l.29 Sardanapalus, Act I, Scene i, lines 9–13.
p.897, l.36 LJ, V, 177.
p.898, l.7 LJ, V, 223. Letter of Jan. 11, 1821.
p.898, l.16 LJ, V, 227–8.
p.898, l.23 LJ, V, 183.
p.898, l.29 LJ, V, 183–4.
p.899, l.2 LJ, V, 186.
p.899, l.4 LJ, V, 234. Letter of Jan. 28, 1821.
p.899, l.15 LJ, V, 186–7.
p.899, l.29 Astarte, p. 304. Letter of Jan. 11, 1821.
p.899, l.32 LJ, V, 185. Diary entry of Jan. 24, 1821.
p.899, l.37 LJ, V, 189.
p.900, l.5 LJ, V, 190.
p.900, l.14 MS. note at the end of the proof, Morgan Library.
p.900, l.34 Letter to . . . , p.16.

p.900, l.38 Bowles: *Invariable Principles.* . . . (*LJ*, V, 532.)

p.901, l.5 Letter to . . . , pp. 34, 47n.

p.901, l.11 Letter to . . . , pp. 54–5.

p.901, l.21 LJ, V, 200. Diary entry of Feb. 9, 1821.

p.901, l.27 Green, p. 101.

p.902, l.6 LJ, V, 203.

p.902, l.27 LJ, V, 242–3. Letter of Feb. 16, 1821.

p.903, l.2 LJ, V, 206.

p.903, l.12 LJ, V, 208.

p.903, l.25 LJ, V, 272. Letter of April 28, 1821.

p.903, l.33 Gatteo, pp. 63, 65, 67. The old Camaldolese monastery of San Giovanni, founded in the fourteenth century and abandoned in the eighteenth, was taken over by the Capuchin nuns in 1817. An exception to the rules of entrance was made for Allegra, who, at four years and less than two months, was the youngest girl in the school.

p.903, l.38 Gatteo, p. 65.

p.904, l.1 Gatteo, p. 74. The record of the payment by Lega Zambelli, secretary of the noble Lord Byron, for the semester ending Aug. 30 is quoted from a document dated March 1, 1821.

p.904, l.8 Letter of Felice Tellarini to Byron, March 2, 1821. I have given the translation of the Marchesa Origo (Origo, p. 237), but she has misread the date as March 11 (see Origo, note 4, p. 505). The manuscript, in the Murray collection, shows it as clearly March 2. This letter and the record of Lega's payment of the semester's tuition effactually date Allegra's arrival at the convent as March 1, 1821.

p.904, l.13 "Vie," pp. 483–4.

p.904, l.19 On March 20 and March 22 Claire records having written to Byron, but these letters may have been first drafts of her long letter of March 24. (*LJ*, V, 498–9.)

p.904, l.30 LJ, V, 500–1.

p.905, l.12 LJ, V, 264. Some omitted portions are here filled in from quotations from the original letter in H. B. Smith: *A Sentimental Library*, p. 41.

p.905, l.20 Gatteo, p. 69. The source is given as Nino Massaroli in an article in *La Piè*, Anno VII, N. 3.

p.905, l.30 LBC, II, 168–9.

p.906, l.5 LJ, V, 267. Letter of April 26, 1821.

p.906, l.16 B-SP, II, 597. Letter of March 23, 1821.

p.906, l.23 LJ, V, 271. Letter of April 26, 1821.

p.906, l.25 LJ, V, 212. Letter of Jan. 2, 1821. In a postscript of this letter Byron told Moore: "From the second part of the Memoirs cut what you please." (*LJ*, V, 216.) He did not give the same permission with the first part, which dealt with the events of his marriage and separation.

p.906, l.28 LJ, V, 272. Letter of April 28, 1821.

p.906, l.36 Bowles had erroneously supposed Gilchrist, a grocer at Stamford, to have been the writer of the review of Spence's *Anecdotes* in the *Quarterly Review* for Oct. 1820, in which Bowles had been taken to task for his strictures on Pope, for he knew him to have written the anonymous review of Spence in the *London Magazine*, of Feb. 1820.

Bowles wrote a reply to Gilchrist, dated Oct. 25, 1820, and published in *The Pamphleteer* (Vol. XVII, pp. 73–96). On Dec. 2, Gilchrist answered in a pamphlet full of personalities. Bowles in turn became even more acrimonious in a rejoinder dated Feb. 17, 1821, entitled "Observations on the Poetical Character of Pope: further elucidating the 'Invariable Principles of Poetry,' etc., with a Sequel in reply to Octavius Gilchrist." (*The Pamphleteer*, Vol. XVII, pp. 369–84, and Vol. XVIII, pp. 213–58). It was probably Bowles's last attack on Gilchrist which inspired Byron's second letter, entitled: *Observations upon 'Observations.' A Second Letter to John Murray, Esq., on the Rev. W. L. Bowles's Strictures on the Life and Writings of Pope.*

p.907, l.13 LJ, V, 588.

p.907, l.21 LJ, V, 276–7. Letter of May 10, 1821.

p.907, l.34 LJ, V, 279. Letter of May 11, 1821.

p.907, l.36 Smiles, I, 420.

p.908, l.3 LJ, V, 285. Letter of May 14, 1821.

p.908, l.11 Memoirs of Robert William Elliston, 1845, Concluding Series, p. 270. The play was performed first on April 25 and again on April 30 on the authority of the Lord Chancellor and was acted a total of seven times, pending a hearing before the court of King's Bench.

p.908, l.20 LJ, V, 290.

p.908, l.28 LJ, V, 297. Letter of May 25, 1821.

p.909, l.13 LJ, V, 306–7.

p.909, l.18 LJ, V, 323. Letter of July 14, 1821, to Murray. The story is in Daru's *Histoire de la République de Venise* and Sismondi's *Histoire des Républiques Italiennes du Moyen Age.* (See Appendix of first edition of *The Two Foscari*.)

p.909, l.23 Poetry, V, 115.

p.909, l.38 Marchand: "Lord Byron and Count Alborghetti," p. 1000.

p.910, l.18 Ibid., p. 1001.

p.910, l.36 Ibid., p. 1002.

p.911, l.6 See Strout, pp. 50–6.

p.911, l.21 Strout, p. 82.

p.911, l.31 Strout, pp. 90–1. The last reference is to Murray's having been afraid to put his name on the title page of the first edition.

p.912, l.20 LJ, V, 318.

p.912, l.7 LJ, V, 421.

p.913, l.2 Origo, p. 238.

p.913, l.4 "Vie," p. 640.

p.913, l.7 "Vie," p. 640.

p.913, l.11 LJ, V, 321. Letter of July 6, 1821.

p.913, l.15 Origo, p. 256.

p.914, l.11 "Vie," p. 660.

p.914, l.22 LJ, V, 239–40. This letter is misdated Feb. 15, 1821, in *LJ*, no doubt because Byron's "Fy" and "Jy" looked much alike.

p. 914, l.29 Byron's letter of July 15 was returned to him and he sent it on to Spa. The Duchess's reply, dated Aug. 17, 1821, is given in *LJ*, V, 238–9n.

p.915, l.12 Origo, pp. 260–1.

p.915, l.14 Marchand: "Lord Byron and Count Alborghetti," p. 1005. Letter of July 6, 1822.

p.915, l.20 "*Vie,*" p. 678.

p.916, l.10 Origo, p. 263. Letter of July 26, 1821.

p.916, l.18 Origo, pp. 263–4.

p.917, l.14 LJ, V, 336. Letter of Aug. 2, 1821.

p.918, l.4 LJ, V, 189.

p.918, l.8 LJ, V, 190.

p.918, l.21 *Cain,* Act II, Scene i.

p.919, l.2 *Cain,* Act I, Scene i.

p.919, l.10 *Poetry,* V, 209.

p.919, l.26 B-SP, II, 658–9. Letter of July 14 [?], 1821. (Corrected from Murray MSS.)

p.920, l.8 *Mary Shelley's Journal,* p. 159.

p.920, l.10 Dowden, II, 420.

p.921, l.28 Shelley: *Works,* Julian ed., X, 296–9. Letter of Aug. 7, 1821.

p.922, l.5 Ibid., X, 302.

p.922, l.17 Origo, p. 264.

p.922, l.29 See Shelley: *Works,* Julian ed., X, 12–13. Letter of Dec. [22], 1818.

p.922, l.32 Ibid., X, 306. Letter of Aug. [10?], 1821.

p.922, l.38 LJ, V, 342–3. Letter of Aug. 10, 1821, to Murray.

p.923, l.8 Shelley: *Works,* Julian ed., X, 304. Letter of Aug. [10], 1821.

p.923, l.21 Ibid., X, 306–7. Letter of Aug. [10?], 1821.

p.923, l.24 Ibid., X, 308. Letter of [Aug. 11, 1821].

p.924, l.7 Ibid., 311–12. Letter of [Aug. 15, 1821].

p.924, l.17 Ibid., X, p. 310.

p.925, l.5 LBC, II, 188. Mary's letter, printed first with omissions by Dowden (II, 425–7), was among Byron's papers in the Dorchester collection which came to John Murray on Lady Dorchester's death in 1914, but it has since disappeared. (See *Letters of Mary W. Shelley,* I, 150.)

p.926, l.12 Shelley: *Works,* Julian ed., X, 314. Letter of [Aug. 16, 1821].

p.926, l.21 Ibid., X, 315. Letter of [Aug. 16, 1821].

p.926, l.33 Origo, p. 277.

p.927, l.5 Shelley: *Works,* Julian ed., X, 332. Letter of Oct. 22, 1821. The spy who reported to the "Buon Governo" spelled the name "Filicchi." Archivio di Stato, Firenze. Buon Governo. Serie Commune. Filza LVIII. Affari 2885. Report of Andạ Bandelloni, Sept. 26, 1821. (From copy in Keats-Shelley Memorial, Rome.)

p.927, l.7 Pietri, pp. 34–5.

p.927, l.25 Archivio di Stato, Firenze. Buon Governo. Serie Commune. Filza LVIII. Affari 2885. Report of the spy Andạ Bandelloni, at Pisa, Sept. 26, 1821. (From a copy in the Keats-Shelley Memorial, Rome.)

p.928, l.20 Shelley: *Works,* Julian ed., X, 318–19.

p.928, l.25 See Hunt: *Lord Byron,* I, 31–3, where Hunt speaks frankly of some of his peculiar notions concerning money.

p.928, l.30 Shelley: *Works,* Julian ed., X, 319–20.

p.928, l.34 Ibid., X, 320. Undated letter, but probably early Sept.

p.929, l.14 Ibid., X, 321.

p.929, l.17 Origo, p. 282.

p.929, l.22 LJ, V, 338. By Sept. 20 he told Murray it was "never meant for publication." (*LJ*, V, 369.) It was finally published in the third number of *The Liberal*, April 26, 1823.

p.929, l.23 Byron sent the manuscript of *Cain* to Murray on Sept. 10, 1821, with the stipulation that it might be printed with the other two tragedies if it arrived in time. (*LJ*, V, 360.)

p.929, l.27 B-SP, II, 663n.

p.929, l.37 LJ, V, 348. Letter of Aug. 23, 1821.

p.930, l.6 LJ, V, 357, 359. Letter of Sept. 4, 1821.

p.930, l.18 The couplet, misquoted from memory, is from Pope's "Sober Advice from Horace," (2nd Sermon), lines 151–2:

> Or, when a tight, neat Girl, will serve the Turn,
> In errant Pride continue stiff, and burn?

p.930, l.23 B-SP, II, 664–6. Letter of Sept. 5, 1821. (I have made some corrections from the original manuscript in the Huntington Library.)

p.930, l.28 LBC, II, 197.

p.930, l.33 Scott did not hesitate to accept the dedication, and Murray's decision to publish the drama along with *Sardanapalus* and *The Two Foscari* (on Dec. 19) may have been influenced by Scott's high praise of it. The volume appeared with only one dedication, that to Sir Walter Scott at the head of *Cain*. Kinnaird had not had time to get Goethe's permission, and he probably squelched the dedication to himself, for it did not appear until 1832 in Murray's collected edition of Byron's works (XII, 50).

p.931, l.5 Poetry, IV, 555–6n. The Queen died on Aug. 7, 1821. On the 17th, George IV made his triumphal entry into Dublin. On the 18th, the Queen's body was embarked for her native Brunswick.

p.931, l.8 Medwin printed the poem in 1824 in his *Conversations,* but omitted twelve of the more libelous stanzas. The whole thirty-two stanzas, however, were published in a new edition of Medwin the same year, with the omission of a few words. (See *Athenaeum*, July 27, 1901, p. 113.) Murray included it in Byron's works after the death of George IV.

p.931, l.9 Moore, II, 527n.

p.931, l.22 LJ, V, 364–5.

p.931, l.36 LJ, V, 373–6. Letter of Sept. 24, 1821.

p.932, l.14 LJ, V, 384, 386.

p.932, l.27 Byron called the poem "*The Vision of Judgment,* by Quevedo Redivivus." He chose for his pseudonym the name of the great Spanish satirist Francisco Gomez de Quevedo y Villegas (1580–1645), whose *Sueños* (1627) marked the climax of his ridicule of the vices and foibles he had witnessed as an attaché of the Spanish courts of Philip III and Philip IV. Byron had a considerable admiration for this Spaniard, who came to be known as "the scourge of silly poets." The suggestion to revive him as his spokesman on this occasion perhaps came from Quevedo's first "Vision," *El Sueño de las Cavalleras* (*The Vision of the Skulls*), a satire on human follies and vices depicted in a story of the Last Judgment.

p.932, l.33 LJ, V, 386–7.

p.933, l.4 LJ, VI, 381–3.

p.933, l.21 Southey: *Poetical Works*, V, 195–6.

p.934, l.30 At the end of the poem Byron wrote the date "Rⁿ Oct. 4,

1821," and then a memorandum: "This poem was begun on May 7, 1821, but left off the same day—resumed about the 20th of September of the same year, and concluded as dated." (*Poetry*, IV, 525n.) Byron had no sooner finished it than he began another poetic drama, on the dangerous subject of the love of angels (fallen) with earthly women. Medwin (I, 189) says Byron told him *Heaven and Earth* was commenced at Ravenna on Oct. 9, and that the composition occupied him for about fourteen days.

p.935, l.2 LJ, V, 387. Letter of Oct. 6, 1821.

p.935, l.17 Lord Lovelace notes: "Erased (apparently not by the writer) and hardly legible." (*Astarte*, p. 308n.)

p.935, l.22 *Astarte*, pp. 307–8. Letter of Oct. 5, 1821.

p.935, l.25 Origo, p. 284.

p.935, l.30 Luzio, I, 173–4. (Origo, pp. 284–5.)

p.936, l.3 "Vie," p. 725.

p.936, l.32 LBC, II, 203–4. The last sentence quoted is here corrected from the Murray MSS.

p.937, l.19 LJ, V, 439.

p.937, l.28 LJ, V, 446–7.

p.938, l.9 LJ, V, 456–8.

p.938, l.22 LJ, V, 392–3. Letter of Oct. 20, 1821.

p.938, l.34 Shelley: *Works*, Julian ed., X, 331.

p.939, l.6 Ibid., X, 330.

p.939, l.14 Diary of Claire Clairmont, Ashley 2819 (3).

p.939, l.25 Origo: *Allegra*, p. 118. The original Italian letter is reproduced opposite p. 84.

p.939, l.30 Ibid., p. 119.

p.940, l.12 Origo, p. 290.

p.940, l.20 LJ, V, 372. Letter of Sept. 20, 1821.

p.940, l.24 LJ, V, 395. Letter of Oct. 21, 1821.

p.940, l.25 LJ, V, 397–8. Letter of Oct. 28, 1821.

p.940, l.33 Moore, II, 550.

p.941, l.1 Translated from a deposition of Ghigi to the executors of Byron's estate. (Murray MSS.) The story of Ghigi's trials with these animals is told in his letters to Lega Zambelli in the months that followed. Copies of these letters are in the Public Library at Forlì. The originals are now in the Zambelli papers, recently acquired by the British Museum. One after one the animals sickened and died, and Ghigi feared that he would be required to replace them. The badger was the first to go of a "violent inflammation" caused by too much fat around the kidneys, as he reported on Dec. 15. "The monkeys are well and the heron [crane?] eats many fish."

p.941, l.18 LJ, V, 463.

p.941, l.30 Rogers, p. 237.

p.942, l.4 Moore: *Memoirs*, II, 638. They also visited together the Uffizzi Gallery, but Byron wandered apart to avoid the "jostling starers and travelling talkers." (*LJ*, V, 464.)

p.942, l.14 Clayden, I, 321.

p.942, l.18 Claire Clairmont's diary, Ashley 2819 (3). Entry of Nov. 1, 1821.

p.942, l.28 LJ, V, 466.